TRUTH FOR TODAY

COMMENTARY

Eddie Cloer, D.Min.
General Editor

David Stewart, M.A.R.
Managing Editor

Timothy Paul Westbrook, M.Div.
Assistant Editor

Don Shackelford, Th.D.
Associate Old Testament Editor

Duane Warden, Ph.D.
Associate New Testament Editor

Truth for Today Commentary

An Exegesis & Application of the Holy Scriptures

Exodus

Coy D. Roper, Ph.D.

Resource Publications
2205 S. Benton
Searcy, AR 72143

Truth for Today Commentary
Exodus

2205 S. Benton, Searcy, AR 72143

ISBN: 978-0-9818128-1-6

Photographs in this volume were provided by:
David Stewart, p. 213
Brian Metz, p. 423
Todd Bolen / BiblePlaces.com, pp. 588, 599, 600, 601, 606, 608, 622, 624
Kim Guess / BiblePlaces.com, p. 597
Becky Bardon / BiblePlaces.com, p. 640
A full-size model of the tabernacle is on view at Timna Park in Israel's southern desert (the Negev).

Contents

Charts and Maps

Photographs

Editor's Preface

This volume on Exodus continues the series of commentaries that, we trust, will eventually cover every book in God's divine revelation to us. With this book, fourteen volumes in the series will have been completed: *Exodus; Psalms 1—50; Psalms 51—89; Isaiah; Ezekiel; The Life of Christ, 1; The Life of Christ, 2; Acts 1—14; Acts 15—28; Colossians and Philemon; 1 & 2 Thessalonians; Hebrews; Revelation 1—11;* and *Revelation 12—22.*

A major undertaking of this kind is obviously ambitious, but no one denies its value or timeliness. Our hope is to prepare three or four commentaries each year until the set has been completed. May the Lord in His gracious providence allow us to achieve the effort that is envisioned. More important, may the works stand as faithful servants to the will of God.

A reliable commentary is a profitable assistant for diligent Bible study. Any study of the Scriptures, however, should be predicated upon the realization that God's Word—and His Word alone—is our guide to an accurate understanding of His revelation. A commentary must never be seen as taking the place of God's precious Word; it must be viewed as a printed teacher that seeks to guide the reader to a better understanding of the Word that God has given.

The author of this commentary does not intend for his comments to be regarded as infallible; he knows that he is subject to mistakes, as is the case with every scholar. In writing a commentary, the author only wishes to share with others the fruits of his lifelong study of the Scriptures. We hope that this sharing will aid and encourage every reader in the pursuit of knowledge about God as revealed in the Bible.

Coy D. Roper, the author of this volume, has distinguished himself as one of our finest Old Testament scholars. He graduated from Abilene Christian University with the B.S. degree in Bible, completed the M.T. in secondary education at Northeastern State University, and returned to Abilene Christian University and earned the M.S. degree in Bible and missions. He finished his Ph.D. at the University of Michigan's Department of Near

Eastern Studies with an Old Testament concentration. Recently, he earned the M.A. degree from Heritage Christian University with an emphasis in Greek.

With diligence and faithfulness, he has served as a professor of the Old Testament and New Testament in four of our Christian colleges and one school of preaching: Western Christian College (Canada), Macquarie School of Preaching (North Ryde, Australia), Michigan Christian College (now Rochester College), Lipscomb University, and Heritage Christian University.

In addition to his love for teaching, brother Roper has continually manifested a missionary heart. He served as a missionary and teacher in Australia for ten years. Preaching for and working with local congregations has also been a predominant passion. Wherever he has been, he has continued to preach and assist in building up congregations of the Lord's people. He has preached for churches in Texas, Oklahoma, Tennessee, Michigan, Canada, and Australia. Currently, he is preaching for the church in Trent, Texas, and serving half-time as a staff writer for Truth for Today World Mission School.

His work on Exodus will take its place among the great commentaries on the Bible. May his treatment of this section of the Scriptures be a blessing to the church until Jesus comes.

Bible scholars from the churches of Christ are seeking to provide this multi-authored series on the entire Bible to our generation and to future generations. We can leave to those who will follow us no finer legacy than presentations on every book of the Scriptures. A project of this magnitude requires many faithful laborers, much time, and great persistence. Let us join, as brothers and sisters bought by Christ's blood, and work together until the task is completed.

Eddie Cloer
General Editor

Abbreviations

OLD TESTAMENT

Genesis	Gen.	Ecclesiastes	Eccles.
Exodus	Ex.	Song of Solomon	Song
Leviticus	Lev.	Isaiah	Is.
Numbers	Num.	Jeremiah	Jer.
Deuteronomy	Deut.	Lamentations	Lam.
Joshua	Josh.	Ezekiel	Ezek.
Judges	Judg.	Daniel	Dan.
Ruth	Ruth	Hosea	Hos.
1 Samuel	1 Sam.	Joel	Joel
2 Samuel	2 Sam.	Amos	Amos
1 Kings	1 Kings	Obadiah	Obad.
2 Kings	2 Kings	Jonah	Jon.
1 Chronicles	1 Chron.	Micah	Mic.
2 Chronicles	2 Chron.	Nahum	Nahum
Ezra	Ezra	Habakkuk	Hab.
Nehemiah	Neh.	Zephaniah	Zeph.
Esther	Esther	Haggai	Hag.
Job	Job	Zechariah	Zech.
Psalms	Ps.	Malachi	Mal.
Proverbs	Prov.		

NEW TESTAMENT

Matthew	Mt.	1 Timothy	1 Tim.
Mark	Mk.	2 Timothy	2 Tim.
Luke	Lk.	Titus	Tit.
John	Jn.	Philemon	Philem.
Acts	Acts	Hebrews	Heb.
Romans	Rom.	James	Jas.
1 Corinthians	1 Cor.	1 Peter	1 Pet.
2 Corinthians	2 Cor.	2 Peter	2 Pet.
Galatians	Gal.	1 John	1 Jn.
Ephesians	Eph.	2 John	2 Jn.
Philippians	Phil.	3 John	3 Jn.
Colossians	Col.	Jude	Jude
1 Thessalonians	1 Thess.	Revelation	Rev.
2 Thessalonians	2 Thess.		

AB	Amplified Bible
ASV	American Standard Version
CEV	Contemporary English Version
ESV	English Standard Version
KJV	King James Version
NAB	New American Bible
NASB	New American Standard Bible
NCV	New Century Version
NEB	New English Bible
NIV	New International Version
NJB	New Jerusalem Bible
NKJV	New King James Version
NLT	New Living Translation
NRSV	New Revised Standard Version
REB	Revised English Bible
RSV	Revised Standard Version
TEV	Today's English Version

Hebrew Transliteration

Studying the Word of God in the original languages brings out more fully the richness of the biblical texts. This series attempts to incorporate a healthy number of Greek and Hebrew words that help clarify the passages under investigation. Although translating and transliterating are difficult tasks with any language, Hebrew poses a particular challenge. First, it is an old language, and spelling and pronunciation have evolved over time. Second, there are multiple methods for transliterating Hebrew words into English. Therefore, the editorial committee has discussed how we will transliterate Hebrew, and we have adapted our own method for the series. It is assumed that not all of our readers will have a working knowledge of Hebrew. Our system attempts to present a transliteration that will simplify pronunciation and assist in word studies. In order to accomplish this, we have applied the following rules throughout the commentary.

Rule 1. No difference is indicated by the hard / soft pronunciation of "Begad Kapath" letters: דּדגּגבּב תּתפּפכּכ. The meaning of a word is not affected by whether or not these letters are hard or soft.

Rule 2. When the *Daghesh Forte* indicates a doubling of consonants, the letter is doubled in the transliteration.

Rule 3. The Tetragrammaton (יְהוָה) is transliterated *YHWH* and written "Yahweh" in the text. Since the original vowel pointings are unknown for this word, they have been left out when it appears in the commentary, thus forming יהוה.

Rule 4. The transliteration distinguishes between ה when used as a consonant and ה when used as a vowel letter to lengthen the vowel *Qamets*.

Rule 5. The vocalized *sheva* is indicated by ^{e}.

Rule 6. Since the word "torah" (law) is a commonly known word, the ת that begins this word is transliterated as *t* rather than *th*.

Examples of transliterated words:

לְדָוִד, *l^edawid*; חַטָּאִים, *chatta'im*, תּוֹרָה, *torah*; אַשְׁרֵי, *'ashrey*; and אִישׁ, *'ish*

Consonants

There are twenty-three consonants in the Hebrew text. They are listed below by name, Hebrew symbol, and transliteration.

Name	Hebrew	Transliteration
Aleph	א	'
Beth	ב	*b*
Gimel	ג	*g*
Daleth	ד	*d*
He	ה	*h*
Vav	ו	*w*
Zayin	ז	*z*
Heth	ח	*ch*
Teth	ט	*t*
Yodh	י	*y*
Kaph	כ ך	*k*
Lamedh	ל	*l*
Mem	מ ם	*m*
Nun	נ ן	*n*
Samekh	ס	*s*
Ayin	ע	'
Pe	פ ף	*p*
Tsadhe	צ ץ	*ts*
Qoph	ק	*q*
Resh	ר	*r*
Sin	שׂ	*ś*
Shin	שׁ	*sh*
Tav	ת	*th*

Vowels

The vowels in Hebrew are used more for determining the form of a word rather than the root meaning. We have tried to differentiate between these vowels to help guide their pronunciation and grammatical function. They are listed here by name, Hebrew symbol, and transliteration.

Name	Hebrew	Transliteration
Qamets	ָ	*a* (long)
Patach	ַ	*a* (short)
Tsere	ֵ	*e* (long)
Segol	ֶ	*e* (short)
Hireq Yodh	ִי	*i* (long)
Hireq	ִ	*i* (short)
Qamets Yodh	ָי	*ay*
Segol Yodh	ֶי	*ey*
Tsere Yodh	ֵי	*ey*
Holem	וֹ	*o* (long)
Qamets-Hatuph	ָ	*o* (short)
Shureq	וּ	*u* (long)
Qibbuts	ֻ	*u* (short)
Hatep-Patach	ֲ	^{a}
Hatep-Segol	ֱ	^{e}
Hatep-Qamets	ֳ	^{o}

Suggested Hebrew Grammar Books

For further study of the Hebrew language, we recommend the following books:

Kelly, Page H. *Biblical Hebrew: An Introduction Grammar*. Grand Rapids, Mich.: Wm. B. Eerdmans Publishing Co., 1992.

Pratico, Gary D. and Miles Van Pelt. *Basics of Biblical Hebrew Grammar*. Grand Rapids, Mich.: Zondervan, 2001. This book includes an interactive CD-ROM.

Seow, Choon Leong. *A Grammar for Biblical Hebrew*. Nashville: Abingdon Press, 1987.

Weingreen, J. *A Practical Grammar for Classical Hebrew*, 2d ed. New York: Oxford University Press, 1959.

Introduction

Exodus records the birth of a nation under God, the beginning of a theocratic kingdom. The descendants of Abraham became God's people redeemed for God's purposes.

The book links Genesis with the rest of the Old Testament. If one were to read only Genesis, he would ask, "What happened next? Were the promises to Abraham, Isaac, and Jacob ever fulfilled?" Exodus helps to answer these questions. It tells the reader that Abraham's descendants became a great nation in Egypt and then were delivered out of bondage by God. They became His people, governed by His law. On the other hand, if a student were to read only the historical books (Joshua—Esther) or the writings of the prophets, he would wonder, "Who are these people? Where did they come from? Why were they often condemned by the prophets? Why did God care so much about them?" Exodus answers these questions by proclaiming that these were the people whom God delivered out of Egypt. In this way, Exodus bridges the gap between the patriarchs and the prophets.

THE NAME AND CLASSIFICATION

In the English Bible, the name "Exodus" is derived from the Septuagint (LXX), the ancient Greek version of the Hebrew Bible. The Greek word ἐξόδου (from ἔξοδος, *exodos*), which is found in Exodus 19:1, means "departure." Therefore, the book is named after its major event—the departure of the Israelites from Egypt.

In the Hebrew Bible, this book is called after the first two words of the text, וְאֵלֶּה שְׁמוֹת (*w*[e]*'elleh sh*[e]*moth).* This Hebrew title could be translated "And these are the names," or simply "Names."[1]

Exodus is the second book of the Pentateuch. Derived from two Greek words meaning "five scrolls,"[2] the term "Pentateuch" refers to the first five books of the Old Testament (Genesis—Deuteronomy). These five books are referred to by both Jews and Christians as "the Law," or "Torah" (תּוֹרָה) in the Hebrew Bible.[3] These books are also known as the Books of Moses since Moses is regarded as their author.

THE EMPHASIS

The Book of Exodus is primarily about the Israelites' exodus, or departure, from Egypt. The exodus was the most important event in Israelite history. It defined Israel as a people especially called and blessed by God. "Who were the Israelites?" They were the people God delivered out of Egypt. "Who was their God, Yahweh?"[4] He was the God who delivered them out of Egypt.

"Exodus" may not be the best word for this event. It is not as if the Israelites one day decided to leave Egypt and simply "exited." Rather, God brought them out of Egypt by His power and might. "Deliverance," therefore, is a better term to use in speaking of what happened when the Israelites left Egypt. The Book of Exodus makes it clear that Israel's "going out" was not their own doing, but God's.

Further, the book does not end with Israel's deliverance; it

---

[1]William Sanford LaSor, David Allan Hubbard, and Frederic William Bush, *Old Testament Survey: The Message, Form, and Background of the Old Testament* (Grand Rapids, Mich.: Wm. B. Eerdmans Publishing Co., 1982), 131.

[2]John Taylor, "The 'Five Books,'" in *Eerdmans' Handbook to the Bible,* ed. David Alexander and Pat Alexander (Grand Rapids, Mich.: Wm. B. Eerdmans Publishing Co., 1973), 122.

[3]The Torah is one of the three divisions of the Hebrew Bible. The other two are the Prophets and the Writings.

[4]The word "Yahweh" is used in this commentary for the four-letter name of God (יהוה, *YHWH*). This name is translated "Jehovah" in a few English versions of the Bible.

goes on to tell how God made a covenant with Israel. This covenant included laws and ordinances for living. Instructions for building the tabernacle were also given.

Exodus describes how God, in His mercy, delivered His people from Egyptian bondage, made a covenant with them, gave them His law, and provided the tabernacle as the place where He would dwell among them.

THE AUTHOR

Moses is undoubtedly the author of Exodus. Although he is not identified in Exodus as the author of the book, he is said to have written down the laws that were given by God (24:4; 34:27; see 17:14). Likewise, he is spoken of as the writer in other places in the Pentateuch (Num. 33:1, 2; Deut.1:1). Jesus Himself referred to Moses as having written about Him: "For if you believed Moses, you would believe Me, for he wrote about Me. But if you do not believe his writings, how will you believe My words?" (Jn. 5:46, 47).

The fact that the New Testament attributes the Law to Moses (Mt. 19:8; Jn. 7:19; Acts 3:22; Rom. 10:5) provides grounds for accepting him as the author of the entire Pentateuch, including Exodus. Philip said concerning Jesus, "We have found Him of whom Moses in the Law and also the Prophets wrote—Jesus of Nazareth, the son of Joseph" (Jn. 1:45). The Gospels refer to statements of Moses and to "the book of Moses" (see Mk. 7:10; 12:26; Lk. 2:22, 23; 20:37).

Of course, accepting Moses as the author of the Pentateuch does not rule out the possibility that, in a few instances, some changes in the text may have been made by scribes who succeeded Moses. In addition, Moses himself may have used earlier documents in writing the Law. (For more information, see *Appendix: The Author of Exodus.*)

THE DATE

The book dates to approximately the time of the exodus from Egypt. Ronald F. Youngblood has said, "The period when Moses composed the book is roughly the same as the period during which the Israelites were making their way through the Sinai desert."[5] Scholars today are divided on the question of the date of the exodus. Based on archaeological evidence, many commentators date the exodus at about 1290 B.C. (the late date). Due to the biblical evidence, other writers favor a date around 1445 B.C. (the early date). (For more information, see *Appendix: The Date of the Exodus*.)

THE HISTORICAL SITUATION

Exodus is part of a larger whole. Its story follows, without a break, the events recorded in Genesis. The Hebrew text of Exodus begins with a conjunction (וְאֵלֶּה שְׁמוֹת, *w^{e}'elleh sh^{e}moth,* "And these are the names"), indicating that the book was intended to be a continuation of Genesis. Leviticus, Numbers, and Deuteronomy then carry the story forward. In fact, the first twelve books of the Old Testament (Genesis—2 Kings), with the exception of Ruth, tell a continuous story.

The book itself begins with the family of Jacob (the Israelites) in Egypt. These people became so numerous that they were enslaved by the Egyptians. The book tells how God delivered Israel, using Moses as His spokesman and miraculous signs (the ten plagues) as His means to convince Pharaoh, the king of Egypt, to let the people go. God delivered the nation through the Red Sea and brought them to Mount Sinai, meeting their needs all along the way. There He made a covenant with Israel. The stipulations of the covenant are the laws found in the rest of the book (and in the rest of the Pentateuch), along with instructions for building the tabernacle. The book continues by telling the story of the building of the tabernacle—a narrative that is interrupted by the Israelites' apostasy in worshiping a golden calf—and ends with the building and erection of the tabernacle.

---

[5]Ronald F. Youngblood, *Exodus*, Everyman's Bible Commentary (Chicago: Moody Bible Institute, 1983), 12.

THE RELATIONSHIP OF EXODUS TO THE REST OF THE PENTATEUCH

Terence E. Fretheim said, "Exodus does not stand alone but is an integral 'chapter' in the larger Pentateuch. . . . Exodus may be considered the center of the Pentateuch."[6] Exodus is linked to Genesis in a number of ways:

1. Exodus 1:1–5 identifies the people in Egypt with the patriarchs in Genesis; this text appears to be a shortened form of the genealogy found in Genesis 46:8–27.
2. Abraham's earlier journey to Egypt in Genesis 12:10–20 foreshadowed Israel's experiences recorded in Exodus.
3. Israel's bondage and deliverance are foretold in Genesis 15:13, 14 and again in 46:3, 4.
4. Israel's God in Exodus identifies Himself with the God of Abraham, Isaac, and Jacob (Ex. 6:2, 3).
5. The promises to the patriarchs—especially the promise of land—are referred to frequently in Exodus (see Ex. 2:24; 6:4, 5, 8).
6. Joseph, who plays so prominent a role in Genesis, is spoken of in Exodus 1. The fact that his bones were carried back to Canaan—in keeping with his wishes, according to Genesis 50:24, 25—is noted in Exodus 13:19.[7]

Exodus is linked closely with the rest of the Pentateuch as well.[8] Leviticus continues the story of the giving of the Law at Sinai and records the consecration of the priesthood, for which instructions are found in Exodus 29. Numbers relates how Israel left Sinai to travel to the promised land. In Deuteronomy Moses reminded the people of the experiences recorded in Exodus.

---

[6]Terence E. Fretheim, "Exodus, Book of," in *Dictionary of the Old Testament: Pentateuch*, ed. T. Desmond Alexander and David W. Baker (Downers Grove, Ill.: InterVarsity Press, 2003), 249.

[7]For these examples and additional ones, see Ibid., 249–50.

[8]Ibid., 250.

THE PURPOSE

What is the purpose of Exodus? The book serves a threefold purpose.

First, it proclaims Israel's redemption[9] as part of the ongoing story of God's plan to save mankind[10] by keeping His promises to Abraham. Exodus relates how God made Abraham's seed into a great nation, delivered the people from Egyptian bondage, and came to dwell among them. The structure of the book provides a clue as to its purpose. As it opens, The Israelites are depicted as an enslaved people. By the end of the book, Israel is portrayed as a people delivered by God who are ready for Him to dwell in the completed tabernacle. The last paragraph of the book says, "Then the cloud covered the tent of meeting, and the glory of the LORD filled the tabernacle" (40:34). Exodus ends on the high note that God would dwell with Israel.

Second, it records the covenant that served as the basis for all of God's dealings with Israel from that point forward. The rest of the Old Testament is to be understood in terms of this covenant. Exodus 19:3–6 says,

> Moses went up to God, and the LORD called to him from the mountain, saying, "Thus you shall say to the house of Jacob and tell the sons of Israel: 'You yourselves have seen what I did to the Egyptians, and how I bore you on eagles' wings, and brought you to Myself. Now then, if you will indeed obey My voice and keep My covenant, then you shall be My own possession among all the peoples, for all the earth is Mine; and you shall be to Me a kingdom of priests and a holy nation.' These are the words that you shall speak to the sons of Israel."

---

[9]Redemption is a major theme of the book (6:6, 7; 15:13). (Wilbur Fields, *Exploring Exodus*, Bible Study Textbook Series [Joplin, Mo.: College Press, 1976], 2.)

[10]Therefore, the main purpose of Exodus is to provide another chapter in what has been called "salvation history."

The people responded, "All that the LORD has spoken we will do!" (19:8). This is the covenant: God said that Israel would be His people if Israel would do His will. Israel agreed to those terms. Whenever Israel, later in its history, is spoken of as making a covenant with God, the idea is not that Israel was making a new or different covenant, but that Israel was reaffirming its commitment to the Sinai covenant.

The covenant found in Exodus 19 is so important that the rest of the Old Testament is to be understood on the basis of this agreement. Old Testament history demonstrates that, as long as Israel kept the covenant by obeying God, He faithfully blessed Israel. When Israel disobeyed (which happened frequently), then God punished Israel. God's covenant relationship with Israel provided the basis for the exhortations and condemnations given to Israel by the prophets.[11] (For more information, see *Appendix: The Covenant.*)

Third, it contains the law of God, which resulted from the covenant. Since the making of the covenant and the giving of the Law followed the miraculous deliverance from Egypt, the Book of Exodus reminded Israel that responsibilities came with their redemption. Israel accepted those responsibilities when the people agreed to the terms of the covenant. The responsibilities themselves are spelled out in the Law given by God through Moses at Sinai.

THE TYPE OF LITERATURE

In order to understand the book properly, we must recognize that Exodus is primarily a narrative. The book contains poetry and lengthy legal passages, but both the poetry and the laws are set in a narrative framework. The student, therefore, must consider the narrative techniques that the author used. The techniques found in the book are as follows:

---

[11]A book on interpreting the Bible contains a chapter entitled "The Prophets: Enforcing the Covenant in Israel." (Gordon D. Fee and Douglas Stuart, *How to Read the Bible for All Its Worth,* 2d ed. [Grand Rapids, Mich.: Zondervan, 1993], 165.)

(1) *The use of introductory sentences (similar to topic sentences) and summary statements.* Like a careful author today, the writer usually told his readers at the beginning of a paragraph or section *who* did *what,* and *when* and *where* he did it. At the conclusion of the paragraph or section, he usually summed up what he had just described.

(2) *The use of literary techniques,* such as key words and phrases, and chiasmus. Key words and phrases are employed to indicate where narrative sections begin and end. Chiastic structures are used for emphasis. "Chiasmus," or inverted parallelism, is "a Latinized word based on the Greek letter χ (Chi) to symbolize the inverted sequence or crossover of parallel words or ideas in a . . . literary unit."[12] In a chiastic structure, parallel thoughts are arranged in an ABBA pattern, as in Mark 2:27: "The Sabbath [A1] was made for man [B1], and not man [B2] for the Sabbath [A2]."

(3) *The use of repetition.* The writer, like other ancient authors, used repetition. For example, he repeated the Sabbath commandment six times and, including brief summary statements, gave details regarding the building of the tabernacle five times.[13] Readers today often see repetition as ineffective. However, the writer of Exodus saw it as necessary. Why? One reason is that repetition is valuable for emphasis; readers today can assume that what was repeated was considered important. Another reason is that, in ancient times, writings were not readily accessible to the general public. People lived, for the most part, in an oral culture where messages were spoken and heard. The Israelites were the intended recipients of the message of Exodus. When they first "read" Exodus, they did not themselves read it, but heard it read to them. In such a situation, repetition is essential if the message is to be remembered by those for whom it is intended. Consequently, these repetitions, which are sometimes thought

---

[12]Richard N. Soulen and R. Kendall Soulen, *Handbook of Biblical Criticism,* 3d ed., rev. and exp. (Louisville: Westminster John Knox Press, 2001), 32.

[13]Sabbath instructions are given in Exodus 16:23–30; 20:8–11; 23:12; 31:13–16; 34:21; 35:1–3. The listing of items for the tabernacle is given in Exodus 25:8—30:38; 31:6–11; 35:10–19; 36:8—39:32; 39:33–43.

to be indications of different sources, simply reflect the author's narrative style and his effort to achieve his literary purpose.

THE VALUE FOR MODERN READERS

The Book of Exodus has considerable value for readers today.

Without it, we could not understand much that is found in the New Testament. Jesus Christ was a prophet like Moses (Acts 3:19–23). Without Exodus, would anyone understand that idea? The tabernacle, with its sacrificial system, was a "shadow" of the Christian system (Heb. 10:1). Could that fact be appreciated without an understanding of what was involved in building the tabernacle? Christians are a "people for God's own possession" (1 Pet. 2:9), just as the Israelites were in Old Testament times. Without Exodus, could that fact be appreciated?

Without Exodus, people today could not have a proper understanding of God. The Bible was written to help mankind understand God. Exodus teaches much about God: about His holiness and justice and concern for the oppressed, about His love and grace and mercy, about His longsuffering and patience, about His wrath and His punishment of sin.

Without Exodus, it would be more difficult to understand what God requires of His people. Even though the specific laws of Exodus are not bound on people in the Christian age, we can rightfully deduce from Exodus that God requires people of all ages to be faithful and obedient to Him and to show love toward fellow human beings.

OUTLINES

The book can be divided into two parts:

I. The Deliverance (1—18)
II. The Covenant (19—40)
  A. The Covenant and the Commandments (19—24)
  B. The Building of the Tabernacle (25—40)

Other outlines are possible. Warren W. Wiersbe divided the book by aspects of the relationship between God and His people:

I. Redemption: The Lord Delivers His People (1—18)
II. Covenant: The Lord Claims His People (19—24)
III. Worship: The Lord Dwells with His People (25—40)[14]

Another possibility is to organize the book "according to the experiences shared by God's people Israel," as follows:[15]

I. God's People Delivered (1:1—13:16)
II. God's People Led (13:17—18:27)
III. God's People Made into a Covenant Nation (19—24)
IV. God's People Given Instructions for the Tabernacle (25—31)
V. God's People in Sin: the Golden Calf (32—34)
VI. God's People Constructing the Tabernacle (35—40)

---

[14]Warren W. Wiersbe, *Be Delivered* (Colorado Springs, Colo.: Victor, 1998), 8.
[15]Adapted from Fields, 5.

The Expanded Outline

I. DELIVERANCE (1—18)
- A. The Israelites Enslaved in Egypt (1:1–22)
  1. Their entrance into Egypt and prosperity there (1:1–7)
  2. Oppressed but not destroyed (1:8–22)
- B. The Deliverer: Moses (2:1—4:26)
  1. His birth and early life (2:1–10)
  2. His attempts at deliverance (2:11–15)
  3. His life in Midian (2:16–22)
  4. The Israelites' cry to God (2:23–25)
  5. Moses' call by God (3:1—4:17)
     - a. Moses' encounter with God (3:1–6)
     - b. God's intentions (3:7–9)
     - c. God's initial call and Moses' first response: "Who am I?" (3:10–12)
     - d. Moses' second response: "Who are You?" (3:13–15)
     - e. A preview of the deliverance (3:16–22)
     - f. Moses' third response: "They will not believe me" (4:1–9)
     - g. Moses' fourth response: "I am not eloquent" (4:10–12)
     - h. Moses' fifth response: "Send someone else" (4:13–17)
  6. Moses' acceptance of God's call and his departure for Egypt (4:18–26)
- C. Initial Failure (4:27—6:13)

1. Aaron, Moses, and the people (4:27–31)
2. First appeal to Pharaoh (5:1–21)
   a. Moses' request and Pharaoh's negative response (5:1–4)
   b. Consequences of the request: gathering straw (5:5–14)
   c. The foremen's complaint to Pharaoh (5:15–19)
   d. The foremen's complaint to Moses (5:20, 21)
3. Moses' plea to God and God's response (5:22—7:7)
   a. Moses' complaint to God (5:22, 23)
   b. God's response: His name revealed and His promise repeated (6:1–8)
   c. The people's refusal to listen (6:9)
   d. God's renewed call to Moses (6:10–13)

D. Moses and Aaron's Genealogy (6:14–27)
E. Successful Attempt Begun (6:28—7:7)
   a. God's command for Moses to speak to Pharaoh (6:28–30)
   b. God's promise of success (7:1–7)
F. Deliverance by Means of the Plagues (7:8—13:16)
   1. The miracle of the staff (7:8–13)
   2. The first nine plagues (7:14—10:29)
      a. Water turned to blood (7:14–25)
      b. Frogs (8:1–15)
      c. Gnats (8:16–19)
      d. Flies (8:20–32)
      e. Pestilence on the cattle (9:1–7)
      f. Boils (9:8–12)
      g. Hail (9:13–35)
      h. Locusts (10:1–20)
      i. Darkness (10:21–29)
   3. The last plague: death of the firstborn (11:1—12:36)
      a. The plague announced (11:1–10)
      b. The Passover instituted (12:1–28)
      c. The firstborn killed and the Israelites freed (12:29–36)
   4. The day the exodus begun (12:37—13:16)
      a. The Israelites' departure from Egypt (12:37–42)

b. The law of the Passover (12:43–51)
c. The dedication of the firstborn (13:1, 2)
d. The speech of Moses (13:3–16)

G. Deliverance Through the Red Sea (13:17—15:21)
1. The journey to the Red Sea (13:17–22)
2. Crossing the Red Sea (14:1–31)
a. Pursuit by Pharaoh and his army (14:1–9)
b. The Israelites' panic (14:10–14)
c. God's instruction to Moses (14:15–20)
d. The Israelites delivered (14:21–25)
e. Pharaoh's army drowned (14:26–31)
3. Praise for deliverance (15:1–21)

H. Journey to Sinai (15:22—18:27)
1. At Marah, bitter water made sweet (15:22–25a)
2. At Marah, a preview of the covenant (15:25b–27)
3. In the wilderness of Sin, food provided by God (16:1–36)
a. The grumbling of the Israelites (16:1–3)
b. God's promise of provision (16:4–8)
c. The appearing of God's glory (16:9–12)
d. Quail and manna (16:13–21)
e. Resting on the Sabbath (16:22–30)
f. Manna preserved (16:31–36)
4. At Rephidim, water from a rock (17:1–7)
5. At Rephidim, victory over Amalek (17:8–16)
6. Jethro's visit with Moses in the wilderness (18:1–27)
a. His coming to Moses (18:1–7)
b. His rejoicing at God's deliverance (18:8–12)
c. His advice to Moses (18:13–27)

II. THE COVENANT (19—40)

A. The Institution of the Covenant Between the Lord and Israel (19:1—24:18)
1. The covenant made (19:1–25)
a. Their calling from God (19:1–9)
b. Their consecration to God (19:10–15)
c. Their coming before God (19:16–25)

2. The Ten Commandments and Israel's reaction (20:1–21)
3. The Book of the Covenant (20:22—23:33)
    a. Prologue: the Giver of the Law (20:22)
    b. Laws related to the worship of God (20:23–26)
    c. Laws related to slavery (21:1–11)
    d. Laws regarding personal injuries (21:12–27)
    e. Laws regarding oxen (21:28–36)
    f. Crimes against property (22:1–17)
    g. Capital crimes related to idolatry (22:18–20)
    h. Laws requiring compassion (22:21–27)
    i. Laws honoring God (22:28–31)
    j. The demands of justice (23:1–9)
    k. Keeping the Sabbath (23:10–13)
    l. Three annual feasts (23:14–17)
    m. Laws concerning sacrifices (23:18, 19)
    n. Epilogue: entering the promised land (23:20–33)
4. Ratification of the covenant (24:1–11)
5. Receiving the Law (24:12–18)

B. The Tabernacle for Israel's Worship of the Lord (25:1—40:38)
1. Plans for the tabernacle (25:1—31:18)
    a. Contributions and commission for building (25:1–9)
    b. Instructions for building (25:10—27:21)
        (1) The ark of the covenant (25:10–16)
        (2) The mercy seat (25:17–22)
        (3) The table of showbread (25:23–30)
        (4) The golden lampstand (25:31–40)
        (5) The tent (26:1–37)
        (6) The bronze altar (27:1–8)
        (7) The court (27:9–19)
        (8) The oil for the lamp (27:20, 21)
    c. Instructions concerning the priests (28:1—29:46)
        (1) The priestly garments (28:1–43)
            (a) The priests identified (28:1–5)
            (b) The ephod and the onyx stones (28:6–14)

(c) The breastpiece and the Urim and Thummim (28:15–30)
(d) The robe (28:31–35)
(e) The gold plate, tunic, turban, and sash (28:36–39)
(f) Tunics, sashes, caps, and linen breeches (28:40–43)
(2) The consecration of the priesthood (29:1–30)
(a) The priestly garments (29:1–9)
(b) The consecration ceremony (29:10–37)
(c) The continual daily offerings (29:38–42)
(d) The results of consecration: God's presence (29:43–46)
d. Further instructions for building (30:1–38)
(1) The altar of incense (30:1–10)
(2) The tax required (30:11–16)
(3) The bronze laver (30:17–21)
(4) The anointing oil (30:22–33)
(5) The incense (30:34–38)
e. A summary of the instructions (31:1–18)
(1) The builders and the building plans (31:1–11)
(2) The Sabbath command repeated (31:12–17)
(3) The conclusion of the Law (31:18)
2. Apostasy and restoration (32:1—34:35)
a. Apostasy: the golden calf (32:1–35)
(1) Israel's sin: worshiping a calf idol (32:1–6)
(2) God's response: the threat to destroy Israel (32:7–10)
(3) Moses' intercession (32:11–13)
(4) God's reconsideration (32:14)
(5) Israel's punishment (32:15–35)
(a) Drinking polluted water (32:15–24)
(b) Three thousand slain by the Levites (32:25–29)
(c) Forgiveness and punishment (32:30–35)
b. Restoration: God's promise of His presence (33:1–23)

- (1) God's withdrawal from the people (33:1–6)
- (2) Assurance that God would manifest Himself (33:7–23)

c. Restoration: God's renewal of the covenant (34:1–35)
- (1) God's willingness to renew the covenant (34:1–4)
- (2) God's name and nature proclaimed (34:5–9)
- (3) The covenant renewed (34:10)
- (4) The Law reissued (34:11–26)
  - (a) God's warning against a covenant with any nation (34:11–17)
  - (b) God's emphasis on Israel's responsibilities in worship (34:18–26)
- (5) The Ten Commandments given a second time (34:27, 28)
- (6) The Lord's grandeur displayed (34:29–35)

3. Building the tabernacle (35:1—39:43)

a. Preparations for building the tabernacle (35:1—36:7)
- (1) The Sabbath command (35:1–3)
- (2) Call for a contribution (35:4–9)
- (3) A summons to build the tabernacle (35:10–19)
- (4) The freewill offering (35:20–29)
- (5) The construction foremen (35:30–35)
- (6) Call for workers (36:1, 2)
- (7) The abundant offering (36:3–7)

b. The construction of the tabernacle (36:8—38:31)
- (1) The tent (36:8–38)
- (2) The ark of the covenant (37:1–5)
- (3) The mercy seat (37:6–9)
- (4) The table of showbread (37:10–16)
- (5) The golden lampstand (37:17–24)
- (6) The altar of incense (37:25–28)
- (7) The anointing oil and incense (37:29)
- (8) The bronze altar (38:1–7)
- (9) The bronze laver (38:8)

(10) The court (38:9–20)
(11) The cost of the tabernacle (38:21–31)
(a) The leaders (38:21–23)
(b) The amount given (38:24–31)
c. The making of the priestly garments (39:1–31)
(1) The ephod and the onyx stones (39:1–7)
(2) The breastpiece (39:8–21)
(3) The robe (39:22–26)
(4) The tunics, turban, caps, linen breeches, and gold plate (39:27–31)
d. The presentation of the tabernacle (39:32–43)
4. Erecting and consecrating the tabernacle (40:1–38)
a. Directions for setting up the tabernacle (40:1–8)
b. Directions for consecrating the tabernacle and the priests (40:9–15)
c. Setting up the tabernacle (40:16–33)
d. The Lord's indwelling of the tabernacle (40:34–38)

Part I

Deliverance

(1—18)

1. The Israelites Enslaved in Egypt (1:1–22)
2. The Deliverer: Moses (2:1—4:26)
3. Initial Failure (4:27—6:13)
4. Moses and Aaron's Genealogy (6:14–27)
5. Successful Attempt Begun (6:28—7:7)
6. Deliverance by Means of the Plagues (7:8—13:16)
7. Deliverance Through the Red Sea (13:17—15:21)
8. Journey to Sinai (15:22—18:27)

Chapter 1

The Israelites Enslaved in Egypt

Exodus is about the deliverance of the Israelites from Egypt. The book begins with a reminder of how and when "the sons of Israel" came into Egypt (1:1–5). Jacob and his family had taken refuge in the fertile Nile area during a severe famine. Egypt had stored a large supply of grain, having been warned of the approaching famine by God through Joseph, one of Jacob's sons (Gen. 41).

The story continues with an account of how God's people came to need deliverance. They had been enslaved because the Egyptians had become afraid of them. Over time, the Israelites had multiplied (1:6, 7). A new king arose, and he "knew not Joseph" (1:8; KJV); that is, he did not remember or recognize what Joseph had done to help Egypt during the famine in earlier years. The Egyptians feared that the Hebrews, whose strength and number were greater than their own, would turn against them if Egypt were attacked by their enemies (1:9, 10).

After that, the Egyptians—especially Pharaoh—tried to solve the "Israelite problem." Nothing they did worked; in spite of everything, Israel continued to prosper.

First, the Egyptians oppressed Israel. Nevertheless, the more God's people were oppressed, the more they prospered. Pharaoh then made Israel serve with even greater rigor, which apparently did not solve the problem (1:11–14).

Second, Pharaoh commanded the Hebrew midwives to kill the male children. However, the midwives thwarted Pharaoh's purposes. They did not kill the children, and they lied to Pharaoh to explain why the children still lived. As a result, the people multiplied and God blessed the midwives (1:15–21).

Third, Pharaoh required that all newborn Hebrew boys be thrown into the river. The ultimate result of this strategy was that the child who was to become the deliverer was brought up in the court of Pharaoh himself (1:22—2:10).

The theme of this narrative is that nothing works when man opposes God. Even Pharaoh was no match for God. No one can win over God.

THE ISRAELITES' ENTRANCE INTO EGYPT AND PROSPERITY THERE (1:1–7)

1Now these are the names of the sons of Israel who came to Egypt with Jacob; they came each one with his household: 2Reuben, Simeon, Levi and Judah; 3Issachar, Zebulun and Benjamin; 4Dan and Naphtali, Gad and Asher. 5All the persons who came from the loins of Jacob were seventy in number, but Joseph was already in Egypt. 6Joseph died, and all his brothers and all that generation. 7But the sons of Israel were fruitful and increased greatly, and multiplied, and became exceedingly mighty, so that the land was filled with them.

Verses 1–5. This list links the opening of Exodus with Genesis 46:8–27. It begins in the same way with the phrase **Now these are the names** and concludes with the same number of people. Listed here are the eleven **sons of Israel** besides Joseph, since he already lived in Egypt. God's chosen people became known as "Israel" (יִשְׂרָאֵל, *Yiśra'el*), the name given to **Jacob** (Gen. 32:38; 35:10), whose sons were the progenitors of the twelve tribes. These sons are listed here in birth order according to their respective mothers: Leah, Rachel, Bilhah, and Zilpah (Gen. 35:23–26).

The text says that **seventy** went into Egypt, whereas Stephen mentions seventy-five (Acts 7:14). What is the reason for the difference? Gleason L. Archer, Jr., suggested that Stephen "may have intended to include the expanded number in the Septuagint,"[1]

---

[1]Gleason L. Archer, Jr., *Encyclopedia of Bible Difficulties* (Grand Rapids, Mich.: Zondervan Publishing House, 1982), 378.

which has seventy-five rather than seventy in Exodus 1. He also said that the number in the Septuagint probably included some of Joseph's grandchildren.[2] Either number—seventy or seventy-five—is correct, depending on who is counted in the total.

Verses 6, 7. At first, the members of Jacob's family were honored guests in Egypt and prospered there. When God blessed them by multiplying them as He did, His promise to Abraham was being fulfilled (Gen. 12:2; 15:5; 17:1–8). How many people made up the Israelite nation? Enough that about 600,000 men were numbered after the deliverance (12:37; 38:26).

Commentators point out the similarity between Exodus 1:7 and Genesis 1:28: "God blessed them; and God said to them, 'Be fruitful and multiply, and fill the earth.'" The Israelites **were fruitful . . . and multiplied . . . so that the land was filled with them.** This reminder of God's will for man at the beginning suggests that God was involved in Exodus in a "new creation," the creation of a people to be His own. It is noteworthy that the same Hebrew word (אֶרֶץ, *'erets*) is translated "earth" in Genesis 1:28 and "land" in Exodus 1:7.

"The land was filled with them" probably refers to that part of Egypt in which Israel lived, known as the land of Goshen (Gen. 45:10). This was the "best of the land . . . the land of Rameses" (Gen. 47:11).

The result of Israel's stay in Egypt was that one of God's promises was fulfilled: Abraham's descendants became numerous. It seems likely that God brought Israel to Egypt for that very purpose. The settled lifestyle in Egypt provided a better environment for the Israelites to grow and multiply than did the wandering shepherd life of the patriarchs. The Israelites themselves later remembered their time in Egypt—or at least their food in Egypt—with fondness, saying that there they "sat by the pots of meat, when [they] ate bread to the full" (16:3). As they wandered in the wilderness, they said, "We remember the fish which we used to eat free in Egypt, the cucumbers and the melons and the leeks and the onions and the garlic" (Num. 11:5). While they probably exaggerated the pleasure they had in Egypt, it is likely

---

[2]Ibid., 379.

that they had enjoyed much about their life there. For God's purposes, Egypt was a good land to produce a numerous people.

THE ISRAELITES OPPRESSED BUT NOT DESTROYED (1:8–22)

Forced Labor Decreed (1:8–14)

**[8]Now a new king arose over Egypt, who did not know
Joseph. [9]He said to his people, "Behold, the people of the sons
of Israel are more and mightier than we. [10]Come, let us deal
wisely with them, or else they will multiply and in the event
of war, they will also join themselves to those who hate us, and
fight against us and depart from the land." [11]So they appointed
taskmasters over them to afflict them with hard labor. And they
built for Pharaoh storage cities, Pithom and Raamses. [12]But the
more they afflicted them, the more they multiplied and the
more they spread out, so that they were in dread of the sons of
Israel. [13]The Egyptians compelled the sons of Israel to labor
rigorously; [14]and they made their lives bitter with hard labor
in mortar and bricks and at all kinds of labor in the field, all
their labors which they rigorously imposed on them.**

Verse 8. The enthronement of **a new king . . . who did not know Joseph** probably means that, as time passed, there arose a king (or pharaoh) who did not remember or appreciate what Joseph had done for the Egyptians. He had, after all, saved the entire nation from the seven years of famine. Who was this king? Although the answer depends on the date of the exodus, two truths can be stated about him: (1) God did not think it necessary to reveal his name to the readers, and (2) he was alive at the time of the oppression but died before the deliverance (2:23).

Regarding the identity of this pharaoh, there are two main possibilities. If the late date for the exodus (c. 1290 B.C.) is accepted, then the pharaoh when Moses left Egypt was Seti I and the pharaoh of the exodus was Rameses II. If the early date (c. 1445 B.C.) is accepted, then the pharaoh at the time when

Moses fled from Egypt was Thutmose IV and the pharaoh during the exodus was Amenhotep II.[3]

Some have thought that this "new king" had something to do with the Hyksos, who ruled Egypt from about 1670 to 1550 B.C. One view is that Jacob's family had been welcomed there because the Hyksos, who were Semites, were ruling Egypt at the time. Then, when a non-Semite—an Egyptian "who did not know Joseph"—came to the throne, he was not favorably disposed towards the Israelites and so enslaved them. Others have argued that the pharaoh "who did not know Joseph" was a Hyksos ruler, and that the family of Jacob was welcomed by the native Egyptians but enslaved by the Hyksos.

Verse 9. When Pharaoh said that the Israelites were **more and mightier** than the Egyptians, he was undoubtedly speaking in hyperbole. Nevertheless, his fear was real. Why was he worried? Some scholars believe that Egypt's paranoia about Israel may have been the result of having previously been overrun by foreigners, perhaps the Hyksos. This had left the Egyptians with a legacy of fear; they were afraid of being conquered again by a foreign nation. If an enemy nation—especially a Semitic nation related to Jacob's descendants—attacked Egypt, then the Israelites living among them might join with that nation to defeat the Egyptians.

Verse 10. In response to such rapid growth, the king proposed to **deal wisely** (חָכַם, *chakam*) with the people of Israel by enslaving them. How could such an unrighteous act be done "wisely"? The Old Testament concept of "wisdom" involved the ability to accomplish some task successfully. While the wise man is often assumed to be a righteous man, wisdom can also be used for unrighteous purposes. For this reason, the Hebrew term can also be translated "shrewd" (2 Sam. 13:3). From the Egyptian standpoint, enslaving the Israelites was the wise thing to do because it accomplished their purposes.

Verse 11. What real-life incidents were behind the **hard labor** of the Israelites? Did the Egyptian army suddenly appear, bat-

---

[3]Gleason L. Archer, Jr., *A Survey of Old Testament Introduction*, rev. and exp. (Chicago: Moody Press, 1994), 244–46.

tering down doors and hauling the able-bodied men away to work camps? Were notices posted, requiring men to show up for work and prescribing punishment if they failed to do so? The text does not provide these details. It does, however, reveal that the Israelite slaves **built** [two] **storage cities, Pithom and Raamses.** Both of these cities were located in the eastern delta, although their exact sites are disputed. Those who favor a late date for the exodus often identify "Raamses" with the city that Rameses II built and named after himself. Others who support an early date point out that the name "Rameses" was used to identify the land where Jacob and his family settled (Gen. 47:11), an event which significantly predated the Rameside dynasty. Some authors identify "Pithom" with the biblical Succoth (12:37; 13:20; Num. 33:5, 6), while others distinguish the two cities.

Verse 12. The oppression had the opposite effect of what Pharaoh intended. The Israelites **multiplied and . . . spread out** instead of diminishing in number. Here is the first statement of a major theme of Exodus: God was with His people and would accomplish His will. Nothing that Pharaoh or the Egyptians could do would thwart His purposes.

Verses 13, 14. The rulers of Egypt redoubled their efforts to cripple Israel. The writer used several expressions to emphasize all that was done to hurt the Israelites. **The Egyptians compelled the sons of Israel to labor *rigorously*; and they made their lives *bitter* with *hard* labor . . . all their labors which they *rigorously* imposed on them** (emphasis added). However, "hard" and "bitter" service did not keep Israel from growing, and Pharaoh thought it necessary to take another step.

Death Decreed for Newborn Sons (1:15–22)

[15]Then the king of Egypt spoke to the Hebrew midwives, one of whom was named Shiphrah and the other was named Puah; [16]and he said, "When you are helping the Hebrew women to give birth and see them upon the birthstool, if it is a son, then you shall put him to death; but if it is a daughter, then she shall live." [17]But the midwives feared God, and did not do as the king of Egypt had commanded them, but let the boys live.

[18]So the king of Egypt called for the midwives and said to them, "Why have you done this thing, and let the boys live?" [19]The midwives said to Pharaoh, "Because the Hebrew women are not as the Egyptian women; for they are vigorous and give birth before the midwife can get to them." [20]So God was good to the midwives, and the people multiplied, and became very mighty. [21]Because the midwives feared God, He established households for them. [22]Then Pharaoh commanded all his people, saying, "Every son who is born you are to cast into the Nile, and every daughter you are to keep alive."

Verse 15. To this point, God's chosen people have been referred to as "the sons of Israel" (1:7, 9, 12, 13) or "the Israelites" (NRSV). Throughout the rest of the chapter, the term **Hebrew** is used to refer to the **midwives** and the women (1:15, 16, 19). ("Hebrews" is also found in verse 22 of the NRSV.) The name "Hebrew" literally means "one from the other side" and may reflect Abraham's migration from Ur, east of the Euphrates River (see Josh. 24:2, 3).[4] Other sources suggest that "Hebrew" is "an older and broader term than 'Israelite,'" that it "was often used when foreigners spoke to or about Abraham's people (Gen. 39:14, 17; 40:15)," and that the name "Hebrew" (עִבְרִי, *'ibri*) can be traced to the name "Eber" (עֵבֶר, *'eber*), the son of Shem, in Genesis 10:21.[5] Nahum M. Sarna, however, disagreed with this last thought, saying that the origin of the name "must remain a mystery."[6]

---

[4]Francis Brown, S. R. Driver, and Charles A. Briggs, *The Brown-Driver-Briggs Hebrew and English Lexicon* (Boston: Houghton, Mifflin and Co., 1906; reprint, Peabody, Mass.: Hendrickson Publishers, 1997), 720.

[5]Note on Exodus 1:15, Bruce M. Metzger and Roland E. Murphy, eds., *The New Oxford Annotated Bible with the Apocrypha*, rev. and enl. (New York: Oxford University Press, 1991), 70; Alfred Haldar, "Hebrew," in *The Interpreter's Dictionary of the Bible*, ed. George Arthur Buttrick (Nashville: Abingdon Press, 1962), 2:552. Anson F. Rainey wrote that the term "was clearly meant to be the designation of an ethnic or national group." (Anson F. Rainey, "Hebrews," in *Harper's Bible Dictionary*, ed. Paul J. Achtemeier [San Francisco: Harper & Row, 1985], 379.)

[6]Nahum M. Sarna, *Exploring Exodus: The Origins of Biblical Israel* (New York: Schocken Books, 1996), 54–55.

One curious aspect of this story is that only two midwives, **Shiphrah** and **Puah**, are named. Did a group of people numbering in the millions need only two midwives? The most common explanation is that these two women were in charge of the midwives of the Israelites.

Verse 16. In addition to enslavement, Pharaoh's next strategy was to require the Hebrew midwives to kill the Israelites' baby boys when they were born. **Upon the birthstool** (עַל־הָאָבְנָיִם, *'al ha'abnayim*) is literally "upon the stones," apparently signifying "the seat on which the woman about to give birth was customarily placed."[7] **Son**[s] were to be killed because they were "potential warriors and rebels," whereas the **daughter**[s] who were left could bear children for the Egyptians, increasing the Egyptian population.[8]

Verse 17. The midwives disobeyed Pharaoh because they **feared God**. Since these women are called "Hebrew midwives" and had Semitic names (1:15), they were probably Israelites; therefore, it is not surprising that they "feared God." This verse contains the first specific reference to "God" by name in Exodus, but God's providential hand certainly was behind all that had happened before. Because the people believed in God, Pharaoh lost again!

Verses 18, 19. When Pharaoh asked why they had not carried out his order, the midwives apparently lied by telling him that the **Hebrew women** delivered their babies **before the midwife** [could] **get to them**. Pharaoh apparently accepted the midwives' unlikely story, which adds a touch of ironic humor to the narrative. Pharaoh had intended to act "wisely" (1:10), but he was foolish enough to believe the midwives' shrewd response to his question. Terence E. Fretheim said, "Two lowly Hebrew women silence the king of Egypt, that paragon of wisdom, with a single remark! This is ironic, of course, for no king worth his

---

[7]Umberto Cassuto, *A Commentary on the Book of Exodus*, trans. Israel Abrahams (Jerusalem: Magnes Press, 1997), 14.

[8]Waldemar Janzen, *Exodus*, Believers Church Bible Commentary (Scottdale, Pa.: Herald Press, 2000), 38.

scepter would have considered the response satisfactory, let alone from midwives."[9]

Verses 20, 21. Consequently, Pharaoh's plan did not work. The Israelites **multiplied**, and God blessed the midwives in a special way: He **was good to the midwives** and **established households for them**. The NRSV says that God "gave them families," which may suggest that earlier they had been unable to have children.

This passage is about population increase. The Israelites had multiplied; the Egyptians had tried to keep them from increasing further, but Pharaoh's measures had not worked. When the midwives "promote[d] God's plan to make Israel a large people . . . they insure[d] large families for themselves."[10] A subtle suggestion of God's approval is found in the fact that they are named in the text. This lends them "dignity and importance,"[11] in contrast to Pharaoh, who remains unnamed. The plan of Pharaoh, king of Egypt, mighty monarch of the greatest nation of the ancient Near East, was thwarted by two insignificant midwives who were regarded as very significant by God.

What can be said about the midwives' lie? Possibly, this was not a lie at all; perhaps the Hebrew women did have their children before the midwives arrived to help them. Commentators point out that archaeological evidence suggests the Hebrew women were larger and hardier than the Egyptian women, but this does not prove that the midwives did not intend to deceive the king. Another possibility is that the midwives delayed their coming to help the women who were about to bear children until the children had in fact already been born. Yet, such a solution might have created more problems than it solved.

One might argue that God will excuse a lie in such a situation, that He takes into account the circumstances and the motives involved when one tells something less than the truth in such a time of crisis. However, it is enough to acknowledge that the

---

[9]Terence E. Fretheim, *Exodus*, Interpretation: A Bible Commentary for Teaching and Preaching (Louisville: John Knox Press, 1991), 34.

[10]Janzen, 39.

[11]Ibid.

midwives told a lie. The Bible does not pronounce its blessings upon that lie, but relates it as part of the narrative. From this viewpoint, we can say that God did not reward the midwives because they told a lie, but because they refused to kill the Israelite babies. There is no need to justify the lie (since the inspired writer did not justify it), nor does this lie set a precedent which allows Christians today to lie under certain circumstances.

Verse 22. The text in the NASB, following the Masoretic text[12] does not specify that the **son**[s] who were to be **cast into the Nile** were the sons of the Hebrews. However, some versions, following other witnesses to the Old Testament text,[13] specify that the boys were to be Hebrew children. The NRSV reads, "Every boy that is born to the Hebrews you shall throw into the Nile, but you shall let every girl live."

Pharaoh thus gave the fateful orders that would lead, on the one hand, to great mourning on the part of Israel and, on the other hand, to the development of the one man whom God would use to bring Israel out of captivity. The later death of the firstborn of the Egyptians (12:29, 30) may be seen as a just punishment for the crime Pharaoh had committed so many years earlier by having all those innocent Israelite babies killed. On a later occasion, another king had young children killed in order to prevent a rival king from growing to manhood (Mt. 2:16)!

APPLICATION

The Futility of Fighting Against God (Ch. 1)

James Weldon Johnson began a poem—a sermon in verse—on the prodigal son with these words: "Young man, young man,

---

[12]The term "Masoretic text" (MT) refers to "the received text of the Hebrew [Old Testament] as annotated for punctuation (with accents) and vocalization (with 'points') by the Masoretes (or Masorites), the authoritative teachers of scriptural tradition." (Richard N. Soulen and R. Kendall Soulen, *Handbook of Biblical Criticism*, 3d ed., rev. and exp. [Louisville: Westminster John Knox Press, 2001], 109.)

[13]As the basis for its reading, the NRSV cites the Samaritan Pentateuch, the Septuagint, and the Aramaic Targums (translations of the Hebrew Scriptures that reflect rabbinical interpretation).

your arm's too short to box with God."[14] Those lines stick in the memory because of their vivid imagery. Picture a boxer with short arms trying vainly to hit an opponent who has much longer arms. Imagine two men from the Middle Ages wearing armor and mounted on horses for a jousting contest. One has a lance twelve feet long, and the other's lance is only six feet long! Similarly, we might think of two athletic teams that are completely mismatched. For instance, in the 2003 rugby World Cup series, the Australian team defeated Namibia 142–0. The poet Johnson was saying that when we fight against God, our situation is like that. There is no way we can win.

The futility of fighting against God is well illustrated in Exodus. The story told in this book is basically a story of the one true God versus the many false gods of Egypt. We might also view it as the one true God versus Pharaoh, who was regarded as a god. Ultimately, of course, God won the battle. Israel was delivered, and Pharaoh himself acknowledged God's power.

The first chapter of Exodus gives us a preview of the story. Here, Pharaoh made a concerted effort to defeat God's people, and thus to defeat God, but he was beaten in every attempt.

(1) *Pharaoh enslaved them.* Why? Because he was afraid of them. What was the result? The people of Israel multiplied and spread out (1:12).

(2) *Pharaoh made their work more rigorous.* When he saw that his first effort did not accomplish his purpose, Pharaoh made the people work even harder (1:13, 14). Apparently, that did not work either, since Pharaoh took further steps.

(3) *Pharaoh told the Hebrew midwives to kill the baby boys* (1:15, 16). The midwives refused to obey Pharaoh because they "feared God" (1:17–21), and God honored these midwives. He "established households for them" (1:21) by giving them "families" (NRSV). In addition, He preserved their stories and their names for posterity. (Notice that these women are named in Exodus while Pharaoh remains nameless.) The mighty pharaoh's plan was thwarted by two lowly midwives!

---

[14]James Weldon Johnson, *God's Trombones* (New York: Viking Press, 1927; reprint, New York: Penguin Books, 1976), 21.

(4) *Pharaoh next commanded that the baby boys be thrown into the Nile* (1:22). In a sense, Pharaoh succeeded this time in that his orders were carried out. Later, however, the Egyptians would pay for these murders with the lives of their firstborn (4:23)! In another sense, the strategy backfired, for it allowed God to raise up the deliverer of Israel in Pharaoh's household, being nursed by his own Hebrew mother at Pharaoh's expense! God was working behind the scenes during all of this to bring about the fulfillment of His plan.

Fighting against God is futile. All the forces of evil in this world, though they seem to be winning now, will be defeated in the end! (That is the theme of the Book of Revelation.) Pharaoh's futile efforts to beat God proves that human beings cannot fight against God and win. We fight against Him when we act as if we can sin with impunity, as if we can sin against God and not get caught. We cannot "get away with" anything where God is concerned. He set a law of consequences in operation in His universe: "Whatever a man sows, this he will also reap" (Gal. 6:7). We *will* be called to account for our rebellion against the Creator of the Universe.

God's law of sowing and reaping is inexorable. However, He gave us something that supersedes that law. We can avoid reaping the ultimate consequences of our sin because Christ died for us. By repenting and coming to Christ in obedience, we can have our debt cancelled by the grace of God and the blood of Christ.

The Israelites' Captivity and God's Providence (1:1–14)

Why was Israel in Egypt? Joseph said that when his brothers sold him into Egypt, they intended evil but "God meant it for good in order to . . . preserve many people alive" (Gen. 50:20). God arranged providentially for Joseph and the rest of Jacob's family to be in Egypt during the years of famine. However, Joseph's answer is not the whole story. If God wanted to preserve His people alive, He could have prevented the famine. God wanted His people in Egypt. Why? (1) So that there they could multiply. (2) So that He could deliver them out of Egypt to help them understand His grace and power.

The Importance of Women (1:15–22)

Exodus indicates that women played important roles in the preservation and deliverance of God's people. Two midwives thwarted Pharaoh's plan to kill the Hebrew baby boys (1:15–22). Moses' mother put her son in an ark on the river to save his life. An Egyptian princess found the baby and decided to keep him. Moses' sister watched over the little boy until he was found (2:1–10). To this might be added the role of Jethro's daughters in providing a home for Moses in the wilderness (2:16–22) and Zipporah's circumcising her son which resulted in the saving of Moses' life (4:24–26). Perhaps God was trying to communicate to us the importance of women, especially in sustaining and preserving life.

Chapter 2

Moses' Early Life

Chapter 2 continues the narrative of chapter 1 concerning Israel's humiliation by the Egyptians. It narrows the story to one family and to a child born of that family. From this point to the end of Exodus, the book revolves around Moses. It is possible, in fact, to see the entire Pentateuch as the story of Moses, with Genesis and Exodus 1 serving as a preface to the story. Moses lived 120 years, and his life may be viewed as three forty-year periods (Acts 7:23; Ex. 7:7; Deut. 34:7). For the first forty years, he lived as royalty in Egypt (2:1–15). During the second period of his life, he was a shepherd in Midian (2:16—4:17). He spent the final period of his life as the leader of the Israelites (Ex. 4:18—Deut. 34:8).

Moses, a beautiful child, was born during the time when the male infants of Israel were condemned to die (2:1, 2; 1:22). His parents were both from the house of Levi. Moses' mother hid him as long as she could, then placed him in a basket among the reeds by the riverbank, where the daughter of Pharaoh found him (2:2–6). Moses' sister offered to obtain a nurse from among the Hebrew women for the child. When her offer was accepted, Moses' own mother became his nurse (2:7–9).

Moses was then reared in Pharaoh's household until he killed an Egyptian who was beating an Israelite slave. The day after killing and burying the Egyptian, when he attempted to separate two quarreling Israelites, Moses discovered that his crime was known. He fled from Egypt, barely escaping the pharaoh's wrath (2:10–15).

Upon leaving Egypt, Moses fled to Midian. There, he protected seven daughters of the priest of Midian. As a result, the priest gave his daughter Zipporah to Moses to be his wife, and they had a son, Gershom (2:16–22).

Meanwhile, back in Egypt, the pharaoh who had sought Moses' life died. The Hebrew people were groaning under their bondage, but God was making preparations to deliver them (2:23–25).

MOSES' BIRTH AND EARLY LIFE (2:1–10)

**1Now a man from the house of Levi went and married a
daughter of Levi. 2The woman conceived and bore a son; and
when she saw that he was beautiful, she hid him for three
months. 3But when she could hide him no longer, she got him
a wicker basket and covered it over with tar and pitch. Then
she put the child into it and set it among the reeds by the bank
of the Nile. 4His sister stood at a distance to find out what would
happen to him.**

**5The daughter of Pharaoh came down to bathe at the Nile,
with her maidens walking alongside the Nile; and she saw the
basket among the reeds and sent her maid, and she brought it
to her. 6When she opened it, she saw the child, and behold, the
boy was crying. And she had pity on him and said, "This is
one of the Hebrews' children." 7Then his sister said to Pha-
raoh's daughter, "Shall I go and call a nurse for you from the
Hebrew women that she may nurse the child for you?" 8Pha-
raoh's daughter said to her, "Go ahead." So the girl went and
called the child's mother. 9Then Pharaoh's daughter said to her,
"Take this child away and nurse him for me and I will give you
your wages." So the woman took the child and nursed him.
10The child grew, and she brought him to Pharaoh's daughter
and he became her son. And she named him Moses, and said,
"Because I drew him out of the water."**

Verses 1, 2. The text reveals several facts about Moses. First, he was descended from the tribe of **Levi**. His ancestry is traced through both parents, which emphasizes his lineage. Levi was later chosen by God to become the priestly tribe of Israel.

Second, as an infant, Moses was **beautiful** (טוֹב, *tob*). The Hebrew word has many nuances of meaning, including "pleasant," "agreeable," and "good."[1] The NRSV says that he was "a fine baby."

Third, Moses was born during Israel's time of trouble. Pharaoh had ordered the Egyptians to destroy all of the baby boys born to the Hebrews (1:22). To save her baby, Moses' mother (so far unnamed[2]) **hid him for three months**.

Verses 3, 4. When Moses was too old to be kept hidden, his mother put him in **a wicker basket**. She set the basket afloat near the shore on **the Nile**. This action is filled with irony: Pharaoh had commanded the Egyptians to throw the Hebrew infants into the river to destroy them (1:22), whereas Moses' mother placed him in the river to save him. She then instructed **his sister** (also unnamed so far[3]) to see **what would happen to him**. The writer of Hebrews gave Moses' parents credit for exercising faith in these actions (Heb. 11:23).

The KJV refers to the "wicker basket" as "an ark of bulrushes," while the NRSV calls it "a papyrus basket." The word translated "basket" or "ark" is תֵּבָה (*thebah*), the same word used for Noah's ark in Genesis 6—9. In fact, the word is found only in these two passages in the Hebrew Bible. The author apparently intended for the reader to remember that other life-saving boat when he read of the little boat that saved the baby Moses. Both of these "arks" were coated with **pitch** in order to make them waterproof (see Gen. 6:14).

Verse 5. Moses, in his little ark, was put into the water **among the reeds** (סוּף, *sup*) and was found by **the daughter of Pharaoh**. Who this Egyptian princess was, the text does not say. No doubt, Pharaoh had many wives and many children. While the Bible makes it clear that Moses was brought up at court with the privileges of royalty, it does not suggest either that Moses was found

---

[1]See Francis Brown, S. R. Driver, and Charles A. Briggs, *The Brown-Driver-Briggs Hebrew and English Lexicon* (Boston: Houghton, Mifflin and Co., 1906; reprint, Peabody, Mass.: Hendrickson Publishers, 1997), 373–75.

[2]Moses' parents, Amram and Jochebed, are identified in Exodus 6:20.

[3]Moses' sister, Miriam, is first named in Exodus 15:20 as a prophetess and the sister of Aaron.

by Hatshepsut, who was later queen of Egypt, or that Moses was destined to become the next king of Egypt.

Was Moses' mother wise in her placement of the baby? Did she know that this was a place where Pharaoh's daughter came to bathe? At least, it is possible that Moses' mother knew where the princess bathed. She may have placed the child where she did in the hope that the princess would have compassion on her son.

Verses 6–9. Whether or not Moses' mother foresaw the outcome, the child's **crying** produced **pity** in the heart of the king's daughter. The result was that this daughter of Pharaoh raised the boy as her own. It is remarkable that, because of the sister's suggestion, Moses' **mother** was able to **nurse him**, feeding him at her own breast. More than this, she was paid to do it! She was apparently allowed to take care of him in her own home for several years. Children were not weaned as early then as they are now, a fact demonstrated by the story of Hannah and her son Samuel (1 Sam. 1:20–28; 2:11).

Verse 10. After being weaned, Moses was raised as the **son** of **Pharaoh's daughter**. Given his association with his own mother, Moses almost certainly grew up knowing that he was an Israelite by birth and believing in the one true God of heaven and earth. The irony is heavy in this narrative: Not only did Pharaoh fail to keep Israel from multiplying, but, because of his attempts to cripple Israel, the person who would eventually lead Israel to freedom was raised in his own household. As an infant, the deliverer was even nursed by his own Hebrew mother at Pharaoh's expense.

The name **Moses** was given to the boy by his Egyptian mother. In Hebrew, this name means "drawn out of the water." However, the word "Moses" is an Egyptian word, found in such names as "Rameses" and "Thutmose." This provides additional evidence for the Egyptian background of the exodus. According to Nahum M. Sarna, the name "Moses" in Egyptian means "to be born" or "to be a son"; but its Hebrew form, מֹשֶׁה (*Mosheh*), was interpreted in terms of the verb מָשָׁה (*mashah*), meaning "to draw out (from the water)." The name perhaps suggests not only how Moses was saved but also how God used Moses to save

Israel through the Red Sea, drawing them out of the water to safety.[4]

Many commentators assume that the Hebrew meaning of the word was added by the writer, based on the similarity of the word for "drawn out" with the sound of the Egyptian word "Moses." The problem with this view is that it appears to discount the text, which says that the daughter of Pharaoh said she named him Moses **because** [she] **drew him out of the water**. If one accepts exactly what the text says, the best solution of how an Egyptian could give Moses a name based on a Hebrew wordplay is to assume that the princess spoke Hebrew as well as Egyptian and gave him a name which was significant in both languages. R. Alan Cole said, "An Egyptian mistress might well understand and use the tongue of her domestic servants to give orders."[5]

Stories from other nations in the ancient Near East are similar in some respects to the story of Moses' being put in the basket and found by a princess. For instance, a legend concerning Sargon, a king of Akkad who lived in the third millennium B.C., claimed that he was put in a basket of rushes, left in the Euphrates, and later found and adopted by a "drawer of water" before eventually becoming a king.[6]

However, Sarna pointed out great differences between that story (and similar ones from other cultures) and the story of Moses. For example, "Sargon [was] exposed to the river because he [was] the unwanted child of an illicit relationship"; in contrast, Moses was put in the river by a loving mother only when she was forced to do so, and even then his mother continued to show her love by having his sister watch over him. Sargon was found by a commoner, but Moses was found by a princess. In addition, in the case of Sargon, the hero of the legend learned his true royal identity only later in life; but Moses, because he

---

[4]Nahum M. Sarna, *Exploring Exodus: The Origins of Biblical Israel* (New York: Schocken Books, 1996), 32–33.

[5]R. Alan Cole, *Exodus: An Introduction and Commentary*, Tyndale Old Testament Commentaries (Downers Grove, Ill.: Inter-Varsity Press, 1973), 59.

[6]Sarna, 29–30.

was nursed by his own mother, knew who he was from his early childhood (and had no royal blood to discover). In other words, as Sarna said, "The supposed close affinities between this folkloristic composition and our Exodus narrative are fanciful."[7] To claim that such tales prove the story of Moses to be a mere legend rather than historical fact is invalid.

MOSES' ATTEMPTS AT DELIVERANCE (2:11–15)

Exodus 2:11–22 tells the story of the beginning of the next forty years of Moses' life. This phase of his life was initiated by two events: First, he killed an Egyptian and had to flee from Egypt, losing his home there (2:11–15). Second, he defended the daughters of Reuel and consequently gained a wife and a home (2:16–22).

11Now it came about in those days, when Moses had grown up, that he went out to his brethren and looked on their hard labors; and he saw an Egyptian beating a Hebrew, one of his brethren. 12So he looked this way and that, and when he saw there was no one around, he struck down the Egyptian and hid him in the sand. 13He went out the next day, and behold, two Hebrews were fighting with each other; and he said to the offender, "Why are you striking your companion?" 14But he said, "Who made you a prince or a judge over us? Are you intending to kill me as you killed the Egyptian?" Then Moses was afraid and said, "Surely the matter has become known." 15When Pharaoh heard of this matter, he tried to kill Moses. But Moses fled from the presence of Pharaoh and settled in the land of Midian, and he sat down by a well.

Verses 11, 12. The text implies that **Moses** felt called, out of compassion, to deliver his people from oppression. That is why he killed **an Egyptian** who was mistreating **a Hebrew**. Then he **hid** [the body] **in the sand**. Though Moses may have been angry,

---

[7]Ibid., 30.

he was not out of his mind. His was a premeditated act: **He looked this way and that.** The text does not defend his actions; therefore, readers are under no obligation to conclude that Moses did right. Neither should we assume that the passage provides a precedent for engaging in murder to right a wrong.[8]

Verses 13–15. The next day Moses tried to stop a fight between **two Hebrews**, saying to the one who was mistreating the other, **"Why are you striking your companion?"** The **offender** responded, **"Who made you a prince or a judge over us? Are you intending to kill me as you killed the Egyptian?"** These questions, most likely spoken in sarcasm, demonstrate the man's rejection of Moses' authority. Nevertheless, according to God's own timing, Moses later became the leader of all the people of Israel.

When **Moses** realized that others knew he had killed an Egyptian, he **was afraid**. He had reason to be, since **Pharaoh**, when he learned about Moses' deed, **tried to kill Moses**. "Egyptians maintained a substantial sense of ethnic pride that caused them to consider foreigners inferior. For a foreigner to kill an Egyptian was a great crime."[9]

Stephen elaborated on this event (Acts 7:23–29), as did the writer of Hebrews (Heb. 11:24–27). These New Testament writers added the following information in their interpretations of the occurrence: (1) Moses was about forty years old at the time (Acts 7:23). (2) "Moses was educated in all the learning of the Egyptians, and he was a man of power in words and deeds" (Acts 7:22), and had access to "the treasures of Egypt" (Heb. 11:26). (3) Moses consciously chose to cast his lot with Israel rather than continuing to enjoy the life of an Egyptian prince (Heb. 11:24–26). (4) Moses specifically saw himself as Israel's

---

[8]In the narratives throughout the Old Testament, usually the aim of the writer was to tell the story to achieve some purpose, not to moralize over the actions of the participants in the story, even if they were among the "heroes of faith." Therefore, readers should not assume that if some otherwise godly person did something that seemed to be bad, it must really have been good.

[9]John H. Walton and Victor H. Matthews, *Genesis—Deuteronomy,* The IVP Bible Background Commentary (Downers Grove, Ill.: InterVarsity Press, 1997), 87.

deliverer. This is hinted in Exodus 2:11, but it is specifically stated in Acts 7:23–25. (5) According to Hebrews 11:27, Moses was not afraid of the Egyptian king's wrath.

The mention of Moses' lack of fear creates a problem. Although Hebrews says that Moses by faith "left Egypt, not fearing the wrath of the king" (Heb. 11:27), Exodus 2:14 says that after Moses learned that others knew he had killed the Egyptian, he "was afraid" **and said, "Surely the matter has become known."**

How could one inspired writer say that Moses was afraid and another writer say that he was unafraid? It should be emphasized that the author of Hebrews was well acquainted with the Old Testament and had no intention of contradicting Exodus. While Exodus 2:14 says that Moses was afraid, the text does not say that Moses left Egypt because of his fear. Presumably, Moses could have dealt with Pharaoh's wrath in other ways. Further, Hebrews does not deny that Moses was afraid but says that it was faith, rather than fear, that caused him to abandon Egypt.[10]

Moses fled to **the land of Midian**. The people there, the Midianites, were descendants of Abraham, through his wife Keturah (Gen. 25:2). The land of Midian at that time included part of the Sinai Peninsula (see comments on 3:1). In this area—the same land into which he was eventually to lead the Israelites—Moses would spend the next forty years of his life.

MOSES' LIFE IN MIDIAN (2:16–22)

16Now the priest of Midian had seven daughters; and they came to draw water and filled the troughs to water their father's flock. 17Then the shepherds came and drove them away, but Moses stood up and helped them and watered their flock. 18When they came to Reuel their father, he said, "Why have you come back so soon today?" 19So they said, "An Egyptian

[10]F. F. Bruce, *The Epistle to the Hebrews*, The New International Commentary on the New Testament (Grand Rapids, Mich.: Wm. B. Eerdmans Publishing Co., 1964), 321–22.

delivered us from the hand of the shepherds, and what is more, he even drew the water for us and watered the flock." [20]He said to his daughters, "Where is he then? Why is it that you have left the man behind? Invite him to have something to eat." [21]Moses was willing to dwell with the man, and he gave his daughter Zipporah to Moses. [22]Then she gave birth to a son, and he named him Gershom, for he said, "I have been a sojourner in a foreign land."

Verses 16, 17. In Midian Moses "sat down by a well" (2:15) and there defended **seven daughters** of **the priest of Midian** from some **shepherds** who prevented them from watering their sheep. Moses apparently was a man with a passion for the oppressed; this is the third time in this chapter that he helped one who was being victimized. First, he killed an Egyptian who was beating an Israelite, and then he sought to save an Israelite who was being mistreated by a fellow Israelite. Perhaps his compassion for the oppressed was one of the characteristics that made him the ideal deliverer.

Verse 18. The girls' father is referred to as "the priest of Midian" in verse 16, but is here identified by the name **Reuel**. The priest of Midian is usually called either "Jethro" (3:1; 4:18; 18:1) or "Hobab" (Num. 10:29). The Hebrew text in Numbers 10:29 is ambiguous, making it possible to identify either Reuel or Hobab as Moses' father-in-law. However, Judges 4:11 identifies Hobab as Moses' father-in-law, and Reuel was most likely Hobab's father.[11] Other interpretations of these passages are possible; usually Jethro and Reuel are thought to be alternative names for Moses' father-in-law.

Verse 19. After Reuel's surprise at his daughters' early return (2:18), they replied that **an Egyptian** had helped them. The portrait of Moses that emerges from this chapter is that of an Israelite who had been thoroughly Egyptianized—at least in appearance and speech. Still, he was concerned for the oppressed and

[11]Note on Exodus 2:18, Bruce M. Metzger and Roland E. Murphy, eds., *The New Oxford Annotated Bible with the Apocrypha*, rev. and enl. (New York: Oxford University Press, 1991), 71.

was willing to take action to deliver them. He was physically strong; otherwise, he would not have been able to kill the Egyptian or drive off **the shepherds**. He was also able to adapt to living in a foreign land.

Verse 20. In all of the excitement, Reuel's daughters had forgotten to extend hospitality to their rescuer. As a result, their father chided them with repetitive questions: **"Where is he then? Why is it that you have left the man behind?"** Reuel then concluded with a direct command: **"Invite him to have something to eat."**

Verses 21, 22. The result of Moses' good deed was that he was invited to the home of the girls' father, who gave him **his daughter Zipporah** in marriage. They had a **son**, whom they named **Gershom** (גֵּרְשׁוֹם, *Gershom*). This name is related to the Hebrew word *ger* (גֵּר), which means "alien" or "stranger," emphasizing that Moses saw himself as a "stranger in a strange land" (2:22; KJV) during his years in Midian.[12]

Brevard S. Childs pointed out interesting similarities and differences between Moses' attempts at delivering Israel in Egypt (2:11–15) and his rescue of Reuel's daughters in Midian (2:16–22). Both stories emphasize Moses' "active concern to the weak which transcends the narrow bounds of nation and people," and both emphasize Moses' being forced to "live apart from his people whom he [had] not succeeded in delivering." However, the accounts are different in three ways. (1) In the first story, Moses' enemy was an Egyptian who oppressed Moses' people; in the second, Moses himself was mistaken for an Egyptian who oppressed people. (2) In the first, the strife was between an Egyptian and a Hebrew; the second involved strife between non-Israelites. (3) In the first, Moses fled from his home; in the second, he found a home.[13]

---

[12]John I. Durham, in contrast to most commentators, asserted that Moses was referring to Egypt as the land in which he had been a stranger. (John I. Durham, *Exodus*, Word Biblical Commentary, vol. 3 [Waco, Tex.: Word Books, 1987], 23–24.)

[13]Brevard S. Childs, *The Book of Exodus: A Critical, Theological Commentary*, The Old Testament Library (Louisville: Westminster Press, 1974), 32.

THE ISRAELITES' CRY TO GOD (2:23–25)

[23]Now it came about in the course of those many days that the king of Egypt died. And the sons of Israel sighed because of the bondage, and they cried out; and their cry for help because of their bondage rose up to God. [24]So God heard their groaning; and God remembered His covenant with Abraham, Isaac, and Jacob. [25]God saw the sons of Israel, and God took notice of them.

Verses 23–25. The scene at the end of chapter 2 shifts back to **Egypt**. **The king** who had sought Moses' life had **died**, but that did not make life easier for the Israelites. In their slavery, they **cried out** to **God** for relief. **God heard their groaning** and **remembered His covenant** with the patriarchs. At last, the time had come for God to act on behalf of His people, the descendants of **Abraham**.

Cole wrote, "To say that God 'remembers' is to assert that He repeats His acts of saving grace towards His people Israel again and again, and in this way fulfils His promises, and shows His own self-consistency."[14] To understand what it means when God "remembers" Israel, we should note that God could also "forget" Israel, as in the following passages:

> Why do You forget us forever?
> Why do You forsake us so long? (Lam. 5:20).

> Since you have forgotten the law of your God,
> I also will forget your children (Hos. 4:6).

To "forget," then, is to "forsake." To "remember" is to act in such a way as to bless the one remembered. Truly, **God saw the sons of Israel, and God took notice of them**.

---

[14]Cole, 24.

APPLICATION

Moses and Christ (Ch. 2)

The lives of Moses and Jesus Christ have striking similarities. The Bible invites us to compare the two, especially in view of the fact that Moses said, "God will raise up for you a prophet like me" (Deut. 18:15), a passage fulfilled by the coming of Jesus (Acts 3:22; see Jn. 1:21, 25; 6:14; 7:40). In what ways were they alike? How were they different? What can we learn from these comparisons?

Both Moses and Christ were born at times of persecution. When we read about the decree of Pharaoh to kill all the male babies in Egypt, our minds leap ahead to another occasion—the time when Herod issued the order that all boys two years of age and under be put to death (Mt. 2:16). In both situations, God's messenger—with God's help—escaped death. When Moses was born, the Egyptian ruler was attempting to kill all the Hebrews' baby boys. Not long after Jesus was born, the Judean ruler Herod attempted to kill all the male infants of Israel. Both Moses and Jesus escaped death, with God's help.

Both Moses and Christ lived exemplary lives. Both are spoken of as "humble" (Num. 12:3; Mt. 11:28–30). Both loved their people, gave up personal glory for them, and interceded on their behalf (see Ex. 32:11–14; Mt. 23:37–39; Jn. 17).

Of course, there are differences. While Moses lived an admirable life (Heb. 11:23–29), he was guilty of sin (Ex. 2:11–15; Num. 20:1–13). Jesus, in contrast, lived a sinless life (Heb. 4:15). Moses offered to bear the guilt of the people—an offer God refused (Ex. 32:32). Yet, Jesus could and did bear the people's sins. He did this not for the Jews only, but for all people (Mt. 26:28; 2 Cor. 5:21).

Both Moses and Christ were God's spokesmen. Through Moses came the Law (Jn. 1:17); but when Christ came, He became God's spokesman (Heb. 1:1, 2; Jn. 3:34; 7:16–18). In one sense, Christ is the giver of a new law (Gal. 6:2), even though He did not institute a "legalistic" system. The two laws were given in different ways: One came through Moses, from a blazing mountain (Heb. 12:18–24); the other was given as Christ taught quietly from the top of another mountain (Mt. 5—7). Today, we are to hear Christ rather than Moses (Mt. 17:5; Jn. 1:17; Heb. 1:1, 2).

Both Moses and Christ performed miracles. As God's spokesman and deliverer, Moses needed the ability to perform signs so that both the Israelites and the Egyptians would know that he was God's messenger. Similarly, Jesus performed miracles to confirm that He was a teacher and prophet from God (Acts 2:22; Jn. 3:1, 2; 20:30, 31). The difference between the two is that Moses died and stayed dead. Jesus was raised from the dead after three days.

Both Moses and Christ delivered God's people. Moses came as the great deliverer, the messenger God used to deliver God's people out of slavery. Christ also came as a deliverer, to free mankind from the slavery of sin (Lk. 19:10; Jn. 8:32). Moses accomplished his task (in part) by sacrificing unblemished lambs (Ex. 12); Christ accomplished His work by sacrificing Himself (Jn. 10:15–18).

Both Moses and Christ received a heavenly reward for faithful service. We cannot doubt Moses' eternal salvation, since he appeared with Jesus at the transfiguration. In a similar way, Jesus, after His death and resurrection, was glorified (Acts 2:36; Phil. 2:9–11). Of course, a further difference between Christ and Moses is that God never promised that anyone could share Moses' eternal salvation by following him, but Jesus is able and willing to share His glory with those who follow Him (Rev. 3:21).[15]

Conclusion. Just as many followed Moses and were loyal to the Law, we should be determined to follow—to be loyal to—our Lord Jesus Christ and the revelation which came through Him! If we fail to do so, we are in greater danger than those who failed to heed Moses' words (Heb. 2:1–4).

---

[15]There are other ways in which Moses and Christ can be compared and contrasted. In the introduction to his commentary, James Burton Coffman listed twenty similarities between Christ and Moses. Under the heading "Moses the Type of Christ," he noted these parallels in their births: "Both Jesus and Moses were the sons of virgin princesses, Jesus by miraculous birth, Moses by adoption. Both forsook great joys to be identified with the poor. Jesus forsook heaven; Moses left Pharaoh's palace. Both were rejected, Jesus by his own nation, Moses by his brethren." (James Burton Coffman, *Commentary on Exodus, The Second Book of Moses* [Abilene, Tex.: ACU Press, 1985], xx–xxi, 23–24.)

God's Providence in Israel's Deliverance (Ch. 2)

Because of God's providence, the Israelites were in Egypt. God's providential care is evident in the failure of Pharaoh's attempts to thwart Israel's growth and in Moses' being raised in Pharaoh's house and then spending forty years in the deserts of Midian. Two truths should be noticed, however, about God's providence. (1) While God does not cause evil (sin), He can bring good even out of man's sinful acts (Rom. 8:28). Killing the Israelite babies was sinful, but God brought good out of that sin. (2) People play a role in God's providence. Think about the way Moses' mother placed her baby so that he was saved. This surely was an instance in which God providentially used human wisdom to accomplish His work. When our wisest, most skillful efforts meet the opportunities God provides, God's providence works through us.

Moses' Mother—An Example Of Selfless Motherhood (2:1–10)

Moses' mother loved her baby and, with God's help, successfully saved his life and became his nurse. Like Samuel's mother, when she had finished nursing him, she was willing to give him up for God's purpose. Moses' mother also took him to Pharaoh's daughter for his good and for the ultimate good of Israel. Mothers need to realize that their task is to look after their children while they are young but then to give them up when they are older, allowing them to grow up and serve the Lord on their own.

Moses' Decision (2:11–22)

Exodus 2 provides excellent details for a sermon on Moses' decision to give up the pleasures and glories of Egypt so that he could serve God. The main ideas for this sermon can be taken from Hebrews 11:24–27.

Man's Talents and God's Call (2:11–22)

Exodus 2 presents Moses as a man concerned for justice, determined to deliver the oppressed. God recognized his talents and concerns and so called him to be the deliverer of His people.

Here is another way to look at the situation: God gave Moses talents to use as the deliverer, and Moses manifested those talents early in his life. Each person should ask himself or herself, "What talents has God given me? Considering my talents, what has God called me to do?"

CHAPTER 3

MOSES' CALL BY GOD (PART 1)

Chapters 3 and 4 contain Moses's call by God. Moses was serving his father-in-law, Jethro, as a shepherd in the land of Midian. At Mount Horeb, God appeared to Moses in a burning bush. Because of His great compassion for His people, He called on Moses to deliver the Israelites from Egypt (3:1–10).

First, Moses asked, "Who am I?" suggesting that he was unable to do the job. God responded by saying that He would be with Moses (3:11, 12). Second, Moses asked by what name he should identify God when he went to the people. God responded by saying that His name was "I AM," adding that He was the same God whom their forefathers had worshiped (3:13–15). God then again called Moses to the task of delivering the people, predicting what would happen when he did: Pharaoh would refuse to hear, but would finally be persuaded by God's miracles, and eventually the Israelites would leave Egypt, taking with them gifts from the Egyptians (3:16–22).

MOSES' ENCOUNTER WITH GOD (3:1–6)

[1]Now Moses was pasturing the flock of Jethro his father-in-law, the priest of Midian; and he led the flock to the west side of the wilderness and came to Horeb, the mountain of God. [2]The angel of the LORD appeared to him in a blazing fire from the midst of a bush; and he looked, and behold, the bush was burning with fire, yet the bush was not consumed. [3]So Moses said, "I must turn aside now and see this marvelous sight, why the bush is not burned up." [4]When the LORD saw

that he turned aside to look, God called to him from the midst of the bush and said, "Moses, Moses!" And he said, "Here I am." [5]Then He said, "Do not come near here; remove your sandals from your feet, for the place on which you are standing is holy ground." [6]He said also, "I am the God of your father, the God of Abraham, the God of Isaac, and the God of Jacob." Then Moses hid his face, for he was afraid to look at God.

Verse 1. Chapter 3 begins by describing the situation of **Moses** in Midian. He served **his father-in-law** as a shepherd. His father-in-law is here called **Jethro . . . the priest of Midian**; Jethro may also have been referred to as "Reuel" (2:18). Moses had left his own people and family in Egypt; he had become a part of Jethro's family. Jethro may have been more like a father to him than a father-in-law.

Jethro, or Reuel, was "the priest of Midian." In what sense and of what religion was he a priest? While the text does not say, one possibility is that he was a worshiper of the Lord. This may be further evidence, along with the account of Melchizedek (Gen. 14:18, 19), that people outside Israel believed in and worshiped the one true God.[1] The Midianites were descendants of Abraham; among them might have been found people who shared Abraham's faith.

Since Jethro is identified as a priest, some believe that Moses learned about God from this source and that the worship of the God who was known as "Yahweh" originated with the Midianites. However, Moses had the opportunity to develop his faith among his own people in Egypt. To assign to the Israelites in Egypt some other religion or faith in some other god, one would have to deny the accuracy of the biblical account. Further, since the Midianites were descendants of Abraham (Gen. 25:1–6), they could have been worshipers of the one true God, with some kind of priesthood—although the priesthood would not necessarily

[1]Some might add Balaam (Num. 22—24) to the list of non-Israelite religious leaders in ancient times who were believers in the one true God. However, it is more likely that Balaam was a diviner who would speak in the name of any god from whom a customer might seek an answer.

have been authorized by God. The religions of Israel and Midian could very well have originated from a common source: Abraham's faith.

Moses had **led the flock . . . to Horeb, the mountain of God**. Apparently, this mountain was called both Horeb and Sinai.[2] God's providence is evident in that He led Israel to the very place where Moses had been tending sheep. Horeb is here called "the mountain of God," in view of what was about to take place. The Lord would appear to Moses on this mountain, and later He would give the Law on the same mountain. The use of the term at this point in the narrative with a view to events yet to happen is proleptic.[3]

Verses 2, 3. The story continues with what is technically known as a "theophany," an appearance of God. God **appeared** to **Moses** in a **bush** that burned but **was not consumed** by the **fire**. God's appearance came to constitute a part of the calling of Old Testament prophets (Is. 6; Jer. 1; Ezek. 1). Moses' call has much in common with other narratives, such as, the call of Gideon (Judg. 6:11–24) and the call of Jeremiah (Jer. 1:4–9). It became, in effect, a pattern for the calling of later prophets.[4]

The angel of the Lord who appeared to Moses has occasioned considerable comment. He is mentioned a number of times in the Old Testament. Here he is God Himself; according to verse 6 this angel said, "I am the God of your father, the God of Abraham. . . ." One source notes that in this passage "the angel of the Lord is not a heavenly being subordinate to God but the Lord (Yahweh) in earthly manifestation."[5]

---

[2]Note on Exodus 3:1, Bruce M. Metzger and Roland E. Murphy, eds., *The New Oxford Annotated Bible with the Apocrypha*, rev. and enl. (New York: Oxford University Press, 1991), 72; Nahum M. Sarna, *Exploring Exodus: The Origins of Biblical Israel* (New York: Schocken Books, 1996), 38.

[3]Ibid., 38–39. A "prolepsis" is a "figure of speech by which what is to follow is taken as already effective." (*The New Lexicon Webster's Encyclopedic Dictionary of the English Language*, deluxe ed. [Danbury, Conn.: Lexicon Publishers, 1992], 800.)

[4]Terence E. Fretheim, *Exodus*, Interpretation: A Bible Commentary for Teaching and Preaching (Louisville: John Knox Press, 1991), 51.

[5]Note on Genesis 16:7, Metzger and Murphy, 20. Compare Gen. 16:13; 21:17, 19; Ex. 14:19.

The burning bush is the first of the miracles connected with the exodus. Miracles are not common in Old Testament history. They are "bunched together" at certain points in Israel's history: at the exodus and conquest of Canaan, for example, and during the prophetic ministries of Elijah and Elisha. Miracles occurred at times of crisis for Israel—at times when the nation's existence was threatened. The centerpiece of this miracle, the fire that burned in the bush but did not consume it, was probably a symbol of God or a manifestation of His presence, for God's presence is often represented by fire.[6]

Verse 4. From the burning bush, **God called . . . and said, "Moses, Moses!"** Calling Moses' name twice rather than once probably indicated the significance of the moment and the importance of the summons. Moses answered, **"Here I am,"** demonstrating his willingness to hear what God had to say. Moses' affirmative response does him credit. It is similar to an earlier reply to God's call by Abraham (Gen. 22:1) and to later replies to His call, such as those by Samuel (1 Sam. 3:4–8) and Isaiah (Is. 6:8).

Verse 5. God went on to say that the place was **holy ground**. It was not "holy ground" because of some prior consecration to the Lord; it was holy because it was where the Lord appeared. In a sense, God transferred holiness to the ground—holiness that no longer adhered to the place after He was through with it. The Lord's command to Moses to **remove** [his] **sandals** emphasized the holiness of the area. Removing one's sandals before entering a holy place was an ancient custom (see Josh. 5:15).[7]

Verse 6. God identified Himself to Moses by saying that He was the same God who was worshiped by the patriarchs, **Abraham**, **Isaac**, and **Jacob**. This emphasizes that the Exodus account is a continuation of the narrative found in Genesis.

As God introduced Himself, He said, **"I am,"** which is the usual way He began His conversations with His people. For example, He said, "I am the LORD who brought you out of Ur of the Chaldeans" (Gen. 15:7); "I am God Almighty [אֵל שַׁדַּי, *'El Shadday*]" (Gen. 35:11); "I am the God of your father Abraham"

[6]Sarna, 41.

[7]Note on Exodus 3:5, Metzger and Murphy, 72.

(Gen. 26:24); "I am the LORD, the God of your father Abraham and the God of Isaac" (Gen. 28:13). In the Old Testament, God frequently referred to Himself as the "God of your fathers" or "the God of Abraham [and / or Isaac and / or Jacob]," but He never said to Abraham that He was the God of Abraham's fathers. Nahum M. Sarna therefore noted that there was a distinct break between Abraham and those who came before him.[8]

Moses reacted to God's appearance by **hid**[ing] **his face, for he was afraid to look at God**. Sarna explained, "The overwhelming, awesome intensity of the experience of the encounter with the Divine Presence typically, in the Bible, evokes trauma and dread."[9] The Scriptures give several examples of the danger involved in looking on the face of God (see Gen. 32:25, 31; Ex. 33:20; Judg. 6:22, 23; 13:22). Besides the danger associated with being in the presence of the One who is altogether holy and powerful, the person who comes into God's presence cannot help but feel his or her own insignificance and unworthiness. Therefore, the usual and correct response to the Lord's presence is an attitude of humility and penitence. This disposition was exemplified by Isaiah in his encounter with God (Is. 6:5).

GOD'S INTENTIONS (3:7–9)

7The LORD said, "I have surely seen the affliction of My people who are in Egypt, and have given heed to their cry because of their taskmasters, for I am aware of their sufferings. 8So I have come down to deliver them from the power of the Egyptians, and to bring them up from that land to a good and spacious land, to a land flowing with milk and honey, to the place of the Canaanite and the Hittite and the Amorite and the Perizzite and the Hivite and the Jebusite. 9Now, behold, the cry of the sons of Israel has come to Me; furthermore, I have seen the oppression with which the Egyptians are oppressing them."

Verses 7, 8a. God set forth His intentions as He commissioned

---

[8]Sarna, 44.
[9]Ibid., 45.

Moses to be His agent in bringing Israel out of **Egypt**. Two considerations evidently motivated God as He began executing His plan to deliver His people. One was His compassion for His suffering people. He said, **"I have surely seen the affliction of My people."** The other consideration was His longstanding plan to deliver the people out of Egypt and bring them to the land of Canaan (Gen. 15:13–16; 46:1–4; 48:21; 50:24, 25). Consequently, God intended to **deliver** [Israel] **from the power of the Egyptians** and **bring them . . . to a land flowing with milk and honey**.

The expression "land flowing with milk and honey" was used to suggest the richness of the land; these were "foods that made it a paradise in the eyes of semi-nomads."[10] Sarna said that this expression is found about twenty times and suggests the fertility of the land; it is, he asserted, a "metaphor of fertility."[11] He expressed the view that "honey" (דְּבַשׁ, *d^e^bash*) does not refer to "bees' honey" but to "the sweet syrup produced from the juice of the grape and especially the date."[12] Other commentators say that the "honey" is in fact the honey of bees.[13] In several contexts *d^e^bash* can only refer to bees' honey (Judg. 14:8; 1 Sam. 14:27; Ps. 19:10; Prov. 16:24; Song 4:11; 5:1).

Verse 8b. The land is also spoken of as the home of six peoples: **the Canaanite, Hittite, Amorite, Perizzite, Hivite,** and **Jebusite.** The good news for Israel was that Canaan was a fruitful land; the bad news was that the land was fully inhabited, which implied that Israel would have to deal with those nations in some way when God brought them into Canaan. Sarna commented on the extreme "ethnic complexity" in Canaan, evidenced not only by the number of nations mentioned in Exodus, but also by the fact that Joshua conquered thirty-one royal city-states (Josh. 12). This complexity was due, in part, to Palestine's geographical features. The inclusion of the list of nations in the

---

[10]Note on Exodus 3:8, Metzger and Murphy, 72.

[11]Sarna, 46–47.

[12]Ibid, 47.

[13]R. Alan Cole, *Exodus: An Introduction and Commentary,* Tyndale Old Testament Commentaries (Downers Grove, Ill.: Inter-Varsity Press, 1973), 66–67.

account of God's appearance to Moses "means that the people of Israel [were] destined to defy and to overcome all these powerful disintegrative forces that . . . made the land a home to so many diverse ethnic groups."[14]

The names for Canaan's inhabitants are found in the same order in 3:17 and Judges 3:5. These same names appear, although in a different order, in 23:23, 33:2, 34:11, and Joshua 12:8. According to Numbers 13:29, the Amalekites lived in the land of the Negev, which was in the south; the Hittites, Jebusites, and Amorites lived in the hill country; and the Canaanites lived by the sea and along the Jordan. R. Alan Cole noted that Deuteronomy 7:1 gives a list of seven nations, while Genesis 15:19–21 mentions ten nations.[15] After saying that there is no evidence that these nations shared "common historical traditions," he went on to describe the six peoples listed in Exodus 3:8 as follows:

> *Canaanite* was the term still used long afterwards by the Phoenicians to describe themselves; it may mean "traders". *Hittites* probably means immigrant groups from the old Hittite empire in the north . . . (*cf.* Gn. 23). Sihon and Og, the semi-settled kings of east Jordan, are called *Amorite* (Nu. 21:21); so is the coalition of five kings in the Judaean hills (Jos. 10:5). By origin the word *amurru* means "Westerner" and was given originally by the settled Mesopotamians to their nomadic neighbours to the west. *Perizzite* may be "villager", perhaps used in a derogatory sense like modern "pagan," but the suffix may be of Hurrian origin (*cf.* "Kenizzite"). *Hivites* appear [to be used for] "Horites". If so, they would preserve the name, if not the blood, of the Hurrian conquerors of half a millennium before. . . . The Gibeonite confederacy is described as Hivite (Jos. 9:7). *Jebusites* are the aboriginal inhabitants of Jebus or Jerusalem (also called Amorites, Jos. 10:5).[16]

---

[14]Sarna, 49.
[15]Cole, 67.
[16]Ibid.

Verse 9. The Israelites' **cry** had been heard by God, and He had **seen the oppression** they experienced at the hands of the **Egyptians**. This section seems repetitious: verses 7 and 9 are roughly equal. Critical scholars see in these repetitions the use of two different sources.[17] However, these verses utilize a literary device known as "chiasm," in which parallel elements are found in a passage in an ABBA pattern. This pattern is used for emphasis and especially focuses attention on any statement(s) found in the center of the pattern. Dividing these verses according to this method yields the following structure:

A1: "I have . . . seen the affliction of My people who are in Egypt" (3:7).
  B1: "[I] have given heed to their cry . . . I am aware of their sufferings" (3:7).
    C1: "So I have come . . . to deliver them from . . . the Egyptians" (3:8).
    C2: "[I have come] to bring them up . . . to a good . . . land" (3:8).
  B2: "The cry of the sons of Israel has come to Me" (3:9).
A2: "I have seen the oppression [they are receiving from] the Egyptians" (3:9).

The statement labeled A2 adds information to the statement labeled A1: The Egyptians were the source of the affliction. B1 includes information not found in B2: God's awareness of Israel's sufferings. Further, the A and B statements serve to focus attention on the C statements. Therefore, the central thought of the passage is that God intended to deliver the Israelites and bring them into a better land. This structure should make it clear that what might be considered repetitious—perhaps based on different written sources—is in reality a carefully crafted literary device.

---

[17]John Gray, for example, attributed verses 7 and 8 to J (the Yahwist) and verses 9 through 15 to E (the Elohist). (John Gray, "The Book of Exodus," in *The Interpreter's One-Volume Commentary on the Bible*, ed. Charles Laymon [Nashville: Abingdon Press, 1971], 34.)

GOD'S INITIAL CALL AND MOSES' FIRST RESPONSE: "WHO AM I?" (3:10–12)

10"Therefore, come now, and I will send you to Pharaoh, so that you may bring My people, the sons of Israel, out of Egypt."
11But Moses said to God, "Who am I, that I should go to Pharaoh, and that I should bring the sons of Israel out of Egypt?"
12And He said, "Certainly I will be with you, and this shall be the sign to you that it is I who have sent you: when you have brought the people out of Egypt, you shall worship God at this mountain."

Verse 10. God called Moses to lead **the sons of Israel . . . out of Egypt**, a task which would require him to appear before **Pharaoh**. God referred to the Israelites as **My people**. They were His in the sense that He had initially called Abraham, and then He watched over and blessed the patriarchs (Abraham, Isaac, and Jacob) and their descendants (the Israelites).

Verse 11. Moses responded to God's commission with the question **"Who am I . . . ?"** Moses had attempted to deliver his people forty years earlier, but he was rejected by them and failed. His sense of unworthiness or inability was characteristic of true prophets.[18] The biblical evidence seems to indicate that God can better use an individual who believes he is inadequate than one who is over-confident.

Verse 12. God responded by saying, **"I will be with you**." God's reply, according to commentators, probably reflects the name of God: "I will be" is similar in Hebrew to "Yahweh"[19] (see comments on 3:14). God was the answer to Moses' feeling of lacking worth and ability. He seemed to say, "I am with you; if I am on your side, you have nothing to worry about." This important principle is taught throughout the Old Testament and is repeated in the New (see Rom. 8:31, 32).

---

[18]Sarna, 49.
[19]Cole, 68.

God then gave Moses a **sign**: Israel was to **worship God** on the very **mountain** where Moses was standing—a sign that could only be seen after the fact. God was saying, "When it happens, you will know that I did it." Terence E. Fretheim wrote,

> Is it God . . . who has sent him? It cannot be absolutely clear in advance that God is the one who stands behind this call to action. It will become clear to Moses that God has sent him only when all this has been accomplished and Moses stands with Israel (the 'you' is plural) and serves God at the very place at which they are now standing. God's assurance of being with Moses is as much as Moses can know at this moment. But when these events have taken place, God's presence will be seen to have been effective and Moses will know that it is indeed God who stands behind the commission.[20]

Other examples of signs to be realized only in the future include 1 Samuel 2:34 and Isaiah 37:30.

MOSES' SECOND RESPONSE: "WHO ARE YOU?" (3:13–15)

[13]Then Moses said to God, "Behold, I am going to the sons of Israel, and I will say to them, 'The God of your fathers has sent me to you.' Now they may say to me, 'What is His name?' What shall I say to them?" [14]God said to Moses, "I AM WHO I AM"; and He said, "Thus you shall say to the sons of Israel, 'I AM has sent me to you.'" [15]God, furthermore, said to Moses, "Thus you shall say to the sons of Israel, 'The LORD, the God of your fathers, the God of Abraham, the God of Isaac, and the God of Jacob, has sent me to you.' This is My name forever, and this is My memorial-name to all generations."

Verse 13. It has been said that the first response of **Moses** was "Who am I?" and his second response was "Who are You?"

---

[20]Fretheim, 62.

Moses knew that the people would ask for the **name** of the deity who had commissioned him. Cole explained,

> To ask the question, "Under what new title has God appeared to you?" is equivalent to asking, "What new revelation have you received from God?" Normally, in patriarchal days, any new revelation of the ancestral God will be summed up in a new title for Him (Gn. 16:13) which will in [the] future both record and recount a deeper knowledge of God's saving activity. We may therefore assume that, in asking this question, they were expecting a new title for the patriarchal God.[21]

Verses 14, 15. God answered by using a play on words. In Hebrew the being verb **I AM** (הָיָה, *hayah*) is similar to the divine name (יהוה, *YHWH*). Since this name consists of four consonants, it is sometimes called the "Tetragrammaton." Modern scholars usually transliterate the divine name as "Yahweh" in English.[22] However, in most English versions of the Bible, the Hebrew word *YHWH* is translated as LORD, being printed with small capital letters. This tradition reflects the Jewish practice of reading "Lord" (אֲדֹנָי, *'Adonay*) when *YHWH* is found in the Hebrew text.

When God uses the word as His name, He is saying, **"I AM WHO** [or what] **I AM."** Another possibility is "I will be who [or what] I will be." Scholars say that the meaning of the phrase suggests that God is the essence of being, the "ground of being." However, since *YHWH* is "a third person form and may mean 'He causes to be,'" the name may not "indicate God's eternal being but God's action and presence in historical affairs."[23]

God indicated emphatically that He intended to be known by the name "Yahweh" ("LORD"). Previously, He had been known by a number of designations; but He chose, from this point for-

---

[21]Cole, 69.

[22]Some English versions have transliterated the Tetragrammaton as "Jehovah," which reflects earlier German scholarship that used the letters "j" and "v" for the Hebrew *yod* (י) and *waw* (ו). Current English scholarship prefers the letters "y" and "w" for these consonants.

[23]Note on Exodus 3:14, Metzger and Murphy, 72.

ward, to be known by His personal name, the covenant name "Yahweh." In fact, "Yahweh" was to be God's **memorial-name to all generations**. The NRSV says, "This is my name forever, and this my title for all generations." The NIV renders it, "This is my name forever, the name by which I am to be remembered from generation to generation." Also, God emphasized that He was the same God who was worshiped by Israel's forefathers: **Abraham**, **Isaac**, and **Jacob**.

A PREVIEW OF THE DELIVERANCE (3:16–22)

**16"Go and gather the elders of Israel together and say to them,
'The LORD, the God of your fathers, the God of Abraham, Isaac
and Jacob, has appeared to me, saying, "I am indeed concerned
about you and what has been done to you in Egypt. 17So I said,
I will bring you up out of the affliction of Egypt to the land of
the Canaanite and the Hittite and the Amorite and the Perizzite and the Hivite and the Jebusite, to a land flowing with milk
and honey."' 18They will pay heed to what you say; and you
with the elders of Israel will come to the king of Egypt and you
will say to him, 'The LORD, the God of the Hebrews, has met
with us. So now, please, let us go a three days' journey into the
wilderness, that we may sacrifice to the LORD our God.' 19But I
know that the king of Egypt will not permit you to go, except
under compulsion. 20So I will stretch out My hand and strike
Egypt with all My miracles which I shall do in the midst of it;
and after that he will let you go. 21I will grant this people favor
in the sight of the Egyptians; and it shall be that when you go,
you will not go empty-handed. 22But every woman shall ask of
her neighbor and the woman who lives in her house, articles
of silver and articles of gold, and clothing; and you will put
them on your sons and daughters. Thus you will plunder the
Egyptians."**

A synopsis of the story, a preview of the upcoming deliverance, is given in 3:16–22. In fact, Exodus 4:29—12:36 can be outlined using the main ideas found in these verses:

1. Moses' presentation to the elders (3:16, 17; compare 4:29–31)
2. The appearance before Pharaoh (3:18; compare 5:1–3)
3. Pharaoh's refusal (3:19; compare 5:4—7:7)
4. God's miracles (3:20a; compare 7:8—12:29)
5. Pharaoh's acquiescence (3:20b; compare 12:30–32)
6. Gifts from the Egyptians (3:21, 22; compare 12:33–36).

Verses 16, 17. At the beginning of the preview, God told Moses to assemble **the elders** and speak to them. The elders were "a kind of representative judicial body in Israel."[24] Moses was to bring them a message from God. In this way, he would act as a prophet, for a prophet is one who delivers a message for another. God's message for His people began with the fact that He was **concerned** about them and their suffering (see 2:24, 25; 3:7, 9). Because of His compassion, God promised to deliver the Israelites from **the affliction of Egypt** and bring them to another **land** (see comments on 3:7, 8a, 8b).

Verse 18. The people of Israel would listen to Moses and ask **the king** to allow them to **go a three days' journey into the wilderness** in order to **sacrifice** to Yahweh. However, Pharaoh would not listen to their request. Was it deceitful to ask for three days when the Israelites really wanted to leave Egypt permanently? Nahum M. Sarna said that their request was "a stratagem designed to outmaneuver the pharaoh's intransigence [uncompromising spirit]."[25]

Verse 19. Pharaoh would not let Israel leave, **except under compulsion** (וְלֹא בְּיָד חֲזָקָה, *w^{e}lo' b^{e}yad ch^{a}zaqah*). The KJV translates the phrase more literally, "not by a mighty hand." The NRSV has "unless compelled by a mighty hand." The deliverance of Israel would be accomplished by God's mighty hand. "The image of an outstretched or mighty hand or arm is common in Egyptian inscriptions to describe the power of Pharaoh. It is used throughout the exodus narratives to describe God's power over Pha-

---

[24]Sarna, 53. Elders are also mentioned in Exodus 4:29; 12:21; 17:5, 6; 18:12; 19:7; 24:1, 9, 14.

[25]Ibid., 55.

raoh."[26] (See 13:9, 14, 16.) God did not just deliver Israel; He *powerfully* delivered them.

This preview prepared Moses for what was ahead, and especially for the fact that his initial efforts to free Israel would be ineffectual. In this respect, as well as others, Moses' call was similar to that of later prophets who were told that the people to whom they spoke would refuse to hear them (see Is. 6:9, 10). This was the first of several occasions when God let Moses know that Pharaoh would initially refuse to let the people go (see 4:21; 7:1–5; 10:1, 2; 11:9, 10).

Verse 20. Since the king of Egypt would not let the Israelites go initially, God would perform **miracles**, an obvious reference to the ten plagues (7:14—12:30). These wonders would bring judgment on the Egyptians, but they would provide redemption for the Israelites. As a result of the plagues, Pharaoh would **let** [them] **go**.

Verses 21, 22. Not only would the Israelites be allowed to leave, but they would also take with them as gifts many of the treasures of Egypt—**articles of silver and articles of gold, and clothing**. These items would be acquired from the neighbors and servants of the Israelites: **every woman shall ask of her neighbor and the woman who lives in her house** (see 11:2, 3; 12:35, 36). This language suggests that the Israelites had their own slaves, a relationship later governed by the law of Moses. Although God's people were under the control of Pharaoh and had to endure hard labor, apparently some of them were prosperous. They possessed "flocks and herds" and "a very large number of livestock" (12:38; see 9:6). The fact that Israel would **plunder the Egyptians** must have been good news to Moses: He would ultimately succeed in the task God was giving him. Further, God's promise to Abraham would be fulfilled as He judged the nation of Egypt and led Israel out "with many possessions" (Gen. 15:14).

---

[26]John H. Walton and Victor H. Matthews, *Genesis—Deuteronomy*, The IVP Bible Background Commentary (Downers Grove, Ill.: InterVarsity Press, 1997), 89.

APPLICATION

How God Prepares a Man (Chs. 1—4)

Israel was greatly oppressed in Egypt. God heard His people's cry and determined to deliver them. While deliverance was undoubtedly God's work, He used a human being—Moses—to accomplish His purposes. The tasks God wants to accomplish on earth, He accomplishes by using human instruments. How does He do this? The story of Moses' preparation for the job of leading Israel out of the wilderness can help to answer that question. The first few chapters of Exodus reveal how God prepares someone through whom He can do His will.

God chose Moses. There is no doubt that Moses, like Jeremiah after him, was chosen from before his birth. This does not, of course, detract from Moses' need to choose God (see Heb. 11:24–26). Still, Moses was born to do a certain job. What about us? It is possible that God has a special purpose in mind for each of us. What is that purpose? It may be a special role in a local congregation. You may be able to reach someone with the gospel when no one else can; you may have a unique ability to take the gospel to a particular country or people. Perhaps there is some service only you can render. How can we know what God wants us to do? To find out, we must be willing to be used by God. We may never know what God has in mind for us to do until we begin to choose Him.

God preserved Moses. Whom God has chosen, God protects. God would not allow Moses to be killed as a baby, so Moses' parents saved him. People who have come close to death but have been saved ask, "Why? Why did God choose to save me?" Often, they answer, "God must have a mission for me." We would not disagree with them, but would encourage them to look around to discover that mission. Maybe we should also ask ourselves, "Has not God preserved us all? Why did He allow us to be born? Why has He kept us safe in our travels?" It may be that God has preserved us because He has a special place for us to serve in His vineyard.

God prepared Moses. Moses' preparation was providential. He did not know what he was being prepared for or that he was being prepared for anything. His preparation came in three stages. (1) His mother was his nurse. From her, he must have learned about the God of Abraham, Isaac, and Jacob, as well as the plight of Israel. He got his faith from his people. (2) He was prepared through the time he spent in Egypt. Because of that time, he could go into the court of Pharaoh and talk to him on his own terms. He knew the Egyptian court, Egyptian customs, and the Egyptian language. (3) He was prepared through the time he spent in the wilderness as a shepherd. In Midian he learned what wilderness living was like, he came to know the territory in which Israel was to travel, and he grew accustomed to life as a shepherd. Moses especially learned the kind of attitudes he needed to lead God's people in the wilderness. Moses at eighty was not the brash, impulsive, and (perhaps) arrogant person he was at forty; he was wiser, more patient, and probably gentler. He was ready to be a leader who trusted in God rather than self; he was a selfless shepherd, a servant leader—the kind of leader Israel needed.

What about your preparation? God has been preparing you through your schooling, your heritage, your home life, your work, your relationships, your successes, and even your failures (Rom. 8:28). Perhaps God has been preparing you for a special task. A preacher who had incurable cancer, instead of bemoaning that fact, began ministering to others with cancer. A Christian who used to be an alcoholic and a drug addict turned his life around, got an education, and became a counselor of others who were in the same predicament he had overcome.

God called Moses. He called Moses when He spoke to him at the burning bush. Maybe the first part of His call was Moses' realization of the majesty and holiness of God. Still, Moses was reluctant to hear God's call! He objected: (1) "Who am I?"; (2) "Who will I say sent me?"; (3) "They will not believe me"; (4) "I am not eloquent"; (5) "Send someone else." However, God would not take no for an answer. He had a response for every objection that Moses made.

Does God still call? He does. Not miraculously, but providentially, through circumstances. God prepares us to meet challenges and then presents us with those challenges. When our hearts are moved to accept such challenges, that is when and how God calls us.

Does God take no for an answer? Yes, He does. If we choose not to accept His call, He can still accomplish His purposes—but He will not do so through us (see Esther 4:14). Paul said, "I did not prove disobedient to the heavenly vision" (Acts 26:19), implying that it is possible to be disobedient to God's call.

God empowered Moses. The Lord's primary answer to Moses' reluctance was "I will be with you." That is God's answer to us today (Mt. 28:18–20). God never gives us a task to do without also giving us the ability to do it (Eph. 3:20; Phil. 4:13). "When (or where) God guides, God provides." When we are trying to do God's will, to respond to God's call, He will empower us to accomplish His purposes.

Moses stood before Pharaoh and told him, "God says, 'Let My people go!'" What a change had come over Moses! He was not the Israelite slave he might have been if Pharaoh's decree had not caused him to be placed in the river. He was not the brash, arrogant, Egyptianized prince he would have been without his experiences in Midian. He was not the scared fugitive from Egypt or the smelly shepherd of Midian that he would have been if God had not called him. He was not any of these, yet he was all of them and more. He was God's person, God's spokesman, God's prophet—the equal, even the superior, of Pharaoh—unafraid, ready to do God's will, and prepared for the trying task of leading a rebellious people for forty years in the wilderness. What great deeds God accomplished through him!

Similar statements can be made of us. However poor we are, however inadequate we feel, God can accomplish great things through us. We must seek His will for our lives and then move out to answer His calling!

The Great "I AM" (Ch. 3)

Almost any chapter in Exodus can be used to preach on the characteristics of God. A sermon on "The Great 'I AM'" from Exodus 3 could point out the following characteristics of God: (1) God is "I AM," the One who is, who has always been, and who causes to be. (2) God is holy—too holy for His face to be seen, so holy that one must recognize his own sinfulness in God's presence. (3) God has condescended to enter into a relationship with man; He is the God of the fathers. (4) God is the compassionate deliverer: of Israel in the past, but of all mankind today.

Holy Ground (3:1–6)

The ground on which Moses stood when God appeared to him was "holy ground" only because God was associated with it and only as long as God was associated with it. No ground on this earth is "holy ground" today. The "Holy Land" is not "holy" in the same sense that the ground in Exodus 3:5 was. The closest thing in our world to "holy ground" is the church for which Christ died. Abraham Lincoln, in his Gettysburg Address, said that the men who had died on that battlefield in Gettysburg, Pennsylvania, consecrated it (made it, in a sense, "holy"). We should learn to give greater reverence to those things associated with God, such as the church, the Bible, worship, and God's name.

Jesus, the Great "I AM" (3:14)

In the New Testament Jesus used the phrase "I am" (see Jn. 8:24, 58), identifying Himself with the God who called Himself "I AM" in Exodus 3:14. Who and what God was and is, Jesus also was and is. It is possible to connect Jesus' seven "I am" sayings in the Gospel of John with the characteristics of God found in the Old Testament. The aim of such a sermon would be to proclaim Jesus' deity and to illustrate that He cares for us just as God cared for His people in the past.

Chapter 4

Moses' Call by God (Part 2)

Chapter 4 continues the story of the call of Moses. He offered two more excuses as to why he could not lead God's people out of Egypt. His first excuse was that the people of Israel would not believe him. In answer to this objection, God gave Moses three signs that he could perform: (1) his staff would become a serpent (4:1–5); (2) his hand would become leprous (4:6–8); and (3) when he poured out water, it would become blood (4:9). Moses' second excuse was that he was not eloquent, but was slow of speech (4:10, 11). The Lord answered by saying that He would be with Moses when he spoke (4:12). Finally, Moses said, "Send someone else," a response which greatly angered God (4:13, 14). The Lord then provided Aaron to be Moses' spokesman (4:14–17).

The narrative next turns to Moses' exit from Midian. Moses sought and received permission from his father-in-law, Jethro, to return to Egypt (4:18). After the Lord recommissioned him for his task (4:19), Moses left, taking with him his wife and two sons (4:20). As he went, God again related to Moses what he was to do, adding further information about what would happen afterwards (4:21–23). Then, on the way, the Lord would have killed him, but his life was saved when Zipporah circumcised their son (4:24–26).

The chapter closes with the beginning of Moses' mission. He met his brother Aaron in the wilderness, and the two of them went to the Israelites in Egypt. When the people saw Moses' signs, they believed what he had to say. After hearing about God's great concern for them in their affliction, they worshiped Him (4:27–31).

MOSES' THIRD RESPONSE: "THEY WILL NOT BELIEVE ME" (4:1–9)

[1]Then Moses said, "What if they will not believe me or listen to what I say? For they may say, 'The LORD has not appeared to you.'" [2]The LORD said to him, "What is that in your hand?" And he said, "A staff." [3]Then He said, "Throw it on the ground." So he threw it on the ground, and it became a serpent; and Moses fled from it. [4]But the LORD said to Moses, "Stretch out your hand and grasp it by its tail"—so he stretched out his hand and caught it, and it became a staff in his hand—[5]"that they may believe that the LORD, the God of their fathers, the God of Abraham, the God of Isaac, and the God of Jacob, has appeared to you."

[6]The LORD furthermore said to him, "Now put your hand into your bosom." So he put his hand into his bosom, and when he took it out, behold, his hand was leprous like snow. [7]Then He said, "Put your hand into your bosom again." So he put his hand into his bosom again, and when he took it out of his bosom, behold, it was restored like the rest of his flesh. [8]"If they will not believe you or heed the witness of the first sign, they may believe the witness of the last sign. [9]But if they will not believe even these two signs or heed what you say, then you shall take some water from the Nile and pour it on the dry ground; and the water which you take from the Nile will become blood on the dry ground."

Verse 1. Moses' concern at this point was not getting Pharaoh to **believe** him, but getting the Israelites to believe him! After all, he had left Egypt with a stained reputation and had apparently not returned for forty years. If the people were not convinced that **the LORD**, "the God of their fathers" (4:5) had **appeared** to Moses, then they would not **listen** to him or follow him even if Pharaoh allowed them to leave. In fact, throughout their time in the wilderness, the people's trust in Moses continued to be a major issue.

Verses 2, 3. God's response to Moses' question was to provide him with what he needed to make the Israelites believe him:

Moses' ability to perform signs. From that time forward, one of the marks of a true prophet was that he could perform authentic signs. Jesus was a prophet like Moses (Deut. 18:15–22; Acts 3:22) in that He also performed signs so that people would hear and believe.

For the first sign, the Lord commanded Moses to **throw** down his **staff** (מַטֶּה, *matteh*), a shepherd's rod. Moses had been tending his father-in-law's sheep in Midian (3:1), so it was natural to carry this instrument in his **hand** (יָד, *yad*). The term "hand" is often repeated in this chapter for emphasis. The "mighty hand" of God would work through the human "hand" of Moses (see comments on 3:19). When Moses threw the staff down, it turned into **a serpent**. Naturally, he reacted in fear and **fled from it.**

Verses 4, 5. Then the Lord told Moses to **grasp** [the serpent] **by its tail**. Moses' faith in God's protection is evident since such an act could have resulted in being bitten. When he obeyed, the serpent changed back into **a staff**. Later, Moses demonstrated this sign before the Israelites and it caused them to **believe** (4:29–31). The same sign was also presented before Pharaoh, but he would not listen (7:8–13).

Verse 6. The second sign also involved Moses' **hand**, which God told him to place in his **bosom** (חֵיק, *cheyq*). In this case, the term refers to the fold of the garment covering his chest (see Ps. 74:11; Prov. 6:27; 16:33). When Moses removed his hand, it **was leprous like snow**. This same description appears in Numbers 12:10 where Miriam was judged by God. The severity of this skin disease can be seen from Aaron's response: "Oh, do not let her be like one dead, whose flesh is half eaten away when he comes from his mother's womb!" (Num. 12:12).

Verses 7, 8. Next, the Lord commanded Moses to repeat the process. After doing so, **his hand . . . was restored like the rest of his flesh.** Moses must have felt relief to have his hand returned to its previous condition. God then explained that if the Israelites did not accept **the first sign**, the staff being changed into a serpent, then they would accept **the last sign**, Moses' hand becoming leprous. No doubt this latter sign was among those performed before the Israelites which resulted in their belief (4:29–31).

Verse 9. The third sign involved Moses' taking **water from the Nile.** This important river was used for irrigating the fields of Egypt, and its annual flooding also replenished the soil. Further, the river was utilized as a convenient mode of transportation. Due to all of these benefits, the Nile was viewed as a god. Whenever Moses **pour**[ed] the water from the Nile **on the dry ground**, it would **become blood**. This precious resource would become utterly useless.

God gave Moses these three signs to perform in order to encourage His people to accept Moses as God's spokesman. All three were sufficiently spectacular to produce the faith the people needed. Also, each of the three involved destructive, negative consequences: For a staff to become a snake was dangerous, for a man's hand to become leprous was horrible, and for water to be turned into blood was devastating. However, in the first two cases, the circumstances were reversed. These signs prefigured the plagues, while the third sign actually became the first plague (7:14–25).

MOSES' FOURTH RESPONSE: "I AM NOT ELOQUENT" (4:10–12)

[10]Then Moses said to the LORD, "Please, Lord, I have never been eloquent, neither recently nor in time past, nor since You have spoken to Your servant; for I am slow of speech and slow of tongue." [11]The LORD said to him, "Who has made man's mouth? Or who makes him mute or deaf, or seeing or blind? Is it not I, the LORD? [12]Now then go, and I, even I, will be with your mouth, and teach you what you are to say."

Verse 10. The next excuse that Moses offered was that he was not **eloquent**, that is, "a man of words" (אִישׁ דְּבָרִים, *'ish d^{e}barim*). He also claimed to be **slow of speech and slow of tongue** (כְבַד־פֶּה וּכְבַד לָשׁוֹן, *k^{e}bad peh uk^{e}bad lashon*). This phrase can more literally be rendered "heavy of mouth and heavy of tongue." What did Moses mean when he said these things? Sarna suggested three possibilities: He may have had a speech defect, may have lost his fluency in the Egyptian language, or perhaps just thought he was inadequate as a speaker.[1] However, Sarna said that Moses' own lack of eloquence was irrelevant because his message came from God (see Jer. 1:6–9).

Verse 11. God affirmed that He is the One who makes man **mute or deaf, or seeing or blind**. While believers are generally willing to agree that God makes man to see, they are not inclined to affirm that God makes a man "mute or deaf . . . or blind." However, the Old Testament uniformly teaches that everything that happens is either caused or permitted by God (see Job 1:21, 22; Amos 4:6).

Verse 12. The Lord's rebuttal of Moses' excuse makes it clear that God would enable Moses to accomplish what He had called him to do. As a result of divine aid, Moses is remembered in the New Testament as a man who was "powerful in speech" (Acts 7:22; NIV).

MOSES' FIFTH RESPONSE: "SEND SOMEONE ELSE" (4:13–17)

13But he said, "Please, Lord, now send the message by whomever You will." 14Then the anger of the LORD burned against Moses, and He said, "Is there not your brother Aaron the Levite? I know that he speaks fluently. And moreover, behold, he is coming out to meet you; when he sees you, he will be glad in his heart. 15You are to speak to him and put the words in his mouth; and I, even I, will be with your mouth and his mouth, and I will teach you what you are to do. 16Moreover, he shall speak for you to the people; and he will be as a mouth for you and you will be as God to him. 17You shall take in your hand this staff, with which you shall perform the signs."

Verse 13. Moses continued in his reluctance to accept God's commission. When he replied to God's renewed call, he addressed God as **Lord**, using the Hebrew word אֲדֹנָי (*'Adonay*) rather than

[1]Nahum M. Sarna, *Exploring Exodus: The Origins of Biblical Israel* (New York: Schocken Books, 1996), 54–61.

the name "Yahweh," which God had said He preferred.[2] He declined God's commission, suggesting that God choose someone else for the job.

When Moses, a mere man, was called by God, the eternal Creator, he hesitated and made excuses, trying to find a way not to obey. Contrary to what the reader might anticipate, God was very patient with Moses, meeting each excuse and each objection with comforting words intended to take care of Moses' problems. Moses' excuses reflected a "thinly veiled lack of faith. . . . [Consequently,] it is remarkable how patiently and accommodatingly God respond[ed] to Moses' questions and objections throughout 3:1— 4:17."[3]

Verse 14. After Moses asked God to send someone else, **the anger of the Lord burned against Moses**. God is patient to a point, but He can and does become angry. In spite of His anger, God responded to Moses' excuses by providing his brother **Aaron** to be his spokesman. Aaron is introduced into the narrative for the first time; to this point, the reader has only been informed about Moses' parents and older sister (2:1, 4). Aaron is described as **the Levite**, which sets the stage for his future service as high priest (see comments on 2:1, 2). God informed Moses that Aaron was already on his way to meet him, and that his brother would be **glad** to see him.

Verses 15–17. Moses made excuses as to why he could not lead God's people out of Egypt, but the Lord provided assurance that He would **be with** him and Aaron. God commanded Moses **to speak** to his brother Aaron and to **put the words in his mouth**. It was Moses' responsibility to relay to his brother all of the words that God had spoken to him. Aaron would, in turn, **speak for** [Moses] **to the people**. The chain of command was clear: God, Moses, Aaron. Finally, God reminded Moses that he was to take along his **staff** through which God would perform miraculous **signs**.

---

[2]This difference was deliberate, according to Waldemar Janzen, *Exodus*, Believers Church Bible Commentary (Scottdale, Pa.: Herald Press, 2000), 72.

[3]Ibid., 70–71.

MOSES' ACCEPTANCE OF GOD'S CALL AND HIS DEPARTURE FOR EGYPT (4:18–26)

Moses' Departure (4:18–20)

[18]Then Moses departed and returned to Jethro his father-in-law and said to him, "Please, let me go, that I may return to my brethren who are in Egypt, and see if they are still alive." And Jethro said to Moses, "Go in peace." [19]Now the LORD said to Moses in Midian, "Go back to Egypt, for all the men who were seeking your life are dead." [20]So Moses took his wife and his sons and mounted them on a donkey, and returned to the land of Egypt. Moses also took the staff of God in his hand.

Verse 18. Moses left the mountain where he had encountered the Lord and **returned** to get permission from **his father-in-law** to leave the land where he had been living for about forty years. Even though Moses was a grown man, advanced in years, he still showed respect for the authority of his father-in-law. In response, **Jethro** gave him his blessing: **"Go in peace."**

Verse 19. God deemed it necessary to speak to **Moses** again, appointing him to fulfill the mission He had originally called him to accomplish. Liberal critics see in such repetitions evidence of an editor's use of different sources. However, these apparently repetitious passages can be explained in at least three other ways:

(1) Ancient writers valued fullness of expression, using repetition, in contrast to writers today who value economy in the use of words.

(2) The repetitions may be necessary. Humans tend to be forgetful and need to be reminded again and again.

(3) The repetitions are not merely repetitious, since more information is added in each account. Compare these verses, for instance:

- In 3:10 the Lord said, "I will send you to Pharaoh, so that you may bring My people, the sons of Israel, out of Egypt."

- In 4:19 the Lord said, **"Go back to Egypt, for all the men who were seeking your life are dead."**
- In 4:21 the Lord said, "When you go back to Egypt see that you perform before Pharaoh all the wonders which I have put in your power."

In the first passage, the Lord said that He would send Moses to Egypt to deliver His people. In the second, He added the information that those who sought Moses' life had died (see 2:15, 23). In the third, He further instructed Moses to use the signs that He had given him to accomplish the mission.

Verse 20. In response to God's calling, **Moses** left for Egypt, taking with him **his wife and his sons**. This is the first mention of a second son. The first, Gershom, is identified by name in 2:22; the name of the second, Eliezer, is not revealed until 18:4. The text says that **Moses also took the staff of God in his hand**. This shepherd's staff had become God's staff, a symbol of authority and the means by which Moses would perform signs throughout the rest of his ministry.

Further Instruction from the Lord (4:21–23)

[21]The Lord said to Moses, "When you go back to Egypt see that you perform before Pharaoh all the wonders which I have put in your power; but I will harden his heart so that he will not let the people go. [22]Then you shall say to Pharaoh, 'Thus says the Lord, "Israel is My son, My firstborn. [23]So I said to you, 'Let My son go that he may serve Me'; but you have refused to let him go. Behold, I will kill your son, your firstborn."'"

Verses 21–23. God prepared **Moses** for the task at hand. First, the Lord reminded Moses of the **wonders** which He had already enabled him to **perform** and said that he was to perform them for **Pharaoh**. This use of those signs expanded their purpose; initially they were given so that the Israelites might see them and believe Moses. Second, He let Moses know that Pharaoh would not listen, saying that **the Lord** would **harden his heart**. Third, He foretold the final plague—the death of the **firstborn**—in terms which declared that the death of the firstborn of Egypt was a just punishment for the mistreatment that God's firstborn (**Israel**) had suffered at the hand of Pharaoh. This illustrates the biblical principle that "whatever a man sows, this he will also reap" (Gal. 6:7). God made it clear to Moses, as He did to later prophets, that his message would not be gladly received.

A Bridegroom of Blood (4:24–26)

[24]Now it came about at the lodging place on the way that the LORD met him and sought to put him to death. [25]Then Zipporah took a flint and cut off her son's foreskin and threw it at Moses' feet, and she said, "You are indeed a bridegroom of blood to me." [26]So He let him alone. At that time she said, "You are a bridegroom of blood"—because of the circumcision.

Verses 24–26. This paragraph about the **bridegroom of blood** is one of the most difficult passages in Exodus. Interpreters have offered a wide range of explanations for the event. The following notes from a study Bible are typical:

> [Exodus 4:24–26 is] an archaic tradition that traces the origin of circumcision (compare Gen 17.9–14) to the Midianite wife of Moses. . . . [Ex. 4:24] reflects an ancient belief in demonic attack . . . warded off by the timely performance of the rite. Originally circumcision was a puberty or marriage rite.[4]

Other suggested explanations of the passage include the following: (1) Before Moses and his family could be allowed to leave Midian, he had to appease the god of the Midianites by circumcising the child who had been born in Midian.[5] (2) The story

---

[4]Notes on Exodus 4:24–26 and 4:24, Bruce M. Metzger and Roland E. Murphy, eds., *The New Oxford Annotated Bible with the Apocrypha*, rev. and enl. (New York: Oxford University Press, 1991), 74.

[5]Julian Morgenstern, "The 'Bloody Husband' (?) (Exod. 4:24–26) Once Again," *Hebrew Union College Annual* 34 (1963): 66–70.

is actually Midianite. It has a Midianite background and belongs earlier in the book; the god in the story is a Midianite deity who bears the name "Yahweh."[6] (3) Moses had not circumcised his first son because he had promised that son to the local idol, as part of the agreement when Jethro gave him his daughter; therefore, God required him to circumcise that son as a way of showing he had renounced idolatry.[7] (4) The angel of the Lord sought to kill Moses because of his lack of faith and willing obedience when the Lord called him.[8] None of these explanations seem likely, and most of them must be rejected if the biblical narratives are accepted as historical accounts.

The variety of interpretations does indicate that the passage is both grammatically and theologically difficult. For example, the story begins with this information: **The Lord met him and sought to put him to death.** This statement is problematic. (1) Whom did the Lord seek to kill? Most commentators agree that Moses was the object of God's wrath, but the antecedent of the pronoun is unclear; the pronoun "him" could refer to Moses or to one of his sons. (2) If Moses was the person whom God sought to put to death, why would He do this immediately after commissioning him to bring His people out of Egypt? (3) Why does the text say that "the Lord met him"? Could the Lord not do from heaven whatever He wanted to do? (4) Why does the passage say, "The Lord *sought* to put him to death" or "*tried* to kill him"? (NRSV; emphasis added). Is anything too great for the Lord to do? If the Lord wanted to kill him, why did He not do so? Why only "seek" or "try"? Does the wording imply that God tried and failed?

To understand the meaning of the passage, the first question that needs to be answered is "What happened?" What historical reality is represented by the words? The writer was using anthro-

---

[6]Hans Kosmala, "The 'Bloody Husband'," *Vetus Testamentum* 12 (1962): 20–22.

[7]Gregory B. Smith, "An Exegesis of Exodus 4:24–26," unpublished paper for a graduate class on Exodus (Nashville: David Lipscomb University, 1991), 5. Smith cited Rabbinic sources.

[8]C. Houtman, "Exodus 4:24–26 and Its Interpretation," *Journal of Northwest Semitic Languages* 11 (1985): 88–89.

pomorphic language; that is, he was putting what God did in terms of what a man might do, so that men might more readily understand it (as when Genesis 11:5 says that God came down and saw the tower that men were building). "The LORD . . . sought to put him to death" refers, then, to Moses' being stricken suddenly with some potentially fatal disease or attacked in some other way so that his life was endangered. He was about to die. Who kills people by means of disease or injury? In Old Testament theology, God did. Whatever happened, good or bad, God did it. If it was bad, then repentance and making amends would cause God to change His actions toward the afflicted person.

Therefore, it may be said that God sent an affliction or injury which resulted in Moses' being on the brink of death. Since **circumcision** solved the problem, it was surely Moses' failure to circumcise one of his sons that caused the affliction. God had made a covenant with Abraham and his descendants that required them to be circumcised (Gen. 17), and Moses was a descendant of Abraham. If Moses had not circumcised one of his sons, he was guilty of failing to obey God.

The circumcision was performed by Moses' wife, **Zipporah,** who **cut off her son's foreskin**. Moses' life was therefore saved by his wife. After the circumcision, she **threw** [the foreskin] **at Moses' feet**. Most commentators believe that her response indicated her anger at having to perform the operation.

No one knows for certain what Zipporah meant when she called Moses **a bridegroom of blood** after the circumcision. Guesses range from speculation that she was saying Moses was a guilty bridegroom, having killed the Egyptian long before, to the idea that this was a traditional Midianite saying used when the bridegroom was circumcised in connection with his wedding.[9] An attractive suggestion was provided by John Smith: "Zipporah is simply saying to Moses, 'You are my husband brought back to me from the dead by a blood covenant—mine twice over now.'"[10] The last sentence in verse 26 appears to have

---

[9]Smith, 10–11.

[10]John Smith, *The Permanent Message of Exodus and Studies in the Life of Moses* (Cincinnati: Jennings and Pye, 1903), 83.

been added because Zipporah's saying was well known to the readers. The author anticipated that they needed to be told *why* she made the statement.

The second question to be answered in regard to Moses' near death and his son's circumcision is "Why?" Why did God try to kill Moses, and why is the incident recorded in the Book of Exodus? The "why" of the story probably relates to (1) the importance of circumcision and (2) the importance of Israel's leader providing a good example of faithful obedience for those whom he was called to lead. Moses could not have successfully led God's people in God's way if he had not himself been obedient to God's law. His disobedience would have been evident in his son's lack of circumcision. Warren W. Wiersbe commented, "Moses couldn't lead the people of Israel if he was disobedient to one of the fundamental commandments of the Lord (Gen. 17:10–14)."[11] For the first readers, the story emphasized the importance of obedience and especially "serve[d] to dramatize the tremendous importance of circumcision."[12]

This story seems to relate to other events in the book. For instance, it involves the circumcision of Moses' son just after the text records that God threatened Egypt's firstborn sons. Moses' life was saved by an operation which involved the shedding of blood, and Moses was then called a "bridegroom of blood." In a similar way, Israel escaped the ravages of the tenth plague by the shedding of the blood of a lamb and was then, in a sense, "married" to God, although Exodus does not picture Israel's election in those terms. Furthermore, when this incident occurred, Moses was leaving the wilderness to enter Egypt, having received permission from the priest of Midian. Later, when blood was shed and the firstborn died, Moses was leaving Egypt to enter the wilderness. He had obtained permission from Pharaoh, who was regarded as a god in Egypt and may have had priestly functions. These parallels may not be coincidental.

---

[11]Warren W. Wiersbe, *Be Delivered* (Colorado Springs, Colo.: Victor, 1998), 21.

[12]Brevard S. Childs, *The Book of Exodus: A Critical, Theological Commentary*, The Old Testament Library (Louisville: Westminster Press, 1974), 104.

AARON, MOSES, AND THE PEOPLE (4:27–31)

[27]Now the LORD said to Aaron, "Go to meet Moses in the wilderness." So he went and met him at the mountain of God and kissed him. [28]Moses told Aaron all the words of the LORD with which He had sent him, and all the signs that He had commanded him to do. [29]Then Moses and Aaron went and assembled all the elders of the sons of Israel; [30]and Aaron spoke all the words which the LORD had spoken to Moses. He then performed the signs in the sight of the people. [31]So the people believed; and when they heard that the LORD was concerned about the sons of Israel and that He had seen their affliction, then they bowed low and worshiped.

Verses 27, 28. God sent **Aaron** to meet **Moses** at **the mountain of God**—apparently Mount Sinai, or Mount Horeb. Midian, the land from which Moses was traveling, must have been east of that mountain. Aaron was no doubt "glad" to be reunited with his brother (4:14) and greeted him with a customary **kiss**. Moses related to Aaron all that God had told him, and together they returned to Egypt to bring news of forthcoming deliverance to the people of Israel.

Verses 29–31. After gathering the **elders** together, **Moses and Aaron** revealed to them **the words** [of] **the LORD** and also **performed the signs** that God had given them. As a result, they responded appropriately by believing what Moses and Aaron had to say. Since Moses' arrival was evidence that God had heard their cries (2:23), **they bowed low and worshiped**. Chapter 4, therefore, ends on a high note. God had heard His people's cries! He was aware of their distress, and He had sent a miracle-working deliverer! The people of Israel had high hopes! Unfortunately, their hopes would not quickly be realized.

APPLICATION

Excuses (Chs. 3; 4)

Moses' questions to God could be used to introduce a sermon on excuses. The lesson could proceed from his excuses to those offered by other Bible characters—Adam, Aaron, Saul, those invited to the feast (Lk. 14:16–24), and others—and then go on to excuses people offer today for not becoming Christians or for not being faithful as Christians.

Another possibility is to devote an entire lesson to Moses' excuses as compared to excuses people offer today. (1) Moses asked, "Who am I?" Some people believe they are inadequate, not realizing that God's power can make them adequate. (2) "Who are you?" Some people do not respond because they do not understand God's nature. (3) "They will not believe." Perhaps the closest thing to this excuse today is "Why should I believe?" God offers us signs, which are recorded in the Bible, to help us believe. (4) "I am not eloquent." The "I can't" syndrome keeps many people from becoming Christians or fulfilling their potential as Christians. (5) "Send someone else." The heart of the matter is that some people do not want to answer God's call. They need to learn that *no one else* can do for you what God wants you to do.

Talking Back to God (Chs. 3; 4)

Is it right to "talk back to God" or to argue with Him? Should we try to talk Him out of what He plans to do? Moses did, and God was patient with him. Job did, and God was patient with him. Perhaps we are too reluctant to express the true feelings of our hearts when we go to God in prayer. We may need to speak more openly and boldly to God, as Moses did. To speak to God boldly shows faith, not the lack of it. In the end, the major question is not "Did we 'talk back' to God?" but "Did we at last submit to God's will?" Moses submitted, and Job submitted. We must do the same.

God's Call Today (Chs. 3; 4)

Are we called by God as Moses was? In a sense, all are called by the gospel to become Christians (1 Thess. 2:14). Waldemar Janzen wrote, "The call of God has been extended through Jesus Christ to every person."[13] After we are Christians, we are spo-

[13]Janzen, 79.

ken of as those who have been "called" (1 Cor. 1:9; Eph. 4:1; Col. 3:15). We are then referred to as the "elect" of God (Col. 3:12; KJV). In another sense, each of us is "called" providentially to serve in a special capacity in the church, using the specific gifts we have been given. Each person needs to heed God's call to become a Christian and then accept God's "calling" for his or her life.

"What Is That in Your Hand?" (4:2)

God had called Moses to lead His people out of Egypt, but Moses was reluctant to accept God's calling. In part, this was because he thought he was incapable of doing the job. In 4:1 he asked, "What if they will not believe me . . . ?" God's reply was "What is that in your hand?" It was not much—just a shepherd's staff. Nevertheless, this became the instrument God used to deliver Israel. Moses needed to learn that, no matter how inadequate we may be or feel, God can use whatever we have to accomplish the task He wants us to do. We need to learn the following truths:

Everyone has something in his hand. We all have some talent or gift that can be used in the service of God. The parable of the talents teaches us that there are "five-talent" people, "two-talent" people, and "one-talent" people; but there are no "zero-talent" people in God's kingdom. (Talents were sums of money, but the teaching can be applied to "talents" in the sense of "abilities," as we use the word.) God has given to every member of the church a talent, or talents, that can be used in His service (Rom. 12:3–8). The lack of a particular gift or ability does not mean that we have nothing to give (see Acts 3:6).

Whatever we have in our hands, God intends for us to use it in His service. The talents we have are to be used to build up the body of Christ (see Rom. 12:3–8; 1 Cor. 12; Eph. 4:11–16; 1 Pet. 4:10, 11). Whatever we have, God can use it in His service to His glory. If God could use a shepherd's staff to deliver His people, He can use our abilities, our education, our occupations, our possessions, and our relationships to accomplish His purposes. If you are inclined to say, as Moses was, "God cannot use me because I am unable to do anything," think about this: If God could use a donkey to speak to Balaam, He can certainly use you in some meaningful way.

Whatever we give to God, He can multiply its use. If someone had asked Moses, before God spoke to him, "What is that rod good for?" he would have said, "It is good for looking after sheep." He would never have dreamed how God could expand its usefulness, yet God could and did. In the same way, He can expand your usefulness to Him. Just as Jesus could multiply the boy's loaves and fish to feed five thousand men (Jn. 6:8–14), God can multiply the use of whatever you give to Him.

What is that in your hand? Whatever it is, let me urge you to give it to God—but first, you need to give *yourself* to the Lord, holding nothing back (Rom. 12:1, 2; 2 Cor. 8:5).

CHAPTER 5

FAILURE IN EGYPT

Moses' first effort to deliver the Israelites is recorded in chapters 5 and 6. Perhaps it is surprising that the attempt ended in failure. Moses and Aaron appeared before Pharaoh to ask his permission for the people to worship the Lord in the wilderness (5:1). Pharaoh refused, dismissed the message from God, and even commanded that the Israelites' burdens be increased (5:2–9). The result seen by the people was heavier work and greater suffering (5:10–14). When the Israelites complained to Pharaoh, he refused to lighten their load (5:15–19). Consequently, they complained to Moses and Aaron (5:20, 21), and Moses in turn complained to the Lord (5:22, 23).

MOSES' REQUEST AND PHARAOH'S NEGATIVE RESPONSE (5:1–4)

**1And afterward Moses and Aaron came and said to Pha-
raoh, "Thus says the LORD, the God of Israel, 'Let My people
go that they may celebrate a feast to Me in the wilderness.'"
2But Pharaoh said, "Who is the LORD that I should obey His
voice to let Israel go? I do not know the LORD, and besides, I
will not let Israel go." 3Then they said, "The God of the
Hebrews has met with us. Please, let us go a three days' jour-
ney into the wilderness that we may sacrifice to the LORD our
God, otherwise He will fall upon us with pestilence or with
the sword." 4But the king of Egypt said to them, "Moses and
Aaron, why do you draw the people away from their work?
Get back to your labors!"**

Verse 1. After Moses and Aaron met with the people, they went to see Pharaoh. How were they able to arrange such an interview? Did Moses' former position make it possible for him to be granted the right to approach Pharaoh? Or, had he, in the forty years since he had left Egypt, been forgotten by the court? Was it enough that he and Aaron represented a slave people of considerable size and importance to the Egyptians?

Moses and Aaron addressed Pharaoh with the prophet's preface: **"Thus says the Lord."** Then they requested permission for the **people** to go into **the wilderness** to **celebrate a feast** in honor of the Lord. The Egyptians may have heard similar appeals from other peoples who worked for them. The phrase "celebrate a feast" is translated from the verb חָגַג (*chagag*) and denotes a pilgrim festival. The term appears later in Exodus in reference to the annual celebrations of the Israelites: the Passover, Feast of Unleavened Bread, Feast of Harvest, and Feast of Ingathering (12:14; 23:14–16).

Verse 2. Pharaoh summarily denied their request, saying, **"Who is the Lord that I should obey His voice to let Israel go? I do not know the Lord, and besides, I will not let Israel go."** Pharaoh revealed his hardheartedness from the beginning. Apparently, he had no experience with the Lord and no respect for the deity of an oppressed people. To Pharaoh, who was himself considered a god, the Lord's demand seemed absurd.

This verse can be seen as a key to understanding the Exodus narrative: The purpose of God's dealings with the Egyptians was to teach Pharaoh who the Lord was and to impress upon him that all mankind—even the king of Egypt—should obey Him. Pharaoh would come to know the Lord well in the events that followed!

Verse 3. Moses and Aaron appealed to Pharaoh again, emphasizing that this pilgrimage was commanded by their **God** (see 3:18). The festival required **a three days' journey**, as well as **sacrifice**. The reason for this traveling distance is that the Egyptians considered the sacrifices of the Israelites to be detestable (see comments on 8:26). Moses and Aaron warned Pharaoh that his failure to let God's people leave could result in dire consequences for them.

Verse 4. When Moses and Aaron persisted in asking permission, Pharaoh accused them of taking **the people away from their work**. Then, with a show of malice and defiance, he made the people work even harder (5:5–14). He responded, in effect, "How dare you make such a request of me? I'll show you that you can't even think about taking off from your work!" This king had no more compassion for Israel than the previous one.

CONSEQUENCES OF THE REQUEST: GATHERING STRAW (5:5–14)

Pharaoh's Harsh Orders (5:5–9)

**5Again Pharaoh said, "Look, the people of the land are now
many, and you would have them cease from their labors!" 6So
the same day Pharaoh commanded the taskmasters over the
people and their foremen, saying, 7"You are no longer to give
the people straw to make brick as previously; let them go and
gather straw for themselves. 8But the quota of bricks which
they were making previously, you shall impose on them; you
are not to reduce any of it. Because they are lazy, therefore they
cry out, 'Let us go and sacrifice to our God.' 9Let the labor be
heavier on the men, and let them work at it so that they will
pay no attention to false words."**

Verse 5. Once more the king replied, **"Look, the people of the land** [the Israelites] **are now many, and you would have them cease from their labors!"** The first part of this statement is translated in the NRSV, "Now they [the Israelites] are more numerous than the people of the land [the Egyptians]."[1] The difference lies in the interpretation of "people of the land" (עַם הָאָרֶץ, *'am ha'arets*). If the phrase means "Egyptians," a reasonable inference, then the NRSV translation, which follows the Samaritan Pentateuch, is possible. However, "people of the land" can also mean "peasants" and more likely refers to the Israelites, as sug-

[1]The REB is similar to the NRSV: "Your people already outnumber the native Egyptians."

gested by the Hebrew text, which is followed by the NASB and most other major versions.[2]

Verse 6. In response to the request of Moses and Aaron, the king gathered **the taskmasters over the people and their foremen**. "The taskmasters over the people" were the Egyptians in charge of the production of bricks and "their foremen" were the Israelites they had placed over the work groups. The Hebrew word for "foremen," from שֹׁטֵר (*shoter*), literally means "scribes." Part of their job probably included keeping a tally of the bricks that were made each day.[3]

Verse 7. Pharaoh told these men that, from then on, the Israelites had to **gather straw for themselves** to manufacture the bricks. That would, of course, be a time-consuming and labor-intensive process.

An Egyptian painting from the tomb of Rekhmire, a royal adviser (c. 1470–1445 B.C.), illustrates the process of brick manufacturing.[4] Water was carried from a pool and then added to a mud mixture with a hoe. From there, the mud was transported to another place where the brickmaker worked. A wooden mold was pressed to the ground over the mud. After removing the mold, a newly formed brick was left to dry in the sun. Rows of these bricks were made and later stacked in preparation for their use. Alfred J. Hoerth explained why straw was to be added to the bricks: "Straw acts as a binder when the mud is poor in clay. Conversely, straw is added when the mud is too rich in clay, to prevent the bricks from warping and cracking while drying."[5]

Ruins have been found in Egypt in which buildings were made, at least in part, with bricks which contained no straw. These strawless bricks have been cited as evidence of the truth-

---

[2]John I. Durham, *Exodus,* Word Biblical Commentary, vol. 3 (Waco, Tex.: Word Books, 1987), 64–65.

[3]George Rawlinson, "Exodus," in *The Pulpit Commentary,* vol. 1, *Genesis and Exodus,* ed. H. D. M. Spence and Joseph S. Exell (Grand Rapids, Mich.: Wm. B. Eerdmans Publishing Co., 1950), 124.

[4]Alfred J. Hoerth, "Brick," in *The International Standard Bible Encyclopedia,* rev. ed., ed. Geoffrey W. Bromiley (Grand Rapids, Mich.: Wm. B. Eerdmans Publishing Co., 1979), 1:546.

[5]Ibid., 545.

fulness of the Exodus account.[6] However, it should be noted that Exodus neither says nor implies that the Israelites ever made bricks without straw.

Verse 8. Further, Pharaoh commanded that the same **quota of bricks** be required of the people. The time spent searching for straw could not be spent in the actual making of bricks, but the Israelite workers would still be required to produce the same number. The king attributed the Israelites' request to their being **lazy**. He mimicked Moses and Aaron, saying, **"Therefore they cry out, 'Let us go and sacrifice to our God'"** (see 5:3).

Verse 9. Pharaoh concluded, **"Let the labor be heavier on the men, and let them work at it so that they will pay no attention to false words."** He reasoned that if the Israelites were busy, then they would have no time to think about holding a festival to the Lord. Further, the people would disregard any speech delivered to them by Moses and Aaron. Pharaoh referred to the message that the two men previously received from God as "false words" or "lies" (NIV).

Israel's Inability to Comply (5:10–14)

[10]So the taskmasters of the people and their foremen went out and spoke to the people, saying, "Thus says Pharaoh, 'I am not going to give you any straw. [11]You go and get straw for yourselves wherever you can find it, but none of your labor will be reduced.'" [12]So the people scattered through all the land of Egypt to gather stubble for straw. [13]The taskmasters pressed them, saying, "Complete your work quota, your daily amount, just as when you had straw." [14]Moreover, the foremen of the sons of Israel, whom Pharaoh's taskmasters had set over them, were beaten and were asked, "Why have you not completed your required amount either yesterday or today in making brick as previously?"

Verses 10, 11. The **taskmasters** and **foremen** gave this news

---

[6]Henry H. Halley, *Halley's Bible Handbook*, 24th ed., rev. (Grand Rapids, Mich.: Zondervan, 1965), 120.

to the Israelites: They would have to find their own **straw** while producing the same amount of **labor** making bricks. It is probably no accident that they introduced Pharaoh's message in the same way Moses and Aaron had introduced God's message, saying, **"Thus says Pharaoh"** (see 5:1). The implication was that Pharaoh's word was equal to—indeed more powerful than—the word of Yahweh.

Verse 12. The result was that **the people scattered through all the land of Egypt to gather stubble for straw**. "Through all the land of Egypt" is probably a hyperbole intended to convey the idea of a widespread, time-consuming search for the stubble that was necessary to make bricks. (For a similar use of hyperbole, see 1:9.)

Verses 13, 14. Predictably, the Israelites fell short of delivering their allotment of bricks, with the result that the Israelite foremen **were beaten**.

THE FOREMEN'S COMPLAINT TO PHARAOH (5:15–19)

15Then the foremen of the sons of Israel came and cried out to Pharaoh, saying, "Why do you deal this way with your servants? 16There is no straw given to your servants, yet they keep saying to us, 'Make bricks!' And behold, your servants are being beaten; but it is the fault of your own people." 17But he said, "You are lazy, very lazy; therefore you say, 'Let us go and sacrifice to the LORD.' 18So go now and work; for you will be given no straw, yet you must deliver the quota of bricks." 19The foremen of the sons of Israel saw that they were in trouble because they were told, "You must not reduce your daily amount of bricks."

Verse 15. The Israelite **foremen** then complained to **Pharaoh**. It is interesting that the foremen had access to Pharaoh. The passage implies that this king of Egypt had a personal style of governance, that he was very much involved in the daily affairs of state, or at least in his building projects.

Verse 16. The foremen spoke politely, implying that they had done nothing in the past to deserve bad treatment, and claimed that their beatings were **the fault** of the Egyptians. They said that they were being treated unfairly by being forced to gather their own raw materials and still produce the same number of **bricks**. The foremen were caught in the middle between Pharaoh (and his task masters), who gave the orders, and the Israelites, who were incapable of fulfilling such unreasonable demands.

Verses 17, 18. Pharaoh's reply repeated the charge that their being **lazy** was behind their request to **sacrifice to the Lord** (see 5:8). He then said that he would not change his mind; they still had to gather their own **straw** and yet make the same number of **bricks**. Pharaoh turned their own words against them: They had said, **"Let us go,"** whereas he responded, **"So go now and work."** He meant that they would have to gather their own straw, for he reiterated that they would "be given no straw."

Verse 19. At that point, the **foremen** knew—given Pharaoh's belligerent attitude—that **they were** [really] **in trouble**. The word "trouble" (רַע, *ra'*) could also be translated "evil" (see KJV; ASV). Concerning this Hebrew term, Umberto Cassuto wrote,

> [It] may contain . . . an allusion to the name *Re'* the chief deity of the Egyptian pantheon, as though to express two thoughts simultaneously: they saw themselves in an *evil* [רַע *ra'*] plight because they had been delivered into the hands of the worshippers of the god *Re'*.[7]

The narrative style of this account is noteworthy. Here, as in other narratives, a story is repeated. In this case, the account is given four times, almost in the same words. In verses 7 and 8, Pharaoh told the taskmasters that the people were not to be given straw. In verses 10 and 11, the taskmasters relayed this message, in the same words, to the Israelites. Verse 16 records the Israelites' complaint to Pharaoh about having to gather their own straw to make bricks. Pharaoh's reply, a repeat of the command, is given in verses 18 and 19.

---

[7]Umberto Cassuto, *A Commentary on the Book of Exodus*, trans. Israel Abrahams (Jerusalem: The Magnes Press, 1997), 72.

THE FOREMEN'S COMPLAINT TO MOSES (5:20, 21)

[20]When they left Pharaoh's presence, they met Moses and Aaron as they were waiting for them. [21]They said to them, "May the LORD look upon you and judge you, for you have made us odious in Pharaoh's sight and in the sight of his servants, to put a sword in their hand to kill us."

Verse 20. As the Israelite foremen left the throne room, **they met Moses and Aaron**, who were presumably **waiting** to hear how the interview had gone. The foremen were greatly distressed by what they had just heard. When they encountered Moses and Aaron, they undoubtedly remembered the days before these two had begun to "deliver" them. Those bygone days seemed to be a sweet dream compared to the troubles they were currently experiencing.

Verse 21. The foremen complained to Moses and Aaron; they even blamed them for the trouble they were enduring. They were saying, "You have made us stink to the Egyptians—you have caused them to dislike us—and you have given them an excuse to kill us." When they spoke of **a sword . . . to kill us**, they were most likely thinking of severe mistreatment as slaves, being beaten or even being worked to death. **"May the LORD look upon you and judge you"** was a way for one who was unable to avenge himself to say, "You have wronged me; may God punish you!"

MOSES' COMPLAINT TO GOD (5:22, 23)

[22]Then Moses returned to the LORD and said, "O Lord, why have You brought harm to this people? Why did You ever send me? [23]Ever since I came to Pharaoh to speak in Your name, he has done harm to this people, and You have not delivered Your people at all."

Verses 22, 23. The text does not record how **Moses** answered the foremen. However, he must have understood and been touched by their feelings and embarrassed by their accusation against him. He took their complaint to God. Usually, he served as a mediator from God to man, bringing God's word and God's law to the people; in this case (and in others), he served as a mediator from man to God, bringing Israel's concerns to God.

Just as the people accused him of not doing what he said he would do, Moses accused God of not doing what He had promised. Moses said, in effect, "You called me to deliver the people. I came and did what You said, but You have not done what You said You would do; You have not delivered the people. In fact, their situation is worse than it was before! Why have You brought harm to this people?" It may seem presumptuous for God's servant to speak so frankly to God, but Moses often addressed God in such terms. Concerning Moses' complaint, Terence E. Fretheim commented,

> What [Moses] does not understand is why this particular effect [God's treatment of the Israelites] had to occur; this episode has only delayed the deliverance. God does not chide Moses for his hard questions. God receives them for what they are: complaints at a difficult moment in life. God simply responds by assuring Moses that his purposes are on track. . . . God's resolve is clear; Israel will be delivered. In fact, Pharaoh himself will send, indeed drive, them out with a mighty hand.[8]

Chapter 5 ends with Moses' question asked but not answered; the dilemma has been posed but not solved. God's answer is not given until the next chapter.

APPLICATION

"Who Is the LORD?" (5:2)

Pharaoh asked the question "Who is the LORD?" From our standpoint, his question sounds arrogant. It was a question asked by a stubborn, hardhearted, cruel ruler who had no love for God

---

[8]Terence E. Fretheim, *Exodus*, Interpretation: A Bible Commentary for Teaching and Preaching (Louisville: John Knox Press, 1991), 88.

or man. From Pharaoh's standpoint, it was probably a reasonable question. The Israelites were a lowly slave people, yet their representative was making demands of Pharaoh, the god-king of the greatest nation in the world! How dare he! Since Moses was speaking in the name of a deity whom Pharaoh did not recognize, he was asking, "Who is this god who presumes to make such demands?" No wonder he snarled, "Who is the LORD?" and went on to refuse Moses' demands.

Of course, Pharaoh came to know the Lord—so well, in fact, that he was brought to his knees and sought the Lord's blessings himself (12:32). Still, Pharaoh's question is a fair question. The Lord Himself frequently announced in the Book of Exodus that the purpose of His actions was to show Israel, the Egyptians, and indeed all men that He is the Lord (6:7; 7:3–5; 8:10; 8:22). Therefore, it is a good idea for us to see how the Book of Exodus answers that question. *Who is the Lord?* It is impossible to discuss all of God's characteristics in one lesson, but let us examine some of the truths taught in Exodus.

The Lord is the God of Abraham, Isaac, and Jacob (3:6, 15; 6:2, 3; 32:13). Exodus is a continuation of Genesis; everything that God did in Exodus was done to fulfill the promises God made to Abraham. God planned to bring a Savior into the world through the descendants of Abraham. He began to fulfill that plan by making Israel His people. In Exodus the God of Abraham, Isaac, and Jacob became the God of a chosen nation and began to dwell with His people Israel (19:5, 6; 29:45, 46).

The Lord is the great "I AM" (3:13, 14). The Hebrew word translated "I AM" (הָיָה, *hayah*) is closely related to the word translated "LORD" or "Yahweh" (יהוה, *YHWH*). The implication is that the Lord always is, always has been, and always will be—He is the Eternal One. God dwells not in time, but in eternity.

The Lord is the holy One (Lev. 11:45; Is. 6:3). Because He is holy, the place where He appeared to Moses became holy (3:5). The place where He was worshiped, the tabernacle, was holy (28:29, 35), and all things connected with the tabernacle—even the high priest's garments—were holy (28:2; 29:29; 30:25–29). His people were declared holy (19:6). R. Alan Cole said, "The law was a verbal expression of God's holiness, the Tent was a visible parable of it, and the nation of Israel was intended to be a walking illustration of it."[9] Just as the people of God then were to be holy (Lev. 11:45), His people today are to be holy (1 Pet. 1:15, 16).

The Lord is the all-powerful God who can defeat anyone who stands against Him. Exodus is the story of the conflict between God and the gods of Egypt, and of God's victory over those gods—a victory spoken of in Exodus 14:30 and celebrated in Exodus 15. God was superior to the gods of the greatest nation under heaven in Moses' day, and He remains greater than any other power in the universe. Cole explained, "Pharaoh stands for the height of human power, ranged against God and the people of God: therefore his fall is a fitting symbol for all time of the impossibility of striving against God, or of thwarting His plans."[10] He is, indeed, "King of kings and Lord of lords" (1 Tim. 6:15).

The Lord is a merciful and gracious God. He proclaimed Himself to be "compassionate and gracious, slow to anger, and abounding in lovingkindness" (34:6). The Book of Exodus emphasizes God's grace, providing abundant evidence of His compassion and mercy.

The Lord is the defender of the helpless. When God required the Israelites to deal fairly with the weak and defenseless, He specifically gave His character and His concerns as the reason (22:21–27; see Lev. 19:9–14).

The Lord is the God who gives commands, requires obedience, and punishes sinners. While God is gracious and merciful, He is also severe (see Rom. 11:22). He gives commands (chs. 20—24), requires obedience (19:5), and punishes disobedience (ch. 32; see Num. 15:32–36). Even the passage that speaks most clearly of His grace and mercy also says that He will not "leave the guilty unpunished" (34:7).

The Lord is a God who changes His mind. In one sense, He is changeless (see Heb. 13:8). In another sense, however, He can change His mind (see 32:14). He changed the way He dealt with Israel in accordance with their behavior. Likewise, God changes

---

[9]R. Alan Cole, *Exodus: An Introduction and Commentary*, Tyndale Old Testament Commentaries (Downers Grove, Ill.: Inter-Varsity Press, 1973), 23.

[10]Ibid., 29.

toward us when our circumstances change. As sinners, we were under the sentence of death; but when we changed our circumstances by turning to Christ and being saved, He changed His behavior toward us. We were delivered from the sentence of death and became children of God (Rom. 3:23, 24; 5:1; 6:17–23).

How would you answer the question "Who is the LORD?" Our understanding of God determines how we live. God is too holy to accept people in their sins. He is so just that He must punish sins, yet He is so merciful that He will forgive sins. We must understand this: His mercy can only be extended to those who meet the conditions He has set forth.

The God of Exodus (5:2)

In his commentary on Exodus, R. Alan Cole included an excellent section on "The Theology of Exodus." He said that the God of Exodus is:

1. "The God Who Controls History"
2. "[The God Who Says,] 'I Am Yahweh'"
3. "The God Who Is Holy"
4. "The God Who Remembers"
5. "The God Who Acts in Salvation"
6. "The God Who Acts in Judgment"
7. "The God Whose Anger May Be Averted"
8. "The God Who Speaks"
9. "The God Who Is Transcendent"
10. "The God Who Lives Among His People."[11]

Discouraged Messengers (5:20–23)[12]

At the end of chapter 5, Moses (along with the rest of Israel) was discouraged. He was not the only messenger of God to become discouraged; so did Elijah (1 Kings 19:1–18) and Jeremiah (Jer. 20:7–9). It is not wrong to be discouraged. What should God's messenger do when he becomes discouraged? Go to God,

---

[11]Ibid., 19–40.

[12]Waldemar Janzen, *Exodus*, Believers Church Bible Commentary (Scottdale, Pa.: Herald Press, 2000), 92.

as Moses did. God will comfort and encourage those who take their fears and concerns to Him (see Acts 18:9; 1 Cor. 2:3).

Initial Failure, Ultimate Success (5:20–23)

Moses' experience in Exodus 5 reminds us that initial failure does not necessarily mean ultimate defeat. At the end of the chapter, Moses apparently had lost the battle; but eventually the circumstances changed, and Moses was on the winning side! Many great men have experienced failures before finally succeeding. Many teams have come from behind to win competitions. Many Christian endeavors started from insignificant beginnings and had to overcome initial failures before their eventual success. What is the moral of the story? Keep trying, and remember that God can ultimately help us to succeed.

CHAPTER 6

BEGINNING AGAIN

Exodus 6 tells of a new beginning for the Israelites' deliverance from Egypt. In their first attempt to get Pharaoh to let the people go, Moses and Aaron had met with failure: Pharaoh had refused their request to hold a feast to the Lord and made life even more difficult for the Israelites (ch. 5). When they complained to Moses, he took their complaint to the Lord.

In response, God assured Moses of the ultimate success of the mission (6:1). Then God emphasized His name, "Yahweh," and told Moses to remind the people of the covenant He had made with Abraham, Isaac, and Jacob. Because of this covenant, He had heard the cries of the Hebrew slaves. He would deliver them, make them His people, and bring them to the land of Canaan (6:2–8). However, the Israelites were so discouraged that they took no comfort from Moses' words (6:9). God again commissioned a reluctant Moses to go before Pharaoh to demand Israel's release (6:10–13).

At this point, the account pauses to give the genealogy of the Levites, the family of Moses and Aaron (6:14–27). Then, the text says that God called Moses to deliver the people. Nevertheless, Moses again tried to resign from the mission by protesting that he was not eloquent (6:28–30). God's response to this protest is found in chapter 7.

GOD'S RESPONSE: HIS NAME REVEALED AND HIS PROMISE REPEATED (6:1–8)

1Then the LORD said to Moses, "Now you shall see what I

**will do to Pharaoh; for under compulsion he will let them go,
and under compulsion he will drive them out of his land."**
**2God spoke further to Moses and said to him, "I am the
LORD; 3and I appeared to Abraham, Isaac, and Jacob, as God
Almighty, but by My name, LORD, I did not make Myself known
to them. 4I also established My covenant with them, to give
them the land of Canaan, the land in which they sojourned.
5Furthermore I have heard the groaning of the sons of Israel,
because the Egyptians are holding them in bondage, and I have
remembered My covenant. 6Say, therefore, to the sons of Israel,
'I am the LORD, and I will bring you out from under the burdens of the Egyptians, and I will deliver you from their bondage. I will also redeem you with an outstretched arm and with
great judgments. 7Then I will take you for My people, and I
will be your God; and you shall know that I am the LORD your
God, who brought you out from under the burdens of the Egyptians. 8I will bring you to the land which I swore to give to
Abraham, Isaac, and Jacob, and I will give it to you for a possession; I am the LORD.'"**

Verse 1. God was answering Moses' questions which are found in 5:22: "Why have You brought harm to this people?"; "Why did You ever send me?" God's reply was, in effect, "Wait! The story is not over; I will deliver Israel in the end, and you yourself will observe what I will do to Pharaoh." God's answer suggested that the reason He permitted Pharaoh to thwart Moses' first attempt was that when God succeeded, it would be obvious that it was only **under compulsion** that **Pharaoh** had **let** [the people] **go**. Those who looked back on this event would not say, "Wasn't Pharaoh a kind king? He felt sorry for us and let us leave Egypt." The more Pharaoh resisted Moses' requests, the more glory God would receive when Israel finally escaped from Pharaoh's control.

The Hebrew wording in verse 1 is more literally reflected in the NRSV: "By a mighty hand he will let them go; by a mighty hand he will drive them out of his land." God, using "a mighty hand," would force Pharaoh to release Israel. Pharaoh, in turn, would drive the Israelites out of Egypt with "a mighty hand."

Verses 2, 3. God (אֱלֹהִים, *'Elohim*) again identified Himself as **the LORD** or "Yahweh" (see comments on 3:14, 15). He said that the patriarchs had known Him as **God Almighty** (אֵל שַׁדַּי, *'El Shadday*; see Gen. 17:1; 28:3; 35:11; 48:3), but not by His **name, LORD.** The problem for the interpreter of the Scriptures is that the word "LORD" or "Yahweh" (יהוה, *YHWH*) is found frequently in Genesis. Often, the patriarchs themselves used this name for God. How, then, could God say that He was not known as "LORD" or "Yahweh" to **Abraham, Isaac, and Jacob**?

One view is based on the false Documentary Hypothesis which assumes that four ancient sources were combined to form the Pentateuch. (For more information on this hypothesis, see *Appendix: The Author of Exodus*.) According to one of these alleged sources (the "E" document), the descendants of Abraham did not use the name "Yahweh" for God until the time of Moses.[1] Furthermore, according to this view, "Yahweh" was the name of "the God of the tribe to which Moses, on his flight from Egypt, joined himself."[2] Thus, at the time of Moses, the name "Yahweh," the name of the Kenites' god, was connected to the God whom the patriarchs had worshiped.

The most likely explanation of the text is that the full significance of the name "Yahweh" was not known to the fathers. In ancient times, a name was more than just a way of identifying an individual. To it were attached important meanings indicating something about the character, place, or work of the individual who bore it. Therefore, the name "Yahweh" may have been known as a name of God from the first, but its covenantal significance did not become clear until Yahweh delivered His people and established a covenant relationship with them.

The name was not new but was infused with new meaning at the time of the exodus, since Yahweh was entering into a new relationship with His people Israel. Ronald F. Youngblood noted, "Not until the time of Moses would the descendants of the patri-

---

[1]J. Philip Hyatt, *Exodus*, The New Century Bible Commentary (Grand Rapids, Mich.: Wm. B. Eerdmans Publishing Co., 1971), 93.

[2]Karl Budde, *Religion of Israel to the Exile*, American Lectures on the History of Religions, 4th Series, 1898–1899 (New York: G. P. Putnam's Sons, 1899), 19.

archs come to know that name in all of its rich meaning and application."[3] "Yahweh" was not only the unique personal name for God, but also the "relational" name for God. It was the name God used in establishing a relationship with human beings.

According to Exodus, to "know" God by the name "Yahweh" did not mean merely being able to identify the God of Israel as a deity named "Yahweh." After all, both the Egyptians and the Israelites already knew the name of Israel's God. One purpose of the plagues was to make it possible for the Egyptians to "know" the Lord. For example, in 7:17, Moses said, "Thus says the LORD, 'By this you shall know that I am the LORD: behold, I will strike the water that is in the Nile . . . and it will be turned to blood.'" In 10:2, God said that He performed His signs among the Israelites "that you may know that I am the LORD." In neither case did God say, "I have performed signs that you may believe that I am God." Therefore, He did not mean that they needed to know that Yahweh existed, to believe in Him, or to be able to identify Him by the right name. Rather, He meant that the people needed to know who He is, what He is like, and what He can do—as part of beginning or continuing a relationship with Him.

Verses 4, 5. God said that He had two reasons for delivering the Israelites. First, He had made a **covenant** with Abraham, Isaac, and Jacob. God had not only promised Abraham that his descendants would become numerous, but He also said that they would be delivered from bondage and inherit the land of Canaan (Gen. 12:7; 15:12–16, 18; 17:8). This promise was repeated to Isaac and Jacob (Gen. 24:7; 28:4, 13; 48:4; 50:24).

Second, God had **heard** [their] **groaning** (see 2:23–25) and **remembered** [that] **covenant**. To say that God "remembered" is not to imply that God can forget. Rather, it means that God determined to act to bless those remembered in accordance with His previously revealed purposes.

Verse 6. God then told Moses to announce His intentions to the people, prefacing the message with **"I am the LORD,"** an

---

[3]Ronald F. Youngblood, *Exodus*, Everyman's Bible Commentary (Chicago: Moody Bible Institute, 1983), 42.

expression frequently used in Exodus and throughout the Pentateuch. In every context where the expression is found, it provides the basis for a command, a promise, or a threat. Because God is the Lord—because God is Yahweh, with all the meaning attached to that name—there was something Israel must do, some promise they could rely on, or some threat they needed to fear. The name "Yahweh" involves the character of God. Since Yahweh is what He is, there is a certain way people must act, a reason they should be comforted or warned. The name "Yahweh" equals the character or person of the Lord; to know the Lord as "Yahweh" is to know what the Lord is like. In order that they might know Him, God intended to **bring** them out of Egypt, remove their **burdens**, **deliver** them from **bondage**, and **redeem** them by means of **great judgments**.

Verse 7. God told Moses to announce His name to the people so that they would know for certain who was responsible for their deliverance. He would take them to be His **people**, and He would **be** [their] **God**. He said, **"You shall** [then] **know that I am the LORD your God, who brought you out from under the burdens of the Egyptians."** These words of comfort foreshadowed the covenant that God would make with Israel at Mount Sinai (see 19:3–6). However, at this point in their history, they had much to learn about the Lord. God's announcement probably did not bring them the assurance it should have.

Verse 8. God would guide them to **the land** that He had promised to **Abraham, Isaac, and Jacob** (see comments on 6:4, 5). Verses 6 through 8 provide an outline for Israel's experiences from this point through the entrance into Canaan: (1) God delivers Israel from Egypt (Ex. 1—18); (2) God makes Israel His people (Ex. 19—Lev.); (3) God gives Israel a land (Num.—Josh.).

THE PEOPLE'S REFUSAL TO LISTEN (6:9)

9 So Moses spoke thus to the sons of Israel, but they did not listen to Moses on account of their despondency and cruel bondage.

Verse 9. Moses took God's message to the people. However, rather than being thrilled with a new word from God and embracing the added assurance He provided, the people remained in their **despondency**. Their spirits had been broken by Pharaoh's **cruel bondage**. Pharaoh's aim when he increased their workload had been achieved (5:9). In his contest with the God of Israel, Pharaoh seemed to be winning.

GOD'S RENEWED CALL TO MOSES (6:10–13)

**10 Now the LORD spoke to Moses, saying, 11 "Go, tell Pharaoh
king of Egypt to let the sons of Israel go out of his land." 12 But
Moses spoke before the LORD, saying, "Behold, the sons of
Israel have not listened to me; how then will Pharaoh listen to
me, for I am unskilled in speech?" 13 Then the LORD spoke to
Moses and to Aaron, and gave them a charge to the sons of
Israel and to Pharaoh king of Egypt, to bring the sons of Israel
out of the land of Egypt.**

Verses 10–13. God instructed His servant **Moses** to appear before the king again in order that His people might leave that place (see 5:1). The people of Israel were apparently not the only ones discouraged; Moses was depressed as well. It was as if he had forgotten his dialogue with the Lord at the burning bush. He reverted to the old excuses he had previously offered (4:10), but this time he added evidence to support his claim: "Even my own people will not listen to me. How, then, can you expect Pharaoh to pay me any heed? I told you I cannot speak persuasively!" God responded by repeating His commission to Moses and Aaron, telling them again that He had called them to **bring the sons of Israel out of the land of Egypt**.

MOSES AND AARON'S GENEALOGY (6:14–27)

**14 These are the heads of their fathers' households. The sons
of Reuben, Israel's firstborn: Hanoch and Pallu, Hezron and
Carmi; these are the families of Reuben. 15 The sons of Simeon:
Jemuel and Jamin and Ohad and Jachin and Zohar and Shaul
the son of a Canaanite woman; these are the families of Sim-**

eon. [16]These are the names of the sons of Levi according to their generations: Gershon and Kohath and Merari; and the length of Levi's life was one hundred and thirty-seven years. [17]The sons of Gershon: Libni and Shimei, according to their families. [18]The sons of Kohath: Amram and Izhar and Hebron and Uzziel; and the length of Kohath's life was one hundred and thirty-three years. [19]The sons of Merari: Mahli and Mushi. These are the families of the Levites according to their generations. [20]Amram married his father's sister Jochebed, and she bore him Aaron and Moses; and the length of Amram's life was one hundred and thirty-seven years. [21]The sons of Izhar: Korah and Nepheg and Zichri. [22]The sons of Uzziel: Mishael and Elzaphan and Sithri. [23]Aaron married Elisheba, the daughter of Amminadab, the sister of Nahshon, and she bore him Nadab and Abihu, Eleazar and Ithamar. [24]The sons of Korah: Assir and Elkanah and Abiasaph; these are the families of the Korahites. [25]Aaron's son Eleazar married one of the daughters of Putiel, and she bore him Phinehas. These are the heads of the fathers' households of the Levites according to their families. [26]It was the same Aaron and Moses to whom the LORD said, "Bring out the sons of Israel from the land of Egypt according to their hosts." [27]They were the ones who spoke to Pharaoh king of Egypt about bringing out the sons of Israel from Egypt; it was the same Moses and Aaron.

The function of the genealogies in Genesis, in part, was to narrow the line of mankind to Abraham, and then to narrow the line of Abraham to Jacob, in order to focus on the seed through whom God would bless the world. In Exodus, one genealogy (of a kind) has already been presented: "These are the names . . ." (1:1–5). That passage draws attention to the men who became the heads of the tribes of Israel. It answers the question "Who were the people who were delivered?" The answer is "Those who were descended from the sons of Jacob." The genealogy in chapter 6 serves a function similar to that of the listings in Genesis. Of the descendants of the people named in chapter 1, who delivered Israel? Chapter 6 answers that question: Israel's deliverers were Moses and Aaron, two men descended from Levi.

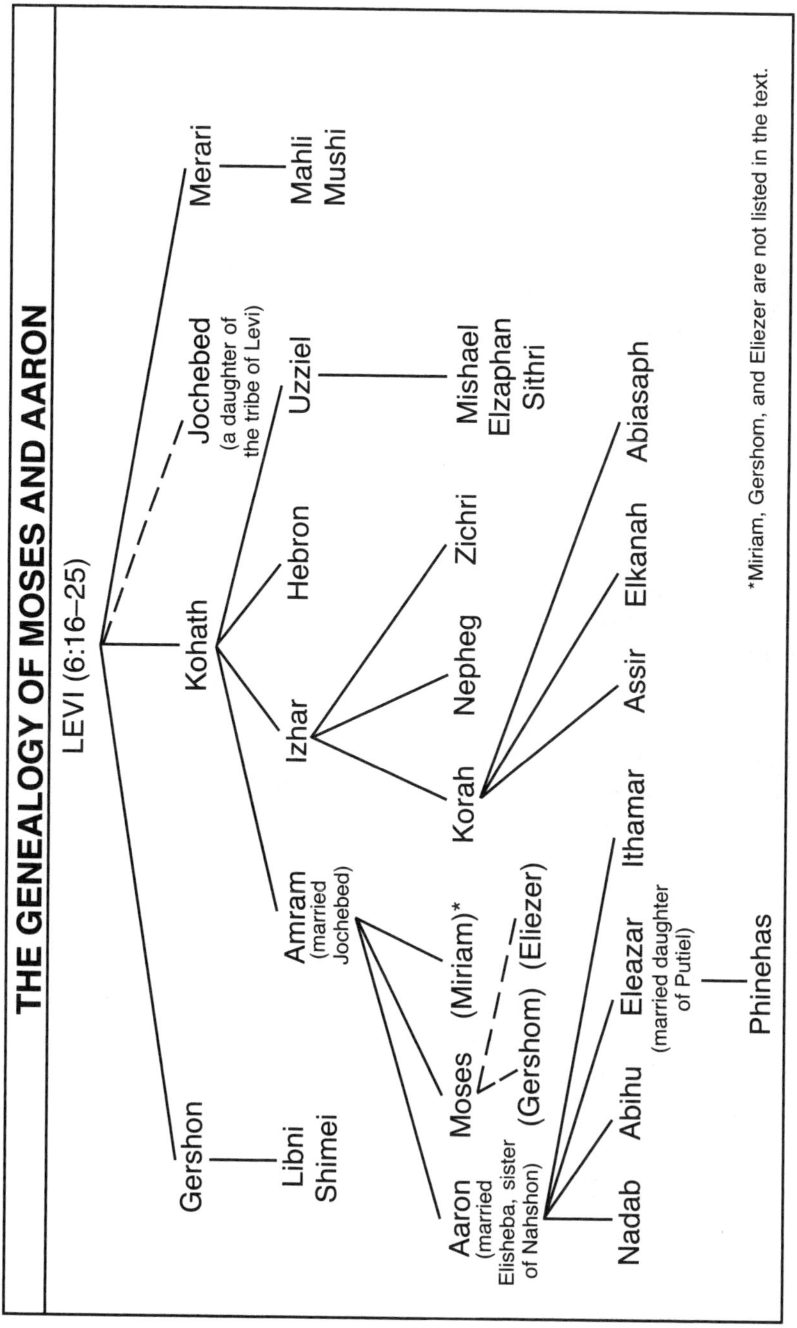
THE GENEALOGY OF MOSES AND AARON
LEVI (6:16–25)
Gershon
Kohath
Jochebed (a daughter of the tribe of Levi)
Merari
Libni
Shimei
Amram (married Jochebed)
Izhar
Hebron
Uzziel
Mahli
Mushi
Aaron (married Elisheba, sister of Nahshon)
Moses
(Miriam)*
(Gershom)
(Eliezer)
Korah
Nepheg
Zichri
Mishael
Elzaphan
Sithri
Nadab
Abihu
Eleazar (married daughter of Putiel)
Ithamar
Assir
Elkanah
Abiasaph
Phinehas
*Miriam, Gershom, and Eliezer are not listed in the text.

One question that arises from a consideration of the genealogy is: Why, in the middle of a narrative about the deliverance of Israel from Egypt, did the writer of Exodus interrupt the flow of the story to include a genealogy? The genealogy was placed between two phases of the story. Moses' first attempt to get Pharaoh to let the people go is in 4:27—6:12. It ended in failure, with Pharaoh triumphant, but with God still insisting that Moses and Aaron deliver Israel (6:10–13). In the second phase, Moses started over, so the writer included a review of what had happened earlier. This time, Moses' efforts were successful (6:28—12:51).[4]

The genealogy in chapter 6 focuses attention on the Israelites who were to become the priestly line. Since Levi was the father of the priestly tribe, the genealogy features him. Aaron was the first high priest, so the genealogy highlights him and his family rather than Moses. After Aaron, the emphasis is on Eleazar, who succeeded Aaron as high priest. Finally, Phinehas is listed in the next generation, no doubt because later the Lord gave him and his descendants "a covenant of a perpetual priesthood" (Num. 25:13).

To say that the passage emphasizes the priestly role of Aaron and his descendants does not mean, as some commentators claim, that it was written by the author(s) of the "P" document later in Israelite history because there was doubt about which family should serve as priests.[5] Even when the book was written, during the time in the wilderness, the people needed to understand the importance of the Aaronic priesthood (see Num. 16; 17).

Verses 14–16. Obviously, this genealogy is not a comprehensive listing of all the sons of Jacob. The author gave the names of **the sons of Reuben**, Jacob's oldest son, and then the names of **the sons of Simeon**, the second oldest. Next, he gave **the names of the sons of Levi**, Jacob's third oldest son. (The names

---

[4]In Genesis also, genealogies were sometimes used to separate two narratives or two parts of a narrative. For instance, the genealogy of Esau in Genesis 36 is inserted between the story of Isaac (which is largely the story of Jacob) and the story of Jacob (which is primarily the story of Jacob's sons, especially Joseph).

[5]John I. Durham, *Exodus*, Word Biblical Commentary, vol. 3 (Waco, Tex.: Word Books, 1987), 83–84.

in these lists are consistent with the record in Genesis 46:9–11.) Then the author continued by giving the genealogy of Levi's family. He provided no information about the other sons of Jacob. Therefore, the genealogy of Exodus is a selective one, focusing on the family of Levi, and especially on the family of Moses and Aaron. It was important to remind readers that these men who were leading God's people were descendants of Levi, the son of Jacob. At that time, it was much more important to know from what family a person descended than it is now.

Verses 17–19. The three sons of Levi introduced in verse 16 are now highlighted, along with their descendants. The names of these men were **Gershon**, **Kohath**, and **Merari**. Although all of the descendants of these men were considered **Levites**, only those coming from Kohath (through Amram and Aaron) would serve as priests in the tabernacle. Thus, the genealogy focuses on Kohath's descendants: **Amram and Izhar and Hebron and Uzziel.**

Verse 20. Although previously introduced as descendants of Levi (2:1), Moses' parents are identified here for the first time: His father was **Amram** and his mother was **Jochebed**. Amram **married his father's sister**, that is, his aunt. Later, marriage between a man and his aunt was forbidden in the Law (Lev. 18:12). Jochebed gave birth to two sons, **Aaron and Moses**. Their sister, Miriam (15:20), is not mentioned in the genealogy.

A question that arises from a consideration of the genealogy relates to the numbers found in it. For one thing, only two generations separate Levi from Moses. Levi was the father of Kohath; Kohath, of Amram; Amram, of Aaron and Moses. Therefore, Levi was Moses' great-grandfather—assuming that the term "son" should always be interpreted literally in this context. On the surface, it is difficult to understand how 430 years (12:40) could transpire in just four generations (see Gen. 15:16) and Israel could increase from about seventy people who entered Egypt with Jacob to about two million who left with Moses.

Furthermore, the text says that Levi lived 137 years (6:16), Kohath lived 133 years (6:18), and Amram lived 137 years (6:20). The total number of years the three men lived is 407 years, which would be close to the amount of time that Israel spent in Egypt.

However, Levi was an older man when Israel went into Egypt, and Kohath also went from Canaan into Egypt (Gen. 46:6, 7, 11). Since the lives of the sons and their fathers would have overlapped, the years, if taken literally, cannot be added together to determine the length of the Egyptian sojourn. Four generations would more likely add up to one hundred, or, at the most, two hundred years, rather than four hundred.

Umberto Cassuto said that the numbers in a genealogy are not to be taken literally, either here or in Genesis. Adding the figurative meanings he proposed for these numbers, he arrived at "a period of 430 years, which is the number recorded in [12:40]."[6] However, the problem is solved by most conservative commentators by assuming that generations were left out of this genealogy, just as they are passed over in other biblical genealogies.[7] Based on the genealogies found in 1 Chronicles, Gleason L. Archer, Jr., pointed out that "there were nine or ten generations between the sons of Jacob and the generation of Moses."[8] For example, 1 Chronicles 7:22–27 lists ten generations from Jacob's grandson Ephraim to Moses' assistant Joshua.[9]

Verses 21, 22. In addition to Amram, two other sons of Kohath, **Izhar** and **Uzziel**, are highlighted by their descendants. One of the **sons** of Izhar was **Korah**, who is mentioned again in verse 24. No descendants are named for Kohath's son Hebron.

Verse 23. Instead of featuring Moses, the genealogy emphasizes his brother **Aaron**, Amram's firstborn son (see 7:7). Aaron **married Elisheba, the daughter of Amminadab, the sister of Nahshon.** Elisheba's family came from the lineage of Judah. Her brother Nahshon was a prominent leader for that tribe during

---

[6]Umberto Cassuto, *A Commentary on the Book of Exodus*, trans. Israel Abrahams (Jerusalem: Magnes Press, 1997), 87.

[7]R. Alan Cole, *Exodus: An Introduction and Commentary*, Tyndale Old Testament Commentaries (Downers Grove, Ill.: Inter-Varsity Press, 1973), 87; Wilbur Fields, *Exploring Exodus*, Bible Study Textbook Series (Joplin, Mo.: College Press, 1976), 149–50; Peter Enns, *Exodus*, The NIV Application Commentary (Grand Rapids, Mich.: Zondervan, 2000), 177.

[8]Gleason L. Archer, Jr., *Encyclopedia of Bible Difficulties* (Grand Rapids, Mich.: Zondervan Publishing House, 1982), 111.

[9]Ibid., 111-12.

the wilderness wandering (Num. 1:7; 2:3; 7:12, 17; 10:14). The names of Amminadab and Nahshon both appear in the genealogies of King David (Ruth 4:20) and Jesus Christ (Mt. 1:4).

Aaron and Elisheba had four sons: **Nadab and Abihu, Eleazar and Ithamar.** The first two sons, Nadab and Abihu, are infamous for the "strange fire" they offered to God which resulted in their deaths (Lev. 10:1, 2). In contrast, Eleazar and Ithamar are remembered for their godliness. After Aaron's death, Eleazar took his place as high priest (Num. 20:28; Deut. 10:6).

Verse 24. The descendants of **Korah** (6:21) are listed here, interrupting Aaron's family line. Korah was one of the leaders of the rebellion against Moses and Aaron in the wilderness. He challenged the idea that only Aaron and his sons could serve as priests, claiming that the whole congregation was holy to God. As a result, the Lord brought judgment on Korah and the other rebels by swallowing some of them up in the earth and sending down fire from heaven to consume the rest (Num. 16:1–40).

Verse 25. The attention returns to the priestly lineage of Aaron, whose third **son Eleazar** became the father of **Phinehas**. Phinehas is remembered for his great zeal, which stopped the plague that God had brought on Israel for their idolatry and immorality (Num. 25).

The genealogy ends as it began in verse 14: **These are the heads of the fathers' households.** However, the added reference to **the Levites** indicates that the purpose of the record was to highlight the priestly tribe.

Verses 26, 27. The fact that the genealogy is about the ancestry of Aaron and Moses is punctuated in these verses. The author's use of repetition forms a chiasm:

A1: **It was the same Aaron and Moses**
  B1: **to whom the LORD said, "Bring out the sons of Israel from the land of Egypt according to their hosts."**
    C: **They were the ones who spoke to Pharaoh king of Egypt**
  B2: **about bringing out the sons of Israel from Egypt;**
A2: **it was the same Moses and Aaron.**

This structure begins and ends with Aaron, who was featured in the genealogy.

GOD'S COMMAND FOR MOSES TO SPEAK TO PHARAOH (6:28–30)

[28]Now it came about on the day when the LORD spoke to Moses in the land of Egypt, [29]that the LORD spoke to Moses, saying, "I am the LORD; speak to Pharaoh king of Egypt all that I speak to you." [30]But Moses said before the LORD, "Behold, I am unskilled in speech; how then will Pharaoh listen to me?"

Verses 28–30. The verses which immediately follow the genealogy raise a question: When did **the LORD** [speak] **to Moses** on this occasion? The problem again is repetition; 6:28–30 repeats the thoughts found in 6:10–12, using almost the same words. In 6:28–30, was the writer speaking of the same occasion or of a different occasion than that spoken of in 6:10–12? If he was speaking of the same occasion, why did he believe it necessary to repeat the same information in almost the same words?

Perhaps the best way to understand 6:28–30 is to see these words as the beginning of a new chapter in the narrative of the deliverance. The previous chapter consisted of 4:27—6:13, a passage that can be read from first to last as an exciting story. The story tells of the failure of Moses' mission, but it makes sense. Then, as a dividing line between the two parts of the story, we have the genealogy of 6:14–27. This new part begins with 6:28 and continues through 12:51; in it the writer told how the second attempt at deliverance succeeded. Walter C. Kaiser, Jr., said, "Many regard this section [6:14–27] as an 'interruption' of the narrative. But the narrative itself is at a turning point. The stage has been set in 1:1—6:12, and now the main action begins."[10]

In verse 28 Moses indicated that God had commissioned him in **Egypt** (without denying that He had also spoken to him at

---

[10]Walter C. Kaiser, Jr., "Exodus," in *The Expositor's Bible Commentary*, vol. 2, *Genesis—Numbers* (Grand Rapids, Mich.: Zondervan, 1990), 344.

Sinai) and said **on** [that] **day** He gave instructions to Moses to speak to Pharaoh on His behalf. Apparently, 6:10–13 and 6:28–30 refer to the same occasion.[11] The account provides a fitting conclusion to the story that ends in verse 13 and a suitable beginning to the story that begins in verse 28.

As in verse 12, the text once again notes that Moses claimed to be **unskilled in speech** (עֲרַל שְׂפָתָיִם, *ʿaral śepathayim*), a phrase that can be literally translated "uncircumcised lips" (KJV; NKJV). This expression is an idiom obviously meaning "unskilled in speech" or something similar. The NRSV has "poor speaker," and the NIV has "faltering lips." "Uncircumcised lips" probably refers to "lips that are not adequate and capable of saying the words necessary to get a needed job done," just as "uncircumcised hearts and ears" depicts "ears and hearts that will not hear and comprehend."[12] Implied in this figure of speech is the idea that being "uncircumcised" means being inferior or inadequate or unclean—a view which reflects the Israelites' understanding of themselves as the "circumcised," especially called and blessed by God, in contrast to the "uncircumcised" (everyone else), who were not so blessed. God provided a solution to Moses' problem in the next chapter; in fact, it is the same solution He had provided earlier (4:14–16).

APPLICATION

Dealing with Discouragement (Ch. 6)

Warren W. Wiersbe noted that Moses became discouraged but did what all God's leaders ought to do: Moses took his problems to the Lord. Wiersbe asked, "How did the Lord encourage His struggling servant?" and answered this question with four statements. (1) "God spoke to him and gave him great promises" (6:1–8)." (2) "God . . . reminded Moses of His covenant name 'Jehovah'" (6:3). (3) "The Lord assured Moses that He felt the

---

[11]Enns, 176.

[12]Fields, 147. Leviticus 26:41 uses the phrase "uncircumcised hearts" (see Ezek. 44:7, 9), and Jeremiah 6:10 (KJV) speaks of an uncircumcised ear. Moses described his inability to speak well with different words in 4:10.

burdens of His people and was working on their behalf" (6:5; see 2:24). (4) "The Lord commanded Moses to speak to Pharaoh again" (6:9–13). Then he declared that the genealogy which follows "isn't there by accident, for it's the Lord's way of reminding us, the readers, that God had prepared Moses and Aaron for their ministry in Egypt."[13]

Strengthened by God (Ch. 6)

Moses surely needed strengthening after the resistance described in chapter 5. Wilbur Fields showed that "God's man" was strengthened by the following: (1) God's name (6:2, 3, 6, 29); (2) God's promises (6:1, 6–8); (3) God's covenant (6:4, 5); (4) God's command (6:10–13, 28, 29); and (5) past examples (family associations) (6:14–27).[14]

How God Deals with Disappointment (6:1–13)

The beginning of Exodus 6 depicts Moses as being discouraged. He had done what God had told him to do. He had done everything he could for his people. He had attempted to deliver Israel from Egyptian slavery, but none of his efforts had succeeded. Pharaoh had spurned him, mocked his God, and rejected his request. Worse, Pharaoh had made life harder for the Israelites. As a result, the Israelites—who had once welcomed Moses (4:29–31)—had turned against him (5:19–21). Moses' bright hope for Israel's release had been extinguished. He must have been wondering, "Where is God in all this? Did He not promise to be with us, to make our efforts successful? What happened to those promises?" Therefore, Moses complained to God (5:22, 23).

Did you ever feel as if everything you were doing—even what you were trying to do for God—was going wrong? What should you do in such a situation? You should do what Moses did: Even though he complained, he made the right choice in taking his problem to God. Then the story turns to what God did. As we consider what God did for Moses, we can find com-

---

[13]Warren W. Wiersbe, *Be Delivered* (Colorado Springs, Colo.: Victor, 1998), 25–27.

[14]Fields, 140.

fort in our own situations. Let us see how God deals with discouragement by thinking about what God did for Moses.

God did not rebuke Moses. Moses complained to God. However, from God's standpoint, his complaint did not deserve a rebuke. Sometimes we are too timid when we approach God. We must be willing to speak our minds to God, to share with Him our deepest thoughts. The more direct and personal and heartfelt our prayers are, the more meaningful they will be.

God encouraged Moses. God first reassured Moses that his mission would ultimately be successful (6:1). Second, God encouraged him by giving a further revelation about Himself (6:2–4). He reminded Moses that He was "the LORD," the God of the patriarchs. Third, God encouraged him by telling Moses of His concern for the people and repeating the promises He had made to them (6:5–8).

When we are discouraged, we need to remember these truths: (1) Though we may experience temporary and temporal failures, ultimately, if we are faithful to God, permanent and eternal success will be ours. (2) God loves us and has a personal interest in us. We should take courage in His nature—in His love, His compassion, His power, and His might. Our faith regarding the future is based not on our ability, but on God's strength. (3) God has promised to be with us. We are His covenant people, as were the Israelites, and we can depend on His promises. He will strengthen us so that we can indeed accomplish everything He wants us to do (Eph. 3:20; Phil. 4:13).

God recommissioned Moses. Moses brought good news to Israel: God had not forgotten or forsaken His people. He would deliver them. However, the Israelites, mired in despondency, refused to hear. That must have deepened Moses' own discouragement. God's response to Moses was, in effect, "Do what I originally called you to do" (see 6:10, 11). Regardless of how he felt, Moses was to carry out his commission.

When times of discouragement come to us, what should we do? We should not quit! We should carry out our commission, the Great Commission, doing all we can to fulfill God's will.

God met Moses' need. Moses, in his discouragement, thought himself inadequate for the job; apparently his old feelings of inferiority returned (6:12; see 4:10). Again, the Lord did not rebuke Moses. Rather, He met Moses' need for help and reminded him of his call (6:13). Likewise, God will take care of our inadequacies, whether real or imagined. We simply need to remember who is on our side. "If God be for us, who can be against us?" (Rom. 8:31; KJV).

Do you ever get discouraged because of your failures or because of the way others treat you? If you do, you are in good company—the company of Moses and Elijah, for instance. What should you do when you are discouraged? (1) Turn to God. Tell Him your problems, and then leave the matter in His hands. (2) Carry out the commission He has given you. "Let us not lose heart in doing good, for in due time we will reap if we do not grow weary" (Gal. 6:9).

The Names of God (6:2, 3)

The names of God in the Old Testament have great meaning and significance. Three of those names are given in this text: (1) "The LORD" (*YHWH*), (2) "God" (*'Elohim*), and (3) "God Almighty" (*'El Shadday*). Additional names are found in other texts. Among them are *'Adon* (or *'Adonay*), meaning "Lord," and *'El 'Elyon*, which is translated as "God Most High."[15]

God's Promises (6:6–8)

God promised deliverance from the burdens of Egypt, deliverance from bondage, redemption, the opportunity to become God's people, and entrance into the promised land. These promises sound similar to God's promises to mankind today (see Mt. 11:28; Jn. 8:32; 14:3; Gal. 3:26, 27).

Why People Will Not Hear Good News (6:9)

Moses brought the people good news, but they would not listen because of their "despondency and cruel bondage." Some people will not hear the good news of the gospel today because

---

[15]These names are discussed in J. Alec Motyer, "The Names of God," in *Eerdmans' Handbook to the Bible*, ed. David Alexander and Pat Alexander (Grand Rapids, Mich.: Wm. B. Eerdmans Publishing Co., 1973), 157–58. Most Bible dictionaries explain the various names used for God.

they also are despondent and in bondage. (The preacher or teacher may want to give other examples of people who would not hear the good news for reasons that are given in the Bible or are easily deduced. For example, see Acts 12:12–16.)

Children of God (6:14–27)

In ancient times, great importance was attached to sonship. This tendency is evidenced in the genealogy of Moses and Aaron in Exodus 6. Many people today are interested in tracing their genealogies, hoping to discover that they are descended from someone great. More important than who our ancestors are is the fact that we are children of God. He is our Father, and we are in His family (see 1 Jn. 3:1, 2).

Chapter 7

The Plagues: Water Turned to Blood

After the failure of Moses' first attempt to free Israel from Pharaoh's dominion (chs. 5; 6), chapter 7 reports the beginning of the successful effort to persuade the king of Egypt to let God's people go. The deliverance was accomplished by means of ten plagues. Therefore, the story of Israel's release is largely a story of the plagues, as told in chapters 7 through 13.

Chapter 7 begins with God's response to Moses' complaint that he was "unskilled in speech" (6:30). As He had arranged at Sinai, God provided for Moses' weakness by giving him Aaron to be his spokesman (7:1, 2). Again, He indicated what would happen when Moses and Aaron spoke to Pharaoh (7:3–5).

Next, the text reveals how Moses and Aaron obeyed God's instructions (7:6, 7). They appeared before Pharaoh, demanded that he let Israel go, and worked a miracle before him: Aaron's rod became a serpent. However, Egypt's magicians imitated the sign, and Pharaoh refused Israel's request (7:8–13).

Then, at the Lord's urging, Moses and Aaron went to Pharaoh and warned him that God would turn the water of Egypt into blood. The first plague followed (7:14–21). When the magicians did a trick to imitate this miracle, Pharaoh's heart was hardened, and he refused the Israelites' request (7:22–25).

GOD'S PROMISE OF SUCCESS (7:1–7)

**1Then the Lord said to Moses, "See, I make you as God to
Pharaoh, and your brother Aaron shall be your prophet. 2You
shall speak all that I command you, and your brother Aaron**

shall speak to Pharaoh that he let the sons of Israel go out of his land. 3But I will harden Pharaoh's heart that I may multiply My signs and My wonders in the land of Egypt. 4When Pharaoh does not listen to you, then I will lay My hand on Egypt and bring out My hosts, My people the sons of Israel, from the land of Egypt by great judgments. 5The Egyptians shall know that I am the LORD, when I stretch out My hand on Egypt and bring out the sons of Israel from their midst." 6So Moses and Aaron did it; as the LORD commanded them, thus they did. 7Moses was eighty years old and Aaron eighty-three, when they spoke to Pharaoh.

Verses 1, 2. The LORD started over with **Moses**. Considerable time may have elapsed after the failed attempt to free Israel (4:29—6:9) and the renewed call to Moses (6:10–13, 28, 29). Moses seemed to have forgotten his prior objection and God's prior provision (4:10–16; see 6:12, 30). Nevertheless, God was patient with Moses. He did not reproach Moses for his forgetfulness or faithlessness, but simply repeated what He had said before (3:10; 4:15, 16, 22, 23). **Aaron** would be Moses' spokesman, just as a **prophet** is God's spokesman, and **Pharaoh** was to be the recipient of the message.

Verses 3, 4. God went on to warn Moses that He would **harden Pharaoh's heart** so that the king would **not listen** to Israel's request for release. This message echoed the previous warnings that God had given to Moses (3:19–22; 4:21). Apparently, God wanted Moses to understand that he was not called to an easy task; he was to speak to an unreceptive king. Perhaps God wanted to forewarn Moses about Pharaoh's stubbornness in order to keep Moses from becoming depressed or giving up. When God called certain prophets on later occasions, He also let them know that their primary audience would not listen to their message.

The statement "I will harden Pharaoh's heart" and similar expressions appear throughout the narrative of the ten plagues (9:12; 10:1, 20, 27; 11:10; 14:4, 8, 17). Do these expressions mean that God hardened Pharaoh's heart against his will, taking away his freedom of choice and making him merely a pawn in the divine plan? While the text here attributes the hardening of Pharaoh's heart to God, other verses in Exodus say that Pharaoh hardened his own heart (7:13, 14, 22, 23; 8:15, 19, 32; 9:7, 34, 35). Apparently, Pharaoh made a choice to react negatively to Moses' demands. Having demonstrated a hard heart, Pharaoh then became the object of God's additional hardening. When one hardens his heart and chooses the downward way, God allows—and even turns him over to—his downward slide to perdition.

When Pharaoh's heart was hardened, God intended to send **signs** (אוֹת, *'oth*), **wonders** (מוֹפֵת, *mopeth*), and **judgments** (שֶׁפֶט, *shepet*) to deliver Israel. Throughout the Exodus account, the plagues are called "signs and wonders" or simply "signs" (7:3; 8:23; 10:1, 2) and "judgments" (7:4; 12:12), as well as "plagues" (9:14; 11:1; 12:13). These descriptive words suggest a "blow" or a "stroke" that God planned to deliver against Pharaoh.

Eventually, God would **bring out** [His] **hosts**, who are identified as **My people the sons of Israel.** The term "hosts" (צָבָא, *tsaba'*) suggests "armies." While the escaping captives did not look like armies, the people of Israel had the potential to become a powerful fighting force. Enabled by God's might, they would eventually defeat every nation that stood in the way of their conquest of the land that He had given to them.

Perhaps the most important lesson to be learned from this passage is that *God is in control.* God spoke through Moses; He hardened Pharaoh's heart; He sent the plagues; He delivered the people; and He, in the end, was magnified, even by the Egyptians. They at last recognized the inability of their many gods to protect them against the mighty hand of Moses' God. Throughout Exodus, Yahweh is the "only prime mover in the narratives of revelation and deliverance, and even of the offering of [the] covenant."[1] Moses played a role in the drama of the book, but God was the author, director, and main character!

Verse 5. As a result of God's "signs," "wonders," and "judgments" (7:3, 4), **the Egyptians** would **know** God to be **the Lord.** This does not mean merely that the Egyptians were to recognize

[1]John I. Durham, *Exodus*, Word Biblical Commentary, vol. 3 (Waco, Tex.: Word Books, 1987), 86.

that Yahweh had enabled the Israelites to escape captivity. Rather, the Egyptians would know something about Yahweh that they had not known before. "To know" Yahweh is to know more than God's name; it is to understand something about Him—about His nature, His character, His power, and His might. God was sending these plagues to enable the Egyptians "to know" Him, that is, to reveal great truths about Himself to the Egyptians. God wanted to be known even by the heathen Egyptians.

Verse 6. God's servants complied with His orders: **So Moses and Aaron did it; as the LORD commanded them, thus they did.** Not only does this statement serve as a fitting conclusion to the paragraph (7:1–7), it also functions as a preface to the narrative that follows and introduces a theme found frequently in the Pentateuch—namely, the obedience of God's people (see 7:20; 39:43). From this point on, Moses and Aaron followed God's orders.

Verse 7. The statement that **Moses was eighty years old and Aaron eighty-three** should be considered as parenthetical, inserted to provide personal information about the two major characters of the narrative. This, too, is typical of the Pentateuch. Frequently in Genesis, and to a lesser extent in the other books of the Torah, the writer inserted the age of the individual about whom he was writing. The passage may also indicate that "Moses and Aaron [had] earned the right to some respect by virtue of their survival to the age of experienced wisdom."[2] At an age when many people today have retired, the eighty-year-old Moses was about to begin the adventure of a lifetime and the work for which he will forever be remembered.

THE MIRACLE OF THE STAFF (7:8–13)

[8]Now the LORD spoke to Moses and Aaron, saying, [9]"When Pharaoh speaks to you, saying, 'Work a miracle,' then you shall say to Aaron, 'Take your staff and throw it down before Pharaoh, that it may become a serpent.'" [10]So Moses and Aaron came to Pharaoh, and thus they did just as the LORD had commanded; and Aaron threw his staff down before Pharaoh and

---

[2]Ibid., 88.

his servants, and it became a serpent. [11]Then Pharaoh also called for the wise men and the sorcerers, and they also, the magicians of Egypt, did the same with their secret arts. [12]For each one threw down his staff and they turned into serpents. But Aaron's staff swallowed up their staffs. [13]Yet Pharaoh's heart was hardened, and he did not listen to them, as the LORD had said.

Verses 8–10. The first time **Moses and Aaron** appeared before **Pharaoh**, they worked no miracle (5:1–4). The next time they went before him, God told them to demonstrate their credentials by turning Aaron's **staff** into **a serpent** (see 4:1–5). Following God's orders, they met with **Pharaoh**, and Aaron's staff became a serpent.

Two questions arise from verse 10. First, the text specifies that **Aaron threw his staff down**; but when God first appeared to Moses, it was Moses' staff that was turned into a snake (4:3). Were both Moses and Aaron's staffs turned into serpents? Probably, this rod was the same one used by Moses; it became common property when God endowed it with power in the hands of Moses and Aaron. It could be spoken of as Moses' staff (9:23; 10:13; 14:16), Aaron's staff (7:10–12), or God's rod (4:20).

Second, the words for **serpent** are different in 4:3 (נָחָשׁ, *nachash*) and 7:10 (תַּנִּין, *thannin*). In fact, the word *thannin* in 7:10 can mean "crocodile" and is so translated by Umberto Cassuto.[3] John I. Durham translated it as "a monstrous snake."[4] Was a different kind of creature produced in chapter 7 than in chapter 4? While it is possible that in chapter 7 a crocodile or some larger reptile was produced, it is also possible that the author was using a synonym.[5] Regardless of the answers to these questions, the meaning of the passage is not affected: God provided a miracle to show Pharaoh that Moses and Aaron were His messengers.

---

[3]Umberto Cassuto, *A Commentary on the Book of Exodus*, trans. Israel Abrahams (Jerusalem: Magnes Press, 1997), 94.

[4]Durham, 89.

[5]George Rawlinson, "Exodus," in *The Pulpit Commentary*, vol. 1, *Genesis and Exodus*, ed. H. D. M. Spence and Joseph S. Exell (Grand Rapids, Mich.: Wm. B. Eerdmans Publishing Co., 1950), 166.

Verses 11–13. Whatever effect that miracle might have had on **Pharaoh** was nullified when **the magicians of Egypt** were able to duplicate this feat **with their secret arts**. However, God proved the authenticity of the sign done by Moses and Aaron by causing **Aaron's staff** to swallow up the magicians' **staffs**. Nevertheless, Pharaoh remained unconvinced. His **heart was hardened, and he did not listen** to Moses and Aaron's request, just **as the LORD had said**.

How could the magicians duplicate Moses and Aaron's signs, since the text makes it clear that Moses and Aaron performed real miracles? Some believe that the magicians were able, by some demonic power, to perform supernatural feats. Some Bible passages seem to suggest that Satan has at times been given such power (see 2 Thess. 2:9–12; Rev. 13:14; 16:14; 19:20).

A more likely explanation is that the Egyptian magicians were good at doing what magicians have always done: making people believe that they could do the impossible, and, therefore, the miraculous. Nahum M. Sarna supported this opinion by stating that "the trick was a standard item in their [the magicians'] professional repertoire."[6]

In either case, the text makes it clear that God's powers were more impressive than the magicians' apparent powers. By His divine strength, Aaron's snake swallowed the other snakes. As the story progresses, the preeminence of God's power becomes even more evident when the magicians are unable to duplicate the majority of the plagues. Although unnamed here, later Jewish, Christian, and pagan literature identifies two of these magicians as Jannes and Jambres (see 2 Tim. 3:8).

WATER TURNED TO BLOOD (7:14–25)

The Lord's Directions (7:14–19)

[14]Then the LORD said to Moses, "Pharaoh's heart is stubborn; he refuses to let the people go. [15]Go to Pharaoh in the

---

[6]Nahum M. Sarna, *Exploring Exodus: The Origins of Biblical Israel* (New York: Schocken Books, 1996), 67.

morning as he is going out to the water, and station yourself to meet him on the bank of the Nile; and you shall take in your hand the staff that was turned into a serpent. [16]You shall say to him, 'The LORD, the God of the Hebrews, sent me to you, saying, "Let My people go, that they may serve Me in the wilderness. But behold, you have not listened until now." [17]Thus says the LORD, "By this you shall know that I am the LORD: behold, I will strike the water that is in the Nile with the staff that is in my hand, and it will be turned to blood. [18]The fish that are in the Nile will die, and the Nile will become foul, and the Egyptians will find difficulty in drinking water from the Nile."'" [19]Then the LORD said to Moses, "Say to Aaron, 'Take your staff and stretch out your hand over the waters of Egypt, over their rivers, over their streams, and over their pools, and over all their reservoirs of water, that they may become blood; and there will be blood throughout all the land of Egypt, both in vessels of wood and in vessels of stone.'"

Verses 14, 15. Since the miracle of turning the staff into a serpent failed to convince Pharaoh to let Israel leave (7:13), **the LORD** gave **Moses** directions concerning the next sign. This was the first plague: turning water into blood. God made the reason for the plague clear: Pharaoh was **stubborn** and **refuse**[d] **to let the people go**. Moses was told when and how to announce the plague. He was to **go . . . in the morning**, to **take in** [his] **hand the staff that was turned into a serpent**, and to speak to **Pharaoh**.

Verses 16–18. When he spoke, Moses was to specify the following:

1. *Who sent him*—Moses was sent by **the LORD**, Yahweh, **the God of the Hebrews**.
2. *The Lord's demand*—God said, **"Let My people go,"** that Israel might **serve** the Lord **in the wilderness**.
3. *Pharaoh's previous response*—Pharaoh had refused to listen.
4. *God's purpose in sending the plague*—He wanted Pharaoh and all of Egypt to **know** that God is **the LORD**, Yahweh.

5. *What the plague would involve*—**The water** would **be turned to blood**, the **fish** would **die**, and **the Egyptians** would **find difficulty in drinking water from the Nile.**

This plague was not accompanied by an appeal for Israel's freedom, but was rather announced as a consequence of Pharaoh's previous refusal to permit Israel to leave Egypt. God did not tell Moses to say to Pharaoh, "Unless you let the people of Israel go, you will experience this plague." Instead, He instructed Moses to say something like this to Pharaoh: "Because you have refused to allow Israel to leave, because of the hardness of your heart, you will experience this plague."

Verse 19. After **Moses** announced the coming of the plague, he instructed **Aaron** to **stretch out** [his] **hand** with the **staff**, causing the **waters** throughout **Egypt** to become **blood**. The plague would affect everyone in **Egypt**; the water would be turned to blood in the **rivers** ("streams"; NIV), **streams** ("canals"; NIV), **pools** ("ponds"; NIV), **reservoirs of water**, and **vessels of wood and . . . vessels of stone**. The term "vessels" is not in the original Hebrew text. Instead, it merely says "in wood and stone" (וּבָעֵצִים וּבָאֲבָנִים, *uba'etsim uba'ᵃbanim*). The NIV interprets this phrase to mean "wooden buckets and stone jars." Rawlinson suggested that the text refers to tanks of wood and stone which were used in homes for storing water from the Nile.[7]

Moses and Aaron's Obedience (7:20–25)

[20]So Moses and Aaron did even as the LORD had commanded. And he lifted up the staff and struck the water that was in the Nile, in the sight of Pharaoh and in the sight of his servants, and all the water that was in the Nile was turned to blood. [21]The fish that were in the Nile died, and the Nile became foul, so that the Egyptians could not drink water from the Nile. And the blood was through all the land of Egypt. [22]But the

[7]Rawlinson, 172.

magicians of Egypt did the same with their secret arts; and Pharaoh's heart was hardened, and he did not listen to them, as the LORD had said. [23]Then Pharaoh turned and went into his house with no concern even for this. [24]So all the Egyptians dug around the Nile for water to drink, for they could not drink of the water of the Nile. [25]Seven days passed after the LORD had struck the Nile.

Verse 20. The writer again said that **Moses and Aaron** were obedient to **the LORD.** Just as God **had commanded**, and as Moses had said, Aaron **lifted up the staff and struck the water that was in the Nile** and **the water . . . was turned to blood**. Moses and Aaron had an audience for this demonstration; not only was **Pharaoh** present, but also many of Pharaoh's **servants** were there. These servants probably included high government officials, such as might be found in a king's advisory council.

Verse 21. One consequence of the plague was that **the fish** in the **Nile died** and it **became foul**, presumably because of the decaying fish. The magnitude of the blow that this plague struck upon the Egyptian psyche is almost inconceivable. The Nile was the source of life for Egypt; without its water, Egypt could not exist. R. Alan Cole wrote, "The Nile was worshipped as a god, and . . . its water was the life-blood of Egypt."[8] This plague made the Nile almost useless. It could not provide **the Egyptians**, most of whom lived within a few miles of the river, with their basic necessities. They could not eat its fish, which they relied on as a food staple. Further, they **could not drink** [its] **water** or use it for irrigating their crops.

One question that arises with regard to this first plague is "Was the water turned into real **blood**?" Could something like sand, red dirt, or algae have been added to the water so that it turned red like blood and caused the fish to die? Some assert that since the text says "blood," it means "blood" and any attempt to make anything else out of the word is misguided. The word translated "blood" (דָּם, *dam*) is the usual word for "blood" in the

---

[8]R. Alan Cole, *Exodus: An Introduction and Commentary*, Tyndale Old Testament Commentaries (Downers Grove, Ill.: Inter-Varsity Press, 1973), 90.

Old Testament. Further, those who believe in God have no difficulty accepting the fact that He could change real water into real blood, if He chose to do so. After all, Jesus demonstrated His power by changing real water into real wine (Jn. 2:6–10).

Those who believe that the water did not become real blood may have this opinion without doing any injustice to the text or denying God's ability to work miracles. The people of ancient times were incapable of performing modern chemical analyses on substances. It is possible, therefore, that to the writer—and to the people affected by the plague—the substance looked like blood; therefore, the author called it blood (see 2 Kings 3:22, 23). In other words, "The thought is not one of clinical analysis but of outward resemblance."[9] According to 7:20, the Nile was turned to blood, but 7:24 says that because of the plague "the Egyptians . . . could not drink of the water of the Nile." The water had been turned to blood, but the passage says that the Nile was still water. Apparently, the best way to interpret this paragraph is to say that the writer was telling his readers that the water was turned into something that looked like blood and perhaps tasted like blood, but was understood to be red, foul-smelling, undrinkable water, polluted to the extent that the fish in the river died.

Verses 22, 23. For the Nile to be stricken was a disaster; but when **the magicians** were able to do what seemed like **the same** thing (no doubt on a smaller scale), **Pharaoh's heart was hardened**. He went back to his palace with **no concern** for what **the Lord had said** or the problems his own people faced.

Verses 24, 25. The writer did not say that this plague left **the Egyptians** altogether without water. They were able to dig shallow wells **around the Nile** to get **water to drink**. The notice that **seven days passed after the Lord had struck the Nile** may indicate that the first plague lasted seven days.

APPLICATION

How God Works in the World (7:1–10)

Exodus, like the other books in the Bible, was written to reveal

---

[9]Ibid.

God so that we might know Him better. One thing the book reveals is how God works in the world. Exodus shows that God does get involved with humanity. He is not, as Deism suggests, a God who is far off, removed from the world and unconcerned about His creation. He is not an uninvolved, uncaring God who made the universe and then removed Himself to let it function and deteriorate on its own. Both the Old and the New Testaments teach that God has intervened in human history. He intervened to rescue the Israelites from slavery. He intervened by sending Jesus Christ, in accordance with His promises to Abraham, to rescue mankind from sin and its consequences.

How has God worked in the world in the past? How does He work today?

First, in the past God worked through miracles. God is capable of performing miracles, and He has done so in human history. The Bible often speaks of the miracles God has performed; Exodus abounds in miracles. Among them are the burning bush, the ten plagues, the miraculous crossing of the Red Sea, the provision of manna and quail, and water that came forth from a rock. To reject these as miracles, one would have to reject the Bible as a reliable historical record, and, therefore, reject the inspiration of the Scriptures.

God no longer works miraculously as He did in Bible times. Many people use the word "miracle" to refer to marvelous events or beneficial occurrences which they attribute to God. We should not deny that everything good that happens in the world is, in fact, God's doing (Jas. 1:17). However, to state that whatever God does through natural means is a "miracle" is to use the word in a way that the Bible does not use it. The Scriptures teach that the age of the miraculous—the time of God's performing the biblical kind of miracles—is over.

Second, God works through natural laws. The Bible teaches that events we regard as "natural"—the sun rising, the rain falling, and the grass growing—are God's doing. Jesus said, "[God] causes His sun to rise on the evil and the good, and sends rain on the righteous and the unrighteous" (Mt. 5:45). Notice that *God* "causes His sun to rise" and "sends rain." Indeed, anything that happens by "natural" laws is God's work (see Ex. 4:10, 11). When a person gets sick and takes medicine prescribed by a doctor, someone might claim, "The doctor [or the medicine] made him well." Someone else might argue, "He got well according to the laws of nature; in a sense, 'nature' made him sick and 'nature' made him well." However, the Christian can declare, without denying the working of natural law, "God made him well."

Third, God works through providence. When we say that God works "through providence," we are asserting that God works in the world in non-miraculous ways. The best statement of God's providence is found in Romans 8:28. That fact is evident in Exodus, especially in the life of Moses. He grew up in Pharaoh's household. If Pharaoh had not attempted to wipe out a generation of baby boys, Moses would not have been reared in Pharaoh's court and would not have been as well prepared to lead Israel out of Egypt. Should we attribute the things that happened to Moses during the first eighty years of his life to coincidence? The Christian sees all these events as God's working through providence, non-miraculously, to accomplish His purposes.

Most readers can see God's providence in Moses' life. The question is, Does God still work providentially today? Romans 8:28 says so, and the history of mankind and the accounts of the early church—perhaps even our own history—provide evidence that He does. That fact should comfort and encourage us, especially when our outlook is grim.

Fourth, God works through people. God wanted something done: He wanted His people delivered out of Egypt. He could have accomplished that task without human intervention. (Since God had the power to create the universe, nothing is impossible for Him.) Instead, He chose to use a human agent, Moses, to do what He wanted done. The work was God's, and God was given the credit; yet God used a fallible human being to get it done. Likewise, in the Christian age, God wants people to be saved. He accomplishes that work using human agents—people who preach and teach the gospel to all the world (Mt. 28:18–20; Rom. 10:12–17). The work is God's, and God gets the credit. Nevertheless, human beings must answer the call and allow God to work through them (Acts 14:27). We must be willing to hear God's call and use our heads, hands, feet, and mouths in His service, to accomplish His work. When God works through us, we are to give Him the glory.

Conclusion. God is active in the world today, through nature and through providence, but He also wants to accomplish His will through us. Are we willing to be used by God today? We sing, "Our God, He Is Alive." Let us believe it and act as if we believe it!

Aaron Illustrates the Role of a Prophet (7:1, 2)

What was the role of a prophet? God put the words in his mouth, and he spoke for God; he was God's mouthpiece. Moses was to be "as God," and Aaron was to be Moses' "prophet" (7:1, 2). In other words, Moses was to "put the words in his mouth" (4:15). Aaron was to speak for Moses "to the people," serving as a "mouth" for Moses (4:16).

Counterfeit Religion (7:22)

Pharaoh's magicians could duplicate Moses' signs (7:22). How? Probably, by doing magic tricks. Although their signs were counterfeit, they were convincing. In New Testament times, some apparently performed counterfeit miracles (Acts 8:9–11; 2 Thess. 2:8–12; Rev. 13:14; 16:13, 14; 19:20). Imitation of New Testament Christianity was also possible in other ways. In particular, false teachers presented a perverted form of Christ's teaching. Jesus warned about the coming of false teachers (Mt. 7:15) and so did His apostles (1 Jn. 4:1). Counterfeit forms of Christianity exist today and may be very convincing, as were the magicians' tricks. To avoid being deceived by those who claim to perform miracles today, we must know that counterfeit religion exists and know how to distinguish the counterfeit from the real thing. Ultimately, God will convincingly demonstrate the difference between false religion and the true way (Mt. 7:21–23).

Chapter 8

The Plagues: Frogs, Gnats, and Flies

Chapter 8 records the second plague (frogs), the third plague (gnats), and the fourth plague (flies). In connection with the second plague, Moses and Aaron appeared before Pharaoh to demand Israel's release and to announce the plague that would come if he refused their request (8:1, 2). By the power of God, Moses and Aaron produced the frogs; yet, the Egyptian magicians duplicated the feat (8:3–7). Pharaoh relented and called for Moses and Aaron. He said that if they would remove the plague, he would let the people go. Consequently, the plague was removed (8:8–14), but Pharaoh hardened his heart and refused to let the people go (8:15).

According to God's word, Moses and Aaron then produced gnats which spread throughout the land. The magicians were convinced that this sign was done by "the finger of God." However, Pharaoh remained unmoved and unwilling to let Israel leave Egypt (8:16–19).

Prior to the next plague, Moses confronted Pharaoh and warned him that swarms of flies would afflict Egypt if he did not let the Israelites go. He added that God would make a distinction between Egypt and Israel: Goshen, the land where the Israelites lived, would not experience the plague. God sent the plague, just as Moses had said (8:20–24). Pharaoh responded by trying to bargain with Moses, first suggesting that Israel worship within the land. Then, he gave permission for Israel to go only a short distance to hold their feast (8:25–29). After the swarms of flies departed, Pharaoh hardened his heart again and refused to let the people go (8:30–32).

FROGS (8:1–15)

Frogs Cover Egypt (8:1–7)

[1]Then the LORD said to Moses, "Go to Pharaoh and say to him, 'Thus says the LORD, "Let My people go, that they may serve Me. [2]But if you refuse to let them go, behold, I will smite your whole territory with frogs. [3]The Nile will swarm with frogs, which will come up and go into your house and into your bedroom and on your bed, and into the houses of your servants and on your people, and into your ovens and into your kneading bowls. [4]So the frogs will come up on you and your people and all your servants."'" [5]Then the LORD said to Moses, "Say to Aaron, 'Stretch out your hand with your staff over the rivers, over the streams and over the pools, and make frogs come up on the land of Egypt.'" [6]So Aaron stretched out his hand over the waters of Egypt, and the frogs came up and covered the land of Egypt. [7]The magicians did the same with their secret arts, making frogs come up on the land of Egypt.

Verses 1, 2. The account of the second plague relates what Moses was to say to **Pharaoh** but does not record Moses' actual encounter with the Egyptian king. **The LORD** said that the second plague was to be prefaced by an appeal—**"Let My people go"**—and a threat—**"But if you refuse to let them go, behold, I will smite your whole territory with frogs."** The verb "smite" (נָגַף, *nagap*) sometimes refers to a blow that causes serious injury or even fatality. It is also used for the overwhelming defeat of an army in battle. In ancient Egypt, "frogs" were used as a symbol of the goddess Heket (or Heqet), who supposedly aided women in childbirth. Women wore charms bearing her image to protect them while giving birth. Instead of being a symbol of aid, the frog would become a devastating menace to Egyptian society.

Verses 3, 4. The effect of the plague is vividly described. The **frogs** would be found in Pharaoh's **house** and **bedroom**, on his **bed**, and in the **houses of** [his] **servants** ("officials"; NIV) and the rest of his **people**, the Egyptians. They would even pollute the **ovens** and **kneading bowls** throughout the land. By mentioning such personal places, the author emphasized that no one would escape their foul presence.

Ancient "ovens" were mostly utilized for baking bread. They were made from clay and were shaped like either a cylinder or an egg. Ovens could be placed in the ground or above it, either indoors or outside.[1] "Kneading bowls" or "kneading troughs" (NIV) were used for mixing water and flour in order to make bread. These cooking utensils could be large in size, a fact illustrated by a clay figurine of an ancient Phoenician woman kneading her dough (ninth to sixth centuries B.C.).[2] However, the type of trough used by the Israelites "must have been a small, light wooden box, for it could be bound up in clothes and carried on the shoulders (Ex. 12:34)."[3]

Verses 5–7. Since nothing is said about Pharaoh's reaction to Moses' demands, the reader must assume that the king again refused Israel's appeal. What is certain is that the Lord told Aaron to **stretch out** [his] **hand** (see 7:19), and the result was that **frogs came up and covered the land of Egypt**. However, **the magicians** were able, probably by means of some conjuror's trick, to duplicate to a small degree the miracle God performed through Aaron.

The Frogs Die Out (8:8–15)

8Then Pharaoh called for Moses and Aaron and said, "Entreat the LORD that He remove the frogs from me and from my people; and I will let the people go, that they may sacrifice to the LORD." 9Moses said to Pharaoh, "The honor is yours to tell me: when shall I entreat for you and your servants and your people, that the frogs be destroyed from you and your houses, that they may be left only in the Nile?"

---

[1]David M. Howard, Jr., "Oven," in *The International Standard Bible Encyclopedia*, rev. ed., ed. Geoffrey W. Bromiley (Grand Rapids, Mich.: Wm. B. Eerdmans Publishing Co., 1986), 3:622.

[2]Adrianus van Selms, "Bread," in *The International Standard Bible Encyclopedia*, rev. ed., ed. Geoffrey W. Bromiley (Grand Rapids, Mich.: Wm. B. Eerdmans Publishing Co., 1979), 1:541.

[3]Ibid.

[10]Then he said, "Tomorrow." So he said, "May it be according to your word, that you may know that there is no one like the LORD our God. [11]The frogs will depart from you and your houses and your servants and your people; they will be left only in the Nile." [12]Then Moses and Aaron went out from Pharaoh, and Moses cried to the LORD concerning the frogs which He had inflicted upon Pharaoh. [13]The LORD did according to the word of Moses, and the frogs died out of the houses, the courts, and the fields. [14]So they piled them in heaps, and the land became foul. [15]But when Pharaoh saw that there was relief, he hardened his heart and did not listen to them, as the LORD had said.

Verse 8. If the magicians hoped to convince Pharaoh that they were as capable of working wonders as Moses and Aaron, they should have demonstrated their ability to remove the frogs, rather than pretending to be able to produce more frogs. Pharaoh saw that, in spite of their secret arts and trickery, he could not depend on his magicians to end the plague. Therefore, he invited **Moses and Aaron** to come before him and asked Moses to **entreat the LORD** [to] **remove the frogs**. He agreed that he would **let the people go, that they** [might] **sacrifice to the LORD.** Pharaoh's attitude had already changed since he asked, "Who is the LORD . . . ?" (5:2); but he had not yet arrived at the point of surrender that he would reach later in the story (12:32).

Verses 9, 10. Moses gave **Pharaoh** the opportunity to choose when the plague of frogs would end. When Pharaoh named the time (**"Tomorrow"**) and the plague was removed at that exact time, there could be no doubt that the plague had been sent and then taken away by **the LORD**, the **God** of Israel. The king would then become convinced of the unique power of the Lord, realizing that **there is no one like** Him.

Verse 11. Moses assured Pharaoh that **the frogs** would be removed from him, his officials, and the Egyptian people; **they** [would] **be left only in the Nile.** This river served as a natural habitat for these creatures. Frogs tended to be more plentiful in Egypt after the annual flooding of the Nile; the receding waters left ponds which served as a breeding ground for them.

Verses 12–14. After **Moses and Aaron** departed from **Pharaoh**, Moses prayed for **the LORD** to remove **the frogs. The LORD** heard Moses' intercession and **did according to the word of Moses,**[4] illustrating that, as James said, "The effective prayer of a righteous man can accomplish much" (Jas. 5:16).

However, the removal of the plague was almost as unpleasant as the plague itself. Walter C. Kaiser, Jr., said, "This 'relief' [רְוָחָה, *r^ewachah;* 8:15] was worse than the plague for this proud king."[5] The offending frogs did not just hop back into the river. Rather, they died wherever they were—in **the houses, the courts, and the fields**. In an effort to clean up, the Egyptians **piled them in heaps**. The aftermath of the plague may have been its worst aspect: **the land became foul**. The land was filled with the stench of decaying frogs.[6] This same language previously occurred in 7:21 where the fish "died, and the Nile became foul." Whether or not the Egyptians realized it, the smell was the consequence of Pharaoh's refusal to heed God's directions.

Verse 15. Nevertheless, after **Pharaoh saw that there was relief, he hardened his heart** (וְהַכְבֵּד אֶת־לִבּוֹ, *w^ehakbed 'eth libbo*). Three different Hebrew verbs, with various shades of meaning, are used in the statements made about the hardening of Pharaoh's heart. One frequent word, used here in verse 15, is כָּבֵד (*kabed*), which means "be heavy." Another verb that commonly occurs is חָזַק (*chazaq*), meaning "grow strong." In 7:3 and 13:15, the word is actually קָשָׁה (*qashah*), which means "make hard."

Pharaoh's perversity is evident again. He had seen Moses and Aaron perform miracles, had seen Egypt troubled by two plagues, and had seen his people suffer from those plagues. Still, when relief came, he forgot his pledge to Moses and refused to let God's people go. Pharaoh's failure to **listen** happened just as

---

[4]Almost the same words are used to describe God's response to Moses' prayer as are used to describe Moses' obedience to God's instructions (7:6, 10, 20).

[5]Walter C. Kaiser, Jr., "Exodus," in *The Expositor's Bible Commentary*, vol. 2, *Genesis—Numbers* (Grand Rapids, Mich.: Zondervan, 1990), 352. Verse 15 is numbered as verse 11 in the Hebrew text.

[6]These details suggest that the account was written by an eyewitness and therefore provide evidence of its authenticity.

God had predicted, and these circumstances would still work out so that God would be glorified.

GNATS (8:16–19)

[16]Then the Lord said to Moses, "Say to Aaron, 'Stretch out your staff and strike the dust of the earth, that it may become gnats through all the land of Egypt.'" [17]They did so; and Aaron stretched out his hand with his staff, and struck the dust of the earth, and there were gnats on man and beast. All the dust of the earth became gnats through all the land of Egypt. [18]The magicians tried with their secret arts to bring forth gnats, but they could not; so there were gnats on man and beast. [19]Then the magicians said to Pharaoh, "This is the finger of God." But Pharaoh's heart was hardened, and he did not listen to them, as the Lord had said.

Verses 16, 17. As a result of Pharaoh's hardening his heart, God sent the third plague, the plague of **gnats**, which affected both **man and beast**. The Hebrew word translated "gnats" in the NASB is from כֵּן (*ken*). Exactly what insect is represented by this word is difficult to determine since the term rarely appears in the Old Testament.[7] While several versions besides the NASB also have "gnats" (NRSV; NIV; ESV; NAB), others translate *ken* as "lice" (KJV; NKJV), "maggots" (REB), and "mosquitoes" (NJB).

The Jewish philosopher Philo described the "gnats" of this plague as entering the nostrils and ears, as well as flying into the eyes and injuring the pupils.[8] R. Alan Cole said that the word *ken* probably referred to mosquitoes: "Mosquitoes will breed in unbelievable numbers; when disturbed they rise in a black cloud, and the air is full of their shrill buzz."[9] Whatever the plague involved, the insects were innumerable and widespread **through**

---

[7]In addition to Exodus 8:16–18, the term *ken* appears in Psalm 105:31, which refers back to this third plague. Further, some scholars think the word is also found in Isaiah 51:6; the NIV renders the term "flies" in that passage.

[8]Philo *On the Life of Moses* 1.19.

[9]R. Alan Cole, *Exodus: An Introduction and Commentary*, Tyndale Old Testament Commentaries (Downers Grove, Ill.: Inter-Varsity Press, 1973), 92–93.

all the land of Egypt. "All" does not necessarily mean that these pests affected every square foot of Egyptian territory; rather, the word suggests that the gnats (or mosquitoes) were dispersed throughout the country.

Verses 18, 19. The **magicians** had, to this point, appeared to match Moses' miracle-working. However, they could not duplicate the production of the **gnats**. Therefore, they concluded that Moses was more than a magician and what he was doing was more than just a magic trick. Moses' miracles were real.

The context implies a meeting called by Pharaoh after the plague, at which Pharaoh asked his counselors whether or not he should give in to Moses' demands. The magicians had been invited to this meeting, and they advised **Pharaoh**, saying, **"This is the finger of God."** In other words, they said, "This is the real thing; this is not just a trick." The implication was that Pharaoh ought to listen to Moses and Aaron, for they truly came from the God who works miracles.

The expression "finger of God" is similar to those concerning His mighty "hand" and "arm" (see comments on 3:19). Even though God is a spiritual being, He is described in human terms to help people understand Him better. The power of God's finger(s) is applied to the Creation (Ps. 8:3), the writing of the Ten Commandments on tablets of stone (Ex. 31:18; Deut. 9:10), and Jesus' driving out demons (Lk. 11:20).

Pharaoh refused to heed the magicians' advice and **hardened** his **heart** again, with the result that Israel was again forbidden to exit the land of their slavery. Nothing is said about the removal of the third plague. The gnats, or mosquitoes, were a temporary problem that may have solved itself. Just as God had turned the Nile into blood for a short time, He had temporarily sent the plague of gnats upon Egypt.

FLIES (8:20–32)

Flies Swarm Egypt (8:20–24)

20Now the LORD said to Moses, "Rise early in the morning and present yourself before Pharaoh, as he comes out to the

water, and say to him, 'Thus says the LORD, "Let My people go, that they may serve Me. [21]For if you do not let My people go, behold, I will send swarms of flies on you and on your servants and on your people and into your houses; and the houses of the Egyptians will be full of swarms of flies, and also the ground on which they dwell. [22]But on that day I will set apart the land of Goshen, where My people are living, so that no swarms of flies will be there, in order that you may know that I, the LORD, am in the midst of the land. [23]I will put a division between My people and your people. Tomorrow this sign will occur."'" [24]Then the LORD did so. And there came great swarms of flies into the house of Pharaoh and the houses of his servants and the land was laid waste because of the swarms of flies in all the land of Egypt.

Verse 20. After **Pharaoh** changed his mind and refused to allow the people of Israel to go, God sent the fourth plague. He instructed **Moses** to confront the king **early in the morning . . . as he comes out to the water**, just as Moses had done before the first plague (7:15). Moses was also told to go to Pharaoh "early in the morning" before the seventh plague (9:13). Moses' message from God was the same as it had been before: **"Let My people go."**

Verse 21. Coupled with the message was the threat of the fourth plague. If Pharaoh refused to listen, God would **send swarms of flies** on him, his officials, and the Egyptian people. What was this plague? The original text reads merely "swarms" (הֶעָרֹב, *he'arob*). In addition to the NASB, most other translations also assume that "swarms of flies" are meant (KJV; NKJV; NRSV; NIV; ESV; REB; NAB). The NJB translates the term as "horseflies." Some editions of the NASB have "swarms of insects." Cole indicated that the word means "mixture" and could refer to a mixture of insects, "swarms of all sorts of flying creatures," but added that if one species is meant, the Septuagint translation suggests the offending insect was the "modern gadfly or March-fly," which has a painful bite.[10] The psalmist later wrote that God

---

[10]Cole, 93–94. See Philo *On the Life of Moses* 1.23.

"sent among them swarms of flies which devoured them" (Ps. 78:45). To the ancient Egyptians, the biting fly symbolized tenacity and persistence. A military decoration known as the "Order of the Golden Fly" or "Fly of Valor" was awarded to their soldiers for bravery in battle.

Verses 22, 23. The plague was to affect everyone and every place in Egypt, except God's people in **the land of Goshen** (Gen. 45:10; 47:27). In exempting the Israelites from this plague, God made it clear that He differentiated between His people and the Egyptians. He apparently did the same thing in the rest of the plagues (9:4, 11, 26; 10:6, 23; 11:7). While punishing the Egyptians, God protected His people. In doing so, He emphasized His presence: **"I, the LORD, am in the midst of the land."**

Moses was to set a time for the plague to begin: **"Tomorrow."** Then, when it happened, Pharaoh and his servants would know that the Lord had brought the plague upon Egypt. The arrival of the "swarms" could not be seen as merely coincidental.

Verse 24. The author recorded what God instructed Moses to tell Pharaoh and then skipped to the coming of the plague. He omitted Moses' actual encounter with Pharaoh, when Moses presented God's word to Pharaoh and the king refused to hear. The writer assumed that the reader would understand what had happened.

The plague first affected **the house of Pharaoh**, and then **the houses of his servants** ("officials"; NIV). The fact that **the land was laid waste because of the swarms of flies** has led some commentators to identify the "swarms" as insects which were not only annoying but also spread infectious diseases, such as skin anthrax.[11]

The Flies Removed (8:25–32)

25Pharaoh called for Moses and Aaron and said, "Go, sacrifice to your God within the land." 26But Moses said, "It is not

---

[11]John H. Walton and Victor H. Matthews, *Genesis—Deuteronomy*, The IVP Bible Background Commentary (Downers Grove, Ill.: InterVarsity Press, 1997), 92.

right to do so, for we will sacrifice to the LORD our God what is an abomination to the Egyptians. If we sacrifice what is an abomination to the Egyptians before their eyes, will they not then stone us? 27We must go a three days' journey into the wilderness and sacrifice to the LORD our God as He commands us." 28Pharaoh said, "I will let you go, that you may sacrifice to the LORD your God in the wilderness; only you shall not go very far away. Make supplication for me." 29Then Moses said, "Behold, I am going out from you, and I shall make supplication to the LORD that the swarms of flies may depart from Pharaoh, from his servants, and from his people tomorrow; only do not let Pharaoh deal deceitfully again in not letting the people go to sacrifice to the LORD."

30So Moses went out from Pharaoh and made supplication to the LORD. 31The LORD did as Moses asked, and removed the swarms of flies from Pharaoh, from his servants and from his people; not one remained. 32But Pharaoh hardened his heart this time also, and he did not let the people go.

Verse 25. The swarms of flies bothered **Pharaoh** so much that, for the first time, he agreed to Moses' demands. He called **Moses and Aaron** and gave them permission to take a religious holiday **within the land** of Egypt. This was the first in a series of compromises proposed by Pharaoh.

Verses 26, 27. Moses replied that they could not **sacrifice to the LORD** within the land what was **an abomination to the Egyptians** (see Gen. 43:32; 46:34). Cole commented, "Moses refuses on the grounds that to sacrifice in Egypt would be like killing a pig in a Muslim mosque, or slaughtering a cow in a Hindu temple. . . . [R]ioting would break out at once."[12] James K. Hoffmeier suggested that the Egyptians might have objected to Israel's sacrificing for any one of three reasons: (1) They might have objected to sacrificing cattle because they viewed them as sacred; (2) they might have objected to sacrificing sheep because of their aversion to shepherds (Gen. 46:34); or (3) they might have

---

[12]Cole, 95.

simply objected to the sacrificial rites of Israel.[13] Whatever the reason for the objection, Moses' protest implied "that it would be inappropriate to offer Yahweh pure offerings in a pagan land."[14] Moses therefore insisted on Israel's going on **a three days' journey into the wilderness** in order to make their sacrifices to the Lord.

Verses 28, 29. Pharaoh apparently agreed to Moses' terms, adding only that Israel should **not go very far away**. Then Pharaoh entreated **Moses** to ask **the LORD** to remove the **flies**. Moses agreed, saying that he would take care of the matter the next day; but he stipulated that **Pharaoh** must not **deal deceitfully again** with the Israelites, as he had done in the case of the frogs (8:8, 15). In other words, Pharaoh had to keep his part of the bargain when the plague was removed.

Was Moses telling the truth when he told Pharaoh that Israel wanted to go into the wilderness **to sacrifice** to God? One answer to that question is that, in fact, Israel did go three days into the wilderness (and beyond), and they did sacrifice to the Lord. Some might say that Moses told the truth, even though it was not the whole truth. A better answer is that if Pharaoh had granted Israel such a privilege, the exodus might have been unnecessary. However, God knew that the king would not. Therefore, the request was merely one step which, combined with others, led to God's complete triumph over Egypt and Israel's miraculous deliverance.

Verses 30–32. The result of Moses' appearance before the pharaoh on this occasion was similar to what had happened after the plague of frogs (8:12–15). **Moses** prayed, **the LORD** heard, and the plague was **removed**. Nevertheless, **Pharaoh hardened his heart** and did not allow the Israelites to leave Egypt. The king was arrogant, cruel, selfish, and deceitful. He was a covenant breaker. For such a ruler, one can have no pity—only disdain. The narrative compels the reader to look forward to Pharaoh's ultimate defeat.

---

[13]James K. Hoffmeier, "Exodus," in *Evangelical Commentary on the Bible,* ed. Walter A. Elwell (Grand Rapids, Mich.: Baker Book House, 1989), 46.

[14]Ibid.

APPLICATION

"Let My People Go" (8:1)

God's people were in bondage, and God demanded through His spokesman Moses, "Let My people go" (8:1). Today, many people are in bondage. They may be enslaved, for instance, by the effects of poverty, alcoholism, drug addiction, or racial prejudice. Such people need to be freed! Furthermore, God wants them to be free.

We are God's agents to do His work in the world. While freeing people from the bondage that blights their lives is not the primary mission of the church, it should be part of our mission. Helping others physically, socially, and mentally is doing good to all people as we have opportunity (Gal. 6:10). This includes visiting orphans and widows in their affliction (Jas. 1:27), doing to others as we would have them do to us (Mt. 7:12), and loving our neighbors as ourselves (Mt. 22:39).

Most significant, however, is recognizing that people are in bondage to sin and need to be freed (Rom. 3:23; 6:23). The primary mission of the church is to do all we can, in the name of Christ, to free those who are in bondage to sin and Satan (Jn. 8:34–36; Heb. 2:14, 15). Just as Moses contended with Pharaoh for the freedom of Israel, we are in a constant battle, trying to free people from the devil's grip as we demand, in God's name, "Let My people go!"

The Incomparable God (8:10)

Various lessons could be developed using 8:10 as a text.

(1) The plagues demonstrated conclusively that the gods of Egypt were not to be compared with the Lord God. The prophets often taught the same truth, contrasting the Lord with the people's idols. We need to understand that "there is no one like the LORD."

(2) "There is no one like the LORD" today to direct our steps, to heal our hurts, to bless our lives, and to save us from sin.

(3) Another possibility is to concentrate on the characteristics of God: "There is no one like the LORD," for example, in holiness, love, or wrath.

God Answers Prayer (8:12, 13)

"Moses cried to the LORD," and "the LORD did according to the word of Moses" (8:12, 13). When righteous people cry out to God, He hears them (Mt. 7:7, 8; Jas. 5:16).

The Most Dangerous Disease: Hardening of the Heart (8:15)

Some people suffer from a dangerous condition called "hardening of the arteries." The medical term for this condition is "arteriosclerosis," and it is defined as "a chronic disease in which thickening and hardening of the arterial walls impair blood circulation."[15] A person who has this disease is in danger of suffering a stroke or a heart attack.

An even more deadly disease is the "hardening of the heart." Pharaoh had this problem. Exodus 8:15 says that Pharaoh "hardened his heart and did not listen" to God's messengers. The Lord had just sent the second plague, frogs, upon the land of Egypt, as Moses had predicted. Pharaoh relented and asked Moses to remove the frogs, saying that he would let Israel go (8:8). Moses agreed, Pharaoh named the time, and the frogs died. However, Pharaoh did not honor his word; he refused to let the people go. He "hardened his heart."

As we consider the hardening of Pharaoh's heart, we will note how people today can be afflicted by the same problem.

How was Pharaoh's heart hardened? Exodus sometimes says that Pharaoh hardened his heart (8:15), while other times it says that God hardened Pharaoh's heart (4:21; 7:3; 9:12; 10:1). Which one is right? Did God harden Pharaoh's heart, or did he harden his own heart? If we say that God hardened Pharaoh's heart, does that mean that Pharaoh had no will of his own, that he was unable to make any choice except the one which God imposed upon him?

The best solution to the problem is to recognize that Exodus first emphasizes that Pharaoh hardened his heart and then states that God hardened Pharaoh's heart. Both 4:21 and 7:3 speak of what God would do in the future; only after Pharaoh had hard-

---

[15]*The American Heritage Dictionary*, 4th ed., s.v. "arteriosclerosis."

ened his heart does the text say that God hardened it. In other words, after Pharaoh had hardened his own heart, then God further hardened it. Pharaoh had decided on the road he would take, but God perhaps gave him a push down that road. We can be sure that Pharaoh had free will, just as we do. He was responsible for his own choices, and God will hold him accountable for the choices he made.

When we consider more carefully what happened when Pharaoh hardened his heart, we conclude that Pharaoh's disease involved the following: (1) persistence and stubbornness, (2) refusal to hear God's word, (3) unwillingness to accept abundant evidence of the truth of that word, (4) arrogance and pride, and (5) a lack of compassion for people.

How can our hearts be hardened? "Hardening of the heart" is also a problem today. The New Testament says that some have their consciences "seared with a hot iron" (1 Tim. 4:2; KJV). Furthermore, it speaks of people who hardened their hearts (Mk. 6:52; Acts 19:9) and warns us against the hardening of the heart (Heb. 3:8, 13, 15; 4:7).

Second Thessalonians 2:10–12 describes some who will "perish" because "God will send upon them a deluding influence so that they will believe what is false." Who are these people who are sent along the path to destruction by God Himself? They are individuals who "did not receive the love of the truth so as to be saved" and "did not believe the truth, but took pleasure in wickedness." In other words, if a person does not love or believe the truth but takes pleasure in wickedness, then God may send him a "deluding influence" so that he will believe a lie and perish eternally! If we, like Pharaoh, deliberately choose the wrong path, God will not hinder us from taking it. Indeed, He may speed us on our way.

If we persistently refuse to hear the Word of God in spite of the evidence for its truth, then we have hard hearts. If we are full of pride and lack compassion for others, then we are like Pharaoh.

Conclusion. We must remember that the hardening of the heart is more dangerous than the hardening of the arteries because it can lead to *eternal* death! God's Word can soften a hard heart. The story of the cross and the Christ who died for us can dissolve that wall we have erected between us and God's mercy. Let us come to Him in faith and obedience.

"This Is the Finger of God" (8:19)

When the magicians of Egypt said, "This is the finger of God" (8:19), they were acknowledging God as the source of the plague of gnats. We sometimes speak of natural disasters as "acts of God," but are not other things that we experience also "acts of God"? Do we see the "finger of God" in our lives? We must acknowledge that God is working in our world. We should learn to see the "finger of God" as He works in our lives.

Chapter 9

The Plagues: Cattle Disease, Boils, and Hail

Exodus 9 records the next three plagues—plagues number five (cattle disease), six (boils on man and beast), and seven (hail). The Lord instructed Moses to go before Pharaoh again and ask him to let Israel go. He was to tell Pharaoh that, if he refused the request, God would send a fatal pestilence on Egypt's livestock but would spare Israel's animals (9:1–4). Just as God said, the plague fell upon the Egyptians the next day (9:5, 6). However, Pharaoh still refused to release Israel (9:7).

Next, without warning the Egyptians ahead of time, God sent the plague of boils on man and beast. This plague was so pervasive that it also affected Egypt's magicians and kept them from taking their place at court. Even this painful experience did not convince Pharaoh to let the Israelites leave Egypt (9:8–12).

The third plague in the chapter is prefaced by God's declaration of His purposes. After again demanding Israel's freedom, God threatened to send another plague. Yet, this time He declared that the plague would teach Egypt to know the Lord and His unique power, so that God's name might be proclaimed (9:13–16). Because of Pharaoh's stubbornness, God said He would send a plague of hail which would destroy crops and kill any man or beast left in the open. This prior warning made it possible for believers, even among the Egyptians, to escape the hail (9:17–21).

The threat became a reality, and the hail fell on all of Egypt, except in the area where the Israelites resided (9:22–26). Consequently, Pharaoh admitted for the first time that he was in the wrong. Then he said (again) that he would let Israel go (9:27, 28). Moses stopped the hail, but he said he knew that Pharaoh did not really fear the Lord (9:29–33). Again, after he received relief from the plague, Pharaoh changed his mind and denied Moses' request (9:34, 35).

PESTILENCE ON THE CATTLE (9:1–7)

[1]Then the LORD said to Moses, "Go to Pharaoh and speak to him, 'Thus says the LORD, the God of the Hebrews, "Let My people go, that they may serve Me. [2]For if you refuse to let them go and continue to hold them, [3]behold, the hand of the LORD will come with a very severe pestilence on your livestock which are in the field, on the horses, on the donkeys, on the camels, on the herds, and on the flocks. [4]But the LORD will make a distinction between the livestock of Israel and the livestock of Egypt, so that nothing will die of all that belongs to the sons of Israel."'" [5]The LORD set a definite time, saying, "Tomorrow the LORD will do this thing in the land." [6]So the LORD did this thing on the next day, and all the livestock of Egypt died; but of the livestock of the sons of Israel, not one died. [7]Pharaoh sent, and behold, there was not even one of the livestock of Israel dead. But the heart of Pharaoh was hardened, and he did not let the people go.

Verses 1–3. After the swarms of flies had departed and **Pharaoh** had again hardened his heart, God sent word to him through **Moses** that he must let Israel leave the land or face the consequences of **a very severe pestilence** on the **livestock** of Egypt. The Hebrew word דֶּבֶר (*deber*), translated "pestilence" or "murrain" (KJV), is a vague term used for a widespread epidemic, giving no hints as to the specific nature of the disease. The word "livestock" (מִקְנֶה, *miqneh*), also rendered "cattle" (KJV), is a comprehensive term which includes all of the animals that would be impacted:[1] **horses, donkeys, camels, herds** ("cattle"; NIV), and **flocks** ("sheep and goats"; NIV). Again, the narrator related what God told Moses to tell Pharaoh, then left it to the reader to con-

---

[1]J. Philip Hyatt, *Exodus*, The New Century Bible Commentary (Grand Rapids, Mich.: Wm. B. Eerdmans Publishing Co., 1971), 116.

clude that Moses actually took that message to Egypt's king (see comments on 8:1, 2).

Verses 4, 5. Evidence that this plague came from **the LORD** was abundant. First, God's hand was seen in the severity of the plague, since it caused the death of all kinds of livestock (9:3). Second, the miraculous nature of the plague was obvious in its selectivity: God afflicted the Egyptians, but not the Israelites (see comments on 8:22). Third, the timing of the plague indicated that God was in control of it: Moses said that it would happen **"tomorrow"**—and it did.

This plague differed from those which had gone before in that, for the first time, it resulted in the loss of life (the life of animals) and in the Egyptians' means of livelihood. They needed their animals, both for meat and to farm the land. If their animals died, their source of food was endangered. John J. Davis noted that this plague "was unique from the standpoint of its relationship to their personal property. Prior to this time the plagues had had the effect of irritation and pain, but not the widespread loss of personal property."[2]

Many animals in the Egyptian culture were used to represent gods. The animals were probably not viewed as gods themselves, but rather as manifestations or vessels of the gods. A few examples which correspond to the present text include the cow (representative of Hathor), the bull (representative of Apis, Mnevis, or Ptah), and the ram (representative of Amun or Khnum). Sacred animals were often associated with temples and cared for by the priests. Many of these animals were mummified after their death, a ritual paid for by worshipers who were seeking a blessing from their respective deities.

Verse 6. No one can know for sure what disease afflicted the livestock in Egypt. Some scholars suggest that it was anthrax.[3] However, John I. Durham argued against the speculation in-

---

[2]John J. Davis, *Moses and the Gods of Egypt: Studies in Exodus*, 2d ed. (Grand Rapids, Mich.: Baker Book House, 1986), 119.

[3]Ibid.; Nahum M. Sarna, *Exploring Exodus: The Origins of Biblical Israel* (New York: Schocken Books, 1996), 72; R. Alan Cole, *Exodus: An Introduction and Commentary*, Tyndale Old Testament Commentaries (Downers Grove, Ill.: Inter-Varsity Press, 1973), 96.

volved in identifying the pestilence with any specific disease because to do so discredits "the theological tenor of the biblical narrative, which will admit no naturalistic and hence nonmiraculous 'explanations.'"[4] Whatever it was, it was deadly to the livestock of the Egyptians. However, the statement that **all the livestock of Egypt died** must mean something like "a great number," since at least some of the livestock were still alive later when the plague of hail fell upon Egypt (9:19–21). Wilbur Fields wrote, "It would seem that the term *all* in 9:6 (as in 8:17) is not to be taken in an absolute sense, but as referring to such a large portion that what remained was as nothing in comparison."[5] The word "all" is often used hyperbolically in the account of the plagues, just as people today use "all" or "everyone" to refer to "many," "most," or "a large number."

Verse 7. When the Egyptians' livestock died, the Israelites' animals were spared.[6] Pharaoh had been told that the Lord would "make a distinction between the livestock of Israel and the livestock of Egypt" (9:4). He had undoubtedly heard rumors that Israel's livestock had not been affected. In response, **Pharaoh sent** messengers to Goshen to confirm the rumors. However, his servants' report that **not even one of the livestock of Israel** [was found] **dead** did not convince him to change his mind about Israel. His **heart . . . was hardened**, and he refused again to **let the people go**.

The common Hebrew word used to say that Pharaoh "sent" (שָׁלַח, *shalach*) to see whether or not the Israelites' animals were still alive is the same one that was used when Moses demanded that Pharaoh let the people go in verse 1. Durham translated that phrase as "*Send out* my people" (emphasis added).[7] He said that Pharaoh's hardened heart explains why "Pharaoh would send out those whom he had no need to send out, his factfinders to

---

[4]John I. Durham, *Exodus*, Word Biblical Commentary, vol. 3 (Waco, Tex.: Word Books, 1987), 118.

[5]Wilbur Fields, *Exploring Exodus,* Bible Study Textbook Series (Joplin, Mo.: College Press, 1976), 201–2.

[6]The fact that the Israelites owned livestock may be significant in determining the nature of the slavery that they endured.

[7]Durham, 116.

Goshen, and refuse to send out those whom Yahweh had commanded him to send out, the sons of Israel to their religious commitment."[8]

BOILS (9:8–12)

[8]Then the Lord said to Moses and Aaron, "Take for yourselves handfuls of soot from a kiln, and let Moses throw it toward the sky in the sight of Pharaoh. [9]It will become fine dust over all the land of Egypt, and will become boils breaking out with sores on man and beast through all the land of Egypt." [10]So they took soot from a kiln, and stood before Pharaoh; and Moses threw it toward the sky, and it became boils breaking out with sores on man and beast. [11]The magicians could not stand before Moses because of the boils, for the boils were on the magicians as well as on all the Egyptians. [12]And the Lord hardened Pharaoh's heart, and he did not listen to them, just as the Lord had spoken to Moses.

Verses 8–10. The fifth plague had affected the physical bodies of Egypt's animals; the sixth struck the bodies of the Egyptians themselves, as well as injuring their livestock again. **Moses** threw **soot from a kiln** into the air, and the dust he scattered became **boils . . . on man and beast**. According to William A. Shell, the Hebrew term כִּבְשָׁן (*kibshan*) used in this text "denotes a kiln for firing pottery or reducing lime to the desired form."[9] The word "boil" (שְׁחִין, *sh*[e]*chin*) can refer to a variety of skin inflammations which cause uncleanness, great suffering, and potentially death (Lev. 13:18–20; Job 2:7; 2 Kings 20:1, 7). These boils sometimes covered a man's whole body, "from the sole of his foot to the crown of his head" (Job 2:7; see Deut. 28:35). The term "beast" (בְּהֵמָה, *b*[e]*hemah*) may encompass both domesticated and wild animals.

It is probably better to think of Moses' action primarily as a

---

[8]Ibid., 119.

[9]William A. Shell, "Furnace," in *The International Standard Bible Encyclopedia*, rev. ed., ed. Geoffrey W. Bromiley (Grand Rapids, Mich.: William B. Eerdmans Publishing Co., 1982), 2:371.

visual aid than to think that a cloud of dust spread throughout the land, afflicting man and beast as it went. Likely Moses threw the soot into the air, those who were touched by the dust were afflicted immediately, and from there the plague spread. Some scholars suggest that Moses' "symbolic sprinkling of ashes in the air (9:10) demonstrated the helplessness of the Egyptian air-deity (Show [or Shu]) in the face of coming events."[10] Perhaps the festering boils also exposed the weakness of Imhotep, the god of medicine.

The text does not record Moses' audible demand or threat to **Pharaoh**, just as in the case of the fourth plague that brought swarms of flies (see comments on 8:24). However, the absence of the mention of a verbal confrontation between Moses and Pharaoh does not prove that there was none. The fact that verse 12 says that Pharaoh "did not listen to them" suggests that Moses and Aaron had, in fact, spoken to him and again requested Israel's release.

Verse 11. The potency of the plague is emphasized by the fact that **the magicians** themselves were infected with **the boils**, to the extent that they **could not stand before Moses**. This statement implies that when Moses appeared before Pharaoh, the magicians were there to counteract his efforts. The evidence from the Book of Exodus suggests that they were part of Pharaoh's court (see Gen. 41:8, 24). An impartial observer would have been forced to conclude that whatever powers the magicians commanded were not the equal of those connected with Moses, Aaron, and Israel, since the magicians' powers could not protect them from the attack by Moses' God. This verse records the last appearance of the magicians in Exodus.

Verse 12. When the writer described Pharaoh's refusal after the sixth plague, he said for the first time in the series that **the Lord hardened Pharaoh's heart**. Only after Pharaoh had demonstrated his rebellious, arrogant nature did the Lord harden his heart, presumably by worsening his already stubborn traits.

---

[10]Alexander Macalister and R. K. Harrison, "Boil," in *The International Standard Bible Encyclopedia*, rev. ed., ed. Geoffrey W. Bromiley (Grand Rapids, Mich.: Wm. B. Eerdmans Publishing Co., 1979), 1:532.

Again, the text emphasizes the fact that Pharaoh's refusal should not have come as a surprise, since God had foretold it (see comments on 7:3, 4; 8:15).

HAIL (9:13–35)

Warning About Hail (9:13–21)

[13]Then the LORD said to Moses, "Rise up early in the morning and stand before Pharaoh and say to him, 'Thus says the LORD, the God of the Hebrews, "Let My people go, that they may serve Me. [14]For this time I will send all My plagues on you and your servants and your people, so that you may know that there is no one like Me in all the earth. [15]For if by now I had put forth My hand and struck you and your people with pestilence, you would then have been cut off from the earth. [16]But, indeed, for this reason I have allowed you to remain, in order to show you My power and in order to proclaim My name through all the earth. [17]Still you exalt yourself against My people by not letting them go. [18]Behold, about this time tomorrow, I will send a very heavy hail, such as has not been seen in Egypt from the day it was founded until now. [19]Now therefore send, bring your livestock and whatever you have in the field to safety. Every man and beast that is found in the field and is not brought home, when the hail comes down on them, will die."'" [20]The one among the servants of Pharaoh who feared the word of the LORD made his servants and his livestock flee into the houses; [21]but he who paid no regard to the word of the LORD left his servants and his livestock in the field.

Verse 13. As He had with the first and fourth plagues (7:15; 8:20), **the LORD** instructed **Moses** to announce to **Pharaoh** the seventh plague **early in the morning**. This time God did not specify that the interview was to take place near the water. The text does not state that Moses carried out the Lord's directions, but the reader may assume that he did. Moses' request did not vary: **"Thus says the LORD, the God of the Hebrews, 'Let My people go, that they may serve Me.'"**

Verse 14. The explanation Moses was to provide went far beyond any message he had so far relayed to Pharaoh. First, God made it clear that other calamities would come, a fact He had not specifically revealed to Pharaoh previously. In speaking of **all My plagues**, God was probably referring to "all" the plagues that still lay in the future. Second, God revealed why He was sending plagues upon Pharaoh and his land: **so that you may know that there is no one like Me in all the earth.** Pharaoh would learn that the Lord was unique, not to be compared with the gods of Egypt.

Verses 15, 16. In fact, God said that He could have completely destroyed the Egyptians—and would have done so, except that it was His intention to use the plagues to demonstrate His **power** before them. As a result of that demonstration, the Lord's **name** would be proclaimed **through all the earth**. Waldemar Janzen commented,

> God's aim is not only to free Israel from its present oppression, something God could have achieved quickly, but to make God's name (God's character as Deliverer; cf. 3:13–15; 20:1–2) known worldwide. Not only Egypt and Israel, but all nations are to recognize the cosmic rule of a God who opposes oppression.[11]

Indeed, the mighty works of God in Egypt greatly impressed the Gentile nations that Israel encountered in the years that followed (18:1; Josh. 2:10, 11; 9:9; 1 Sam. 4:8). In the New Testament, the apostle Paul quoted verse 16 as a gripping illustration of God's sovereign power (Rom. 9:17).

Verse 17. God then diagnosed Pharaoh's sin: **"Still you exalt yourself against My people by not letting them go."** Pharaoh's problem was pride and arrogance; he refused to take orders from the God of a people he considered inferior.

Verse 18. Then Moses announced the coming plague, the most destructive **hail** that **Egypt** had ever seen. The phrase **from**

---

[11]Waldemar Janzen, *Exodus*, Believers Church Bible Commentary (Scottdale, Pa.: Herald Press, 2000), 126.

the day it was founded until now portrays a linear view of history, as opposed to a cyclical one. Similar expressions appear throughout the Scriptures (10:6; Num. 14:19; Ezra 9:7; Jer. 7:25; 32:31; Mt. 24:21; Phil. 1:5).

Verse 19. This particular announcement was different. On this occasion Moses offered the Egyptians the opportunity to save the lives of their people and **livestock**. Knowing that the hail was coming (and when it was coming), the Egyptians could provide shelter for their servants and stock in barns and houses and so save their lives.

Verses 20, 21. The writer then skipped to the end of the story to tell what happened. Some who believed in and revered God saved the lives of their **servants** and **livestock**. Others did not pay attention to the Lord's message; presumably, their people and their animals died when the hail came.

A surprising statement is made here: Some Egyptians **feared the word of the Lord**. These same Egyptians are called **the servants of Pharaoh**. God had, in effect, made converts out of some of Pharaoh's servants! Both earlier and later in the account, Pharaoh's "servants" are distinguished from "the people" of Egypt (8:3, 21; 9:14; 10:6; 11:3; 12:30). These were most likely government officials who served as Pharaoh's advisers and members of his court (7:10, 20; 9:30, 34; 10:7; 11:8; 14:5). As such, they "were privy to whatever Pharaoh learned."[12] On this occasion, some of the king's officials who heard Moses' warning acted accordingly.

Hail Rains Down (9:22–26)

[22]Now the Lord said to Moses, "Stretch out your hand toward the sky, that hail may fall on all the land of Egypt, on man and on beast and on every plant of the field, throughout the land of Egypt." [23]Moses stretched out his staff toward the sky, and the Lord sent thunder and hail, and fire ran down to the earth. And the Lord rained hail on the land of Egypt. [24]So there was hail, and fire flashing continually in the midst of the

---

[12]Durham, 129.

hail, very severe, such as had not been in all the land of Egypt since it became a nation. [25]The hail struck all that was in the field through all the land of Egypt, both man and beast; the hail also struck every plant of the field and shattered every tree of the field. [26]Only in the land of Goshen, where the sons of Israel were, there was no hail.

Verses 22, 23a. After the announcement of the coming plague, **Moses**, at God's command, **stretched out his staff toward the sky** so that there would be no doubt that **the Lord** was the cause of the **hail**. When he made this gesture, the hail began. This plague was as widespread as the others had been: The hail fell **on all the land of Egypt, on man and on beast and on every plant . . . throughout the land.**

Verses 23b–25. The plague did not consist solely of **hail**; it also involved **thunder**, lightning, and rain (9:33). "Thunder" is translated from a plural form of קוֹל (*qol*), a term which often refers to one's "voice." It is the power of the Lord's voice that rumbles as thunder (Ps. 29:3). Within the descriptive phrases **fire ran down to the earth** and **fire flashing continually**, the term "fire" (אֵשׁ, *'esh*) should be understood as "lightning" (NIV; CEV; NCV). This was the worst hailstorm the country had ever seen, striking and even killing **man and beast** (9:19), and destroying **every plant** and **tree** (see comments on 10:5). The gods worshiped by the Egyptians could do nothing to protect the people—whether Nut (the sky goddess), Isis (the goddess of life), or Seth (the protector of the crops).

Verse 26. As with the plagues of the swarms of flies (8:22, 23) and the diseased livestock (9:4), **the land of Goshen** where the Israelites resided was spared. God made a distinction between His people and their oppressors.

The Hail and Thunder Cease (9:27–35)

[27]Then Pharaoh sent for Moses and Aaron, and said to them, "I have sinned this time; the Lord is the righteous one, and I and my people are the wicked ones. [28]Make supplication to the Lord, for there has been enough of God's thunder and hail;

and I will let you go, and you shall stay no longer." [29]Moses said to him, "As soon as I go out of the city, I will spread out my hands to the LORD; the thunder will cease and there will be hail no longer, that you may know that the earth is the LORD's. [30]But as for you and your servants, I know that you do not yet fear the LORD God." [31](Now the flax and the barley were ruined, for the barley was in the ear and the flax was in bud. [32]But the wheat and the spelt were not ruined, for they ripen late.) [33]So Moses went out of the city from Pharaoh, and spread out his hands to the LORD; and the thunder and the hail ceased, and rain no longer poured on the earth. [34]But when Pharaoh saw that the rain and the hail and the thunder had ceased, he sinned again and hardened his heart, he and his servants. [35]Pharaoh's heart was hardened, and he did not let the sons of Israel go, just as the LORD had spoken through Moses.

Verse 27. The plague of hail must have been the most frightening blow the Egyptians had experienced to this point. For the first time, **Pharaoh** confessed that he had **sinned**[13]—that he and his **people** were **the wicked ones** and **the LORD** was **the righteous one**. Later events, however, cast doubt on Pharaoh's repentance. Possibly, his confession was motivated merely by the desire to get relief from the plague. If he did realize that he was in the wrong in this contest against the Lord, he later reverted to his arrogant ways. Pharaoh's words serve as a reminder that just saying, "I have sinned" does not guarantee one's salvation.

Why did Pharaoh associate his people with himself in his confession, saying, "I and my people are the wicked ones"? One way that the people had been "wicked" was in their enslavement of the Israelites. Israel's oppression could not have been accomplished by Pharaoh alone. Probably, they also shared his guilt by encouraging his hardhearted decisions against letting Israel go. In verse 34, for instance, the text says not only that Pharaoh

[13]Of what sin was Pharaoh guilty? It must have been pride, which led to disobedience. If this interpretation is correct, the conclusion must follow that even in Old Testament times God expected all people—those of unbelieving nations as well as the Israelites—to obey Him.

sinned and hardened his heart, but that his servants did also.

Verse 28. When he called Moses and Aaron to come before him, Pharaoh was anxious for the hail to be removed. Therefore, he asked them to intercede with God in Egypt's behalf. He promised once again to **let** [Israel] **go**.

Verse 29. Moses agreed, making sure that the Egyptians knew that, just as the hail had started at his command, it was ending at his direction. He then reiterated that God had sent the plague and would remove it in order that Pharaoh might **know** the Lord. On this occasion he specified that Pharaoh would learn that **the earth is the LORD's**. The plague demonstrated this truth: Since the earth is the Lord's, He is the controller of all nature and can send hail where and when He chooses. Pharaoh should have learned that lesson from the hailstorm.

Verse 30. Moses went on to say that he was aware that Pharaoh and his **servants** did not **yet fear the LORD God**. Even if Pharaoh had been sincere at that moment, Moses knew by divine inspiration that Pharaoh's heart would be further hardened and that additional plagues would be sent.

Verses 31, 32. At this point in the narrative, the writer paused to add a parenthetical note telling when the hail came: **(Now the flax and the barley were ruined, for the barley was in the ear and the flax was in bud. But the wheat and the spelt were not ruined, for they ripen late.)** W. H. Gispen noted, "Flax was grown in Egypt to make linen for clothing (linen was also used to wrap mummies). Spelt is a type of coarse wheat and is harvested after the barley. The Egyptians used spelt to bake bread."[14] Commentators agree that the time mentioned must have been about January. The time of the final plague and the deliverance was about April, the date of the Passover. Therefore, approximately three months remained for the final three plagues.

Verse 33. Moses then **spread out his hands to the LORD**. Again, this gesture made it obvious that Moses was the means by which the plague ended. At the same time, Moses was illus-

---

[14]W. H. Gispen, *Exodus*, trans. Ed van der Maas, Bible Student's Commentary (Grand Rapids, Mich.: Regency Reference Library, Zondervan Publishing House, 1982), 103.

trating that he could stop the hail only by appealing to the Lord. In ancient times, men often prayed with their hands outstretched to God (1 Kings 8:22, 38, 54; Ezra 9:5; Ps. 44:20; 88:9; 143:6; Is. 1:15; 1 Tim. 2:8). After Moses prayed, the **thunder** and **hail** must have ended abruptly.

Verses 34, 35. Seeing that the plague had ended and feeling relieved, **Pharaoh** rethought his position. Perhaps he said something like the following to himself: "The hail has stopped; the land is saved. Maybe it only happened to come when it did. Perhaps Moses and his God had nothing to do with it. In any case, we cannot afford to lose our slave labor. We have lived through the worst thing that could happen to us. Why should I let Israel go? I will not do it!" The text simply says that Pharaoh, when he saw that the storm had ended, **sinned again** by **harden**[ing] **his heart**, along with **his servants**, and did not **let the sons of Israel go**. All this, of course, was exactly what the Lord had consistently predicted.

APPLICATION

"God of the Nations" (9:16)

In the narrative about the plagues, we find this surprising statement: "For this reason I have allowed you to remain, in order to show you My power and in order to proclaim My name through all the earth" (9:16). This verse may be surprising because we are not accustomed to thinking that the God of the Old Testament was concerned about "all the earth," that is, about nations other than Israel. This passage teaches that God desires to be known, to have His name—which implies His power and might—proclaimed "through all the earth." Even though God had a special relationship with Israel in the Old Testament, He was still God of all the nations.

God blesses all nations. This fact was a major theme of New Testament evangelists when they spoke to Gentiles (Acts 14:16, 17; 17:25; see Rom. 1:19–21).

God controls the destinies of nations. In 9:16 God stated clearly that He was in charge of Pharaoh's destiny: "This is why I have let you live" (NRSV). God rules—not just over His obedient people, but also over all the kingdoms of the earth (Deut. 10:14; Dan. 4:17, 25, 32). One way of expressing this concept is to say that God is the "Ruler of all history."[15] He uses even the mightiest empires as tools to do His will, even to punish His own people (see Hab. 1—3). He is the "just and holy Ruler" who "presides, governs and guides (see 2 Kings 19:25, 28; Ezekiel 38:3–4, 10–11, 16; 39:2–3)."[16]

God holds the nations accountable. Egypt was punished for enslaving and mistreating God's people, for killing Israelite babies, and for the hardheartedness of its king (4:22, 23). God also held other nations accountable for their failure to observe laws common to all humanity—for their mistreatment of His people and for their cruelty and inhumanity toward one another (see Amos 1; 2).[17]

God wants His people to treat other nations fairly. The descendants of Abraham were to "be a blessing" to others (Gen. 12:2). The Israelites were restricted from intermarrying or making covenants with non-Israelites, and non-Israelites could not own land in Israel or become king. However, God's people were never forbidden to associate with other peoples. In fact, non-Israelites (later called Gentiles) were among the Israelites when they left Egypt (12:38). That there were non-Israelites living among the Israelites from the beginning of Israel as a nation is evident from the fact that laws were given to regulate Israel's behavior towards "strangers," that is, foreigners (12:48, 49; 20:10; 22:21; 23:9, 12; Lev. 19:10). Just as Israel was commanded to "love your neighbor as yourself" (Lev. 19:18), so the people were required to "love

---

[15]J. Alec Motyer, "The Prophets," in *Eerdmans' Handbook to the Bible*, ed. David Alexander and Pat Alexander (Grand Rapids, Mich.: Wm. B. Eerdmans Publishing Co., 1973), 372.

[16]Ibid.

[17]Douglas S. Huffman summarized God's interaction with nations other than His people in the Old Testament in the following way: "God exercises sovereignty over the unbelieving gentile nations, using them as tools to discipline Israel (Habakkuk) and calling them to repentance (Jonah) and declaring judgment upon them (Nahum, Obadiah)." (Douglas S. Huffman, "Gentile," in *The Eerdmans Dictionary of the Bible*, ed. David Noel Freedman [Grand Rapids, Mich.: Wm. B. Eerdmans Publishing Co., 2000], 494–95.)

[the stranger] as yourself" (Lev. 19:34). Basically, the same laws that applied to the Israelites also applied to the "strangers" who lived among them (12:49; Num. 15:30; 35:15).

In later times, the Jews developed traditions that depicted the Gentiles as unclean. Jews avoided Gentiles as much as possible, and faithful Jews were not to eat with Gentiles. Such traditions were not a part of God's law. The law of Moses anticipated that unbelievers would always live among God's people and required God's people to treat them as well as they did one another.

God wants all nations to know and worship Him. God let Pharaoh live through the plagues—and ultimately brought all of the ten plagues upon Egypt—in order to show the king His power and to proclaim His name throughout "all the earth" (9:16). God's mighty acts in Exodus became known to the peoples of other lands (Josh. 2:9, 10), with the result that God's name was proclaimed in "all the earth." God's plan was to bless "all the families of the earth" through Abraham's seed (Gen. 12:3). Israel became the nation through whom that plan was to be fulfilled. God chose Israel to be a "light [to] the nations" (Is. 49:6) so that through God's people others would come to know Him who is the "God of gods and the Lord of lords" (Deut. 10:17). Ultimately, God used Israel to bring the Savior of the nations into the world.

Conclusion. We misunderstand the Old Testament if we think that God was concerned only with the Jews. God loved the other nations too (Jon. 1—4), and He wanted the Jews to be the means by which others came to know Him. If the Israelites had a responsibility to be a "light to the nations," how much more do we have that responsibility? God's concern for the nations, then, is a missionary call for us today!

Why God Allows Evil to Exist (9:16)

God allowed Pharaoh to remain in power in order to achieve His own ends (9:16). The Most High God is ruler over the realm of mankind and sets over it whomever He wishes (see Dan. 4:17, 25, 32; 5:21). Sometimes God may allow evil to exist or evil rulers to remain in power so that ultimately His purpose will be served. What is God's purpose? He wants people throughout the world to know His power and proclaim His name.

Believers in Pharaoh's Service (9:20)

Some "among the servants of Pharaoh . . . feared the word of the LORD" (9:20). Perhaps these believers were part of Pharaoh's inner council, for that is how the word "servant" is used in the book (see 7:10, 20; 8:3, 4). In the New Testament, some "saints" were members of "Caesar's household" (Phil. 4:22). We should not assume that those whom we regard as enemies (as the Israelites must have viewed the Egyptians) or those in positions of authority cannot be convinced of and convicted by the truth of God's Word.

Pharaoh's Lack of Repentance (9:27–35)

After the plague of hail, Pharaoh confessed his sin, as well as that of his people. God has always wanted people to recognize and confess their sinfulness (Ps. 32:1–5; 51:1–4; Lk. 15:18; 18:13; Jas. 5:16; 1 Jn. 1:9). However, something was wrong with Pharaoh's confession. It may have been insincere, or it may have been prompted by the wrong motive. He may have confessed his sin solely because of his discomfort. Whether or not the confession was sincere, it was not followed by a change of life. He immediately returned to his old ways. To be pleasing to God, a confession of sin must be accompanied by repentance and must lead to a change of behavior (Lk. 3:10–14; 2 Cor. 7:9, 10).

Chapter 10

The Plagues: Locusts and Darkness

The eighth plague (locusts) and the ninth (darkness) are described in chapter 10 as the story moves toward its climax. The tenth plague (the death of the firstborn) is the subject of chapters 11 through 13.

In this chapter, God instructed Moses to go to Pharaoh and explain that He was sending the plagues to teach Israel to know the Lord (10:1, 2). Moses and Aaron appeared before Pharaoh, demanded that Israel be allowed to leave, and announced that God would send a plague of locusts on Egypt if Pharaoh refused. Then they left Pharaoh's presence (10:3–6).

At the urging of his servants, Pharaoh brought back Moses and Aaron and agreed to let Israel go; but he asked who would be going (10:7, 8). When the two Israelite leaders responded that everyone—including the children and the flocks and herds—would go, Pharaoh changed his mind again and refused to allow God's people to leave (10:9–11).

Next, at the Lord's command, Moses held out his hand and the devastating locust plague began (10:12–15). Never had there been so many locusts in Egypt! Pharaoh quickly called for Moses and Aaron. He confessed his sin and asked that the plague might be removed (10:16, 17). Moses prayed, and the locusts were removed; but Pharaoh's heart was hardened, and he refused to let Israel go (10:18–20).

Apparently without warning the Egyptians, God then sent the ninth plague, darkness, over all the land. A thick darkness lasted for three days in Egypt, but it did not affect the Israelites (10:21–23). Pharaoh responded by telling Moses that the people could go, but they would have to leave their livestock behind (10:24). Moses insisted that they all must go, including the animals (10:25, 26). Pharaoh's heart was hardened again, and he drove Moses away with strong words, to which Moses replied in kind (10:27–29).

LOCUSTS (10:1–20)

Warning About Locusts (10:1–6)

[1]Then the LORD said to Moses, "Go to Pharaoh, for I have
hardened his heart and the heart of his servants, that I may per-
form these signs of Mine among them, [2]and that you may tell
in the hearing of your son, and of your grandson, how I made
a mockery of the Egyptians and how I performed My signs
among them, that you may know that I am the LORD."
[3]Moses and Aaron went to Pharaoh and said to him, "Thus
says the LORD, the God of the Hebrews, 'How long will you
refuse to humble yourself before Me? Let My people go, that
they may serve Me. [4]For if you refuse to let My people go,
behold, tomorrow I will bring locusts into your territory. [5]They
shall cover the surface of the land, so that no one will be able
to see the land. They will also eat the rest of what has escaped—
what is left to you from the hail—and they will eat every tree
which sprouts for you out of the field. [6]Then your houses shall
be filled and the houses of all your servants and the houses of
all the Egyptians, something which neither your fathers nor
your grandfathers have seen, from the day that they came upon
the earth until this day.'" And he turned and went out from
Pharaoh.

Verse 1. The eighth plague began with **the LORD** directing **Moses** to speak to **Pharaoh**. The text does not specify that Moses was to threaten Pharaoh with another plague. Since, in fact, that is what Moses did (10:4–6), it can be assumed that God gave him those instructions.

God indicated that it was He who had **hardened** [Pharaoh's] **heart**, as well as **the heart**[s] **of his servants**, his closest advisers.

This passage, along with 9:34, indicates that Pharaoh was not alone in his obstinate refusal to obey the Lord; his advisers shared his guilt. As before, the Lord's hardening of Pharaoh's heart should be understood as God's allowing and encouraging the king to follow the rebellious tendencies that he had previously exhibited.

Verse 2. God told Moses what He was planning. By hardening Pharaoh's heart and performing miraculous signs, God would achieve two results. First, God's actions would give the Israelites something to remember—a story of redemption to pass on to future generations (**your son, and . . . your grandson**). It was important for the Israelites to remember what God had done for His chosen people so that they would be grateful and not forsake the covenant (12:26, 27; 13:8; Deut. 4:9; 6:7; Ps. 77:11–20; 78:4–6, 43–53; 105:26–38; 106:7–12; 135:8, 9; 136:10–15). That salvation story would be told in terms of how God **made a mockery of the Egyptians** and how He **performed** [His] **signs among them**. Perhaps the meaning here is how God made a mockery of the Egyptians *by* performing His signs among them. The Egyptians—with their gods, their king, and their power—were mocked by the ten plagues.

Second, God's signs would lead the people of Israel to **know that** [He is] **the Lord**. Obviously, the Israelites already knew God's name and knew that the God who was performing these miracles was Yahweh. To "know" God as "Yahweh" meant more than just knowing His name. It meant knowing something more about His character, His person, than they knew before. This passage, therefore, may shed light on 6:3, where God said that by the name "Yahweh" He did not make Himself known to the patriarchs. Probably, the passage in chapter 6 means that, although they knew His name, they did not know Him as intimately as they would after He had rescued them from bondage.

Verse 3. Again, **Moses and Aaron** stood before **Pharaoh**, and again they threatened Egypt with a plague unless Pharaoh allowed the **people** to go into the wilderness to worship **the Lord**. They indicated as they had before that Pharaoh's refusal amounted to pride, the opposite of humility. He had **refuse**[d]

to humble himself and had disobeyed the Lord's commands. Humility before God always leads to obedience to His will.

Verse 4. The plague that God's servants threatened was almost certainly the worst of the plagues to that point. **Locusts** brought famine in their wake, for the locusts would eat every living plant. Both the people and the livestock would perish for lack of food. It is no wonder that, when Pharaoh asked Moses and Aaron to remove the plague, he said, "Remove this death from me" (10:17). A locust plague meant death—if not immediately, then eventually.

The coming plague was described in detail. Initially, Moses told when it would happen: **"tomorrow."** This time marker appears throughout the account of the plagues, whether given by Pharaoh, the Lord, or Moses (8:10, 23, 29; 9:5, 18).

Verse 5. Next Moses indicated how many locusts there would be: They would **cover the surface of the land**. The word "surface" (עַיִן, *'ayin*) can literally be translated "eye." "The eye of the land" is an unusual expression that only appears a few other times in the Scriptures (10:15; Num. 22:5, 11). It refers to the "visible *surface* of earth."[1]

Moses further described how the locusts would affect Egyptian life: They would **eat** all the crops **left** alive after the **hail**. This description suggests that the use of "all" and "every" in reference to the destruction of plants and trees from the previous hailstorm should be interpreted as hyperbole (9:25). The text itself reveals that other crops were not ruined, namely the wheat and the spelt (9:31, 32).

Verse 6. None of Israel's oppressors would be exempt from the plague: The locusts would swarm every place, including the **houses** of Pharaoh, his **servants**, and **all the Egyptians**.

Finally, Moses predicted the magnitude of the plague: It would be more severe than any locust plague before or after this time in Egypt (see 9:18, 24). Mention of **your fathers** and **your grandfathers** is parallel to "your son" and "your grandson" in

---

[1]Francis Brown, S. R. Driver, and Charles A. Briggs, *The Brown-Driver-Briggs Hebrew and English Lexicon* (Boston: Houghton, Mifflin and Co., 1906; reprint, Peabody, Mass.: Hendrickson Publishers, 1997), 744.

verse 2. The grouping from verse 2 refers to Israelite descendants, whereas the grouping in verse 6 points to Egyptian ancestors. These terms serve as bookends for the section (10:1–6).

The text shifts from saying "Moses and Aaron" (10:3) to using **he**, which presumably refers to Moses. Once Moses had announced the plague, he apparently turned without waiting for a response and left.

Pharaoh Negotiates with Moses (10:7–11)

7Pharaoh's servants said to him, "How long will this man be a
snare to us? Let the men go, that they may serve the LORD their
God. Do you not realize that Egypt is destroyed?" 8So Moses
and Aaron were brought back to Pharaoh, and he said to them,
"Go, serve the LORD your God! Who are the ones that are
going?" 9Moses said, "We shall go with our young and our old;
with our sons and our daughters, with our flocks and our herds
we shall go, for we must hold a feast to the LORD." 10Then he
said to them, "Thus may the LORD be with you, if ever I let you
and your little ones go! Take heed, for evil is in your mind.
11Not so! Go now, the men among you, and serve the LORD, for
that is what you desire." So they were driven out from Pharaoh's presence.

Verse 7. Moses' departure produced alarm in the hearts of **Pharaoh's servants** (advisers). They immediately asked Pharaoh, **"How long will this man be a snare to us?"** "How long . . . ?" echoes Moses' question in verse 3. A "snare" (מוֹקֵשׁ, *moqesh*) is a trap set for a bird or an animal (Amos 3:5; Job 40:24). Pharaoh's men saw Moses as one who was leading Egypt into a trap and so was bringing about the nation's destruction. That he was a "snare" to them meant that he was dangerous to them. One translation reads, "How long must he be a menace to us?" (NAB), and another says, "How much longer are we to be tricked by this fellow?" (NJB).

The servants' statement **"Egypt is destroyed"** is obviously an exaggeration or an anticipation of what would happen if Moses continued to plague their country: "Egypt will be completely destroyed." The acknowledgment of Moses' success in destroying Egypt is a tribute to the reality and ferocity of the "signs" which God had done through Moses. Then the servants urged Pharaoh to **"let the men go."** The term "men" is translated from a plural form of the Hebrew word אִישׁ (*'ish*), which can also be rendered "people" (NIV).

Verses 8, 9. Pharaoh listened to his advisers and recalled **Moses and Aaron**. He agreed to allow the Israelites to leave the land but asked **who** would be **going**. His question implied that he was unwilling to let everyone go. Moses and Aaron answered that everyone would go: **"We shall go with our young and our old; with our sons and our daughters, with our flocks and our herds."** All of the Israelites would leave, regardless of their age or gender, and their animals would go too.

Verse 10. Pharaoh told Moses and Aaron, **"Thus may the Lord be with you, if ever I let you and your little ones go!"** His tone must have been sarcastic. Perhaps he was saying, "I will never let all of you go! If you ever get your request, it will be your God who does it. No one else will help you." John I. Durham suggested that Pharaoh was using a clever play on words. Since the name "Yahweh" is related to the word translated "be" (see comments on 3:14, 15), he presented Pharaoh as saying something like "Yahweh will indeed *be* with you when I agree to such a request as that!"[2]

The reason for Pharaoh's refusal is obvious. His suspicions were aroused by Moses' request. To ask that everyone be allowed to leave, and that the Israelites be permitted to take all their property with them, suggested that they were doing more than just going on a three-day journey to hold a feast (5:1, 3; 8:27). They were trying to leave Egypt permanently. That was the **evil** (or "evil purpose") Pharaoh believed was in their **mind**,[3] and he did not intend to allow that to happen.

Verse 11. Pharaoh then offered his next compromise. His pre-

---

[2]John I. Durham, *Exodus*, Word Biblical Commentary, vol. 3 (Waco, Tex.: Word Books, 1987), 136.

[3]H. L. Ellison, *Exodus*, The Daily Study Bible Series (Philadelphia: Westminster Press, 1982), 57.

vious compromise, consisting of two parts, is found in 8:25–29: The Israelites could sacrifice "within the land," and then they could leave but "not go very far away." This time Pharaoh said that he would let **the men** (הַגְּבָרִים, *hagg*[e]*barim*) leave, but not the women and children. To him and others in the court, it seemed that he was making a reasonable offer, since generally only men were involved in worship at religious festivals (23:17; 34:23; Deut. 16:16). Further, by keeping the women and children, Pharaoh could ensure that the men would return. Since Moses and Aaron refused Pharaoh's terms, they did not just leave **Pharaoh's** court but were **driven out from** [his] **presence**.

Locusts Cover the Land (10:12–20)

12Then the LORD said to Moses, "Stretch out your hand over
the land of Egypt for the locusts, that they may come up on the
land of Egypt and eat every plant of the land, even all that the
hail has left." 13So Moses stretched out his staff over the land
of Egypt, and the LORD directed an east wind on the land all
that day and all that night; and when it was morning, the east
wind brought the locusts. 14The locusts came up over all the
land of Egypt and settled in all the territory of Egypt; they were
very numerous. There had never been so many locusts, nor
would there be so many again. 15For they covered the surface
of the whole land, so that the land was darkened; and they ate
every plant of the land and all the fruit of the trees that the hail
had left. Thus nothing green was left on tree or plant of the
field through all the land of Egypt. 16Then Pharaoh hurriedly
called for Moses and Aaron, and he said, "I have sinned against
the LORD your God and against you. 17Now therefore, please
forgive my sin only this once, and make supplication to the
LORD your God, that He would only remove this death from
me." 18He went out from Pharaoh and made supplication to the
LORD. 19So the LORD shifted the wind to a very strong west wind
which took up the locusts and drove them into the Red Sea;
not one locust was left in all the territory of Egypt. 20But the
LORD hardened Pharaoh's heart, and he did not let the sons of
Israel go.

Verses 12, 13. After Moses and Aaron left Pharaoh's court, God directed **Moses** to **stretch out** [his] **hand.** This gesture would provide visual evidence that the plague came from God through him (see 7:20; 9:22, 23; 10:21, 22). When Moses acted in obedient faith, the locust plague began.

To achieve His purposes in this case, God used natural phenomena: a plague of **locusts** and **an east wind**. As J. Philip Hyatt noted, "An east wind would bring the locusts from the desert regions of Sinai and Arabia, where the desert locusts breed under favourable conditions."[4] However, the fact that it was the work of God—a supernatural event, a miracle—was obvious for the following reasons: (1) it was predicted (10:4–6); (2) it happened on command, when **Moses stretched out his staff**; and (3) it was the worst locust plague in Egypt's history (10:14). Pharaoh's reaction proved that the Egyptians saw the plague as something more than just another natural disaster (10:16).

Verse 14. The description of the plague emphasizes the number of the locusts: **The locusts came up over all the land of Egypt and settled in all the territory of Egypt.** The text also says that the locusts **were very numerous**; there were more than Egypt had ever seen before (see 9:18, 24; 10:6) or would ever see **again**.

Verse 15. As previously predicted (10:5), the locusts **covered the surface of the whole land.** The fact that **the land was darkened** suggests that there were so many locusts that the swarm in flight cast a great shadow over the land. This darkness exposed the weakness of the various sun gods that were worshiped by the Egyptians, especially their chief deity Re (or Ra).

The final focus is on the effect of the locusts: **They ate every plant** that remained after **the hail** (see comments on 10:5). The terrible destruction that can be caused by an army of locusts is vividly portrayed in the Book of Joel. The prophet described them as having "the appearance of horses," making the sound "of chariots," and having "the teeth of a lion." They are so destructive that they lay waste the vines and strip the bark from the trees. They turn a lush paradise into a "desolate wilderness" (Joel

---

[4]J. Philip Hyatt, *Exodus*, The New Century Bible Commentary (Grand Rapids, Mich.: Wm. B. Eerdmans Publishing Co., 1971), 124.

1:4–12; 2:1–11). As in the case of the hailstorm, the damage from the locust plague demonstrated the frailty of the Egyptian gods who supposedly gave life to the crops and protected them.

Verse 16. Convinced by this plague, **Pharaoh hurriedly called for Moses and Aaron.** Again, as he had done in the case of the hail (9:27), Pharaoh confessed sin. This time he focused solely on himself, omitting any reference to his people. **He said, "I have sinned against the LORD your God"**; but he did not confess the Lord as *his* God. Apparently, he recognized that the Lord had the right to command him and that he had the obligation to obey the Lord. He had sinned, therefore, by disobeying the Lord.

Pharaoh had also sinned, he said, **"against you."** He may have had in mind his mistreatment of Moses and Aaron. For instance, at their last meeting, he had driven them out of his presence (10:11). More likely, he was speaking of his sin against the people of Israel. Since he was, at least temporarily, acknowledging God's sovereignty, he also had to acknowledge that he had mistreated God's people by oppressing them. To dishonor God's people was to dishonor God.

Did Pharaoh's confession indicate his repentance? If so, it was short-lived (see 10:20). Probably, Pharaoh provides a good example of what the apostle Paul called "the sorrow of the world [which] produces death." Worldly sorrow is sorrow prompted by the fact that the sinner is caught and punished. It provides no spiritual reward, in contrast to "godly sorrow," which leads to repentance (a change of life) and brings about salvation (2 Cor. 7:9, 10).

Verse 17. After confessing his sin, Pharaoh asked for Moses to **forgive** him and to pray that **God** might **remove this death** from him. The locusts, if they continued to plague the land, would bring famine and death in their wake. Indeed, the sight, the sound, and the smell of the locusts must have created images of death in the minds of the Egyptians.

Verses 18, 19. Again the text shifts its focus from "Moses and Aaron" (10:16) to Moses: **He went out from Pharaoh and made supplication to the LORD.** Moses consented to Pharaoh's request. He prayed to the Lord, with the result that **the LORD** removed **the locusts** by the same means He had used to bring them against Egypt—**a very strong . . . wind**. This time, the wind blew from the **west** and **drove them into the Red Sea**, where they perished.

Verse 20. Pharaoh lost his religion as quickly as he had found it. When he saw that the plague was lifted, he hardened his heart (or **the Lord hardened Pharaoh's heart**), and he again rejected Moses' request.

DARKNESS (10:21–29)

21Then the Lord said to Moses, "Stretch out your hand toward the sky, that there may be darkness over the land of Egypt, even a darkness which may be felt." 22So Moses stretched out his hand toward the sky, and there was thick darkness in all the land of Egypt for three days. 23They did not see one another, nor did anyone rise from his place for three days, but all the sons of Israel had light in their dwellings. 24Then Pharaoh called to Moses, and said, "Go, serve the Lord; only let your flocks and your herds be detained. Even your little ones may go with you." 25But Moses said, "You must also let us have sacrifices and burnt offerings, that we may sacrifice them to the Lord our God. 26Therefore, our livestock too shall go with us; not a hoof shall be left behind, for we shall take some of them to serve the Lord our God. And until we arrive there, we ourselves do not know with what we shall serve the Lord." 27But the Lord hardened Pharaoh's heart, and he was not willing to let them go. 28Then Pharaoh said to him, "Get away from me! Beware, do not see my face again, for in the day you see my face you shall die!" 29Moses said, "You are right; I shall never see your face again!"

Verses 21–23. The darkness of the ninth plague is thought by most commentators to have been brought on by a sandstorm. The fact that it was **a darkness which may be felt** seems to give credence to that point of view, as does the effect of the darkness: **Nor did anyone rise from his place for three days.** Darkness brought on by the absence of sunlight does not keep people in their houses, but a terrible sandstorm would. A sandstorm or dust storm could be so severe that it would produce darkness and prevent people from seeing.[5]

One might object, "If the darkness was only a sandstorm, then how could it have been recognized as an act of God, as a miracle?" It would have been recognized as the work of God for three reasons: (1) the storm's *timing* (it happened when **Moses stretched out his hand**); (2) its *intensity* (it was a darkness "which may be felt," a **thick darkness** which continued **for three days**); and (3) its *selectivity* (it did not affect **the sons of Israel**). Other explanations for the darkness are possible: It could have been brought on by "a superabundance of aqueous vapors floating in the atmosphere,"[6] or it may simply have been a "supernatural darkness . . . which has no natural explanation."[7]

The previous locust plague also produced darkness (10:15). Both of these plagues were an affront to the Egyptian sun deities, especially the god Re (Ra). The fact that the Israelites possessed light while the Egyptians remained in darkness demonstrated the superior power of the Lord. Throughout the Bible, darkness symbolizes judgment from God (Is. 8:22; Joel 2:1, 2; Zeph. 1:15; Amos 5:20; Mt. 8:12; 2 Pet. 2:17; Jude 13).

Verse 24. Pharaoh knew that this plague also came from God, whether or not Moses had appeared before him to announce it. Therefore, he sent for **Moses** and offered to let the people **go**, including their **little ones**, with the only restriction being that they must leave behind their **flocks** and **herds**. Perhaps the king thought that, if the Israelites left their possessions behind, they would surely return. This was Pharaoh's third attempt to get Moses to agree to a compromise (see 8:25–29; 10:8–11).

Verses 25, 26. Moses was adamant; the Israelites would all go, and they would take all of their flocks and herds with them. He said, **"Not a hoof shall be left behind."** He told Pharaoh that,

---

[5]James Burton Coffman, *Commentary on Exodus, The Second Book of Moses* (Abilene, Tex.: ACU Press, 1985), 127–28.

[6]Adam Clarke, *The Holy Bible with a Commentary and Critical Notes*, vol. 1, *Genesis—Deuteronomy* (Cincinnati: Hitchcock & Walden, n.d.), 341.

[7]Ronald E. Clements, *Exodus*, The Cambridge Bible Commentary (Cambridge: University Press, 1972), 63.

until they got into the wilderness, they did not know what **sacrifices** would be required by **the Lord**. They therefore needed to have all of their **livestock** with them.

Verses 27–29. Again, **the Lord hardened Pharaoh's heart**, and he refused to allow Israel to leave. Angrily, the king commanded Moses to leave his presence, saying that he would kill him if Moses saw him again. **Moses** replied that he would **never see** [Pharaoh's] **face again**.

How could Moses' statement be true since he apparently did see Pharaoh's face again in 12:31, 32? One possibility is that Pharaoh's words were spoken at the height of his exasperation and later, with good reason, he changed his mind. Therefore, Moses changed his mind also. Another way of understanding the two passages is to recognize that both men spoke angrily. R. Alan Cole said, "It would be unfair to hold either Moses or pharaoh to words spoken in the heat of anger."[8] A third, less likely, possibility is that on the occasion recorded in 12:31, 32, Moses did not personally confront Pharaoh but rather sent him a message.[9]

APPLICATION

Telling Our Children (10:2)

The religion of Israel was, to a great extent, home-based. Their children were "home-schooled" in their faith. Their deliverance was to be rehearsed before their children at the Passover Feast and at other times as well (see Deut. 6:6, 7). Should we not also rehearse our deliverance before our children? How often do we tell our children at home what the Lord has done for us?

"Who Is Going?" (10:9–11)

Moses' answer to Pharaoh's question "Who is going?" was "Everyone!" (10:9–11). We, too, are "bound for the promised land." Whom shall we take with us? Everyone! We should make sincere efforts to bring people of all kinds into the church and

---

[8]R. Alan Cole, *Exodus: An Introduction and Commentary*, Tyndale Old Testament Commentaries (Downers Grove, Ill.: Inter-Varsity Press, 1973), 101.

[9]Ibid.

encourage them to be happy and busy in the church. Let us not leave out the young (our children, our sons and daughters), the old (our seniors), the men, the women, or anyone we can persuade to join us on the way to Zion. "No child left behind" has been a slogan used in connection with public education. "No soul left behind" would be a good motto for the church.

"Not a Hoof Shall Be Left Behind" (10:26)

If Satan cannot lure us to reject Christ's claims outright, he will tempt us to compromise with the Lord. Three or four times in the plague narrative, Pharaoh tried to convince Moses to compromise what God had instructed him to do. He said that he would allow Israel to leave if they would not go far, or if they would leave their families or their possessions behind.

"Go, but not far away." After the plague that brought swarms of flies, Pharaoh said, "Go, sacrifice to your God within the land" (8:25). Moses insisted that the Israelites must journey three days into the wilderness (8:27). Pharaoh responded, "I will let you go . . . only you shall not go very far away" (8:28). However, Pharaoh hardened his heart (8:32). In a similar way, Satan today says, "Be part of the church, but don't go too far from the world; don't get too involved with the church."

"Go, but leave your children." After the hail, Pharaoh agreed to let the people go (9:27, 28) but then hardened his heart (9:34, 35). Before the next plague, he agreed to let the people go but asked who would be going. Moses replied, "We shall go with our young and our old; with our sons and our daughters, with our flocks and our herds we shall go, for we must hold a feast to the LORD" (10:9). Pharaoh then refused to let them go, saying that he would never allow the children to leave with their parents (10:10). Satan still says, "If you must be a Christian, go ahead, but leave your children. You have no business trying to influence them to be Christ's followers."

"Go, but leave your possessions." Later came the plague of darkness. Pharaoh responded, "Go, serve the LORD, only let your flocks and your herds be detained. Even your little ones may go with you" (10:24). Moses replied that the Israelites needed the animals for sacrifice (10:25) and then said, "Our livestock too

shall go with us; *not a hoof shall be left behind,* for we shall take some of them to serve the LORD our God. And until we arrive there, we ourselves do not know with what we shall serve the LORD" (10:26; emphasis added). The Lord again hardened Pharaoh's heart (10:27). If Satan cannot keep you from the Lord, he will try to convince you not to use your possessions for God's cause.

The proper response to all of Satan's temptations to compromise is "Not a hoof shall be left behind." There shall be no compromise! Just as great athletes do not quit and great soldiers do not surrender, great Christians are never willing to compromise or bargain with the enemy.

Conclusion. If we do not give up, we will ultimately have victory. Finally, after the death of the firstborn, Pharaoh surrendered: "Rise up, get out from among my people, both you and the sons of Israel, and go, worship the LORD, as you have said. Take both your flocks and your herds, as you have said, and go" (12:31, 32). Even so, if we persevere, without compromise, we can win over Satan.[10]

---

[10]This sermon idea is from Claude Guild, who served as a missionary in Brisbane, Australia, in the 1970s.

Chapter 11

Announcement of the Last Plague: Death of the Firstborn

Exodus 11 narrates the beginning of the end of Israel's captivity. The prediction of the tenth and last plague, the death of the firstborn, is presented.

The Lord spoke to Moses to announce that He planned to bring one more plague on Egypt, after which Pharaoh would allow Israel to leave (11:1). Then He told the Israelites to ask their neighbors for gifts before they left (11:2). The writer added that the Israelites in general, and Moses in particular, were highly esteemed by the Egyptians (11:3).

In verses 4 through 7, the scene shifts back to Pharaoh's court. Moses told Pharaoh that God would kill all the firstborn of Egypt, sparing the Israelites. As a result, the Israelites would be urged to leave the land. After announcing this final plague, Moses left Pharaoh "in hot anger" (11:8).

The chapter concludes with two statements about the plagues: First, God told Moses that Pharaoh would not listen in spite of the plagues (11:9). Second, the reader is reminded that Pharaoh consistently refused to hear because of his hard heart (11:10).

THE LORD'S ANNOUNCEMENT TO MOSES (11:1–3)

**1Now the Lord said to Moses, "One more plague I will
bring on Pharaoh and on Egypt; after that he will let you go
from here. When he lets you go, he will surely drive you out
from here completely. 2Speak now in the hearing of the people
that each man ask from his neighbor and each woman from**

her neighbor for articles of silver and articles of gold." [3]The LORD gave the people favor in the sight of the Egyptians. Furthermore, the man Moses himself was greatly esteemed in the land of Egypt, both in the sight of Pharaoh's servants and in the sight of the people.

In light of the conclusion of the previous chapter, in which Pharaoh and Moses declared that they would not see one another again (10:28, 29), many commentators have interpreted 11:1–3 as a parenthesis.[1] At some time prior to the confrontation with Pharaoh reported in 10:24–29 and 11:4–8, the Lord had spoken to Moses and told him to announce the last plague. The opening line of verse 1 can be translated, "Now the LORD had said to Moses" (NIV).[2] Umberto Cassuto suggested that, during this conversation with Pharaoh, Moses recalled the message recorded in 11:1–3, a message which he had previously been given by the Lord.[3]

Why would the author choose to insert such a parenthesis at this point in the narrative? The Lord's prior appearance to Moses explains Moses' announcement in 11:4–8. Without 11:1–3, the reader might wonder where Moses heard the information he conveyed to Pharaoh, why Moses was so bold in announcing the final blow on the Egyptians, or why Pharaoh did not just do away with Moses if he found him so offensive. (This might have been unwise because "Moses . . . was greatly esteemed.")

Verses 1 through 3, therefore, serve as an introduction to what follows by informing the reader that the Lord intended to send one more plague. When Pharaoh allowed Israel to leave, the Egyptians would give the Israelites generous presents to take with them.

---

[1]James Burton Coffman, *Commentary on Exodus, The Second Book of Moses* (Abilene, Tex.: ACU Press, 1985), 130; W. H. Gispen, *Exodus*, trans. Ed van der Maas, Bible Student's Commentary (Grand Rapids, Mich.: Regency Reference Library, Zondervan Publishing House, 1982), 111.

[2]See Walter C. Kaiser, Jr., "Exodus," in *The Expositor's Bible Commentary*, vol. 2, *Genesis—Numbers* (Grand Rapids, Mich.: Zondervan, 1990), 369.

[3]Umberto Cassuto, *A Commentary on the Book of Exodus*, trans. Israel Abrahams (Jerusalem: Magnes Press, 1997), 131–32.

Verse 1. In the prior revelation, **the LORD** had informed **Moses** that **one more plague** would cause **Pharaoh** to allow Israel to exit the land. Rather than just allowing God's people to leave, the Egyptians would **drive** [them] **out . . . completely**. In other words, the Egyptians wanted so much to get rid of the Israelites that they would forcibly eject them (see 6:1; 12:31–36).

Verse 2. God then told Moses to have the Israelites **ask** their **neighbor**[s] for gifts—**articles of silver and articles of gold**. This is exactly what He had predicted when He first called Moses (3:22). Later in Exodus, God's command was obeyed; the Israelites asked, and the Egyptians gave (12:35, 36). In addition to items made of silver and gold, the Israelites also requested clothing (3:22; 12:35).

Ethical questions arise in connection with the Israelites' obtaining these gifts from their Egyptian neighbors.[4] Was it ethical for the Israelites to "borrow" (KJV) jewelry from the Egyptians when they were leaving and knew they could not pay it back? While the Hebrew word שָׁאַל (*sha'al*) can mean "borrow" (22:14 [13]), the term is better translated as "ask" in this context (NASB; NKJV; NRSV; NIV). Again, some may wonder whether or not it was ethical even to ask for such gifts, in view of the fact that Exodus later says that Israel "plundered the Egyptians" (12:36; see 3:22). These gifts could simply be viewed as payment which the Israelites had not received during their long years of servitude.

Verse 3. Why did **the Egyptians** so readily give to their Israelite neighbors? The answer appears to be that they wanted to get rid of them.[5] They connected Israel with the plagues they had experienced, and the gifts seemed a small price to pay to remove the source of their problems.

The text makes it clear why the Egyptians were so surpris-

---

[4]A summary of theories concerning the "theft" of the Egyptians' valuables is given in John I. Durham, *Exodus*, Word Biblical Commentary, vol. 3 (Waco, Tex.: Word Books, 1987), 148.

[5]This idea is implied in R. Alan Cole, *Exodus: An Introduction and Commentary*, Tyndale Old Testament Commentaries (Downers Grove, Ill.: Inter-Varsity Press, 1973), 102.

ingly bountiful: **The LORD gave** [His] **people favor**. The Israelites did not earn the Egyptians' respect, but rather they received it as a gift from God—a fact that is repeated in 12:36. Indeed, it was the Lord who "brought them out with silver and gold" (Ps. 105:37).

Furthermore, **Moses himself was greatly esteemed** by everyone in **Egypt**. Why? Perhaps some still remembered his royal upbringing. More likely, he was esteemed because he was the human instrument through whom Yahweh had brought Egypt to its knees.

MOSES' ANNOUNCEMENT TO PHARAOH (11:4–8)

**4Moses said, "Thus says the LORD, 'About midnight I am
going out into the midst of Egypt, 5and all the firstborn in the
land of Egypt shall die, from the firstborn of the Pharaoh who
sits on his throne, even to the firstborn of the slave girl who is
behind the millstones; all the firstborn of the cattle as well.
6Moreover, there shall be a great cry in all the land of Egypt,
such as there has not been before and such as shall never be
again. 7But against any of the sons of Israel a dog will not even
bark, whether against man or beast, that you may understand
how the LORD makes a distinction between Egypt and Israel.'
8All these your servants will come down to me and bow themselves before me, saying, 'Go out, you and all the people who follow you,' and after that I will go out." And he went out from Pharaoh in hot anger.**

As previously noted, this paragraph probably continues the scene found in 10:24–29. Moses, as he had done before, spoke to Pharaoh to warn him about this final plague. The prelude to the plague differed from similar warnings, however, in that Moses did not attach an "if clause"; he did not say, in effect, "The plague will happen *if* you do not let the people go." Rather, he announced in advance the sure outcome of the catastrophe: The Israelites were to leave the land!

Verse 4. Chapter 10 ended with Moses saying, "You are right;

I shall never see your face again!" (10:29). Before he left Pharaoh's presence, Moses announced the final plague, prefacing his words with the prophet's declaration **"Thus says the Lord."** In other words, Yahweh was the One who had given him his message.

In a number of cases in the narrative about the plagues, the text describes God's revelation to Moses but does not specifically narrate Moses' transmission of the message to Pharaoh, though it is clear that Moses does indeed faithfully present God's word to the king. In this case, the text presents the transmission of the message without describing God's original revelation of that message to Moses. The writer assumed that the reader would "fill in the blanks" when reading the story.

At this point, Moses presented the Lord's preview of the plague. He began by telling when it would take place and who would be responsible: **"'About midnight I** [the Lord] **am going out into the midst of Egypt.'"** J. Philip Hyatt labeled this description as "vivid anthropomorphic language," that is, imagery which describes God's actions in human terms (see Gen. 3:8; 11:5; 18:22; Ex. 7:17; 8:19).[6]

Verse 5. Next Moses revealed what the plague would involve: **"All the firstborn in the land of Egypt shall die."** The fact that the "firstborn" males were to die made the tragedy doubly horrible. The firstborn were regarded as the most precious members of the family. A firstborn son was considered the first fruit of his father's strength (Ps. 78:51; 105:36). He received "a double portion" of his father's inheritance (Deut. 21:17), and he was expected to carry on the family name. Nevertheless, for God to kill Egypt's firstborn was just, since Egypt had killed Israel's sons (1:22) and mistreated God's firstborn, Israel (4:23). The death of the firstborn sons was a measure-for-measure punishment on the Egyptians.[7]

Moses also noted who would be affected: The plague would kill all of the firstborn of the Egyptians. God would not discrim-

---

[6]J. Philip Hyatt, *Exodus*, The New Century Bible Commentary (Grand Rapids, Mich.: Wm. B. Eerdmans Publishing Co., 1971), 130.

[7]Nahum M. Sarna, *Exploring Exodus: The Origins of Biblical Israel* (New York: Schocken Books, 1996), 94.

inate based on wealth, social status, or power. The plague would impact the greatest of the Egyptians, even **Pharaoh who sits on his throne.** Although Pharaoh was honored as a god, he would be powerless to save his own firstborn son—the prince of Egypt.

Further, the plague would reach down to the least, **the slave girl who is behind the millstones.** In a parallel passage, the least is described as "the captive who was in the dungeon" (12:29). Grinding grain was the lowliest of jobs fit for a slave or a prisoner (Judg. 16:21; Is. 47:2). Carl G. Rasmussen explained that "millstones" were typically two stones that had been carved from basalt, "a rough black volcanic rock." The miller would kneel behind the lower stationary stone, which was usually shaped like a rectangle and had a slight downward slope of 15 degrees. After placing grain on this stone, he would vigorously rub the smaller upper stone against the lower one. As a result, the ground grain would run down the incline and fall into a heap.[8]

The devastating plague would even kill **the firstborn of the cattle.** The term בְּהֵמָה (*b^ehemah*), rendered "cattle," is broader than bulls and cows. This Hebrew word is usually rendered "beast" in Exodus, and is translated this way twice in the narrative of the last plague (11:7; 12:12).

Verse 6. Moses then revealed how the people would react: **"There shall be a great cry in all the land of Egypt."** This cry of horror, sorrow, and pity was to be greater than any other ever heard in Egypt (see 9:18, 24; 10:6, 14).

Verse 7. After describing who would be affected and how they would react, Moses noted who would be spared. **The sons of Israel** were not to be affected by the plague so that the Egyptians could see that **the LORD makes a distinction between Egypt and Israel** (see 8:22, 23; 9:4).

---

[8]Carl G. Rasmussen, "Mill; Millstone," in *The International Standard Bible Encyclopedia*, rev. ed., ed. Geoffrey W. Bromiley (Grand Rapids, Mich.: Wm. B. Eerdmans Publishing Co., 1986), 3:355. See the picture of an Egyptian model dated to the Old Kingdom (c. 2700–2200 B.C.) in James B. Pritchard, *The Ancient Near East in Pictures Relating to the Old Testament* (Princeton, N. J.: Princeton University Press, 1954), 46 (no. 149).

When Moses said concerning Israel that **a dog will not even bark, whether against man or beast,** he was saying that God's people were in no danger at all.[9] A barking (or snarling) dog is not particularly dangerous, but Israel would not even have to contend with that minor problem. John I. Durham explained, "The Israelites will remain unharmed and undisturbed. Not even the empty snarl of a dog will interrupt the quiet of the Israelite settlement, while among the Egyptians the air will be torn by the piercing cries of lament."[10] The people of Israel had nothing to fear, even though the death of the firstborn was bringing grief and horror to the Egyptians.

In Hebrew, the phrase "a dog will not even bark" is literally "a dog will not sharpen his tongue" (לֹא יֶחֱרַץ־כֶּלֶב לְשֹׁנוֹ, *lo' yech^{e}rats keleb l^{e}shono*). The precise background and meaning of the idiom "sharpen his tongue" is unclear, but it does appear elsewhere in reference to humans (Josh. 10:21). In both cases, *not* "sharpening the tongue" refers to remaining silent. In the present text, the KJV says that a dog shall not "move his tongue," whereas the NRSV says that he will not "growl." Wilbur Fields suggested that verse 7 means "[God's] protection would be so total that not even a dog would bark at the hordes of departing Israelites and their cattle."[11]

Verse 8. Finally, Moses proclaimed to Pharaoh the outcome of this plague: **"All these your servants will come down to me and bow themselves before me."** Pharaoh's officials, who normally spent a good part of each day bowing down to Pharaoh, would, when the plague struck, go to Moses and bow down before him. The narrative of the plagues relates a contest between Yahweh and the Egyptian gods, represented especially by Pharaoh. This passage predicted unequivocal victory for Yahweh. Even Pharaoh's closest supporters would bow down—not to Pharaoh, but to Yahweh's ambassador!

When Pharaoh's servants bowed down to Moses, they would

---

[9]Cole, 103.

[10]Durham, 149.

[11]Wilbur Fields, *Exploring Exodus*, Bible Study Textbook Series (Joplin, Mo.: College Press, 1976), 231.

urge the Israelites to **go out**. "Going out" is a theme throughout this passage. Pharaoh had told Moses to "get away" (10:28). Then Moses said that the Lord was "going out" into Egypt (11:4). Afterwards, Pharaoh's own servants told Israel to "go out" (11:8). When they did, Moses said that he would "go out," and then he "went out" from Pharaoh's presence (11:8).[12]

Moses punctuated his announcement by leaving Pharaoh's court abruptly, **in hot anger**, matching the anger Pharaoh had displayed in 10:28. The term "anger" (אַף, *'ap*) can also be translated "nostril." This association of meanings came about because when a person is angry, his nostrils flare.

SUMMARY STATEMENT (11:9, 10)

[9]Then the LORD said to Moses, "Pharaoh will not listen to you, so that My wonders will be multiplied in the land of Egypt." [10]Moses and Aaron performed all these wonders before Pharaoh; yet the LORD hardened Pharaoh's heart, and he did not let the sons of Israel go out of his land.

At this point in his narrative, a summary statement is inserted to complete the story of the first nine plagues, just as the story began with an overview of what was about to happen (7:1–5; see 3:18–22; 4:21–23).

Verse 9. Some versions make it clear that this verse does not continue the story told in 11:4–8 (NIV; NLT; CEV; NCV). For example, the NLT says, "Now the LORD had told Moses earlier," indicating that everything that had happened with regard to the plagues had been predicted by the Lord from the beginning.

Verse 10. What the Lord had predicted in verse 9 had happened. **Moses and Aaron** [had] **performed all these wonders before Pharaoh.** "These wonders" included not only the first nine plagues, but also the sign which Moses and Aaron had done

---

[12]The same Hebrew word, יָצָא (*yatsa'*), is used for "going out" four times in 11:4, 8. A different word, הָלַךְ (*halak*), is used for "get away" in 10:28.

before Pharaoh (7:9–13). However, **the Lord hardened Pharaoh's heart** by encouraging him to follow the path he had already chosen. The result was Pharaoh's refusal to allow the Israelites to leave Egypt. However, the tenth plague changed the ending to the story.

Chapter 11, then, is transitional. It concludes the narrative of the first nine plagues and introduces the story of the final and most significant plague.

APPLICATION

"Greatly Esteemed" (11:3)

"The Lord gave the people favor in the sight of the Egyptians," and "Moses himself was greatly esteemed in the land of Egypt" (11:3). This esteem could be linked to the plagues which demonstrated the Lord's power and indicated that the Lord favored His people. The Israelites may have been looked upon with fear or respect, as those of a defeated land might view the people of a conquering nation. Still, the esteem in which they were held reminds us of the fact that the early church also had "favor with all the people" (Acts 2:47). Today, we cannot depend on miracles to gain the esteem of those outside the church. What we can do is live the right kind of lives (1 Pet. 2:12; 3:15, 16). When we do, we will, as a group of people, probably also be "greatly esteemed" by our societies.

No Favoritism in Wrath (11:5)

To punish the Egyptians for mistreating Israel and for killing the Israelite babies, God sent a plague to kill the Egyptians' firstborn. In expending His wrath upon them, He showed no favoritism, slaying all the firstborn—from the king's firstborn to the slave girl's firstborn. Similarly, in the Day of Judgment, God will punish without showing favoritism: All who have rejected Him will be expelled from His presence, from the highest to the lowest. The rich or famous will not be favored by God and be saved if they have not obeyed Him. Neither will God have pity on the poor just because they are poor.

"A Dog Will Not Even Bark" (11:7)

Exodus 11:7 says, "Against any of the sons of Israel a dog will not even bark." Egyptian families were about to be devastated by the tenth plague, the death of the firstborn. Moses said, "There shall be a great cry in all the land of Egypt, such as there has not been before and such as shall never be again" (11:6). While all this was happening, the Israelites were to be spared; they would not even be threatened by a dog's bark. An alternate understanding of verses 6 and 7 is suggested by the REB, which says, "From all over Egypt there will go up a great cry. . . . But throughout all Israel no sound will be heard from man or beast, not even a dog's bark. Thus you will know that the LORD distinguishes between Egypt and Israel."

The main point was plain: "The LORD makes a distinction between Egypt and Israel." Of course, it was not just with regard to the tenth plague that the Lord distinguished between Egypt and Israel. In addition to the death of the firstborn (11:7; 12:13), the Israelites escaped the effects of the swarms of flies (8:21–23), the plague on livestock (9:4), the plague of hail (9:26), and the plague of darkness (10:23).

God's sparing Israel proved to Pharaoh that the people of Israel were the Lord's people and that, since they had such a powerful God, Pharaoh should allow them to leave. It also demonstrated to the Israelites God's love and concern for them. Because God spared them, because of the fact that "a dog [did] not even bark," they must have felt "special." In fact, they were special—so special that God made "a distinction between Egypt and Israel."

God made a distinction between His people and others. God continued to "make a distinction" between Israel and others in the Old Testament. He promised to give the Israelites specific blessings if they obeyed His commands (Lev. 26; Deut. 27; 28). God fulfilled those promises, providing food and water in the wilderness, giving Israel victory (for example, in the conquest of Canaan), and protecting His people from their enemies (see 2 Kings 19:35–37).

However, God also held Israel accountable for the special privileges which the people enjoyed; with these great privileges came great responsibilities. If the people gloried in the privileges but failed to live up to the responsibilities (as in Jeremiah's day [Jer. 7]), they would be cursed. That, in fact, is what eventually happened. As a result, both the northern kingdom (Israel) and the southern kingdom (Judah) were destroyed. Nevertheless, anyone who encountered Israel in Old Testament times could see without a doubt that God made a distinction: Israel was God's chosen nation.

God makes a distinction today between His people and others. God makes no distinction between people today in regard to how they are saved (Acts 10:34, 35), but does He in other ways? Do Christians have God's promise that, while all the rest of the world may be groaning in travail, "a dog will not even bark" at us? Can Christians expect serene lives, blessed by God, protected from the harm that others experience in this world?

We wish it were so. Passages in both the Old Testament and the New seem to promise prosperity and health to those who do the Lord's will. Some interpret these Scriptures as a promise that Christians will never experience the problems that unbelievers know. Some preachers make such promises, preaching a "health and wealth" gospel. However, our experience teaches us that God's people today are not exempt from the disasters and pain that are common to mankind. A closer look at the Scriptures tells us that neither in the Old Testament nor the New is there any absolute promise of "health and wealth" for believers. Righteous Job suffered. If the perfect man Jesus was crucified, if early Christians were martyred, if the blessings of following Christ are accompanied by persecution (Mk. 10:29–31), why should we expect to escape problems and pain?

God does distinguish between His people and others, but the blessings He provides are spiritual. We are today, as was Israel, "a chosen race, a royal priesthood, a holy nation, a people for God's own possession" (1 Pet. 2:9). The church consists of those who have been saved (Acts 2:47; see 1 Cor. 12:13; Eph. 5:23). Christ loved and died for the church (Eph. 5:23–25). No other group can make that claim! Indeed, God "makes a distinction" today: One is either in the church because he has been saved, or he is not in the church and is not saved.

For those who are in the church, God promises providential care, help in temptation, answered prayer, constant forgiveness, and other blessings. While God does not keep us from experiencing troubles just because we are Christians, He is always available to help and comfort us. He does not desert His faithful followers in times of trouble.

Along with His blessings come responsibilities (1 Pet. 2:9, 10). We cannot rejoice in the blessings and forget the responsibilities, or expect to continue to receive the blessings if we constantly fail to live up to the responsibilities.

God illustrated the protection He would give His people by assuring them that when all of Egypt was wailing, among the Israelites "a dog [would] not even bark." Christians can depend on a similar promise: Throughout eternity—outside heaven, across that great gulf—there will be wailing and gnashing of teeth. Inside the heavenly city, however, there will "no longer be any death; there will no longer be any mourning, or crying, or pain" (Rev. 21:4). There will not even be a dog's threatening bark to disturb the peace of those within. If you are in the church, that city is your destination.

Pharaoh: The Deterioration of a Soul (11:9, 10)

Warren W. Wiersbe, in a chapter on the plagues, concentrated on "the moral and spiritual deterioration" of Pharaoh. He focused on Pharaoh's responses to the last seven plagues: (1) "Bargaining" (8:20–32); (2) "Resisting" (9:1–12); (3) "Deceiving" (9:13–35); (4) "Appealing" (10:1–20); and (5) "Threatening" (10:21–29). He then said,

> The hardening of Pharaoh's heart is a warning to all of us. If the sinful human heart doesn't respond by faith to God's Word, it cannot be transformed by the grace of God (Ezek. 36:26–27; Heb. 8:7–13). Instead it will become harder and harder the longer it resists God's truth.[13]

We must heed what God has told us (Heb. 3:7, 8; 10:31).

---

[13]Warren W. Wiersbe, *Be Delivered* (Colorado Springs, Colo.: Victor, 1998), 35–47.

Chapter 12

The Passover, the Last Plague, and the Departure

Chapter 12 tells the story of the last plague and the institution of the Passover feast. Repetition in this chapter and the next can be explained as reflecting the same instructions recounted on different occasions.

God gave directions for preparing a Passover lamb and sprinkling its blood on the doorposts and lintel of a house (12:1–7). Each Israelite family was to roast a lamb and eat all of it, with "unleavened bread and bitter herbs" (12:8–11). The reason for the feast was given before it happened: The Lord would go through the land and strike down the Egyptian firstborn, but would pass over the houses where He saw the blood (12:12, 13).

The Passover was to be an annual feast, a "memorial" to commemorate Israel's deliverance from Egypt (12:14–20). Moses relayed God's instructions to the elders (12:21–23). He announced that this feast would teach the Israelite children about their deliverance from Egypt (12:24–27). To their credit, the Israelites obeyed the Lord (12:28).

At the appointed hour, the Lord struck Egypt so that all their firstborn died (12:29, 30). Pharaoh then urged Moses and Aaron to leave—to go with everything they owned. He was joined in his request by the rest of the Egyptians, who readily gave the Israelites the gifts they requested (12:31–36).

The chapter gives details about Israel's exodus (12:37–41) and records further instructions about their observance of the Passover (12:42–49). It concludes with a summary statement about Israel's obedience and affirms the people's deliverance by the Lord (12:50, 51).

THE PASSOVER INSTITUTED (12:1–28)

The Passover Explained (12:1–13)

**[1]Now the LORD said to Moses and Aaron in the land of
Egypt, [2]"This month shall be the beginning of months for you;
it is to be the first month of the year to you. [3]Speak to all the
congregation of Israel, saying, 'On the tenth of this month they
are each one to take a lamb for themselves, according to their
fathers' households, a lamb for each household. [4]Now if the
household is too small for a lamb, then he and his neighbor
nearest to his house are to take one according to the number
of persons in them; according to what each man should eat,
you are to divide the lamb. [5]Your lamb shall be an unblem-
ished male a year old; you may take it from the sheep or from
the goats. [6]You shall keep it until the fourteenth day of the
same month, then the whole assembly of the congregation of
Israel is to kill it at twilight. [7]Moreover, they shall take some
of the blood and put it on the two doorposts and on the lintel
of the houses in which they eat it. [8]They shall eat the flesh that
same night, roasted with fire, and they shall eat it with unleav-
ened bread and bitter herbs. [9]Do not eat any of it raw or boiled
at all with water, but rather roasted with fire, both its head and
its legs along with its entrails. [10]And you shall not leave any
of it over until morning, but whatever is left of it until morn-
ing, you shall burn with fire. [11]Now you shall eat it in this man-
ner: with your loins girded, your sandals on your feet, and your
staff in your hand; and you shall eat it in haste—it is the LORD's
Passover. [12]For I will go through the land of Egypt on that night,
and will strike down all the firstborn in the land of Egypt, both
man and beast; and against all the gods of Egypt I will execute
judgments—I am the LORD. [13]The blood shall be a sign for you
on the houses where you live; and when I see the blood I will
pass over you, and no plague will befall you to destroy you
when I strike the land of Egypt.'"**

This first paragraph of Exodus 12 gives instructions regarding the Passover. In anticipation of the actual event—their deliverance from the death of the firstborn and their subsequent escape from Egypt—the Israelites were told how they were to commemorate the occasion.

Verse 1. The author of Exodus noted that God gave these instructions **in the land of Egypt**, implying that neither he nor his original readers were any longer in Egypt. These instructions are thus distinguished from the additional commands that God gave concerning the Passover after Israel left Egypt (Num. 9:9–14; Deut. 16:1–8).

Verse 2. The Lord gave the date for the annual memorial feast, but He did more than that. Regardless of which month of the year had been the Hebrews' first month, from that point forward the month in which the Passover was held would begin the new year.[1] **The first month of the year**, Abib (Nisan), coincides with "the latter part of March and first part of April"[2] (see comments on 13:4). The time of the last plague and the exodus is easy to remember: Jesus was killed on or about Passover, and many observe Easter at that time today.

Further, the exodus marked the "birth of a nation." Just as the United States celebrates July 4 as its birthday, Israel would celebrate Passover night as its birthday. Peter Enns explained,

> The deliverance from Egypt is a new beginning for Israel; from now on, every glance at the calendar will remind them of this fact. It also provides a connection to Genesis and creation. At the Exodus, God's people are being "recreated"; they are starting over with a fresh slate.[3]

Verses 3, 4. After explaining the significance of the day of

---

[1]Something similar is done by people who date their calendars from the beginning of their religion—by followers of Christ whose calendar is dated from the birth of Jesus (in the use of B.C. / A.D.) and by Muslims whose calendar is dated from the Hejira ("flight") of Muhammed in A.D. 622.

[2]Harold Lindsell, note on Exodus 12:2, *NRSV Harper Study Bible*, ed. Verlyn D. Verbrugge (Grand Rapids, Mich.: Zondervan Publishing House, 1991), 94.

[3]Peter Enns, *Exodus*, The NIV Application Commentary (Grand Rapids, Mich.: Zondervan, 2000), 247.

THE JEWISH CALENDAR

Number of Month		Hebrew Name	Modern Equivalent	Feasts	Agriculture
Sacred sequence	*Civil sequence*				
1	7	Abib (Nisan)	March–April	Passover Unleavened Bread First fruits	Spring (later) rains; barley and flax harvest begins
2	8	Ziv (Iyyar)	April–May		Barley harvest; dry season begins
3	9	Sivan	May–June	Weeks (Pentecost)	Wheat harvest
4	10	Tammuz	June–July		Tending vines
5	11	Ab	July–August		Ripening of grapes, figs, and olives
6	12	Elul	August–September		Processing grapes, figs, and olives
7	1	Ethanim (Tishri)	September–October	Trumpets Day of Atonement Tabernacles (Booths)	Autumn (early) rains begin; plowing
8	2	Bul (Marcheshvan)	October–November		Sowing of wheat and barley
9	3	Kislev	November–December	Hanukkah (Dedication)	Winter rains begin; snow in some areas
10	4	Tebeth	December–January		
11	5	Shebat	January–February		
12	6	Adar	February–March	Purim	Almond trees bloom; citrus fruit harvest
		Second Adar (Adar Sheni)	*Month added every three years so that the lunar calendar corresponds to the solar year.*		

their deliverance, the Lord gave instructions for the Israelites regarding how they were to keep the feast. His reference to them as **the congregation of Israel** marks the first usage of this expression in the Scriptures. When God delivered the descendants of Jacob out of Egypt, they became a "congregation" (עֵדָה, *'edah*), an organized community of His people. The assembled Israelites were indeed "the congregation of the LORD" (Num. 27:17; 31:16; Josh. 22:17).

Each household among the people of Israel was to select **a lamb** or a kid. The term שֶׂה (*śeh*), translated "lamb," can refer to the young offspring of either a sheep or goat. This selection was to take place **on the tenth** of Abib. **If the household** [was] **too small** [to eat] **a lamb** by itself, then two households were to join together. One family was to share with the closest **neighbor**, preventing an unnecessary waste of food.

Verse 5. The Passover lamb had to be **an unblemished male a year old**. To be "unblemished" meant that the animal could not be blind, lame, deformed, or diseased (see Deut. 15:21; Mal. 1:8). Such defects detracted from the lamb's value and made it an unacceptable sacrifice to God (see Lev. 22:19–21; Deut. 17:1). As previously noted, the animal could be taken **from the sheep or from the goats.**

Verse 6. God commanded the Israelites to **keep it until the fourteenth day** of Abib, four days after it was selected.[4] On this day, all of the Israelite households were to **kill** their chosen lambs. This slaughter was to take place **at twilight**. The Hebrew text literally says "between the evenings" (בֵּין הָעַרְבָּיִם, *beyn ha'arbayin*). This expression refers to the brief period of time between sunset and darkness. The NEB has "between dusk and dark." A parallel passage says "at even[ing], at the going down of the sun" (Deut. 16:6; KJV).

Verse 7. The blood from the lamb was to be placed **on the two doorposts and on the lintel** of the home where the Passover lamb would be eaten (see 12:4). The "lintel" (מַשְׁקוֹף, *mashqop*)

---

[4]On the occasion of the first Passover, apparently there were not four days between the time these instructions were given and the time the plague struck, since the Israelites had no time to prepare to leave (12:39).

refers to the horizontal beam over the top of a doorway. This part of a structure could have been a wooden beam or a slab of stone. The blood put on the doorframe served as a protective mark (see Gen. 4:15; Ezek. 9:4; Rev. 7:2, 3). Although not offered on an altar, the Passover lamb still served as a substitutionary sacrifice (12:27; 34:25). Its lifeblood had to be taken in order to preserve the lives of those gathered in the house (see Lev. 17:11).

Verses 8, 9. The Israelites were also commanded to **eat the flesh that same night.** God specified that the lamb was to be **roasted with fire**. The meat could not be eaten **raw**; it had to be thoroughly cooked because the Israelites were not to eat any of the animal's blood (see Gen. 9:4; Lev. 3:17; 7:26, 27; 17:10–14; 1 Sam. 14:31–33), nor could the meat be **boiled . . . with water**.

Along with the roasted lamb, the Israelites were told to eat **unleavened bread and bitter herbs**. In the additional instructions that God gave Israel at Mt. Sinai, the "unleavened bread" is referred to as "the bread of affliction." Its purpose was to remind the people that they "came out of the land of Egypt in haste" (Deut. 16:3; see Ex. 12:11, 39). The "bitter herbs" would also remind the Israelites of the "bitter" experiences they had in Egyptian bondage (1:14). According to the Mishnah, these particular herbs consisted of lettuce, chicory, pepperwort, endives, and dandelion.[5]

Verse 10. The Passover lamb was to be consumed by the whole household. Since it was consecrated for that special occasion, whatever was not eaten by **morning** was to be **burn**[ed] **with fire**.

Verse 11. Those who ate were to eat it hastily, dressed for a quick exit: **with your loins girded, your sandals on your feet, and your staff in your hand.** To have "your loins girded" meant to have "your cloak tucked into your belt" (NIV) in order to make walking or running easier (see 1 Kings 18:46). The "staff" (מַקֵּל, *maqqel*) would serve as a walking stick on the journey. A different Hebrew word is used here than for the unique "staff" (מַטֶּה, *matteh*) used by Moses and Aaron. By eating the Passover meal in this way, the Israelites would demonstrate their faith in the

---

[5]Mishnah *Pesahim* 2.6.

Lord that He would soon deliver them out of Egypt.

The point of the Passover was to remember what the Lord had done on the night of the final plague. Therefore, the feast was appropriately designated **the Lord's Passover**. The noun "Passover" (פֶּסַח, *pesach*) is related to the verb פָּסַח (*pasach*), translated "pass over" in verses 13, 23, and 27.

Verse 12. By this plague, God would (1) kill **the firstborn** of **both man and beast** in **Egypt** (4:23; 11:5; 12:29) and (2) **execute judgments** on **all the gods of Egypt**. The text of Exodus does not specifically state which deities were targeted in the first nine plagues; almost every plague has multiple possibilities (see comments on 7:21; 8:1, 2; 9:4, 5, 10, 23b–25; 10:15, 21–23). Nevertheless, this verse clearly states that the last plague was intended to strike at "all the gods" of Egypt. When the firstborn of Egypt died, in a sense, the Egyptian gods died. At least, it became evident that they were lifeless, powerless, and ineffective against the wrath of the one true God.

Verse 13. At the same time, God showed that He was alive and powerful. He differentiated between His people and the Egyptians (8:22, 23; 9:4; 11:7) by sparing those who were in homes protected by **the blood**.

The Feast of Unleavened Bread Explained (12:14–20)

14"'Now this day will be a memorial to you, and you shall celebrate it as a feast to the Lord; throughout your generations you are to celebrate it as a permanent ordinance. 15Seven days you shall eat unleavened bread, but on the first day you shall remove leaven from your houses; for whoever eats anything leavened from the first day until the seventh day, that person shall be cut off from Israel. 16On the first day you shall have a holy assembly, and another holy assembly on the seventh day; no work at all shall be done on them, except what must be eaten by every person, that alone may be prepared by you. 17You shall also observe the Feast of Unleavened Bread, for on this very day I brought your hosts out of the land of Egypt; therefore you shall observe this day throughout your generations as a permanent ordinance. 18In the first month, on the fourteenth

day of the month at evening, you shall eat unleavened bread, until the twenty-first day of the month at evening. [19]Seven days there shall be no leaven found in your houses; for whoever eats what is leavened, that person shall be cut off from the congregation of Israel, whether he is an alien or a native of the land. [20]You shall not eat anything leavened; in all your dwellings you shall eat unleavened bread.'"

After God told Moses and Aaron what they were to say to the congregation of Israel regarding the Passover (12:1–13), He informed them about another feast (12:14–20). Along with the Passover feast itself, the Israelites were to observe "the Feast of Unleavened Bread" (12:17).

Verse 14. This day probably refers to the day when the Israelites began their exodus from Egypt (see 12:17). The Feast of Unleavened Bread was to serve as **a memorial** whereby the Israelites would remember God's mighty work in delivering them from Egyptian bondage. The celebration was to be **a permanent ordinance**. References to the Passover and the Feast of Unleavened Bread occur throughout the Scriptures (Num. 9:1–5; Josh. 5:10; 2 Chron. 30:1–27; 35:1–19; Ezra 6:19–22; Lk. 2:41; Jn. 2:13; 6:4; 11:55; Acts 12:3, 4; 20:6). These feast days are still observed by many Jews in modern times.

Verse 15. The Feast of Unleavened Bread was to be held in conjunction with the Passover for **seven days**. God required the people to **eat unleavened bread** during that period; He even told them to rid their homes of **leaven**. "Leaven" is a substance added to dough to produce fermentation, which causes the bread to rise. The Israelites customarily reserved a pinch of leavened dough from the previous day of baking and kneaded it into the new batch. Over time, leaven came to symbolize corruption and evil that quickly spread (Mt. 16:6; Lk. 12:1; 1 Cor. 5:6–8; Gal. 5:9). Those who did not obey God's command to rid their homes of leaven were to **be cut off from Israel**. They were to be excluded from the community, either by banishment or by execution (31:14; Lev. 20:2, 3).

Verse 16. The Feast of Unleavened Bread was to begin and end with a **holy assembly** or "holy convocation" (KJV). **On the**

first day and **on the seventh day** of this festival, the Israelites were to gather together in worship before the Lord. **No work** could be performed on those days, other than making the necessary food preparations.

Verse 17. The Feast of Unleavened Bread would remind the people of the deliverance of their **hosts** from Egyptian bondage. The term "hosts" (**צָבָא**, *tsaba'*) often refers to an army organized for battle. This description is fitting, since the Israelites were headed to Canaan where they would fight numerous battles in order to conquer the land. The fact that the Feast of Unleavened Bread was to become **a permanent ordinance** is repeated for emphasis (see 12:14).

Verse 18. This feast was to be observed from **the fourteenth day** to **the twenty-first day** of **the first month**. "The fourteenth day" designates the Passover (12:6), whereas the fifteenth to "the "twenty-first day" marks the Feast of Unleavened Bread.

Verse 19. The Israelites' **houses**, which had been cleansed of leaven (12:15), were to remain this way for **seven days**—the full duration of the feast. The judgment for the offender is repeated from verse 15: **that person shall be cut off from the congregation of Israel.** Such an individual would receive this punishment regardless of his status, **whether he is an alien or a native of the land.** This law anticipated the Israelites' conquering of Canaan and their possession of the land. Therefore, "a native of the land" refers to an Israelite. In contrast, an "alien" (גֵּר, *ger*) denotes a non-Israelite living in Israel (see comments on 12:48).

Verse 20. The last sentence of the paragraph summarizes and emphasizes what God has already said: **"You shall not eat anything leavened; in all your dwellings you shall eat unleavened bread."**

The First Passover Observed (12:21–28)

21Then Moses called for all the elders of Israel and said to them, "Go and take for yourselves lambs according to your families, and slay the Passover lamb. 22You shall take a bunch of hyssop and dip it in the blood which is in the basin, and apply some of the blood that is in the basin to the lintel and

the two doorposts; and none of you shall go outside the door of his house until morning. [23]For the LORD will pass through to smite the Egyptians; and when He sees the blood on the lintel and on the two doorposts, the LORD will pass over the door and will not allow the destroyer to come in to your houses to smite you. [24]And you shall observe this event as an ordinance for you and your children forever. [25]When you enter the land which the LORD will give you, as He has promised, you shall observe this rite. [26]And when your children say to you, 'What does this rite mean to you?' [27]you shall say, 'It is a Passover sacrifice to the LORD who passed over the houses of the sons of Israel in Egypt when He smote the Egyptians, but spared our homes.'" And the people bowed low and worshiped.

[28]Then the sons of Israel went and did so; just as the LORD had commanded Moses and Aaron, so they did.

Moses began his instructions to the people by telling them what to do to be delivered from the plague of the death of the firstborn (12:21–24). Therefore, 12:1–20 gives details about the memorial, while 12:21–28 returns to the story of the tenth plague and of Israel's deliverance, a narrative which paused after 11:8. If a person were to read 11:1–8 and then continue reading at 12:21, he would not miss any of the story.[6]

Moses received God's word concerning the feast (12:1–20) and relayed the instructions to Israel (12:21–27a). In response, the people of Israel bowed down and worshiped and then did what the Lord had told them to do (12:27b, 28). After that, the event about which they had been warned occurred (12:29–32).

Verse 21. Moses instructed **the elders** of the people to select the **lambs**, just as God had directed him (12:3). Furthermore, at the right time, they were to **slay the Passover lamb**.

Verse 22a. Next, Moses told the Israelites to put the lamb's

---

[6]This fact does not, as many commentators think, prove the existence of sources which were used by the author or editor of Exodus. Rather, the insertion of instructions concerning the feast prior to the actual account of the plague can be seen as a characteristic of the author's narrative style. For his own purposes, he chose to insert instructions and laws into the narrative sections.

blood on **the lintel and the two doorposts** (see 12:7). To accomplish this task, they were to use **a bunch of hyssop**. R. Alan Cole said that, according to tradition, "hyssop" is the herb marjoram (see NEB). He added, "Its use is purely utilitarian: it is a common Palestinian herb which, when fastened in a bunch, would make a good sprinkler."[7] Hyssop was used in other sacrificial rites as well (Lev. 14:4–7, 49–52; Num. 19:6, 18; see Ps. 51:7).

Verses 22b, 23. Furthermore, Moses commanded the people to stay inside **until morning**. Those who were within the houses that had the lamb's blood on the doorframes would be safe throughout the night. God would **pass through** to kill the firstborn of Egypt, but He would **pass over** the firstborn of Israel. The Lord would prevent **the destroyer** from entering the homes of His faithful people.

A common understanding is that a "death angel" killed the firstborn in Egypt. The text indicates that the Lord was responsible for these deaths; it was He who struck the Egyptians (12:29) and passed over the houses of the Israelites (see 11:4; 12:12). The mention of a "destroyer" suggests that God used a destroying angel (or "death angel") to execute Egypt's firstborn.[8] Other passages in the Bible also refer to destroying angels who act as God's agents (2 Sam. 24:16; 2 Kings 19:35; Ps. 78:49; 1 Cor. 10:10).

Verses 24, 25. Moses emphasized, just as the Lord had instructed him (12:14, 17), that the Passover **event** was to be continually commemorated. The celebration was to be handed down from generation to generation. **This rite** was to be perpetuated in **the land** that God had promised Israel, the land of Canaan.

Verses 26, 27. He added that the purpose of the feast was for parents to teach their **children** how the Lord had delivered His people, killing **the Egyptians** but sparing **the sons of Israel**. Since children are naturally inquisitive, the question would arise, **"What does this rite mean to you?"** This teachable moment afforded parents—primarily fathers—an opportunity to tell their sons and daughters about God's work in redeeming their nation

---

[7]R. Alan Cole, *Exodus: An Introduction and Commentary*, Tyndale Old Testament Commentaries (Downers Grove, Ill.: Inter-Varsity Press, 1973), 110.

[8]Ibid.

(see 13:8, 14; Deut. 4:9; 6:6–9, 20–25; Josh. 4:6, 7, 21–24). Marvin R. Wilson wrote, "From this practice of ritual questioning the term *Haggadah* (lit. 'explaining, telling') took on increased importance in the life of the community. (Today the term is used for the book that explains the meaning of the Passover meal.)"[9] (For **Passover sacrifice** and **passed over**, see comments on 12:7, 11.)

After hearing Moses' words, **the people bowed low and worshiped**. This signified their submission to the will of God, even though it would mean great loss of life in Egypt and great changes in their own lives.

Verse 28. After the Israelites indicated that they accepted God's directions when they bowed and worshiped, they showed their respect for His word by obeying the commands He had given through **Moses and Aaron**. A flurry of activity must have followed in the Hebrews' homes as they prepared to sacrifice the lambs and to leave Egypt.

THE FIRSTBORN KILLED AND THE ISRAELITES FREED (12:29–36)

**29Now it came about at midnight that the LORD struck all
the firstborn in the land of Egypt, from the firstborn of Pharaoh who sat on his throne to the firstborn of the captive who
was in the dungeon, and all the firstborn of cattle. 30Pharaoh
arose in the night, he and all his servants and all the Egyptians, and there was a great cry in Egypt, for there was no home where
there was not someone dead. 31Then he called for Moses and
Aaron at night and said, "Rise up, get out from among my people, both you and the sons of Israel; and go, worship the
LORD, as you have said. 32Take both your flocks and your herds,
as you have said, and go, and bless me also." 33The Egyptians
urged the people, to send them out of the land in haste, for they said, "We will all be dead." 34So the people took their
dough before it was leavened, with their kneading bowls**

[9]Marvin R. Wilson, "Passover," in *The International Standard Bible Encyclopedia*, rev. ed., ed. Geoffrey W. Bromiley (Grand Rapids, Mich.: Wm. B. Eerdmans Publishing Co., 1986), 3:676. See Mishnah *Pesahim* 10.4.

bound up in the clothes on their shoulders.

35Now the sons of Israel had done according to the word of Moses, for they had requested from the Egyptians articles of silver and articles of gold, and clothing; 36and the Lord had given the people favor in the sight of the Egyptians, so that they let them have their request. Thus they plundered the Egyptians.

Verse 29. What the Lord had promised, He performed. It was **at midnight** (11:4), presumably on the day that Moses left Pharaoh, that God **struck all the firstborn in the land of Egypt**. This plague impacted all of society, from the greatest (**Pharaoh**) to the least (**the captive**), and even the **cattle** (see comments on 11:5). The contrast made between the king and the prisoner is emphasized by their respective positions: Pharaoh was elevated **on his throne**, whereas the captive was cast down **in the dungeon**. "Dungeon" is the translation of the Hebrew phrase בֵּית הַבּוֹר (*beyth habbor*), which literally means "house of the pit" (see Gen. 40:15; Is. 24:22; Jer. 37:16).

Verse 30. So extensive was the plague that death came to every **home** in **Egypt**. To see the significance of this event, the reader must picture the awful scenes that dominated that dreadful night—the fear, the loss, and the **great cry** of grief (compare Mt. 2:16–18).

Verse 31. After this last plague, Pharaoh finally drove the people from Egypt (6:1; 11:1). He wasted no time, calling for **Moses and Aaron** in the middle of the **night**. This invitation is ironic because Pharaoh had warned Moses that if he saw the king's face again he would surely die (10:28). However, this final plague sent by God brought the king to his knees. Pharaoh used a rapid fire of imperatives to emphasize his point: **"Rise up, get out . . . and go."** One commentator put it like this: "Get up, get out, and go on."[10]

Verse 32. Pharaoh urged the Israelites to leave with everything they had, saying, **"Take both your flocks and your herds."**

---

[10]John I. Durham, *Exodus*, Word Biblical Commentary, vol. 3 (Waco, Tex.: Word Books, 1987), 167.

He commanded them to do just as they had previously requested (10:9, 26). Pharaoh even asked Moses and Aaron to **bless** him. This is ironic, since he wanted a blessing from the very God whom he had earlier said he did not know. He had been defeated, his gods had been defeated, and he knew it. He surrendered unconditionally.

Verse 33. The rest of **the Egyptians** joined Pharaoh in urging the Israelites to leave. They all had been affected by the plagues; every family had experienced death because of the tenth plague. They could see nothing but more death in the future if the Israelites remained in the land. Therefore, as the Egyptians had shared Pharaoh's guilt and punishment, they shared his impassioned plea that Israel leave or **"We will all be dead."**

Verse 34. Consequently, as God had predicted, the Israelites left hurriedly. They left **their dough** in **their kneading bowls**, wrapped these utensils in their **clothes**, and carried them **on their shoulders**. (For "kneading bowls," see comments on 8:3, 4.) They gathered their belongings and departed.

Verse 35. At this point in the story, the narrator told about the requests the Israelites made of their neighbors. References to this request and the Lord's favor (11:2, 3; 12:35, 36) are used to introduce and conclude the tenth plague (11:1—12:36). In verse 35, the NASB uses the past perfect tense, which denotes action completed in the distant past: The Israelites **had done** just as they had been instructed, and they **had requested** their neighbors' valuables (see NKJV; NRSV; REB). The "tense" of a verb in the Hebrew language does not strictly signify the "time" of the action of the verb. Therefore, a verb can be translated in one of several ways, depending on the context. In this context, the past tense, which conveys action completed in more recent time, seems to be called for. For example, the NIV uses the past tense: "did . . . asked" (see KJV; NAB; NJB).

Verse 36. The Israelites asked for gifts from the Egyptians, and the Egyptians bestowed those gifts on them liberally. They would have done anything to rid themselves of the people who had brought such trouble to Egypt! Was the fact that the Israelites **plundered the Egyptians** ethical? One could say that the Israelites had earned these riches through their slave labor.

THE ISRAELITES' DEPARTURE FROM EGYPT (12:37–42)

[37]Now the sons of Israel journeyed from Rameses to Succoth, about six hundred thousand men on foot, aside from children. [38]A mixed multitude also went up with them, along with flocks and herds, a very large number of livestock. [39]They baked the dough which they had brought out of Egypt into cakes of unleavened bread. For it had not become leavened, since they were driven out of Egypt and could not delay, nor had they prepared any provisions for themselves.

[40]Now the time that the sons of Israel lived in Egypt was four hundred and thirty years. [41]And at the end of four hundred and thirty years, to the very day, all the hosts of the LORD went out from the land of Egypt. [42]It is a night to be observed for the LORD for having brought them out from the land of Egypt; this night is for the LORD, to be observed by all the sons of Israel throughout their generations.

The writer next gave details of the beginning of their journey: where and how the Israelites went, how many went, in what manner they went, and when they left Egypt.

Verse 37. The first stage of the journey into the wilderness was **from Rameses to Succoth**. "Rameses" most likely refers to the storage city "Raamses" mentioned earlier, although the spelling is slightly altered (see comments on 1:11). The name "Succoth" means "booths." Scholars differ on the locations of both places.

About six hundred thousand men left Egypt, not counting women and **children**. This round number agrees with the more exact figure 603,550 given in 38:26 and with the totals found in Numbers (Num. 1:46; 2:32; 11:21). Counting two or three people (a wife and children) for every man, the total number of the group which left Egypt would have been greater than two million.

To many interpreters, this number seems too large. They ask several questions: "How could so large a group have crossed the Red Sea in one night?"; "How could such a great number of people have survived for forty years in an inhospitable wilderness?"; "Where could they have found enough food and water?" The Bible believer sees no problem here because the Scriptures state that *it was only because God miraculously supplied their needs that Israel survived.*

The biggest problems relate to what the Scriptures themselves say. The Israelites were not prepared to fight hostile nations on their way to Canaan, but with such a large army, one might think they could have overwhelmed any foe. However, the Bible speaks of the Israelites as being few in number (Deut. 7:7; 9:1, 2).

What can be said about these problems? Some affirm that the numbers can be taken literally and the apparent difficulties can be solved. This position is supported ably by Gleason L. Archer, Jr.[11] Others think that Israel's exodus occurred over a period of time and was nothing like the exodus and sojourn described in the Old Testament. Skeptics completely reject the event, claiming that Israel was never in Egypt and therefore never came out of Egypt.

The numbers themselves have been explained in various ways. For example, it has been suggested that the figures in Exodus and Numbers came from a displaced census list which dated to the time of David.[12] One popular approach is to say that the word אֶלֶף (*'elep*), rendered "thousand," can have different meanings, such as "tribe," "clan," or "group."[13] Though problematic, this idea has even been accepted among conservatives. Symbolic or theological meanings for the numbers have also been offered.

The consistency of the biblical record must not be overlooked. The Israelites had become so numerous in Egypt that the Egyptians were afraid of them (1:9), and the total number is the sum

---

[11]Gleason L. Archer, Jr., *A Survey of Old Testament Introduction*, rev. ed. (Chicago: Moody Press, 1974), 236–38.

[12]Nahum M. Sarna, *Exploring Exodus: The Origins of Biblical Israel* (New York: Schocken Books, 1996), 102. This theory seems unlikely. It is difficult to conceive that a writer would say that Moses numbered the Israelites and then give numbers from more than four hundred years later.

[13]Cole, 112; Bruce C. Birch, "Number," in *The International Standard Bible Encyclopedia*, rev. ed., ed. Geoffrey W. Bromiley (Grand Rapids, Mich.: Wm. B. Eerdmans Publishing Co., 1986), 3:557–58.

of a series of smaller numbers (Num. 1; 2). The best course for the believer is to accept exactly what the text says: that about 600,000 men left the land of Egypt. This large number is significant in the narrative in two ways: (1) It illustrates to what extent God had multiplied the chosen family, and (2) it would, in days to come, demonstrate God's great power as He met the needs of this vast multitude.

Verse 38. When the Israelites left, they did not go alone. They took with them **a very large number of livestock**. This fact suggests that they were not all, or altogether, poverty-stricken during their years in Egypt. They also took with them **a mixed multitude** of people. The word "mixed" (עֵרֶב, *'ereb*) is related to the term "swarm" (עָרֹב, *'arob*), which is used for the flies of the fourth plague (8:17). Among this swarm of people may have been Egyptians who had become their friends or who, because of the mighty signs and wonders they had seen, had come to believe in the Lord (see 9:20). Other slaves, especially Semites, may have taken advantage of the chaotic conditions in Egypt at the time to make their escape with the Israelites. During the wilderness period, at least some of these non-Israelites were called "rabble" when they complained (Num. 11:4).

From the first, non-Israelites ("strangers") lived among the people of God. The Lord gave directions regarding whether or not, and under what circumstances, "a stranger" could participate in the Passover (12:43–49). Later, He included numerous statutes in the Law to protect strangers (see 22:21; 23:9, 12). These facts demonstrate that the attitudes and practices of the Jews towards the Gentiles in New Testament times were not based on the law of God. Rather, their aversion to Gentiles and their refusal to have any association with them developed as part of later traditions and prejudices.

Verse 39. The horde of Israelites and the mixed multitude with them left in haste, without having time to thoroughly prepare for the journey. Moses told Pharaoh that the plague would occur "about midnight" (11:4). If he meant midnight of the same day, then the Israelites had only a few hours to prepare the lamb and the Passover meal, and no time at all to get ready for their exit from Egypt.

Whenever the Israelites stopped to rest or make camp, **they baked the dough** that they had carried in their kneading bowls on their shoulders (12:34). Since no leaven had fermented the dough, they made **cakes of unleavened bread** (see the NIV).

Verses 40, 41. The text, after describing Israel's departure, gives details to help the reader understand the significance of the story. **Israel** was not **in Egypt** for one year or two, but for **four hundred and thirty years**. The people's exodus was a matter of great importance. The emphasis on the phrase **to the very day** suggests that the writer saw both the length of the sojourn and the day of deliverance as significant.

The 430-year stay in Egypt raises several questions.

(1) Can the 430 years of 12:40, 41 be reconciled with the 400 years predicted in Genesis 15:13, 16? All that is needed to reconcile the two passages is to understand that the prophecy in Genesis gave the time in round numbers, whereas Exodus is more exact (see Acts 7:6; 13:17–20; Gal. 3:17).

(2) Exodus 6:16–20 names only two generations between Levi and Moses, a fact which appears to agree with the prediction in Genesis 15:16 that in the "fourth generation" the Israelites would leave Egypt. Levi was the father of Kohath, Kohath was the father of Amram, and Amram was the father of Moses. How could these four generations cover a 430-year period?

That question has two possible answers. First, these men lived a long time: Levi, 137 years; Kohath, 133 years; and Amram, 137 years. Since Abraham's son Isaac was not born until Abraham was one hundred years old, a "hundred years" may have been used to represent a generation in Genesis 15.[14] A second possibility is that, since biblical genealogies are sometimes abridged, one or more individuals may have been omitted from the genealogy in Exodus 6 (see comments on 6:20).

(3) Does this 430-year period apply only to the time Israel spent in Egypt, or does it include the time of the patriarchs as well? Wording in the Samaritan Pentateuch and the Septuagint indicates that the 430 years includes time "in the land of Canaan"

---

[14]Ronald F. Youngblood, *Exodus*, Everyman's Bible Commentary (Chicago: Moody Bible Institute, 1983), 70.

as well as "in the land of Egypt."[15] These texts may suggest that Israel was actually in Egypt only about 215 years.[16] Nevertheless, all English versions follow the Hebrew text and say that Israel was in Egypt for 430 years, which generally agrees with God's promise made to Abraham (Gen. 15:13).

Verse 42. After providing information about Israel's departure, the writer returned to the subject of the Passover. He emphasized that the **night** of their deliverance from the tenth plague was one to be remembered by **all** Israelites **throughout their generations** as they observed the Passover.

The Hebrew word שִׁמֻּר (*shimmur*), which is rendered **observed,** appears twice in verse 42. In both cases, the NASB suggests that the Israelites are the ones observing the night in honor of God (see KJV). In contrast, some other versions understand the first occurrence of *shimmur* as a reference to God's watching, thus making a play on words (NIV; REB; NAB; NJB). For example, the NIV translates, "Because *the LORD kept vigil* that night to bring them out of Egypt, on this night *all the Israelites are to keep vigil* to honor the LORD for the generations to come" (emphasis added).[17] In other words, because **the LORD** watched over His people on the night of the tenth plague, **the sons of Israel** were to keep watch one night each year by observing the Passover.

THE LAW OF THE PASSOVER (12:43–51)

43The LORD said to Moses and Aaron, "This is the ordinance of the Passover: no foreigner is to eat of it; 44but every man's

---

[15]Durham, 172.

[16]For a chart that compares various views regarding the length of Israel's stay in Egypt and the date of the exodus, see "Comparison of Chronological Systems," in John H. Walton, *Chronological and Background Charts of the Old Testament* (Grand Rapids, Mich.: Zondervan Publishing House, 1994), 99.

[17]In his commentary, John I. Durham translated, "It was a night of keepings for Yahweh, to bring them out from the land of Egypt—so it is, the night for Yahweh, a night of keepings for all the sons of Israel, generation after generation." Durham connected Yahweh's "keepings" with God's keeping His promises to His people. (Durham, 169, 173.) Cole called the Lord's vigil a "watchnight service." (Cole, 113.)

slave purchased with money, after you have circumcised him, then he may eat of it. [45]A sojourner or a hired servant shall not eat of it. [46]It is to be eaten in a single house; you are not to bring forth any of the flesh outside of the house, nor are you to break any bone of it. [47]All the congregation of Israel are to celebrate this. [48]But if a stranger sojourns with you, and celebrates the Passover to the LORD, let all his males be circumcised, and then let him come near to celebrate it; and he shall be like a native of the land. But no uncircumcised person may eat of it. [49]The same law shall apply to the native as to the stranger who sojourns among you."

[50]Then all the sons of Israel did so; they did just as the LORD had commanded Moses and Aaron. [51]And on that same day the LORD brought the sons of Israel out of the land of Egypt by their hosts.

The narrative again pauses, and additional information is provided about the Passover. In particular, 12:43–47 gives directions about who could participate in the feast. This revelation was especially necessary in light of the "mixed multitude" who left Egypt among the Israelites.

Verse 43. God revealed to His people that **no foreigner** was to **eat** of the Passover. A "foreigner" (נֵכָר, *nekar*) was a non-Israelite from another land. After the Israelites were settled in Canaan, this person might visit there for a short time. The "foreigner" should be distinguished from the "sojourner" (12:45) and the "stranger" (12:48) who actually lived among the Israelites for extended periods of time and had close associations with them.[18]

Verse 44. In contrast to the foreigner's not being able to eat the Passover, an Israelite master could circumcise a **slave**, making the slave eligible to eat it. The slave's circumcision identified him with God's covenant people (Gen. 17:10). The descriptive

---

[18]For a discussion of these various terms, see Daniel I. Block, "Sojourner; Alien; Stranger," in *The International Standard Bible Encyclopedia*, rev. ed., ed. Geoffrey W. Bromiley (Grand Rapids, Mich.: Wm. B. Eerdmans Publishing Co., 1988), 4:561–64.

phrase **purchased with money** distinguishes this kind of slave from one born in the master's house (Gen. 17:12, 23).

Verse 45. In addition to the "foreigner" (12:43), the **sojourner** and **hired servant** were barred from sharing in the Passover feast. The Hebrew word תּוֹשָׁב (*thoshab*), translated "sojourner" or "temporary resident" (NIV), also appears in conjunction with the word for "hired servant" (שָׂכִיר, *śakir*) in other passages (Lev. 22:10; 25:6, 40). These terms most likely refer to temporary laborers who moved among the people of Israel looking for work. The "sojourner" was apparently "more temporary and dependent" than the "stranger" in verse 48.[19]

Verse 46. At this point, three rules regarding the Passover Feast were given: The sacrificial lamb had **to be eaten in a single house**, all of it had to be eaten, and none of its bones were to be broken. The full significance of these guidelines became known many years later (see Num. 9:12; Ps. 34:20; Jn. 19:36).

Verses 47, 48. The basic rule was that the Passover was a memorial for Israel: **All the congregation of Israel** was to observe the feast. However, if a **stranger** (גֵּר, *ger*) and **all** the **males** in his household would **be circumcised**—in other words, if they would become as **native** Israelites—then they would be eligible to participate in the religious services along with the rest of the Israelites. Once the "stranger" accepted circumcision, he was bound by the same rules (and, presumably, protected by the same laws) as the native Israelite.

Verse 49. There was not to be a double standard—one **law** for the **native** Israelite and another for the **stranger**. When a "stranger" or an "alien" (NIV) was circumcised, he was regarded as an Israelite himself. He could join with the native Israelites in speaking of Abraham, Isaac, and Jacob as "our fathers." Israel's history became his history. He was eligible for the same rewards and was responsible for the same requirements as were other Israelites (12:19; Lev. 16:29; 17:8, 15; 18:26; 19:33, 34; 20:2; 22:18; 24:16, 22; Num. 9:14; 15:14–16, 26, 29, 30). In later times, such

---

[19]Francis Brown, S. R. Driver, and Charles A. Briggs, *The Brown-Driver-Briggs Hebrew and English Lexicon* (Boston: Houghton, Mifflin and Co., 1906; reprint, Peabody, Mass: Hendrickson Publishers, 1997), 444.

converts to Judaism were referred to as "proselytes."

Verses 50, 51. After the break to present additional instructions for the Passover, the author again, as he had done in 12:28, included a statement to sum up what had happened so far in his account. The Israelites had obeyed the words of **the Lord** given to them by **Moses and Aaron**.

On that same day (the day specified in 12:41) God delivered the Israelites out of Egypt. The people were, in fact, led out according to **their hosts**. Other possible translations include "armies" (NKJV), "companies" (NRSV), and "divisions" (NIV). The Hebrew word צָבָא (*tsaba'*), translated "hosts," is "a technical term of organization, primarily, in the [Old Testament], for military purposes. [In 6:26], the reference seems to be to a logistical apportionment of the sons of Israel by tribal and clan subdivision."[20] Since the word emphasizes military organization, it likely anticipates that the people of God would ultimately have to fight for the territory that He was giving to them (see comments on 12:17).

APPLICATION

"Christ, Our Passover" (Ch. 12)

James Burton Coffman noted that the Passover lamb was a type of Christ, "our Passover" (1 Cor. 5:7), in the following ways: (1) It was innocent. (2) The innocent suffered for the guilty. (3) It was submissive and uncomplaining in death. (4) Not a bone of it was broken. (5) The lamb was offered from the foundation of the world. God purposed to send Christ "before the world" existed. (6) It was in eating the Passover that the Israelites were rescued from death. It is by figuratively "eating" of Christ's body (Jn. 6:56) that people today are saved. (7) The lamb was kept for four days before it was killed. Christ was in Jerusalem four days before the crucifixion. (8) The lamb was a male in the prime of life without spot or blemish, that is, perfect. So was Jesus Christ. (9) Both the lamb (in the first century A.D.) and the Lord Jesus

---

[20]Durham, 81.

Christ suffered death at 3:00 p.m. (10) Both the lamb and Jesus suffered death on the fourteenth of Abib (Nisan). (11) The great ordinances commemorating the two deliverances, the Lord's Supper and the Jewish Passover, were instituted *before* the events they were designed to commemorate.[21]

"When I See the Blood" (12:13, 23)

A "scarlet thread" of redemption runs through the Bible. Blood has been the God-ordained means of man's salvation from the earliest times to the present. In Exodus, also, it is blood that saves. The story of Israel's deliverance parallels the story of our salvation.

Israel's Story. (1) Death was imminent. The tenth plague was the death of the firstborn. The purpose of the plague was to convince Pharaoh and the Egyptians to allow Israel to leave. The plague served its purpose. Death came that night to every house in Egypt. When the Egyptians felt the force of the plague, they not only let the Israelites go, but they begged them to leave. They even gave the Israelites valuable gifts to encourage them to go.

(2) God provided a way of escape. At the same time that He determined to kill the firstborn of Egypt, God provided a way of escape for the Israelites. To be saved from the plague, each family was to kill a lamb—an unblemished lamb—and smear its blood on the doorposts and lintel of their house. God said, "When I see the blood, I will pass over you" (12:13).

(3) Israel had to do something. The Israelites had a role to play in their salvation. They had to do what God said. They showed that they believed God by following His instructions. They killed the lambs, and they stayed in the houses protected by the blood.

(4) Then Israel was saved. That night, the destroyer did not touch their firstborn sons. Throughout the land, there was weeping for those who were dead, but in the Israelite homes, all were alive.

(5) God provided a memorial. God instituted a feast—the

---

[21]Adapted from James Burton Coffman, *Commentary on Exodus, The Second Book of Moses* (Abilene, Tex.: ACU Press, 1985), 162.

Passover Feast—to help the people remember what He had done for them on that night.

Our Story. (1) Death is imminent. The wages of sin is death (Rom. 6:23); death is deserved by sinners. Those who have sinned are, in fact, under the sentence of death. Ultimately, unrepentant sinners will be subject to the second death, eternal death.

(2) God has made a way to escape the sentence of death. That way involves blood. Jesus is the "Lamb of God who takes away the sin of the world" (Jn. 1:29). He is our Paschal Lamb, our "Passover" (1 Cor. 5:7), whose blood was shed for our salvation. The New Testament teaches that we are not saved by the blood of bulls and goats (Heb. 10:4), but by the blood of Jesus Christ!

(3) We have something to do. Do we have a role to play in our salvation? Yes, we show our faith in God and in His provisions for our salvation by following His instructions. We are saved by the blood of Christ when, after we have confessed our belief in Him and repented, we are baptized into Christ, into the death of Christ (see Acts 2:38; Rom. 5:9; 6:3; 10:9, 10).

(4) Then we are saved. When we obey the Lord's instructions, we can rejoice, knowing that all our sins have been washed away by the blood of the Lamb!

(5) God provides a memorial. As in the story of the Israelites' salvation, God has instituted a memorial feast to be kept—not annually, but weekly. The Lord's Supper, the memorial of Christ's sacrificed body and blood, was given so that we will constantly remember what God did through Christ to save us.

God still says, "When I see the blood, I will pass over." When we are covered by the blood of Christ, He will not hold us accountable for our sins, whatever they are! Surely, you want that blessing! "Have you been to Jesus for the cleansing power? Are you washed in the blood of the Lamb?"[22]

Removing the Leaven (12:15)

The Israelites had to remove the leaven from their homes during the Feast of Unleavened Bread. Today, when Jews observe

---

[22]E. A. Hoffman, "Have You Been to Jesus?" *Songs of Faith and Praise,* comp. and ed. Alton H. Howard (West Monroe, La.: Howard Publishing Co., 1994).

the Passover, they ceremonially remove from their houses anything that might be used as leaven. The Old Testament requirement makes Paul's instructions in 1 Corinthians 5:6–8 understandable. We "clean out the old leaven" by practicing church discipline, and we practice discipline to keep the old "leaven" from corrupting the "dough." That is, we must keep the church from being negatively influenced by an impenitent sinful member. We may also apply Paul's instructions to the individual Christian's life: All of us should get rid of the evil influences in our lives.

Chapter 13

Remembering The Day of Deliverance And the Journey to the Red Sea

Chapter 13 continues the story of the exodus, first revealing further instructions related to the remembrance of the occasion and then giving details regarding the next step on Israel's journey into the wilderness. The chapter could be thought of as presenting the results of redemption. Because Israel had been redeemed, the people had responsibilities: (1) to give their firstborn to the Lord, (2) to worship at the Feast of Unleavened Bread, and (3) to travel on toward the promised land.

The Lord spoke to Moses as the Israelites were leaving Egypt, saying that Israel was to set apart the firstborn of both man and animals for Him and to remember the day of their deliverance (13:1, 2). Moses then spoke to the people to tell them to keep the Passover (13:3). He gave other instructions regarding the observance of the Feast of Unleavened Bread, including a command to use the occasion of the feast to tell the Israelite children about God's deliverance of Israel (13:4–10). God then, through Moses, gave more specific directions regarding the dedication of Israel's firstborn—what was to be offered, how it was to be offered, and why it was to be offered. Again, the occasion would serve as a means of teaching Israelite children their redemptive history (13:11–16).

The narrative continues by telling what route the people of Israel took out of the land of Egypt ("the way of the wilderness to the Red Sea"), what they took with them ("the bones of Joseph"), where they went (from Succoth to Etham), and how they were led (by "a pillar of cloud by day" and "a pillar of fire by night") (13:17–22).

REMEMBERING THE DAY OF DELIVERANCE (13:1–16)

The Dedication of the Firstborn (13:1, 2)

[1]Then the Lord spoke to Moses, saying, [2]"Sanctify to Me every firstborn, the first offspring of every womb among the sons of Israel, both of man and beast; it belongs to Me."

Verses 1, 2. Either after they had traveled to Succoth (12:37)[1] or as they were preparing to leave Goshen, **the Lord** gave **Moses** instructions concerning the **firstborn** of Israel. The "firstborn" is defined as **the first offspring of every womb** (פֶּטֶר כָּל־רֶחֶם, *peter kol rechem*). This phrase can more literally be translated "whatever first opens every womb" (see KJV; NKJV). Verse 15 further describes the firstborn as "the males." The Israelites were to **sanctify** their firstborn to the Lord. The term "sanctify" (קָדַשׁ, *qadash*) means "set apart" or "make holy." The rationale for setting apart the firstborn was that, since God had spared the firstborn children and animals of Israel, they belonged to Him (13:15; Num. 3:13; 8:17, 18).

Possibly, the report of God's revelation to Moses in verses 1 and 2 is an overview: The text says that God spoke to Moses concerning the dedication of the firstborn. Then, in the next sections, Moses told the people how to observe the feast (13:3–10) and how to "devote" or "give over" (NIV) the firstborn (13:11–16).

The Speech of Moses (13:3–16)

[3]Moses said to the people, "Remember this day in which you went out from Egypt, from the house of slavery; for by a powerful hand the Lord brought you out from this place. And nothing leavened shall be eaten. [4]On this day in the month of Abib, you are about to go forth. [5]It shall be when the Lord

---

[1]Succoth was thought to be the place for this revelation by Walter C. Kaiser, Jr., "Exodus," in *The Expositor's Bible Commentary*, vol. 2, *Genesis—Numbers* (Grand Rapids, Mich.: Zondervan, 1990), 382, and Wilbur Fields, *Exploring Exodus*, Bible Study Textbook Series (Joplin, Mo.: College Press, 1976), 277.

**brings you to the land of the Canaanite, the Hittite, the Amor-
ite, the Hivite and the Jebusite, which He swore to your fathers
to give you, a land flowing with milk and honey, that you shall
observe this rite in this month. 6For seven days you shall eat
unleavened bread, and on the seventh day there shall be a feast
to the Lord. 7Unleavened bread shall be eaten throughout the
seven days; and nothing leavened shall be seen among you,
nor shall any leaven be seen among you in all your borders.
8You shall tell your son on that day, saying, 'It is because of
what the Lord did for me when I came out of Egypt.' 9And it
shall serve as a sign to you on your hand, and as a reminder on
your forehead, that the law of the Lord may be in your mouth;
for with a powerful hand the Lord brought you out of Egypt.
10Therefore, you shall keep this ordinance at its appointed time
from year to year.**

**11"Now when the Lord brings you to the land of the Canaan-
ite, as He swore to you and to your fathers, and gives it to you,
12you shall devote to the Lord the first offspring of every womb,
and the first offspring of every beast that you own; the males
belong to the Lord. 13But every first offspring of a donkey you
shall redeem with a lamb, but if you do not redeem it, then you
shall break its neck; and every firstborn of man among your
sons you shall redeem. 14And it shall be when your son asks
you in time to come, saying, 'What is this?' then you shall say
to him, 'With a powerful hand the Lord brought us out of Egypt,
from the house of slavery. 15It came about, when Pharaoh was
stubborn about letting us go, that the Lord killed every first-
born in the land of Egypt, both the firstborn of man and the
firstborn of beast. Therefore, I sacrifice to the Lord the males,
the first offspring of every womb, but every firstborn of my
sons I redeem.' 16So it shall serve as a sign on your hand and
as phylacteries on your forehead, for with a powerful hand the
Lord brought us out of Egypt."**

Verse 3. Formerly, the Lord had spoken to Moses (12:1) and Moses had spoken to the elders (12:21), who in turn relayed Moses' words to the people (12:28). In chapter 13, **Moses** apparently spoke directly to **the people**. The emphasis of his speech was the need for the people to **remember** continually what had happened when **the Lord** brought them out of Egypt **by a powerful hand**. They were to remember that occasion by keeping the Feast of Unleavened Bread.

Verse 4. The section begins with Moses telling the people, **"On this day . . . you are about to go forth,"** and it concludes with his explanation that the memorial feast was to be an annual observance at the same time (13:10). They were to remember their deliverance **in the month of Abib** when the event first occurred. The "month of Abib" corresponds to the "first month of the year" in 12:2. The Hebrew word אָבִיב (*'abib*) refers to "fresh, young ears"[2] (9:31; Lev. 2:14); the barley ripened and harvest began during this month. "Abib" was the older name for the first month, and the later name was "Nisan." "Nisan" evidently was taken from the Babylonian calendar, as is true of the names of other Hebrew months. It only appears in the Old Testament in books written after the Babylonian exile (Neh. 2:1; Esther 3:7).

Verse 5. The Israelites were to remember their redemption in **the land** to which they were going. It was a land occupied by at least five different nations: **the Canaanite, the Hittite, the Amorite, the Hivite and the Jebusite** (see comments on 3:8b). The fact that it was inhabited suggested that it would not fall easily into Israel's hands. At the same time, the fact that it was a land **flowing with milk and honey** indicated that it was fertile and prosperous, worth the effort required to take it (see comments on 3:7, 8a). God had promised the Israelites' **fathers** (Abraham, Isaac, and Jacob) that He would give the land to their descendants (the Israelites).

Verse 6. The people were to remember the great event they were now experiencing by observing the Feast of Unleavened Bread. **For seven days** they were to **eat unleavened bread** (see 12:15). On **the seventh day** they were to hold **a feast to the Lord.** In the previous instructions, a "holy assembly" was mentioned on both "the first day" and "the seventh day" (12:16).

---

[2]Francis Brown, S. R. Driver, and Charles A. Briggs, *The Brown-Driver-Briggs Hebrew and English Lexicon* (Boston: Houghton, Mifflin and Co., 1906; reprint, Peabody, Mass.: Hendrickson Publishers, 1997), 1.

Verse 7. Beyond eating **unleavened bread** for **seven days, nothing leavened** was to be found among the Israelites. Earlier they had been told to remove the leaven from their homes; failure to comply would result in being "cut off from Israel" (12:15). After settling the land of Canaan, nothing leavened was to be found **in all** [their] **borders**.

Verse 8. As in the case of the Passover (12:26, 27), the Feast of Unleavened Bread was to serve as a teaching tool. A father would say to his **son**: **"It is because of what the LORD did for me when I came out of Egypt."**

Verse 9. The feast would provide opportunity for all Israel to know and teach **the law of the LORD**; it would both symbolize and remind the people of what God had done. The phrases **as a sign . . . on your hand** and **as a reminder on your forehead** in verse 9 are parallel to "as a sign on your hand" and "[frontals] on your forehead" in verse 16 (see Deut. 6:8; 11:18). From the time of the return from Babylonian captivity to the days of Jesus (Mt. 23:5), and even in modern times, Jews have interpreted these words literally, wearing on their foreheads and left arms leather bands with small boxes ("phylacteries") containing cer-

Jews with Phylacteries at the Western Wall (Jerusalem)

tain Scriptures (Ex. 13:1–10, 11–16; Deut. 6:4–9; 11:13–21).[3] However, these words were probably intended to be taken figuratively.[4] If so, they meant something like this: "Hold these words close. Let the Law be part of your daily lives, both in your actions and in your thoughts."

Verse 10. The Feast of Unleavened Bread was to be celebrated annually. Once a **year**, the memorial feast would encourage the Israelites to remember constantly their redemption and to live by God's law.

Verse 11. In addition to keeping the feast, the Israelites were to remember their deliverance from Egypt by the dedication of their firstborn males to the Lord. This institution was to begin when they received **the land** of Canaan which **the LORD** had promised to their forefathers.

Verse 12. The firstborn **males** of animals that were "clean"—that is, suitable for sacrifice—were to be offered to God. Other passages in the Law define "clean" and "unclean" animals (Lev. 11:3–7; Deut. 14:3–8). This was an ancient distinction, for clean animals were distinguished from unclean animals at the time of the flood (Gen. 7:2, 8). Exodus 22:30 further clarifies that the firstborn of clean animals ("oxen" and "sheep") were to remain with their mothers for seven days and then be sacrificed to the Lord on the eighth day. The blood of the firstborn would be sprinkled on the altar, its fat burned to the Lord, and the meat consumed by the priests (Num. 18:17, 18).

Verse 13. If an animal was unclean and could not be sacrificed, such as **a donkey**,[5] then it was to be **redeem**[ed] **with a**

---

[3]For more information, see Roger L. Omanson, "Phylactery," in *The International Standard Bible Encyclopedia*, rev. ed., ed. Geoffrey W. Bromiley (Grand Rapids, Mich.: Wm. B. Eerdmans Publishing Co., 1986), 3:864–65.

[4]R. Alan Cole spoke of them as "pure metaphor." (R. Alan Cole, *Exodus: An Introduction and Commentary*, Tyndale Old Testament Commentaries [Downers Grove, Ill.: Inter-Varsity Press, 1973], 114.)

[5]John I. Durham proposed a different interpretation of this law. He asserted that "there is no firm [Old Testament] evidence (see Lev 11:1–8) that the he-ass was considered unclean—it was a valuable burden carrier (note Exod 9:3)." Because of its practical value, it was excepted from the general rule stated in verse 12. (John I. Durham, *Exodus*, Word Biblical Commentary, vol. 3 [Waco, Tex.: Word Books, 1987], 179.) However, while the donkey was an extremely

lamb. In other words, a lamb or a kid was to be given as a substitute for it (see comments on 12:3, 4). As an alternative, it could be killed so that the owner would not profit from it. He was commanded to **break its neck**, perhaps so none of the animal's blood would be shed. Later in the Law, a redemption price was set for unclean animals at five shekels of silver to be paid when they were a month old (Num. 18:15, 16).

The **firstborn** of Israel's **sons** were also to be **redeem**[ed]. Although human sacrifices were offered by the Canaanites, God never approved of such a practice (Lev. 18:21; 20:2–5; Deut. 12:31; 18:10).[6] Since God had spared the Israelite children when He "passed over" their houses, in a sense those firstborn males now belonged to Him. As a reminder of this, the Israelites were to "redeem" them—in effect, to buy them back. The price of redemption was five shekels of silver to be paid when the firstborn son was a month old (Num. 18:15, 16). This practice of consecrating the firstborn son is illustrated in the birth narrative of Jesus, who was taken to the temple after he was a month old (Lk. 2:23, 24).

Verses 14, 15. The sacrificing of the firstborn animals and the redeeming of firstborn sons also provided occasions for teaching the Israelite children (see 12:26, 27; 13:8). The text suggests that a young **son** would gaze in wonder as his father sacrificed a firstborn lamb or broke a donkey's neck, and the child would ask, "Why are you doing this?"

The answer would be similar to the teaching presented when the family observed the Passover. The father would say, "Son, it is because **the Lord** delivered us from **Egypt**." He would then proceed to tell the whole story: "**Pharaoh** refused to let the people **go**. Therefore, God **killed** the Egyptian **firstborn** but spared Israel. Consequently, Israel dedicates its **firstborn** to the Lord. God delivered Israel by **a powerful hand**. The people did not sneak out or barely get away. Instead, Israel marched out trium-

---

valuable asset to the Israelites (20:17), it clearly fell under the category of unclean animals since it did not have a split hoof (see Lev. 11:3–7; Deut. 14:3–8).

[6]In later history, the Israelites did engage in this detestable practice (2 Kings 16:3; 17:31; 21:6; Ezek. 16:20, 21; see 2 Kings 3:27). For this reason, they were severely chastised by the prophets (Is. 57:4, 5; Jer. 7:30–34; 19:4–9; Ezek. 16:20, 21).

phantly as a result of God's great signs and wonders!"

Verse 16. In this manner, through questions and answers at teachable moments, the Israelite faith was to be passed on from one generation to the next. The goal of the instruction connected to the giving of the firstborn was that the redemptive history of Israel might be kept close to the minds of the people: **So it shall serve as a sign on your hand and as phylacteries** [frontals] **on your forehead** (see comments on 13:9).

THE JOURNEY TO THE RED SEA (13:17–22)

[17]Now when Pharaoh had let the people go, God did not lead them by the way of the land of the Philistines, even though it was near; for God said, "The people might change their minds when they see war, and return to Egypt." [18]Hence God led the people around by the way of the wilderness to the Red Sea; and the sons of Israel went up in martial array from the land of Egypt. [19]Moses took the bones of Joseph with him, for he had made the sons of Israel solemnly swear, saying, "God will surely take care of you, and you shall carry my bones from here with you." [20]Then they set out from Succoth and camped in Etham on the edge of the wilderness. [21]The LORD was going before them in a pillar of cloud by day to lead them on the way, and in a pillar of fire by night to give them light, that they might travel by day and by night. [22]He did not take away the pillar of cloud by day, nor the pillar of fire by night, from before the people.

The exodus narrative continues with details of Israel's route out of Egypt, what they took with them, where they went, and how they were led by God (13:17–22).

Verse 17. God did not lead the people **by the way of the land of the Philistines**, a way spoken of "in Isaiah 9:1 [as] the 'Way of the Sea,' which corresponds to the Latin name of *Via Maris*, used since Roman times."[7] This northern "way" along the Med-

---

[7]Nahum M. Sarna, *Exploring Exodus: The Origins of Biblical Israel* (New York: Schocken Books, 1996), 105.

iterranean coast would have been the shortest route from Egypt to Canaan. The text gives the reason God selected a different route: He knew that **the people** were not yet ready for battle and that facing Philistine warriors would discourage them, making them want to **return to Egypt**.[8] Their tendency to become discouraged when facing superior military forces is evident from the later incident involving the twelve men sent to spy out Canaan (Num. 13:32—14:4). The Israelites, therefore, were to travel by a different path.

The mention of "Philistines" in this verse and others (15:14; 23:31) poses some difficulty. The Philistines did, in fact, inhabit the coastal areas of Palestine, but most of the archaeological evidence suggests that they did not settle in the area until about 1200 B.C. There have been various solutions offered to explain this problem.

First, a few might argue that the exodus had to occur after 1200 B.C. However, this time frame is later than most scholars are willing to date it—even those who support the "late date" of 1290 B.C.

Second, many have asserted that Exodus was written much later than the time of Moses and that the term "Philistines" is an anachronism. However, the Bible itself testifies to Mosaic authorship of the Pentateuch.

Third, some have supported the idea that, many years after Moses wrote the Pentateuch, an editor or scribe updated his work with the more modern designation "Philistines." This change would have been made to aid the reader in his understanding.[9]

The fourth and final explanation is that some Philistines were already in the land at the time, even though archaeologists have not yet found much evidence of their presence.[10] In other words, the Philistines migrated to Canaan in waves over a long period of time. It is noteworthy that references to the Philistines also

---

[8]Another possible enemy might have been the Egyptian soldiers stationed in the garrisons along this important road.

[9]The same argument has been made for the reference to "Dan" in Genesis 14:14. This town was not known by that name until it was later conquered by the Danites in the Judges period (Judg. 18:29).

[10]Kaiser, 385.

appear in the narratives of Abraham and Isaac (Gen. 21:32; 26:1), who lived several hundred years prior to the exodus.

Verse 18. Instead of going "by the way of the land of the Philistines," the Israelites exited Egypt **by the way of the wilderness to the Red Sea**. (For information on the "Red Sea," see *Appendix: The Route of the Exodus*.) Further, they went up in **martial array** (חֲמֻשִׁים, *chamushim*). The NIV says that they were "armed for battle," while the NRSV describes them as being "prepared for battle." This may mean that the Israelites were armed, but not heavily armed. Perhaps they possessed some slings and stones, bows and arrows, and spears. However, Exodus 17:13 indicates that the Israelites also had some swords which they used to defeat the Amalekites. John I. Durham explained that the Israelites went forth "in fighting formation, that is, with the armed men in the vanguard, their more vulnerable dependents in the protection of their lead."[11] God's people must have known that they would eventually face opponents and have to fight.

Verse 19. As they departed, they **took** [with them] **the bones of Joseph**, probably his mummified body. This was in keeping with Joseph's last wishes in Genesis 50:25, which is quoted here in verse 19: **"God will surely take care of you, and you shall carry my bones from here with you."** He spoke these words in faith (Heb. 11:22), believing the promises made to his forefathers (Gen. 50:24). Joseph's bones being taken from Egypt testified to the fact that God keeps His promises, for God had said that He would bring Israel out of Egypt and take them to Canaan (Gen. 15:13–16). In the exodus, He was keeping that pledge. After the conquest of Canaan, the remains of Joseph were laid to rest at Shechem (Josh. 24:32).

Verse 20. After **Succoth**, the next stop on Israel's itinerary was **Etham**, located **on the edge of the wilderness**. This was the final stop before reaching the shore of the Red Sea (see 14:2).

Verses 21, 22. As they went, **the Lord** used **a pillar of cloud by day** and **a pillar of fire by night** to show them the way and to allow them to travel at **night** (see Num. 9:15–23). At every juncture on their journey, the Israelites could see God's guid-

---

[11]Durham, 185.

ance. In the Old Testament the Lord is often represented by a cloud and/or by fire.

APPLICATION

Lessons from the Passover (13:3)

God said to Israel through Moses, "Remember this day" (13:3). The day to remember was the day when God's people were saved from the tenth plague and delivered out of Egypt.

At its inception, the Passover emphasized the family aspect of Israel's religion. Each family was commanded to choose a lamb, kill it at twilight without breaking any of its bones, roast it, and eat it in its entirety. If there were too few people living in a house to eat a whole lamb, then two families could join together to eat it. The blood of the lamb was to be sprinkled on the doorposts and lintel of each house. When God saw the blood on a house, He "passed over" and did not allow the destroyer to enter. Those eating the Passover meal wore their robes and sandals and kept their staffs (12:11), ready to leave hurriedly.

As the years passed, this celebration allowed the Israelites to teach their children about their deliverance. Each requirement for the feast was a reminder of how God had delivered them from bondage, passing over the Israelite homes when the firstborn of Egypt died.

What lessons can Christians today learn from the Passover? Thinking about the Passover should cause Christians to do the following:

Recognize the importance of family worship. Of course, when we come together to worship, we do so as a family, God's family. In addition, we ought to worship the Lord at home with our families. We can sing and pray with our children and instruct them at home, as Israel did in observing the Passover.

Remember the role of Christ in salvation. Paul spoke of Christ as "our Passover" (1 Cor. 5:7). Jesus was the "Lamb of God" (Jn. 1:29, 36), the "Lamb that was slain" (Rev. 5:12). Christ was like the Passover lamb in that He was unblemished (Ex. 12:5; 1 Pet. 1:18, 19), not one of His bones was broken (Ex. 12:46; Jn. 19:36), and His blood was a sign before God (Ex. 12:13). Like the Passover, His memorial feast includes unleavened bread (Ex. 12:18; 1 Cor. 5:8).[12]

Realize the value of commemorating our redemption. The Passover Feast was designed to remind Israel of their rescue from Egypt. In a similar way the Lord's Supper, instituted during the Passover, is intended to serve as a memorial of Jesus' death and our salvation through His death (Lk. 22:19; 1 Cor. 11:24, 25). We need to be reminded constantly of what Jesus has done for us.

Remind one another that we are on a journey. Just as the Israelites were dressed for travel when they ate the Passover, so Christians should always keep in mind that we are strangers and pilgrims on the earth. Remembering Jesus' death by taking the Lord's Supper should cause us to look away from this world and to look forward to His second coming.

Conclusion. Only Israelites could participate in the Passover. This should remind people today that the Lord's Supper is to be observed on the Lord's Day in the Lord's church by the Lord's people. Those who desire to participate in the benefits provided by our Passover Lamb and to have fellowship in the Lord's Supper must be a part of spiritual Israel, the church of the Lord.

"A Powerful Hand!" (13:3, 9, 14, 16)

Israel was delivered by the "powerful hand" of God. His power is described in various translations as a "mighty hand" (NIV), as a "strong hand" (NRSV), or as "strength of hand" (KJV; NRSV). These images help us to understand the matchless strength God uses to help His people. However, we must remember that God's hand was mighty for disaster (against Egypt) as well as deliverance (for Israel). As we think about God's hand punishing the Egyptians, we should also keep in mind Hebrews 10:31, which says, "It is a terrifying thing to fall into the hands of the living God."

Letting God Lead (13:17, 18)

God led the children of Israel, and He wants to lead us today.

---

[12]John D. Davis, "Passover," in *A Dictionary of the Bible*, 4th rev. ed. (Grand Rapids, Mich.: Baker Book House, 1957), 572.

God leads His people in many different ways.

God often leads us by way of detour (13:17, 18). The easiest way is not always the best way. God led the Israelites by way of a detour to protect and prepare them.

Sometimes God leads us by way of a dead end (14:8–10). Dead ends force us to turn to God for direction and deliverance. As the song says, "Where could I go but to the Lord?"

God leads us by way of a dry place (15:22–27). God tested Moses and Israel to see if they would trust Him. He uses dry places to test us today as well.

When we begin to question God's leading, we should remember that He is in control and our Father knows best (Deut. 8:2). God is the way-maker (Jn. 14:6), the mountain-mover (Mt. 17:20), the problem-solver, and the burden-lifter (1 Pet. 5:7).[13]

Keeping Promises (13:19)

Moses kept Israel's promise to Joseph by bringing his bones out of Egypt in order to bury them in the promised land (13:19). God kept His promise to Israel to bring them out of Egypt and into Canaan. "God is faithful"; He always keeps His promises (1 Cor. 10:13; 2 Pet. 3:9). Christians should be people of integrity who always keep their promises (Mt. 5:37).

[13]Melvin Whitlock, speech in chapel, Heritage Christian University (Florence, Ala.) in 2000.

Chapter 14

Crossing the Red Sea

Chapters 14 and 15 contain the final episode in the story of Israel's deliverance from Egypt. In chapter 14 the people experience God's powerful salvation, whereas in chapter 15 they celebrate it.

God directed Israel to journey to Pi-hahiroth and to camp near the Red Sea (14:1, 2). He then predicted what would happen: Pharaoh's heart would be hardened, and he would pursue the Israelites; but God would be honored in the end (14:3, 4).

As God had foretold, when Pharaoh learned that the Israelites had escaped, he changed his mind about releasing them. Taking six hundred chariots, he followed them into the wilderness, presumably intending to force them to return. The Egyptians caught up with God's people at Pi-hahiroth (14:5–9).

When the Israelites saw the Egyptian army, they became frightened and accused Moses of bringing them into the wilderness to die. Moses tried to assure the people that the Lord would save them (14:10–14). God then instructed Moses what to do next, declaring that He would be "honored" (14:15–18).

While "the angel of God" held back the Egyptians with the pillar of cloud (14:19, 20), Moses stretched out his hand. The sea divided, and the Israelites crossed on dry land (14:21, 22, 29). When Pharaoh's army attempted to follow, the Lord made it impossible (14:23–25). With a gesture from Moses, the waters returned upon the pursuing chariots, and the army perished (14:26–28).

When the Israelites saw that they had been delivered and witnessed the dead bodies of the Egyptians, they "feared the

LORD" and also "believed in the LORD and in His servant Moses" (14:30, 31).

PURSUIT BY PHARAOH AND HIS ARMY (14:1–9)

[1]Now the LORD spoke to Moses, saying, [2]"Tell the sons of Israel to turn back and camp before Pi-hahiroth, between Migdol and the sea; you shall camp in front of Baal-zephon, opposite it, by the sea. [3]For Pharaoh will say of the sons of Israel, 'They are wandering aimlessly in the land; the wilderness has shut them in.' [4]Thus I will harden Pharaoh's heart, and he will chase after them; and I will be honored through Pharaoh and all his army, and the Egyptians will know that I am the LORD." And they did so.

[5]When the king of Egypt was told that the people had fled, Pharaoh and his servants had a change of heart toward the people, and they said, "What is this we have done, that we have let Israel go from serving us?" [6]So he made his chariot ready and took his people with him; [7]and he took six hundred select chariots, and all the other chariots of Egypt with officers over all of them. [8]The LORD hardened the heart of Pharaoh, king of Egypt, and he chased after the sons of Israel as the sons of Israel were going out boldly. [9]Then the Egyptians chased after them with all the horses and chariots of Pharaoh, his horsemen and his army, and they overtook them camping by the sea, beside Pi-hahiroth, in front of Baal-zephon.

Verses 1, 2. In the previous chapter, the Israelites were encamped at Etham (13:20). From there, God instructed them **to turn back and camp before Pi-hahiroth . . . in front of Baal-zephon**, by the Red Sea. The location of these places is uncertain. (See the map in *Appendix: The Route of the Exodus.*)

Verse 3. To **Pharaoh**, the route that the Israelites were taking would not have made any sense; it would seem like the people were lost, **wandering aimlessly in the land.** The CEV says, "The king will think they were afraid to cross the desert and that they are wandering around, trying to find another way to leave the country." While this strategy seems strange, it suited the Lord's purpose: It baited the trap in which He would catch Pharaoh's army so that He might free Israel and show His power.

Verse 4. God Himself explained His motives, saying that His purpose was to **harden Pharaoh's heart**. Exodus sometimes says that Pharaoh hardened his own heart; but toward the end of the plagues narrative, the language indicates that God was hardening Pharaoh's heart in order to fulfill His purpose. As He sent the plagues and freed His people, He demonstrated that He is indeed God over all. When Pharaoh came after the Israelites and was defeated, God would be **honored** and **the Egyptians** would **know** that He was **the Lord**.

Verse 5. Upon learning that the Israelites had left Egypt, **Pharaoh and his servants** asked, **"What is this we have done?"** Maybe his advisers reported that Israel was trying to flee the land, as he had feared, rather than just going into the wilderness to worship.[1] Possibly, Pharaoh changed his mind about letting **the people** go, as he had after earlier plagues. In any case, the Egyptians realized that they had lost a valuable asset; no longer would they have the Israelites to provide them with free labor for their building projects.

Verses 6, 7. Consequently, Pharaoh determined to go after his lost property. **His chariot** was accompanied by **six hundred select chariots**, along with **all the other chariots of Egypt**. The chariots had **officers over all of them.** The term "officer" (שָׁלִישׁ, *shalish*) originally referred to the third man in a chariot crew; this group often consisted of a driver, a shield-bearer, and a warrior. The text may indicate that there were three men in each chariot. However, the term later came to be used for a high ranking "officer," which is how most versions render the word.[2] Since the chariot was the deadliest implement of war available at the time

---

[1]This possibility was suggested by Umberto Cassuto, *A Commentary on the Book of Exodus*, trans. Israel Abrahams (Jerusalem: Magnes Press, 1997), 161, and Peter Enns, *Exodus*, The NIV Application Commentary (Grand Rapids, Mich.: Zondervan, 2000), 271.

[2]J. Philip Hyatt, *Exodus*, The New Century Bible Commentary (Grand Rapids, Mich.: Wm. B. Eerdmans Publishing Co., 1971), 152.

(the equivalent of a modern-day tank), Pharaoh's forces were formidable indeed.

Verse 8. A summary of the situation is presented at this point. Not only had Pharaoh had a "change of heart" (14:5), but **the LORD** had also **hardened** [his] **heart**. Therefore, Pharaoh **chased after** the Israelites as they **were going out boldly**. The phrase בְּיָד רָמָה (*b^e^yad ramah*), translated "boldly," literally means "with a high hand." The expression "suggests confidence on Israel's part, probably due to ignorance of the danger that threaten[ed] them."[3]

Verse 9. The narrative resumes from verse 7, adding that **Pharaoh** pursued the Israelites with **his horsemen and his army**. This pursuit was successful; the Egyptian force caught up with the Israelites as they were camped by the Red Sea.

THE ISRAELITES' PANIC (14:10–14)

10As Pharaoh drew near, the sons of Israel looked, and behold, the Egyptians were marching after them, and they became very frightened; so the sons of Israel cried out to the LORD. 11Then they said to Moses, "Is it because there were no graves in Egypt that you have taken us away to die in the wilderness? Why have you dealt with us in this way, bringing us out of Egypt? 12Is this not the word that we spoke to you in Egypt, saying, 'Leave us alone that we may serve the Egyptians'? For it would have been better for us to serve the Egyptians than to die in the wilderness." 13But Moses said to the people, "Do not fear! Stand by and see the salvation of the LORD which He will accomplish for you today; for the Egyptians whom you have seen today, you will never see them again forever. 14The LORD will fight for you while you keep silent."

Verse 10. When the Egyptians approached, the Israelites **became very frightened**. How could they escape from the king when he had at his command such a great army? The people's

---

[3]Waldemar Janzen, *Exodus*, Believers Church Bible Commentary (Scottdale, Pa.: Herald Press, 2000), 176.

first reaction was to cry out to **the LORD** for help.

Verses 11, 12. The Israelites' second reaction was to complain to Moses (see 16:3; 17:3). They ironically asked why **Moses** had brought them into **the wilderness** to **die**. They asked, **"Is it because there were no graves in Egypt . . . ?"** Obviously, there were plenty of graves in Egypt. Part of the irony in their question is that Egypt emphasized death, burial, and monumental tombs perhaps more than any other culture of the day. The people were saying, "If we were going to die, we should have just died in Egypt." They added that they had asked Moses to **leave** [them] **alone** when he first came to **Egypt** to deliver them. The people would have rather suffered as slaves for the rest of their lives than to be killed in battle.

Why did the Israelites not think about the signs which Moses and Aaron had done? Had they already forgotten the ten plagues which God had sent upon the Egyptians? Did they not realize that God had humbled Pharaoh and his servants to the point that they had permitted Israel to leave? Where were the gifts which God had moved the Egyptians to give to their slaves as they left? If God's people had thought about all that He had done, they surely would have trusted Him to protect them in their present situation, just as He had previously met their needs. However, their faith proved inadequate.

Verse 13. Moses, in contrast, spoke words that demonstrated faith and the courage that comes from faith. He quieted their fears by affirming that the Lord would save them. Of course, when he said that they would **see the salvation of the LORD,** he was not talking about salvation from their sins. Rather, he meant salvation from Egypt and the slavery Israel had experienced there. The Israelites had nothing more to **fear** from **the Egyptians**. They would **never see them again forever**, which meant, at least, that the Egyptians would not succeed in enslaving them again.

This salvation would be accomplished by the Lord. Moses said that the people's role would be merely to **stand by** and observe what the Lord was about to do. Instead of "stand by," some versions have "stand still" (KJV; NKJV), while others have "stand firm" (NRSV; NIV).

Verse 14. When God fights for someone, all that person has to do is to **keep silent**—to watch quietly and see Him win the battle. **The Lord will fight for you** is a key idea in this passage and a major theme of the Old Testament.[4] Even though the Israelites had gone out "in martial array" (13:18), the Lord was the "warrior" who fought for them (15:3). Later in the chapter, when the Egyptians saw that they were defeated, they cried out, "The Lord is fighting for them [Israel] against the Egyptians" (14:25). Only because the Lord fought for them—not because of their superior forces, weaponry, or military ability—did the Israelites win their freedom.

GOD'S INSTRUCTION TO MOSES (14:15–20)

15Then the Lord said to Moses, "Why are you crying out to
Me? Tell the sons of Israel to go forward. 16As for you, lift up
your staff and stretch out your hand over the sea and divide it,
and the sons of Israel shall go through the midst of the sea on
dry land. 17As for Me, behold, I will harden the hearts of the
Egyptians so that they will go in after them; and I will be hon-
ored through Pharaoh and all his army, through his chariots
and his horsemen. 18Then the Egyptians will know that I am
the Lord, when I am honored through Pharaoh, through his
chariots and his horsemen."

19The angel of God, who had been going before the camp
of Israel, moved and went behind them; and the pillar of cloud
moved from before them and stood behind them. 20So it came
between the camp of Egypt and the camp of Israel; and there
was the cloud along with the darkness, yet it gave light at night.
Thus the one did not come near the other all night.

Verse 15. In this verse, **the Lord** was responding to an unrecorded petition of **Moses**. Either before or after Moses spoke

---

[4]See Deut. 1:30; 3:22; 20:4; Josh. 10:14; 10:42; 2 Chron. 20:29. For examples of the Lord's people depending on Him to fight for them or to give them victory, see Josh. 6:1–21; Judg. 6:13–16; 1 Sam. 17:45–47; 2 Kings 6:16, 17; 19:32–37.

encouraging words to the people, he spoke to God, apparently asking for God's help. God's initial response was **"Why are you crying out to Me?"** It was as if He were saying "Do you not trust Me to deliver you? You need not cry out or complain." Then God gave an amazing order: **"Go forward."** Israel was "between a rock and a hard place"—between "the pursuing Egyptians and the impassable sea."[5] They had Pharaoh's army behind them, the desert on both sides of them, and the Red Sea in front of them. What were they to do? God said, "Go forward."

Verse 16. Next, God explained how the people could go forward. Moses was to **lift up** [his] **staff and stretch out** [his] **hand over the sea**, and the sea would be divided. The Israelites would pass through **on dry land**.

Verses 17, 18. God would again **harden the hearts of the Egyptians**, and they would attempt to follow. When they did so, God would be **honored** through them. This is a reference to the fact that God would destroy the Egyptian **army** in the sea. "I will be honored" is translated from כָּבֵד (*kabed*), which means "be heavy, weighty, or honored." The word is sometimes used in reference to wealthy and influential people who possessed the respect and admiration of others. Moreover, the term is often used for giving God the honor that He deserves. In this text, the NIV says "I will gain glory" (see NRSV; NEB; NAB; NJB). The CEV says, "I will be praised." Both the Israelites and **the Egyptians** would **know** God to be **the Lord**.

Verse 19. To protect Israel during the time required for the path through the sea to be prepared, God placed a barrier between the Egyptians and the Israelites: **The angel of God, who had been going before the camp of Israel, moved and went behind them.** The text adds that the **cloud** moved as well, from the front of the camp to the back.

Both the angel and the cloud represented God's presence. **The pillar** of cloud and fire hovered over the Israelite camp and led Israel on their journeys. In this way, the Lord provided the Israelites with a visible reminder of His constant presence. In

---

[5]John I. Durham, *Exodus*, Word Biblical Commentary, vol. 3 (Waco, Tex.: Word Books, 1987), 198.

13:21, 22, the Lord is associated with the pillar of cloud and the pillar of fire, as in this passage "the angel of God" is associated with the "pillar of cloud." In some sense, then, "the LORD," "the angel of God," and "the pillar" all signify God and His presence among the Israelites.

Verse 20. The cloud that stood between the two camps gave off some **light**, but its primary function was to keep the Egyptians away from God's people as the night passed and the wind blew a valley through the sea.

THE ISRAELITES DELIVERED (14:21–25)

21Then Moses stretched out his hand over the sea; and the
LORD swept the sea back by a strong east wind all night and
turned the sea into dry land, so the waters were divided. 22The
sons of Israel went through the midst of the sea on the dry
land, and the waters were like a wall to them on their right
hand and on their left. 23Then the Egyptians took up the pur-
suit, and all Pharaoh's horses, his chariots and his horsemen
went in after them into the midst of the sea. 24At the morning
watch, the LORD looked down on the army of the Egyptians
through the pillar of fire and cloud and brought the army of
the Egyptians into confusion. 25He caused their chariot wheels
to swerve, and He made them drive with difficulty; so the Egyp-
tians said, "Let us flee from Israel, for the LORD is fighting for
them against the Egyptians."

Verse 21. Moses continued to follow the Lord's instructions. He **stretched out his hand**, and God **divided** the **waters** by means of **a strong east wind** which blew **all night**. What a dramatic event this must have been! There should be no doubt that this was a miracle—a spectacular act of God unexplainable in any other way. God used a natural force, "a strong east wind," to perform a supernatural act, a miracle. In the eighth plague, He had also used "an east wind" that blew all day and night to cover the land of Egypt with locusts (10:13, 14). The "strong east wind" that parted the Red Sea is poetically called "the blast of [God's] nostrils" (15:8). In looking back at what had happened, Old Testament books which recall Israel's deliverance through **the sea** focus more on God's parting of the water than on His destruction of the Egyptians.[6]

Verse 22. With **the waters** divided, the Israelites were able to walk through **the sea on the dry land**. The waters that were piled up on either side of God's people are compared to **a wall**. Presumably, since the wind blew all night (14:21), it took that long for the Israelites to cross the sea. The text specifies that at daybreak the waters came back together (14:27).

Verses 23–25. The Egyptians followed the Israelites into **the sea** during **the morning watch**, sometime between 2:00 and 6:00 a.m. Apparently, **the LORD**, who had been preventing Pharaoh's army from approaching the Israelites by means of the cloud, allowed them to go forward. Pharaoh probably thought that his war chariots could quickly catch the slow-moving Israelites with all their goods, their families, and their livestock.

However, when they drove their chariots into the sea, following the path of the Israelites, the Egyptians discovered that they could not move as easily as the people they were pursuing. From His presence in **the pillar of fire and cloud**, the Lord **brought the army of the Egyptians into confusion**, causing **their chariot wheels to swerve** and making **them drive with difficulty**. Exactly how the Lord confused the Egyptians is not known. Some commentators speculate that the heavy war chariots of the Egyptians tended to break through the dry surface over which the Israelites had passed, causing the chariot wheels to move slowly, to become stuck, or even to fall off. The relevant verses can be translated in various ways:

> The LORD . . . threw the Egyptian army into panic. He clogged their chariot wheels so that they turned with difficulty (NRSV; see REB; NAB; NJB).

> . . . the LORD . . . made them panic. Their chariot wheels got stuck, and it was hard for them to move (CEV).

---

[6]Nahum M. Sarna, *Exploring Exodus: The Origins of Biblical Israel* (New York: Schocken Books, 1996), 114–16. Sarna cited Josh. 4:22–28; Ps. 66:5, 6; 77:15–21; 78:13, 53; 106:9–11, 22; 114:3, 5; 136:13–15; Is. 51:9, 10; 63:11–13.

> The LORD . . . threw [the army] into confusion. He made the wheels of their chariots come off so that they had difficulty driving (NIV; see NKJV).

At that point, Pharaoh's soldiers realized that they would be unable to overtake Israel. They concluded that their problems originated with **the LORD**, the God of the Hebrews. Perhaps they thought about what they had previously forgotten: all that the Lord had done in Egypt to bring about Israel's escape. Remembering, they became frightened, and their thoughts turned from capturing Israel to **flee**[ing] **from Israel**.

Imagine the confusion within the ranks of Egypt's army. The soldiers had driven into the sea, but now some were struggling to get their chariots to move. Others may have been trying to control their horses after their chariot wheels had been damaged. Some were no doubt attempting to press forward, while others were shouting, "Turn back!" and trying to return to the western shore. At the height of their panic, disaster struck.

PHARAOH'S ARMY DROWNED (14:26–31)

26Then the LORD said to Moses, "Stretch out your hand over the sea so that the waters may come back over the Egyptians, over their chariots and their horsemen." 27So Moses stretched out his hand over the sea, and the sea returned to its normal state at daybreak, while the Egyptians were fleeing right into it; then the LORD overthrew the Egyptians in the midst of the sea. 28The waters returned and covered the chariots and the horsemen, even Pharaoh's entire army that had gone into the sea after them; not even one of them remained. 29But the sons of Israel walked on dry land through the midst of the sea, and the waters were like a wall to them on their right hand and on their left.

30Thus the LORD saved Israel that day from the hand of the Egyptians, and Israel saw the Egyptians dead on the seashore. 31When Israel saw the great power which the LORD had used against the Egyptians, the people feared the LORD, and they believed in the LORD and in His servant Moses.

Verses 26, 27. Again, **the LORD** spoke **to Moses**, telling him to **stretch out his hand** so that **the waters** would return to their place and drown **the Egyptians**. Moses did as God had said, and the waters **returned**. Panicked and confused, the charioteers continued to drive into the sea as it crashed down upon them. The verb נָעַר (*na'ar*), translated **overthrew** in verse 27, is also rendered "swept" (NIV) and "tossed" (NRSV).[7] One commentator explained,

> The verb "tossed" . . . can also mean "shake oneself free, shake off." Thus we could think of this statement, not as a literal descriptive, but as a metaphorical clincher: "The Lord shook off the Egyptians into the sea." With the sea miracle, the Lord is saying to the Egyptians, as it were, "Enough of you! Be gone!" and shaking himself free of their clinging presence once and for all.[8]

Verses 28, 29. As a consequence of God's "shaking them off," all of the Egyptians who **had gone into the sea** died in the sea. A parallel can be drawn between the army of locusts and the **army** of **Pharaoh** as both groups all perished in the Red Sea (10:19). With the destruction of the Egyptian army, the fear and threat of Egypt was finally removed from Israel.[9]

Verses 28 and 29 contrast Israel's experience with the Egyptians' fate. The Egyptians died in the midst of the water; but God saved **Israel** by enabling them to pass through the Red Sea **on dry land**, with **the waters** held back **like a wall** on either side of them (see 14:22). Just as the death of the firstborn meant death for Egypt while the Passover preserved life for Israel, so the Red Sea brought death to the Egyptians but gave new life to the Israelites.

---

[7]The NIV says that "the sea went back to its place. The Egyptians were fleeing toward it, and the LORD swept them into the sea." The NRSV translates, ". . . at dawn the sea returned to its normal depth. As the Egyptians fled before it, the LORD tossed the Egyptians into the sea."

[8]Janzen, 180.

[9]Sarna, 113.

Verse 30. The chapter concludes with a statement summarizing the results of Israel's passing through the sea. By bringing His people safely between the divided waters, God saved them. The Israelites were certain of their salvation and of Egypt's defeat because, with their own eyes, they **saw the Egyptians dead on the seashore**. This is a masterpiece of understatement by an eyewitness. Never could the people doubt that God had delivered them from the Egyptians through the Red Sea, for they had seen the evidence with their own eyes.

Verse 31. This deliverance by the mighty **power** of God produced both fear and faith. The people **feared the Lord**! One must live in awe, respect, and obedience before a God who can do such wonders and destroy His enemies so completely. The Israelites also had faith in God and faith in Moses as His representative and spokesman: **They believed in the Lord and in His servant Moses.**[10] The people's trust in Moses, both before and after this time, was closely linked to their faith in God. To believe Moses' words was to believe in God; to believe in God was to believe in—to have trust and confidence in—Moses, the one whom God had appointed to lead His people.

APPLICATION

When Our Faith Is Tested (Ch. 14)

James 1:3 says, "The testing of your faith produces endurance." Probably, the "testing" James meant was persecution. The idea is that when a Christian's faith is tested and he still remains faithful, he grows spiritually. Unfortunately, not everyone passes the test.

Is our faith ever tested? Are we ever tempted to give up on God? When life is going badly for us—because of personal sickness, bereavement, financial difficulties, family conflicts, or per-

---

[10]Moses is called God's "servant" in other passages (Num. 12:7, 8; Deut. 34:5; Josh. 1:2, 7; Mal. 4:4). This honorary designation was usually given to those who were chosen by God for a special purpose and were obedient to Him, such as: Abraham, Job, Caleb, Joshua, David, Elijah, Isaiah, and the Messiah.

sonal problems—our faith is tested. Sometimes this is true even when our lives are going well. Prosperity can tempt us to be materialistic, for instance. What do we do then? The experience of the Israelites as they stood on the shore of the Red Sea provides some guidelines.

When our faith is tested, we should remember that matters are not as bad as they seem. That was true for the Israelites. They thought they had escaped. Imagine their jubilation! Then they reached the edge of the sea, and their joy turned to despair. They faced the sea in front of them, the desert was on both sides, and behind them was Pharaoh's army (14:9). The forces against them seemed to be overwhelming. They saw no way out. However, since we know the rest of the story, we know that there *was* a way out. Ultimately, God delivered them.

Like the Israelites, we tend to look at the negative, imagine the worst, and fail to see the positive possibilities when we are faced with problems. We must have faith that the situation is not as dark as it seems.

When our faith is tested, we should look to God. The Israelites "cried out to the LORD" (14:10). That much they got right—but then they started to complain. In doing so, they exhibited two negative attitudes that continued to characterize them: forgetfulness and ingratitude. They forgot what God had done for them, and they were ungrateful for His blessings. Nevertheless, God responded to their cry by promising them deliverance. Moses assured them that God would rescue them: "Do not fear! Stand by and see the salvation of the LORD" (14:13, 14).

Turning to God when our faith is tested should become natural for us. In God—through prayer, through the Scriptures, and through our fellow Christians—we can find the help and comfort we need in times of trial. Sometimes people move farther away from God instead of drawing closer to Him, even turning away from the church. May that never be said of us!

When our faith is tested, we should move forward. We must press on in the upward way, heading for the promised land. The most remarkable thing about the story in Exodus 14 is found in God's instructions. After Moses said, "Stand by and see" (14:13), God said, "Go forward" (14:15). Their faith was tested! To their credit, despite their misgivings, they did indeed "go forward" into the sea. As the sea opened, they marched through on dry ground. By doing so, they were saved, delivered from their peril.

What about us? When our faith is tested, we usually know what we ought to do. The question is whether or not we will do it—in spite of our misgivings, fears, and problems.

Frequently, when our faith is tested by trying circumstances or difficult situations, we need to do what Israel was told to do: (1) Depend on God: "Stand by and see the salvation of the LORD" (14:13). (2) Then "go forward" (14:15). Paul said, "Forgetting what lies behind and reaching forward to what lies ahead, I press on toward the goal for the prize of the upward call of God in Christ Jesus" (Phil. 3:13, 14). Is there a sea in front of us? God can open the sea. Is there a wall in front of us? God can help us tear down that wall. Have we encountered a closed door? God can open that door. We should walk through the sea, tear down the wall, or enter through the door. The solution to the testing of our faith is simply to "keep the faith," to keep doing what the Lord would have us to do.

Conclusion. God has the answer for our individual lives and for the corporate life of the church. We must hear His instructions and press on, even when the way ahead seems impossible. The God who could open the Red Sea can open a door for us that will result both in our being blessed and in our being a blessing to others.

Freedom at Last! (Ch. 14)

"Freedom" is a word that people hold dear. Many nations have fought to become free or to remain free. That is why we enjoy listening to the story of the Israelites' deliverance from Egyptian captivity. God heard the cries of the people in slavery and made them free indeed! He can do the same in our lives (Jn. 8:32, 36).

They were enslaved. God heard Israel's cries because of their bitter affliction (Ex. 3:7). Through His spokesmen He commanded the king of Egypt, "Let My people go!" Then, by His mighty hand, He delivered them from their slavery. We are—or were—enslaved to sin (Rom. 6:19–23). This slavery is also bitter, with the only wages being death. While we are enslaved by sin, we are without God, separated from Christ, and without hope (Eph. 2:12).

They were powerfully delivered by God. The good news for Israel was that God interceded in human history to bring them out of their slavery (3:8). Though the language is accommodative, it is also especially meaningful: God said, "I have come down to deliver them." Is it not wonderful that God intervened personally in human affairs to provide their salvation? God delivered them by means of the plagues. Sometimes Pharaoh was moved to promise the Israelites they could go. Each time the plague was removed, he would harden his heart and deny them freedom. Finally, God killed Egypt's firstborn (11:4, 5; 12:29), but He passed over the homes of obedient Israelites who had put blood on their doorposts (see 12:7, 13). Pharaoh released the slaves but later changed his mind and pursued them (14:5–9). Then God delivered the Israelites through the Red Sea. When Pharaoh's soldiers attempted to follow, they perished (14:24–28). Israel was at last free from Egyptian bondage. The Israelites were not set free by their own goodness or might, but by God's power and mercy and grace. They were set free by blood—because they had applied the blood to their doorposts and lintels.

The good news for people today is that God has again intervened in human history to deliver mankind. This time He came down as Jesus Christ, who was born, lived, died, was resurrected, and ascended to heaven so that we might be delivered from our spiritual slavery! He has made it possible for us to apply His blood to our lives, by being baptized (Rom. 6:3, 4). Paul likened Israel's passing through the cloud and the sea to baptism (1 Cor. 10:1, 2). Therefore, we can compare our baptism to their experience. As they stood on the eastern shore of the sea and rejoiced in their freedom, so we can rejoice when we have passed through the waters of baptism.

Conclusion. No one can deny that we must do something to be set free. We must consent to being baptized, just as the Israelites had to put the blood on their doors. We must believe in Jesus, be willing to confess our faith in Him, repent of our sins, and be buried with Him in baptism. When we obey the gospel, we are free from the guilt, slavery, and condemnation of sin (Acts 2:38; Rom. 6:22; 8:1). The cause of our deliverance is not our obedience, but the blood of Christ and the grace of God.

"Stand By . . . Go Forward" (14:13, 15)

When the Israelites faced an impossible situation, the Lord's instruction was first "Stand by" and then "Go forward." Sometimes we may need to stand still, waiting on the Lord's providence to show the way while we pray, study, meditate, and seek His will. In other situations, we need to "go forward" in faith, taking action to do the Lord's will. We must be prepared to do both.

"Baptized into Moses" (14:21, 22; 1 Cor. 10:1, 2)

We are justified in using the story of the Israelites' deliverance through the Red Sea as a figure of baptism because Paul compared the two in 1 Corinthians 10:1, 2. How was passing through the Red Sea like what we did when we became Christians? (1) Both baptisms involved immersion: The Israelites were immersed in the cloud and the sea; we were immersed in water. (2) Both brought salvation: The Israelites gained deliverance from bondage, and we experienced new birth. (3) Both gave reason for rejoicing afterwards. (4) Both made God's deliverance possible. (5) Both required faith. The Israelites had to trust God and walk through the water; because of our faith we obeyed God's command in order to be saved. (6) Both offered deliverance from something and to something. Israel became God's people, responsible to do God's work and God's will; so did we.

Chapter 15

Praise for Deliverance And Bitter Water Made Sweet

In chapter 15 the song that Moses and the Israelites sang after the Lord had delivered them through the Red Sea is given (15:1–21). It also includes the account of their initial experiences on their wilderness journey (15:22–27).

Moses and the Israelites praised the Lord in song—for who and what He is, and for what He had done by destroying the Egyptian army in the sea. The song depicts the Lord as Israel's strength, song, and salvation (15:2); He is a warrior with majestic power, who in His anger overthrows His enemies (15:3, 6, 7). Furthermore, He is the God above all gods, "majestic in holiness," and a wonder-worker (15:11).

He destroyed the Egyptians in the sea (15:1); they drowned in its depths (15:4, 5). To accomplish His victory, He caused the waters to be heaped up and then used the wind to cover the enemy in the waters (15:8–11).

The Lord is the One who in lovingkindness would lead His people to His holy habitation (15:13). The neighboring peoples—the Philistines, the Edomites, the Moabites, and the Canaanites—would hear of the destruction of the Egyptian army, and they would fear the Lord (15:14–16a). Consequently, Israel would be able to settle in the promised land (15:16b, 17). The song ends with a note of praise (15:18). After a brief summary of the recent events (15:19), the text adds that Miriam and the women danced and sang similar praises (15:20, 21).

Then the journey to Sinai begins. The Israelites traveled to the wilderness of Shur and came to Marah, where the water was too bitter to drink (15:22, 23). As a result, they complained to

Moses. Having received instruction from the Lord, he threw a tree into the water and the water became sweet (15:24, 25a). God then stated the terms on which He would make a covenant with them (15:25b, 26). The chapter concludes by stating that Israel moved on to a place called Elim, where there was an abundance of water and food (15:27).

THE REJOICING OF THE ISRAELITES (15:1–21)

Moses and the Sons of Israel Rejoice (15:1–19)

The song that Moses and the Israelites sang provides a poetic account of the miracle at the sea, enclosed within two prose accounts (14:13–31; 15:19). The poem, known in Judaism as *Shirat ha-Yam*, "The Song of the Sea," "assumed a special place in the Jewish liturgy quite early," eventually being incorporated "into the fixed, daily morning service" of Jewish synagogues.[1] Archaic characteristics in the language of the song have led scholars to believe that this song "may be the oldest piece of sustained poetry in the Hebrew Bible."[2] However, its archaic forms do not necessarily prove that the poem was written earlier than the narrative in which it is found since poetry frequently uses archaic style and language.

The poem's structure—along with the fact that "Moses and the sons of Israel" are said to have sung the song—has led to the conclusion that the hymn was performed antiphonally, with two groups singing the words alternately to one another. However, there is no agreement as to the antiphonal arrangement of the song.[3] All agree that the song eloquently expresses the praise

---

[1]Nahum M. Sarna, *Exodus*, The JPS Torah Commentary (New York: Jewish Publication Society, 1991), 76.

[2]Ibid., 75.

[3]"One view was that the people repeated or completed the phrase or verse that Moses initiated. Another held that the verses were recited by them in alternation. Still another view had the people reciting the entire song after Moses had finished it." (Ibid., 76.) One more possibility is that Miriam and the women sang the chorus (15:21) after each line or two.

Israel must have felt on the occasion of their deliverance. Nahum M. Sarna said that the song is "a paean of praise to God, the biblical way of expressing gratitude. It is not an epic narrative but a spontaneous, lyrical outpouring of emotion on the part of the people who experienced the great events of the Exodus."[4] Typical of the high regard with which scholars view the poem is S. R. Driver's tribute: "The ode of triumph [15:1–18] is one of the finest products of Hebrew poetry, remarkable for poetic fire and spirit, picturesque description, vivid imagery, quick movement, effective parallelism, and bright, sonorous . . . diction."[5]

The most important point to remember in understanding this passage is that, unlike the preceding chapters, these verses are written as poetry and need to be interpreted as such. The poetic nature of the passage means, for one thing, that the passage contains more figures of speech than prose generally does.

In addition, the structure of the text should be considered carefully. The song can be divided into two stanzas.[6] The first stanza (15:1b–12) alternates between praising God for who He is and praising Him for what He had done for Israel:

Introduction (15:1b): The Lord is highly exalted because He has hurled the horse and its rider into the sea.

Praise to the Lord for who He is (15:2, 3): He is my strength, song, and salvation. He is my God and a warrior.

Praise to the Lord for what He has done (15:4, 5): He has cast Pharaoh's chariots and army into the sea.

---

[4]Ibid., 75.

[5]S. R. Driver, *The Book of Exodus,* The Cambridge Bible for Schools and Colleges (Cambridge: University Press, 1953), 129.

[6]While the NASB does not divide the poem into stanzas, other versions do, although they differ in where they place the divisions. For example, the NIV divides the poem into the following stanzas: 15:1–5, 6–8, 9–10, 11–12, 13–18; the NKJV, 15:1–10, 11–13, 14–17, 18; the NRSV, 15:1–3, 4–10, 11–12, 13–18; the NCV, 15:1–8, 9–10, 11–13, 14–18. It is difficult to determine whether verse 13 belongs in the first stanza or in the second.

Praise to the Lord for who He is (15:6, 7): He is majestic in power, overthrowing His enemies.

Praise to the Lord for what He has done (15:8–10): He has used the waters and the wind to defeat Pharaoh's army.

Praise to the Lord for who He is (15:11): He is greater than all the gods, majestic in holiness, a worker of wonders.

Praise to the Lord for what He has done (15:12): He caused the earth to swallow His enemies, and He has brought His people to His holy habitation.

The second stanza (15:13–18) emphasizes the results of what the Lord had done:

The consequences for Israel (15:13): They will be guided to God's holy habitation.

The consequences for the nations (15:14–16): The Philistines, Edomites, Moabites, and Canaanites will be afraid.

The consequences for Israel (15:17): They will be planted in the place God has chosen for them.

The conclusion (15:18): Let God be praised forever!

The poem is an effective, unified work of literary art. Therefore, we have no reason to think, as some scholars have suggested, that it is a combination of poems put together long after the exodus.[7]

---

[7]The view that the poem is unified contrasts with that of John I. Durham, for example, who said, "This poem is a composite of at least two . . . and perhaps three . . . poems." (John I. Durham, *Exodus*, Word Biblical Commentary, vol. 3 [Waco, Tex.: Word Books, 1987], 205.)

The Introduction (15:1a)

[1a]Then Moses and the sons of Israel sang this song to the LORD, and said. . . .

Verse 1a. The chapter commences by setting the stage for the celebration of God's deliverance. The text informs the reader of the basic facts about the event. (1) *When did it occur?* **Then,** that is, after the deliverance through the sea recorded in chapter 14. (2) *Who participated?* **Moses and the sons of Israel.** Later, Miriam and the women are also spoken of as celebrating (15:20, 21). (3) *What did they do?* They **sang this song,** the words in 15:1b–18. (4) *Who was honored in the celebration?* **The LORD,** to whom they sang the song.

Nahum M. Sarna pointed out that the hymn has a prose introduction and concludes "with another prose statement summarizing the victory" (15:19). It thus provides the first biblical example of this genre, or type of literature—"the combination of prose narration with a laudatory hymn extolling the victory." Another example is provided by the song of Deborah (Judg. 4; 5).[8]

The song of Moses underscores the fact that worship in general, and praise in song in particular, is always an appropriate response to being saved. This is seen in other passages in both the Old and New Testaments (Ps. 98:1–5; 149:1–4; Acts 16:25; Rom. 15:9; Eph. 5:18–20; Col. 3:16; Heb. 13:15; Rev. 15:3).

The First Stanza (15:1b–12)

[1b]"I will sing to the LORD, for He is highly exalted;
The horse and its rider He has hurled into the sea.
[2]The LORD is my strength and song,
And He has become my salvation;
This is my God, and I will praise Him;
My father's God, and I will extol Him.

---

[8]Nahum M. Sarna, *Exploring Exodus: The Origins of Biblical Israel* (New York: Schocken Books, 1996), 113–14.

[3]The LORD is a warrior;
The LORD is His name.
[4]Pharaoh's chariots and his army He has cast into the sea;
And the choicest of his officers are drowned in the Red Sea.
[5]The deeps cover them;
They went down into the depths like a stone.
[6]Your right hand, O LORD, is majestic in power,
Your right hand, O LORD, shatters the enemy.
[7]And in the greatness of Your excellence
You overthrow those who rise up against You;
You send forth Your burning anger, and it consumes them as chaff.
[8]At the blast of Your nostrils the waters were piled up,
The flowing waters stood up like a heap;
The deeps were congealed in the heart of the sea.
[9]The enemy said, 'I will pursue, I will overtake, I will divide the spoil;
My desire shall be gratified against them;
I will draw out my sword, my hand will destroy them.'
[10]You blew with Your wind, the sea covered them;
They sank like lead in the mighty waters.
[11]Who is like You among the gods, O LORD?
Who is like You, majestic in holiness,
Awesome in praises, working wonders?
[12]You stretched out Your right hand,
The earth swallowed them."

Verse 1b. At this point, the theme of the song is introduced: **The LORD** is to be praised because of what He has done. He is called **highly exalted** because **the horse and its rider He has hurled into the sea.** Since this is figurative language, the reader should not expect exactness. That the poem speaks of horses and riders rather than chariots should not be taken to mean that there were no chariots present. In fact, the poem later says that both the chariots and the army perished (15:4), and the prose account of the event mentions horses as well as chariots (15:19).

The poem's statement that the Lord **hurled** the riders into the sea does not contradict the description of their drowning found in the previous chapter. Why did Moses say that God "hurled" horses and riders if He really flooded chariots by returning the waters of the sea to their place? The answer is simply that Moses was speaking poetically. "Horses and riders" and "hurling" are more vivid, effective ways of expressing the feelings attached to the facts of God's deliverance of Israel. The text speaks of the destruction of the Egyptians in the sea in a number of different ways in the chapter:

> The Lord hurled the horse and its rider into the sea (15:1b).
>
> The Lord cast Pharaoh's chariots and army into the sea and drowned his officers (15:4).
>
> The Lord blew with His wind, the sea covered them, and they sank (15:10).
>
> The Lord stretched out His right hand and the earth swallowed them (15:12).

The Israelites were singing about the same event in all four verses; the use of the figurative language of poetry allowed them to speak of that event in four different ways.

Verses 2, 3. These verses *praise the Lord for who He is*. The poet provided the first installment of his portrayal of the Lord's person. Each description that is given adds something to the reader's understanding of God. As the **strength** of the believer, the Lord is both the protector and the power source for His people. As his **song**, the Lord is both the source of worship (the One who makes it possible for His people to sing) and the object of worship (the One who receives the praise which His people offer).

Further, the poet described God as his **salvation**, no doubt referring to the salvation Israel had just experienced in gaining their freedom from Egypt. He claimed the Lord as his **God**, even as He was his **father's God** (see 3:6; 18:4). This means that the poet and the Israelites had a personal relationship with God and were both obligated and privileged to worship Him.

Perhaps the most intriguing description in these verses is the Lord as a **warrior**—or, more literally, "a man of war" (KJV). God is pictured as a warrior who goes out to fight against His enemies (see 14:14, 25; Deut. 1:30; Is. 42:13; Jer. 20:11). The entire song celebrates His success in battle. The Lord as a "warrior" is "a concept that remains significant throughout the Old Testament and even into the New Testament. It is especially prominent in the books of Samuel, where the title 'Yahweh of Armies' (Lord of Hosts) is common."[9]

As the poet completed this section of his song, he said, **"The Lord** [Yahweh] **is His name."** The poet was not merely identifying his God with this list of attributes; rather, he was describing what it means to be Yahweh. To "know" Yahweh is to understand Him in all these ways.

Verses 4, 5. These verses *praise the Lord for what He had done*. Here, the destruction of Pharaoh's army is described for the first time in the poem. The verses emphasize, first, the extent of the destruction: It included **Pharaoh's chariots**, **his army**, and **the choicest of his officers**. They emphasize, second, the place and manner of the destruction: It occurred **in the Red Sea**, into which the Egyptians were **cast**. The reader can imagine the sight of the water sweeping over the chariots and throwing their occupants into the sea. The Egyptians sank **into the depths** of the water **like a stone** where they drowned (see 14:28; Jer. 51:63, 64).

Verses 6, 7. These verses again *praise the Lord for who He is*. The song returns to the nature of **the Lord** as a reason for praising Him. The characteristics mentioned in these verses are God's power and justice. Since He is **majestic in power**, no one can withstand His might—not even the greatest military force in the world. Moreover, God is just and will not allow His enemies to go unpunished. He **shatters the enemy**, **overthrow**[s] **those who rise up against** Him, and His **burning anger . . . consumes them as chaff**. In this comparison, the term "chaff" (קַשׁ, *qash*), or "stubble" (NIV), refers to the heavier straw that was not carried away

[9]John H. Walton and Victor H. Matthews, *Genesis—Deuteronomy*, The IVP Bible Background Commentary (Downers Grove, Ill.: InterVarsity Press, 1997), 101.

by the wind in the winnowing process; it was often gathered up and consumed in the fire (Is. 5:24; Joel 2:5; Mal. 4:1; Mt. 3:12). Since God is sovereign over all the earth, He has the right to destroy His enemies.[10] In fact, He would be unjust if He did not do so.

Verses 8–10. These three verses return to giving *praise to the Lord for what He had done*. They add to the description of the outpouring of God's wrath on the Egyptians as Pharaoh's army perished in the sea (15:4, 5). The text poetically describes the part the sea played in their destruction. By **the blast of** [His] **nostrils**, the Lord caused **the waters** to pile up **like a heap** (see 14:29). To an onlooker, the waves might have appeared almost solid, or **congealed in the heart of the sea**. Pharaoh's people determined to overtake the Israelites,[11] planning to plunder their goods (**"I will divide the spoil"**) and **destroy them**. Nevertheless, the Lord defeated His enemies by blowing with His **wind** (רוּחַ, *ruach*) or "breath" (NIV). The image of the Egyptians sinking like **lead** in the sea parallels that of the sinking "stone" in verse 5.

The imagery of "nostrils" and "breath" are examples of God being described in human terms (anthropomorphism). Other instances in the song include God as a "warrior" or "man of war" (15:3), as well as the references to His "right hand" (15:6, 12), "hands" (15:17), and "arm" (15:16). Such vivid expressions help humans relate to God, who is a purely spiritual being.

Verse 11. The climax of this description of Yahweh is reached in this verse, which again gives *praise to the Lord for who He is*. The song affirms that God has no counterpart among the gods of the nations. The question **"Who is like You among the gods, O LORD?"** is intended to be answered, "No one!" The fact that God is unique, altogether different from man-made gods, is a major emphasis in the Old Testament.

This verse gives three ways in which Yahweh has no equal.

---

[10]God is indeed a God of wrath or vengeance: "'Vengeance is Mine, I will repay,' says the Lord" (Rom. 12:19; see Deut. 32:35; Ps. 94:1).

[11]The poet was selective; he was not simply retelling the story. The singers (and, later, the readers) already knew the story. Therefore, he did not mention the fact that the Israelites had previously passed through the sea.

(1) None is like Him in His majestic **holiness**. Those who worshiped other gods did not even claim that their gods were holy. (2) Yahweh alone is **awesome** and praiseworthy. No idol deserves to be worshiped. (3) Only God possesses wonder-working power. The false gods of Egypt could do nothing, either good or evil; certainly they could not work wonders as the Lord had just done at the Red Sea. God had exposed the weakness of these deities, bringing judgment on them through the ten plagues (see comments on 12:12).

Verse 12. This verse concludes the first stanza with *praise to the Lord for what He had done*. By God's mighty power, **the earth swallowed them**. A progression may be seen in the poet's three mentions of the Egyptians' destruction. The Lord cast them into the sea (15:4, 5) by causing the sea to come upon them so that they sank into it (15:8–10). The final outcome was that "the earth swallowed them." Since the sea is a part of "the earth," when they sank into the sea, they were "swallowed" by the earth. Another possibility is that "the earth" refers to "the underworld," or "Sheol."[12]

The Second Stanza (15:13–18)

13"In Your lovingkindness You have led the people whom You have redeemed;
In Your strength You have guided them to Your holy habitation.
14The peoples have heard, they tremble;
Anguish has gripped the inhabitants of Philistia.
15Then the chiefs of Edom were dismayed;
The leaders of Moab, trembling grips them;
All the inhabitants of Canaan have melted away.
16Terror and dread fall upon them;
By the greatness of Your arm they are motionless as stone;

---

[12]Wilbur Fields, *Exploring Exodus*, Bible Study Textbook Series (Joplin, Mo.: College Press, 1976), 324; Sarna, *Exodus*, 80.

Until Your people pass over, O LORD,
Until the people pass over whom You have purchased.
[17]You will bring them and plant them in the mountain of Your inheritance,
The place, O LORD, which You have made for Your dwelling,
The sanctuary, O Lord, which Your hands have established.
[18]The LORD shall reign forever and ever."

The second stanza of the poem emphasizes the results of God's action at the Red Sea on behalf of Israel. Apparently, in 15:13–16, the people sang of what would happen in the future as if it had already occurred. R. Alan Cole said that the past tense in these verses may be "'prophetic perfects': future events are described as if they had already taken place. This is common in early days, and particularly familiar in the prophetic books of the Old Testament."[13] Even though Israel's arrival at Mount Sinai and the nations' fear of Israel because of the events at the Red Sea were still in the future, Moses and the Israelites sang as if they were already at Sinai (though not yet in Canaan) and as if the nearby peoples were already voicing their fear of Israel.

Verse 13. The second stanza begins with *the consequences for Israel*. God's deliverance of Israel meant redemption and leadership for His people. Having **redeemed** Israel, God acted in **lovingkindness** and **strength**, demonstrating both His mercy and His might. He **led** and **guided** Israel to His **holy habitation**, probably a reference to Mount Sinai (see Deut. 33:2; Judg. 5:5). Others see "holy habitation" as an allusion to the land of Canaan, the promised land, which is also referred to in 15:17.[14] The NIV has "will lead" and "will guide," indicating that these events would occur in the future.

---

[13]R. Alan Cole, *Exodus: An Introduction and Commentary*, Tyndale Old Testament Commentaries (Downers Grove, Ill.: Inter-Varsity Press, 1973), 125.

[14]James Burton Coffman, *Commentary on Exodus, The Second Book of Moses* (Abilene, Tex.: ACU Press, 1985), 208.

Verses 14–16. These verses focus on *the consequences for the nations*. The peoples of **Canaan** and surrounding nations (**Philistia,**[15] **Edom**, and **Moab**) are said to **have heard** about what God did to the Egyptians, which caused them to **tremble** (see Num. 22:1–6; Josh. 2:8–11). The various nations were in **anguish** and were **dismayed**; they experienced **trembling**, their courage **melted away**, and **terror and dread** came upon them. They were **motionless as stone**, as if frozen in place, incapable of preventing Israel from entering the land. They remained in this condition until Israel passed into their promised land. Israel, in contrast, moved freely into the land as **the people . . . whom** [God] **purchased**. Again, the NIV uses the future tense ("will") to show that these events had not yet happened. These verses echo the emphasis of the first part of the poem: God overcomes His enemies and blesses His people.

Verse 17. This verse returns to *the consequences for Israel*. It speaks of the final result of Israel's redemption through the Red Sea: God's people would be **plant**[ed] in the land which He would give them. This vivid agricultural imagery frequently appears in the Old Testament, demonstrating the sovereignty of the Lord (2 Sam. 7:10; Ps. 44:2; 80:8; Jer. 24:6; 32:41; 42:10; Amos 9:15). Here, the land is metaphorically described as **the mountain of** [God's] **inheritance, the place** of His **dwelling**, and the **sanctuary** which He **established**. All three of these expressions refer to the same place—the promised land.[16] The people sang this song to celebrate the fact that God had delivered them from Egypt through the sea. God had (speaking prophetically) brought them to His "holy habitation" (15:13), Mount Sinai, and He would (in the future) ultimately bring them to the promised land.

Verse 18. This final verse of the hymn serves as *the conclusion*. The song ends the same way it began: with praise to **the Lord**. These final words of praise picture the Lord as a king—the absolute ruler of Israel, a king who **reign**[s] **forever and ever.**

---

[15]The mention of Philistia in this context is sometimes thought to be an anachronism (see comments on 13:17).

[16]Martin Noth, *Exodus*, trans. J. S. Bowden, The Old Testament Library (Philadelphia: Westminster Press, 1962), 126.

Although the expression "forever and ever" in the Old Testament does not always mean what Christians understand as "eternally," this passage may suggest that the poet understood something about the concept of eternity. He praised God for the fact that He has always existed and will always exist as the Sovereign One over all the earth.

A Summary Statement (15:19)

19For the horses of Pharaoh with his chariots and his horsemen went into the sea, and the LORD brought back the waters of the sea on them, but the sons of Israel walked on dry land through the midst of the sea.

Verse 19. Another summary statement, in prose, explains what the Israelites were celebrating. They were rejoicing because God had destroyed the army of **Pharaoh** but had enabled **Israel** to pass through the Red Sea **on dry land**.

Miriam and the Women Rejoice (15:20, 21)

20Miriam the prophetess, Aaron's sister, took the timbrel in her hand, and all the women went out after her with timbrels and with dancing. 21Miriam answered them,
"Sing to the LORD, for He is highly exalted;
The horse and his rider He has hurled into the sea."

Verses 20, 21. The celebration after Israel's deliverance also involved **the women**, who were led by **Miriam** in **dancing** and in **sing**[ing] a version of (or a part of) the same song the men sang (15:1b). Dancing was a way of expressing joy in ancient times. Certainly, the Israelites had good reason to rejoice.[17] Later in Israel's history, the women came out of the cities to meet the

---

[17]The dancing that Miriam and the other women engaged in was not the equivalent of modern dancing. Neither does their dancing and using timbrels while singing provide a precedent which justifies dancing or using instrumental music in the worship of the church today. (Coffman, 210–11.)

men who were victorious in battle; they greeted them with singing, dancing, and the sound of tambourines and other musical instruments (Judg. 11:34; 1 Sam. 18:6–8).

Miriam is called a **prophetess** in verse 20. She is one of only a few prophetesses identified in the Old Testament.[18] Usually, a prophet is defined as one who speaks for another. A prophet of God speaks for God or by the inspiration of God. Possibly, Miriam was a prophetess in this sense. God may have at times given her messages to relay to the people. He may have revealed this poem to Miriam.[19]

AT MARAH, BITTER WATER MADE SWEET (15:22–25a)

22Then Moses led Israel from the Red Sea, and they went out into the wilderness of Shur; and they went three days in the wilderness and found no water. 23When they came to Marah, they could not drink the waters of Marah, for they were bitter; therefore it was named Marah. 24So the people grumbled at Moses, saying, "What shall we drink?" 25aThen he cried out to the LORD, and the LORD showed him a tree; and he threw it into the waters, and the waters became sweet.

After the celebration of their salvation, the Israelites began their long trek, first to Sinai and then to the promised land. In the narrative of their journey to Sinai, as the story is recorded in 15:22—18:27, two facts are emphasized: (1) The Israelites complained about everything. Over and over again, they gave evidence of their forgetful and ungrateful nature.[20] (2) God provided

---

[18]Others were Deborah (Judg. 4:4); Huldah (2 Kings 22:14); Noadiah, a false prophetess (Neh. 6:14); and Isaiah's wife (Is. 8:3).

[19]Music and prophecy were often associated in the Old Testament, since music was sometimes "used to induce the trances from which prophetic utterances proceeded (1 Sam 10:5; 2 Kings 3:15)" (Walton and Matthews, 102).

[20]The specific word for "murmur" (לוּן, *lun*) is found in seven chapters of the Old Testament: Ex. 15; 16; 17; Num. 14; 16; 17; Josh. 9. (Harry M. Orlinsky, *Notes on the New Translation of the Torah* [Philadelphia: Jewish Publication Society of America, 1969], 171; quoted in Coffman, 212.)

for Israel's every need. Rather than punishing them for their ingratitude, God patiently endured their grumbling and responded graciously to their requests.

Verse 22. The Israelites left **the Red Sea** behind them and journeyed **into the wilderness of Shur**. This region was also known as "the wilderness of Etham" (Num. 33:8). They traveled for **three days**, which is reminiscent of Moses' original request to Pharaoh to take "a three days' journey" (3:18; 5:3; 8:27). During this time, however, they were unable to locate any **water**.

Verse 23. The Israelites' first occasion to complain came at **Marah**. When they arrived there, they discovered that **they could not drink the water** because it was **bitter**. The name **Marah** literally means "bitterness."[21] While the place could have been called that before the Israelites arrived,[22] it may have received its name at this time, because of this event. Possibly, it was known as "Marah" only by the Israelites.[23]

Verses 24, 25a. Consequently, the Israelites **grumbled**, or complained ("murmured"; KJV), to **Moses** (see 16:2; 17:3). Moses, in turn, **cried out to the Lord**, petitioning Him on behalf of the people. The Lord answered his prayer by showing him **a tree** to cut down and throw **into the waters** in order to make them **sweet**.[24] Whether the tree provided a "natural" solution to the problem or was simply a symbol of God's "supernatural" (miraculous) sweetening of the water does not really matter. The message is that God cared for His people and provided water for them to drink.

---

[21]In the Book of Ruth, Naomi said she should be called "Mara" when she returned to Bethlehem bereft of her husband and sons (Ruth 1:20). According to Cole, the word "myrrh" seems to be from the same root word. (Cole, 128.)

[22]Ibid.

[23]Different peoples may give different names to the same event, two armies may call the same battle by different names, and different names may refer to the same place.

[24]Writers speculate about what kind of tree this was and how it could have neutralized the bitter taste of the water. A good discussion is given in Cole, 129. A similar story involves the prophet Elisha (2 Kings 2:19–22).

AT MARAH, A PREVIEW OF THE COVENANT (15:25b–27)

[25b]There He made for them a statute and regulation, and there He tested them. [26]And He said, "If you will give earnest heed to the voice of the LORD your God, and do what is right in His sight, and give ear to His commandments, and keep all His statutes, I will put none of the diseases on you which I have put on the Egyptians; for I, the LORD, am your healer."

[27]Then they came to Elim where there were twelve springs of water and seventy date palms, and they camped there beside the waters.

Verses 25b, 26. At Marah, the Lord gave Israel a preview of the covenant He would make with them at Mount Sinai. Apparently, He wanted them to know from the beginning what He would require of them as God's people and what they could expect from Him as their God.

The **statute and regulation** is equivalent to the means by which **He tested them** in verse 25b. They were "tested" in that they were asked to accept and obey God's laws. Another possibility is that they were "tested" at Marah in connection with the "bitter waters" and failed the test. However, the first interpretation seems more likely. R. Alan Cole explained, "It is possible . . . that the 'testing' refers to the conditional nature of the promise in verse 26. . . . God's blessing is always dependent on the obedience of His children to His revealed will."[25]

The terms are specified in verse 26. They were required to obey **God**: to **heed** His **voice**, to **do what is right in His sight**, to listen to **His commandments**, and to **keep all His statutes**. God, in turn, would bless them by putting on them **none of the diseases** which he had **put on the Egyptians**. In fact, **the LORD** said that He was their **healer**; He would heal them and not hurt them if they obeyed Him.

In general, this preliminary covenant corresponds with the covenant which God would make with Israel at Sinai. If Israel

[25]Ibid.

would obey the Lord, then the Lord would bless Israel. However, too much could be made of the promise that "none of the diseases" of Egypt would trouble the Israelites. In this context, the Lord was probably talking about the damage He had brought upon the Egyptians through the plagues, followed by their destruction at the Red Sea.[26] Israel would not experience such disasters if the people would give "earnest heed to the voice of the LORD." While the laws of the Old Testament tended to protect Israel from some diseases, Israel was never given a guarantee that no one would get sick if the nation (or that individual) obeyed God.

Verse 27. The chapter ends on a happy note. The people **came to Elim where there were twelve springs of water and seventy date palms**. In other words, food and water were plentiful. After the bitter waters of Marah, Elim must have seemed like a paradise.

APPLICATION

Singing Because We Have Been Delivered (15:1–21)

Just as the Israelites sang because they had been saved (15:1–21), so those in heaven will sing "the song of Moses . . . and the song of the Lamb" (Rev. 15:3) because of their deliverance. Christians today should sing with "thankfulness in [their] hearts to God" (Col. 3:16; see Rom. 15:9; Eph. 5:19, 20; Heb. 13:15).

The Nature of God (15:1–18)

A lesson on the nature of God could be entitled "This Is My God" (15:2) or "Who Is Like You?" (15:11). The song of deliverance (15:1–18) provides numerous descriptions of the Lord which could serve as the basis for a sermon on what God is like. According to this text, God is (1) His people's strength, (2) His people's song, and (3) His people's salvation. He is (4) a warrior, (5) the Lord, (6) the deliverer, (7) majestic in power, (8) the conqueror

---

[26]Cole said that "these diseases" refers "in the first place to the plagues in general, but in particular to the turning of the water into blood, which made it undrinkable." (Ibid.)

of His enemies, and (9) the controller of nature. God is (10) unique; no other god can be compared with Him. He is (11) majestic in holiness, (12) awesome in praises, (13) a wonder-worker, (14) a guide and (15) a redeemer of His people, and (16) King over all. "The LORD shall reign forever and ever" (15:18).

The Lord Is a "Man of War" (15:3; KJV)

As a "man of war" or "warrior," the Lord fights against His enemies. The song of deliverance proclaims that He always wins the battle; He is always triumphant over His enemies. Let us make sure that we are not His enemies so that He will not destroy us! Put enmity with God behind you; "be reconciled to God" (2 Cor. 5:20).

The Bitter Is Made Sweet (15:23–25)

Christians may face "bitter water"—trying times, temptation, problems, and personal difficulties. God can make our lives "sweet" if we will trust in Him. He may either change the circumstances or change our attitude toward the circumstances. Naomi said that she was no more to be called "Naomi" ("pleasant"), but to be called "Mara" ("bitter") (Ruth 1:20, 21). At the end of the Book of Ruth, however, Naomi was blessed again by God (Ruth 4:14–17). If we trust in God, He will cause all things to work together for good (Rom. 8:28).

The Lord Is Your Healer (15:26)

The Lord heals people physically, even when He does not heal miraculously. Doctors and medicines optimize the conditions for healing, but the Lord does the actual healing. God can also heal in other ways: He can heal our broken hearts and our wounded spirits; He can make us whole emotionally. Above all, the Lord can heal our sick, hell-bound souls of the deadly disease of sin.

Chapter 16

No Food in the Wilderness

Chapter 16 contains the account of the second occasion when the Israelites murmured in the wilderness and the second time that God met their needs. At Marah (15:22–25) they complained because the water was bitter; in the wilderness of Sin (ch. 16), they complained because of a lack of food.

A month after the Israelites left Egypt, they came to the wilderness of Sin; there they grumbled because they did not have enough to eat (16:1, 2). They looked back longingly on their days in Egypt, when they had possessed plenty of food (16:3).

God responded to their complaints by telling Moses that He would provide the people with "bread from heaven" (16:4a). They were to gather this bread every morning, just enough for one day (16:4b), but on the sixth day they were to gather enough for two days (16:5).

Moses and Aaron gathered the people and explained God's plan to them (16:6–8). As Aaron spoke to the people, the glory of the Lord appeared in a cloud. God announced that He was providing the people with meat and bread (16:9–12).

The meat came in the form of quails that covered the camp in the evening (16:13a). The bread was present each morning except for the seventh day. The people called it "manna," a word which means "What is it?" The manna stayed fresh only for a day, except for that which was gathered on the sixth day and lasted for two days (16:13b–26). The Israelites were forbidden to gather food on the seventh day, the Sabbath, for it was proclaimed a holy day and became a day of rest (16:22–30). As God instructed, Moses had Aaron save a pot of manna to be kept "before the Testimony" (16:31–34). The Israelites ate the manna throughout their forty years in the wilderness (16:35, 36).

THE GRUMBLING OF THE ISRAELITES (16:1–3)

[1]Then they set out from Elim, and all the congregation of the sons of Israel came to the wilderness of Sin, which is between Elim and Sinai, on the fifteenth day of the second month after their departure from the land of Egypt. [2]The whole congregation of the sons of Israel grumbled against Moses and Aaron in the wilderness. [3]The sons of Israel said to them, "Would that we had died by the LORD's hand in the land of Egypt, when we sat by the pots of meat, when we ate bread to the full; for you have brought us out into this wilderness to kill this whole assembly with hunger."

Verse 1. After leaving **Elim**, the Israelites **came to the wilderness of Sin**. The exact location of this area is uncertain.[1] Though the Hebrew names are similar, "the wilderness of Sin" is not Mount Sinai. The Israelites arrived there **on the fifteenth day of the second month** after leaving **Egypt**. Assuming that the final plague and the Passover had occurred on the evening of the fourteenth day of the first month (12:2, 6, 12), one month had passed since their departure from Egypt. Much of that time may have been spent at Elim, and they may have made other stops before arriving in the wilderness of Sin (see Num. 33:11–14).

Verse 2. When the Israelites ran out of food, they **grumbled against Moses and Aaron**. The provisions they had brought with them were inadequate for an extended journey. They had animals with them, but they could not afford to eat their breeding livestock. That the **whole congregation** participated in this grumbling is emphasized; apparently, it was not just their leaders who complained, but everyone. They held Moses and Aaron responsible for their lack of food. While hunger is understandable, the

---

[1]W. H. Gispen, *Exodus*, trans. Ed van der Maas, Bible Student's Commentary (Grand Rapids, Mich.: Regency Reference Library, Zondervan Publishing House, 1982), 155.

people's complaints went beyond the boundary of acceptable behavior.

Verse 3. The Israelites again claimed that they would have preferred to remain in **Egypt**, even to die there (see 14:11, 12). They reasoned that, back in Egypt, there had been plenty of food: **"We sat by the pots of meat . . . we ate bread to the full."** On a later occasion, the rabble among the Israelites also complained that they no longer enjoyed the food they had eaten in Egypt: fish, cucumbers, melons, leeks, onions, and garlic (Num. 11:5).

The people's **hunger** apparently blurred their memory of slavery, made them forget their deliverance, and emptied their hearts of gratitude. As a result, they accused Moses and Aaron of leading them into the **wilderness** in order to **kill** them. Despite all of the wonders that God had performed, the people failed to trust that He would provide for their needs.

GOD'S PROMISE OF PROVISION (16:4–8)

4Then the LORD said to Moses, "Behold, I will rain bread
from heaven for you; and the people shall go out and gather a
day's portion every day, that I may test them, whether or not
they will walk in My instruction. 5On the sixth day, when they
prepare what they bring in, it will be twice as much as they
gather daily." 6So Moses and Aaron said to all the sons of Israel,
"At evening you will know that the LORD has brought you out
of the land of Egypt; 7and in the morning you will see the glory
of the LORD, for He hears your grumblings against the LORD;
and what are we, that you grumble against us?" 8Moses said,
"This will happen when the LORD gives you meat to eat in the
evening, and bread to the full in the morning; for the LORD
hears your grumblings which you grumble against Him. And
what are we? Your grumblings are not against us but against
the LORD."

Verses 4, 5. The LORD heard the people's complaints and, rather than punishing them as they probably deserved, He provided for their needs. Peter Enns commented on the absurdity of the charge the people brought against Moses and Aaron and then said, "The only thing more surprising, perhaps, is the response God gives. Rather than punish them, he rains down bread from heaven (v. 4). If any need convincing of the grace of God in the Old Testament, they need only to look here!"[2]

God told **Moses** that He would **rain bread from heaven** on the Israelites. They would then have the responsibility to **gather** this bread for themselves. Each day they were to gather just enough for that **day**, except **on the sixth day** they were to gather enough for two days so that they would not have to do this work on the Sabbath (16:22–26).

God's provision of bread would be a **test** for the people, in that He would see **whether or not they** [would] **walk in** [His] **instruction**. Would they trust the Lord to provide the bread every day, or would they try to gather more than enough for one day? Would they trust Him to provide enough bread on the sixth day to last through the seventh day? Those who failed to follow God's "instruction" showed they did not trust the Lord; they failed the test (16:20, 27). The Hebrew word used for this "instruction" is תּוֹרָה (*torah*), the word for "law." Therefore, this passage brings to mind the Law which would soon be given to Israel at Mount Sinai.

Verses 6–8. Moses and Aaron spoke to the people and told them that **the Lord** had heard their **grumblings**. In the **evening**, they would know that the Lord had **brought** [them] **out of . . . Egypt**, when they received the **meat** He sent their way. **In the morning** they would **see the glory of the Lord.** This prediction may have been fulfilled when they received the food God provided for them,[3] or it may have been fulfilled when the Lord appeared to them "in the cloud" (16:10). The words of Moses and Aaron contain at least a mild rebuke or warning. They made sure that **Israel** knew that the God who brought them out of Egypt had heard their grumblings and that their dissatisfaction was not only against Moses and Aaron, but also against God (16:18).

---

[2]Peter Enns, *Exodus*, The NIV Application Commentary (Grand Rapids, Mich.: Zondervan, 2000), 324.

[3]Wilbur Fields, *Exploring Exodus*, Bible Study Textbook Series (Joplin, Mo.: College Press, 1976), 345.

THE APPEARING OF GOD'S GLORY (16:9–12)

[9]Then Moses said to Aaron, "Say to all the congregation of the sons of Israel, 'Come near before the LORD, for He has heard your grumblings.'" [10]It came about as Aaron spoke to the whole congregation of the sons of Israel, that they looked toward the wilderness, and behold, the glory of the LORD appeared in the cloud. [11]And the LORD spoke to Moses, saying, [12]"I have heard the grumblings of the sons of Israel; speak to them, saying, 'At twilight you shall eat meat, and in the morning you shall be filled with bread; and you shall know that I am the LORD your God.'"

Verses 9, 10. Either at that same gathering or at a later meeting ("in the morning"), **Moses** instructed **Aaron** to tell the people to **come near before the LORD.** As they drew near to Him, **the glory of the LORD appeared in the cloud**, and God Himself spoke.

The appearance of God's glory in a cloud looks both backward and forward. Looking backward, it recalls the fact that the Lord went before Israel in a cloud (13:21, 22; 14:19). Looking forward, it anticipates both God's appearance on Mount Sinai in a "thick cloud" (19:16; 20:21) and His presence in a cloud in the completed tabernacle (40:34–38). God's appearance to the people in Exodus 16 may have been to impress the Israelites with the importance of keeping God's word. It may also have been to confirm Moses' and Aaron's authority in the presence of the people who had complained about them.[4]

Verse 11. Although **the LORD spoke to Moses**, the text makes better sense if it is understood to mean that on this occasion, when "the glory of the LORD appeared," God's words to Moses could be heard by the whole congregation. This interpretation would allow for the following sequence of events: (1) The people murmured (16:2, 3). (2) God spoke to Moses in private, giving instructions about the manna (16:4, 5). (3) Moses and Aaron gath-

---

[4]Gispen, 159. Compare this occasion with the revolt against Moses' authority in Numbers 16 and 17.

ered the congregation and spoke to them (16:6–8). (4) After the congregation had gathered, or at a later meeting, Moses told Aaron to bring the people "near before the LORD" (16:9). (5) At this point, the Lord appeared to the people in a cloud (16:10). (6) In the hearing of the people, God spoke to Moses for the benefit of the people (16:11, 12).

Verse 12. God's message to Moses—and, through Moses, to the people—was that God's provision of food (**meat** and **bread**) for Israel would accomplish the same thing the plagues were intended to accomplish: the people would **know that** [God was] **the LORD** [their] **God**. Again, there may be an implied rebuke in these words. The people should already have "known" God; they should have realized that Yahweh would continue to provide for His people and that their complaint showed a lack of faith.

QUAIL AND MANNA (16:13–21)

13So it came about at evening that the quails came up and
covered the camp, and in the morning there was a layer of dew
around the camp. 14When the layer of dew evaporated, behold,
on the surface of the wilderness there was a fine flake-like
thing, fine as the frost on the ground. 15When the sons of Israel
saw it, they said to one another, "What is it?" For they did not
know what it was. And Moses said to them, "It is the bread
which the LORD has given you to eat. 16This is what the LORD
has commanded, 'Gather of it every man as much as he should
eat; you shall take an omer apiece according to the number of
persons each of you has in his tent.'" 17The sons of Israel did
so, and some gathered much and some little. 18When they mea-
sured it with an omer, he who had gathered much had no excess,
and he who had gathered little had no lack; every man gath-
ered as much as he should eat. 19Moses said to them, "Let no
man leave any of it until morning." 20But they did not listen to
Moses, and some left part of it until morning, and it bred worms
and became foul; and Moses was angry with them. 21They gath-
ered it morning by morning, every man as much as he should
eat; but when the sun grew hot, it would melt.

Verse 13a. After God had told Israel that He would meet their needs by providing them with meat at evening and with bread in the morning, He began to fulfill His promise by sending **quails**. The quails are a relatively minor part of the story. The account uses only half of a verse to tell about them, whereas it uses the rest of the chapter (about twenty-three verses) to relate details about the bread which was called "manna" (16:31). The provision of quails differed from that of the manna. Apparently, the quails were not provided for the Israelites throughout the wilderness wanderings,[5] but the manna continued to appear regularly until the Israelites reached the border of Canaan (16:35).

Commentators sometimes suggest a natural explanation for Israel's feast of quails. Quails in large numbers migrated at this time of year over the Sinai peninsula and would have been easy to catch.[6] However, even if there may have been a natural aspect to this occurrence, the number of quails necessary to feed the Israelite multitude and the significant timing of the event made it obvious that God was responsible for providing the quails for His people.

Verses 13b, 14. After mentioning the quails, the text turns to the bread. The bread is described as **a layer of dew around the camp** which became, after the **dew evaporated, a fine flake-like thing,** as **fine as the frost**. Later it is described as being "like coriander seed, white, and its taste was like wafers with honey" (16:31). This substance could be baked (16:23). Numbers 11:7, 8 adds this information:

> The manna was like coriander seed, and its appearance like that of bdellium. The people would . . . grind it between two millstones or beat it in the mortar, and boil it in the pot and make cakes with it; and its taste was as the taste of cakes baked with oil.

If it was gathered but not eaten or used that day, it "bred worms

---

[5]Another occasion, about a year later, on which God provided quails is described in Numbers 11:4–6, 18–23, 31–35.

[6]Fields, 346–47.

and became foul" (16:20). If it was not gathered before "the sun grew hot, it would melt" (16:21). In Psalm 78:24, 25, it is spoken of as "food from heaven" and "the bread of angels." In Psalm 105:40 it is called "the bread of heaven" (see Neh. 9:15).

Verse 15. The manna was obviously something which the Israelites had not seen before: When they **saw it**, they asked each other, **"What is it?"** (מָן הוּא, *man hu'*). Consequently, they named it "manna" (מָן, *man*), which means "What [is it]?"[7] (The English spelling is a transliteration of the Greek word μάννα [*manna*].) R. Alan Cole explained the word as meaning "the what's-its-name."[8] Moses told the people it was **the bread which the LORD** had provided for them.

Scholars have sought a natural explanation for the manna, either in a substance produced by insects that can be found on tamarisk trees or in a kind of moss or lichen that grows on rocks in the Sinai peninsula.[9] However, even if any naturally occurring substance had anything to do with the manna of which the Bible speaks, it was provided by God for His people. Consider the following: (1) the amount which had to be produced to feed the Israelites, (2) the consistency with which it had to be produced (six days a week for fifty-two weeks a year, for forty years), (3) the fact that it was available every day except the Sabbath, and (4) the fact that it stopped when Israel arrived in the promised land. The production of manna was clearly a supernatural phenomenon, rather than a purely natural one.[10]

---

[7]Considerable scholarly discussion has been devoted to the origin and meaning of the name "manna," as in John J. Davis, *Moses and the Gods of Egypt: Studies in Exodus*, 2d ed. (Grand Rapids, Mich.: Baker Book House, 1986), 189–90, and Brent A. Strawn, "Manna," in *Dictionary of the Old Testament: Pentateuch*, ed. T. Desmond Alexander and David W. Baker (Downers Grove, Ill.: InterVarsity Press, 2003), 560.

[8]R. Alan Cole, *Exodus: An Introduction and Commentary*, Tyndale Old Testament Commentaries (Downers Grove, Ill.: Inter-Varsity Press, 1973), 131.

[9]These substances are described in F. S. Bodenheimer, "The Manna of Sinai," *The Biblical Archaeologist* 10 (February 1947): 2–6, and Nahum M. Sarna, *Exploring Exodus: The Origins of Biblical Israel* (New York: Schocken Books, 1996), 117–18.

[10]Arguments against a "natural" explanation are given in Gispen, 156–57, and Davis, 191–93.

Verse 16. Besides describing the manna, this section provides three rules related to its gathering and consumption. The first rule concerned how much was to be gathered. The people were told to **gather** as much as they needed for one day—**an omer** for each person, which equals about $1^2/_3$ liters, or two quarts.[11]

Verses 17, 18. The Israelites obeyed, although **some gathered** more than the amount specified and some gathered less. This was "not from disobedience but rather because they had, of necessity, to estimate how much they gathered."[12] Nevertheless, the result was that all had exactly enough. The text emphasizes that the total amount of manna provided by the Lord was exactly the right amount for the number of people in the camp. W. H. Gispen said, "The miracle was that when they measured it by the omer there was exactly enough for each person."[13]

Verses 19, 20. A second rule concerned how they were to eat the manna: All that they gathered in the morning of one day, they were to eat before the **morning** of the next day. **Some** of the people broke this rule, perhaps wanting to put some aside and save it in case the manna was not there the next day. When this happened, the manna spoiled, and **Moses** became **angry** with those who had disobeyed God's instruction.

Verse 21. The third rule required a daily harvesting of the manna. The people gathered the manna each **morning**. If they failed to collect their food before **the sun grew hot**, it dissolved. Therefore, if they were lazy and decided that it was too much trouble to get up early to get the manna, they went hungry (see Prov. 6:9–11).

Obviously, by the provision of the manna and the giving of these rules, God intended not only to meet Israel's needs, but also to teach His people several lessons. They needed to learn (1) to depend on and trust in God (see Deut. 8:3), (2) to obey Him for the good of the nation and each individual, and (3) to appreciate the value of regular, diligent work.

---

[11]John I. Durham, *Exodus*, Word Biblical Commentary, vol. 3 (Waco, Tex.: Word Books, 1987), 225.

[12]Gispen, 161.

[13]Ibid. Paul used this passage in 2 Corinthians 8:14, 15.

RESTING ON THE SABBATH (16:22–30)

[22]Now on the sixth day they gathered twice as much bread, two omers for each one. When all the leaders of the congregation came and told Moses, [23]then he said to them, "This is what the LORD meant: Tomorrow is a sabbath observance, a holy sabbath to the LORD. Bake what you will bake and boil what you will boil, and all that is left over put aside to be kept until morning." [24]So they put it aside until morning, as Moses had ordered, and it did not become foul nor was there any worm in it. [25]Moses said, "Eat it today, for today is a sabbath to the LORD; today you will not find it in the field. [26]Six days you shall gather it, but on the seventh day, the sabbath, there will be none."

[27]It came about on the seventh day that some of the people went out to gather, but they found none. [28]Then the LORD said to Moses, "How long do you refuse to keep My commandments and My instructions? [29]See, the LORD has given you the sabbath; therefore He gives you bread for two days on the sixth day. Remain every man in his place; let no man go out of his place on the seventh day." [30]So the people rested on the seventh day.

Verse 22a. Another rule regarding the manna overshadowed the others: the Sabbath rule. **On the sixth day** [the people] **gathered twice as much bread, two omers for each** [person]. On that day alone, they not only ate the manna provided for the day but also put aside manna for the next day. The Lord made these arrangements possible by preventing the manna from spoiling when it was gathered on the sixth day and kept overnight.[14] Moreover, He provided no manna on the seventh day, so that no one would be tempted to break the Sabbath law.

---

[14]Some commentators suggest that the manna was preserved by baking or boiling it (16:23). While the Israelites were told to do this on the sixth day in preparation for the seventh, the cooking of the manna was not key to its preservation. If it had been, then the Israelites could have preserved it any day of the week. The preservation of the manna was something God did miraculously.

Verses 22b, 23. The leaders of the congregation went to **Moses** and reported that the people were gathering twice as much bread as they previously had done. John I. Durham suggested that these men were alarmed that the people were exceeding the one-omer limit. In response, Moses reassured them that gathering double the amount of manna on the sixth day was according to God's will.[15]

The Sabbath is mentioned here for the first time in the Scriptures, although a hint of it is seen in verse 5. It is called **a sabbath observance, a holy sabbath to the Lord**, "a sabbath to the Lord" (16:25), and "the seventh day, the sabbath" (16:26). The term "Sabbath" (שַׁבָּת, *shabbath*) is related to the verb שָׁבַת (*shabath*), which means "cease" or "rest"; the Sabbath became a day of rest for the Israelites. In preparation for the seventh day, the Israelites were commanded to **bake** or **boil** their food on the sixth day and keep it overnight.

Some people believe that the Sabbath day is a continuing ordinance, in effect from the days of Genesis to the present time. Although its pattern was based on creation (20:11; Gen. 2:3), the Old Testament contains no example of anyone keeping the Sabbath before Exodus 16. In this chapter, its observance serves as a foreshadowing of the Sabbath commandment given as part of the Ten Commandments in Exodus 20:8–11, just as the preliminary statement of the covenant in Exodus 15:25b, 26 serves as a precursor to the covenant given in Exodus 19. Besides this, the Sabbath observance was instituted in order to help the Israelites remember their deliverance from Egyptian bondage (Deut. 5:15).

Verse 24. The people obeyed **Moses** by preparing their food on the day before the Sabbath and saving it overnight. **They put it aside until morning**, and there were no bad effects: **It did not become foul nor was there any worm in it.** Previously, the food had spoiled when the Israelites had saved it overnight in violation of Moses' command (16:20). However, God did not allow this to happen on the Sabbath, in accordance with His instructions (16:5).

---

[15]Durham, 225.

Verses 25, 26. Moses told the Israelites to **eat** what they had saved overnight. Since that day was **a sabbath to the Lord**, the people would **not find** [any manna] **in the field.** God was not going to supply this miraculous bread on a day that He commanded them to rest. They had **six days** to collect it, but **on the seventh** there would not be any.

Verse 27. As with the rule against leaving any of the manna until morning (16:19, 20), **some of the people** chose to break the Sabbath law concerning its gathering. Whether from greed or a lack of trust in the Lord, these people were unwilling to listen to Moses. Obviously, some of the Israelites did not pass the Lord's test (16:4, 5). They were no doubt surprised when they **went out to gather** manna, but did not find any.

Verse 28. In response to their disobedience, **the Lord said to Moses, "How long do you refuse to keep My commandments and My instructions?"** God directed this question to Moses as the leader of Israel. However, it is important to notice that the Hebrew verb ending translated "you" is plural. For this reason, some versions have "you people" (CEV; NCV) or "these people" (NLT).

Verses 29, 30. The Lord was obviously displeased, but in this case He chose not to punish the wrongdoers. Rather, He strongly rebuked the people for breaking His law and expanded it by telling them, **"Let no man go out of his place on the seventh day."** In other words, they were not to leave the camp to look for manna or for any other reason on the seventh day of the week. He may even have implied that each family was to stay "at home"—in the vicinity of their own tent. Implied in this command was the requirement that the people not work on the Sabbath day. That was, in fact, the way Israel understood God's law, so they **rested on the seventh day**.

What was implicit in the law regarding the manna became explicit in the Ten Commandments, which were given to Israel about a month later.[16] God commanded the people to "remem-

---

[16]The command in Exodus 20:10 expands upon the manna requirement because it does not merely say, "You shall not gather manna on the sabbath"; rather, it states, "You shall not do any work."

ber the sabbath day, to keep it holy" (20:8). He added specifically how they were to make the day holy, or to set it apart from the other days: "The seventh day is a sabbath of the LORD your God; in it you shall not do any work" (20:10).

MANNA PRESERVED (16:31–36)

**31The house of Israel named it manna, and it was like cori-
ander seed, white, and its taste was like wafers with honey.
32Then Moses said, "This is what the LORD has commanded,
'Let an omerful of it be kept throughout your generations, that
they may see the bread that I fed you in the wilderness, when
I brought you out of the land of Egypt.'" 33Moses said to Aaron,
"Take a jar and put an omerful of manna in it, and place it
before the LORD to be kept throughout your generations." 34As
the LORD commanded Moses, so Aaron placed it before the Tes-
timony, to be kept. 35The sons of Israel ate the manna forty
years, until they came to an inhabited land; they ate the manna
until they came to the border of the land of Canaan. 36(Now an
omer is a tenth of an ephah.)**

Verse 31. The text informs the reader that the Israelites called this bread from heaven **manna** (see comments on 16:15). It also gives a description: **it was like coriander seed, white, and its taste was like wafers with honey** (see comments on 16:13b, 14). "Coriander" was an annual herb known for its pleasant aroma, and its seeds were used as a condiment.

Verse 32. From this point, the text speaks of events which happened considerably later than those previously described. It relates what **the LORD** told **Moses** to do after the tabernacle was completed, more than a year later. God instructed His servant to save an **omerful** of manna to remind future **generations** of how He miraculously provided food for Israel during their years in the **wilderness**.

Verses 33, 34. Moses told Aaron that the **jar** of manna was to be placed **before the LORD**. Aaron consequently placed it **before the Testimony**. "The Testimony" is a reference to the tablets of the Law (31:18; 32:15; 34:29) which were placed in the "ark of the covenant" in the inner compartment of the tabernacle. The ark was also known as "the ark of the testimony" (25:22; 26:33) due to the tablets it held (25:16). The jar of manna was placed in the ark after the tabernacle was built. Hebrews 9:4 specifies that the jar was made from gold, and that it was kept inside the ark with the tablets of the covenant and Aaron's staff that budded.

Verse 35. The account skips ahead in time, speaking of what happened with regard to **the manna** over the next **forty years. The sons of Israel** ate this bread throughout their forty years in the wilderness, **until they came to the border of the land of Canaan**. These details all indicate that the author saw the events from a later date. However, since this verse does not speak of the manna's ceasing, the passage could still have been written by Moses.[17] The manna did not cease until Israel had actually entered Canaan (Josh. 5:12).

This verse was written in poetic style, as its lines form an ABAB pattern:

A1: "The sons of Israel ate the manna forty years,"
  B1: "until they came to an inhabited land;"
A2: "they ate the manna"
  B2: "until they came to the border of the land of Canaan."

Verse 36. The discussion of the manna concludes by specifying that an **omer** was **a tenth of an ephah.**[18] The term "omer," only occurs in this chapter of the Bible (16:16, 18, 32, 33, 36). This unfamiliar word may have referred to a small cup or bowl.

APPLICATION

Lessons from the Manna (Ch. 16)

One of the most significant events in Israel's wilderness experience occurred in Exodus 16. The Israelites ran short of food,

---

[17]Enns believed that the contents of this paragraph indicate that Moses could not have written it. (Enns, 327–28.)

[18]An ephah is equal to "about one-half bushel." (Durham, 227.)

and God provided manna. The story presents several lessons for us to learn.

(1) *Remember God's Blessings* (16:1–3). The people "grumbled" (16:2); the KJV says that they "murmured," and the NRSV has "complained." They grumbled eight times in this context (16:2, 7, 8, 9, 12)! This was neither the first nor the last time that God's people complained; they were, in fact, constantly complaining. They had a genuine need, but it was wrong for them to complain. Why did they complain? They were forgetful, ungrateful, and lacking in faith. They forgot that they had been in bondage and had cried out to God. (Egypt had not seemed so attractive back then!) They were ungrateful for what God had already done for them. They also lacked faith: They failed to appreciate the fact that a God who was able to split the sea so that they could walk through on dry ground could also provide them with food in a barren wilderness. They grumbled against Moses and Aaron, but their complaint was really against God (16:7, 8).

Let us learn to complain less. Paul said about this same group of people, though regarding a different occasion, "Nor [let us] grumble, as some of them did, and were destroyed by the destroyer" (1 Cor. 10:10). Philippians 2:14 says, "Do all things without grumbling or disputing." Sometimes, when I ask someone how he is, he will answer, "I can't complain." I occasionally respond jokingly, "I can." A person can always find something to complain about if he wants to. The question is, Does he choose to complain, or will his memory of what God has done, his gratitude for what God has done, and his faith in God keep him from complaining?

(2) *Trust God's Provisions* (16:4–16). God met Israel's need. He provided manna in the morning and meat (quails) at night. He helped Israel, in spite of the fact that these complaining, faithless, forgetful, ungrateful people did not deserve to be helped. One reason He provided the manna was to help Israel learn that "man does not live by bread alone . . . but by everything that proceeds out of the mouth of the LORD" (Deut. 8:3).

Let us learn that God graciously meets our needs, even when we do not deserve His blessings. Although we cannot claim that we deserve His favors, God meets our needs for food, clothing, and shelter. He continues to bless us in many ways, even when we are forgetful, ungrateful, and faithless. Why? It is His nature to be compassionate, gracious, and loving (34:6; 1 Jn. 4:8).

Especially, we must understand that God meets our greatest need—our need for spiritual food and life—through Jesus Christ, the Bread of Life. Jesus claimed to be the true "bread out of heaven," which gives eternal life. That is something the manna in the wilderness could not do (Jn. 6:31–35).

(3) *Obey God's Commands* (16:16–36). Though God provided the manna, the people had to take advantage of God's gracious provision. They had to gather the manna according to His command in order to have food for each day.

God gave specific commands regarding how the manna was to be gathered. The Israelites were to gather a certain amount each day, twice as much on the sixth day, and nothing on the seventh day. The Sabbath day was to be a day of rest. This instruction tested their industry, their faith, and their loyalty. Would they perform this daily task? Would they trust God to give enough on the sixth day to sustain them on the seventh day? Would they obey God exactly? Some did not. Those who did not follow God's directions were not blessed.

Let us learn that we also must take action to receive God's gift. God provides our food, for instance, but that does not relieve us of the responsibility of working to earn a living. When Jesus, the Bread of Life, walked the hills of Palestine, those who wanted to be blessed by Him, to partake of the Bread of Life, had to go out wherever He was. They had to believe in Him and follow Him. Today, if we would receive the Bread of Life into our lives, we also must do something. We must "receive Christ as our Savior" the way people did in Acts 2: by believing in Him, repenting of our sins, and being baptized into Christ for the forgiveness of sins.

If we are to be blessed by God's provisions, we must follow God's directions. In Old Testament times, it was never acceptable to disobey God's laws deliberately. We must understand that God still requires us to obey Him today (Mt. 7:21; Heb. 5:8, 9). To fail to obey God is to deny ourselves His blessings and to invite His punishment.

What was written in earlier times was written for our instruction (Rom. 15:4). Let us learn from the account of the manna. (1) We should not complain and show ingratitude and a lack of faith. (2) Even though we do not deserve it, God provides for us and meets our needs—especially our need for salvation through Jesus Christ. (3) We must do something to take advantage of God's provision of salvation. (4) It is important for us to obey God's commands unquestioningly and completely.

Israel's "Bread from Heaven"—
And Ours (16:4, 15; Jn. 6)

God called manna "bread from heaven" (16:4). The Lord gave the people this bread to eat. In New Testament times, the Jews regarded the manna as "bread out of heaven" given by God (Jn. 6:31). Jesus said that He was the "true bread out of heaven" (Jn. 6:32). Our Bread of Life (Jn. 6:35) is like manna in that (1) He came from God, just as the manna was given by God. (2) He meets humanity's needs, just as the manna met the Israelites' needs. However, Jesus differs from the manna because those who come to Him will never hunger again (Jn. 6:35). Those who ate of the manna died, but those who partake of "the bread which comes down out of heaven" will live forever (Jn. 6:47–51).

"Our Daily Bread" (16:16–21; Mt. 6:11)

God's provision of manna may help us to understand what Jesus meant when He said we should pray, "Give us this day our *daily* bread" (Mt. 6:11; emphasis added). The people had to depend on God daily for their food; trying to store manna for the future did not work. Even so, we should do our work each day, believing that God will provide for us. We need to depend on God to take care of our tomorrows (Mt. 6:34).

The Need to Work (16:16)

The Lord's requirement that the Israelites gather the manna daily illustrates the fact that God expects His people to work, regularly and industriously, to make a living (Eph. 4:28). God gives us every good gift (Jas. 1:17), including our daily bread; but we still have to work for it.

CHAPTER 17

MORE CRISES IN THE WILDERNESS

Two more crises confronted the Israelites as they traveled toward Mount Sinai. In chapter 17 they found themselves without water and being attacked by the Amalekites.

The Israelites continued their journey until they arrived at Rephidim. There they found no water. As before, they complained, accusing Moses of bringing them into the wilderness to kill them of thirst (17:1–3). Moses, in turn, cried out to the Lord, asking what he should do and protesting that the people were almost ready to stone him (17:4). God instructed him to pass before the people and, using the same rod he had used in Egypt, to strike the rock at Horeb so that water would "come out of it" (17:5, 6). Moses followed God's orders, and water flowed from the rock. Moses renamed the place Massah and Meribah to reflect the people's quarrelsome attitude (17:7).

Another crisis occurred when the Amalekites fought against Israel at Rephidim (17:8). Moses put Joshua in charge of the Israelite forces. Then, accompanied by Aaron and Hur, Moses went to the top of a hill overlooking the battlefield (17:9, 10). When he held up his hands, the battle favored Israel; when he became tired and lowered his hands, Amalek prevailed (17:11, 12a). So Aaron and Hur provided him with a stone to sit on and held up his hands for him (17:12b), and Israel won the battle (17:13).

God decreed that Israel would be at war with Amalek continually and instructed Moses to write that fact in a book; Israel was told that God would blot out the memory of Amalek altogether (17:14). Moses erected an altar in memory of Israel's victory (17:15, 16).

AT REPHIDIM, WATER FROM A ROCK (17:1–7)

[1]Then all the congregation of the sons of Israel journeyed by stages from the wilderness of Sin, according to the command of the LORD, and camped at Rephidim, and there was no water for the people to drink. [2]Therefore the people quarreled with Moses and said, "Give us water that we may drink." And Moses said to them, "Why do you quarrel with me? Why do you test the LORD?" [3]But the people thirsted there for water; and they grumbled against Moses and said, "Why, now, have you brought us up from Egypt, to kill us and our children and our livestock with thirst?" [4]So Moses cried out to the LORD, saying, "What shall I do to this people? A little more and they will stone me." [5]Then the LORD said to Moses, "Pass before the people and take with you some of the elders of Israel; and take in your hand your staff with which you struck the Nile, and go. [6]Behold, I will stand before you there on the rock at Horeb; and you shall strike the rock, and water will come out of it, that the people may drink." And Moses did so in the sight of the elders of Israel. [7]He named the place Massah and Meribah because of the quarrel of the sons of Israel, and because they tested the LORD, saying, "Is the LORD among us, or not?"

Verse 1. The journey from Egypt to Sinai was accomplished in **stages**, as the Israelites camped in different places. Having left **the wilderness of Sin**, where God had met their need for food, the Israelites moved on to **Rephidim**. Apparently, Rephidim was not far from Mount Sinai, since it was near "Horeb" (17:6). Horeb and Sinai are used interchangeably to refer to the mountain where Israel received the Law. Commentators do not agree on the location of Rephidim.[1]

---

[1]Possible locations of Rephidim are discussed in S. R. Driver, *The Book of Exodus*, The Cambridge Bible for Schools and Colleges (Cambridge: University Press, 1953), 155–56; R. Alan Cole, *Exodus: An Introduction and Commentary*, Tyndale Old Testament Commentaries (Downers Grove, Ill.: Inter-Varsity Press, 1973), 133–34; and Ronald F. Youngblood, *Exodus*, Everyman's Bible Commentary (Chicago: Moody Bible Institute, 1983), 85.

At Rephidim the Israelites found **no water**. The place may have disappointed the people because it had the appearance of an oasis, but when they arrived they discovered that all the wells were dry.

Verses 2, 3. If Rephidim did not provide what it seemed to promise, the Israelites' frustration, anger, and fear are more understandable, although still inexcusable. They responded to this crisis as they had to all the others. For the fourth time since leaving their homes in Egypt, they **quarreled with Moses**.[2]

Moses first tried to reason with the people, urging them, in effect, to change their behavior. They were not only protesting against Moses, but they were also **test**[ing] **the Lord**—a dangerous thing to do.

The people could not be dissuaded. **They grumbled against Moses**, accusing him again—as they had before (16:3)—of delivering them **from Egypt** and bringing them into the wilderness just to **kill** them.

Verse 4. Moses, who was apparently more concerned about this latest protest than he had been about the earlier complaints, took the matter to God. He **cried out to the Lord**, asking **what** he should do. Moses thought the **people** were so upset that they were about to **stone** him.

Verse 5. The Lord responded with a plan to show that it was He who gave the people water to drink. Everything about the occasion was designed to make that message clear. **Moses** was to **pass before the people** with **some of the elders of Israel**. In other words, the bringing forth of the water was to be a solemn public occasion; no one could miss its importance. The miracle was not to be done in secret; there were to be reliable eyewitnesses (the elders) to report what had happened.

For this ceremony, Moses was to **take in** [his] **hand** the **staff** which he had used in Egypt to perform wonders. By touching

---

[2]While still in Egypt, they complained to Moses when the Egyptians refused to allow them to leave and instead increased their burdens (5:21). After leaving Egypt, they complained when they were trapped between Pharaoh's army and the sea (14:11, 12). They complained because of the bitter water at Marah (15:23, 24) and because there was no food in the wilderness of Sin (16:2, 3). They said almost the same thing every time they complained.

the Nile with this staff, he had begun the first plague, turning the water to blood (7:17, 20). The rod had been the means by which God had done mighty works, and the people who saw Moses with it could expect God to work further wonders.

Verse 6. The Lord also told Moses that He would **stand before** [him] **there on the rock at Horeb**. In some sense, the Lord Himself was there when the rock was split. It may be that the cloud of His presence that hovered over the camp in the daytime had on this occasion moved to the rock.[3] However God made His presence known, the people were aware that Yahweh was there; Moses was not producing water on his own.

The mention of "Horeb" at this point is problematic because 19:2 indicates that the Israelites had to leave Rephidim in order to travel to Mount Sinai. Probably, the best way to reconcile the two accounts is to assume that Horeb refers to a range of mountains. Israel may have arrived there but still had some distance to travel to arrive at the specific place where they would receive the Law.

The Lord directed Moses to **strike the rock**, promising him that **water** would come forth for **the people** to **drink**. The text says nothing about drilling for the water or finding a hidden spring. The manner in which the water was produced made it obvious to the Israelites that their thirst was being quenched by God Himself. Afterwards, they would know that they had not been fooled by a magician's trick; they had observed another mighty work of God. Wilbur Fields suggested that the rock may have been some distance away, perhaps even miles from the camp. He cited Psalm 78:15, 16: ". . . He brought forth streams also out of the rock, and caused waters to run down like rivers."[4] Paul referred to this incident in 1 Corinthians 10:4, where he said that Christ was the rock which produced the waters.

The story concludes with these encouraging words: **And Moses did so.** At least one of the Israelites was obedient to the

---

[3]Walter C. Kaiser, Jr., "Exodus," in *The Expositor's Bible Commentary*, vol. 2, *Genesis—Numbers* (Grand Rapids, Mich.: Zondervan, 1990), 407.

[4]Wilbur Fields, *Exploring Exodus*, Bible Study Textbook Series (Joplin, Mo.: College Press, 1976), 365.

Lord. Moses struck the rock, water came forth, the people drank, and **the elders** were eyewitnesses to all that had happened.

Verse 7. The text includes a postscript: Moses **named** the place **Massah** (meaning "test") and **Meribah** (meaning "quarrel") because of Israel's experience there. **Israel** had **quarrel**[ed] and **tested the Lord** at this place. The people had doubted the Lord's presence and power among them. Whether or not anyone had verbally said, **"Is the Lord among us?"** their complaining about the lack of water demonstrated their doubt. If they had trusted the Lord, they would not have questioned that He would provide for their needs. To doubt and question the Lord is to "test" Him.

The fact that the place was named "Massah and Meribah" has generated much discussion.[5] After a similar incident in Kadesh toward the end of the wilderness wanderings, the text mentions "the waters of Meribah" (Num. 20:13). Most liberal commentators suggest that the two narratives in Exodus 17 and Numbers 20 are separate accounts of the same incident.[6] If not, why would the places be given the same name? In response to this manner of reasoning, R. Alan Cole wrote, "Of course, if the same event happened twice, there is no reason why the same name should not be used twice."[7]

If the biblical narratives are accepted as they are written, then one must conclude that the two stories are dealing with separate events. The details are very different, making the possibility that they are two accounts of the same incident impossible. They happened at different places and at different times. In addition, the results were different, for God was displeased with Moses after the second incident. The stories are remembered in the rest of Scripture as distinct accounts.[8]

---

[5]See Cole, 133–34.

[6]For example, see Martin Noth, *Exodus*, trans. J. S. Bowden, The Old Testament Library (Philadelphia: Westminster Press, 1962), 140.

[7]Cole, 134.

[8]The first miracle of striking the rock and bringing forth water is typically referred to in more general language (Deut. 8:15; 33:8; Ps. 78:15, 16, 20; 95:8; 105:41; 114:8; Is. 48:21). The event in Numbers is usually referenced with more detail (Num. 20:24; 27:14; Deut. 32:51; 33:8; Ps. 106:32).

AT REPHIDIM, VICTORY OVER AMALEK (17:8–16)

The Victory Given (17:8–13)

[8]Then Amalek came and fought against Israel at Rephidim.
[9]So Moses said to Joshua, "Choose men for us and go out, fight against Amalek. Tomorrow I will station myself on the top of the hill with the staff of God in my hand." [10]Joshua did as
Moses told him, and fought against Amalek; and Moses, Aaron, and Hur went up to the top of the hill. [11]So it came about when
Moses held his hand up, that Israel prevailed, and when he let his hand down, Amalek prevailed. [12]But Moses' hands were
heavy. Then they took a stone and put it under him, and he sat on it; and Aaron and Hur supported his hands, one on one side and one on the other. Thus his hands were steady until the sun set. [13]So Joshua overwhelmed Amalek and his people with the
edge of the sword.

Verse 8. This time, the Israelites faced a man-made problem. **Amalek**, a people who dwelt in the wilderness of Sinai and in the southern part of Canaan, **came and fought against Israel at Rephidim**. Perhaps they viewed Israel as a threat to their territory and livelihood, as did the Edomites at a later time (see Num. 20:14–21).[9] However, Amalek's attack is not described as an attempt to defend their own territory, but as an attempt to plunder Israel. Therefore, God declared that Israel was to "blot out the memory of Amalek." Deuteronomy 25:17–19 says,

> Remember what Amalek did to you along the way when you came out from Egypt, how he met you along the way and attacked among you all the stragglers at your rear when you were faint and weary; and he did not fear God. Therefore it shall come about when the LORD your God has given you rest from all your surrounding

---

[9]Driver, 158.

> enemies, in the land which the LORD your God gives you as an inheritance to possess, you shall blot out the memory of Amalek from under heaven: you must not forget.

Verse 9. Moses put **Joshua** in charge of mustering a military force from among the Israelites to fight against the Amalekites. Joshua is mentioned here in the narrative for the first time, without explanation or further identification. Obviously, Moses believed that his readers would already be familiar with him. Joshua was Moses' young assistant (24:13; 33:11; Num. 11:28) who later took Moses' place as the leader of Israel (Deut. 31:3, 7, 23; 34:9). His early experiences in battle in the wilderness prepared him to lead the conquest of Canaan forty years later.

As Joshua fought against the Amalekites, Moses himself would stand on a **hill** overlooking the battle, **with the staff of God in** [his] **hand**. The "staff of God" in the hands of Moses was the tool God had frequently used to accomplish great things. Moses apparently intended not only to watch the battle, but also to encourage the Israelite troops and secure God's help by using this staff.

Verse 10. Joshua went out with his soldiers the next day to fight against the Amalekites. **Moses**, accompanied by **Aaron** and **Hur**, **went up to the top of the hill**. Hur was one of Moses' lieutenants, who, along with Aaron, could be left in charge when Moses was away (24:14). According to one tradition recorded by Josephus, Hur was Miriam's husband—and therefore Moses' brother-in-law.[10]

Verses 11–13. At his place on the hill, **Moses held his hand up**, most likely with the staff in it. When he did, **Israel** had the advantage in the battle. Eventually, **Moses** grew tired and had to lower his **hands**. When he did, Amalek began to win. Therefore, in order to ensure victory for Israel, **Aaron and Hur** provided **a stone** for Moses to sit on and held **his hands** up the entire day, **until the sun set**. The battle ended with an overwhelming victory for **Joshua** and Israel over the Amalekites.

---

[10]Josephus *Antiquities* 3.2.4.

What part did Moses' holding up his hands play in the victory? Nahum M. Sarna suggested three possibilities: (1) Moses' outstretched hands represented prayer or supplication. However, as Sarna said, "We can hardly assume that Moses ceased to pray when his hands flagged." (2) Since, in the ancient Near East, the hand connoted power or strength, Moses' upraised hand mediated "divine power to the Israelite warriors." If this explanation is correct, Sarna said, there is "neither magical ritual nor magical formula involved." (3) A third possibility, which Sarna found persuasive, is the suggestion "that Moses held up an ensign that served to rally the Israelite forces and to bolster morale." Evidence for this possibility may lie in the fact that the altar Moses built to commemorate the event was named "The LORD is My Banner [or Ensign]."[11]

The primary purpose of Moses' holding up his hands was to demonstrate that the victory was won by the power of the Lord, not by the power of Israel's army. The truth that the Lord was the real victor in the battle would have been even more evident if Moses was holding the "staff of God" in his upraised hand. That staff might then have become the "ensign" or "banner" which, when seen by the troops, caused them to rally and fight with even greater determination and confidence.

The Victory Recorded (17:14–16)

[14]Then the LORD said to Moses, "Write this in a book as a memorial and recite it to Joshua, that I will utterly blot out the memory of Amalek from under heaven." [15]Moses built an altar and named it The LORD is My Banner; [16]and he said, "The LORD has sworn; the LORD will have war against Amalek from generation to generation."

Verse 14. In the first mention of writing in the Bible,[12] **the LORD** told **Moses** to record in a book that He would destroy **Amalek**. God's instruction for Moses to **recite** what he had written

---

[11]Nahum M. Sarna, *Exploring Exodus: The Origins of Biblical Israel* (New York: Schocken Books, 1996), 122–23.

[12]Ibid., 123.

to **Joshua** indicates that Joshua was to be his successor.

After this incident, references to the people of Amalek are found only in the context of being Israel's enemies. Two cases are especially prominent. (1) In Numbers 14:39–45, the Israelites had sinned in connection with the report of the twelve spies and were condemned to spend a generation in the wilderness. However, the people were determined to enter the land anyway. When they sought to do so without God's approval or help, they were defeated by the "Amalekites and the Canaanites." (2) In 1 Samuel 15:2 the Lord told Saul through Samuel, "I will punish Amalek for what he did to Israel, how he set himself against him on the way while he was coming up from Egypt." Saul was then instructed to destroy the Amalekites completely, but he failed to do so (1 Sam. 15:3–9).

Verses 15, 16. To commemorate the victory over Amalek, **Moses built an altar and named it The Lord is My Banner**. Israel often erected a monument or an altar or heaped up stones to commemorate great events in the lives of God's people (see Josh. 4:1–7). Apparently on the occasion of the dedication of the altar, Moses repeated what **the Lord** [had] **sworn**: that He would be at **war against Amalek from generation to generation**.

APPLICATION

Testing the Lord (17:2, 7)

When the Israelites "quarreled with Moses" and "grumbled against Moses" (17:2, 3), they were really testing the Lord (17:2, 7). They tested the Lord by showing doubt that He was among them. When we complain and grumble about our situations, are we not testing the Lord? Do we doubt that He is "among us"? Do we act as though He were far away and unconcerned about our problems? Let us not "test" the Lord as the Israelites did!

Holding Up One Another's Hands (17:8–16)

Aaron and Hur held up Moses' hands, and the Israelites won the battle over Amalek. This is a good example for us. Aaron and Hur encouraged the encourager! Similar situations may occur in our lives as Christians. We are in a spiritual battle (Eph. 6:10–

13). We need divine help and encouragement from others to win this battle. Therefore, we should both give encouragement and receive encouragement (Heb. 3:12, 13; 10:19–25).

We ought to put a high priority on assembling to worship together because the assembly is where we receive encouragement. Spiritual danger is all around us. Because discouragement could affect our eternal destinies, assembly time with our fellow Christians is crucial. There is no life in Christ without life in the church.

God encourages us through the Helper (Jn. 14:1–9, 16), the Holy Spirit. "Helper" is from the Greek word παράκλητος (*paraklētos*), which means "advocate, helper, encourager." Let us encourage one another. We can hold up one another's hands as we live from day to day.

Holding Up Moses' Hands (17:12)

Aaron and Hur's holding up Moses' hands has become proverbial for the support that helpers give to great men. A great evangelist speaks eloquently to congregations throughout the brotherhood, but someone else makes it possible for him to do so by scheduling his appointments or arranging transportation for him. A preacher does a great work in a congregation, but others help him by, for instance, doing secretarial work. A writer achieves fame, but others help him with his spelling and grammar. The speaker, preacher, or writer gets the accolades, but his helpers make it possible for him to do his work. If we cannot be great leaders, let us be great at holding up the hands of those who are. If we do, we will ourselves be blessed by God, though our deeds may not be noticed by others.

When God "Holds a Grudge" (17:14–16)

The words of Exodus 17:14–16 imply that the Lord held a grudge against Amalek. His animosity toward that nation would continue until they were altogether destroyed. That sounds strange, especially since God forbids us to hold grudges (Lev. 19:18; Col. 3:13). Let us consider how He dealt with Amalek in Moses' day and what His attitude toward the Amalekites means for those who are like them today.

How did God deal with Amalek? In Exodus 17 Israel had been delivered out of Egypt. They were traveling through the wilderness on their way to Mount Sinai, where they would receive God's law. Along the way they had encountered difficulties which led them to complain, but God had met their needs for water (ch. 15) and for food (ch. 16). Then they came to Rephidim, a place where "there was no water for the people to drink" (17:1). Again, they complained and God responded graciously, this time by giving them water from a rock.

Next comes the setting for our text. Amalek attacked Israel. Moses responded by commissioning Joshua to put together a force to fight against the Amalekites. The next day, Joshua led his men onto the field while Moses, accompanied by Aaron and Hur, took his place on the top of a nearby hill. As the two armies engaged in battle, Moses held up his hand. As long as he held up his hand, Israel prevailed over its enemy. Eventually, however, he tired and had to rest his hand. "When he let his hand down, Amalek prevailed" (17:11). Aaron and Hur brought a stone for him to sit on, and they "supported his hands," holding them up until the sun went down. We read that "Joshua overwhelmed Amalek and his people with the edge of the sword" (17:12, 13). After that, God declared that He would "utterly blot out the memory of Amalek" and that He would "have war against Amalek from generation to generation" (17:14–16).

If we wonder why God would threaten Amalek with constant punishment and ultimate destruction, the question is answered in Deuteronomy 25:17–19, where Moses wrote that Amalek "met you along the way and attacked among you all the stragglers at your rear when you were faint and weary; and he did not fear God" (Deut. 25:18). The Amalekites were not defending their homeland. Like predators of the desert, they were preying on the weakest of God's chosen people, who were as a whole "faint and weary." They deserved the wrath of God!

God continued to be at war with Amalek. Later, after the Amalekites' sin in connection with the evil report of the twelve spies, Israel tried to go up into the promised land on their own, against God's orders. On that occasion they were defeated by "the Amalekites and the Canaanites" (Num. 14:45). However, other passages in the Pentateuch predicted the ultimate destruction of Amalek (Num. 24:20) and required Israel to "blot out the memory of Amalek from under heaven" (Deut. 25:17–19). First Samuel 15 relates that Saul was given the task of completely destroying the Amalekites. Saul did not fully obey God's orders, so David still had to fight against the Amalekites (1 Sam. 27:8; 30). They were eventually destroyed during Hezekiah's reign (1 Chron. 4:41–43).

Why did God deal with Amalek as He did? The history of God's animosity toward Amalek does not answer the question "Why?" Why would God, for hundreds of years, continue to hold against the Amalekites the sin of their forefathers?

We cannot know with certainty why God does what He does. What He does is right because He is God, but we cannot be sure of His reasons unless He reveals those reasons. Still, we can make these observations: (1) God's continuing punishment of Amalek's descendants may illustrate what He meant when He said He would visit the "iniquity of fathers on the children and on the grandchildren to the third and fourth generations" (34:7). (2) The Amalekites' attack on Israel in Exodus 17 may not have been their only sin. As a warlike tribe which preyed on its neighbors, they deserved destruction. (3) To say the least, God's animosity toward Amalek illustrates that God did not take lightly the mistreatment of His people (as other Old Testament Scriptures demonstrate). To attack Israel was to attack God. Those who attacked Israel could therefore expect to be destroyed sooner or later.

Does God hold grudges today? Has He condemned certain nations to ultimate destruction? God no longer has a physical nation which He claims as His own. He determines the destiny of nations and may decide to bring a nation down because of its cruelty. However, if He does, He does not communicate that decision to man. We cannot be sure exactly what He is doing or why He is doing it, but we can be sure that God is working in the world. Because of what He has told us in His Word, we can rely on two truths about destruction by God.

God will destroy those who persecute His people. Revelation teaches that truth plainly, as does 2 Thessalonians 1:6–9. God "holds a grudge" against those who oppose His people. He will destroy the enemies of His people without our help. We, as God's people, the church, do not need to take up arms to destroy the enemies of Christ. God will do it Himself.

God will ultimately destroy unrepentant sinners. God remembers our sins and condemns us because of them. As long as we remain in a sinful state, God "holds a grudge" against us. If He continues to do so, we will ultimately be destroyed in eternal fire.

Wait! There is good news! Through the blood of Christ, we can be forgiven. When we turn to Christ—by believing in Him, repenting of our sins, and being baptized for the forgiveness of sins—God will forgive us. Then we can experience the comfort of Hebrews 8:12: "'For I will be merciful to their iniquities, and I will remember their sins no more.'"

The Value of a Memorial (17:15, 16)

After great occasions, God's people frequently built memorials to help them remember what had happened. God Himself instituted memorials (the Passover and the Lord's Supper) to help His people remember their deliverance. Perhaps as individuals, families, and congregations, we should build "memorials" to great events in our lives. We must not dwell on the past so much that we fail to move forward, but "memorials" can help us to teach younger generations what the Lord has done for us.

Chapter 18

Jethro's Visit with Moses In the Wilderness

After the Israelites arrived at the "mount of God," Jethro, Moses' father-in-law, came to see him, bringing Zipporah, his wife, and their two sons, Gershom and Eliezer. Exodus 18 describes Jethro's visit with Moses (18:1–6).

After Moses and Jethro exchanged greetings (18:7), Moses recounted to his father-in-law how the Lord had delivered Israel from Egypt and from the perils of the journey (18:8). Hearing this, Jethro rejoiced with his son-in-law, praised the Lord, and brought sacrifices to Him (18:9–12).

The next day Jethro observed Moses' sitting all day judging the people, a procedure which wearied both Moses and the people (18:13). That evening Jethro talked with Moses concerning his method of leadership. He urged him to make it his task to intercede with God on behalf of the people and to teach the people the law. However, Jethro suggested that he appoint good men to judge minor disputes, dealing only with major cases himself (18:14–23).

Moses took his father-in-law's advice (18:24–26). Then "Moses bade his father-in-law farewell," and Jethro returned to his own land (18:27).

JETHRO'S COMING TO MOSES (18:1–7)

1Now Jethro, the priest of Midian, Moses' father-in-law, heard of all that God had done for Moses and for Israel His people, how the LORD had brought Israel out of Egypt. 2Jethro, Moses' father-in-law, took Moses' wife Zipporah, after he had

sent her away, [3]and her two sons, of whom one was named Gershom, for Moses said, "I have been a sojourner in a foreign land." [4]The other was named Eliezer, for he said, "The God of my father was my help, and delivered me from the sword of Pharaoh."

[5]Then Jethro, Moses' father-in-law, came with his sons and his wife to Moses in the wilderness where he was camped, at the mount of God. [6]He sent word to Moses, "I, your father-in-law Jethro, am coming to you with your wife and her two sons with her." [7]Then Moses went out to meet his father-in-law, and he bowed down and kissed him; and they asked each other of their welfare and went into the tent.

Verse 1. Moses received a visitor at the "mount of God" (18:5), that is, Horeb or Mount Sinai (3:1; 4:27; 24:13). His **father-in-law, Jethro,** who is elsewhere called Reuel (2:18; 3:1; 4:18), came to visit him. He figured in the narrative earlier in the book when Moses fled from Egypt and found refuge, a wife, and a vocation in his home. As **the priest of Midian**, Jethro may have been a worshiper of Yahweh, the only true God. Jethro came because he had **heard** what **God had done for Moses and for Israel**. God's plan—to cause the nations to "know" Him through His powerful deliverance of Israel—was working.

Verse 2. Jethro brought with him **Moses' wife Zipporah**. The text informs the reader only that Moses had **sent her away**, not when or why he had done so. The word שָׁלַח (*shalach*), translated "sent . . . away," is used for divorce later in the Old Testament. Here it has a neutral meaning, as in 18:27, where it is used in regard to Jethro's departure.[1]

Since Zipporah was last mentioned in 4:24–26, in the "bridegroom of blood" incident, scholars often assume that Moses had sent her and the two sons back to Jethro, her father, from there. Perhaps he understood how dangerous his mission was and wanted to protect his family. Another possibility is that Zippo-

---

[1]R. Alan Cole, *Exodus: An Introduction and Commentary*, Tyndale Old Testament Commentaries (Downers Grove, Ill.: Inter-Varsity Press, 1973), 137, 142.

rah had been in Egypt with Moses and experienced the exodus, but Moses had recently sent her to Jethro in order to report their deliverance.

Verses 3, 4. Jethro and his daughter Zipporah were accompanied by **her two sons**. The first son was named **Gershom**, which means "A stranger there." This name was given because of Moses' statement, **"I have been a sojourner in a foreign land"** (see comments on 2:22). The second son, not previously mentioned in the book, was named **Eliezer**, which means "My God is help." This name was based on Moses' declaration, **"The God of my father was my help, and delivered me from the sword of Pharaoh."**

Verses 5–7. Moses' father-in-law announced his intention to visit by sending a message that was to arrive before he did. When Jethro reached the Israelite camp, bringing Moses' **wife** and two **sons**, Moses was glad to see him and greeted him in the usual way, by bowing and then kissing him. Then Moses invited Jethro into his **tent**.

Perhaps the most intriguing question about this visit and its outcome is "When did it happen?" Its placement in the text suggests that it occurred after the battle with the Amalekites but before the giving of the Law on Mount Sinai. However, commentators frequently assert that the Exodus 18 incident is out of chronological order. Biblical narratives were not always written in strict chronological order. This fact is evident in Exodus in the account of the final plague and the institution of the Passover. Two possible ideas should be considered.

(1) References to God's "statutes" and "laws" suggest that Jethro's visit occurred *after the giving of the Law.*[2] Moses said that his job was to "make known the statutes of God and His laws" (18:16), and Jethro advised Moses to "teach them the statutes and the laws" (18:20). Therefore, it seems that Moses must have re-

---

[2]Nahum M. Sarna asserted that "the parallel account of the establishment of the judiciary given in Deuteronomy Chapter 1 specifies that the reorganization took place at the close of their stay at Horeb, which is Sinai." (Nahum M. Sarna, *Exploring Exodus: The Origins of Biblical Israel* [New York: Schocken Books, 1996], 127.)

ceived the Law already. In favor of this interpretation is the fact that the event happened at the **mount of God** (18:5), or Mount Sinai. Further, the account does not have the characteristics of the "travel stories" which precede it, telling about the journey and the Israelites' arrival in a new place. (Even the story about the making of the covenant in chapter 19 has these characteristics.)

If the reported incident is not in chronological order—that is, if it happened sometime during the year that Israel spent at Sinai while the tabernacle was being constructed—why was it included at this point? The obvious answer is that it served the writer's purpose to include it here rather than putting it later. What that purpose was, it is impossible to know for sure. Perhaps the event was inserted here to provide a further demonstration of how the Lord provided for Israel. He had provided deliverance, guidance (by the cloud and the fire), water, food, and protection (victory over enemies). By relating this incident, the text shows that the Lord also provided organization for His people.

Nahum M. Sarna suggested two possible reasons for placing the narrative out of sequence. First, the account provides "much-needed relaxation of tension" from the frantic pace at which the narrative has been moving. Second, the friendly relations between the Midianites (or Kenites) in the first part of the chapter tie the narrative to—and contrast sharply with—the treacherous behavior of the Amalekites in chapter 17. Likewise, the emphasis on "the statutes and the laws" (18:20) in the latter part of the chapter creates a bridge to the covenant and the Law, which will be introduced in chapter 19.[3]

(2) Jethro's visit could have occurred *before the giving of the Law* on Mount Sinai. If Moses had not yet received the Ten Commandments, then the phrase "the statutes and the laws" may be a reference to laws that had been given by God but had not been written down. James Burton Coffman took this position, affirming that the expression "the statutes and the laws" has "no reference to the Decalogue, which was not yet given, but is a refer-

[3]Ibid., 128–29.

ence to that vast body of rules and regulations that Moses had already communicated to the people upon the commandment of the Lord."[4] In other words, if the incident occurred before Moses received the Law, then he must have been judging the people according to what he knew of God's will at the time. Later, "the statutes and the laws" would be given more fully on Mount Sinai.

Another possibility is that the expression is "proleptic," speaking of what was yet to come as if it already existed. Other examples of this "proleptic" usage may be found earlier in Exodus, where "commandments" and "statutes" (15:26) and "instruction" (*torah,* or "law"; 16:4) are spoken of before the Law was given.

JETHRO'S REJOICING AT GOD'S DELIVERANCE (18:8–12)

8Moses told his father-in-law all that the LORD had done to Pharaoh and to the Egyptians for Israel's sake, all the hardship that had befallen them on the journey, and how the LORD had delivered them. 9Jethro rejoiced over all the goodness which the LORD had done to Israel, in delivering them from the hand of the Egyptians. 10So Jethro said, "Blessed be the LORD who delivered you from the hand of the Egyptians and from the hand of Pharaoh, and who delivered the people from under the hand of the Egyptians. 11Now I know that the LORD is greater than all the gods; indeed, it was proven when they dealt proudly against the people." 12Then Jethro, Moses' father-in-law, took a burnt offering and sacrifices for God, and Aaron came with all the elders of Israel to eat a meal with Moses' father-in-law before God.

Verse 8. Moses told Jethro **all that the LORD had done** for Israel in delivering them out of Egypt, through the Red Sea, and

---

[4]James Burton Coffman, *Commentary on Exodus, The Second Book of Moses* (Abilene, Tex.: ACU Press, 1985), 247. This idea was also supported by Peter Enns, *Exodus,* The NIV Application Commentary (Grand Rapids, Mich.: Zondervan, 2000), 371.

from **all the hardship** along the way. These difficulties would include their lack of food and water, as well as being attacked by the Amalekites.

Verses 9–11a. Jethro was impressed. He repeated what Moses said God had done, using similar words to praise **the LORD** and to proclaim His greatness. He then acknowledged that Yahweh was **greater than all the gods**. John I. Durham said, ". . . implicit in this statement is that Jethro believes, as he *has* believed, that Yahweh is a God among gods. He has believed indeed, that Yahweh is greater than the others. Now he has confirmation that in that belief he was right."[5] Jethro's words do not reflect the monotheism that later characterized the Israelite religion, since monotheism means a belief in one God and the denial of all others. Rather, Jethro's statement may exhibit monolatry or henotheism. Monolatry is the worship of one God who *alone* is worthy of praise, although other gods are thought to exist. Henotheism is the belief in one God, without denying the existence of *others* who may be worthy of praise.

Verse 11b. The second half of verse 11 is more difficult. When the text says that **they dealt proudly against the people**, it is apparently speaking of the gods of the Egyptians, expressing the idea that those gods were arrogant in their dealings with Israel (see NRSV; NIV; CEV). Durham translated, "They have acted rebelliously against them" and said that the Egyptian gods had "acted rebelliously in regard to Yahweh by working against his people Israel."[6] W. H. Gispen said that the intended meaning is "that the Lord is greater than all the gods precisely in those things where the Egyptians were arrogant against the Israelites."[7] The description of the "arrogant" treatment of Israel by Egypt's gods probably is just a way of referring to the mistreatment of Israel by Pharaoh (who was viewed as one of Egypt's gods) and the people who worshiped those gods. According to

---

[5]John I. Durham, *Exodus*, Word Biblical Commentary, vol. 3 (Waco, Tex.: Word Books, 1987), 244.

[6]Ibid., 239, 244.

[7]W. H. Gispen, *Exodus*, trans. Ed van der Maas, Bible Student's Commentary (Grand Rapids, Mich.: Regency Reference Library, Zondervan Publishing House, 1982), 174.

10:3, Pharaoh's sin was that he refused to humble himself before the Lord. In other words, he was prideful or arrogant.

Verse 12. Then Jethro . . . took sacrifices to Yahweh. He gave **a burnt offering**, one in which the entire animal was consumed in the fire. He also made **sacrifices**, presumably the equivalent of what would later be called "peace offerings," in which part of the sacrifice was offered on the altar and the rest was eaten by the worshipers.[8] This offering has raised several questions.

(1) Did Jethro offer the sacrifices himself? The Hebrew word לָקַח (*laqach*), translated "took" (NASB; KJV; NKJV), is ambiguous and would allow, but not require, that possibility. Some versions render the verb as "brought" (NRSV; NIV; REB; NAB), while others translate it as "offered" (NJB; CEV). Jethro could have offered the sacrifices himself, or he could have brought the animals to be sacrificed by someone else, although he himself was present for the ritual and the meal that followed.

(2) If Jethro offered the sacrifices himself, what authorized him to do so? While the Law may not yet have been given to Moses, sacrifices were offered throughout the age before the giving of the Law. Perhaps, as the head of a family, as the priest of Midian, and as an honored guest, Jethro would have had the privilege of offering sacrifices himself if he chose to do so.[9]

(3) Does the offering of these sacrifices conclusively demonstrate that Jethro was a believer in the Lord God alone? No, for it was customary in the ancient Near East to honor gods who were considered powerful, and even to speak of an individual god (while worshiping it) as if it were the only god.[10] Nevertheless, as indicated earlier, Jethro may have been a true believer in Yahweh. Even if he had not been previously, on this occasion—after hearing of all that Yahweh had done for His people Israel—

---

[8]Durham, 245.

[9]Coffman argued forcibly that Jethro was, like Melchizedek, a legitimate priest of the Lord who had every right to offer sacrifices, since the Mosaic Law had not yet been given. (Coffman, 244–46.)

[10]John H. Walton and Victor H. Matthews, *Genesis—Deuteronomy*, The IVP Bible Background Commentary (Downers Grove, Ill.: InterVarsity Press, 1997), 104–5.

perhaps he became a believer in the one true God.[11]

After the offering of the sacrifices, Jethro ate **a meal** with **Aaron** and **all the elders of Israel**. Moses is not mentioned in regard to this meal but must have been present. The sharing of the meal may be significant. The sacrifices, assuming they were the equivalent of peace offerings, almost certainly provided the meat for the meal. Since all the elders were present, and since the elders were "the representative extension of the whole people of Israel,"[12] in a sense "all" of Israel was present.

Furthermore, the meal was eaten **before God**, which suggests that it had a solemn purpose. That purpose may have been to ratify a covenant between the two peoples—Jethro's people and the Israelites—just as a meal later became part of the process of ratifying the covenant God made with Israel (24:11).[13] If this meal sealed a covenant between the two peoples, that would help to explain the good relationship which existed later between the Kenites and Israel (Judg. 4:11–22; 1 Sam. 15:6). The Kenites were apparently the family of the Midianites to which Moses' father-in-law belonged (Judg. 4:11).

JETHRO'S ADVICE TO MOSES (18:13–27)

13It came about the next day that Moses sat to judge the people, and the people stood about Moses from the morning until the evening. 14Now when Moses' father-in-law saw all that he was doing for the people, he said, "What is this thing that you are doing for the people? Why do you alone sit as judge and all the people stand about you from morning until evening?" 15Moses said to his father-in-law, "Because the people come to me to inquire of God. 16When they have a dispute, it comes to me, and I judge between a man and his neighbor and make known the statutes of God and His laws." 17Moses' father-

---

[11]Some believe that on this occasion Jethro became a convert to Yahwism. (Coffman, 245.)

[12]Durham, 245.

[13]Sarna, 128–29. For other examples of covenant meals, see Gen. 26:30; 31:54.

in-law said to him, "The thing that you are doing is not good.
[18]You will surely wear out, both yourself and these people who
are with you, for the task is too heavy for you; you cannot do
it alone. [19]Now listen to me: I will give you counsel, and God
be with you. You be the people's representative before God,
and you bring the disputes to God, [20]then teach them the stat-
utes and the laws, and make known to them the way in which
they are to walk and the work they are to do. [21]Furthermore,
you shall select out of all the people able men who fear God,
men of truth, those who hate dishonest gain; and you shall
place these over them as leaders of thousands, of hundreds, of
fifties and of tens. [22]Let them judge the people at all times; and
let it be that every major dispute they will bring to you, but
every minor dispute they themselves will judge. So it will be
easier for you, and they will bear the burden with you. [23]If you
do this thing and God so commands you, then you will be able
to endure, and all these people also will go to their place in
peace."

[24]So Moses listened to his father-in-law and did all that he
had said. [25]Moses chose able men out of all Israel and made
them heads over the people, leaders of thousands, of hundreds,
of fifties and of tens. [26]They judged the people at all times; the
difficult dispute they would bring to Moses, but every minor
dispute they themselves would judge. [27]Then Moses bade his
father-in-law farewell, and he went his way into his own land.

Verses 13, 14. The **day** after he shared the meal with the elders, Jethro observed Israel's judicial system in operation. **Moses sat to judge the people** single-handedly, hearing cases as **the people stood** and waited for their opportunity to appear before him. Moses' judging "in context means arbitrating legal issues between parties based on the standard of 'God's decrees and laws' (v. 16)."[14] Jethro perceived that the system needed to be improved. His first step toward improvement was to ask Moses **why** he **alone** judged **the people** so that it was necessary for some of them to wait all day to be heard.

---

[14]Enns, 371.

Verses 15, 16. Moses replied, in effect, that he had been chosen as God's representative. Therefore, if **the people** needed to know God's thinking on any matter, they had to come and ask him. To **inquire of God** was to inquire of Moses. If the people had **a dispute** against one another, Moses was equipped to determine who was right. If God had not already revealed the answer to Moses through some prior revelation, Moses would ask God and God would give him an answer. Moses carried out his duties by making known to Israel **the statutes of God and His laws**.

Verses 17, 18. Jethro responded by saying, **"The thing that you are doing is not good."** The system needed improvement because it was difficult for Moses to handle a job that big by himself and because it was difficult for the **people** to wait for hours to have their cases heard.

Verses 19, 20. Consequently, Jethro suggested that Moses be more selective in the role he played. He made two recommendations. First, he said, **"Be the people's representative before God."** In prayer, Moses could bring their problems and **disputes** to the Lord. Second, he said, in effect, "Be God's representative to the people." Moses could **teach them the statutes and the laws, and make known to them the way . . . to walk and the work . . . to do.**

Verse 21. Jethro further recommended that Moses leave the settlement of everyday disputes to others, to men whom he would appoint to be over the people. Apparently, Israel was to have the equivalent of higher and lower courts, since the men appointed would be placed over **thousands**, **hundreds**, **fifties**, and **tens**.

These men were to be qualified for the job. They were to be **able men**, or competent and intelligent men, **who fear**[ed] **God**. Such leaders would never knowingly wrong anyone. As **men of truth**, they would seek God's will when hearing a case. Being men **who hate dishonest gain**, they could not be bribed.

Verses 22, 23. These appointed men were to take Moses' place in hearing most cases, which would be classified as **minor dispute**[s]. When a **major dispute** arose, the case would be brought to Moses for judgment. The system of sharing his burdens with others would make the work easier for Moses, and he would **be able to endure**. In addition, the new arrangement would benefit the **people**, for their cases would be heard in a timely fashion, and so the people would **go to their place in peace**. They would go home feeling satisfied, in contrast to the disgruntled attitude they must have developed when they had to wait for hours to get an audience with Moses.

While the advice came from him, Jethro insisted that Moses should act on his suggestions only if **God** commanded him to do so.[15] Therefore, the institution of this new organization must have had God's approval (see Num. 11:16, 17, 24, 25).

Verses 24–26. To **Moses'** credit, he **listened to his father-in-law and did all that he had said** (18:17–23). He could easily have reasoned: "I am the leader of the Israelites. I have talked with God, and He has revealed His will to me. I brought Israel out of Egypt, and I know what I am doing. Who is this Midianite who thinks he can tell me what to do?" Moses' willingness to accept others' suggestions is evidence of his humility (see Num. 12:3).

A noteworthy feature of this narrative is the affirmation that Israel's judicial system originated from a suggestion by a non-Israelite, the Midianite priest Jethro.[16] No Israelite author would have made up such a story; the only rational explanation for its inclusion in the Pentateuch is that the incident actually happened.

Verse 27. After Jethro had given his advice and it had been accepted, **Moses bade his father-in-law farewell**. Jethro then returned to Midian.

Numbers 10 indicates that, after a year at Sinai when Israel was ready to leave the mountain and travel to Canaan, "Hobab the son of Reuel the Midianite, Moses' father-in-law" was with Israel. Moses invited Hobab, his brother-in-law, to accompany the Israelites on their journey (Num. 10:29). He at first refused and insisted on returning to his own land, but Moses urged him to stay and be "eyes" for Israel since he knew the area. In fact, Moses promised that the Lord would treat Hobab as well as He treated the Israelites (Num. 10:30–32). The text does not say whether or not Hobab accepted Moses' offer, although some

---

[15]Coffman, 249.
[16]Sarna, 127.

Kenites were later living among the Israelites in Canaan (Judg. 1:16; 4:11; 1 Sam. 15:6; 27:10).[17]

Some commentators assume that Numbers 10 and Exodus 18 tell of the same occasion.[18] While that is possible, these could have been different incidents. One possibility is that Jethro returned to Midian earlier and left Hobab with Israel at Sinai, where he stayed until the Israelites were ready to depart for Canaan.

APPLICATION

Jethro: Help in Strange Places (Ch. 18)

Did you ever find help in a strange place, from a surprising source? Perhaps you were in a strange city, lost, wondering what to do next, and someone you never met before stopped to help you. Perhaps you found yourself falsely accused, and it seemed everyone was against you, but then someone whom you considered your enemy stood up for you by telling the truth. In Jethro, Moses found help in a strange place—in Midian, from a non-Israelite.

He gave Moses a home when he had none. When Moses fled from Egypt after killing and burying the Egyptian, he was homeless and alone. By God's providence, Moses helped the daughters of Jethro when they led their flock to the well to water the sheep. Subsequently, Jethro extended to Moses his hospitality. Eventually, he gave Moses his daughter in marriage, shared his home with Moses, gave Moses a job as a shepherd, and seems to have treated Moses as if he were his own son.

He took care of Moses' family when Moses could not. When Jethro visited Moses at Mount Sinai, he brought with him Moses' wife and two sons (18:1–4). Moses had likely sent his wife away sometime after leaving Midian, probably for her own protection. Jethro had looked after Zipporah and the children until they could join Moses.

---

[17]Cole, 142.

[18]Sarna, 128.

He encouraged Moses when his own people may have discouraged him. When Jethro went to Moses, he had already heard what God had done in bringing Israel out of Egypt. He "rejoiced over all the goodness which the LORD had done to Israel" (18:9), blessed the Lord (18:10, 11), and offered sacrifices to God (18:12). By eating a meal "before God" with the leaders of Israel, Jethro bound his people to Israel in a covenant relationship. Jethro's actions must have been very encouraging to Moses, who was burdened with the gigantic task of leading a stubborn people through an inhospitable wilderness.

He offered good advice when Moses needed it. When Jethro observed the legal system which was being used by Moses, he saw some problems and suggested changes. He advised Moses to delegate the job of judging minor matters to other men who were qualified for the job, so that Moses himself could focus on major issues. To Moses' credit, he accepted his father-in-law's advice.

He may have provided Moses a guide during Israel's wilderness wandering. Numbers 10:29–32 relates that Moses offered the job of guide to Hobab, Jethro's son, but it does not say whether or not he accepted the offer.

Conclusion. God worked providentially through Jethro to provide help for Moses when he needed it. Jethro has a place alongside a number of other non-Israelites who were helpful to God's chosen people. Rahab assisted the Israelite spies in Jericho (Josh. 2). Hegai was in charge of the king's harem and favored Esther (Esther 2:8, 9). The "commander of the officials" showed favor and compassion toward Daniel (Dan. 1:9).

God's cause needs helpers. Great men need helpers. You may not be considered "great" by others, but you may be able to help someone who is "great." You may be a Jonathan who helps a David, a Barnabas who encourages a Paul, an Andrew who brings a Peter to Christ, an Aaron or a Hur who holds up the arms of a Moses, or a Jethro who provides the help a leader needs just when he needs it.

We should be aware that help for God's people can come from unusual places. Also, we must realize that we have the responsibility to provide the help others need when we can.

Getting Organized (Ch. 18)

Exodus 18 teaches several principles which can help us to get organized to do the Lord's work in the local church. (1) Moses listened to Jethro and heeded his advice. In the same way, leaders ought to be willing to listen to others and take advice, even if that advice comes from unlikely sources. (2) Jethro and the Israelite leaders apparently made a covenant. Similarly, leaders of the church should be willing to form partnerships with others who can help them accomplish their purposes. (3) Moses was told to concentrate on what he was uniquely qualified to do. In the same way, leaders today ought to spend most of their time and effort using the specific talents God has given them. (4) Moses delegated responsibility for judging minor disputes to others. Likewise, leaders today should learn to delegate. (5) Those to whom Moses delegated responsibility had to be especially qualified. Even so, the people to whom church leaders delegate responsibility today need to be qualified for the work they are called to do. For a New Testament example of some of these same leadership principles, see Acts 6:1–7.

Jethro, a Good Man (Ch. 18)

Several characteristics possessed by Moses' father-in-law are worthy of our imitation today.[19] Jethro did the following:

1. "Kept informed about God and His people" (18:1)
2. "Recognized Moses' just claims to his wife and sons" (18:2–4)
3. Was "courteous" (18:5–8)
4. "Rejoiced in others' blessings" (18:9)
5. "Praised the Lord" (18:10, 11)
6. "Worshipped" (18:12)
7. "Gave good advice" (18:13–22)
8. "Recognized God's final and supreme authority" (18:23).

---

[19]Wilbur Fields, *Exploring Exodus*, Bible Study Textbook Series (Joplin, Mo.: College Press, 1976), 376–77.

The Names of Moses' Sons (18:3, 4)

Moses' two sons were named "Gershom," which refers to being a "stranger," and "Eliezer," which implies "God is my helper." These names well describe Moses' situation in Midian. He was a "stranger" in a strange land, and God had helped him by delivering him out of Pharaoh's hand. Christians, too, are "aliens and strangers" in this world (1 Pet. 2:11). We, too, have been delivered from death by God.

Things That Are "Not Good" But Are Not Sinful (18:17)

When Jethro said, "The thing that you are doing is not good," he did not mean that Moses' approach to leadership was sinful or wrong. However, it was not good because it was inefficient and ineffective. While some things that we do may not be sinful, we may need to admit that they are "not good" in the sense that they do not achieve the desired results. Imagine, for instance, a Christian who decided to obey the Lord's command to "go . . . preach" (Mk. 16:15) and determined to be a missionary, but he decided to walk to another continent rather than flying, sailing, or driving. That means of travel would not be expedient. The New Testament teaches us that we must always be scriptural, but it also teaches us to use the best means possible. Paul said that we ought to be wise—to use effective methods—as we build up the Lord's church (1 Cor. 3:10). He also urged us to use care and speak wisely as we talk to others about the gospel (see Col. 4:5). To use unfruitful methods or to speak without preparation would not be a sin; but it would be ineffective and unfruitful, and therefore "not good."

Part II

The Covenant (19—40)

1. The Institution of the Covenant
   Between the Lord and Israel (19:1—24:18)
2. The Tabernacle for Israel's Worship
   Of the Lord (25:1—40:38)

CHAPTER 19

THE COVENANT BETWEEN GOD AND HIS PEOPLE

The origin of the covenant between God and Israel is recorded in Exodus 19. This covenant was to govern all of God's dealings with His people from that time forward.

Israel arrived in the wilderness of Sinai in the third month after they left Egypt and camped at the foot of Mount Sinai (19:1, 2). Then Moses went up on the mountain. There God recited what He had already done for the Israelites, and He offered to make them His special people if they would obey His words (19:3–6). Moses repeated God's offer to the people, and they agreed to do all that the Lord commanded (19:7, 8).

The Lord said that He would personally speak to the people, so Moses told the Israelites to consecrate themselves for an encounter with the Lord. However, no one was to come near the sacred mountain (19:9–15). On the third day, God made His presence known to the people (19:16–19). Then He instructed Moses to return to the top of the mountain, taking Aaron with him (19:20–25).

ISRAEL'S CALLING FROM GOD (19:1–9)

**1In the third month after the sons of Israel had gone out of
the land of Egypt, on that very day they came into the wilder-
ness of Sinai. 2When they set out from Rephidim, they came
to the wilderness of Sinai and camped in the wilderness; and
there Israel camped in front of the mountain. 3Moses went up
to God, and the LORD called to him from the mountain, saying,
"Thus you shall say to the house of Jacob and tell the sons of**

Israel: [4]"You yourselves have seen what I did to the Egyptians, and how I bore you on eagles' wings, and brought you to Myself. [5]Now then, if you will indeed obey My voice and keep My covenant, then you shall be My own possession among all the peoples, for all the earth is Mine; [6]and you shall be to Me a kingdom of priests and a holy nation.' These are the words that you shall speak to the sons of Israel."

[7]So Moses came and called the elders of the people, and set before them all these words which the LORD had commanded him. [8]All the people answered together and said, "All that the LORD has spoken we will do!" And Moses brought back the words of the people to the LORD. [9]The LORD said to Moses, "Behold, I will come to you in a thick cloud, so that the people may hear when I speak with you and may also believe in you forever." Then Moses told the words of the people to the LORD.

Verses 1, 2. The Israelites arrived at **the wilderness of Sinai** in **the third month** after they left **Egypt, on that very day.**[1] John J. Davis noted that "Jewish tradition placed this event on the first day of the third month of the Jewish year." He added that "similar tradition assigns the giving of the law to the fiftieth day after the Passover but this appears to be of too recent origin to be considered historical."[2]

Umberto Cassuto calculated the days involved in the Sinai revelation as follows:

---

[1]John I. Durham suggested that the phrase "on that very day" means that on the very day that they arrived at the mountain, Moses went up the mountain to meet with God. (John I. Durham, *Exodus*, Word Biblical Commentary, vol. 3 [Waco, Tex.: Word Books, 1987], 261.)

[2]John J. Davis, *Moses and the Gods of Egypt* (Grand Rapids, Mich.: Baker Book House, 1971, 1986), 202, citing Francis D. Nichol, ed., *The Seventh-Day Adventist Bible Commentary* (Washington, D.C.: Review and Herald Publishing Association, 1953), 593, and C. F. Keil and F. Delitzsch, *The Pentateuch*, vol. 2, trans. James Martin, Biblical Commentary on the Old Testament (Grand Rapids, Mich.: Wm. B. Eerdmans Publishing Co., 1949), 89. James Burton Coffman accepted the theory that the giving of the law occurred exactly fifty days after Passover. (James Burton Coffman, *Commentary on Exodus, The Second Book of Moses* [Abilene, Tex.: ACU Press, 1985], 259.)

19:1 "That very day" was the first day of the month.

19:3 "Moses went up to God" early the next day, the second day of the month. On the same day, Moses brought God's words back to the people.

19:8 "Moses brought back the words of the people to the LORD" on the third day of the month. In return, God gave Moses the directions found in 19:9b; then Moses took those directions back to the people.

19:9b "Moses told the words of the people to the LORD" when he gave the people's assent to God's proposal on the next day, the fourth day of the month.

19:10 "Today and tomorrow" refers to the fourth and fifth days of the month.

19:11 "The third day" in this sequence was the sixth day of the month.[3]

Cassuto concluded his reckoning by saying,

> Consequently the day of the Revelation was on the sixth of the month, which marked the end of the seventh week after the exodus of the Israelites from the land of Egypt. The later tradition that links the Festival of Weeks with the Day of the Revelation on Mount Sinai agrees, apparently, with the actual meaning of the text.[4]

The text indicates that Israel's last stop before Sinai was **Rephidim** (17:1, 8). The passage repeats itself; the facts appear three times. Some attribute this phenomenon to the use of different sources. However, this is not unnecessary repetition; each clause overlaps, adding information to the narrative. The relationship of the three clauses can be illustrated as follows:

---

[3]Adapted from Umberto Cassuto, *A Commentary on the Book of Exodus*, trans. Israel Abrahams (Jerusalem: Magnes Press, 1997), 224–29.

[4]Ibid., 229.

Where they were (general area):
19:1b: **. . . they came into the wilderness of Sinai.**

What they did (they camped):
19:2b: **. . . they came to the wilderness of Sinai and camped in the wilderness . . .**

Where they camped (specific area):
19:2c: **. . . there Israel camped in front of the mountain.**

The repetition may have been intended to emphasize Israel's arrival at the mountain—Mount Sinai, the "mount of God"—to which God had promised to bring the people.[5] In the third month after they left Egypt, the Israelites camped at the foot of Mount Sinai.

Verse 3. When the Israelites had camped at the foot of Mount Sinai, **Moses went up to God** for the first time. While Moses stayed on **the mountain**, God told him to give Israel the opportunity to enter into a covenant relationship with Him. Poetic repetition is found in the phrases **say to the house of Jacob** and **tell the sons of Israel**, expressions which share the same meaning.

Verse 4. God began His offer by speaking of what He had done for Israel. He had triumphed over **the Egyptians** by means of the plagues and by destroying their army in the sea. He had carried the Israelites **on eagles' wings** through the wilderness and **brought** them to Himself at Mount Sinai. The metaphor of "eagles' wings" suggests that God carried the Israelites in the same way that a mother eagle carries her young as they learn to fly (see Deut. 32:11). The image illustrates God's tender care and Israel's complete dependence. By bringing Israel to Himself at the mountain, God fulfilled a promise that He had made earlier (3:12).

In beginning the covenant-making process, God announced the basis of the covenant. He was not entering into a covenant

---

[5]Cassuto, concerning another passage, commented, "The triple reference to an important subject (vv. 12–13; 21–22; 24) accords with a common literary practice." (Ibid., 233.)

MOSES' TRIPS UP MOUNT SINAI[1]

Trip 1. God Offered a Covenant (19:3–7). God offered to make a covenant with Israel, and Moses went down and repeated God's offer to Israel.

Trip 2. The People Accepted the Offer (19:8b–15). Moses took Israel's reply to God and received a message that God would come down on the mountain.

Trip 3. God Prepared the People to Receive the Law (19:20–25). God called Moses up to warn him not to let the people come near, and to tell him to come up with a few others; 19:25 says that Moses went down and told the people. In Exodus 20 God gave the Ten Commandments to the assembly at the foot of the mountain. The people heard the voice of God from their place there. Frightened, they asked Moses to speak to them instead.

Trip 4. God Gave the Law in Greater Detail to Moses (20:21—23:33). The statement that Moses "approached the thick cloud where God was" refers to Moses' next trip up the mountain. God gave him the laws in the Book of the Covenant, and Moses gave the people these laws and wrote them down (24:3, 4). Moses went down in 24:3; but before he went down, he received word that he was to go up again and take others with him (24:1, 2).

Trip 5. God Met with the Leaders of Israel (24:9–11). Moses took a group of leaders up on the mountain, and they had a feast to ratify their covenant with God.

Trip 6. God Gave Instructions Regarding the Tabernacle (24:12—31:18). Moses went up to receive "the stone tablets with the law and the commandment" (24:12). He also received the instructions for building the tabernacle. This time he was there for forty days and nights (24:18). When he returned to the Israelite camp, he had tablets of stone with the commandments written by the finger of God (31:18; Deut. 5:22)—but he discovered the people involved in idolatry (ch. 32).

Trip 7. Moses Received the Law a Second Time, as God Renewed the Covenant (ch. 34). Moses went up with two new stone tablets, saw God, and received the Ten Commandments a second time. He stayed forty days and nights (34:28).

---

[1]Scholars have inferred additional trips from 19:9 and 32:31.

relationship with Israel because of Israel's righteousness. In fact, since Israel had left Egypt, the people had frequently proved themselves to be faithless, forgetful, and ungrateful. By grace, God had chosen Israel because of the promises made to the patriarchs, especially the promises made to Abraham. The covenant was based on God's gracious acts on behalf of Israel—on what God had done for Israel, not on what Israel had done or promised to do for God (Deut. 7:6–8; 9:4–6).

Verse 5. After speaking of His own gracious acts as the basis for the covenant, God spelled out the terms of the covenant. Israel's responsibility was to **obey** [God's] **voice** and **keep** [His] **covenant**—two ways of saying the same thing. In turn, God would bless Israel, by making Israel His **own possession among all the peoples** of the world. This passage affirms that, whatever else might be said about the Israelites, they were God's special people in the Old Testament.[6] God had the right to choose Israel because **all the earth** belongs to Him.

The expression "My own possession" (לִי סְגֻלָּה, *li s^egullah*) is also translated "a peculiar treasure unto me" (KJV), "a special treasure to Me" (NKJV), "my treasured possession" (NRSV; NIV), and "my personal possession" (NJB). The phrase appears in other texts which also describe Israel's relationship to God (Deut. 7:6; 14:2; 26:18; Ps. 135:4). The term *s^egullah* itself is associated with such personal treasures as silver and gold (1 Chron. 29:3; Eccles. 2:8). In the present context, the language refers to a prized possession valued above all others. Therefore, the privilege of being God's "very own people" (CEV) implies special blessings, as God looks after and blesses those who belong to Him.

Verse 6. God added to this idea the fact that Israel would be **a kingdom of priests and a holy nation**. "A kingdom of priests" (מַמְלֶכֶת כֹּהֲנִים, *mamleketh koh^anim*) is translated "priestly kingdom" in the NRSV. Walter C. Kaiser, Jr., said that there are, in fact, four

[6]Israel was God's chosen nation during the Mosaic Era. However, under the new covenant, the distinction between Jews and Gentiles has been removed (Gal. 3:26–29; Eph. 2:13–18). Therefore, in this present age, the Jews as a physical people (or Israel as a nation) are no longer God's chosen ones any more than other peoples of the earth.

defensible translations of the Hebrew phrase: "kings, [that is,] priests," "royal priesthood," "priestly kingdom," and "kings (and) priests."[7]

James Burton Coffman asserted that this passage demonstrates "that the Jewish priesthood which the Lord later gave to Israel was *not* the original intention," that God originally intended for every believer to function as a priest.[8] However, the priestly system could not have been an afterthought or an inferior alternative in God's plan. The priestly system initiated shortly after this time was a "shadow of the good things to come" (Heb. 10:1), enabling people in later days to understand more fully God's dealings with man under the new covenant.

In contrast to Coffman's views, most commentators see the phrase as emphasizing the whole nation as a "kingdom of priests," or a priestly kingdom, rather than individuals as priests. R. Alan Cole, for example, wrote, "It is the universal priestly status of Israel to which attention is called."[9] This understanding emphasizes *the kind of nation Israel was to be*. John I. Durham said that the phrase "describes what Israel was always supposed to be: a kingdom run not by politicians depending upon strength and connivance but by priests depending on faith in Yahweh, a servant nation instead of a ruling nation."[10]

A second emphasis is on *what the nation was to do*. As a kingdom of priests, the people had the responsibility to share their knowledge of the Lord with the people of other kingdoms. Kaiser put it well: "The whole nation was to act as mediators of God's grace to the nations of the earth, even as Abraham had been promised that through him and his seed all the nations of the earth would be blessed (Genesis 12:3)."[11] Durham commented that this expression presents Israel as a nation "committed to the

---

[7]Walter C. Kaiser, Jr., "Exodus," in *The Expositor's Bible Commentary*, vol. 2, *Genesis—Numbers* (Grand Rapids, Mich.: Zondervan, 1990), 417.

[8]Coffman believed that the Israelites, because of sin, forfeited the privilege of the priesthood of all believers. (Coffman, 259.)

[9]R. Alan Cole, *Exodus: An Introduction and Commentary*, Tyndale Old Testament Commentaries (Downers Grove, Ill.: Inter-Varsity Press, 1973), 145.

[10]Durham, 263.

[11]Kaiser, 416.

extension throughout the world of the ministry of Yahweh's Presence."[12]

Israel was to be a "holy nation," that is, a nation set apart from other nations for God's special use. "Holy" (קָדוֹשׁ, *qadosh*) can describe that which is inherently sacred (God), as well as that which has become sacred (in this case, Israel). Holiness is derived from God's divine presence, as well as from divine rituals. "Holy" items, places, and persons stand in stark contrast to those that are common or profane. Since holiness originates with God, it involves goodness and purity. What it meant for Israel to be a "holy nation" was explained in more detail later, especially in Leviticus.

Verses 7, 8a. The next step in the covenant-making process was for the people to agree to the Lord's terms. Although Israel did not deserve to be God's covenant people and could not dictate the terms of the covenant, God offered them the opportunity to accept or reject His proposal. **Moses** called together **the elders**, as representatives **of the people**, and presented to them the **words** of **the Lord**. Probably, the people were present too, or else the elders reported to them what Moses had said. The outcome was this: **All the people answered together and said, "All that the Lord has spoken we will do!"**

This agreement then became the covenant upon which God's dealings with Israel were based. From this time forward, as long as the Israelites remained true to their commitment to do "all that the Lord [had] spoken," God blessed them as His people. When they failed to do "all that the Lord [had] spoken," then God was released from His pledge to be their protector and provider.

Later, as God explained the Law in greater detail, it became clear that the people would experience curses from God when they failed to obey Him. Nevertheless, God would not sever His ties with the Israelites when they sinned. The Old Testament, from Exodus 19 on, is the history of how Israel kept—or, more often, failed to keep—its promise to God and of how God blessed or cursed Israel as a result.

---

[12]Durham, 263.

Verse 8b. In this covenant transaction, **Moses** functioned as an intermediary. As God's representative to Israel, he presented God's word to **the people**. Then, as Israel's representative to God, he gave their response to **the Lord**.

Verse 9. The Lord told **Moses** that He would descend on the mountain **in a thick cloud, so that the people may hear when** He spoke with Moses and **believe in** Moses (see 14:31). While **Moses** was on the mountain, God gave the further instructions contained in 19:10–13.

ISRAEL'S CONSECRATION TO GOD (19:10–15)

**10The Lord also said to Moses, "Go to the people and con-
secrate them today and tomorrow, and let them wash their gar-
ments; 11and let them be ready for the third day, for on the third
day the Lord will come down on Mount Sinai in the sight of
all the people. 12You shall set bounds for the people all around,
saying, 'Beware that you do not go up on the mountain or touch
the border of it; whoever touches the mountain shall surely be
put to death. 13No hand shall touch him, but he shall surely be
stoned or shot through; whether beast or man, he shall not live.'
When the ram's horn sounds a long blast, they shall come up
to the mountain." 14So Moses went down from the mountain
to the people and consecrated the people, and they washed
their garments. 15He said to the people, "Be ready for the third
day; do not go near a woman."**

Verses 10–13. After the covenant had been accepted by the people, their acceptance had to be proclaimed publicly. This formal proclamation would spell out the specific requirements of the covenant which the Israelites had already accepted. Such a solemn occasion required the Israelites to **consecrate** themselves for their meeting with **the Lord**. Because the Lord is altogether holy, careful consideration had to be given to any occasion on which He condescended to meet with human beings. Therefore, after **Moses** told God Israel's response to His offer, God gave him instructions as to how the Israelites should consecrate themselves in order to receive the Law.

The Lord said that the consecration of the Israelites was to take two days, and on **the third day** He would appear **in the sight of all the people**. As part of the consecration process, they were to **wash** their clothes. Further, **the people** were to regard **the mountain** as too holy to be **touch**[ed]; they were to **set bounds** around it and not go near it. If, in fact, any person or animal did touch **the mountain**, he was to be killed. Moreover, his sin was, in a sense, contagious. Just as the offender was not supposed to touch the mountain, those who killed him were not to **touch him**. Rather, they had to put him to death either by stoning him or by shooting him with arrows. Only when the **ram's horn** sounded on the third day were the people to **come up to the mountain**. Even then, they were to gather at the foot of the mountain rather than going up on the mountain.

Verses 14, 15. Moses came back down **the mountain** to give these instructions **to the people**, and they did as the Lord had directed. Moses indicated that, as part of their preparation to experience God's presence, they should refrain from sexual relations (**"do not go near a woman"**) until after His appearance. This temporary abstinence was not required because sexual relations are inherently sinful, but rather because they made the people ceremonially unclean (see Lev. 15:18; 1 Sam. 21:4, 5; 2 Sam. 11:6–11).

ISRAEL'S COMING BEFORE GOD (19:16–25)

16So it came about on the third day, when it was morning, that there were thunder and lightning flashes and a thick cloud upon the mountain and a very loud trumpet sound, so that all the people who were in the camp trembled. 17And Moses brought the people out of the camp to meet God, and they stood at the foot of the mountain. 18Now Mount Sinai was all in smoke because the LORD descended upon it in fire; and its smoke ascended like the smoke of a furnace, and the whole mountain quaked violently. 19When the sound of the trumpet grew louder and louder, Moses spoke and God answered him with thunder. 20The LORD came down on Mount Sinai, to the top of the mountain; and the LORD called Moses to the top of the moun-

tain, and Moses went up. [21]Then the LORD spoke to Moses, "Go down, warn the people, so that they do not break through to the LORD to gaze, and many of them perish. [22]Also let the priests who come near to the LORD consecrate themselves, or else the LORD will break out against them." [23]Moses said to the LORD, "The people cannot come up to Mount Sinai, for You warned us, saying, 'Set bounds about the mountain and consecrate it.'" [24]Then the LORD said to him, "Go down and come up again, you and Aaron with you; but do not let the priests and the people break through to come up to the LORD, or He will break forth upon them." [25]So Moses went down to the people and told them.

Verses 16–19. The final paragraph in chapter 19 describes the theophany, the appearance of God to the people, **on the third day**. The Lord's descent upon **the mountain** must have been awe-inspiring. Words are heaped upon words; images follow one another in rapid succession, intensifying the effect of His appearance. The writer was trying to describe what must have been an indescribable sight. The appearance of the Lord involved the following elements:

1. Thunder and lightning
2. A thick cloud upon the mountain
3. A very loud trumpet sound
4. A smoking mountain
5. The descent of the Lord in fire
6. Smoke ascending as from a furnace
7. A localized earthquake, the quaking of the mountain
8. The trumpet sound growing louder and louder
9. The Lord answering Moses with a sound like thunder.[13]

These sense-shattering phenomena got the people's attention and focused that attention on the One with whom they were entering into a covenant. God was not a human king or an unsee-

---

[13]Such manifestations are typical of God's appearances throughout the Bible.

ing idol, but One who used **thunder and lightning** as His servants, who shook the mountain, who appeared in the **cloud** and in the **fire**! The Israelites should have learned that they could not disobey such a God with impunity. God said that His appearance to the people was intended to allow them to hear when He spoke with Moses and to cause them to "believe in [Moses] forever" (19:9). No doubt, these sights and sounds were also meant to motivate them to keep the Law which God would soon give through Moses.

When the people heard and saw the thunder and lightning, the **trumpet sound**, and the cloud signaling God's presence on the mountain, they **trembled**. Nevertheless, Moses brought them **out of the camp to meet God, and they stood at the foot of the mountain.** God then conversed with Moses: **Moses spoke and God answered him with thunder.**

Verses 20–22. Next, **the LORD called Moses** to come up **the mountain** a third time. He told **Moses** to **warn the people** not to come near the mountain under penalty of death. **The priests** were to **consecrate themselves** when they came **near to the LORD**; if they failed to do so, **the LORD** [would] **break out against them.** In other words, God Himself would kill them.

Who were the "priests"? Since the Law had not yet been given, the Aaronic priesthood had not been initiated (see 28:1). Apparently, these priests were those who served before the establishment of the Aaronic priesthood by the Law. Probably, they were young men, perhaps the firstborn of each family, who had been dedicated to God and who offered sacrifices for the people (see 13:2; 24:5).[14]

Verses 23–25. Moses apparently did not understand why **the LORD** repeated these instructions; he said that **the people** had already been told not to come near the mountain. Moses' puzzled response is understandable in light of the instructions already given (19:12).[15] Nevertheless, God insisted that Moses

---

[14]Kaiser, 419.

[15]Moses' response is not, as many modern commentators assert, evidence that chapter 19 is a collection of sources pieced together by an editor. (Cassuto, 235.)

go down and come up again, bringing **Aaron** with him. Cassuto wrote, "Moses' statement is rejected sharply: 'Go down'—do what I have commanded you, and do not query my orders."[16] He implied that Moses needed to warn the people again not to come near. Then **Moses** did what the Lord had told him to do.

The scene of Israel's meeting with God was majestic. Every detail was in place for the giving of the Law to the people.

APPLICATION

God's Relationship with His People (19:1–8)

No other event in the Old Testament seems more significant than the one recorded in Exodus 19:1–8. In this passage God's covenant with Israel defines His relationship with Israel and provides the setting for the rest of the Old Testament. While this covenant is important in itself, it is also important because God's relationship with Israel in Old Testament times parallels our relationship with Him today (1 Pet. 2:9; Gal. 3:29). The Israelites became God's people by means of a covenant. We, too, have a covenant (Heb. 8:6, 8). God's covenant with Israel may be viewed as a type of God's covenant with us today.

Israel's relationship with God was based on His gracious acts . . . and so is ours. The covenant begins with what God had done: "You yourselves have seen what I did to the Egyptians, and how I bore you on eagles' wings, and brought you to Myself" (19:4). He had delivered Israel from Egypt by sending the plagues in order to force Pharaoh to allow Israel to leave. God then opened and closed the sea to save Israel and destroy Pharaoh's army. He had met the Israelites' needs in the wilderness, providing guidance (13:21, 22), water (15:23–25; 17:2–6), food (16:13–15), victory in battle (17:8–13), and organization (ch. 18). We are reminded that Israel did not deserve God's deliverance or blessings (14:10–12; 15:22–24; 16:19, 20, 28; 17:1–4; Deut. 7:6–8; 9:4–6). Think of all that God had done for Israel, and then ask, "What had Israel done for God? In particular, what had Israel done to deserve to

[16]Ibid., 234.

be delivered?" Nothing! They had murmured and complained. They had been faithless, ungrateful, and disobedient. Israel did not deserve salvation.

In much the same way, the Christian's relationship with God begins with what He has done (Rom. 5:6–9; 2 Tim. 1:9, 10; Tit. 3:5). We are saved by grace. That means that we, like Israel, are undeserving of salvation.

Israel's relationship with God was based on their willingness to accept His terms . . . and so is ours. Consider the terms of God's covenant with Israel. God required something of Israel: to obey His voice and to keep His covenant (19:5, 6). Israel had the right to accept or reject God's offer, but they had no right to change that offer or dictate terms to God. Israel accepted His terms (19:8).

God, having done so much for us, offers us the opportunity to enter into a relationship with Him. We can be His people, but we have a choice. To become His people, we must accept His terms. We cannot change those terms to suit ourselves, dictate the terms of our relationship with God, or do less than God proposes. We must make a commitment to do all that He commands. When we become Christians, we make a promise: "All that the Lord has spoken we will do!" We do not at that moment know everything that He may require of us. Nevertheless, as did Israel, we make an open-ended commitment, saying, in effect, "Lord, I do not yet know all that my commitment will require of me. Still, I pledge that, as I learn Your will for my life, I will do it."

Israel's relationship with God was based on their continuing to keep the covenant . . . and so is ours. As long as Israel was faithful to the covenant, they were God's special people, under His care and protection. However, when the people did not obey God's voice or keep His covenant, He gave Israel over to their enemies.

Various sins were involved in their failure. (1) They forgot what God had done for them—how He had saved them by grace. (2) They closely associated with unbelievers. Rather than driving out the inhabitants of the promised land, they intermarried with them. (3) They remembered their privileges but forgot their responsibilities. They gloried in being God's people and in having His presence among them, but lived as if having God's temple in their midst gave them immunity from punishment for breaking God's law (see Jer. 7). They forgot that the privilege of being God's people came with the great responsibility to live as His people.

The Christian's relationship with God is likewise based on our willingness to be faithful to the covenant. Too often, Christians are unfaithful to their pledge. (1) We forget what God has done for us. (2) We are infected with worldly attitudes. (3) We sometimes remember our privileges but forget our responsibilities. We glory in being "God's people" but forget that this status carries with it responsibilities. Among these is the responsibility to share the light with others, to try to save lost souls (see 1 Pet. 2:9, 10).

Conclusion. What a privilege God has granted us to be His people! That privilege should lead us to respond with gratitude to His commandments. We do this, first, by becoming His children. As His people, we must try to live up to the commitment which we made when we entered into a covenant relationship with Him.

God's People (19:5, 6)

Just as the nation of Israel was God's people under the old covenant, the church is God's people under the new covenant. What does that mean to those who are in the church? The answers to this question are found in 1 Peter 2:9. (1) Like Israel, we are "a chosen race." God's chosen people today are not fleshly Israel, but spiritual Israel. We are chosen because we choose to accept God's gift of salvation. (2) Like Israel, we are "a royal priesthood." As a kingdom of priests, we offer up "spiritual sacrifices" (1 Pet. 2:5; see Rev. 1:6; 5:9, 10). (3) Like Israel, we are "a holy nation." We are to "be holy" as God is holy (1 Pet. 1:15, 16). (4) Like Israel, we are "a people for God's own possession." We are unique, having been purchased with Christ's blood. Our great privileges come with a great responsibility: We are to proclaim the excellencies of our God, even as Israel was to be a "light to the Gentiles."

God's Majestic Holiness (19:10–19)

The people could not come near the mountain when God descended. We must understand the unapproachable "majestic

. . . holiness" of God (15:11). Too many people see Him as a friendly, grandfatherly type who would never hurt anyone. We should see God as loving; at the same time, we are to understand that the One who came down on Mount Sinai inspired fear. "It is a terrifying thing to fall into the hands of the living God" (Heb. 10:31).

God Sets Boundaries (19:12, 23)

Just as God "set bounds" to keep the Israelites from coming too near the mountain, He sets boundaries today around His holy Word (Deut. 4:2; 2 Jn. 9; Rev. 22:18, 19).

Two Mountains: Sinai and Zion (19:16–19)

Hebrews 12 contrasts Mount Sinai with Mount Zion. The church is included in the concept of "Mount Zion." Christians today have not come to something which makes people afraid, but to something much better:

> For you have not come to a mountain that can be touched and to a blazing fire, and to darkness and gloom and whirlwind, and to the blast of a trumpet and the sound of words which sound was such that those who heard begged that no further word be spoken to them. For they could not bear the command, "If even a beast touches the mountain, it will be stoned." And so terrible was the sight, that Moses said, "I am full of fear and trembling." But you have come to Mount Zion and to the city of the living God, the heavenly Jerusalem, and to myriads of angels, to the general assembly and church of the firstborn who are enrolled in heaven, and to God, the Judge of all, and to the spirits of the righteous made perfect, and to Jesus, the mediator of a new covenant, and to the sprinkled blood, which speaks better than the blood of Abel (Heb. 12:18–24).

CHAPTER 20

THE TEN COMMANDMENTS AND THE BOOK OF THE COVENANT (PART 1)

After the Lord had invited Israel into a covenant relationship, the people agreed to do all that He commanded (19:8). In chapter 20, God made His covenant requirements known to them. First, in 20:1–17, He gave them the Ten Commandments. Then, beginning in 20:22, He gave them what has been called "The Book of the Covenant" (20:22—23:33).

THE TEN COMMANDMENTS (20:1–17)

The Ten Commandments given at Mount Sinai were the first stipulations in the covenant that God made with Israel. They are both fundamental to and representative of the rest of the Law. The Ten Commandments are "apodictic" in nature, that is, they are moral absolutes ("You shall" or "You shall not"). This legal form stands in contrast to many of the laws found in "The Book of the Covenant" which are "casuistic," that is, case law. Those particular commands are conditional, dealing with specific circumstances ("if . . . then").

The Ten Commandments are also referred to as the "Decalogue." This designation is derived from a literal rendering of the Hebrew phrase עֲשֶׂרֶת הַדְּבָרִים (*'ᵃśereth haddᵉbarim*), which appears a few times in the Pentateuch (34:28; Deut. 4:13; 10:4). The Septuagint translates the phrase as δέκα λόγους (*deka logous*); it literally means "Ten Words." Beyond giving the number of commands, this designation may also say something about their brevity. Interestingly, a few of the commands appear in Hebrew as just two words (20:13–15).

Which of the laws make up the Ten Commandments? In Judaism, God's announcement of who He is in 20:2 is considered the first of the ten. Others interpret the verse as the preamble, not one of the commandments. The Jews then "group verses 3–6 together, to make the second commandment forbid the worship of other gods, and the use of images of any kind."[1] Roman Catholics "also traditionally group verses 3–6 together, but make them the first commandment" and "then divide the tenth commandment into two, to make up the required number."[2] These differences are relatively insignificant, since the teaching of the text remains the same, no matter how it is divided. This commentary follows the system labeled below that most Protestants use.

NUMBERING THE TEN COMMANDMENTS[3]		
Judaism	Most Protestants Greek Orthodox Philo and Josephus The early church	Roman Catholics Lutherans Augustine
1. I am the Lord (20:2)	I am the Lord (20:2) (Preamble)	I am the Lord (20:2) (Preamble)
2. No other gods and no images (20:3–6)	1. No other gods (20:3) 2. No images (20:4–6)	1. No other gods and no images (20:3–6)
3. Name of the Lord (20:7)	3. Name of the Lord (20:7)	2. Name of the Lord (20:7)
4. Sabbath (20:8–11)	4. Sabbath (20:8–11)	3. Sabbath (20:8–11)
5. Parents (20:12)	5. Parents (20:12)	4. Parents (20:12)
6. Murder (20:13)	6. Murder (20:13)	5. Murder (20:13)
7. Adultery (20:14)	7. Adultery (20:14)	6. Adultery (20:14)
8. Stealing (20:15)	8. Stealing (20:15)	7. Stealing (20:15)
9. False Witness (20:16)	9. False Witness (20:16)	8. False Witness (20:16)
10. Coveting (20:17)	10. Coveting (20:17)	9. Coveting 1 (20:17a) 10. Coveting 2 (20:17b)

---

[1]R. Alan Cole, *Exodus: An Introduction and Commentary*, Tyndale Old Testament Commentaries (Downers Grove, Ill.: Inter-Varsity Press, 1973), 152.

[2]Ibid.

[3]Adapted from B. Davie Napier, *The Book of Exodus*, The Layman's Bible Commentary, vol. 3 (Atlanta: John Knox Press, 1963), 75.

The Ten Commandments can be easily categorized into two groups. The first group of four govern one's vertical relationship with God: (1) "You shall have no other gods before me"; (2) "You shall not make for yourself an idol"; (3) "You shall not take the name of the LORD your God in vain"; and (4) "Remember the sabbath day, to keep it holy." The second group of six govern one's horizontal relationship with other human beings: (5) "Honor your father and mother"; (6) "You shall not murder"; (7) "You shall not commit adultery"; (8) "You shall not steal"; (9) "You shall not bear false witness"; and (10) "You shall not covet."

Throughout the commandments, the pronoun "you" is in the singular form.[4] Most likely God spoke these words to the whole congregation (19:9; 20:19) and used the singular pronoun to emphasize that every individual Israelite was obligated to keep the commandments. An alternative view is that the commandments were addressed to Israel as a group "in the collective second person."[5]

Eight of the Ten Commandments are presented in negative language ("You shall not"), while only two are positive ("Remember" and "Honor"). The adverb "not" (לֹא, *lo'*) emphatically stresses that the action is prohibited. Nevertheless, the negative commands imply their positive counterparts. For example, the prohibition against bearing false witness suggests that an individual should be a person of truth and integrity.

The Ten Commandments were eventually preserved on two stone tablets and stored in the ark of the covenant (34:28; Deut. 10:1–5), symbolizing the close relationship between God and His word. The presence of these tablets in the ark would also remind the people of their obligation to the covenant. The Ten Commandments are repeated, with minor differences, in Deuteronomy 5. In that passage, the words are spoken to a new generation that was ready to enter the promised land; those Israelites were challenged to accept the covenant as their very own.

---

[4]David R. Worley, Jr., "God's Gracious Love Expressed: Exodus 20:1–17," *Restoration Quarterly* 14 (3d–4th Quarter, 1971): 186.

[5]Martin Noth, *Exodus*, trans. J. S. Bowden, The Old Testament Library (Philadelphia: Westminster Press, 1962), 162.

Preamble (20:1, 2)

[1]Then God spoke all these words, saying, [2]"I am the LORD your God, who brought you out of the land of Egypt, out of the house of slavery."

Verses 1, 2. The Ten Commandments were prefaced with a declaration identifying the giver of the Law: **God spoke all these words**. The proclamation of the Law began with a statement of who God is and what He had done for Israel—**"I am the LORD your God, who brought you out of the land of Egypt, out of the house of slavery."** It was important for Israel to remember not only that God had the right to command obedience, but also that He deserved to be obeyed since He had delivered them out of Egypt.

These verses reflect the beginning of the formal covenant between God and Israel. This was a suzerain-vassal covenant, such as was common between a greater power and a lesser power (for example, a sovereign king and a client king). In these treaties, the great king would (1) establish who he was, (2) set out what he had done or would do for the lesser power, and then (3) specify what laws or rules the vassal kingdom must obey. (For more information, see *Appendix: The Covenant.*)

1. Allegiance to God (20:3)

[3]"You shall have no other gods before Me."

Verse 3. The first of the Ten Commandments required the Israelites to give full allegiance to the Lord God. The pagan world around them believed in the existence of **other gods**. This commandment required them to worship the one true God. It made the existence of other gods irrelevant. Israel was to worship the Lord God and Him only. They were to be exclusively committed to Yahweh (see Deut. 6:4, 5).

The phrase **before Me** (עַל־פָּנָ֑י, *'al panay*) can be literally translated "before My face." This phrase has various shades of meaning depending upon the context. It can be rendered in the following ways: (1) "in front of Me" or "in My presence," (2) "before Me" or "in preference to Me," (3) "in addition to Me" or "besides Me," and (4) "in front of Me" or "in defiance to Me."[6] The translation "before Me" may leave some readers with the wrong impression. Contextually, the Lord was not telling the Israelites that it was acceptable to worship other gods as long as they put Him first. Rather, He was demanding their absolute allegiance. The people were not to have any other gods besides Him (20:4–6). This fact is brought out in many translations (NJB; NEB; TEV; CEV; NCV; LB; NLT).

This commandment came first because it was the most basic. A person's attitude toward nature, other human beings, and himself depends on what he thinks about God. This is vividly illustrated in Romans 1:18–32, where Paul accused the Gentiles of hideous sins. Why were they guilty of such terrible things? Because they had quit worshiping the one true God, the Creator, and were worshiping created things.

2. Idolatry (20:4–6)

4"You shall not make for yourself an idol, or any likeness of what is in heaven above or on the earth beneath or in the water under the earth. 5You shall not worship them or serve them; for I, the Lord your God, am a jealous God, visiting the iniquity of the fathers on the children, on the third and the fourth generations of those who hate Me, 6but showing lovingkindness to thousands, to those who love Me and keep My commandments."

Verse 4. The second commandment forbade the making and worshiping of images. The term **idol** (פֶּסֶל, *pesel*) is related to the verb "hew" or "cut" (פָּסַל, *pasal*). It usually refers to an image that

---

6See Francis Brown, S. R. Driver, and Charles A. Briggs, *The Brown-Driver-Briggs Hebrew and English Lexicon* (Boston: Houghton, Mifflin and Co., 1906; reprint, Peabody, Mass: Hendrickson Publishers, 1997), 818–19.

is cut out of wood or stone, that is, a "graven image" (KJV).[7] Moreover, the phrase **any likeness** encompasses any image that might not be covered by the word, such as a molten idol (see 20:23; 34:17; Deut. 27:15).

The prohibition is further clarified by this description: **what is in heaven above or on the earth beneath or in the water under the earth.** This language is reminiscent of creation, when man was given dominion over "the birds of the sky," "the fish of the sea," and "every living thing that moves on the earth" (Gen. 1:26, 28). In essence, God commanded the Israelites not to fashion any idol representing any created being (see Deut. 4:15–19).

Verse 5. The people were not to make, **worship**, or **serve** images. The primary aim of the commandment was to remind the people that God is not material: He cannot be seen, touched, weighed, or measured. God is spiritual (Jn. 4:24) and is not, therefore, to be equated with anything physical. The Israelites were not to worship any god represented by an image, nor were they to make images of **the Lord** [their] **God**. James Burton Coffman wrote,

> The reasons for this are profound. By its very nature any religious image is *false*, being a *lying* presentation of what is allegedly represented. How can that which is material represent anything spiritual? How can that which is helpless represent eternal omnipotence? How can that which decays represent eternal life? How can that which is not intelligent represent omniscience? How can that which is dumb, unfeeling, blind, and *dead* represent any of the vital realities of God and holy religion?[8]

The understanding of God as non-material was unique in the ancient world. People worshiped many gods which were represented by images, or idols, that the people themselves had

---

[7]However, the term *pesel* is used much later in the Old Testament in reference to molten images that were cast by craftsmen (Is. 40:19; 44:10).

[8]James Burton Coffman, *Commentary on Exodus, The Second Book of Moses* (Abilene, Tex.: ACU Press, 1985), 273.

created. As the years passed, Israel often broke this second commandment, as they did the first, by making and worshiping images (see ch. 32). However, the commandment does not absolutely forbid, as some have concluded, the making of pictures or statues representing living things (see 25:18–20). Rather, it forbids *using images as objects of worship.*[9]

God provided a reason for obeying the second commandment, describing Himself as **a jealous God** and saying that He would visit **the iniquity of the fathers on the children, on the third and the fourth generations.** Two questions arise from these statements.

(1) In what sense is God "a jealous God"? The word "jealous" (קַנָּא, *qanna'*) is an adjective that is only used to describe God (20:5; 34:14; Deut. 4:24; 5:9; 6:15). It means that He tolerates no rivals. He alone is to be worshiped, and He demonstrates His intolerance of infidelity by punishing sin. Perhaps God could be thought of as a jealous husband who wants what is best for his wife and refuses to share her with another man. Warren W. Wiersbe explained,

> Just as parents are jealous over their children and spouses over their mates, so God is jealous over His beloved ones and will not tolerate competition (Zechariah 1:14; 8:2). The Scriptures present idolatry as the equivalent of prostitution and adultery (Hosea 1—3; Jeremiah 2—3; Ezekiel 16; 23; James 4:4–5). God desires and deserves the exclusive love of His people (Exodus 34:14; Deuteronomy 4:24; 5:9; 6:15).[10]

(2) How can it be fair for God to punish children for their fathers' sins? The statement that God does this presents a problem, since Deuteronomy 24:16 and Ezekiel 18:20 say that children are not to be punished for their fathers' sins. No contradic-

---

[9]Walter C. Kaiser, Jr., "Exodus," in *The Expositor's Bible Commentary*, vol. 2, *Genesis—Numbers* (Grand Rapids, Mich.: Zondervan, 1990), 422–23.

[10]Warren W. Wiersbe, *Be Delivered* (Colorado Springs, Colo.: Victor, 1998), 110.

tion exists since Exodus 20:5 is speaking of the consequences of sin rather than the guilt of sin. A father's sin can negatively affect his family for three or four generations. His children are likely to learn his bad habits and become like him; then they will suffer for their own sins.

In addition, the consequences of sin—sorrow, sickness, humiliation, incarceration, and early death—can scar a family for generations. The Israelites demonstrated that fact when they were taken into captivity. Innocent children had to suffer the consequences of deportation with their guilty parents and grandparents. Perhaps Israel grasped the principle that children suffer for their parents' sin more easily than the reader today does, since they were familiar with the concept of collective guilt. As W. H. Gispen noted, "In connection with this threat we must remember that in the ancient Near East the ties between the individual and the larger context of tribe, nation, and family had not been devalued as it has been among many people today."[11]

Verse 6. God contrasted His punishment with His kindness. "Those who [demonstrated] hate" toward Him by worshiping idols would suffer for three or four generations (20:5). In contrast, God promised **lovingkindness to thousands, to those who love** [Him] **and keep** [His] **commandments.** Concerning the term "lovingkindness" (חֶסֶד, *chesed*), W. H. Gispen explained,

> It does not refer to kindness to which one has no right or claim; the Hebrew has a different word for this. But the word refers to a goodness, a kindness, a mercy to which one is obligated on the basis of a relationship. . . . In the case of God and Israel the obligation was based on the covenant: covenant love, which expressed itself in a mutual relationship of rights and duties, and in which God binds man to himself.[12]

---

[11]W. H. Gispen, *Exodus*, trans. Ed van der Maas, Bible Student's Commentary (Grand Rapids, Mich.: Regency Reference Library, Zondervan Publishing House, 1982), 192.

[12]Ibid., 192–93.

The contrast between three or four generations and "thousands" emphasizes that God rewards obedience even more generously than He punishes disobedience.

3. The Divine Name (20:7)

7"You shall not take the name of the LORD your God in vain, for the LORD will not leave him unpunished who takes His name in vain."

Verse 7. The third commandment protected the holiness of **God**. It was designed primarily to forbid the use of God's **name** in false oaths, to keep the Israelites from swearing in His name and then breaking the oath (Lev. 19:12). However, it has been and can be applied to prohibiting the use of God's name in swearing or cursing. Nahum M. Sarna pointed out that the Hebrew word translated **take** (נָשָׂא, *naśa'*) means "to take up" or "swear" and is here "an ellipsis for 'to take upon the lips,' that is, 'to utter' the divine name."[13] He also noted that the term **vain** (שָׁוְא, *shaw^e'*) can mean "falsely"; "the ambiguities allow for the proscription of perjury by the principals in a lawsuit, swearing falsely, and the unnecessary or frivolous use of the Divine Name."[14]

Jews later in their history began to believe that God's name, "Yahweh" (יהוה, *YHWH*), was too holy to be pronounced at all. Consequently, the Jews refused to say God's name. Rather than saying the name "Yahweh," they would insert some other word. For instance, "heaven" might be substituted for "Yahweh" or "God." When they read the Scriptures aloud, they would substitute "Adonai" (אֲדֹנָי, *'Adonay*), which means "my Lord," for the name "Yahweh." The English Scriptures generally follow this practice, translating "Yahweh" with **LORD**, using small capital letters, rather than transliterating the name as is usually done with proper names. Nevertheless, it is unlikely that God intended for His personal name to remain unpronounced.

---

[13]Nahum M. Sarna, *Exodus*, The JPS Torah Commentary (New York: Jewish Publication Society, 1991), 111.

[14]Ibid.

4. The Sabbath (20:8–11)

[8]"Remember the sabbath day, to keep it holy. [9]Six days you shall labor and do all your work, [10]but the seventh day is a sabbath of the LORD your God; in it you shall not do any work, you or your son or your daughter, your male or your female servant or your cattle or your sojourner who stays with you. [11]For in six days the LORD made the heavens and the earth, the sea and all that is in them, and rested on the seventh day; therefore the LORD blessed the sabbath day and made it holy."

Verses 8–10. The fourth commandment was given to honor **God** and benefit Israel. God was honored in that Israel, by forgoing **work** on **the sabbath day**, proclaimed faith in God's ability to provide for the nation. For instance, in the case of gathering manna, they demonstrated faith in God to provide enough food in six days so that they could rest on the seventh day (16:22–26). By calling to mind the **six days** of creation, the Sabbath rest reflected on God's sovereignty and His making life possible (Gen. 2:1–3). Israel was benefited in that the Sabbath provided a time of rest and refreshment for them and all those who worked for the Israelites (23:12; see Mk. 2:27).

How was the Sabbath to be **remember**[ed]? Nothing is said in the Ten Commandments about worshiping on the Sabbath. The practice of Sabbath worship and synagogue attendance arose later in the history of Israel. Rather, the Sabbath was a day of rest, not necessarily a day of worship. To **keep** [the Sabbath] **holy** did not require that God's people worship, since the word קָדַשׁ (*qadash*) simply means "separate," "set apart," or "sanctified." One can "set apart" a day for rest just as he can "set apart" a day for worship.

Verse 11. The reason given for the observance of the Sabbath in this passage is that God **made** everything **in six days** and **rested on the seventh day**. That is why God **blessed the sabbath day and made it holy** (see Gen. 2:1–3). To the next generation of Israelites, God gave another reason for keeping the Sabbath: "You shall remember that you were a slave in the land of Egypt, and the LORD your God brought you out of there by a mighty hand and by an outstretched arm; therefore, the LORD your God commanded you to observe the sabbath day" (Deut. 5:15).

The Sabbath was to be observed as a reminder not only of God's creative power, but also of God's redemptive power. The significance of both events—the creation and the deliverance—led Israel to place great emphasis on the observance of this commandment. In later years, the Jews' insistence on keeping the Sabbath, more than anything else, distinguished them from other peoples.

Some who believe that Christians should still observe the Sabbath use this text to say that it was a perpetual commandment given at creation, formally stated in the Ten Commandments, and never revoked. They contend that the clause "remember the sabbath" implies that the Sabbath was already being kept. Further, since God was spoken of as blessing the Sabbath day and making it holy immediately after the creation account (Gen. 2:3), they claim that God *at that time* set the Sabbath aside as a holy day and required people to observe it.

In response to this argumentation, five facts should be noted. (1) At least one Sabbath—and probably more—had already been observed (16:22–30). This occurrence may be what God referred to when He said, "Remember the sabbath." (2) The mention of the sanctification of the Sabbath day in connection with the creation does not necessarily mean that God blessed the seventh day at the time of creation; it may simply suggest that because God rested *then,* God *now* (at the time of the writing of Exodus) was blessing the Sabbath day and making it holy. (3) "Remember" does not necessarily imply that Israel had previously been in the habit of keeping the Sabbath.[15] "*Remember* may simply mean to observe faithfully."[16] (4) There is no biblical record of anyone observing the Sabbath until Exodus. (5) Even if the Sabbath were observed during the patriarchal period, that fact would not require us to observe the Sabbath today.

---

[15]Coffman, 278.

[16]Wilbur Fields, *Exploring Exodus,* Bible Study Textbook Series (Joplin, Mo.: College Press, 1976), 429. (See Mal. 4:4.)

5. Honoring Parents (20:12)

12"Honor your father and your mother, that your days may be prolonged in the land which the LORD your God gives you."

Verse 12. The fifth commandment was designed to promote right relations between parents and children. Children were to **honor** both **father** and **mother**. One honored his or her parents by (1) obeying them (Deut. 21:18–20); (2) speaking respectfully to them and about them (Lev. 19:3); (3) not cursing or striking them (Ex. 21:15, 17; Lev. 20:9); and (4) providing for their needs when they were no longer able to provide for themselves. Jesus indicated that "honoring" parents included this fourth meaning in Mark 7:9–13. He reprimanded the Pharisees for breaking the commandment to honor their parents by claiming that the financial means they should have shared with their parents was "Corban," or "a gift devoted to God" (NIV).

This commandment was applied by Paul to Christians. Ephesians 6:1–3 says, "Children, obey your parents in the Lord, for this is right. 'Honor your father and mother (which is the first commandment with a promise), so that it may be well with you, and that you may live long on the earth.'"

Paul identified this commandment as "the first . . . with a promise." Other commandments had given reasons for obedience, but this command was the first to contain a promise. According to Exodus 20:12, the promise was **that your days may be prolonged in the land which the LORD your God gives you.** To the Israelites, this meant they would be allowed to continue living in Canaan if they honored their parents.[17] Those who honored their parents would keep the covenant between God and their fathers and would not turn away from the Lord. Ultimately, Israel was taken away from the land God had given them because they failed to observe the requirements of the Law which were taught to them by their parents.

---

[17]Ibid., 433–34. The promise was later tied to several other commands (Deut. 4:40; 5:33; 6:1, 2; 11:8, 9; 22:6, 7; 30:15–18; 32:44–47).

Paul's adaptation of the promise implies that the child who obeys his parents will lead a better life ("that it may be well with you") as well as a longer life ("and that you may live long on the earth"). Paul's words should not be taken as an unbreakable promise, but as a principle. In general, children who learn to obey their parents and submit to authority lead better and longer lives than those who do not.[18]

6. Murder (20:13)

[13]**"You shall not murder."**

Verse 13. The sixth commandment was given to protect human life. The more familiar KJV rendering of this verse is "Thou shalt not kill," but the NASB better represents the idea of the commandment.[19] The Hebrew word rendered **murder** is רָצַח (*ratsach*). The translation "kill" is too general in this context, as is evident from the fact that the Law did not ban all killing. For example, the Law regulated but did not prohibit either war or capital punishment. In fact, God sometimes commanded Israel to fight in battle (Num. 10:9; Deut. 20:1), and He required the death penalty for certain crimes—including murder (Ex. 21:12; Num. 35:16–21, 27, 30). Furthermore, the word *ratsach* is "nearly always used of the killing of a personal enemy."[20] What the sixth commandment prohibits is murder, the deliberate and malicious taking of human life.

This prohibition, along with the punishment prescribed elsewhere, underscores the value of life. Human life is precious because it was derived from God. The Lord made man in His own image and likeness and "breathed into his nostrils the breath of life" (Gen. 1:26, 27; 2:7; 9:6).

---

[18]Ibid., 434.

[19]The NKJV, NIV, and NRSV have the same wording as the NASB.

[20]J. Philip Hyatt, *Exodus*, The New Century Bible Commentary (Grand Rapids, Mich.: Wm. B. Eerdmans Publishing Co., 1971), 214. There are, however, some cases where the term *ratsach* is used for either a legal execution by the avenger of blood (Num. 35:27, 30) or an unintentional killing (Deut. 19:3, 4, 6; Josh. 20:3, 5, 6).

The value of human life is evident throughout Mosaic legislation. For example, a thief's right to live superseded his victim's right to his property. According to the Law, if a property-owner killed a thief who was not threatening his life, then the property-owner was guilty of blood (22:3). Furthermore, if a man killed another accidentally and thus did not suffer the penalty of execution, he still had to pay for the act. He could flee to a city of refuge (Num. 35:22–28; Deut. 19:1–10). If he was found innocent of murder, he had to remain in the city of refuge until the death of the high priest. If he was guilty of murder, he was killed by the "blood avenger," who served as an instrument of the court (and society) to punish the murderer. The whole process was regulated by law; it was the legal way to bring a murderer to justice. For a people without a standing army or police force, the procedure was as good a legal system as could have been devised.

7. Adultery (20:14)

[14]**"You shall not commit adultery."**

Verse 14. The seventh commandment was to protect the marriage relationship. This commandment forbade **adultery**—an illicit sexual relationship involving at least one married person. From a human perspective, the sin of adultery in the Old Testament was primarily committed against the married partner of the adulterous person. In other words, if a man committed adultery with another man's wife, he sinned against the man whose wife he had taken.

Ultimately, the sin of adultery was an offense against God (Gen. 20:6; Ps. 51:4). When Potiphar's wife tried to seduce Joseph, he replied, "How then could I do this great evil and sin against God?" (Gen. 39:9). God created the complementary genders and designed the institution of marriage (Gen. 2:18–25). Since He is the One who joins a man and woman together (Mt. 19:6), a violation of that covenant relationship is an affront to Him.

By forbidding adultery, the seventh commandment contributed to the permanency of marriage. To make sure that Israel understood the importance of this commandment, death was prescribed as the punishment for breaking it (Lev. 20:10; Deut. 22:22).

As the various laws were revealed, God had more to say about sexual sins than merely "you shall not commit adultery." He went on to forbid a variety of sexual sins, including homosexuality, bestiality, and incest (Lev. 18:6–18, 22, 23; 20:11–17, 19–21). Probably, these are all related to the seventh commandment; indeed, this commandment may have been intended to include all these sins and others like them (see 1 Tim. 1:10).

8. Theft (20:15)

[15]"You shall not steal."

Verse 15. The eighth commandment protected personal property. It affirmed the right of individuals to own property—in contrast to any view that suggests that all property must be shared communally or owned by the state. The commandment taught that individuals should not be wrongly deprived of their property. Walter J. Harrelson said that "the [Old Testament] conceives of property as a kind of extension of the 'self' of its owner" so that "acts of theft are violations of the person."[21]

Personal property was a gift from God, who owns all things. To **steal** from another person was as if one were stealing from God. Specific laws elaborated on what should be regarded as theft and what should be the penalty for stealing. Theft was never regarded as a capital crime, nor did the Law authorize bodily disfigurement for stealing—as did some other religious codes.[22]

9. False Testimony (20:16)

[16]"You shall not bear false witness against your neighbor."

---

[21]Walter J. Harrelson, "Ten Commandments," in *The Interpreter's Dictionary of the Bible*, ed. George Arthur Buttrick (Nashville: Abingdon Press, 1962), 4:571.

[22]Some believe that the eighth commandment is primarily concerned with stealing a man, or kidnapping (Deut. 24:7; 1 Tim. 1:10). (Worley, 202.)

Verse 16. The setting for the ninth commandment was the court of law. The commandment was intended to protect people from false accusations in court (see 23:1–3). According to David R. Worley, Jr., the commandment deals primarily "with the lying witness who jeopardizes the welfare of another."[23] In the days before fingerprinting and DNA samples, the major evidence for a crime had to be provided by witnesses. There had to be at least two or three; one could not be convicted based on the testimony of just one witness (Deut. 17:6; 19:15). If the witnesses were not truthful, then an injustice would result. False testimony could result in the loss of an individual's reputation, property, and even life (Lev. 19:15, 16; 1 Kings 21:8–14; Mt. 26:59–61). The punishment for **bear**[ing] **false witness** was the same as the harm intended against one's **neighbor** (Deut. 19:16, 17).

This commandment was designed to guarantee the integrity of the judicial process by protecting the accused from false witnesses. Many of the laws which follow in Exodus through Deuteronomy further explain this principle and apply it to individual situations. In addition to its original prohibition of lying in court, the meaning of the commandment was expanded in the Old Testament to forbid all kinds of deceptive speech (Hos. 4:2).[24] Any lying contradicts the nature of God, who Himself is the fountain of all truth and cannot lie (Jn. 17:17; Heb. 6:18).

10. Coveting (20:17)

[17]"You shall not covet your neighbor's house; you shall not covet your neighbor's wife or his male servant or his female servant or his ox or his donkey or anything that belongs to your neighbor."

Verse 17. The tenth commandment relates to the heart of the individual, for it is in the heart that coveting occurs. To **covet** is to desire something which is not one's own. In the New Testament, "coveting" is closely connected to greed—the desire for

[23]Worley, 202.
[24]Fields, 437.

more and more possessions, a passion for "things" that can never be satisfied (Lk. 12:15; Col. 3:5).

Some have interpreted "coveting" as more than a desire for possessions that belong to others; they think that the term relates to unlawful actions to obtain what others have.[25] However, this interpretation may be based on a preconceived idea that the Ten Commandments (indeed, the whole law of Moses) dealt with outward acts and not with man's thoughts or attitudes. Proof that the Law relates to the inner man as well as to the outer man is found here in the tenth commandment, and this is confirmed in other passages throughout the Bible. Even if coveting is the root from which other sins grow, it is in itself a sin (Rom. 7:7–11).

John I. Durham pointed out that coveting could lead to breaking all of the other commandments in the Decalogue. A son's passionate desire to have his own way could drive him to dishonor and harm his parents (21:15, 17). David's lust for Bathsheba resulted in adultery and murder (2 Sam. 11; 12). Ahab's desire to own Naboth's vineyard led to false testimony and murder (1 Kings 21). Coveting merchants who lived in the time of the prophet Amos broke the Sabbath and were guilty of stealing (Amos 8:4–6). The greedy people of Judah who lived in the days of the prophet Jeremiah perhaps violated all of the commandments, trading pure devotion to God and His name for pagan idolatry (Jer. 7:1–15).[26]

In the prohibition against coveting, the **neighbor's house** appears to be a comprehensive term, encompassing all of the valuables that follow in descending order: his **wife, male servant, female servant, ox**, and **donkey**. The phrase **anything that belongs to your neighbor** covers everything else.

ISRAEL'S REACTION (20:18–21)

18All the people perceived the thunder and the lightning flashes and the sound of the trumpet and the mountain smok-

---

25Ibid., 437–38.

26John I. Durham, *Exodus*, Word Biblical Commentary, vol. 3 (Waco, Tex.: Word Books, 1987), 298.

ing; and when the people saw it, they trembled and stood at a distance. [19]Then they said to Moses, "Speak to us yourself and we will listen; but let not God speak to us, or we will die." [20]Moses said to the people, "Do not be afraid; for God has come in order to test you, and in order that the fear of Him may remain with you, so that you may not sin." [21]So the people stood at a distance, while Moses approached the thick cloud where God was.

Verses 18, 19. This text emphasizes the fact that God was present on the mountain. **The thunder and the lightning flashes and the sound of the trumpet and the mountain smoking** all testified to God's presence. The people's reaction of fear and trembling is understandable and even appropriate. When finite, sinful man is confronted by the infinite, holy God, man has reason to be ashamed and afraid. Israel's fear is also understandable because God's holy presence was dangerous. If a person was unprepared or somehow overstepped the bounds of propriety, he could be punished with quick death for coming into contact with God's holy person or with holy things associated with God. As a result of their fear, the Israelites begged **Moses** to speak to them in place of **God** so they would not **die** (see Heb. 12:19, 20).

Verse 20. Moses told the Israelites to **not be afraid**. He also said, **"God has come in order to test you, and in order that the fear of Him may remain with you, so that you may not sin."** According to various commentators, God may have been testing their faith, their obedience, their respect, or their willingness to honor the boundaries that He had set.[27] Perhaps God's aim with this test was to refine His people, to develop in them an appreciation for and understanding of His majesty and power. Then they would fear, or respect, Him and not sin against Him.

Verse 21. Moses returned to his place on the mountain to meet **God** in the **cloud** that enveloped its peak. The fearful people who saw Moses disappear into the cloud must have watched in awe, wondering what would happen to him and to them.

---

[27]Ibid., 303.

PROLOGUE TO THE BOOK OF THE COVENANT: THE GIVER OF THE LAW (20:22)

The second installment of the Law, delivered by God to Moses on the mountain in 20:22—23:33, is referred to as "the book of the covenant" (24:7). These laws, sometimes called in scholarly literature the "covenant code," expanded upon and explained the Ten Commandments.

22Then the LORD said to Moses, "Thus you shall say to the sons of Israel, 'You yourselves have seen that I have spoken to you from heaven.'"

Verse 22. The introduction to this section emphasizes the source of the laws: **the LORD**, Yahweh. Israel should have no doubt about the origin of these laws, for God said, **"You . . . have seen that I have spoken to you from heaven."** This statement provides a clue as to why God spoke to all the people before giving Moses the details of the Law: He wanted to convince them that the One giving these laws was the Lord God Himself.

Although it is difficult to identify an overall organizational scheme for the Book of the Covenant, individual laws do appear in groupings. Each grouping deals with similar situations and seems to have an overall concern (see *The Expanded Outline*).

LAWS RELATED TO THE WORSHIP OF GOD (20:23–26)

23"'You shall not make other gods besides Me; gods of silver or gods of gold, you shall not make for yourselves. 24You shall make an altar of earth for Me, and you shall sacrifice on it your burnt offerings and your peace offerings, your sheep and your oxen; in every place where I cause My name to be remembered, I will come to you and bless you. 25If you make an altar of stone for Me, you shall not build it of cut stones, for if you wield your tool on it, you will profane it. 26And you shall not go up by steps to My altar, so that your nakedness will not be exposed on it.'"

Verse 23. God began giving these "ordinances" (21:1) to expand on the Ten Commandments by restating, in slightly different words, the second commandment (20:4): **"You shall not make other gods besides Me; gods of silver or gods of gold, you shall not make for yourselves."** Why would He begin with the second commandment rather than the first? The wording in this passage is reminiscent of the first commandment in regard to having no other gods "before Me" (20:3); the law forbade making other gods "besides Me." The second commandment was a very practical one, specifying what the Israelites were not to *do*, rather than merely telling them what they were not to think or believe. This is in keeping with the practical nature of all the laws found in the Book of the Covenant.

Verse 24. After specifying what the Israelites were not to make, God explained what they *were* to make: **an altar of earth** where they could **sacrifice** both **burnt offerings** and **peace offerings**. Since regulations for burnt offerings and peace offerings came later in Leviticus, this passage may refer to sacrifices which were already being offered but which had not yet been regulated. The places for making these sacrifices were chosen by God. In those places He would cause His **name to be remembered**. He would **come** to the people and **bless** them there.

Verse 25. The rules regarding the **altar** in this passage have no obvious relation to the later instructions concerning the altar of burnt offering (27:1–8). Possibly, this law applied to the period of time before the building and consecration of the altar of burnt offering, but it remained relevant throughout the period of the wilderness wanderings since the Israelites moved frequently and offered sacrifices in different places. Later, God established only one place for sacrifices to be offered (see Deut. 12:11–14).

This law did not require only earthen altars (20:24), since it added regulations regarding an altar **of stone**. An altar was to be built using natural stones, not **cut stones** that had been shaped by man with a **tool**. One suggestion is that this restriction was for the sake of simplicity. Another possibility is derived from the fact that the Hebrew term חֶרֶב (*chereb*), translated "tool," is a word commonly used for a "sword." A sword (or sharp tool) served as "a symbol of strife, whereas the altar was a symbol of reconciliation."[28] A third idea is that the prohibition was given to distinguish Israelite practice from that of the Canaanites.[29]

Verse 26. Further, the Israelites were not to make an **altar** with **steps**. This law was given to prevent a man's **nakedness** from being seen underneath his garments as he was climbing the stairs (see 28:42). These requirements indicate that the altars made in the wilderness were small, simple structures, rather than the elaborate altars of other nations and the magnificent altar that later stood in front of Solomon's temple (2 Chron. 4:1).

Another possibility, suggested by L. Daniel Hawk, is that the altars spoken of in 20:24–26 were of a different type. He distinguished between "open-air altars and altars connected to the tabernacle,"[30] saying that open-air altars could be constructed anywhere and were used for a variety of purposes. Such altars had been built by Abraham, Isaac, and Jacob, and were also used by Moses (17:14–16; 24:4–8). Moreover, they were still used after the tabernacle was completed, as in the cases of Joshua (Deut. 27:5, 6; Josh. 8:31), Saul (1 Sam. 14:33–35), and Elijah (1 Kings 18:23–38). If such altars were used for a different purpose than that of the altar of burnt offering, then they were not violating the law of Moses. If this interpretation is correct, then the instructions in 20:24–26 may have been intended to regulate how those open-air altars were to be built.

The theme of these instructions might be "Do not emphasize outward structures in your worship." The Israelites needed to remember that they were only passing through the wilderness on their way to the promised land. They were not to tarry, building unnecessarily elaborate altars. Durham commented that this legislation is appropriate near the beginning of the Book of the Covenant since it emphasizes that God was present wherever the people were. This is an important theme in Exodus.[31]

---

[28]F. B. Huey, Jr., *Exodus*, Bible Study Commentary (Grand Rapids, Mich.: Zondervan Publishing House, 1977), 95.

[29]Durham, 320.

[30]L. Daniel Hawk, "Altars," in *Dictionary of the Old Testament: Pentateuch*, ed. T. Desmond Alexander and David W. Baker (Downers Grove, Ill.: InterVarsity Press, 2003), 33.

[31]Durham, 320.

APPLICATION

A Good Law (20:1–17)

In chapter 20 we find the giving of the Ten Commandments, the first part of the law of Moses. These were the first stipulations in the covenant God made with Israel. God had said that if Israel would keep His commandments, then they would be His people. Israel had said that they would do all that God commanded. Now God began to spell out the details of what He wanted Israel to do. The commandments given at Sinai are both fundamental to and representative of the rest of the Law. Through them we can see the Law as God gave it.

Why should we think of the Law as a good law? Looking through the eyes of the New Testament, we may think that the Law was bad: It was but a shadow (Heb. 10:1), and a shadow is surely inferior to the "real thing." The old covenant was inferior; the new is better (Heb. 8:6). The old covenant was faulty (Heb. 8:7). Its purpose was to bring us to Christ; and since Christ has come, it is no longer in effect (Gal. 3:19, 23–25). It brought a ministry of death (2 Cor. 3:7).

At the same time, the New Testament suggests that the law of Moses was a good law. It came with glory (2 Cor. 3:7). Romans 3:1, 2 says that the Jews had an advantage over the Gentiles in that they were "entrusted with the oracles of God." Romans 7:12 says, "So . . . the Law is holy, and the commandment is holy and righteous and good." Hebrews shows Christ and His covenant to be "better" than the old covenant, but that does not mean that the Law was "bad"; rather, it suggests that it was "good."

Jesus did not denounce the Law during His public ministry. Rather, He denounced the traditions which had grown up around the Law. The Law's moral requirements are good. Why, then, was the Law taken away? It was a good law, but it could not take away sin (Gal. 3:19, 22; Heb. 10:4). People did not need better rules to live by; they needed a Savior. That is why the old covenant was fulfilled and the new covenant was established.

In what way was the Law a good law? The goodness of the Law is easy to see. (1) It was based on God's gracious acts toward Israel (19:3, 4; 20:1, 2). It was not law for the sake of law, or decrees imposed by a conqueror who had no interest in the good of the conquered. (2) It provided adequate reasons for obedience (see 20:12). The Law was accompanied by the promise of blessings for obedience and curses for disobedience (Lev. 26; Deut. 28). (3) It was comprehensive. It not only set the standards for Israel's worship, but it also governed all areas of daily life. It was likewise comprehensive in its moral and ethical requirements. Every type of sin is forbidden somehow in the Ten Commandments. (4) It even governed thoughts and attitudes. The tenth commandment is "You shall not covet." Coveting is something that happens in the mind! (5) It protected those who were otherwise defenseless: slaves, strangers or foreigners, widows and orphans, the poor, and the handicapped. (6) It provided capital punishment for crimes against people, but not for crimes against property (21:12; 22:1). The Mosaic law contrasts with the laws of other nations of the ancient Near East, which called for the death penalty even for the theft of property. (7) It required absolute fairness. Exodus 23:2, 3 indicates that witnesses were to be honest and judges were not to be partial. (8) It required a person to treat his enemy well (23:4, 5).

The law of Moses was a good law, but we live under a better law. If the Israelites rejoiced in having the Law, how much more should we rejoice in the new covenant! Let us strive even more to obey the better law which we have through Christ.

Israel never kept the Law perfectly. No matter how good a law is, it cannot save because fallible human beings are unable to keep it perfectly. Let us rejoice that we have a perfect sacrifice—Jesus Christ—who makes it possible for us to be saved, even though we fail to do all that the Lord requires. We must obey God's commandments; yet we must remember that our salvation is not because of our law-keeping, but because of Christ's sacrifice on our behalf.

Preaching the Ten Commandments (20:1–17)

The Ten Commandments furnish abundant material for one or more sermons. The Decalogue could be covered in one sermon, with each commandment serving as a major point. Another possibility is to develop two sermons. One could deal with the first four commandments, while the other would cover the last six. A final approach is to develop a series of ten sermons, each dealing with a separate commandment.

Our Two Great Loves (20:1–17)

Jesus said that to "love God" and to "love your neighbor" were the two great commandments. What do "loving God" and "loving your neighbor" require? Since the Law is based on these two great commandments (Mt. 22:40), the Ten Commandments illustrate what it means to "love God" and "love your neighbor." Even though the Ten Commandments do not apply directly to us, all of them (except the Sabbath commandment) were repeated in the New Testament. Therefore, if we love God, we will obey the first four commandments (or their equivalent). If we love others, we will obey the New Testament equivalent of the last six commandments: We will honor our parents, but we will not murder, steal, commit adultery, bear false witness, or covet.

Why Not Sin? (20:5)

"If God is merciful and gracious and forgives sin, why worry about whether or not we sin?" That question could be answered in several ways, but Exodus 20:5 provides a good answer: Your sin can hurt not only you but also others, including succeeding generations. Illustrations of the consequences of fathers' sins affecting children for three or four generations are abundant.

A Day of Rest (20:10)

One purpose of the Sabbath was to provide a day of rest not only for the Israelites but also for those who depended on them, including their slaves and their working stock. This fact teaches us that we should be concerned about those who depend on us and make sure that their needs are met.

Chapter 21

The Book of the Covenant (Part 2)

In chapter 21, God continued to give Moses the specific laws which make up the Book of the Covenant (20:22—23:33). The chapter begins with a reminder that God is the source of these laws and that Moses was to pass them on to Israel (21:1). Then God gave laws related to slavery, which prescribe when and how a period of slavery would end (21:2–11). He also provided regulations regarding personal injuries, which deal with murder, accidental killing, individual injuries, and other related crimes (21:12–27). The end of the chapter contains laws regarding oxen. These involve situations in which oxen hurt people, as well as circumstances in which the oxen themselves are injured (21:28–36).

LAWS RELATED TO SLAVERY (21:1–11)

Male Slaves Who Serve for Six Years (21:1–6)

1"Now these are the ordinances which you are to set before them:

**2"If you buy a Hebrew slave, he shall serve for six years;
but on the seventh he shall go out as a free man without pay-
ment. 3If he comes alone, he shall go out alone; if he is the hus-
band of a wife, then his wife shall go out with him. 4If his mas-
ter gives him a wife, and she bears him sons or daughters, the
wife and her children shall belong to her master, and he shall
go out alone. 5But if the slave plainly says, 'I love my master,
my wife and my children; I will not go out as a free man,' 6then
his master shall bring him to God, then he shall bring him to**

the door or the doorpost. And his master shall pierce his ear with an awl; and he shall serve him permanently."

Verse 1. God was no longer speaking directly to the people, as He had when He pronounced the Ten Commandments. Rather, He presented these requirements to Moses, who was responsible for making them known to Israel (20:22). The laws in Exodus 21—23 are called **ordinances** (מִשְׁפָּטִים, *mishpatim*) or "judgments" (KJV).[1] The use of this word may signal that the laws being given were different from the previous ones—at least in form, if not in importance. Walter C. Kaiser, Jr., said that it refers to "precedents to guide Israel's civil magistrates in cases of civil dispute."[2] John I. Durham translated the word "guiding decisions" and spoke of the subsequent laws as "case-decisions" or "precedent-decisions," adding that they were applications of the "stated principles" set forth in the Ten Commandments.[3]

Verse 2. The first section of ordinances relates the terms for **buy**[ing] and releasing **a Hebrew slave**. Two situations are considered: a male slave who had served for **six years** (21:1–6) and a female slave purchased as a mate, either for the master or for the master's son (21:7–11).

Slaves were acquired in the ancient world primarily by conquest or by purchase. When one nation overcame another, the conquered people became "spoils of war" and were generally carried away by the conquerors to serve as slaves. To be carried away into slavery seems cruel, but the alternative was to be killed. Slaves were also made by poverty; one might choose to sell himself or his child to pay his debts. Children of slaves acquired in

---

[1]The singular form of the word is found in Micah 6:8 and is translated "justice": "What does the LORD require of you but to do *justice*, to love kindness, and to walk humbly with your God?" (Emphasis added.)

[2]Walter C. Kaiser, Jr., "Exodus," in *The Expositor's Bible Commentary*, vol. 2, *Genesis—Numbers* (Grand Rapids, Mich.: Zondervan, 1990), 429. Kaiser's use of "civil," though understandable to people in modern times, might not be appropriate because Israel probably did not acknowledge a difference between "civil law" and "religious law." All their laws were given by God.

[3]John I. Durham, *Exodus*, Word Biblical Commentary, vol. 3 (Waco, Tex.: Word Books, 1987), 307, 320.

war or of non-Israelite slaves who had been bought were born into a household as slaves.

The slaves discussed in 21:1–11 were those acquired by purchase who were "Hebrew" slaves. Some commentators believe that the designation "Hebrew" (עִבְרִי, *'ibri*) is used with a broader meaning than "Israelite,"—that it perhaps refers to a general category of landless people including, but not limited to, poor Israelites. However, the previous occurrences of the word in Exodus would argue against this idea (1:15, 16, 19; 2:6, 7, 11, 13; 3:18; 5:3; 7:16; 9:1, 13; 10:3). In many of these passages, the Lord is called "the God of the Hebrews," that is, the Israelites. Beyond this, the Hebrew slave is identified as "your kinsman" in a parallel passage (Deut. 15:12). The law gave regulations for Hebrew slaves that did not apply to other slaves. Slaves acquired in war, for example, were not set free after six years of labor.

The general rule is that a slave acquired by purchase remained a slave for only "six years"; in the **seventh** year he left **a free man without payment** or without anyone paying a price to "redeem" him. Slavery in this context, then, was like indentured servanthood: The slave worked for a certain number of years for a set price, and the money was used to pay the debts the man had incurred before becoming a slave. When the six years ended, he was set free. Deuteronomy adds that the slave's owner was not to send him away empty-handed, but was to provide for him liberally from his flock, threshing floor, and wine vat (Deut. 15:13, 14). That text also points out that these rules applied equally to Hebrew women who were slaves (Deut. 15:12). Women might therefore become slaves without any expectation of becoming the mate of the master or his son (see comments on 21:7).

Verses 3–6. Other explanations are provided through a number of "if . . . then" clauses:

(1) If he came in **alone**—that is, if he became a slave in the household in an unmarried state—then he was to leave **alone** (21:3a).

(2) If he came in married, then he was to leave with his **wife** (21:3b).

(3) If he came in unmarried but was given **a wife** during his servitude, then he was to go out **alone**, leaving his **wife** and **chil-**

dren with his **master** (21:4). Though this rule sounds harsh, it was fair, both to the slave and to the master.

(4) If, faced with leaving his **wife** and **children** behind, **the slave** decided that he would prefer to stay with the **master**, then the slave was brought to **God** (אֱלֹהִים, *'elohim*) (21:5, 6). While the plural term *'elohim* (or Elohim) is a designation for God, the word can also refer to rulers or judges of the people. Some versions translate it here as "God" (NASB; NRSV; REB; NAB; NJB), while others translate it "judges" (KJV; NKJV; NIV). In this context, the word probably refers to God's representatives, perhaps the elders or priests of Israel.

At the sanctuary, the slave would swear his continuing allegiance to his master. Then, at **the door or the doorpost**, his ear would be **pierce**[d]. This symbolic act probably took place at the master's house, though some commentators believe the doorpost of the sanctuary is meant. The hole in his ear, in which some think a tag would be placed, was a sign of his master's ownership. What the piercing of the ear signified, other than the slave's status, is uncertain. It may have indicated his willingness to hear and obey his master.

John J. Davis wrote that "there was no such thing as permanent, involuntary servitude for a Hebrew slave to a Hebrew master."[4] However, a Hebrew slave could voluntarily bind himself to serve his master for life. According to legislation given later, all Israelite slaves were to be freed and allowed to return to their land every fiftieth year, in the Year of Jubilee (Lev. 25:10). Nevertheless, Israelites could acquire and permanently possess slaves who were non-Israelites and could pass them on to their children (Lev. 25:44–46).

Female Slaves Bought as Wives (21:7–11)

[7]"If a man sells his daughter as a female slave, she is not to go free as the male slaves do. [8]If she is displeasing in the eyes

---

[4]John J. Davis, *Moses and the Gods of Egypt: Studies in Exodus*, 2d ed. (Grand Rapids, Mich.: Baker Book House, 1986), 227.

of her master who designated her for himself, then he shall let her be redeemed. He does not have authority to sell her to a foreign people because of his unfairness to her. [9]If he designates her for his son, he shall deal with her according to the custom of daughters. [10]If he takes to himself another woman, he may not reduce her food, her clothing, or her conjugal rights. [11]If he will not do these three things for her, then she shall go out for nothing, without payment of money."

Verse 7. If an Israelite sold **his daughter as a female slave**, she was to be treated differently than **male slaves**. The assumption is that the female was bought to become a wife to her master or to her master's son. If the master bought her to be his own wife, she could not go free after six years. Why? No reason is given. Likely, the "business deal" by which she entered into the household was viewed as something more when she married her master. Marriage is not the same as a business relationship between a master and a slave. This provision hints at God's attitude toward divorce: He hates it (Mal. 2:16).

Verses 8–11. Was this restriction fair for the female slave who was not freed after six years? The ordinance seems to anticipate that the purchase would work well for both parties, but such a transaction could have several outcomes.

(1) Even if the master took another wife, this purchased wife would always have **her food, her clothing,** [and] **her conjugal rights** (21:10).

(2) If the master found her displeasing as a wife, then he was to let her be **redeemed** (21:8). In other words, if the purchase was unsatisfactory, the slave's father could buy her back. The master could not sell her to **a foreign people** because that would be unfair to her. While this phrase may refer only to non-Israelites, it may have meant that the man who bought her could not sell her to a third party, a family with whom neither she nor her family were acquainted.

(3) If the master bought her to be the wife of **his son**, he was to treat her as he would a daughter (21:9).

(4) If the master bought her, made her his wife, and then failed to meet his obligations to her, she could go out **for noth-**

ing (21:11). She became a free woman without having to buy her freedom.

Exodus 21:1–11 and the ordinances that follow show that slavery was a way of life in ancient Israel. Before the Law was given, it was already an accepted institution, and the law of Moses did not outlaw it. However, the Law regulated slavery in such a way that its negative effects were, to a great extent, eliminated.

Gordon D. Fee and Douglas Stuart, commenting on Deuteronomy 15:12–17, said that Christians can learn four things from the case laws regarding slaves: (1) God's regulations for slavery under the old covenant were not harsh or brutal. (2) God loves slaves as He loves those who are free. (3) Slavery could be practiced in such a way that slaves were actually better off in bondage than being free. (4) The master did not own the slave in a total sense. God was the owner of both the master and the slave.[5]

LAWS REGARDING PERSONAL INJURIES (21:12–27)

In this section of the Book of the Covenant, there are laws which relate to "personal injuries"—to the killing or injuring of persons. These statutes usually give the general rule first and then apply the rule to specific cases.

Murder (21:12–14)

[12]"He who strikes a man so that he dies shall surely be put to death. [13]But if he did not lie in wait for him, but God let him fall into his hand, then I will appoint you a place to which he may flee. [14]If, however, a man acts presumptuously toward his neighbor, so as to kill him craftily, you are to take him even from My altar, that he may die."

---

[5]Gordon D. Fee and Douglas Stuart, *How to Read the Bible for All Its Worth*, 3d ed. (Grand Rapids, Mich.: Zondervan, 2003), 174.

Verse 12. This verse begins a new section by stating the general rule, just as in 20:23 and 21:2. This one is based on the sixth commandment (20:13), but it differs by adding the penalty to be exacted when someone was guilty of murder. The punishment was the same as that implied in Cain's lament (Gen. 4:14) and specifically called for by God in His covenant with Noah after the flood (Gen. 9:6): The individual who murdered was to be **put to death**.

Verse 13. The general law is followed by situations that illustrate how it should be applied in specific cases. The Law distinguishes between murder and manslaughter. The consideration is motive: If one person killed another but **he did not lie in wait for him**—that is, if the killing was not premeditated—then the person was not guilty of murder. Still, his deed would have consequences. He would **flee** to a city of refuge (see Num. 35),[6] where he was to be tried. If he was not guilty of what is now known as "first degree murder," he could escape death by remaining in the city until the death of the high priest (Num. 35:25, 28; Josh. 20:6).

Verse 14. If, on the other hand, he **presumptuously** struck down **his neighbor**, so as to **kill him craftily**, he was not to be spared. He was to **die**, even if he tried to escape punishment by taking hold of the horns of the **altar** (see 1 Kings 2:28–34). In other words, if one planned to kill another and then deliberately did so, he was guilty of murder and must be put to death.

Other Capital Crimes (21:15–17)

[15]"He who strikes his father or his mother shall surely be put to death.

[16]"He who kidnaps a man, whether he sells him or he is found in his possession, shall surely be put to death.

[17]"He who curses his father or his mother shall surely be put to death."

---

[6]Other commentators view the "place" in verse 13 as a reference to the altar in verse 14. See H. L. Ellison, *Exodus*, The Daily Study Bible Series (Philadelphia: Westminster Press, 1982), 125.

Regulations about striking a man are followed by the requirement of capital punishment for three offenses. Apparently, these crimes were as heinous to God as murder. The first and third related to one's relationship to his parents; the second, to the sanctity of a person's own body.

Verse 15. The fifth commandment to "honor your father and your mother" (20:12) is further explained in this verse. The individual **who strikes** or physically abuses **his father or his mother** would be punished with **death.**

Verse 16. The individual who **kidnaps** another would also suffer capital punishment. Just as murder takes life, the kidnapper steals a person's life—a violation of the eighth commandment (20:15). No matter what happened to the person kidnapped, the kidnapper forfeited his life. No Israelite could forcibly make a slave of another; to steal someone and enslave him would be kidnapping, punishable by **death**.

Verse 17. The fifth commandment is amplified once more. The one **who curses his father or his mother** would also stand guilty. It may be that the sin of cursing one's parents did not refer to a single incident, but to a continuing behavior. John H. Walton and Victor H. Matthews wrote, "The infraction here is not cursing but treating with contempt."[7] Nevertheless, while "curse" (קָלַל, *qalal*) can have the idea of slighting or despising someone (Gen. 16:4, 5), the verb usually refers to cursing someone when it appears in more intensive forms (Gen. 12:3; Lev. 24:14, 23; 2 Sam. 16:5; Prov. 20:20; Eccles. 7:21).

Why are the commands in verses 15 and 17 so important that breaking them made one subject to the **death** penalty? Perhaps the answer to that question is that the authority of parents mirrors God's authority over His children; to strike or curse one's parents is to strike out against God's authority. Such behavior leads to a chaotic society. God regards disobedience and disrespect toward parents as grave sins.

---

[7]John H. Walton and Victor H. Matthews, *Genesis—Deuteronomy*, The IVP Bible Background Commentary (Downers Grove, Ill.: InterVarsity Press, 1997), 112.

Injuries Caused by Striking (21:18–27)

After addressing capital crimes, the text names four situations involving not murder, but hitting. All have in common "striking" or being "struck," either purposely or accidentally (see 21:18, 19, 20, 22, 26).

When Men Fight and One Hurts Another (21:18, 19)

[18]"If men have a quarrel and one strikes the other with a stone or with his fist, and he does not die but remains in bed, [19]if he gets up and walks around outside on his staff, then he who struck him shall go unpunished; he shall only pay for his loss of time, and shall take care of him until he is completely healed."

Verse 18. In the first case presented, one man injures another when the two are fighting; both are apparently equally responsible for the quarrel. No one **die**[s], so the penalty for murder would not apply. The injury is not critical; the man who is struck **remains in bed** but heals later.

Verse 19. If the injured man **gets up and walks around outside on his staff** (the equivalent of walking with crutches), the penalty prescribed was that the one who caused the injury must **pay for his loss of time**. In other words, the injurer was obligated to compensate the injured party for the amount he would have been paid if he had been able to work at his job. The injurer was also required to **take care of him until he** [was] **completely healed.** In other words, he was responsible for meeting the needs of the one he had injured, including food and medical care, until he was healed.

When a Master Strikes His Slave and His Slave Dies (21:20, 21)

[20]"If a man strikes his male or female slave with a rod and he dies at his hand, he shall be punished. [21]If, however, he survives a day or two, no vengeance shall be taken; for he is his property."

The next law anticipated a question: "If I hurt someone else I am liable, but does the law of personal injury apply if I injure my own slave?" The answer is that the law did apply, but with modifications. It spoke of two possibilities.

Verse 20. First, one might strike a **slave with a rod**, causing the slave to die. In such a case, the master was to **be punished**, although the punishment was not specified. The assumption is that the master used excessive force to discipline his slave, or perhaps even intended to kill the slave. Therefore, the master must be punished.

Verse 21. Second, one might strike his slave so that he or she survived for **a day or two** but then died. In such a case, the master was not to be punished. The loss of the slave would be sufficient punishment for him, since a slave was valuable **property**. The assumption in this case is that the master did not intend to kill his slave, as evidenced by the fact that the slave was still alive after the beating.

To people living in the twenty-first century, a law stating that a master could accidentally kill his slave sounds brutal. It should be noted that, while these laws categorize slaves as property, they were not viewed as merely property. Under the Old Testament system, a slave was not the equivalent of a piece of furniture or a domestic animal. There were no laws to keep the owner of a table from breaking it, or the owner of a cow from killing it. However, there were laws limiting what the owner of a slave could do to him. Slaves had limited rights, but they did have rights.

When Men Fight and Strike a Pregnant Woman (21:22–25)

22"If men struggle with each other and strike a woman with child so that she gives birth prematurely, yet there is no injury, he shall surely be fined as the woman's husband may demand of him, and he shall pay as the judges decide. 23But if there is any further injury, then you shall appoint as a penalty life for life, 24eye for eye, tooth for tooth, hand for hand, foot for foot, 25burn for burn, wound for wound, bruise for bruise."

Verse 22. In the third case which does not involve murder, a pregnant **woman** is injured in connection with a fight between men. The penalty for the harm done to her is a payment equal to the injury.

One question that arises concerning these verses is whether the injured woman **gives birth prematurely** or whether she has a miscarriage. Translations differ on the subject. The NRSV, REB, NAB, and NJB all include the word "miscarriage" in their rendering of the verse. The NIV has "she gives birth prematurely" in the text, but puts "she has a miscarriage" in a footnote as an alternative reading. The KJV says "her fruit depart[s] from her."

The Hebrew text literally reads: "They strike a pregnant woman and goes forth the children [plural] and there is no injury." The language is apparently ambiguous: The text does not clearly say whether the child which "comes forth" is the result of a miscarriage or a premature birth. A strong case can be made for the position that a premature birth is meant, rather than a miscarriage. Dónal P. O'Mathúna wrote,

> The verb *yasa'* means "to go out" or "come out" and refers to the ordinary birth of children coming forth from their mother's womb (Gen 25:25–26; 38:27–30) or from their father's loins (Gen 15:4; 46:26). Only in Numbers 12:12 does it describe a stillbirth, and there the subject is not *yeled*, but *mwt*, something dead. The only biblical passage translating *yeled* as anything other than children (or non-human offspring in a few instances) is the Exodus 21 passage. When the Pentateuch elsewhere describes a miscarriage, *sakal* is used (Gen 31:38; Ex 23:26). Thus, the literal reading "her children came out" or "were born" is preferable, with the topic therefore being premature expulsion of the unborn, resulting in different possible injuries depending on the age of the fetus and impact of the blow.[8]

---

[8]Dónal P. O'Mathúna, "Bodily Injuries, Murder, Manslaughter," in *Dictionary of the Old Testament—Pentateuch* (Downers Grove, Ill.: InterVarsity Press, 2003), 93–94.

The alternative view of a miscarriage is supported by parallel legal texts from the ancient Near East. In each of those cases, the woman's baby dies.[9]

The clause **there is no injury** also needs to be considered. Obviously, an injury is involved; otherwise, there would be no need to pay for damages. Thus, many translations add a modifier to "injury" in verse 22: "no *serious* injury" (NIV), "no *lasting* harm" (NKJV), "no *further* harm" (NRSV) (emphasis added). The context clearly implies that if the unborn child is subjected either to a miscarriage or to a premature birth, harm has been done; there has been an injury. The person who caused the harm must pay a fine to recompense the **husband** of the woman. The amount of the fine will be determined by the husband's demands and the judgment of the court. Consequently, the text implies that "no *further* injury" is what is meant by the passage.

If "further injury" does result—if, for instance, the woman is otherwise seriously injured—there is an additional penalty, described in the next three verses.

Verses 23–25. If there is any further injury in connection with the premature birth of the child which was caused by men fighting, the Israelites were commanded to **appoint as a penalty life for life, eye for eye, tooth for tooth, hand for hand, foot for foot, burn for burn, wound for wound, bruise for bruise.**

"Further injury," beyond the minor harm which results from the premature birth of the child, requires additional punishment. How much? These verses establish the principle that the extent of the injury should govern the punishment. Basically, this law teaches that the punishment should vary according to the extent of the harm done.

The "eye for an eye" law is known technically as the *lex talionis*, a Latin phrase meaning "the law of retribution." Some refer to it as the law of "like for like." It is found two other times in

---

[9]James B. Pritchard, ed., *Ancient Near Eastern Texts: Relating to the Old Testament*, 3d. ed. (Princeton, N.J.: Princeton University Press, 1969), 175 (nos. 209–214), 181, 184–85 (nos. 21, 50, 53), 190 (nos. 17, 18); William H. Propp, *Exodus 19—40: A New Translation with Commentary and Introduction*, Anchor Bible, vol. 2a (New York: Doubleday, 2006), 226–27.

other contexts in the Pentateuch. The first is Leviticus 24:19, 20, a context regarding punishment for the infliction of bodily injuries. The other is Deuteronomy 19:21, which deals with the punishment of a false witness. The law is a stereotyped formula meaning, "The punishment shall fit the crime."[10]

Probably the "eye for an eye" law was not meant to be taken literally, any more than the law that said that God's statutes would "be as frontals on your forehead" (Deut. 6:8) was intended to cause the Jews to wear phylacteries. The biblical evidence for being punished by having an eye put out or a hand cut off is minimal; the examples involve the Israelites and their enemies in times of war (Judg. 1:6, 7; 16:21; 2 Kings 25:7). Only one other passage in the Law seems to require bodily mutilation (Deut. 25:11, 12), and it is unlikely that the punishment it prescribes was ever carried out.[11]

In fact, the context in Exodus 21 itself argues against the literal application of the "eye for an eye" formula. The formula calls for a life to be given for a life. What if the premature baby dies? Should the person who caused the child's death be put to death? The context in Exodus 21 relates, not to homicides, but to other crimes involving death. The principle established in this section of the law is that first-degree murder is a capital crime, and other kinds of killing are not. The death of a baby because men are fighting and accidentally injure the baby's mother does not qualify as a homicide; this type of death is accidental, not premeditated.

It would be unfair, therefore, for the retribution for the baby's death to be the death of the person responsible. What, then, would "life for life" mean in this passage? It would have to mean that a payment must be made sufficient to recompense the injured party for the death of the child. In fact, Numbers 35:31 seems to

---

[10]See Martin Noth, *Exodus*, trans. J. S. Bowden, The Old Testament Library (Philadelphia: The Westminster Press, 1962), 182.

[11]Another view is that bodily mutilation did occur in ancient Israel ("it shall be done to him," Lev. 24:19; "you shall do to him," Deut. 19:19), but was eventually replaced by monetary compensation. See Josephus *Antiquities* 4.8.35; Mishnah *Baba Qamma* 8.1, 2. Compare "The Code of Hammurabi" in Pritchard, 175 (nos. 196–201).

say that the only kind of killing for which a ransom could not be paid was murder.[12]

Thus, the "eye for an eye" law was not to be taken literally: If someone knocked out another's eye, he did not have his own eye knocked out. Furthermore, the law was not intended to be used to justify personal retaliation. It does not authorize individuals who have been wronged to respond by saying "an eye for an eye" and then seeking revenge against those who have wronged them.[13] In the Old Testament, as in the New, the Bible teaches that vengeance belongs to God (Deut. 32:35; 1 Sam. 26:32–35; Ps. 94:1; Prov. 24:29; Rom. 12:19). Furthermore, the Law forbade the Israelites to seek vengeance (Lev. 19:18) and taught them to do good to their enemies (23:4, 5; see Prov. 25:21, 22).

The Old Testament does authorize the "avenger of blood" (Num. 35:12–29)—a dead man's nearest relative—to take vengeance on the one who killed his relative. However, it also provided for cities of refuge to which the person who was being pursued by the avenger of blood could flee. There the accused man was tried. If he was innocent, he found refuge in the city. If he was guilty of murder, he was killed by the avenger of blood, who served as *an instrument of the court* (and society) to punish the murderer. The whole process was regulated by law; *it was the legal way to bring a murderer to justice.* For a people without a standing army or police force, the procedure was as good a legal system as could have been devised. Such a system did not involve an individual's taking the law into his own hands and seeking personal revenge.

For those who know the New Testament, the idea that the law did not permit personal revenge may cause some confusion

---

[12]As evidence that the phrase "life for life" was itself a stereotyped expression, consider Leviticus 24:18: "The one who takes the life of an animal shall make it good, life for life." Most would agree that this statute requires the payment of monetary compensation equal to the value of the dead animal. It does not require that another animal be put to death as retribution for the killing of an animal.

[13]See Coy D. Roper, "'An Eye for an Eye': The Problem of Retaliation in Ancient Israel," *The Journal of Biblical Interpretation and Application* 1 (July–September 2002): 21–46.

because they remember the words of Jesus: "You have heard that it was said, 'An eye for an eye and a tooth for a tooth.' But I say to you, do not resist an evil person; but whoever slaps you on your right cheek, turn the other to him also" (Mt. 5:38, 39). They have then assumed that Jesus was contrasting His teachings with those of the old covenant. However, Jesus was not speaking against what the Old Testament actually taught but against the popular misunderstanding of that teaching. Obviously, in Jesus' day, some thought that the "eye for an eye" law justified personal retaliation, but it did not.

When a Master Disfigures His Slave (21:26, 27)

26"If a man strikes the eye of his male or female slave, and destroys it, he shall let him go free on account of his eye. 27And if he knocks out a tooth of his male or female slave, he shall let him go free on account of his tooth."

Verses 26, 27. In the fourth case related to "striking," the penalty was prescribed for destroying a slave's **eye** or knocking out **his tooth**. If the master did either, the penalty was that the slave must be set **free**. The obvious difference between this law and the one in verses 20 and 21 is that, in this case, the beaten slave does not die but is disfigured.

This law is probably included at this point in the Book of the Covenant to explain how the general rule of "eye for eye" would apply to a slave. The phrase "eye for eye" (21:24) presupposes that the offended person is a free man. A slave-master could argue, "If I knock out my slave's eye, I have only hurt my own property. The slave does not own his eye—I do, so he need not be compensated for damage which I do to him." This law refutes such reasoning, declaring that the master who disfigured his slave owed the slave compensation for the injury. In fact, the compensation would equal the value of the slave, which was thirty pieces of silver (21:32). The "payment" of this compensation would give the slave his or her freedom. Again, this law illustrates that slavery did not negate the personhood or value of a slave.

LAWS REGARDING OXEN (21:28–36)

The laws in 21:28–36 have this in common: Each mentions the "ox" (שׁוֹר, *shor*) or "bull" (NIV). The ox was the largest, most expensive, and most dangerous domestic animal. The laws regarding oxen were undoubtedly to be viewed as a pattern for justice regarding any kind of animal. Two basic situations are envisioned: The first involves an ox hurting a person, and the other applies to an ox being hurt.

When an Ox Hurts a Person (21:28–32)

28"If an ox gores a man or a woman to death, the ox shall surely be stoned and its flesh shall not be eaten; but the owner of the ox shall go unpunished. 29If, however, an ox was previously in the habit of goring and its owner has been warned, yet he does not confine it and it kills a man or a woman, the ox shall be stoned and its owner also shall be put to death. 30If a ransom is demanded of him, then he shall give for the redemption of his life whatever is demanded of him. 31Whether it gores a son or a daughter, it shall be done to him according to the same rule. 32If the ox gores a male or female slave, the owner shall give his or her master thirty shekels of silver, and the ox shall be stoned."

Verse 28. As with previous sections of laws, this verse states a general law, and the following verses apply the law to specific cases. The general rule here is that an **owner** is not held accountable for the behavior of his farm animals. A man can control some things, but he is not responsible for what is beyond his control. However, the **ox** which killed a human being was to be killed by stoning, a penalty usually reserved for men guilty of a capital crime. R. Alan Cole wrote that the ox, "like a human being," must be stoned, "for the ox has incurred blood guilt (Gn. 9:5)."[14] Some

[14]R. Alan Cole, *Exodus: An Introduction and Commentary*, Tyndale Old Testament Commentaries (Downers Grove, Ill.: Inter-Varsity Press, 1973), 170.

might consider this unfair to the ox, since it is the nature of the beast to gore. Nevertheless, in keeping with the high priority placed on human life in the Old Testament, anything that took human life must be punished—even an ignorant animal. Further, the fact that the ox was, in effect, a "murderer," rendered its meat unfit to eat.

Verse 29. Another scenario is possible, requiring a different punishment. If the **owner** knew that the **ox** was dangerous—if he had **been warned** but had taken no steps to **confine** the dangerous animal[15]—then he was accountable for what the ox did. **The ox** was still to be **stoned** to death, but in this case the negligent **owner** of the ox was likewise to **be put to death**. In effect, he would be guilty of murder, and the ox would be the equivalent of a weapon used to take another's life.[16]

Verses 30, 31. These verses seem to grant that allowing a goring ox to run loose is not exactly the equivalent of murder. No ransom was allowed in a case of murder (21:12), but a close relative of a person killed by an ox could choose to ask for a monetary settlement. This action would presumably take place in a judicial setting, before the elders of the land. The close relative could request **a ransom** from the person who owned the ox, rather than having the guilty owner killed along with his ox. If he made that choice, the owner of the ox had to pay **whatever** [was] **demanded of him** for the loss of **a son or a daughter**.

Verse 32. This section is completed, as were two previous sections (21:20, 21, 27), with an application regarding slaves. If an **ox** gored a **slave** to death, what was to be done? Again, **the ox** was to be **stoned**, signifying that the ox had, in effect, murdered a human being. In this case, there would be no death penalty for the ox's owner. Rather, he would pay the master of the (deceased) slave the value of the slave: **thirty shekels of silver** (see Zech. 11:12, 13; Mt. 26:15).

---

[15]In comparable legislation, "The Code of Hammurabi" envisions the owner being warned by the city council. Examples of preventative measures included tying up the ox and padding its horns. See Pritchard, 176 (no. 251).

[16]Similar laws are found in modern times. United States law holds the owners of animals responsible for their animals' misdeeds.

When an Ox Is Hurt (21:33–36)

[33]"If a man opens a pit, or digs a pit and does not cover it over, and an ox or a donkey falls into it, [34]the owner of the pit shall make restitution; he shall give money to its owner, and the dead animal shall become his.

[35]"If one man's ox hurts another's so that it dies, then they shall sell the live ox and divide its price equally; and also they shall divide the dead ox. [36]Or if it is known that the ox was previously in the habit of goring, yet its owner has not confined it, he shall surely pay ox for ox, and the dead animal shall become his."

Verses 33, 34. The second set of laws related to oxen speak of conditions in which oxen, rather than hurting others, are themselves injured. Two situations are pictured. The first involves **an ox or a donkey** falling into **a pit** dug or uncovered by someone other than its master. The pit might be a cistern used to hold water or a storage pit for grain. **The owner of the pit**, as the one responsible for the death of the **animal**, would be required to pay for it. If the owner of the pit paid **restitution**, he was allowed to keep the carcass of the animal. Since this animal was not polluted by murder, its meat could be eaten.

Verses 35, 36. What was to be done in the second situation, when **one man's ox** killed another man's ox? The owners of the two oxen were to **sell the live ox and divide its price equally**, as well as dividing the meat of **the dead ox**. Again, an exception was made if the ox that killed the other **was previously in the habit of goring**. If the **owner** of a "goring" ox had allowed it to run loose, then he was to replace the other owner's dead animal—**ox for ox**. After making restitution, he was allowed to keep **the dead animal** and use its meat.

APPLICATION

"Pierce [My] Ear" (21:2–6)

Exodus 21:2–6 teaches that after a slave had served the required number of years, he could leave his master's service as a free man. If he had acquired a wife and children during his years as a slave, and if he loved his master, he could choose not to go free. As a sign of his voluntary lifelong servitude, he would have his ear pierced.

A popular devotional song entitled "Pierce My Ear" is derived from this text.[17] The voluntary devotion of the slave toward his master is used to express the believer's willing service to the Lord. A person can be free of the demands of Christ if he chooses; however, by becoming a Christian, he volunteers for lifelong servitude as a slave to the Lord. Why would he do that? Because he loves his Master (21:5)! Of course, the two situations are not exactly parallel. In truth, one cannot be absolutely free. Everyone is either a slave of sin or a slave of righteousness (Rom. 6:17, 18), and there is a penalty for trying to serve both masters (Rom. 6:23). You have many reasons to say to your Master, "Pierce my ear!"

God's People Are Fair (21:12–36)

The fairness of the Law and its ordinances is impressive (21:12–36). God's people were required to be just, or fair, in their dealings with others (Mic. 6:8). Likewise, Christians are to be just (see Mt. 23:23). Are we? Do we take unfair advantage of others? When we enter into a business transaction, are we only concerned about getting a good "deal" ourselves? Do we brag about profiting at others' expense? Would we sue a large company for an amount disproportionate to our actual injuries?

---

[17]Steve Croft, "Pierce My Ear," © 1980 by Dayspring Music, http://www.mpcofc.org/youth/songs/songbook/song_book_page_3.htm (accessed Oct. 23, 2008).

CHAPTER 22

THE BOOK OF THE COVENANT (PART 3)

The Book of the Covenant (20:22—23:33) continues in this chapter, which contains both negative and positive instruction. Exodus 22 includes ordinances related to theft, idolatry, the need to show compassion, and ways that God must be honored.

The chapter begins with a list of crimes against others' property. These ordinances can be thought of as expansion and application of the eighth commandment, "You shall not steal" (20:15). The laws include regulations regarding theft (22:1–4), carelessness with regard to one's own property (22:5, 6), negligence in the use of others' property (22:7–15), and the misuse of another man's daughter (22:16, 17). Then, after a section on crimes related to idolatry (22:18–20), the chapter provides guidance on how to treat people. The Israelites were to show compassion toward the unfortunate members of society—strangers, widows, orphans, and the poor (22:21–27). Finally, instruction on proper ways to honor God is given (22:28–31).

CRIMES AGAINST PROPERTY (22:1–17)

Theft (22:1–4)

1"If a man steals an ox or a sheep and slaughters it or sells it, he shall pay five oxen for the ox and four sheep for the sheep.

2"If the thief is caught while breaking in and is struck so that he dies, there will be no bloodguiltiness on his account.
3But if the sun has risen on him, there will be bloodguiltiness

on his account. He shall surely make restitution; if he owns nothing, then he shall be sold for his theft. [4]If what he stole is actually found alive in his possession, whether an ox or a donkey or a sheep, he shall pay double."

The first group of laws in this section are connected to theft, to one man's stealing from another. Each example determined whether or not a person was guilty of breaking the eighth commandment (20:15) and, if so, what specific penalty should be imposed.

Several translations reorder these verses in an attempt to smooth out the text (RSV; NRSV; NEB; REB). These versions rearrange the verses in the following order: 1, 3b, 4, 2, 3a. After verse 1 ("If a man steals an ox or a sheep . . ."), the translation continues with verse 3b ("He shall surely make restitution . . ."), then verse 4 ("If what he stole is actually found alive . . ."), followed by verses 2 and 3a ("If the thief is caught while breaking in . . . But if the sun has risen on him . . ."). There is no manuscript evidence, however, to indicate that these verses ever had any other arrangement than that found in the NASB. The seeming disorder is probably an intentional chiastic pattern (ABBA) in the Hebrew text:

A1: "If a man steals an ox or a sheep and slaughters it or sells it, he shall pay five oxen for the ox and four sheep for the sheep" (22:1).

B1: "If the thief is caught while breaking in and is struck so that he dies, there will be no bloodguiltiness on his account" (22:2).

B2: "But if the sun has risen on him, there will be bloodguiltiness on his account" (22:3a).

A2: "He shall surely make restitution; if he owns nothing, then he shall be sold for his theft. If what he stole is actually found alive in his possession, whether an ox or a donkey or a sheep, he shall pay double" (22:3b, 4).

Verse 1. The chapter begins with this principle: If one **steals an ox or a sheep** and then gets rid of it, he must repay fivefold

for the ox and fourfold **for the sheep**. The difference in restitution is probably based on the fact that the ox was more valuable to the family than the sheep. R. Alan Cole wrote, "A trained ox is not only more valuable, but harder to replace" than a sheep.[1]

Perhaps the most important aspect of this punishment is what it did not include. In contrast to other laws of the ancient Near East,[2] the law of Moses never prescribed death or the mutilation of the body for crimes against property—for instance, cutting off a thief's hand. Unlike the penalties required for theft today, the Law did not prescribe confinement or time in prison. After all, there was no police force in ancient Israel, and there were no jails or prisons.

Verse 2. The principle of verse 1 raises this unspoken question: Since the thief was not to be punished by death, what about a thief who was killed during the commission of a crime? The answer is that, if the householder **struck** and killed an intruder at night, he was guiltless. The language may suggest that he did not intend to kill the thief when he struck him (see 21:12).

Verse 3a. However, if the householder killed the thief after **the sun** [had] **risen**, there would be **bloodguiltiness on his account**. Being guilty of the blood of the dead thief made the owner of the house subject to capital punishment.

The difference between the two cases lies in the fact that a thief could not be seen at night. The owner of the house could not judge his intentions, to know whether the intent was to steal or to murder.[3] He had the right to defend himself and his family with deadly force. However, after the "sun has risen," in the light of day, the householder could see what the thief was doing.

---

[1]R. Alan Cole, *Exodus: An Introduction and Commentary*, Tyndale Old Testament Commentaries (Downers Grove, Ill.: Inter-Varsity Press, 1973), 171.

[2]In "The Code of Hammurabi," thieves were sentenced to death in some cases. See James B. Pritchard, ed., *Ancient Near Eastern Texts: Relating to the Old Testament*, 3d ed. (Princeton, N.J.: Princeton University Press, 1969), 166–67 (nos. 6, 7, 21, 22). Law 21 envisioned a man making "a breach" in a house. This act is parallel to 22:2 where the term "breaking in" (מַחְתֶּרֶת, *machthereth*) refers to digging through (see Job 24:16; Ezek. 8:8; 12:5, 7, 12).

[3]Cole, 171. The same idea is presented in Wilbur Fields, *Exploring Exodus*, Bible Study Textbook Series (Joplin, Mo.: College Press, 1976), 484.

Recognizing him as a thief, but not a potential murderer, the owner of the house had no authority to kill him.

This law taught the right of an Israelite to defend himself, even with deadly force, if he seemed likely to be killed.[4] It also upheld the value of the thief's life, which took precedence over property. According to the law of Moses, the life of a person—even a thief—was worth more than any possession.[5]

Verse 3b. Another unspoken question is this: If the thief could not afford to pay the fourfold or fivefold price of the stolen animal, what was to be done? He would **be sold for his theft**, and the money, no doubt, would be given to the offended party.

Verse 4. A final unspoken question appears in verse 4: If the thief had not yet sold or eaten a stolen animal, what was the penalty? If the animal was **actually found alive in his possession**, then the live animal would be returned to the rightful owner. Rather than paying four or five times its value, the thief was then to **pay double** its value.

Carelessness Concerning Fields (22:5, 6)

[5]"If a man lets a field or vineyard be grazed bare and lets his animal loose so that it grazes in another man's field, he shall make restitution from the best of his own field and the best of his own vineyard.

[6]"If a fire breaks out and spreads to thorn bushes, so that stacked grain or the standing grain or the field itself is consumed, he who started the fire shall surely make restitution."

The property laws in the second group relate to damage that is done to a neighbor's field.

Verse 5. Two cases are described here. The first concerns an **animal** getting **loose** and grazing **in another man's field.** In keeping with the ordinances related to the death of an ox (21:33, 34),

---

[4]Peter Enns, *Exodus*, The NIV Application Commentary (Grand Rapids, Mich.: Zondervan, 2000), 449.

[5]James Burton Coffman, *Commentary on Exodus, The Second Book of Moses* (Abilene, Tex.: ACU Press, 1985), 315–16.

the owner of the wandering animal was to pay for what his animal had eaten. In doing so, he could not slight the injured owner. Rather, he had to **make restitution from the best** that he had.

Verse 6. The second case depicts the owner of a field as having started **a fire**, perhaps to burn off the underbrush so that he could plant crops or so that the grass would flourish (see 22:5; NEB). However, because of his carelessness, the fire burned out of control, destroying the **grain** in another man's **field**. In such a case, the man **who started the fire** had to **make restitution**.

In both cases, the offending person was careless, not malicious. When unintentional mistakes occurred, making restitution to the injured party was sufficient. Such situations called for no criminal penalties.

Failures in Keeping Others' Goods Safe (22:7–15)

[7]"If a man gives his neighbor money or goods to keep for him and it is stolen from the man's house, if the thief is caught, he shall pay double. [8]If the thief is not caught, then the owner of the house shall appear before the judges, to determine whether he laid his hands on his neighbor's property. [9]For every breach of trust, whether it is for ox, for donkey, for sheep, for clothing, or for any lost thing about which one says, 'This is it,' the case of both parties shall come before the judges; he whom the judges condemn shall pay double to his neighbor.

[10]"If a man gives his neighbor a donkey, an ox, a sheep, or any animal to keep for him, and it dies or is hurt or is driven away while no one is looking, [11]an oath before the LORD shall be made by the two of them that he has not laid hands on his neighbor's property; and its owner shall accept it, and he shall not make restitution. [12]But if it is actually stolen from him, he shall make restitution to its owner. [13]If it is all torn to pieces, let him bring it as evidence; he shall not make restitution for what has been torn to pieces.

[14]"If a man borrows anything from his neighbor, and it is injured or dies while its owner is not with it, he shall make full restitution. [15]If its owner is with it, he shall not make restitution; if it is hired, it came for its hire."

In the third group, the focus is on a person's failure to safeguard the property entrusted to him. Three situations are pictured this time: one involving "money or goods" kept for someone else, a second involving an animal kept for another, and a third involving the loss of borrowed property.

Verse 7. This first case is about **money or goods** entrusted to a **neighbor**. Such an arrangement was certainly possible in the days before banks. If a **thief** stole something that had been entrusted to another, then he was to repay twice the value of the thing he had stolen (compare 22:4).

Verse 8. If, however, **the thief** [was] **not caught**, then the actual owner of the stolen item would have only the word of **the owner of the house** that the item had been stolen. If this happened, he might believe that the person whom he had trusted with his property had in truth sold his goods and kept the money for himself. In such a circumstance, both men would appear **before the judges** in some kind of court setting.

The word translated "judges" in 22:8, 9 is אֱלֹהִים (*'elohim*) and can be translated "God" (NRSV; NEB; NJB; see comments on 21:6). If "before God" is meant, then the accused person was to appear before God's representatives, probably at the sanctuary. Then the person accused of theft was apparently supposed to swear before Israel's authorities that he was innocent (see 22:11). According to J. Philip Hyatt, "It is assumed here that an oath in the presence of [God] is so strong that the person would not swear to a false oath."[6] John I. Durham contended that the two parties received a divine pronouncement, perhaps through the Urim and the Thummim (see 28:30).[7]

Verse 9. This verse expands the law to include all kinds of property, animals as well as objects. It also includes any situation in which one man believed he had seen a **lost** or stolen item in the possession of his neighbor. When that happened, the owner said, "'**This is it**'; this is my property which was lost." Then the

---

[6]J. Philip Hyatt, *Exodus*, The New Century Bible Commentary (Grand Rapids, Mich.: Wm. B. Eerdmans Publishing Co., 1971), 238.

[7]John I. Durham, *Exodus*, Word Biblical Commentary, vol. 3 (Waco, Tex.: Word Books, 1987), 326.

two men went **before the judges**, or "before God." The one found guilty of deception—whether the man who took what did not belong to him or the man who falsely accused **his neighbor**—was required to **pay** the other party **double** the value of the disputed item.[8]

Verses 10, 11. In this second case, **a man** is depicted as having asked **his neighbor** to **keep** something **for him**, but this time the thing kept was an **animal**. As in the previous cases, that which was entrusted to the neighbor has been lost; in this scenario it either **dies** or **is hurt** or **is driven away while no one is looking**. Again, it is possible that the person keeping the animal might really have taken it himself. In this case, **an oath before the Lord**—made perhaps in the presence of the Lord's representatives—settled the matter. If the keeper of the animal swore such an oath, the **owner** of the animal was to **accept** his word and not require **restitution** of him.

Verse 12. If the animal was **actually stolen**, then the person who was keeping it was to **make restitution** to the animal's **owner**, presumably because he was negligent. However, he did not have to pay double because he was not guilty of a crime.

Verse 13. If the animal was **torn to pieces** by a wild animal, the person who was keeping it was required to show the carcass to the animal's owner **as evidence** (see Amos 3:12). He did **not** have to **make restitution**, since a man could not be blamed for what a wild animal had done.

Verse 14. A third case relates to property borrowed or hired, rather than something entrusted to a **neighbor**. One **man** might, for instance, borrow another's ox to plow his land. If the borrowed animal died or was **injured** while the owner was not with it, the borrower was to **make full restitution** to the **owner**.

Verse 15. If, on the other hand, the **owner** was with the animal when it died or was injured, then the user did not have to **make restitution**. Since the owner of the animal was present, the injury or death was presumably not caused by the user's care-

---

[8]Other law codes in the ancient Near East provided legislation similar to 22:8, 9, such as "The Laws of Eshnunna" and "The Code of Hammurabi." See Pritchard, 163 (nos. 36, 37), 171 (nos. 120–126).

lessness and probably could not have been avoided; therefore, the user was not guilty of any wrongdoing. Moreover, if the animal had been **hired**, the money already spent on hiring it was sufficient to pay for the use of the animal.[9]

Misuse of a Man's Daughter (22:16, 17)

[16]"If a man seduces a virgin who is not engaged, and lies with her, he must pay a dowry for her to be his wife. [17]If her father absolutely refuses to give her to him, he shall pay money equal to the dowry for virgins."

The fourth kind of crime against "property" involves the misuse of a man's daughter. Although it is repulsive to most people today to think of a man's daughter as "property," in ancient Israel the father "owned" his daughter, in a sense, until she was married. Her mistreatment, therefore, could be thought of as a "crime against property." Peter Enns explained that this crime "falls under the category of 'property damage,' not 'social responsibility.'"[10] In the case under consideration, a man "seduces a virgin" who is neither married nor betrothed.

Verse 16. It is important to note that this case deals with an incident of seduction, not rape. Nahum M. Sarna noted that the woman was seduced "by persuasion or deception but not by coercion. There is a presumption of consent on the part of the girl"; "Ibn Ezra points out that the sequence of legal topics is 'from the case of stolen property to that of a stolen heart.' Both are offenses that occasion economic loss and entail payment of compensation."[11]

Furthermore, the girl portrayed here was not spoken for; if she had been married or promised to another, the man would be

---

[9]Similar legislation to this third case is found in "The Code of Hammurabi" and "The Hittite Laws." Ibid., 176 (nos. 245–249), 192 (nos. 75, 76).

[10]Enns, 450.

[11]Nahum M. Sarna, *Exodus,* The JPS Torah Commentary (New York: Jewish Publication Society, 1991), 134–35.

guilty of adultery. Deuteronomy 22:23–27 prescribes the penalty for a betrothed virgin who lies with a man voluntarily (both were to be put to death) and involuntarily (only the man was to be stoned). As it is, the penalty prescribed is that he had to **pay a dowry for her** and marry her. The text suggests that there was a set price for virgins.

Verse 17. If the **father** refused to give his daughter to the man in marriage, the man was still required to **pay** for her.[12] R. Alan Cole expressed the situation as follows:

> This [law concerning the seduction of a daughter] comes under the general heading of robbery. An unmarried girl was, in a sense, her father's property, and he would in due course receive a marriage present or 'bride-price' for her. . . . In this instance, since a man has taken a girl without paying bride-price, bride-price he must pay, for who else will pay it now?[13]

Two things are noteworthy about this law. (1) Fornication—sexual relations with an unmarried person—is not equated with the sin of adultery. In this respect, the moral standard of the New Testament seems to be higher than that of the Old. (2) While the penalty provided fair treatment for the seduced virgin, the offense was primarily against the father, who must be compensated. Unless her father objected, the daughter acquired a husband. The marriage was not the husband's decision, but the father's.

CAPITAL CRIMES RELATED TO IDOLATRY (22:18–20)

[18]"You shall not allow a sorceress to live.

[19]"Whoever lies with an animal shall surely be put to death.

---

[12]See the parallel in "The Middle Assyrian Laws" where a payment was required and the father decided what happened to his daughter (Pritchard, 185 [no. 56]).

[13]Cole, 173.

[20]**"He who sacrifices to any god, other than to the Lord alone, shall be utterly destroyed."**

Three laws in these verses are connected to the first two of the Ten Commandments, which forbade Israel to have gods other than Yahweh (20:3–6).

Verse 18. The first of these laws bans the practice of sorcery. The feminine word for **sorceress** is used rather than the masculine form for "sorcerer," perhaps because more women than men engaged in the practice. The death penalty for sorcery seems harsh until it is remembered that the sorceress was trying to get supernatural help and guidance from someone other than the Lord God (see Deut. 18:9–14). By its very nature, sorcery acknowledges the reality and power of other "gods" and, further, indicates the practitioner's allegiance to those gods rather than to the Lord.

To the extent that this prohibition is applicable today,[14] it would forbid Christians from seeking aid or guidance from mediums, palmists, and fortunetellers. However, the passage does not authorize the death penalty for witches or sorcerers in the Christian age, any more than passages which specify the death penalty for adultery are applicable today.[15] Since Christ's kingdom is "not of this world," members of His church have no authority to punish sinners physically.

Verse 19. The prohibition of bestiality, at first glance, seems to be an expansion of the seventh commandment, "You shall not commit adultery" (20:14). Certainly, it can be seen as related to that commandment. However, its placement in this context suggests another connection. Some of the Canaanite gods were depicted as having sexual relations with animals. This commandment may, therefore, be related not only to sexual misconduct, but also to sexual misconduct connected to the worship of other

---

[14]Several other Old Testament passages condemn sorcery and similar practices (Lev. 19:31; 20:6, 27; Deut. 18:10, 11; 2 Kings 21:6; 1 Chron. 10:13; Is. 8:19; Mic. 5:12). The New Testament also condemns sorcery and witchcraft (Gal. 5:19, 20; Rev. 21:8; 22:15).

[15]Coffman, 321.

gods.[16] Peter Enns, citing Leviticus 18:23–25, asserted that the sin of bestiality was a cultic offense.[17] In any case, the Israelite who was guilty of this sin was to **be put to death** (see Lev. 20:15, 16; Deut. 27:21).[18]

Verse 20. In contrast to other groups of laws in the Book of the Covenant, this group of three laws states the basic principle last rather than first. The general law is stated in verse 20, forbidding sacrifice to any god other than Yahweh. This law goes beyond the penalties announced earlier for *not* worshiping **the Lord alone**, saying that the one who is guilty of worshiping another **god** would **be utterly destroyed**. The verb חָרַם (*charam*), which is translated "utterly destroyed," is different from the verbs translated "put to death." Sarna said that it "implies a greater stringency than does the simple death penalty formula. It implies total annihilation and includes the destruction of the criminal's property."[19]

LAWS REQUIRING COMPASSION (22:21–27)

[21]"You shall not wrong a stranger or oppress him, for you were strangers in the land of Egypt. [22]You shall not afflict any widow or orphan. [23]If you afflict him at all, and if he does cry out to Me, I will surely hear his cry: [24]and My anger will be kindled, and I will kill you with the sword, and your wives shall become widows and your children fatherless.

[25]"If you lend money to My people, to the poor among you, you are not to act as a creditor to him; you shall not charge him interest. [26]If you ever take your neighbor's cloak as a pledge, you are to return it to him before the sun sets, [27]for that is his only covering; it is his cloak for his body. What else shall he sleep in? And it shall come about that when he cries out to Me, I will hear him, for I am gracious."

---

[16]Cole, 174.

[17]Enns, 451.

[18]"The Hittite Laws" also condemned bestiality in most cases as a capital crime. See Pritchard, 196–97 (nos. 187, 188, 199, 200A).

[19]Sarna, 137.

This next section dictates God's laws of compassion. The Israelites were to be compassionate toward strangers (22:21), widows and orphans (22:22–24), and the poor (22:25–27). Sarna wrote,

> These humanitarian stipulations may have been set down after the preceding cultic laws in order to establish a contrast between the moral corruption of paganism (vv. 17–19) and the moral nature of the God of Israel. In addition, they serve to inculcate [reinforce] the idea that the rejection of the non-Israelite religious practices (v. 19) has no bearing on the inalienable right of the alien to civilized treatment free of victimization (v. 20).[20]

These laws differ from the preceding ones in form. While the previous ones were presented as "if/then" clauses ("casuistic" form), these laws are like the Ten Commandments, simply stating "You shall" or "You shall not" ("apodictic" form). Further, while penalties were specified for the offenses named earlier, there was no provision for Israel to punish those who mistreated strangers or charged interest of the poor. These were matters of conscience.

Nevertheless, reasons are given in the text for obeying these categorical imperatives. (1) Since Israel had been strangers in the land of Egypt (22:21), they should be kind to strangers. (2) They should be motivated by their own experiences and the sympathy those experiences should evoke; if the poor man is deprived of his cloak at night, he will have nothing to sleep in and he will be cold (22:27). (3) Most importantly, they were to show compassion for those who could not care for themselves because God had shown compassion to them. Thus, if they afflicted the weak, He would afflict them (22:23, 24). Wilbur Fields noted that God "has a special protective love for the widows and fatherless."[21]

God's concern for the oppressed and powerless, for those on the outskirts of society, is shown frequently in the Old Testament

---

[20]Ibid.
[21]Fields, 493.

(Deut. 14:29; 16:11, 14; 24:17–21; 26:12, 13; 27:19; Ps. 94:6; Is. 1:23; 10:2; Jer. 7:5–7; Zech. 7:10; Mal. 3:5). Christians should likewise show concern toward the disadvantaged.

Verse 21. In the first paragraph on compassion, God required that Israel **not wrong a stranger or oppress him**. He appealed to Israel's memory of their own oppression in **Egypt** to reinforce the lesson. God seems to have been saying, "Surely, you do not want others to suffer as you did." The "stranger" here is the non-Israelite living among the Israelites; the Hebrew word גֵּר (*ger*) refers to a resident alien. Many non-Israelites left Egypt with Israel (12:38), and the law made provision for them. Others would live among them after they reached the promised land.

Verses 22–24. God next warned the Israelites not to take advantage of **any widow or orphan**. Such individuals had no one to take care of them and were therefore vulnerable to human predators. God said that He would **hear** the **cry** of these helpless ones and **kill** their oppressors, leaving the **wives** of the uncompassionate ones as **widows** and their **children fatherless.** In keeping with the Law, God would repay them "like for like." Israel's mistreatment of poor people, widows, and orphans was part of the reason that the kingdom ultimately was taken into exile (Deut. 27:19; 28:49, 50; Is. 1:16–20; Jer. 7:4–7).

Verse 25. The second paragraph on compassion forbade the Israelites to **charge** the **poor** any **interest** (see Lev. 25:35–38; Deut. 23:19, 20). If a poor man needed money, a loan to him was to be thought of as an act of benevolence rather than as a business deal: A brother who had more was simply helping one who had less.[22] "The word for 'poor' [עָנִי, *'ani*] means to be overwhelmed by want, and it is related to the verb 'afflict' [עָנָה, *'anah*] in verse 22."[23]

Verses 26, 27. Apparently, the Israelite who was lending money could accept the poor man's **cloak** as collateral for the

---

[22]Jesus seems to expand this command, saying, "Give to everyone who asks of you, and whoever takes away what is yours, do not demand it back" (Lk. 6:30).

[23]Noel D. Osborn and Howard A. Hatton, *A Handbook on Exodus* (New York: United Bible Societies, 1999), 534.

loan, although he was not required to take it. The fact that a cloak was the only collateral the poor man could offer illustrates how poor he was. If a lender did take the cloak, he had to give it back before nightfall; otherwise, the poor man would have nothing to keep himself warm as he slept. As with the laws concerning widows and orphans, God gave a reason to obey the rule about having compassion on the poor: because He is their protector.

LAWS HONORING GOD (22:28–31)

28"You shall not curse God, nor curse a ruler of your people.

29"You shall not delay the offering from your harvest and your vintage. The firstborn of your sons you shall give to Me.
30You shall do the same with your oxen and with your sheep. It shall be with its mother seven days; on the eighth day you shall give it to Me.

31"You shall be holy men to Me, therefore you shall not eat any flesh torn to pieces in the field; you shall throw it to the dogs."

In addition to the laws regarding property and compassion, chapter 22 gives both negative and positive instruction relating to honoring God. It speaks of sins related to idolatry, which called for the death penalty (22:18–20), and it concludes with a group of laws requiring God's people to honor Him in specific ways (22:28–31). These are framed in terms of "You shall" and "You shall not," without specifying punishments or enforcement procedures.

Verse 28. The first of these laws indicates that it was wrong to **curse God**. The word for "God" is אֱלֹהִים (*'elohim*). Since *'elohim* is a plural form, it is sometimes used for the pagan "gods" of the nations around Israel. In this context, the term refers to the one true God of Israel, not "gods" (KJV). This meaning is evident from the fact that it would be unthinkable for the Law to tell Israel not to curse the "gods" when such gods were not even to be acknowledged. The word *'elohim* can also denote "rulers" or "judges," definitions which some commentators support in verse 28 (see comments on 21:6; 22:8).

To "curse God" would violate the third commandment which prohibits the misuse of the divine name (20:7). The seriousness of this offense can be seen from a story found later in the Pentateuch. While fighting with another, the son of an Israelite woman and an Egyptian man "blasphemed the Name and cursed." As a result, God told Moses that the offender was to "be put to death." In response to the Lord's instructions, the Israelites took the man "outside the camp and stoned him" (Lev. 24:10–16, 23).

To **curse a ruler of your people** was almost the equivalent of cursing God, who was responsible for his becoming a ruler. The gravity of this law is also well illustrated later in the Pentateuch. When some of the Israelites rebelled against Moses and Aaron, God's appointed leaders, God utterly destroyed them (Num. 16). In the New Testament, Paul quoted this verse after he had spoken against the high priest (Acts 23:5).

Verses 29, 30. God had already said that the Israelites were not to sacrifice to other gods, but were to make sacrifices to Him (22:20). In these verses, He specified that the Israelites were to offer their first fruits to Him—the best of the **harvest** (grain) and the **vintage** (wine). The requirement to give their best is specifically stated with regard to the **firstborn** of their **sons** and animals. Therefore, the same principle would be true with regard to their crops (see 23:19; Deut. 18:4; 26:1, 2). The animals and harvested crops were to be offered literally, while the firstborn son was to be redeemed with money or an equivalent sacrifice (13:12, 13; 34:20).

The fact that Israelites were not to sacrifice to other gods but were to sacrifice to Yahweh illustrates an important principle: It was not enough to merely avoid that which was sinful; the Lord's people had to be busy actively doing what He required.

Verse 31. The final requirement in this short series is a prohibition of **eat**[ing] the **flesh** of an animal which was **torn to pieces in the field**. This applied, for example, to the remains of a sheep killed by a wolf. Rather than eating it, the owner was to **throw it to the dogs**, which were known as unclean scavengers (1 Kings 14:11; 16:4; 21:19, 23, 24; 22:38; 2 Kings 9:10, 36; Ps. 59:6, 14, 15; 68:23; Jer. 15:3). Why? One obvious answer is that the animal killed in the field did not have the blood properly drained from the body; therefore, it was impossible to eat its flesh without eating the blood as well. There was already a very old restriction against eating blood (Gen. 9:3, 4; see Deut. 12:16, 23).

What did the Israelites' not eating such an animal have to do with their being **holy men** to God? To be holy is to be "set apart," and refraining from eating blood was one practice that set Israel apart from its neighbors. This was a sign of Israel's "holiness" or "set-apartness"—the fact that Israel was God's special people. Cole said, "All Israel was virtually in the position of priests (Ex. 19:6). It was unthinkable that a priest should defile himself (and so defile God) by eating carrion."[24]

APPLICATION

How Should the Law of Moses Be Used Today? (Chs. 20—23)

In Exodus 20—23 we find the laws that God gave to Moses. When we as Christians read these laws, we may wonder how they could possibly be of any value for us—how this portion of the Scriptures could be "profitable" today (2 Tim. 3:16, 17). We see the value of the Ten Commandments (20:1–17), but the legal details seem irrelevant. How should we as Christians use the legal material found in Exodus 20—23?

Are we to regard the Law as binding on us today? These passages cannot be considered our laws, since the New Testament teaches that the Old Testament has been taken away (Gal. 3:24, 25). Not even the Ten Commandments, as such, are binding on us today.

Are we to assume that God intends for nations today to be governed by the Law? These laws were not for everyone. God wanted Israel to become an ideal society, a "holy nation." We should imitate the principles upon which the laws are based (although not the specific regulations). These principles are the ideals underlying a just society:

---

[24]Cole, 176.

1. Fairness and justice.
2. Compassion and mercy for the care of widows and orphans, the poor, foreigners who lived among the Israelites, the aged, and the handicapped.
3. The value of human beings. Human beings were placed in a different category from animals or property. Human life was so valuable that the only proper punishment for maliciously taking a life was the forfeiture of the murderer's life.
4. The importance of the home and family.
5. The right to own property was protected by laws against theft.
6. Individual responsibility.
7. The centrality of the worship of the one true God.

Christians can learn much from studying the Law (see Rom. 15:4). The laws set forth by God indicate what He values in His people. Applying the following principles in our lives today can help us to please Him.

Make God the central focus of our lives. In Israel, every aspect of life was governed by God's law. Similarly, every aspect of the Christian's life is to be governed by God's law. We must be concerned about doing His will in everything. In worship, in the family, in business, and in recreation, we ought to ask, "What would the Lord have me do?"

Be compassionate to those who are less fortunate than we are. The laws of the Old Testament required that compassion be shown to the poor, to slaves, to widows and orphans, and to strangers. We, too, should be concerned about helping the unfortunate.

Be fair and just. The emphasis on fairness and justice in the Law shows the need for us to be absolutely fair and just in our dealings with others, both within and outside of the church.

Exemplify in the church the principles underlying the Law. We should respect the life of every human being, recognize individual rights and responsibilities, value justice and fairness, show compassion to all, emphasize the importance of the family, and make God and His will the foundation of our society. If we do, the church will be "a light to the nations" (Is. 42:6), "a city set on a hill" (Mt. 5:14), attracting outsiders to its warm fellowship.

Conclusion. We may think that the Old Testament laws are unimportant, that we do not need to study them. However, in them we see what God wanted Israel to be. To a great extent, at least in principle, that is what God wants us to be as His people today.

Our Responsibility to the Unfortunate (22:21–27)

The Law, with its individual ordinances, illustrates principles that will always be true regarding the responsibilities of God's people. One of those principles is that God's people are to help, and never to take advantage of, the unfortunate. Israel was to show consideration for strangers, widows and orphans, and the poor. Based on Leviticus 19:14, we can add to that list the handicapped.

What does the New Testament say? Consider Matthew 25:31–46; Galatians 2:10; 6:10; and James 1:27. Why should we, as Christians, care for the unfortunate? For some of the same reasons God gave Israel:

(1) *Because we have been delivered out of the slavery of sin.* Since we have been so blessed, both spiritually and materially, we ought to be a blessing to others.

(2) *Because we are to show compassion.* Let us do to others what we would have them do to us (Mt. 7:12).

(3) *Because the unfortunate occupy a special place close to the heart of God.* He will avenge their mistreatment (22:23, 24; see Mt. 25:41–46). To be like God and to avoid His wrath, we must care for the unfortunate.

Showing Respect to Rulers (22:28)

To curse a ruler of the people is apparently equivalent to cursing God. Let us show respect to those who rule over us (Rom. 13:1–7; 1 Tim. 2:1, 2; 1 Pet. 2:13, 17). Similarly, we are to honor those who lead in the church (Heb. 13:7, 17).

"You Shall Be Holy Men to Me" (22:31)

To eat the flesh of an animal torn to pieces in the field would pollute Israel; it would make the people "unholy." Just as Israel was a "holy nation," we are to be holy (1 Pet. 1:15; 2:9). Therefore, we need to avoid anything—any activity, any television program or movie, any website—that will keep us from being holy, from being a people set apart from the world for God's service.

Chapter 23

The Book of the Covenant (Part 4)

The Book of the Covenant (20:22—23:33) concludes with laws related to justice, to religious holy days, and to sacrifices. The chapter also gives a number of instructions and promises in regard to entering the promised land.

The focus shifts from what is owed to God (22:28–31) to what is owed to man—namely, justice. To treat one another fairly is man's obligation (23:1–9).

Next, the Lord instructed the people to keep both the Sabbath year and the Sabbath day (23:10–13), to observe the three great national feasts (23:14–17), and to offer acceptable sacrifices to Him (23:18, 19). These laws made no provision for enforcement and prescribed no penalties for disobedience. The chapter ends with an epilogue relating to entering the promised land (20:20–33).

THE DEMANDS OF JUSTICE (23:1–9)

Justice in the Law Courts (23:1–3)

[1]"You shall not bear a false report; do not join your hand with a wicked man to be a malicious witness. [2]You shall not follow the masses in doing evil, nor shall you testify in a dispute so as to turn aside after a multitude in order to pervert justice; [3]nor shall you be partial to a poor man in his dispute."

Verses 1–3. The laws in these verses relate to a court setting.

In ancient Israel, a man might be involved in a trial in one of four ways. He could either be (1) the defendant, (2) the prosecutor, (3) a witness, or (4) a judge. Trials could be held at any time and were generally judged at the city gate by the elders who sat there (Deut. 21:19; 22:15; 25:7; Josh. 20:4). These laws emphasize the fairness of trials by requiring honest testimony from witnesses and impartial decisions from judges.

The laws acknowledge the possibility that a witness or a judge might "bear a false report" or otherwise cause an unfair verdict—a violation of the ninth commandment (20:16). The temptation to **bear a false report** might come from one of three motives. (1) Someone might bear false witness out of malice, or for his own advantage. (2) A false witness might be influenced by public opinion. (3) One might even be tempted to render a wrong judgment out of sympathy for the **poor**. Being concerned about the unfortunate, he might ignore facts or discount testimony damaging to the poor man in the trial and rule in his favor anyway.

According to the law of Moses, all of these temptations must be resisted. Regardless of personal advantage, the belief of the majority, or the status of the person being tried, the witness was to tell the truth (see Lev. 19:15, 16). Whatever the cost, each participant in the trial was responsible for seeing that justice was done. In this way, they would imitate God, who is impartial (Deut. 10:17, 18; Acts 10:34, 35).

Justice Toward an Enemy (23:4, 5)

4"If you meet your enemy's ox or his donkey wandering away, you shall surely return it to him. 5If you see the donkey of one who hates you lying helpless under its load, you shall refrain from leaving it to him, you shall surely release it with him."

Verses 4, 5. Several classes of people were in particular need of justice. First, the Israelites were to be fair to enemies by treating them as friends. Who would not **return** a friend's **ox** or **donkey** if he found it wandering away? Who would not relieve a friend's **donkey** if he found it **lying helpless under its load**? This would be the right thing to do—for an enemy as well as a friend, and for the animal as well as the owner. R. Alan Cole wrote, "*Enemy* in this context probably means 'legal adversary'. Justice demands that we treat him like any other neighbour, and certainly that we do not 'take it out' [on] his helpless livestock."[1] Such action was not a matter of mercy, but of justice (see Deut. 22:1–4; Prov. 25:21, 22).

Although being kind to animals is not the major focus of the requirement, this passage may also suggest the need to treat animals humanely. This principle is also demonstrated by the fact that the Sabbath was to be a day of rest for animals as well as for people (20:10).

Justice for the Unfortunate (23:6–9)

6"You shall not pervert the justice due to your needy brother in his dispute. 7Keep far from a false charge, and do not kill the innocent or the righteous, for I will not acquit the guilty.

8"You shall not take a bribe, for a bribe blinds the clear-sighted and subverts the cause of the just.

9"You shall not oppress a stranger, since you yourselves know the feelings of a stranger, for you also were strangers in the land of Egypt."

Continuing the application of justice, these verses mention the poor, the innocent, and strangers. In the middle of this group of laws is found a prohibition of bribery.

Verse 6. The **needy brother** was to be treated fairly, especially in court cases. Then, as now, those with much money were more likely than the poor to get away with a crime. The rich can almost always take advantage of the poor. However, the message of this law was "You should not do wrong just because you can get away with it!" This ordinance forbade **pervert**[ing] **the justice due** to the needy.

---

[1]R. Alan Cole, *Exodus: An Introduction and Commentary*, Tyndale Old Testament Commentaries (Downers Grove, Ill.: Inter-Varsity Press, 1973), 177.

Verse 7. Then Israelites were forbidden to **kill the innocent or the righteous**. The context suggests that the specific act forbidden was wrongly declaring an innocent or righteous man guilty, with the result that his life was taken; to do so would be the equivalent of killing him.[2] God said that He would intervene on behalf of the innocent man and **not acquit the guilty** man who caused the innocent man's death.

Verse 8. Next, **tak**[ing] **a bribe** was prohibited because a bribe keeps justice from being done; presumably, the same principle applied to offering a bribe. While this law pertained to any official at any time, it was probably especially applicable to the court situations the Israelites experienced. Judges who were chosen from among the elders of the people might have been tempted to rule in favor of whoever could give them the largest gift (see Deut. 16:18–20; 1 Sam. 8:3; 12:3).

Verse 9. In addition, there was a rule against taking advantage of a **stranger**. Again, this rule most likely dealt with oppression in the legal system. Foreigners (resident aliens) would have been at a distinct disadvantage when brought before an Israelite court. Therefore, the Israelites had to be very careful to make sure their judgments were fair. Why should the Israelites care for strangers, for foreigners? Because they themselves had been **strangers** in **Egypt**; their slavery should have made them benevolent toward the foreigners living among them (22:21).

KEEPING THE SABBATH (23:10–13)

10"You shall sow your land for six years and gather in its yield, 11but on the seventh year you shall let it rest and lie fallow, so that the needy of your people may eat; and whatever they leave the beast of the field may eat. You are to do the same with your vineyard and your olive grove.

12"Six days you are to do your work, but on the seventh day you shall cease from labor so that your ox and your donkey may rest, and the son of your female slave, as well as your

---

2Umberto Cassuto, *A Commentary on the Book of Exodus,* trans. Israel Abrahams (Jerusalem: Magnes Press, 1997), 299.

stranger, may refresh themselves. [13]Now concerning everything which I have said to you, be on your guard; and do not mention the name of other gods, nor let them be heard from your mouth."

Near the end of the covenant code, the emphasis turns back to man's relationship to God. The next several laws expand and explain the fourth commandment: "Remember the sabbath day" (20:8).

Verses 10, 11. These verses expand the Sabbath commandment to apply to **the seventh year**, the sabbatical year. **For six years** the Israelites were to work their **land**, but during **the seventh year** they were to let the land **rest and lie fallow**. Whatever grew of its own accord during that year was to be left, first, for the poor of the land and, second, for the animals. What would the Israelites live on during that year? They were to expect sufficiently abundant crops during the sixth year to sustain them during the seventh year (Lev. 25:20–22). This law required the Israelites to have (1) compassion on the land, on the poor, and on the animals, as well as (2) faith that God would provide enough during the sixth year so that they would not need to plant or harvest during the seventh year.

Verse 12. This verse repeats the Sabbath commandment itself (20:9, 10), adding that the purpose of the day was to allow the farm animals, slaves, and foreigners to **refresh themselves** (see Deut. 5:14). Sabbath-keeping was intended to be a humanitarian practice.

Verse 13. The Sabbath section ends with a warning against **mention**[ing] **the names of other gods**. The Lord did not want the Israelites to acknowledge the existence of other gods (20:3). Further, He did not want His people to take oaths in their names or call on them in prayer (Josh. 23:7).

THREE ANNUAL FEASTS (23:14–17)

[14]"Three times a year you shall celebrate a feast to Me. [15]You shall observe the Feast of Unleavened Bread; for seven days you are to eat unleavened bread, as I commanded you, at the

appointed time in the month Abib, for in it you came out of Egypt. And none shall appear before Me empty-handed. [16]Also you shall observe the Feast of the Harvest of the first fruits of your labors from what you sow in the field; also the Feast of the Ingathering at the end of the year when you gather in the fruit of your labors from the field. [17]Three times a year all your males shall appear before the Lord GOD."

The Book of the Covenant follows a natural progression from the observance of the Sabbath to the observance of Israel's three annual feast days: the Feast of Unleavened Bread, the Feast of the Harvest, and the Feast of the Ingathering. These three feasts were connected with the agricultural year, as well as with great historical events in Israel (see 34:18–26; Lev. 23; Deut. 16:1–17).

Verse 14. This section begins and ends by emphasizing that the Israelites were to celebrate **three times a year** (23:14, 17). The general command **you shall celebrate a feast to Me** in verse 14 is clarified in verse 17: "All your males shall appear before the Lord GOD."

Verse 15. The Feast of Unleavened Bread commemorated Israel's deliverance from **Egypt** (12:17–20). **Eat**[ing] **unleavened bread** reminded the people of the fact that they had left Egypt in such a hurry that they did not have time to allow their bread to rise before they departed. This feast followed the Passover and "was observed from the fifteenth through the twenty-first days of Abib, the first month (mid-March to mid-April)," at the "beginning of the barley harvest."[3] The people were not to **appear** in God's presence **empty-handed**; they were to bring "the first fruits of [their] harvest to the priest" (Lev. 23:10).

Verse 16. The Feast of the Harvest was also known as "the Feast of Weeks" (34:22). It "was held seven weeks after the Feast of Unleavened Bread" on "the sixth day of Sivan, the third month (mid-May to mid-June), during the wheat harvest. This celebration commemorated the giving of the law on Mount Sinai."[4] At

---

[3]Ronald F. Youngblood, *Exodus*, Everyman's Bible Commentary (Chicago: Moody Bible Institute, 1983), 107–8.

[4]Ibid., 108.

this feast, the Israelites were commanded to offer **the first fruits** of their wheat harvest to God (34:22; Lev. 23:16, 17). In the New Testament, "the Feast of Harvest" is called "the day of Pentecost" (Acts 2:1; 20:16; 1 Cor. 16:8) because it occurred fifty days after Passover. "Pentecost" is derived from the Greek word πεντήκοντα (*pentēkonta*), meaning "fifty" (see Lev. 23:16).

The Feast of the Ingathering was celebrated "from the fifteenth through the twenty-second days of Tishri, the seventh month (mid-September to mid-October), when the produce of the vines and orchards had been harvested."[5] In addition to the feast's agricultural significance, "it commemorated the desert wanderings after the Exodus and the giving of the law."[6]

The celebration was also known as "the Feast of Booths" or "Tabernacles" (Lev. 23:34; Deut. 16:13; 31:10; see NIV). This name was derived from the fact that God's people lived in "booths" when He brought them out of Egypt. During this feast, the Israelites were commanded to "live in booths" in order to remember their journey through the wilderness (Lev. 23:40–43). Since the civil calendar began in the fall, this feast took place **at the end of the year**; it marked the completion of the agricultural year.

Verse 17. On these three occasions, the adult **males** were to gather together **before the Lord God**. In other words, **three times a year** the men of Israel were to attend a solemn national assembly or convocation. The guidelines for these feasts not only instructed the Israelites in their responsibilities but also reinforced their hope, for they implied the successful completion of Israel's journey. Israel could look forward to celebrating harvests in their own land.

LAWS CONCERNING SACRIFICES (23:18, 19)

18"You shall not offer the blood of My sacrifice with leavened bread; nor is the fat of My feast to remain overnight until morning.

---

[5]Ibid.
[6]Ibid.

[19]"You shall bring the choice first fruits of your soil into the house of the Lord your God.

"You are not to boil a young goat in the milk of its mother."

This brief section expresses Israel's obligations to God. The laws convey what should or should not be done with regard to sacrifices. They relate to the three feasts described in the preceding section (23:14–17). The laws are repeated, with slight variation, in 34:25, 26.

Verse 18. The two laws in this verse both involve negative commandments. The first negative is: **"You shall not offer the blood of My sacrifice with leavened bread."** One of the feasts previously described is the Feast of Unleavened Bread (23:15). During this time, the Israelites were to get rid of any leaven from among them (12:15, 19, 20, 34, 39; 13:3, 7). Further, God commanded His people to offer cakes of unleavened bread along with their animal sacrifices (29:1, 2, 22, 23; Lev. 2:4, 5; 6:14–16; 7:12; 8:2, 26). He instructed Moses, saying, "'No grain offering, which you bring to the Lord, shall be made with leaven, for you shall not offer up in smoke any leaven or honey as an offering by fire to the Lord'" (Lev. 2:11). A few references do mention worshipers bringing leavened bread as an offering to God. However, these cakes were not to be burnt on the altar; instead, they were to be eaten by the priests (Lev. 7:13, 14; 23:17, 20). Perhaps leavened bread was not offered with animal sacrifices on the altar because leaven was viewed as a corrupting force (see comments on 12:15).

The second negative is: **"Nor is the fat of My feast to remain overnight until morning."** This prohibition may mean, as John I. Durham explained, that "the fat was Yahweh's alone and was to be offered to him promptly."[7] After all, the laws regarding sacrifices required that "the fat" (חֵלֶב, *cheleb*) of the animals be offered up by fire on the altar to God (29:13, 22–25; Lev. 3:3, 4, 9, 10). The people were instructed that "all fat is the Lord's" and "you shall not eat any fat or any blood" (Lev. 3:16, 17).

---

[7]John I. Durham, *Exodus*, Word Biblical Commentary, vol. 3 (Waco, Tex.: Word Books, 1987), 334.

Another explanation is that "the fat of My feast" refers to the Passover lamb, the "best" or "choicest" item at that feast.[8] This interpretation is supported by the parallel passage which states, "Nor is the sacrifice of the Feast of the Passover to be left over until morning" (34:25). Moreover, the phrase "remain over night until morning" is reminiscent of the earlier instructions for the Passover (12:10). If the Passover lamb is in view, then perhaps all of verse 18 relates to the Passover and the Feast of Unleavened Bread (see Deut. 16:3, 4).

Verse 19. This verse begins with a positive requirement: The Israelites were told to bring **the choice first fruits of** [their] **soil into the house of the LORD your God.** Before an Israelite provided for himself or saved for the future, he was to give the first and best of his harvest to the Lord. This command relates to the previous feasts (23:14–17) which were connected to the various harvests—barley, wheat, and fruit. These items were used to support the Levitical priests and their families (Num. 18:12, 13; Deut. 18:3–5).

The second part of verse 19 contains a puzzling requirement: **"You are not to boil a young goat in the milk of its mother"** (see 34:26; Deut. 14:21). What was required is clear; why it was required is more difficult. Various explanations have been given. One is that it would be cruel to cook a young goat (or kid) in its mother's milk.[9] The most common and best explanation is that the restriction was placed on Israel because this practice was a feature of pagan Canaanite religion. Umberto Cassuto explained,

> Now we know from the Ugaritic texts that the Canaanites prepared such a dish particularly at festal ceremonies pertaining to the fertility of the soil. In the Ugaritic tablet on 'The gods pleasant and beautiful' it is written

---

[8]C. F. Keil and F. Delitzsch, *The Pentateuch*, vol. 2, trans. James Martin, Biblical Commentary on the Old Testament (Grand Rapids, Mich.: Wm. B. Eerdmans Publishing Co., n.d.), 149–50.

[9]Nahum M. Sarna, *Exodus*, The JPS Torah Commentary (New York: Jewish Publication Society, 1991), 147.

> (line 14): . . . 'boil a kid in milk, a lamb in butter.' The custom of boiling small cattle in milk has been preserved to this day among Bedouins.[10]

If the Israelites engaged in such a practice, it might appear to others that they had adopted the Canaanite religion. The requirement may be tied in some way to the previous law in verse 19. If so, then it may speak of a kid which has been offered as the first fruits of the flock.

Concerning later Judaism, Nahum M. Sarna wrote, "The interdiction of boiling a kid in its mother's milk was generalized to outlaw the mixing of all meat and milk (meaning all dairy products)."[11] Consequently, some Jews keep meat products in one refrigerator and milk products in another, and they do not consume meat and dairy products at the same meal. The law given in 23:19 provides no reason for such a practice.

EPILOGUE: ENTERING THE PROMISED LAND (23:20–33)

Exodus 23:20–33 may be thought of as an epilogue to the Book of the Covenant, in that it contains no additional laws. Rather, it refers to Israel's continued movement toward, and ultimate entrance into, the promised land. The promises and threats in this section urged the people to be faithful as they continued their journey.

The Angel's Guidance (23:20–23)

[20]"Behold, I am going to send an angel before you to guard you along the way and to bring you into the place which I have prepared. [21]Be on your guard before him and obey his voice; do not be rebellious toward him, for he will not pardon your transgression, since My name is in him. [22]But if you truly obey his voice and do all that I say, then I will be an enemy to your

---

[10]Cassuto, 305.
[11]Sarna, 147.

enemies and an adversary to your adversaries. [23]For My angel will go before you and bring you in to the land of the Amorites, the Hittites, the Perizzites, the Canaanites, the Hivites and the Jebusites; and I will completely destroy them."

Verses 20, 21. God promised **to send an angel before** Israel. The angel was to **guard** the people **along the way**, and **bring** them into the land which God had **prepared** for them. He would command or direct Israel, for Israel was to **obey his voice**. In addition, the angel would **pardon** Israel's **transgression** if they were obedient; at least, he would not pardon them if they were disobedient. Israel was to **be on** [their] **guard before him** and to **obey his voice**, not being **rebellious toward him**.

Who was this "angel" (מַלְאָךְ, *mal'ak*)? Since the Hebrew term *mal'ak* simply means "messenger," there are several possibilities as to the identity of this "angel."

One possibility is that he could have been a *human messenger*, or God's representative. Some Jewish commentators believed that the "angel" was first Moses and then Joshua. In a sense, Moses did the things the angel is said to have done for Israel. However, the passage does not sound as if it refers to a human messenger. R. Alan Cole noted that the description of the angel sounds at first like that of a human messenger. Nevertheless, verse 21, which says, **"My name is in him,"** "seems to translate the 'messenger' into the supernatural realm, for God's name is the equivalent of His revealed nature."[12]

A second possibility is that the angel could have been a *heavenly being*, an "angel" in the more usual sense of the word. In favor of this view is the fact that both in this context (23:23) and in others (32:34; 33:2), that interpretation could be taken as the obvious meaning of the passage.

A third possibility is that this angel could have been *Deity*. In other words, the "angel" of God may refer to God Himself. In favor of this view is the fact that God's "name [was] in him." Evidently, the angel had the option to forgive sins, which only God can do. Moreover, the "angel of the LORD" in Exodus 3 was

---

[12]Cole, 181.

undoubtedly a manifestation of God Himself (see comments on 3:2, 3). John I. Durham wrote, "[The angel is] a reference to an extension of Yahweh's own person and Presence" and is "a restatement of the promise and proof of Presence motif that dominates the narrative of Exod 1—20."[13]

A fourth, and closely related, possibility, is that the angel is the *preincarnate Word*, the second person of the Godhead. In favor of this view is the fact that in numerous passages in the Old Testament, the "angel of the LORD" is both identified with and differentiated from the Lord. After considering such evidence, J. Alec Motyer wrote,

> There is only one other in the Bible who is both identical with and distinct from the Lord. One who, without abandoning the full essence and prerogatives of deity or diminishing the divine holiness, is able to accommodate himself to the company of sinners and who, while affirming the wrath of God, is yet a supreme display of his outreaching mercy. Such indeed, is the Angel of the Lord as revealed in the Old Testament, and, consequently, Barton Payne does not hesitate to say these "revelations of the unique Angel . . . can be appreciated only when understood as a preincarnate appearance of Jesus Christ."[14]

Obviously, if the reference to this angel is to the preincarnate Word, that fact could only be known after the Word was made flesh (Jn. 1:1, 14).

Whether the angel was Deity (or the preincarnate Word), a heavenly being, or a human messenger, the message was the same. To Israel came the good news that God would guide, pro-

---

[13]Durham, 335.

[14]J. Alec Motyer, *The Message of Exodus*, The Bible Speaks Today (Downers Grove, Ill.: InterVarsity Press, 2005), 51; citing J. Barton Payne, *The Theology of the Old Testament* (Grand Rapids, Mich.: Zondervan, 1962), 170. See Walter C. Kaiser, Jr., "Exodus," in *The Expositor's Bible Commentary*, vol. 2, *Genesis—Numbers* (Grand Rapids, Mich.: Zondervan, 1990), 446; Wilbur Fields, *Exploring Exodus*, Bible Study Textbook Series (Joplin, Mo.: College Press, 1976), 517.

tect, and forgive them—and eventually give them the promised land. Israel, in turn, had to respect the angel. To be on their "guard before him" suggests that they needed to be aware that disobedience to the angel could be catastrophic.

Verses 22, 23. This part of the chapter concludes with a promise: If Israel did indeed follow the direction of the angel, God would be with them. He would **be an enemy to** [their] **enemies**, lead them **in to the land**, and **destroy** the nations living there—**the Amorites, the Hittites, the Perizzites, the Canaanites, the Hivites and the Jebusites** (see comments on 3:8b).

Warning Against Idolatry (23:24)

24"You shall not worship their gods, nor serve them, nor do according to their deeds; but you shall utterly overthrow them and break their sacred pillars in pieces."

Verse 24. In discussing the people of the land, the Law forbade Israel to participate in the Canaanites' idolatry. Israel was commanded **not** to **worship their gods, nor serve them**; they were not to live as the people of Canaan lived. Further, they were to **overthrow** their idols and **break their sacred pillars in pieces**. Here the term "pillar" (מַצֵּבָה, *matstsebah*) refers to a stone which stood upright at a Canaanite shrine or high place. The stone, often rounded at the top, was closely identified with a deity, usually a male god. Such pillars are sometimes mentioned alongside wooden Asherah poles which symbolized the fertility goddess (34:13; Deut. 7:5; 12:3; 2 Kings 17:10; 18:4; 21:3; 23:14, 15). Archaeologists have discovered many examples of these pillars in Palestine.[15]

Abundant Blessings for Obedience (23:25–31)

25"But you shall serve the LORD your God, and He will bless your bread and your water; and I will remove sickness from

---

[15]R. K. Harrison, "Pillar," in *The International Standard Bible Encyclopedia*, rev. ed., ed. Geoffrey W. Bromiley (Grand Rapids, Mich.: Wm. B. Eerdmans Publishing Co., 1986), 3:870.

your midst. [26]There shall be no one miscarrying or barren in your land; I will fulfill the number of your days. [27]I will send My terror ahead of you, and throw into confusion all the people among whom you come, and I will make all your enemies turn their backs to you. [28]I will send hornets ahead of you so that they will drive out the Hivites, the Canaanites, and the Hittites before you. [29]I will not drive them out before you in a single year, that the land may not become desolate and the beasts of the field become too numerous for you. [30]I will drive them out before you little by little, until you become fruitful and take possession of the land. [31]I will fix your boundary from the Red Sea to the sea of the Philistines, and from the wilderness to the River Euphrates; for I will deliver the inhabitants of the land into your hand, and you will drive them out before you."

Verses 25, 26. The people of God were to only **serve the LORD**. If they did, He promised to **bless** them with food and **water**, with health (by banishing **sickness**), with fertility and fruitfulness (by banishing miscarriages and barrenness), with longevity, and with victory.

Verses 27, 28. God would **send** [His] **terror ahead of** Israel, **throw**[ing] their enemies **into confusion**. He would send **hornets** ahead of Israel to drive the people out of the land. Do these statements refer to the same thing? God's "terror" may be referring to the report of God's mighty deliverance of Israel from Egypt (see 15:14–16),[16] which did, in fact, contribute to Israel's conquest of Canaan (Josh. 2:8–11). Some commentators believe that the "hornets" may be another way of referring to reports about God's powerful demonstrations on behalf of the Israelites. The word for "hornets" (צִרְעָה, *tsir'ah*) is found only three times in the Hebrew Bible (23:28; Deut. 7:20; Josh. 24:12) and its meaning is uncertain, being variously translated as "hornets," "panic-terror," "pestilence," and "depression, discouragement."[17] Others interpret the "hornets" as the armies of Egypt that had

---

[16]Peter Enns, *Exodus*, The NIV Application Commentary (Grand Rapids, Mich.: Zondervan, 2000), 472.

[17]Ibid.

previously gone into Canaan and weakened the forces of the nations there.[18] Perhaps the best explanation is the one given by R. K. Harrison. He wrote,

> Hornets . . . refer to God's miraculous intervention on His people's behalf in dispossessing the indigenous inhabitants of the Promised Land. In these passages the hornet seems to be used in a dramatic metaphorical sense to show how God's onslaught would render the Canaanites immobile, just as the hornet's sting paralyzed its victim.[19]

Interestingly, verse 28 mentions only three of the nations listed in verse 23: **the Hivites, the Canaanites, and the Hittites**. The three listed probably stand for all the peoples of the land. Therefore, no significance should be attached to the fact that nothing is said in verse 28 about driving out the other nations.

Verses 29, 30. One might have expected God to grant Israel a quick victory over the people of Canaan. On the contrary, God said that He would **drive them out** gradually so that **the land** [might] **not become desolate** or the wild **beasts** become **too numerous** before Israel took full possession of the land. Although the Book of Joshua at first appears to relate a quick conquest of the land, Judges reveals that, even after the initial conquest, not all the peoples were subdued nor was all the land occupied (Judg. 1:27–36).

Verse 31. God concluded His message about the conquest by trying to impress upon Israel the extent of the land which He would enable them to occupy. It was to extend **from the Red Sea** (the Gulf of Aqabah[20]) in the east, **to the sea of the Philistines** (the Mediterranean) in the west, and **from the wilderness** in the south, to the **River Euphrates** in the north. "Euphrates" is not in

---

[18]Cole, 183.

[19]R. K. Harrison, "Hornet," in *The International Standard Bible Encyclopedia*, rev. ed., ed. Geoffrey W. Bromiley (Grand Rapids, Mich.: Wm. B. Eerdmans Publishing Co., 1982), 2:757. (See Josh. 10:10; Judg. 4:15; 1 Sam. 5:9, 11; 7:10.)

[20]Kaiser, 447. The Gulf of Aqabah is the body of water on the east side of the Sinai Peninsula.

the Hebrew text but was added by the translators to clarify which river is meant. Cole explained, "'The river' in the Bible is always 'the great river,' i.e., the Euphrates."[21] Israelite "control, if not occupation, actually extended as far as the Euphrates (1 Kings 4:21; 1 Chron. 18:3; 2 Chron. 9:26)"[22] at the height of the kingdoms of David and Solomon.

No Covenants with the Canaanites (23:32, 33)

32"You shall make no covenant with them or with their gods.
33They shall not live in your land, because they will make you sin against Me; for if you serve their gods, it will surely be a snare to you."

Verse 32. However large their kingdom became, the Israelites were not to forget who had given them the land and were not to make a **covenant** with the people of the land **or with their gods**. Covenants were said to be witnessed by the gods of the nations making them. Therefore, if Israel entered into such a covenant, they would, in effect, be acknowledging and making a covenant with the gods of the Canaanites.

Verse 33. Instead, they were to drive all other peoples from the **land**—not because they were antisocial or were haters of mankind, but in order to avoid being tempted to worship the gods of the pagans who lived there. To some extent, the failure of Israel to heed these commands ultimately led to the nation's destruction.

APPLICATION

Not Following a Multitude to Do Evil (23:2; KJV)

While the law in 23:1, 2 was meant especially to ensure fair trials, it can be applied to other situations as well. In general, Christ's disciples should never blindly follow the majority, be-

---

[21]Cole, 184. (See Gen. 15:18; Deut. 1:7; Josh. 1:4.)

[22]Barry J. Beitzel, *The Moody Atlas of Bible Lands* (Chicago: Moody Press, 1985), 10.

cause the majority may be wrong (Mt. 7:13, 14). The fact that a religious belief is widely accepted does not prove that it is scriptural. The fact that "everyone else is doing it" does not make something right.

What About Our Enemies? (23:4, 5, 22, 23)

The Bible teaches that Christians can live righteous lives and still have enemies. Paul had enemies, as did Jesus Himself. What should we, as Christians, do about these enemies?

1. Avoid making enemies (Rom. 12:18).
2. Love, not hate, our enemies (Mt. 5:43–48).
3. Do good to our enemies (Ex. 23:4, 5; Rom. 12:20, 21).
4. Try to be reconciled with our enemies (Mt. 5:23–25).
5. Pray for our enemies (Mt. 5:44).
6. Realize that sometimes what our enemies do to us may turn out for the best (Rom. 8:28; Phil. 1:12).
7. Recognize that, if we are faithful, God will ultimately defeat our enemies (Ex. 23:22, 23; 2 Thess. 1:6–9).

What should we *not* do?

1. Resist these enemies physically (Mt. 5:38–41).
2. Seek revenge on any enemies (Rom. 12:19).
3. Hope for evil to befall our enemies or rejoice when it does (Job 31:29, 30).
4. Speak evil of any enemies (Mt. 5:22).
5. Allow enemies to cause us to reject our Lord, but instead follow the examples of people like Joseph, Job, and Daniel.

Israel and the Promised Land (23:20–33)

From the beginning of the story of the exodus, God intended to guide Israel into a land (3:8), just as He had promised the patriarchs in Genesis. In Exodus 23, as God concluded the Book of the Covenant, He gave Israel two responsibilities with regard to the land.

First, Israel had the responsibility to take the land. It may seem like a misstatement to say that they were to "take" it, since this passage emphasizes God's role in their possessing the land. God would send His "angel" before them to lead them "into the place" which He had "prepared" for them (23:20). Then God said that He would be "an enemy" to Israel's enemies (23:22) and that He would destroy and drive out the inhabitants of the land (23:23, 27–30). He implied that He would enlarge the borders of the land (23:31). Even so, Israel, with God's help, had the responsibility to take the land. The Book of Joshua points out that God gave Israel the land of Canaan, but they still had to "go in to possess" it (Josh. 1:11). The book goes on to tell how Israel had to fight to possess that which God had "given" them.

For Christians, the "promised land" is heaven. We are not required to conquer with swords as did Joshua's army. God will give us the victory, but we still have to do our part.

Second, Israel had the responsibility to drive out the ungodly inhabitants of the land. God would destroy the peoples who lived in Canaan (23:23), throw them into confusion (23:27), and send "hornets" to drive them out (23:28, 29). He told the Israelites, "'You shall utterly overthrow them'" (23:24). God would make them run away when the Israelites attacked (23:27), and Israel was to "drive them out" (23:31–33). The Book of Joshua tells how this conquest was accomplished, but the Book of Judges emphasizes that Israel did not fully carry out God's orders. Their ultimate destruction was brought about by their failure to complete the task of removing the pagans from the land.

God drove out and destroyed the nations that occupied Canaan because they were a wicked people whom He was punishing (Deut. 9:5). Moreover, their pagan practices posed a spiritual threat to His own people (23:24, 31–33). Neither racial prejudice nor national pride had any role in Israel's driving them out; the key purpose was to maintain Israel's faith in God.

Should Christians learn a lesson from Israel's need to drive out the peoples of Canaan? The passage should not be used to teach that Christians should withdraw altogether from the world. At the same time, it does suggest that we must never compromise with the world. We must recognize that people around us can influence us negatively (1 Cor. 15:33). We must be careful to avoid entangling alliances with unbelievers (2 Cor. 6:14–18).

Conclusion. The Israelites were to be a "light to the nations" (Is. 42:6), yet they were still supposed to drive out the nations. Christians experience a similar tension: We are "in the world" but not "of the world." Our task is to reach out to sinners so they might be saved without allowing them to draw us away from Christ. Such a daunting task is possible with God's help!

"He Will Bless Your Bread"—
Blessings in This Life (23:25, 26)

Today Christians are not promised material blessings for doing God's will as the nation of Israel was under the old covenant. Sometimes we will get sick, and sometimes our wives will be barren or will have a miscarriage. However, given the nature of the world as God made it, Christians are likely to receive blessings in this life as well as in that which is to come (Mk. 10:29, 30). Why? Because Christians are industrious, respect authority, develop lasting relationships, build strong healthy homes, treat their bodies as the temple of God, and give their worries to God. One who does these things is more likely to live a long and happy life than someone who does not.

Chapter 24

Ratification of the Covenant

Exodus 24 describes the ratification of the covenant God made with Israel in chapter 19. God told Moses to bring other leaders of Israel back up the mountain to meet with Him (24:1, 2). After Moses presented the Law to the people, they promised to obey God (24:3–8). Then Moses, Aaron, Nadab, Abihu, and seventy of the elders went up the mountain, saw the Lord, and participated in a meal (24:9–11).

The Lord then told Moses to return so that God could Himself write out "the law and the commandment" (24:12). Moses and Joshua went back up the mountain, leaving the elders in the Israelite camp (24:13, 14). Moses entered the cloud of God's glory, where he stayed for forty days and nights (24:15–18).

THE RATIFICATION PROCESS (24:1–11)

The Command to Meet with God (24:1, 2)

1Then He said to Moses, "Come up to the Lord, you and Aaron, Nadab and Abihu and seventy of the elders of Israel, and you shall worship at a distance. 2Moses alone, however, shall come near to the Lord, but they shall not come near, nor shall the people come up with him."

Verse 1. While **Moses** was still on the mountain, God told him to **"come up to the Lord,"** along with **"Aaron, Nadab and Abihu and seventy of the elders."** This command presupposed that Moses would first go down the mountain and then come up again with the leaders that are mentioned.

Verse 2. The other men would remain at a distance, while **Moses alone** would **come near to the LORD**. Although all Israel was holy to God, Moses was set apart as His special servant.

Moses Ratifies the Covenant (24:3–11)

3Then Moses came and recounted to the people all the words of the LORD and all the ordinances; and all the people answered with one voice and said, "All the words which the LORD has spoken we will do!" 4Moses wrote down all the words of the LORD. Then he arose early in the morning, and built an altar at the foot of the mountain with twelve pillars for the twelve tribes of Israel. 5He sent young men of the sons of Israel, and they offered burnt offerings and sacrificed young bulls as peace offerings to the LORD. 6Moses took half of the blood and put it in basins, and the other half of the blood he sprinkled on the altar. 7Then he took the book of the covenant and read it in the hearing of the people; and they said, "All that the LORD has spoken we will do, and we will be obedient!" 8So Moses took the blood and sprinkled it on the people, and said, "Behold the blood of the covenant, which the LORD has made with you in accordance with all these words."

9Then Moses went up with Aaron, Nadab and Abihu, and seventy of the elders of Israel, 10and they saw the God of Israel; and under His feet there appeared to be a pavement of sapphire, as clear as the sky itself. 11Yet He did not stretch out His hand against the nobles of the sons of Israel; and they saw God, and they ate and drank.

These verses describe the ratification of God's covenant with the people. God had said that Israel would be His special people if Israel would obey Him; Israel had responded by saying, "All that the LORD has spoken we will do!" (19:8). However, at that time, the Israelites knew little about what God would require of them. In effect, they accepted any commands God might choose. Beginning in chapter 20, God told Israel in some detail what He expected of them. He revealed to them the Ten Commandments (20:1–21), as well as the laws found in the Book of the Covenant (20:22—23:33). After they had heard the specifics of God's will for them, Israel was given the opportunity to renew their commitment to obey the Lord. The people were being asked, in effect, "Now that you know what God's commandments are, are you still willing to keep them?" The people did not hesitate; again, Israel affirmed, "All the words which the LORD has spoken we will do!" (24:3; see 24:7).

The ratification of God's covenant with Israel involved seven events. (1) Moses recited the Law, and Israel reaffirmed its pledge to obey the Lord (24:3). (2) The words of the Lord were written down, thus giving the covenant permanency (24:4a). (3) An altar was built to serve as a reminder of the occasion (24:4b). (4) Then sacrifices were offered as part of the ratification ceremony, and the altar was sprinkled with blood (24:5, 6). (5) Next, the laws were read from the book, again eliciting an affirmative response from the people (24:7). (6) The blood was sprinkled on the people, signifying the sealing of the covenant (24:8). (7) Finally, the leaders of Israel participated, in the Lord's presence, in a covenant meal (24:9–11).

Verse 3. *The Affirming of the Pledge.* First, when he came down from the mountain, **Moses** orally recited the Law **to the people**. Standing together—united, **with one voice**—the Israelites repeated the pledge of loyalty they had made before God gave the details of the Law. They said, **"All the words which the LORD has spoken we will do!"**

Verse 4a. *The Writing of the Law.* Second, after **Moses** spoke God's words aloud, he **wrote** them **down**, no doubt to be a permanent record of the covenant between God and Israel, and especially to provide a record of the requirements of that covenant. It was usual for covenants in the ancient Near East to be written out and deposited in a special place, from which they could be retrieved and recited from time to time. Presumably, Moses wrote down **all** the laws that the Lord had given him while he was on the mountain.

Verse 4b. *The Building of the Altar.* The third step in the process involved the building of an **altar** at the base of Mount Sinai.

Obviously, the purpose of the altar was not solely to provide a place for sacrifice, since it was built **with twelve pillars for the twelve tribes of Israel**. After the sacrifices, the altar with the pillars would remain as a reminder of the event that had occurred there.

Verses 5, 6. *The Offering of Sacrifices.* Fourth, sacrifices of **burnt offerings** and **peace offerings** were then offered by some of the **young men** of Israel. Apparently, before there was an official priesthood in Israel, young men served in a priestly capacity, officiating during the offering of sacrifices. Why were young men specified? To slaughter, butcher, and transport all the bulls, goats, and lambs would have required considerable strength. Walter C. Kaiser, Jr., suggested that these were the firstborn of the Israelite families and that they served as priests until the Levitical priests were appointed (see Num. 3:41).[1] **Moses** took **half of the blood** that had been drained from the sacrificial animals and **sprinkled** [it] **on the altar**. This ritual was probably performed in order to dedicate or consecrate the altar.[2]

Verse 7. *The Reading of the Law.* Fifth, Moses **read** the laws to the people, and they again affirmed their willingness to do **all that the Lord** [had] **spoken**. As John H. Walton and Victor H. Matthews noted, "A public reading of the terms of the covenant was a part of every covenant-renewal ceremony (see Josh 24:25–27; 2 Kings 23:2; Neh 8:5–9)."[3] **The book of the covenant** refers to the laws which God had given, which Moses had written down, and which the people had agreed to obey. It contains the stipulations, or conditions, upon which the covenant agreement between God and Israel was based. The continuance of the covenant relationship between God and His people depended on their keeping the laws found in that book.

Verse 8. *The Sprinkling of Blood.* Sixth, after **Moses** had read the Law and the people had again agreed to keep the Law, he

---

[1]Walter C. Kaiser, Jr., "Exodus," in *The Expositor's Bible Commentary*, vol. 2, *Genesis—Numbers* (Grand Rapids, Mich.: Zondervan, 1990), 449.

[2]Ibid.

[3]John H. Walton and Victor H. Matthews, *Genesis—Deuteronomy*, The IVP Bible Background Commentary (Downers Grove, Ill.: InterVarsity Press, 1997), 121.

took the remainder of **the blood** and **sprinkled it on the people**, signifying the sealing of the covenant. He said, **"Behold the blood of the covenant."** Just as the altar was sanctified, or set apart, with blood, so were the people. The sprinkled blood witnessed to the fact that God had saved Israel and made them His own special people, and that they now had the responsibility to obey God.

The significance of the blood ritual on this occasion is not revealed. R. Alan Cole suggested two possibilities. (1) Perhaps, by means of the ritual, God was declaring Himself to be related to the people by blood, so that Israel and God were counted as "one blood," and God could be seen as Israel's father and "blood avenger."[4] (2) Another possibility is that, in common with the rituals seen in Genesis 15 and Jeremiah 34:18, this blood ritual "may have been the equivalent of invoking death on oneself if the terms of the covenant [were] not kept."[5] Walter Brueggemann wrote,

> The "blood of the covenant" . . . creates a solidarity between the two parties. This dramatic act is not rationally explicable, but no doubt arises from the recognition that "blood" is the distinctive element that makes life possible. . . . Thus Israel now begins a new life of obedience, signified by sacrifice, the "book of the covenant," and the "blood of the covenant."[6]

Kaiser said that the sprinkling of the blood was "an act of dedication or consecration," that the blood on the altar symbolized "God's forgiveness and acceptance of the offering," and that the blood on the people pointed to "a blood oath" that bound them to be obedient.[7]

---

[4]R. Alan Cole, *Exodus: An Introduction and Commentary*, Tyndale Old Testament Commentaries (Downers Grove, Ill.: Inter-Varsity Press, 1973), 185–86.

[5]Ibid.

[6]Walter Brueggemann, "The Book of Exodus," in *The New Interpreter's Bible*, ed. Leander E. Keck (Nashville: Abingdon Press, 1994), 1:881.

[7]Kaiser, 449.

Verse 9. *The Eating of a Covenant Meal.* This is the seventh and final event of the covenant ratification. At God's invitation (24:1, 2), **Moses** took others up on the mountain—probably only part of the way—to eat in the presence of God. Among those participating in the meal were **Aaron** and his sons **Nadab and Abihu**, who later perished because they offered "strange fire before the LORD" (Lev. 10:1, 2). Also present were **seventy of the elders** who are further identified as "nobles of the sons of Israel" (24:11). These distinguished men probably served as representatives of the twelve tribes.[8]

Verse 10. The text emphasizes that the men who participated in this meal **saw the God of Israel**, a fact which is repeated in verse 11. Since the Bible elsewhere says that no man has ever seen God (33:20; Jn. 1:18; 1 Tim. 6:16), these men probably saw a representation of God rather than God Himself. Kaiser suggested that the men saw a "similitude" of God (see Num. 12:8; Is. 6:1; Ezek. 1:26).[9] James Burton Coffman insisted that "they did not see God 'face to face' in all of his eternal glory" (see Deut. 4:15; 1 Tim. 6:16; 1 Jn. 4:12).[10] Since God is "spirit" (John 4:24)—and since the spiritual cannot be seen with physical eyes—one might argue that one who is in the flesh cannot see God as He actually exists.

The description of the experience speaks only of what the men saw **under His feet**, as if they were afraid or unable to lift their eyes higher than His feet. There they saw something that looked like **a pavement of sapphire, as clear as the sky itself**.

Verse 11. The extraordinary nature of the occurrence is noted. The leaders of Israel "saw" God, **yet He did not stretch out His hand against** them. Brueggemann said that "the scene suggests a stunned, astonished silence. They look and are mesmerized. They do not speak; they do not move. . . . The narrative intends to leave us stunned, bewildered, and awestruck."[11] In other

---

[8]Walton and Matthews, 120.

[9]Kaiser, 449.

[10]James Burton Coffman, *Commentary on Exodus, The Second Book of Moses* (Abilene, Tex.: ACU Press, 1985), 348.

[11]Brueggemann, 881.

words, "They saw God, and He did not strike them dead!"

Those present **ate and drank**, sharing in a meal or a feast to celebrate the covenant which they had just made with the Lord. Although God is not said to have eaten with them, His presence is noted. As one of the parties to the covenant, He was there.

RECEIVING THE LAW (24:12–18)

12Now the LORD said to Moses, "Come up to Me on the mountain and remain there, and I will give you the stone tablets with the law and the commandment which I have written for their instruction." 13So Moses arose with Joshua his servant, and Moses went up to the mountain of God. 14But to the elders he said, "Wait here for us until we return to you. And behold, Aaron and Hur are with you; whoever has a legal matter, let him approach them." 15Then Moses went up to the mountain, and the cloud covered the mountain. 16The glory of the LORD rested on Mount Sinai, and the cloud covered it for six days; and on the seventh day He called to Moses from the midst of the cloud. 17And to the eyes of the sons of Israel the appearance of the glory of the LORD was like a consuming fire on the mountain top. 18Moses entered the midst of the cloud as he went up to the mountain; and Moses was on the mountain forty days and forty nights.

Verse 12. Moses received another directive from the Lord to **come up** to Him **on the mountain**. Moses may have received this message while he was still feasting with the elders. In other words, they had only ascended part way up the mountain and God was calling Moses to come up higher into His presence. The command that "Moses alone . . . shall come near to the LORD" (24:2) could be used to support this position.

Another possibility is that Moses and the elders had returned to the camp when God gave him the command to "come up." The fact that Moses left Aaron and Hur in charge of legal disputes suggests that they were back among the people (24:14; see 18:26). Moreover, when Moses came down from the mountain after forty days, Aaron was in the camp (ch. 32).

The purpose for Moses' trip up the mountain on this occasion was to receive the Law **written** by God Himself on **stone tablets**. Scholars differ concerning what part of the Law was written on the two stone tablets—whether it was just the Ten Commandments or other laws as well. Cole said that "in view of the sequel," **the law and the commandment** must "refer here to the ten words alone."[12] The tablets were also called the "tablets of the testimony" (31:18) and "the tablets of the covenant" (Deut. 9:9).

Verses 13, 14. Moses went up, taking **Joshua** with him. However, before he ascended, he told **the elders** to **wait** for him. If they were still at the place where they had feasted, then perhaps Moses meant for them to "wait" there. However, if they were in the camp, then he may have intended for them to stay among the people. In either case, Moses did not want them to ascend the mountain looking for him.

Moses left **Aaron and Hur** in charge of making decisions regarding **legal matter**[s]. The work of judging was normally Moses' responsibility, but he would not be available. It may be that "the elders," who numbered "seventy" men (24:1), were the judges appointed to decide the easier disputes (see comments on 18:22, 23).

Verse 15. Then Moses **went up to the mountain, and the cloud covered the mountain**. Imagine this scene: Moses "goes where no one has ever gone. He leaves the zone of humanness and enters the sphere of God. And there he stays, forty days and forty nights. . . . No one, not Aaron or Israel . . . knows whether he will ever come out again."[13]

Verses 16–18. Then **the glory of the LORD rested on Mount Sinai . . . for six days.** To the Israelites in the camp below, **the appearance of the glory of the LORD was like a consuming fire on the mountain top.** God's call to Moses came on **the seventh day**. Moses entered into the midst of the **cloud**, into the very presence of God, and there he remained for **forty days and forty**

---

[12]Cole, 187.
[13]Brueggemann, 882.

nights. God's glory reigned as He met with Moses, who received the tablets of stone, "written by the finger of God" (31:18).

APPLICATION

Doing All That the Lord Has Said (24:3, 7)

Moses told the people *all* that the Lord had said, and they *all* said that they would do *all* that the Lord commanded. Are we willing to say that? Sometimes people are unwilling to obey everything the Lord has commanded. They may, for example, overlook or object to the command to be baptized. Let us strive to do everything that the Lord has commanded, seeking His kingdom first (Mt. 6:33).

Cleansed with Blood (24:5–8)

The covenant between God and Israel was ratified by blood. Animals were sacrificed, and blood was sprinkled on the altar and on the people (24:5–8). Hebrews 9:18–20 refers to that occasion. The context also speaks of the use of blood in the dedication of the altar and the tabernacle (Heb. 9:21; see Ex. 29:12, 36; Lev. 8:15, 19). Hebrews 9:22 refers more generally to "all things" being cleansed by blood, speaking probably of the sacrifices made regularly for sins.

What was the writer of Hebrews saying? Under the Law, "without shedding of blood there [was] no forgiveness" (Heb. 9:22). Those who live under the new covenant benefit from a better sacrifice—the sacrifice of Jesus Himself. His sacrifice is better because He entered into the true holy place, heaven (Heb. 9:24); He made His sacrifice only once (Heb. 9:25, 26); He sacrificed Himself to put away sin, in contrast to animal sacrifices (Heb. 9:26; 10:4). His blood bought the church (Acts 20:28). His blood has saved us (Eph. 1:7), it is saving us (1 Jn. 1:7), and it will save us eternally (Rev. 7:14).

"The Blood of the Covenant" (24:8)

Jesus had the Sinai scene in mind as He was instituting the Lord's Supper. He said, "This is My blood of the covenant, which is poured out for many for forgiveness of sins" (Mt. 26:28). When

Jesus died, He brought into existence a "new covenant" (see Jer. 31:31–34). As the Israelites were bound to God by a covenant ratified by blood, so are Christ's disciples. The new covenant was established by the blood of the "Lamb of God."

Eating with God (24:9–11)

In Exodus 24 God confirmed the covenant He made with Israel in chapter 19. The two parties—God and Israel—had already agreed to the terms of the covenant. Through the ceremonies described in Exodus 24, the covenant became effective. Chapter 19 could be likened to the exchange of contracts in a real estate deal today; the ritual in Exodus 24 could be likened to the closing of the agreement.

The ceremonies described in chapter 24 involved the following: (1) Moses' recounting the Law to the people and their repeating their pledge to keep it (24:3); (2) the writing of the Law for posterity (24:4a); (3) the building of an altar (24:4b); (4) the offering of sacrifices and the sprinkling of blood on the altar (24:5, 6); (5) the reading of the Law and the restating of Israel's pledge to keep it (24:7); (6) the sprinkling of the people with blood (24:8); and (7) the eating of a fellowship meal with God (24:9–11). At this time the leaders of Israel are said to have seen God (24:10).

The sharing of a meal was often involved in the sealing of a covenant between two parties in Old Testament times. In this case, the covenant was between Israel and God, so Israel shared this meal with the Lord. They were "eating with God"! Let us think about ways in which we can "eat with God" today.

By becoming Christians, we become partakers of a wedding feast (Mt. 22:1–14). In a sense, then, we are "eating with God" just by being Christians. We have fellowship with Him; we enjoy the "living water" and eat of the "Bread of Life."

As Christians, when we partake of the Lord's Supper, we "eat with God." Jesus said, as He instituted the Lord's Supper, "I will not drink of this fruit of the vine from now on until that day when I drink it new with you in My Father's kingdom" (Mt. 26:29). The implication is that He would eat and drink with us in the kingdom of God. When we participate in the Lord's Supper, we do so not only with our fellow Christians, whom we can see, but also with Christ, whom we cannot see. The Lord's Supper is referred to as "the table of the Lord" (1 Cor. 10:21; see Mt. 18:20).

When we share meals and fellowship with other Christians, we are also, in a sense, eating with God. Eating together was common in the New Testament church (Acts 2:46; 1 Cor. 11). The sharing of meals was the cause, the effect, and the symbol of their closeness to one another in the family of God.

Christian families should see mealtimes as occasions when we "eat with God." We acknowledge His presence when we offer thanks for our food (Lk. 24:30; Jn. 6:11; Rom. 14:6; 1 Tim. 4:4, 5). We advance His cause when we eat together as families because making a habit of such "family fellowship" does more for our children than almost anything else parents can do for them. We enrich our lives and glorify God by talking about spiritual matters as we spend time with our families (Deut. 6:7). We bind ourselves closer to God when we use family meals as opportunities for family worship.

In heaven we will enjoy divine fellowship in an eternal feast; in a sense, we will forever "eat with God." Something like a heavenly banquet is waiting for those who live for God (Lk. 22:30; Rev. 19:9). According to the figurative language of Revelation 22:1, 2, heaven has a beautiful river flowing from the throne of God, which implies pure water to drink. The tree of life bears twelve kinds of fruit, which implies a variety of delicious food to eat. The fact that heavenly Jerusalem is portrayed as descending as a "bride adorned for her husband" (Rev. 21:2) may also suggest that God compares heaven to a marriage feast. Our intimate fellowship there will be like "eating with God."

Conclusion. Israel's leaders had the privilege of eating with God, and we can have that same privilege. Jesus is knocking at the door of our hearts, seeking to come in so that He can eat with us (Rev. 3:20). Let us always be open to His fellowship by obeying His will.

Chapter 25

Instructions for the Tabernacle (Part 1)

Beginning in Exodus 25, the details of building the tabernacle dominate the remainder of the book. The tabernacle was the moveable sanctuary where God met with His people during the years that Israel spent in the wilderness and for centuries afterward. Directions concerning its construction and services were part of the Law given by God to Israel through Moses at Mount Sinai. Since the work of the priests was so closely related to the tabernacle, instructions regarding the priesthood are also included in these chapters.

Exodus 25—31 relates the instructions for building the tabernacle, while Exodus 35—39 describes, often in almost identical language, how those instructions were carried out. In the middle of this narration (chs. 32—34), the text tells about Israel's apostasy with regard to the golden calf, its resultant punishment, and God's gracious renewal of His covenant with His people. The book ends with the completion of the tabernacle and God's blessing it with His presence (ch. 40).

Chapter 25 opens with the Lord's telling Moses how the materials for construction should be obtained. God called for a freewill offering to be given by the Israelites (25:1–7). After He gave the general command to build the tabernacle to His specifications (25:8, 9), He began the instructions by describing how three items of furniture in the tabernacle were to be fashioned: the ark of the covenant (25:10–16), with the mercy seat and the cherubim (25:17–22); the table of showbread (25:23–30); and the lampstand (25:31–39). Instructions about how to build the altar of incense, another piece of furniture in the holy place, are not found

THE BUILDING OF THE TABERNACLE	
Exodus 25—31 **What Was Required**	**Exodus 35—40** **What Was Done**
Offerings for the tabernacle (25:1–9)	Offerings commanded and brought for the tabernacle (35:4–9, 20–29; 36:2–7)
The ark of the covenant (25:10–22)	The ark (37:1–7)
Table of showbread (25:23–30)	Table (37:8–16)
Golden lampstand (25:31–39)	Lampstand (37:17–24)
Curtains, boards, sockets, veil, screen (26:1–37)	Curtains, boards (36:8–38)
Bronze altar for burnt offerings (27:1–8)	Altar of burnt offering (38:1–7)
Court of the tabernacle (27:9–19)	Court of the tabernacle (38:9–20)
Oil for the light (27:20, 21)	Oil for the light [39:37]
Priestly garments (28:1–43)	Priestly garments (39:1–31)
Consecration of the priests and offerings (29:1–43)	
Altar of incense (30:1–10)	Altar of incense (37:25–28)
Atonement money for the tabernacle (30:11–16)	Cost of the tabernacle (38:24–31)
Bronze laver (30:17–21)	Bronze laver (38:8)
Anointing oil and incense (30:22–38)	Oil and incense (37:29)
Choosing the builders (31:1–11)	Builders called and named (35:10–19, 30–35; 36:1, 2; 38:21–23)
Observing the Sabbath (31:12–17)	
	Completion and setting up of the tabernacle; the Lord enters the tabernacle (39:32–43; 40:1–37).

until 30:1–10. The chapter ends with another admonition to make everything "after the pattern" which God had shown Moses on the mountain (25:40).

CONTRIBUTIONS AND COMMISSION FOR BUILDING (25:1–9)

[1]Then the LORD spoke to Moses, saying, [2]"Tell the sons of Israel to raise a contribution for Me; from every man whose heart moves him you shall raise My contribution. [3]And this is the contribution which you are to raise from them: gold, silver and bronze [4]blue, purple and scarlet material, fine linen, goat hair, [5]rams' skins dyed red, porpoise skins, acacia wood, [6]oil for lighting, spices for the anointing oil and for the fragrant incense, [7]onyx stones and setting stones, for the ephod and for the breastpiece. [8]And let them construct a sanctuary for Me, that I may dwell among them. [9]According to all that I am going to show you, as the pattern of the tabernacle and the pattern of all its furniture, just so you shall construct it."

The directions for building the tabernacle begin with a command to take up a contribution (compare 35:4–9). Three facts are noteworthy about this contribution: (1) It was a freewill offering (2) composed of valuable gifts (3) which were to be used for practical purposes.

Verses 1, 2. Freewill offerings were to be given by the people, **from every man whose heart moves him**. Obviously, this **contribution** was not a tithe, a tax, or an obligation imposed by Israel's leadership. Only the people's love, gratitude, and respect for God would compel them to contribute. John I. Durham said that the contribution was to be "a free and joyous offering."[1]

Verses 3–7. The rest of the story relates that they gave liberally (see 35:20–29; 36:2–7). This offering was a one-time contribution. The Law required regular offerings, including tithes (Lev. 27:30–32; Num. 18:21–29; Deut. 12:6, 11; 14:22–28; see 2 Chron.

---

[1]John I. Durham, *Exodus*, Word Biblical Commentary, vol. 3 (Waco, Tex.: Word Books, 1987), 355.

31:5, 6, 12; Neh. 10:37, 38; 13:12; Amos 4:4; Mal. 3:8–10). In addition, 30:11–16 speaks of a contribution to be made when the people were numbered.

What the Israelites gave was valuable. An indication of the worth of some of the gifts they gave voluntarily is seen in 38:24–31. Where did they get such riches to contribute? No doubt, a major portion of what Israel provided for the building of the tabernacle came from the gifts they had requested and received from the Egyptians when they left Egypt (3:21, 22; 11:2; 12:33–36). John J. Davis suggested,

> Additional material was probably also acquired when [Israel] defeated the Amalekites in Rephidim (17:8–16). Whatever materials were needed in addition could have been acquired by trade with caravans which passed through the Sinai Peninsula.[2]

Besides being both valuable and voluntary, the Israelites' gifts of **gold** and **bronze** were practical and useful. The gold that was given was used to overlay the ark of the covenant, and the altar of burnt offering was overlaid with bronze.[3]

Verse 8. God told Moses what the Israelites were to build and how they were to build it (see 35:30—36:2). The Israelites were to **construct a sanctuary**. The word מִקְדָּשׁ (*miqdash*) literally means "holy place" (see 36:1) and is used later in the Old Testament in regard to the temple (Jer. 17:12).[4] It was holy because God made it holy. The passage also provides a clue as to the primary purpose of the tabernacle: It was to be built that God might **dwell among them**.

Of course, the God who made the heavens and the earth does

---

[2]John J. Davis, *Moses and the Gods of Egypt: Studies in Exodus*, 2d ed. (Grand Rapids, Mich.: Baker Book House, 1986), 263.

[3]The KJV translates the Hebrew word "brass." Other translations have "bronze" (NKJV; NASB; NRSV; NIV). R. Alan Cole suggested that the metal was copper. (R. Alan Cole, *Exodus: An Introduction and Commentary*, Tyndale Old Testament Commentaries [Downers Grove, Ill.: Inter-Varsity Press, 1973], 189.)

[4]Ibid., 190.

not dwell in buildings that are made by human hands (Acts 17:24). Neither can He be confined to any one location, since He is omnipresent (Ps. 139:7–12). Nevertheless, the Lord dwelt in the tabernacle in a special sense: There He met with the people, especially at the mercy seat (25:22). In the same way, God later dwelt in the temple (1 Kings 8:10–13).

In the sense that the tabernacle was the dwelling place for God, it became a shadow or type of God's later dealings with mankind.

(1) New Testament writers used similar language to refer to the incarnation of Christ. John wrote that "the Word became flesh, and dwelt among us, and we saw His glory, glory as of the only begotten from the Father, full of grace and truth" (Jn. 1:14). He used the Greek word "dwell" (σκηνόω, *skēnoō*) which means "tabernacle," or "dwell in a tent." (The same word is used in Revelation 21:3.) Therefore, God's dwelling in the tabernacle was a preview of what God the Son, the Word, did as He initiated the new age. Jesus was "God in the flesh," dwelling in human flesh so that He might make His abode among men.

(2) The tabernacle became a shadow or type of the church. In the present age, God is everywhere; but He especially dwells in the church, in which Christians "are being built together into a dwelling of God in the Spirit" (Eph. 2:22; see 1 Cor. 3:16).

(3) Both the tabernacle and the church foreshadow heaven. John wrote, "Behold, the tabernacle of God is among men, and He will dwell among them, and they shall be His people, and God Himself will be among them" (Rev. 21:3).

Verse 9. The Israelites were to build this sanctuary in accordance with God's will. Throughout the story of the tabernacle's construction, there is an emphasis on the importance of Israel's obeying God as they built and on the fact that they did exactly what He commanded. Cole wrote, "Obedience in carrying out God's master-plan [was] essential."[5] The successful completion of their task was due, at least in part, to their careful obedience to God's instructions. Hebrews 8:4, 5 quotes a version of Exodus 25:40: "See that you make all things according to the pattern

---

[5]Ibid., 189.

which was shown you on the mountain." The passage speaks of the Levitical priests as a "copy and shadow" of the "heavenly things" of the new covenant.

When God said that He would **show** Moses **the pattern for the tabernacle and the pattern of all its furniture**, it sounds as if God intended to provide a visual representation of what He wanted the Israelites to build. Durham said that the plan for the tabernacle "may have involved a vision."[6] Another possibility is that God gave Moses some kind of blueprint which would enable the builders to know exactly what He wanted.

THE ARK OF THE COVENANT (25:10–16)

[10]"They shall construct an ark of acacia wood two and a half cubits long, and one and a half cubits wide, and one and a half cubits high. [11]You shall overlay it with pure gold, inside and out you shall overlay it, and you shall make a gold molding around it. [12]You shall cast four gold rings for it and fasten them on its four feet, and two rings shall be on one side of it and two rings on the other side of it. [13]You shall make poles of acacia wood and overlay them with gold. [14]You shall put the poles into the rings on the sides of the ark, to carry the ark with them. [15]The poles shall remain in the rings of the ark; they shall not be removed from it. [16]You shall put into the ark the testimony which I shall give you."

God began His instructions for building the tabernacle by describing the furniture which was to be placed within the tent. Evidently, in giving the plan for His house, He began with that which was most holy—the ark of the covenant with the mercy seat—and moved outward to the furnishings of the holy place. Then, in chapter 26, God gave instructions for the tent itself.

Verses 10, 11. The first item of furniture which God described was the **ark** of the covenant, presumably because this ark served as the central feature of the tabernacle. On top of the ark would be the mercy seat, the place where God actually intended to meet

---

[6]Durham, 355.

with Israel (25:21, 22). However, before the mercy seat could be described, instructions for the building of the ark on which it was to be placed had to be given.

The Hebrew term אֲרוֹן (*'aron*), translated "ark," is not the same word that is rendered "ark" (תֵּבָה, *thebah*) in Genesis 6:14 and Exodus 2:3 (KJV). The word for "ark" here might better be translated "chest."[7] The NRSV retains the traditional "ark," but the NIV has "chest." The ark was a box or chest about 45" long, 27" wide, and 27" high (approximately 4' x 2' x 2'). This measurement assumes the cubit to be about eighteen inches. It was made of **acacia wood** covered with **gold**.

There is a change from the second person ("you") in verse 9 to the third person (**they**) in verse 10. One possible reason for this is that there is a problem with the Hebrew text; the NASB follows the Masoretic text, whereas the Septuagint and Samaritan Pentateuch have "you" in both verses. Some versions use or imply "you" in both verses (REB; NAB; NJB), although others, like the NASB, retain "they" in verse 10 and **you** in verse 11 (KJV; NKJV; NRSV; ESV). For example, the NIV translates, "Have them make a chest" in verse 10 and "[you] overlay it" in verse 11. Probably, the change in person is insignificant.

Verses 12–15. Arrangements had to be made for the ark's transportation as Israel moved about in the wilderness. Consequently, the box had **gold rings** for sockets built into its sides. **Poles** made of **acacia wood** and covered with **gold** were permanently placed within those sockets. This design allowed the ark to be carried by the poles without human beings ever touching the ark itself.

Verse 16. Within the ark would be placed **the testimony**, that is, the two tablets with the Ten Commandments inscribed on them (see 40:20). These tablets were a symbol of the covenant which God had made with Israel. Because of the holiness of God and His law, the ark itself was holy and could not be touched.

God's holy presence so permeated the ark that to misuse it indicated disrespect for God and had lethal consequences (2 Sam. 6:6, 7). As the symbol of God's presence, the ark led the way

---

[7]Cole, 190.

when Israel marched and fought in the wilderness. Each time the ark was raised for travel, it was as if the Lord rose up to take action. When the ark was placed back in the tabernacle, it was as if the Lord returned to rest among His people (Num. 10:35, 36). When the Israelites crossed the Jordan River into Canaan, the ark preceded them. Its position before the people, symbolizing God's presence and power, allowed them to cross the Jordan on dry land (Josh. 4:5–18).

The fact that God's presence was signified by the ark is evident in the incident regarding the twelve spies (Num. 13; 14). After God had told Israel that they would not be allowed to enter the promised land, the Israelites insisted on fighting against the Amalekites anyway. However, neither Moses nor the ark went out of the camp for the battle. Their absence indicated that God was not with Israel, and Israel was defeated (Num. 14:43–45).

The ark came to symbolize God's presence to such an extent that some, Israelites as well as non-Israelites, began to equate the ark with God Himself. The people developed an almost superstitious regard for the ark and attempted to use it as a kind of magic charm to accomplish their purposes, regardless of God's will. In 1 Samuel 4—6, God taught Israel that He was not confined to the ark and could not be compelled to give Israel victory. At the same time, He taught the Philistines that Israel's God was greater than their gods.

The ark remained central to Israel's worship—not only in the wilderness, but also after the nation settled in Canaan. Eventually, it was housed in the temple built by Solomon. "It presumably perished in the sack of Jerusalem in 586 BC."[8]

Through a study of the construction of the ark, several concepts about the tabernacle become evident. The items commissioned by God were characterized by holiness, value, utility, and beauty. (1) *Holiness*. The ark, the centerpiece of the tabernacle, was located in the most holy place, where God met with the high priest. From there outward, the degree of holiness diminished. The furniture and space closer to the ark were holier, while the furniture and space farther from the ark were less holy. (2) *Value*.

---

[8]Ibid., 192.

All of the tabernacle was made of rich and valuable materials. However, the ark, the central and most holy feature of the tabernacle, was made of the most valuable material, gold. (3) *Utility*. While the ark had symbolic and religious value in itself, and while it would have been an impressive box with its gold overlay, it also had a useful purpose: In it were kept the tablets of the Law. (4) *Beauty*. The principle of beauty is likewise seen in the directions for the ark. The box not only served a purpose, but it was designed to be attractive as well. The God who created a beautiful world also planned for His people to build a beautiful place to worship Him.

THE MERCY SEAT (25:17–22)

17"You shall make a mercy seat of pure gold, two and a half cubits long and one and a half cubits wide. 18You shall make two cherubim of gold, make them of hammered work at the two ends of the mercy seat. 19Make one cherub at one end and one cherub at the other end; you shall make the cherubim of one piece with the mercy seat at its two ends. 20The cherubim shall have their wings spread upward, covering the mercy seat with their wings and facing one another; the faces of the cherubim are to be turned toward the mercy seat. 21You shall put the mercy seat on top of the ark, and in the ark you shall put the testimony which I will give to you. 22There I will meet with you; and from above the mercy seat, from between the two cherubim which are upon the ark of the testimony, I will speak to you about all that I will give you in commandment for the sons of Israel."

Verse 17. On top of the ark of the covenant, serving as the lid of the box, was the **mercy seat**. "Mercy seat" is an interpretation rather than a translation of the Hebrew word כַּפֹּרֶת (*kapporeth*), which simply means "covering."[9] The word seems to be used with a double meaning: For one, it obviously refers to the "covering" of the ark. For another, it refers to the fact that Israel's sins

[9]Ibid., 191.

were "covered," or atoned for, when the blood of a sacrifice was sprinkled on the ark's "covering" on the Day of Atonement. A form of the same word is translated "atonement" in Leviticus 7:7, as well as in Leviticus 23:27–32 where the "Day of Atonement" is described. This day is also known by the Hebrew term "Yom Kippur," which means "Day of Covering." It is still observed by Jews today.

Verses 18–21. As was fitting for the place where God would meet with and speak to His people, the "mercy seat" or "covering," along with the **cherubim**, was to be made of pure **gold**. "Cherubim" (כְּרֻבִים) is the plural form of "cherub" (כְּרוּב). Little can be known about the cherubim from the Bible. This text says that they had **faces** and **wings** and were small enough for two of them to face one another from each end of a 45" by 27" space. Since God gave cherubim the task of guarding the Garden of Eden after Adam and Eve had sinned (Gen. 3:24), they were likely not the sweet, angelic beings people imagine them to be:

> The cherubs were not the winged cupids of Renaissance art but were the winged human-headed lions of ancient Mesopotamian and Syro-Palestinian art. Cherubim served as armrests or adorned the sides of royal thrones in the ancient Near East. . . . The Ark, then, was a symbolic throne for the invisible God of Israel (1 Sam. 4:4), who held court between the cherubim and ruled over His people as He met with them there (Exod. 25:22).[10]

Cole said that they "were most likely human-faced winged sphinxes."[11]

The second of the Ten Commandments says, "You shall not make for yourself an idol, or any likeness of what is in heaven above or on the earth beneath or in the water under the earth. You shall not worship them or serve them" (20:4, 5). Some have interpreted the commandment as saying that it is wrong to make

---

[10]Ronald F. Youngblood, *Exodus*, Everyman's Bible Commentary (Chicago: Moody Bible Institute, 1983), 122.

[11]Cole, 191.

an image of any kind for any reason. The fact that God had the cherubim fashioned to put on the mercy seat and embroidered on the inner curtain of the tabernacle (36:35) demonstrates that the commandment forbids making an image for the purpose of worshiping it. The cherubim were not to be worshiped; therefore, the commandment was not broken.

Verse 22. The Lord said, **"There I will meet with you."** The mercy seat was the place where God met with the people. Later in Israel's history, the people understood that the Lord of hosts sat "above the cherubim" (1 Sam. 4:4). From there God directed the people through the revelations He gave to Moses. Once a year, He met with them there for atonement when the high priest went into the most holy place and sprinkled blood on the mercy seat (Heb. 9:5, 7).

The testimony is one way of speaking of God's law, and especially of the two tablets of stone which contained the heart of the Law. Umberto Cassuto said that these tablets must be "the tablets on which the Decalogue is inscribed [34:28], and which are called *testimony* because they testify to the covenant that was made between the Lord and the children of Israel."[12] Perhaps speaking of these tablets as "testimony" also implied that the laws written there would serve as a witness against Israel if the people ignored or broke the Law.

God said that He would speak with Israel from **above the mercy seat** and **from between the two cherubim**. Apparently, in the wilderness, Moses received God's instructions from within the tabernacle. After that, there is no evidence of God's regularly delivering new instructions from "between the two cherubim."

THE TABLE OF SHOWBREAD (25:23–30)

[23]"You shall make a table of acacia wood, two cubits long and one cubit wide and one and a half cubits high. [24]You shall overlay it with pure gold and make a gold border around it.

---

[12]Umberto Cassuto, *A Commentary on the Book of Exodus,* trans. Israel Abrahams (Jerusalem: Magnes Press, 1997), 330.

[25]You shall make for it a rim of a handbreadth around it; and you shall make a gold border for the rim around it. [26]You shall make four gold rings for it and put rings on the four corners which are on its four feet. [27]The rings shall be close to the rim as holders for the poles to carry the table. [28]You shall make the poles of acacia wood and overlay them with gold, so that with them the table may be carried. [29]You shall make its dishes and its pans and its jars and its bowls with which to pour drink offerings; you shall make them of pure gold. [30]You shall set the bread of the Presence on the table before Me at all times."

The rest of chapter 25 describes two of the three items of furniture which were to be kept within the holy place of the tabernacle—the table of showbread and the lampstand. Gold was also used in the manufacture of these items.

Verses 23, 24. The **table** of showbread was about 36" long by 18" wide and 27" high (approximately 3′ x 1½′ x 2′). It was to be made of **acacia wood**, the same wood used in the construction of the ark of the covenant. Moreover, it was to be overlaid with **gold**, as was the ark.

Verses 25–28. Also like the ark, the table was to be made so that it could be carried from one place to another with **gold rings** and **poles**.

Verse 29. The vessels (**dishes**, **pans**, **jars**, and **bowls**) which were to be used in connection with the table were to be made of **pure gold**. These vessels, or ones like them, were later carried away by Nebuchadnezzar and the Babylonians as spoils of war (2 Kings 25:13–17; Ezra 1:7–11).

Verse 30. The **table** was not only beautiful, but it was also useful: On it was kept **the bread of the Presence**. This bread consisted of twelve loaves which remained perpetually on the table. New loaves were substituted for the old each Sabbath, and only the priests were allowed to eat the old loaves (Lev. 24:5–9). Although the text does not explain the symbolism, the loaves probably represented the twelve tribes of Israel. Perhaps this was a reminder that they should see themselves as one people. The constant presence of the bread on the table signified that the people belonged to God and were continually in His presence.

The table of showbread and the lampstand are part of a scene inside the Arch of Titus in Rome. This monument, built later by Titus' brother Domitian, commemorated the Romans' triumph over the Jews in A.D. 70. The table and the lampstand were taken from the Jerusalem temple as plunder and were carried in triumphal procession into Rome.

Lampstand and Table as Depicted on the Arch of Titus (Rome)

THE GOLDEN LAMPSTAND (25:31–40)

**31"Then you shall make a lampstand of pure gold. The lampstand and its base and its shaft are to be made of hammered work; its cups, its bulbs and its flowers shall be of one piece
with it. 32Six branches shall go out from its sides; three branches of the lampstand from its one side and three branches of the
lampstand from its other side. 33Three cups shall be shaped like almond blossoms in the one branch, a bulb and a flower, and three cups shaped like almond blossoms in the other branch, a bulb and a flower—so for six branches going out from
the lampstand; 34and in the lampstand four cups shaped like
almond blossoms, its bulbs and its flowers. 35A bulb shall be under the first pair of branches coming out of it, and a bulb under the second pair of branches coming out of it, and a bulb under the third pair of branches coming out of it, for the six
branches coming out of the lampstand. 36Their bulbs and their**

branches shall be of one piece with it; all of it shall be one piece of hammered work of pure gold. [37]Then you shall make its lamps seven in number; and they shall mount its lamps so as to shed light on the space in front of it. [38]Its snuffers and their trays shall be of pure gold. [39]It shall be made from a talent of pure gold, with all these utensils. [40]See that you make them after the pattern for them, which was shown to you on the mountain."

Verses 31, 32. Another feature of the holy place was the **lampstand**. Like the cherubim and the mercy seat, it was to be made of **pure gold**. It had a single **shaft** coming up from a **base**, with a lamp on the top of it and **six branches** extending from it, each holding a single lamp. Consequently, there were seven lamps (25:37). The Hebrew word for lampstand is מְנוֹרָה (*m^enorah*). A menorah is a "seven-branched lampstand" which "has become the great symbol of the Jewish religion."[13]

Verses 33–36. The lampstand was both functional, giving off light, and beautiful. Artistically designed **almond blossoms** and **flowers**, for example, were not essential to its purpose of giving light. God obviously wanted the place where He met with Israel to be aesthetically pleasing.

Verses 37–39. The **lamps** provided the only **light** within the tabernacle. Symbolically, the lampstand may have functioned as a reminder that God is the only source of light—the light from above that Israel needed to continue to exist.

Verse 40. After describing the lampstand, God warned the people again: **See that you make them after the pattern . . . which was shown to you on the mountain.** The instructions for building the tabernacle found in chapter 25 are sandwiched between two similar exhortations in verses 9 and 40. In speaking of the "pattern," verse 9 says "all that I am *going to show you*," and verse 40 says "which *was shown to you* on the mountain" (emphasis added). Notice the difference in tense. Perhaps God had not yet, in verse 9, started showing the pattern, but He had shown the

[13]Wilbur Fields, *Exploring Exodus*, Bible Study Textbook Series (Joplin, Mo.: College Press, 1976), 579.

pattern—at least for the items of furniture discussed—by the time He spoke to Moses in verse 40.

Cole suggested the following possibilities regarding the significance of the lampstand:

> We are not told the . . . meaning of the symbolism. Some feel that the lampstand stood for Israel's task as a light to the Gentiles (Is. 60:3). Certainly 'seven' is always a symbol of perfection: while oil, at least later, becomes a picture of God's spirit (Zc. 4:1–6). The symbolism might be that of the light which God's presence brings to His people (Nu. 6:25), remembering that light, in the Old Testament, is also a symbol of life and victory (Ps. 27:1).[14]

APPLICATION

The Tabernacle: "A Shadow of Good Things to Come" (25:1–9)

The last sixteen chapters of Exodus are dominated by the story of the building of the tabernacle. Why? Because the tabernacle was the symbol of God's presence. As Exodus ends, the tabernacle is completed and set up. At that time, "the cloud covered the tent of meeting and the glory of the LORD filled the tabernacle" (40:34). So the Book of Exodus is about how the people who had been slaves in Egypt became God's people, among whom God dwelt.

As important as the building of the tabernacle is in its own context, it is also important in terms of its meaning to New Testament Christians. The importance of the tabernacle for Christians is especially pointed out by the writer of Hebrews as he said that the law was "a shadow of good things to come, and not the very image of the things" (Heb. 10:1). The writer points out many specific comparisons between the tabernacle and the New Testament church and implies that others could be made (Heb. 9:1–5). What can Christians learn about the church from the tabernacle?

---

[14]Cole, 193.

What was the tabernacle like—and how is it a shadow of the church? The tabernacle was a tent sitting in a courtyard. Inside the tent there were two compartments, the holy place and the most holy place. Inside the holy place were three items of furniture: the table of showbread, the altar of incense, and the golden lampstand. Inside the most holy place was the ark of the covenant, a chest. The lid of that chest was called the mercy seat. At either end of the mercy seat were two cherubim whose wings overshadowed it. In the courtyard there was an altar of burnt offering and a laver containing water in which the priests washed before they went into the holy place.

How were these items used in worship and sacrifice? Any Israelite could go into the courtyard to bring sacrifices to be offered. The altar of burnt offering was used on a daily basis for the many sacrifices which the Law required. The laver contained water in which the priests washed before they went into the holy place on a daily basis to serve there. Only the high priest could go into the most holy place, and he went there only one day each year, on the Day of Atonement, to make atonement for himself and for the people of Israel.

How does the tabernacle foreshadow the New Testament era? We need to be careful when we apply the Old Testament Scriptures as shadows of the reality which we find in the church. We can abuse this method of Bible study and make the Bible seem to mean something that it does not. How can we use this method safely? We can be sure of what reality the shadow represents if we will remember that the only thing we can say with certainty is what the Bible says.

Several things in the tabernacle appear to be like things in the New Testament era: The table of showbread is like the Lord's Supper; the lampstand is like the Word of God; the altar of incense is like prayer; the washing in the laver is like baptism; the holy place is like the church; and the most holy place is like heaven. We should avoid being dogmatic about these comparisons if they are not clearly stated in Scripture.

However, there are some things about the tabernacle that the New Testament explicitly compares to the Christian age. Hebrews compares Jesus Christ to the high priest of the Old Testament era and compares Jesus' sacrifice of Himself to the sacrifices offered under the old covenant. Moreover, the New Testament teaches us that we as Christians are all priests who offer sacrifices to God (Rom. 12:1, 2). We are also justified in comparing the tabernacle with the church in that the tabernacle was the place where God met with the people; it symbolized the presence of God and He was there in Israel's midst. In a similar way, the New Testament speaks of the church as the dwelling place of God, taking the figure from the temple (which was like the tabernacle in this respect). Therefore, God dwells in us!

How was the tabernacle built—and how can its building relate to the church today? First, it was built according to God's plan (25:9; 40:16). Second, it was built through good leadership. Moses led in making sure that God's directions were followed. God provided men who led in the actual construction of the tabernacle (31:1–6; 35:10, 30–35). Third, it was built with the help and liberal gifts of the whole congregation (35:4–9, 21, 22, 29; 36:1–7). Rather than having to beg the congregation to give more, as is often true today, the leaders then had to beg the people to quit giving! They were giving too much. These all can serve as illustrations related to the church.

Conclusion. We need to thank God for Jesus our high priest, for Jesus' sacrifice, and for the opportunity to approach Him as priests. We need to joyfully offer our sacrifices to God. To build up Christ's church, we need to (1) follow God's instructions, (2) utilize good leadership, and (3) give liberally of the resources with which God has blessed us.

God's Dwelling (25:8)

The tabernacle was to be the place where God dwelt among His people. Today God dwells in the church (1 Cor. 3:16; Eph. 2:21, 22). He also dwells in each Christian (Rom. 8:9; 1 Cor. 6:15–20; Gal. 4:6). Therefore, we need to dedicate our bodies to the Lord (Rom. 12:1, 2), keeping them pure (1 Cor. 16:19, 20).

"Traveling On" (25:12–15, 26–28)

An old song says, "I feel like traveling on." The tabernacle was built for traveling; its portability is evidenced by the rings and poles that were attached to the ark, the table of showbread, and the altar. The Israelites moved about in the wilderness for forty years as strangers in the land, never settling in one place. In a similar way, Christians today are "aliens and strangers" in this world (1 Pet. 2:11). We need to make sure that we do not "settle down" and think of this world as our permanent home. Let us live up to our songs of faith, which declare, "I am a stranger here, within a foreign land; my home is far away upon a golden strand."[15]

Meet with God—Where? (25:22)

The Lord said that He would meet with the Israelites at the mercy seat in the tabernacle (25:22) and that there He would dwell among them (29:43, 45). Where can Christians meet with the Lord today? We meet with Him in the church. It is His church; He is always there. To be in Him, we must be in the church. We also meet with Him in the assembly (Mt. 18:20). However, we can meet with Him at any time or in any place; we do not have to go anywhere special to meet with the Lord (see Jn. 4:21–24). Those who are in the church are in the Lord, and the Lord is in each Christian. If you are a Christian, you always have access to Christ.

---

[15]E. T. Cassel, "I Am a Stranger Here," *Songs of Faith and Praise*, comp. and ed. Alton H. Howard (West Monroe, La.: Howard Publishing Co., 1994).

Chapter 26

Instructions for the Tabernacle (Part 2)

Chapter 26 turns from God's instructions concerning the furnishings to the tabernacle itself, the tent. It focuses, first, on the coverings of the tabernacle (26:1–14), then on the tent's framework (26:15–30), and finally on two veils. One veil separated the holy place from the most holy place, and the other covered the entrance into the holy place (26:31–37).

The floor of the tent is not mentioned at all in Exodus, but a brief reference in Numbers 5:17 indicates that it was bare. In that context, priests were instructed to use "dust that is on the floor of the tabernacle" in a ritual to determine if a man's wife was guilty of adultery.

THE TWO COVERINGS MADE FROM CURTAINS (26:1–13)

1"Moreover you shall make the tabernacle with ten curtains of fine twisted linen and blue and purple and scarlet material; you shall make them with cherubim, the work of a skillful workman. 2The length of each curtain shall be twenty-eight cubits, and the width of each curtain four cubits; all the curtains shall have the same measurements. 3Five curtains shall be joined to one another, and the other five curtains shall be joined to one another. 4You shall make loops of blue on the edge of the outermost curtain in the first set, and likewise you shall make them on the edge of the curtain that is outermost in the second set. 5You shall make fifty loops in the one curtain, and you shall make fifty loops on the edge of the curtain

that is in the second set; the loops shall be opposite each other. [6]You shall make fifty clasps of gold, and join the curtains to one another with the clasps so that the tabernacle will be a unit.

[7]"Then you shall make curtains of goats' hair for a tent over the tabernacle; you shall make eleven curtains in all. [8]The length of each curtain shall be thirty cubits, and the width of each curtain four cubits; the eleven curtains shall have the same measurements. [9]You shall join five curtains by themselves and the other six curtains by themselves, and you shall double over the sixth curtain at the front of the tent. [10]You shall make fifty loops on the edge of the curtain that is outermost in the first set, and fifty loops on the edge of the curtain that is outermost in the second set.

[11]"You shall make fifty clasps of bronze, and you shall put the clasps into the loops and join the tent together so that it will be a unit. [12]The overlapping part that is left over in the curtains of the tent, the half curtain that is left over, shall lap over the back of the tabernacle. [13]The cubit on one side and the cubit on the other, of what is left over in the length of the curtains of the tent, shall lap over the sides of the tabernacle on one side and on the other, to cover it."

Verse 1. Instructions for the building of **the tabernacle** begin with a description of the coverings which comprise the tent. God first spoke of the inner covering of the tent, which was to be made of **ten curtains of fine twisted linen and blue and purple and scarlet material.** In the NASB "material" is in italics, indicating that the word is not found in the original but was added by translators to help the reader understand. The KJV does not add anything to the Hebrew text, but has simply "blue, and purple, and scarlet." The NRSV translates the phrase as "ten curtains of fine twisted linen, and blue, purple, and crimson yarns." The NIV has "ten curtains of finely twisted linen and blue, purple and scarlet yarn." These materials were scarce and expensive. Furthermore, figures of **cherubim** were to be worked into the fabric. These decorations must have made the already beautiful cloth even more impressive.

Verses 2, 3. Then the Lord gave directions for how the material was to be put together. The ten curtains, each **twenty-eight cubits** by **four cubits** (42′ x 6′), were to be put together into two large sheets composed of **five curtains** each. Presumably, the ten curtains were sewed together into two large sheets so that they could be folded and carried from place to place; one large covering would probably have been too bulky to be portable.

Verses 4–6. Then provision was made to fasten these two sheets by attaching **loops** and **clasps** to them. Because this was the innermost covering, closest to the holy furnishings, the clasps were to be made of **gold**.

Apparently, these curtains were to be put together sideways so that the ten curtains, twenty-eight cubits long, would be draped side by side over the ten-cubit-wide, ten-cubit-high tabernacle. The whole covering would not quite have reached the ground on either side; it would have fallen one cubit short. The total length of the covering was forty cubits—long enough to cover the tabernacle from the front to the back (thirty cubits), with ten cubits to cover the inside of the tabernacle (the holy place and the most holy place). However, there would not have been enough material to cover the front of the tabernacle; that was taken care of by the outer curtain or "screen," which is described later in the chapter (26:36).

Verse 7. The second covering for the tent was to be made of **curtains of goats' hair**. The first covering was decorative; the second one would be serviceable. This was the material commonly used for making the tents of desert dwellers; it was probably black, the color of the goats that the people kept.

Verses 8, 9. Besides the material and color, there are two main differences between the second covering and the first covering. One difference was in size. The second covering was larger than the first, consisting of eleven curtains compared to ten (26:7). **Each curtain** was **thirty cubits** long, compared to twenty-eight for the inner covering. The extra material provided covering for the front, back, and sides of the tabernacle. Half, or two cubits, of the extra curtain was to be **double**[d] **over** at the **front of the tent**, that is, folded back from the entrance.

Verses 10, 11. The second difference is in the fastenings which held the two large sheets together. The fastenings for the second covering were **bronze** rather than gold. It was farther removed from the holy place and from the presence of God; therefore, the less precious metal could be used. These **clasps** were to be fitted into the **fifty loops**, which would **join the tent together so that it** [would] **be a unit.**

Verses 12, 13. The other half of the curtain that was not "double[d] over" (26:9) was to **lap over the back of the tabernacle.** As a consequence of these directions, the first covering was altogether covered by the second; it could not have been seen from the outside at all.

THE TWO COVERINGS MADE FROM SKINS (26:14)

14"You shall make a covering for the tent of rams' skins dyed red and a covering of porpoise skins above."

Verse 14. Two other **covering**[s] are then mentioned but not fully described. One was a covering of **rams' skins dyed red**. Probably, the purpose of this third covering was to protect the two inner coverings; rams' skins would have been more water resistant than the two inner coverings, for instance. Since the third covering is not further described (no dimensions are given, for example), it must not have been as significant as the two coverings previously prescribed.

A fourth covering of **porpoise skins** is mentioned. There is some question as to just what kind of skins is meant by the Hebrew word תַּחַשׁ (*thachash*). The KJV renders the term "badgers' skins." However, most commentators favor the view that these were skins of the "sea cow," the dugong, which could be found in the Red Sea.[1] There is also a question as to whether or not this

---

[1]John J. Davis, *Moses and the Gods of Egypt: Studies in Exodus*, 2d ed. (Grand Rapids, Mich.: Baker Book House, 1986), 262; John I. Durham, *Exodus*, Word Biblical Commentary, vol. 3 (Waco, Tex.: Word Books, 1987), 371; see Francis Brown, S. R. Driver, and Charles A. Briggs, *The Brown-Driver-Briggs Hebrew and English Lexicon* (Boston: Houghton, Mifflin and Co., 1906; reprint, Peabody, Mass.: Hendrickson Publishers, 1997), 1065.

was actually another covering for the tabernacle. R. Alan Cole thought that these skins were to be used to make a bag, or bags, in which the coverings of the tabernacle could be carried. He wrote,

> It seems that some sort of leather "tent bag", or wrapper, was provided for transportation. Some think that the phrase denoted a third (or even fourth) tent of leather, placed over the tents of goats' hair and linen, but this would seem to be impossibly heavy and unnecessary.[2]

THE WALLS: THE BOARDS AND THE BARS (26:15–30)

**[15]"Then you shall make the boards for the tabernacle of aca-
cia wood, standing upright. [16]Ten cubits shall be the length of
each board and one and a half cubits the width of each board.
[17]There shall be two tenons for each board, fitted to one another;
thus you shall do for all the boards of the tabernacle. [18]You
shall make the boards for the tabernacle: twenty boards for the
south side. [19]You shall make forty sockets of silver under the
twenty boards, two sockets under one board for its two tenons
and two sockets under another board for its two tenons; [20]and
for the second side of the tabernacle, on the north side, twenty
boards, [21]and their forty sockets of silver; two sockets under
one board and two sockets under another board. [22]For the rear
of the tabernacle, to the west, you shall make six boards. [23]You
shall make two boards for the corners of the tabernacle at the
rear. [24]They shall be double beneath, and together they shall
be complete to its top to the first ring; thus it shall be with both
of them: they shall form the two corners. [25]There shall be eight
boards with their sockets of silver, sixteen sockets; two sock-
ets under one board and two sockets under another board.**

**[26]"Then you shall make bars of acacia wood, five for the
boards of one side of the tabernacle, [27]and five bars for the**

---

[2]R. Alan Cole, *Exodus: An Introduction and Commentary*, Tyndale Old Testament Commentaries (Downers Grove, Ill.: Inter-Varsity Press, 1973), 194.

boards of the other side of the tabernacle, and five bars for the boards of the side of the tabernacle for the rear side to the west. [28]The middle bar in the center of the boards shall pass through from end to end. [29]You shall overlay the boards with gold and make their rings of gold as holders for the bars; and you shall overlay the bars with gold. [30]Then you shall erect the tabernacle according to its plan which you have been shown in the mountain."

Verse 15. After the description of the four coverings for the tabernacle, the text continues by giving instructions for **the boards** which defined the walls of the tabernacle. The boards were to be made of **acacia wood** overlaid with gold (26:29), as was suitable for material that was close to the presence of God. "Acacia," according to Richard E. Averbeck, was "a very hard and durable wood that is also lightweight."[3]

Verses 16, 17. The **board**[s] were **ten cubits** (15′) long, the height of the tabernacle. On the sides, the boards were **one and a half cubits** (27″) wide. These boards were built with **tenons** on the bottom, making it possible for them to stand upright in silver "sockets" (26:19). A "tenon" is "a projection on a piece of wood shaped for insertion into a mortise to make a joint."[4] The "tenons" described in the text were made to fit into "sockets" which were placed on the ground. Umberto Cassuto explained the tenons mentioned as being like door hinges.[5]

Verses 18–21. The directions specified that there were to be **twenty boards** on each side. Side by side, these boards would make up a wall thirty cubits long, the length of the tabernacle.

Verses 22, 23. Instructions for the **rear** [wall] **of the tabernacle** are not as easy to understand, but there seem to have been eight boards, including **two boards** made especially **for the corners**, which would have covered the back in the same way that

---

[3]Richard E. Averbeck, "Tabernacle," in *Dictionary of the Old Testament: Pentateuch*, ed. T. Desmond Alexander and David W. Baker (Downers Grove, Ill.: InterVarsity Press, 2003), 814.

[4]*American Heritage Dictionary*, 4th ed. (2001), s.v. "tenon."

[5]Umberto Cassuto, *A Commentary on the Book of Exodus*, trans. Israel Abrahams (Jerusalem: Magnes Press, 1997), 355.

the other boards covered the sides of the tabernacle.

Verses 24, 25. The text seems to indicate that the **boards** made a solid wall around three sides of the tabernacle. The problem with this interpretation is that if the boards were solid, then the inner covering, if it were draped outside the boards, could not be seen, except on the ceiling. Conversely, if it were draped inside the boards, then the beautiful gold-covered boards could not be seen. The beauty of both the cloth and the cherubim would seem to indicate that God intended the inner covering to be seen by human eyes. Consequently, some scholars conclude that the boards were trellis-like frames which provided a framework for the tabernacle and its coverings but through which the priests could see the inner covering. This interpretation also helps to solve another problem: If the boards were solid and overlaid with gold, their weight would have made their transport difficult. Boards that were frames would not have been as heavy.

Verses 26–30. To hold the **boards** together on the two long **side**[s] of the tent, God indicated that the Israelites were to use **five bars** on each side. **The middle bar** on each side was to be as long as the tent itself. Presumably, the other four bars were not as long. Perhaps each of the other four bars was fifteen cubits long, so that two of them together ran the length of the tent. These bars were to be **gold**-covered and were to be attached to the boards of the **tabernacle** by **pass**[ing] **through . . . rings** placed in the boards for that purpose.

The tent served as the major feature of the tabernacle complex. It was divided into two compartments—the holy place and the most holy place—and housed the tabernacle furniture. Whether or not the individual components of the tent had symbolic significance beyond those specified in the Bible is questionable, but commentators see significance in a number of details given in the plan for the tent. Peter Enns, for instance, noted that the cherubim woven into the inner curtain served as "an ever-present reminder that the tabernacle is an earthly representation of the heavenly tabernacle."[6]

---

[6]Peter Enns, *Exodus*, The NIV Application Commentary (Grand Rapids, Mich.: Zondervan, 2000), 519.

THE VEIL, THE INNER CURTAIN (26:31–35)

**31"You shall make a veil of blue and purple and scarlet ma-
terial and fine twisted linen; it shall be made with cherubim,
the work of a skillful workman. 32You shall hang it on four pil-
lars of acacia overlaid with gold, their hooks also being of gold,
on four sockets of silver. 33You shall hang up the veil under the
clasps, and shall bring in the ark of the testimony there within
the veil; and the veil shall serve for you as a partition between
the holy place and the holy of holies. 34You shall put the mercy
seat on the ark of the testimony in the holy of holies. 35You
shall set the table outside the veil, and the lampstand oppo-
site the table on the side of the tabernacle toward the south;
and you shall put the table on the north side."**

Verse 31. The chapter concludes with instructions for making two curtains, or veils, which were necessary to complete the tabernacle. The first **veil** separated the holy place from the most holy place. It was to be made of **blue and purple and scarlet material and fine twisted linen**, the same material that was used in making the first covering. Like the first covering, it was to have woven into it figures of **cherubim**.

Verse 32. The veil would be hung on **four pillars of acacia overlaid with gold**. If these pillars were placed equidistant from the sides and from one another, there would have been two cubits, or about one yard, between them. These pillars were to have **hooks** and be set in **sockets of silver**.

Verses 33–35. The veil was to be hung **under the clasps**—apparently using the "hooks" referred to in verse 32— to serve as **a partition between the holy place and the holy of holies**. "Holy of holies" is the common way of expressing the superlative degree in Hebrew (קֹדֶשׁ הַקֳּדָשִׁים, *qodesh haqq[a]dashim*). "Holy of holies," therefore, means "most holy," just as "king of kings" means "the greatest king."

The instructions for making the two curtains also tell about the placement of the furniture within the **tabernacle**. Moses and the Israelites were instructed to **bring in the ark of the testimony** into the most holy place, **put the mercy seat on the ark of**

the testimony, and position the **table** and the **lampstand** in the holy place.

The veil separating the holy place and most holy place was lifted only once a year, emphasizing that God is unapproachable because of His holiness. The darkness and quiet of the most holy place, as defined by the veil, spoke of the essential mystery and transcendence of God. At the same time, this stillness proclaimed the good news that the God of creation had chosen to be present with His people in the most holy place. Though invisible, He was there. James Burton Coffman wrote,

> This veil [symbolizes] the mysteries of the [Old Testament]. The purpose of the veil was to hide, to conceal, to deny access; and, as long as that veil was in place, many of the plainest teachings of the [Old Testament] would remain hidden in darkness. The veil is a double symbol of Christ; it represented the *promised* Christ as long as it remained intact; but when it was rent from the top to the bottom at the crucifixion of our Lord, it *then* represented the *revealed* Christ.[7]

Coffman went on to discuss the symbolic significance of the veil at length,[8] referring in particular to the fact that, when Christ died, "the veil of the temple was torn in two from top to bottom" (Mt. 27:51).

THE SCREEN, THE OUTER CURTAIN (26:36, 37)

[36]"You shall make a screen for the doorway of the tent of blue and purple and scarlet material and fine twisted linen, the work of a weaver. [37]You shall make five pillars of acacia for the screen and overlay them with gold, their hooks also being of gold; and you shall cast five sockets of bronze for them."

---

[7]James Burton Coffman, *Commentary on Exodus, The Second Book of Moses* (Abilene, Tex.: ACU Press, 1985), 372.

[8]Ibid., 372–75.

Verse 36. The second curtain is described in the last two verses of the chapter. It was the curtain, or **screen for the doorway** of the tabernacle—the "door," in a sense. It was to be made of the same kind of material as that used for the inner veil.

Verse 37. It was to hang on **five pillars of acacia** with hooks set in **sockets of bronze**. The pillars and the hooks were to be covered with **gold**. If these pillars were set equidistant from one another and from the sides of the tabernacle, they would have been about thirty inches apart.

The outer curtain served as a door into the tabernacle and as a screen, both to keep unauthorized persons from entering the holy place and to keep merely curious eyes from seeing or participating in the holy rites that took place within the tabernacle. The text does not ascribe any symbolic significance to this curtain; but it must have been important, for it was made of the same material that separated the holy place from the most holy place. For Christians, if the holy place symbolizes the church, this screen might symbolize the "door" into the church—faith, repentance, and baptism. When people are baptized into Christ, they are added to the church, Christ's body (Acts 2:47; 1 Cor. 12:13; Gal. 3:26, 27).

The impression left by the text is that, once the materials were collected, the individual parts of the tabernacle were to be constructed. Then, when all was ready, the tabernacle could be put together in a short time. The putting together of a prefabricated building is an imperfect modern analogy. The tabernacle was intended to be portable, so it was designed in such a way that it could be taken down and put up again. Exodus indicates that this was, in fact, what happened (ch. 40).

APPLICATION

"The God of the Tabernacle" (Ch. 26)

The Bible is a book about God. True, it tells us about man—where he came from, what he is doing here, and where he is going—but the Bible is primarily about God. It is intended to reveal Him to us so that we can worship and serve Him now and forever.

When we read the instructions for the building of the tabernacle, therefore, they not only tell us about the tabernacle, but they also tell us something about God. We can know God by what He does and by what He requires us to do, just as we can know God from what He says about Himself.

What is "the God of the tabernacle" like? In this presentation we will not focus on the most obvious characteristics of God, even though the tabernacle reflects them. For instance, the tabernacle teaches us about God's holiness and about both His immanence and His transcendence. However, we will look at some aspects of God's character that are revealed by the details of the tabernacle found in Exodus 26. The characteristics of God say something about what we should be, since we are to take on His nature (2 Pet. 1:4) and be imitators of Him (Eph. 5:1).

He is a God of order. Chapter 26 gives careful instructions for the making of the curtains to cover the tabernacle. God told Moses how long and wide they were to be, how they were to be held together, and how they were to be placed over the framework of the tent. Equally detailed instructions are given for the making of other parts of the tabernacle. God wanted the structure that resulted from Israel's work to reflect the order that is part of His nature. Of course, we should not be surprised that order is reflected in the instructions for the tabernacle, since our God designed and created an orderly world. As people made in the image of God, we tend to be like Him in that we work constantly to bring order out of chaos. In light of this characteristic of God, we need to do things in an orderly way (1 Cor. 14:33).

He is a God of beauty. The tabernacle was intended to be beautiful as well as useful. The curtains that provided the covering for the tent were made of colorful material, and cherubim were woven into the fabric (26:1). Neither the colors nor the cherubim were necessary for the tent to perform its essential function; they were designed for beauty as well as for utility. The gold, silver, and bronze that were used in building no doubt added to the beauty of the tent. Again, the pleasing appearance of the tabernacle should not be surprising, since God made such a beautiful universe. Mankind reflects God's appreciation for what is lovely; people everywhere have engaged in artistic endeavors.

Since God is interested in beauty, Christians should not disdain art and beauty. Above all, however, we should seek and appreciate the beauty of a soul given to God (1 Pet. 3:1–4).

He is a God of utility. The tabernacle was not made merely to look at or to be admired. It was made to be used in the worship of God. The practical value of some of God's instructions are obvious. For instance, the coverings of rams' skins made the tent waterproof. Again, as presented elsewhere in Exodus, the attachment of poles to the furnishings of the tabernacle made it possible for those furnishings to be carried from one place to another. In creation, as well, God made beautiful things useful and useful things beautiful. For instance, the human eye is generally thought of as one of the most attractive features of an individual, but the eye is intended to be useful as well as beautiful. God's interest in usefulness should remind us that Christians have been put into His house as "living stones" (1 Pet. 2:5; see Eph. 2:19–22); we are to be useful in the kingdom, serving God and man (1 Pet. 4:10, 11).

He is a God of mercy. In the mention of the mercy seat (26:34), we are again reminded of God's compassionate nature. God has always wanted to bless and forgive His people, and He used the tabernacle to do so. Of course, God's compassionate nature is also apparent in the world He created. Human beings, in spite of our sinfulness, are often surprisingly merciful and compassionate. Since God is merciful, we as Christians should show gratitude for the mercy bestowed on us by being merciful to others (Mt. 18:21–35; Eph. 4:32; Col. 3:13). The church—the New Testament equivalent of the tabernacle—is to be the means by which the world can come to know God's forgiveness.

He is a God of revelation. Exodus 26 inserts a reminder that God had revealed His law to Israel by mentioning the "ark of the testimony" (26:33). God did not leave Israel without directions. Neither has God, in His created world, ever left people without a witness to His "eternal power and divine nature" (Rom. 1:20). Human beings are interested both in giving and in receiving information. The fact that our God is a God who speaks to people, who has revealed His will to mankind, is significant for us. The same God who spoke to Moses in Exodus is still speaking to us today through His Son (Heb. 1:1, 2) and the New Testament.

Conclusion. God has not changed. He is still a God of order, of beauty, and of utility. He is still a merciful God and a God of revelation. Let us rejoice in His nature, savor His mercy, and follow His directions. We are to be imitators of God. Should we not, then, like God, be orderly? Should we not also be interested in both beauty and utility? Should we not be merciful to others? Finally, should we not recognize our responsibility to pass on to others the revelation which we have received from God?

The Inner Curtain—Invisible Beauty (26:1–6)

The inner curtain of the tabernacle must have been breathtaking; it was made of rich material beautifully decorated with cherubim. However, no one could see it—no one, that is, except the priests who ministered in the tabernacle. If the boards were solid and on the inside of the curtain, even they could not see it! Whether or not anyone else could see the curtain, God could. He could appreciate its beauty and the fact that it had been made as He directed. In a similar way, God sees us as no one else can. He sees and knows the inner man (1 Sam. 16:7). Let us, therefore, not be overly concerned with our outward appearance; instead, let us make sure we are beautiful on the inside (1 Pet. 3:4).

"Fitly Joined Together" (26:4–37)

Exodus describes how the different parts of the tabernacle were to be joined together. The curtains were to be joined with loops and clasps; the boards would be kept in place with tenons and sockets; the veil and screen were to be hung with hooks and sockets. The church today is God's temple, God's building. Each member is a living stone in that building (1 Pet. 2:5). In order for the parts to be held together and for each part of the body to function, the different parts have to be "fitly joined together" (Eph. 4:16; KJV). The members of the Lord's church must be connected. Bricks without mortar binding them together will not make a stable building. In the church, figuratively speaking, we need "loops" and "clasps," "tenons" and "sockets." We can be bound together by being better organized. Above all, we need love, "the perfect bond of unity" (Col. 3:14), the "mortar" which holds the bricks together.

The Most Holy Place—
God's Throne Room (26:31–35)[9]

The most holy place was a type of heaven (Heb. 9:11, 12, 23, 24). (1) God is said to be enthroned in both (Ps. 99:1; Rev. 4:1, 2). (2) Both are said to have the glory of God's presence (Lev. 16:2; Rev. 21:23). (3) Both are depicted as having creatures worshiping God (Ex. 25:18; Rev. 4:6–8). (4) Both are described as being golden (Ex. 25:11, 17, 26–29; Rev. 21:18). (5) Both are said to be "foursquare" (Ex. 28:16; KJV; Rev. 21:16). (6) Both have God's law in them (Ex. 40:20; Ps. 119:89; see 89:14). (7) Both are said to be places where blood atonement is made (Lev. 16:15, 16; Heb. 9:11, 12, 24, 25).

The Torn Veil (26:31–35)

The veil of the tabernacle separated the holy place from the most holy place. The veil was torn from the top to the bottom when Jesus died, indicating that God tore it. This event signified that Christ had opened up the way to heaven for His followers. By dying—by giving His body (His flesh)—Jesus opened up the way for us (Heb. 10:20). All we have to do is enter in through the "new and living way" (Heb. 10:19, 20). However, before we can enter into heaven, one way or another we will have to shed the flesh that we inhabit (1 Cor. 15:50). We will do that either at the moment of death or at Christ's return.

---

[9]Adapted from Wilbur Fields, *Exploring Exodus*, Bible Study Textbook Series (Joplin, Mo.: College Press, 1976), 590.

Chapter 27

Instructions for the Tabernacle (Part 3)

In chapter 27, God provided directions concerning the court of the tabernacle—the space around the tent. He first described how Moses was to make the bronze altar that would stand in the court (27:1–8) and then gave instructions for making the fence of curtains that surrounded and defined the court (27:9–19). The chapter concludes with a brief note concerning the oil which was burned to light the tabernacle (27:20, 21).

Just as the altar of incense is not included in the description of the contents of the tabernacle in chapters 25 and 26, chapter 27 has an interesting omission: the description of the laver. Even though the laver was found in the courtyard, directions for its construction do not appear until 30:17–21.

THE BRONZE ALTAR (27:1–8)

**[1]"And you shall make the altar of acacia wood, five cubits
long and five cubits wide; the altar shall be square, and its
height shall be three cubits. [2]You shall make its horns on its
four corners; its horns shall be of one piece with it, and you
shall overlay it with bronze. [3]You shall make its pails for remov-
ing its ashes, and its shovels and its basins and its forks and
its firepans; you shall make all its utensils of bronze. [4]You shall
make for it a grating of network of bronze, and on the net you
shall make four bronze rings at its four corners. [5]You shall put
it beneath, under the ledge of the altar, so that the net will reach
halfway up the altar. [6]You shall make poles for the altar, poles
of acacia wood, and overlay them with bronze. [7]Its poles shall**

be inserted into the rings, so that the poles shall be on the two sides of the altar when it is carried. [8]You shall make it hollow with planks; as it was shown to you in the mountain, so they shall make it."

Verse 1. Exodus 27:1–8 contains the instructions Moses received for building **the altar** of burnt offering. The structure that is called here simply "the altar" is referred to as the "altar of burnt offering" later in the narrative (30:28; 31:9; 38:1; see Lev. 4:7, 10, 18). This altar was a hollow box (27:8) made of **acacia wood** overlaid with "bronze" (27:2). It measured about **five cubits . . . square** and **three cubits** high (7 1/2′ square and 4 1/2′ high).

The relationship between this altar and the one described in 20:24–26 is uncertain. These two passages may be viewed as supplementary. Perhaps the altar described in chapter 27 provided the framework, while the description in chapter 20 indicates what was to go inside the framework: earth and/or stones.[1] Another possibility is that two different altars are described; perhaps they had different functions or were for use at different times. The altar described in chapter 20 may have been used just until the altar of burnt offering was built or just during the Israelites' time in the wilderness. Later, animals were to be sacrificed only on the altar in the tabernacle (or temple) courtyard. No interpretation is wholly satisfactory.

Verse 2. The **four corners** of the altar had **horns** covered with **bronze**. These were called horns, presumably, because they looked like the horns on cattle. The horns were attached to the altar, being **of one piece with it**. They may have been used to tie sacrifices in position on the altar (Ps. 118:27).[2] When sacrifices were offered, blood was sprinkled on the horns (Ex. 29:12; Lev. 4:7). These horns may have "symbolized power, help, and sanc-

---

[1]Umberto Cassuto, *A Commentary on the Book of Exodus*, trans. Israel Abrahams (Jerusalem: Magnes Press, 1997), 362.

[2]However, the translation of Psalm 118:27 is uncertain. James Burton Coffman's idea that the horns looked like hands extended upward in prayer and symbolized prayer directed to God "for protection and help" is rather fanciful. (See James Burton Coffman, *Commentary on Exodus, The Second Book of Moses* [Abilene, Tex.: ACU Press, 1985], 380–81.)

tuary (cf. 1 Sam 2:1, 10; 2 Sam 22:3; 1 Kings 1:50; 2:28; Pss 89:17; 112:9)."[3] Further, there arose a custom in Israel that one could find refuge by taking hold of the horns of the altar (see 1 Kings 1:49–53; 2:28–34). Archaeologists have discovered stone altars with four horns in Israel at sites such as Megiddo, Gezer, and Beersheba.[4]

Verse 3. Moses was also given instructions for making **utensils** to use with the altar—its **pails, shovels, basins, forks,** and **firepans.** All of these were to be made of **bronze.** John I. Durham wrote,

> The accessories for the Altar . . . included a pot or pail for ash removal, along with a special shovel for that purpose, basins for dashing liquids, pronged forks for the manipulation of the meat and fat being burned, and special pans to hold and transfer coals of fire.[5]

Verses 4, 5. The instructions speak of a **ledge, halfway up,** which may have served as the resting place for the **grating of network of bronze.** If it was on the outside of the box, it may have provided a place for the priests to stand as they offered sacrifices.

It is unclear whether the fire was built under the grate, with the sacrifices placed on top of it, or whether both the wood for the fire and the offerings were placed on the top of the grate. In any case, the metal overlay kept the wooden structure from catching fire. The altar may have been partly or altogether filled with dirt before sacrifices were burned on it, protecting the bronze-covered wood from the flames.

Verses 6–8. The altar must have been big, heavy, and cum-

---

[3]Walter C. Kaiser, Jr., "Exodus," in *The Expositor's Bible Commentary,* vol. 2, *Genesis—Numbers* (Grand Rapids, Mich.: Zondervan, 1990), 462.

[4]See the photos in Edward Ball, "Horns of the Altar," in *The International Standard Bible Encyclopedia,* rev. ed., ed. Geoffrey W. Bromiley (Grand Rapids, Mich.: Wm. B. Eerdmans Publishing Co., 1982), 2:758, and Ralph Gower, *The New Manners and Customs of Bible Times* (Chicago: Moody Press, 1987), 363.

[5]John I. Durham, *Exodus,* Word Biblical Commentary, vol. 3 (Waco, Tex.: Word Books, 1987), 375.

bersome. Nevertheless, it was meant to be carried from place to place. Provision was made for **poles** to fit through **rings**, making it easier to transport (27:4–7).

Chapter 27 does not reveal how the altar was to be used; the reader's familiarity with the sacrifices offered on it is assumed. Additional instructions concerning those sacrifices are given in Leviticus. The sacrifices offered on the altar had a variety of purposes, but their primary function was to make atonement for sin (Lev. 4:18–20). The offering of an animal on the altar was preceded by putting "some of the blood on the horns of the altar" and pouring out the rest of the blood at the base of the altar. On the annual Day of Atonement, the high priest would take some of the blood shed by the sacrificial animal into the most holy place to make atonement for the people (Lev. 16). The altar of burnt offering was an essential part of the process by which Israel sought and received forgiveness.

The New Testament teaches that, in these latter days, Christ is both our sacrifice and our high priest who takes the blood of the sacrifice into the most holy place (Heb. 8:1; 9:11–15). By His blood people are saved today (Eph. 1:7). In addition, altar terminology is used when the Christian is called upon to give himself as a "living . . . sacrifice" to God (Rom. 12:1, 2).

THE COURT (27:9–19)

[9]"You shall make the court of the tabernacle. On the south side there shall be hangings for the court of fine twisted linen one hundred cubits long for one side; [10]and its pillars shall be twenty, with their twenty sockets of bronze; the hooks of the pillars and their bands shall be of silver. [11]Likewise for the north side in length there shall be hangings one hundred cubits long, and its twenty pillars with their twenty sockets of bronze; the hooks of the pillars and their bands shall be of silver. [12]For the width of the court on the west side shall be hangings of fifty cubits with their ten pillars and their ten sockets. [13]The width of the court on the east side shall be fifty cubits. [14]The hangings for the one side of the gate shall be fifteen cubits with their three pillars and their three sockets. [15]And for the other

side shall be hangings of fifteen cubits with their three pillars and their three sockets. [16]For the gate of the court there shall be a screen of twenty cubits, of blue and purple and scarlet material and fine twisted linen, the work of a weaver, with their four pillars and their four sockets. [17]All the pillars around the court shall be furnished with silver bands with their hooks of silver and their sockets of bronze. [18]The length of the court shall be one hundred cubits, and the width fifty throughout, and the height five cubits of fine twisted linen, and their sockets of bronze. [19]All the utensils of the tabernacle used in all its service, and all its pegs, and all the pegs of the court, shall be of bronze."

Verses 9–13. God next gave directions for the construction of the courtyard. The tent was surrounded by a **court** which was **one hundred cubits** (150′) by **fifty cubits** (75′). The court was defined by **hangings** made of **fine twisted linen** which were attached to a series of **pillars.** These pillars were placed five cubits (7$^1/_2$′) apart. The tabernacle was always to be oriented in the same direction—facing east. In the middle of the "wall" on the eastern side there was to be a gate twenty cubits (30′) wide (27:16).

Verses 14, 15. On each side of the **gate** would be a partial wall **fifteen cubits** (22$^1/_2$′) long, with **three pillars.** The Israelites were to make **sockets** to provide footings for the pillars. The sockets were to be made of "bronze," but the "hooks" and "bands" which were used to attach the "hangings" to the pillars were to be made of "silver" (27:17).

The court was not enclosed with a permanent wall. The fence, like the tabernacle, was made to be portable. A fence made of cloth hanging on moveable pillars could be quickly set up and taken down again.

The provision of instructions for the courtyard makes it possible to visualize the entire tabernacle complex. Peter Enns described it as follows:

> The entire structure measured 150′ on the north and south sides and 75′ on the east and west, thus forming a rectangle made up of two squares 75′ by 75′. The one square

> constituted the outer court, in which was placed the altar of burnt offering, roughly a 7′6″ square structure, and the wash basin at the entrance of the Holy Place. Inside the other square was the Holy Place, a rectangle measuring 30′ by 15′, the same proportions as the tabernacle as a whole. The adjoining Most Holy Place measured a perfect 15′ square.[6]

Verses 16, 17. The thirty-foot-wide **gate** (or **screen**) of the courtyard differed from the remainder of the "wall" around the courtyard in that it was covered with a different kind of material. The screen into the court, in fact, had the same kind of material as the curtain that separated the most holy place from the holy place—**blue and purple and scarlet material** along with the **fine twisted linen** that was used for the rest of the courtyard wall. However, the gate had the same kind of **sockets** and **pillars**, set the same distance apart as the rest of the courtyard wall. Presumably, the screen used for the gate could be pulled back, much as a curtain in front of a window or a stage can be pulled back, when the tabernacle was "open for business"—when the Israelites were free to enter and offer sacrifices. Another possibility is that the screen was set back from the rest of the fence so that it provided at each end a way to get into the courtyard, but still have the interior screened from the view of those outside the courtyard. The three or four pillars standing in the gate would not have kept anyone from entering the courtyard.

Verses 18, 19. The **height** of the fence was **five cubits**, or 7½′—considerably lower than the ten-cubit tabernacle. The top of the tabernacle would therefore have been visible from outside the fence, but it would not have been possible for one standing outside the fence to see straight into the tent unless the gate was open.

The text does not speak of the significance or use of the court, except to indicate that it contained the altar. Obviously, the courtyard provided space for offering sacrifices. In addition, it pro-

[6]Peter Enns, *Exodus*, in The NIV Application Commentary (Grand Rapids, Mich.: Zondervan, 2000), 520.

vided an area for the people to gather on special occasions, especially when they brought sacrifices to the Lord. R. Alan Cole said that the courtyard "mark[ed] the outward limits of holiness" and provided "plenty of room" for the crowds, since "men went to YHWH's Tent only for some specific purpose, and usually only on some festal occasion."[7] According to Numbers 15:14, an "alien" (non-Israelite) sojourning with Israel could "make an offering by fire" as did the Israelites. The New Testament does not say anything specifically about the courtyard.

THE OIL FOR THE LAMP (27:20, 21)

[20]"You shall charge the sons of Israel, that they bring you clear oil of beaten olives for the light, to make a lamp burn continually. [21]In the tent of meeting, outside the veil which is before the testimony, Aaron and his sons shall keep it in order from evening to morning before the LORD; it shall be a perpetual statute throughout their generations for the sons of Israel."

Verse 20. The light for the tabernacle was provided by the **lamp**, which most likely refers to the golden lampstand. "Lamp" (נֵר, *ner*) is here referred to in the singular even though seven "lamps" were mounted on the lampstand (25:31–40). Another possibility is that this was a separate lamp from the lampstand specifically designed to provide illumination at night.[8]

The priests were to keep the lamp **burn**[ing] **continually**. Only a certain kind of oil—**clear oil of beaten olives**—was to be used in the lamp. Commentators note that this was the best kind of olive oil.

Verse 21. The fact that the priests were instructed to keep it burning **from evening to morning** emphasizes that it was to burn all night as well as all day. Another view is that the lamp was lit in the evening, was allowed to burn all night, and was

---

[7]R. Alan Cole, *Exodus: An Introduction and Commentary*, Tyndale Old Testament Commentaries (Downers Grove, Ill.: Inter-Varsity Press, 1973), 197.

[8]Ibid., 198.

extinguished in the morning; Exodus 30:8 and 1 Samuel 3:3 are cited in support of this view.[9] This interpretation is possible if "continually" (27:20) is understood as meaning "regularly" or "nightly" or "daily." However, it seems more likely that 30:8 depicts the evening routine in which the priest trimmed the lamps and added oil. The rest of the time the lamps were burning. The light from the lamps was needed during the day as well as at night, since no outside light could have penetrated the curtains covering the tabernacle. The importance of the continually burning light is indicated by the fact that this requirement was spoken of as **a perpetual statute throughout their generations for the sons of Israel**.

The text describes how the oil was to be used and emphasizes the importance of keeping the light burning, but it assigns no symbolic meaning to the oil. Christians, in reading about this light, are likely to remember Jesus' words: "You are the light of the world. . . . Let your light shine before men in such a way that they may see your good works, and glorify your Father who is in heaven" (Mt. 5:14–16).

APPLICATION

Sacrifices Then and Now (27:1–8)

In chapter 27 God gave Moses directions for building the altar of burnt offering. The altar was used to offer sacrifices to God. The passage, therefore, can be used to help us think about the subject of sacrifices, both then and now.

Sacrifices Then. The text does not reveal how the altar was to be used. The first readers did not need that information; they were familiar with the fact that sacrifices were offered on it.

Further instructions concerning those sacrifices are given in the Book of Leviticus. There, we learn that the sacrifices offered on the altar had a variety of purposes. Among the sacrifices were guilt offerings, sin offerings, whole burnt offerings, and peace offerings—including thank offerings and freewill offerings and sacrifices made when vows were taken. For some of the offer-

---

[9]Kaiser, 464.

ings (whole burnt offerings), the whole animal was burned on the altar. For others (such as peace offerings), part of the animal was burned on the altar and the other part was eaten by those who brought the sacrifice. The priests were also given portions of meat from the offerings.

Even though some non-animal sacrifices were offered, the primary purpose of the altar was to burn animal offerings to make atonement for sins (see Lev. 4:18–20). The offering of an animal on the altar was preceded by putting "some of the blood on the horns of the altar" and pouring out the rest of the blood at the base of the altar (Lev. 4:18). On the annual Day of Atonement, the high priest would take some of the blood shed by the sacrificial animal into the most holy place to make atonement for the people (Lev. 16). The altar of burnt offering was an essential part of the process by which Israel sought and received God's forgiveness.

Sacrifices Now. The New Testament teaches that Christ is the sacrifice for those under the new covenant. In addition, He is the high priest who takes the blood of the sacrifice into the most holy place (Heb. 8:1; 9:11–15; see Eph. 5:2; 1 Cor. 5:7). Christians are saved by His blood (Eph. 1:7). No matter what we do for Christ—even if we were to die for Him—in no sense can our sacrifices or our gifts atone for our sins. Only Christ's blood can make atonement for us.

Even though our gifts do not cover our sins, as priests we are to "offer up spiritual sacrifices acceptable to God through Jesus Christ" (1 Pet. 2:5). A sacrifice is an offering; it is anything we offer or give to God.

We are to offer a sacrifice of ourselves. Altar terminology is used when the Christian is called upon to give himself as a "living . . . sacrifice" to God (Rom. 12:1, 2). Jesus called on every Christian to offer himself, even to the point of death, when He said that each one must "take up his cross" and follow Him (Mt. 16:24; see Phil. 2:17).

We are to offer a sacrifice of the praise of our lips. Hebrews 13:15 says, "Let us continually offer up a sacrifice of praise to God, that is, the fruit of lips that give thanks to His name." We are to praise God in song, to "be of the same mind with one another . . . so that with one accord [we] may with one voice glorify the God and Father of our Lord Jesus Christ" (Rom. 15:5, 6). We do not bring animals to offer on an altar; rather, we place before God's heavenly altar the praises of our lips when we join together to sing in the assembly.

We are to offer a sacrifice of good works. Hebrews 13:16 says, "And do not neglect doing good and sharing, for with such sacrifices God is pleased." Doing good to others and sharing what we have with them is considered a sacrifice we make to God. By showing love for others, we manifest our love for God.

We are to offer a sacrifice of money. Paul wrote to the Philippians that he had received from Epaphroditus the gift that they had sent to him. He called that gift "a fragrant aroma, an acceptable sacrifice, well-pleasing to God" (Phil. 4:18). Giving a gift of money to the church for a missionary is, in a sense, a gift to the church and a gift to the missionary—but it is also a gift to God, an offering or sacrifice to the Lord.

We are to offer a sacrifice of saved souls to God. Paul was given the privilege of being "a minister of Christ Jesus to the Gentiles" and wrote of "my offering of the Gentiles" (Rom. 15:16). This imagery depicts Paul as a priest making an offering to God. What was Paul's offering? The Gentiles, the people to whom he preached and who were saved by his preaching. In a similar way, when we preach to others and lead them to salvation, they become our offerings to God.

We cannot give our own blood for our sins. Christ has made the sole sacrifice that takes away sins. Because we have been saved by Christ's blood, we are to make offerings to Him. Are we making the offerings we should, or are we giving Him less than He desires and deserves?

The Christian's Sacrifice (27:1–8)

God does not require animal sacrifices of His children today, but He does require sacrifices. The most basic sacrifice He asks of us is our very lives (Rom. 12:1). He does not say, "Bring a sacrifice and lay it on the altar for Me." Rather, He says, in effect, "Climb onto the altar. You are the sacrifice I want" (see 2 Cor. 8:5; 2 Tim. 4:6).

The Christian's Altar (27:1–8)

Israel had their altar. Do Christians have an altar? In New Testament times, some were saying that Christians were disadvantaged because, unlike the Jews, they had no altar. Hebrews 13:10 says, "We have an altar from which those who serve the tabernacle have no right to eat." What is the Christian's altar? Answers vary, but "altar" probably stands for "sacrifice."[10] As Christians, we have a sacrifice that benefits us alone—the sacrifice of Christ on the cross for our sins. The altar of the Mosaic law reminds us of Christ's sacrifice and calls on us to be willing to give ourselves for Him.

A Lamp Burning Continually—
"This Little Light of Mine" (27:20)

A lamp was to be kept burning in the tabernacle. In a similar way, Christ's disciples are to be "the light of the world" (Mt. 5:14). Just as the light in the tabernacle burned continually, we need to make sure our "lights" never go out. Wherever we are, whatever we do, people should be able to see God's light in our lives at all times. A children's song expresses the idea well: "This little gospel light of mine, I'm going to let it shine. . . ."[11]

---

[10]Neil R. Lightfoot, *Jesus Christ Today: A Commentary on the Book of Hebrews* (Grand Rapids, Mich.: Baker Book House, 1976), 250.

[11]Traditional, "This Little Light of Mine," *Songs of Faith and Praise*, comp. and ed. Alton H. Howard (West Monroe, La.: Howard Publishing Co., 1994).

CHAPTER 28

INSTRUCTIONS FOR THE PRIESTLY GARMENTS

After giving the Israelites directions for the construction of the tabernacle furnishings, the tent, and the court (25:8—27:21), the Lord gave instructions concerning all the priests who would serve in the tabernacle (28:1—29:46). The close connection of the priests with the tabernacle is indicated by the inclusion of directions regarding their service in a long passage otherwise dedicated to the building of the structure (chs. 25—31). Chapter 28 tells how the priests' garments were to be made, and chapter 29 relates how the priests were to be consecrated for the service to which they had been called.

In chapter 28, the Lord specified who would serve as priests, namely Aaron and his sons, and then commanded that special garments be made for them to wear as they served (28:1–5). After this, He gave specific instructions for each of the garments, beginning with those that Aaron the high priest would wear: the ephod with the onyx stones (28:6–14); the breastpiece which carried the Urim and the Thummim (28:15–30); the robe (28:31–35); and the gold plate, tunic, turban, and sash (28:36–39). The chapter ends with the garments that were common to all the priests—tunics, sashes, caps, and linen breeches (28:40–43).

THE PRIESTS IDENTIFIED (28:1–5)

1"Then bring near to yourself Aaron your brother, and his sons with him, from among the sons of Israel, to minister as priest to Me—Aaron, Nadab and Abihu, Eleazar and Ithamar, Aaron's sons. 2You shall make holy garments for Aaron your

brother, for glory and for beauty. [3]You shall speak to all the skillful persons whom I have endowed with the spirit of wisdom, that they make Aaron's garments to consecrate him, that he may minister as priest to Me. [4]These are the garments which they shall make: a breastpiece and an ephod and a robe and a tunic of checkered work, a turban and a sash, and they shall make holy garments for Aaron your brother and his sons, that he may minister as priest to Me. [5]They shall take the gold and the blue and the purple and the scarlet material and the fine linen."

Verse 1. The Lord began by specifying who would serve as **priest**[s]—namely, **Aaron** and **his sons**. Before the priesthood was consecrated, others performed priestly functions. In the Patriarchal period, apparently the heads of families were responsible for offering sacrifices. For example, Abraham built altars and offered sacrifices (Gen. 12:8; 13:18; 22:9, 13), and Job also offered sacrifices (Job 1:5). Earlier in Exodus, the young men performed priestly duties (24:5). They were well suited for this work since butchering animals and handling their carcasses would have been physically demanding.

At this point, one family was appointed to serve as priests: the family of Aaron. No reason is given in the text for the appointment of Aaron. Apparently, God saw in him and his descendants the qualities needed in a priest. Later, men of the Levitical tribe distinguished themselves by their wholehearted devotion to God (32:26–28) and were set aside to serve as the priestly tribe, as helpers for the priests.

The four sons of Aaron are grouped in two pairs: **Nadab and Abihu, Eleazar and Ithamar**. The first pair, "Nadab and Abihu," were killed because they offered "strange fire" on the altar (Lev. 10:1, 2). This event apparently happened not long after they were ordained as priests. The second pair, "Eleazar and Ithamar" are remembered for their godly behavior. Ithamar is mentioned later in connection with the building of the tabernacle (38:21), and Eleazar became high priest after Aaron (Num. 20:24–28). Noting the importance of these family lines in later Israelite history, R. Alan Cole wrote, "The later Zadokite high priests at Jerusalem traced their genealogy to [*Eleazar*] (1 Ch. 6:3–8), while Eli's house, including David's priest Abiathar, traced their ancestry to *Ithamar* (1 Ch. 24:3)."[1]

While the tribe of Levi became the priestly tribe, not all Levites were qualified to serve as priests. Only the descendants of Aaron, who was himself descended from Levi, could become priests; and the high priest was chosen from among them. The Levites served as helpers of the priests and had other duties as well. Therefore, all the priests were Levites (they were descendants of Levi), but not all the Levites were priests (only those descended from Aaron could serve as priests).

Verses 2–5. Then the Lord commanded that special garments be made for the priests to wear as they served. **Aaron**, the high priest, was to serve the Lord in **holy garments** made **for glory and for beauty**. Aaron's role was to be special, set apart from the other priests, and his clothes reflected this distinction. The garments themselves, **a breastpiece**, **an ephod**, **a robe**, **a tunic**, **a turban**, and **a sash**, are described in more detail in 28:6–43.

In chapter 39, which describes the making of the priestly garments, a distinction is made between the high priest, Aaron, and the other priests, who were Aaron's sons. The chapter begins, "Moreover, from the blue and purple and scarlet material, they made finely woven garments for ministering in the holy place as well as the holy garments which were for Aaron" (39:1). The priestly "garments for ministering in the holy place" are distinguished from the "holy garments" which were to be worn by Aaron and succeeding high priests. God told Moses, "You shall make holy garments for Aaron your brother, for glory and for beauty" (28:2). Only the garments of Aaron, the high priest, were designated as "holy."

The distinction is emphasized by the fact that the garments of the high priest are described in detail, while only a few details describe the garments for the other priests. The uniform the high priest was to wear in performing his official duties was elaborately designed, impressive, and symbolic. The garments worn

---

[1]R. Alan Cole, *Exodus: An Introduction and Commentary*, Tyndale Old Testament Commentaries (Downers Grove, Ill.: Inter-Varsity Press, 1973), 199.

by the other priests were much simpler. For them, all that was needed was a tunic, a sash, linen undergarments, and a cap. The high priest wore the same simple garments as the other priests, except for the cap. Yet, in addition, he wore the ephod, the breastpiece, the robe, and the gold plate on a turban, all of which signified his office.

The differences between the uniforms of the high priest and the other priests emphasized the difference in their functions. While the work of the priests was important, the role of the high priest was all-important.

THE EPHOD AND THE ONYX STONES (28:6–14)

**6"They shall also make the ephod of gold, of blue and pur-
ple and scarlet material and fine twisted linen, the work of the
skillful workman. 7It shall have two shoulder pieces joined to
its two ends, that it may be joined. 8The skillfully woven band,
which is on it, shall be like its workmanship, of the same mate-
rial: of gold, of blue and purple and scarlet material and fine
twisted linen. 9You shall take two onyx stones and engrave on
them the names of the sons of Israel, 10six of their names on
the one stone and the names of the remaining six on the other
stone, according to their birth. 11As a jeweler engraves a signet,
you shall engrave the two stones according to the names of the
sons of Israel; you shall set them in filigree settings of gold.
12You shall put the two stones on the shoulder pieces of the
ephod, as stones of memorial for the sons of Israel, and Aaron
shall bear their names before the LORD on his two shoulders
for a memorial. 13You shall make filigree settings of gold, 14and
two chains of pure gold; you shall make them of twisted cord-
age work, and you shall put the corded chains on the filigree
settings."**

Verse 6. The first garment described is the **ephod**. The English word "ephod" is a transliteration of the Hebrew term (אֵפוֹד, *'epod*). The ephod, apparently a kind of vest, has also been depicted as similar to an apron or a kilt.[2] It served as the primary garment characteristic of the high priest's office. It was worn over the robe, and the breastpiece was attached to it. The word "ephod" is used in a variety of ways in the Old Testament. It can refer to an idol (Judg. 8:27; 18:14, 17, 18, 20). It can also refer to a simple linen garment which was evidently the priests' typical daily clothing (1 Sam. 2:18; 14:3; 22:18). The material in the high priest's ephod was the same kind used in making the veil of the tabernacle, with golden threads woven into it to add to its "glory" and "beauty" (28:2).

Exodus 39:2–7 sheds more light on how the Israelites followed these instructions in making the ephod. For instance, 28:6 says that the ephod was to be made **of gold, of blue and purple and scarlet material and fine twisted linen**. How would gold, a precious metal, be used to make a garment that is otherwise made of cloth? Exodus 39:3 explains: "Then they hammered out gold sheets and cut them into threads to be woven. . . ."

Verses 7–11. The front and back of the ephod were joined with **shoulder pieces**. **Two onyx stones**, in **settings** of **gold filigree**, were placed on these shoulder pieces. The word for "onyx" (שֹׁהַם, *shoham*) refers to a very precious stone which could "shine with the lustre of fire"—unlike the onyx known today, "which is neither precious nor brilliant."[3] On each of the stones was to be **engrave**[d] **the names** of **six** of the **sons of Israel**, **according to their birth**. "The sons of Israel" are elsewhere referred to as "the twelve tribes" (24:4; 28:21; 39:14).

Verses 12–14. These onyx **stones** engraved with the names of the **sons of Israel** were to serve as a **memorial**. The stones evidently symbolized all the people of Israel; Aaron was to **bear their names before the Lord on his two shoulders for a memorial** as he sought the Lord's forgiveness and blessings.

---

[2]Walter C. Kaiser, Jr., "Exodus," in *The Expositor's Bible Commentary*, vol. 2, *Genesis—Numbers* (Grand Rapids, Mich.: Zondervan, 1990), 466; Menahem Haran, *Temples and Temple Service in Ancient Israel* (Winona Lake, Ind.: Eisenbrauns, 1985), 166; Cole, 199–200.

[3]Henry W. Soltau, *The Tabernacle: The Priesthood and the Offerings* (Grand Rapids, Mich.: Kregel Publications, 1972), 202.

THE BREASTPIECE AND THE URIM AND THUMMIM (28:15–30)

[15]"You shall make a breastpiece of judgment, the work of
a skillful workman; like the work of the ephod you shall make
it: of gold, of blue and purple and scarlet material and fine
twisted linen you shall make it. [16]It shall be square and folded
double, a span in length and a span in width. [17]You shall mount
on it four rows of stones; the first row shall be a row of ruby,
topaz and emerald; [18]and the second row a turquoise, a sap-
phire and a diamond; [19]and the third row a jacinth, an agate
and an amethyst; [20]and the fourth row a beryl and an onyx and
a jasper; they shall be set in gold filigree. [21]The stones shall be
according to the names of the sons of Israel: twelve, according
to their names; they shall be like the engravings of a seal, each
according to his name for the twelve tribes. [22]You shall make
on the breastpiece chains of twisted cordage work in pure gold.
[23]You shall make on the breastpiece two rings of gold, and shall
put the two rings on the two ends of the breastpiece. [24]You shall
put the two cords of gold on the two rings at the ends of the
breastpiece. [25]You shall put the other two ends of the two cords
on the two filigree settings, and put them on the shoulder pieces
of the ephod, at the front of it. [26]You shall make two rings of
gold and shall place them on the two ends of the breastpiece,
on the edge of it, which is toward the inner side of the ephod.
[27]You shall make two rings of gold and put them on the bot-
tom of the two shoulder pieces of the ephod, on the front of it
close to the place where it is joined, above the skillfully woven
band of the ephod. [28]They shall bind the breastpiece by its
rings to the rings of the ephod with a blue cord, so that it will
be on the skillfully woven band of the ephod, and that the
breastpiece will not come loose from the ephod. [29]Aaron shall
carry the names of the sons of Israel in the breastpiece of judg-
ment over his heart when he enters the holy place, for a memo-
rial before the LORD continually. [30]You shall put in the breast-
piece of judgment the Urim and the Thummim, and they shall
be over Aaron's heart when he goes in before the LORD; and

Aaron shall carry the judgment of the sons of Israel over his heart before the Lord continually."

Verses 15, 16. The most important feature of the high priest's **ephod** was the **breastpiece**. More space is given to it than to any other part of the priest's uniform. It was to be made of the same **material** as the ephod and was **a span in length and a span in width**, that is, about nine inches **square**. A "span" is half a cubit (Ezek. 43:13, 17), or about nine inches.[4] The breastpiece was to be **folded double**, apparently to provide a pocket to hold "the Urim and the Thummim" (28:30). The breastpiece may have formed a kind of sack for the Urim and the Thummim, but this view has been disputed.[5]

Verses 17–20. On the breastpiece were mounted twelve gemstones in **four rows**: (1) **ruby, topaz, emerald**; (2) **turquoise, sapphire, diamond**; (3) **jacinth, agate, amethyst**; and (4) **beryl, onyx, jasper** (see 39:10–14). Commentators have tried to discover symbolic significance in the twelve stones. However, difficulty in identifying the stones and the meager information provided by the text prevent any certainty. In fact, John I. Durham said that "the specific varieties of gemstones employed can only be surmised, as we cannot translate the terms employed for them with any certainty."[6] The problem of identifying the stones represented by the Hebrew words is obvious when various versions are compared. Readers have even tried to compare these twelve stones to the twelve foundation stones of the city wall of New Jerusalem in Revelation 21:19, 20. In English versions of the Bible, however, the lists do not completely coincide: Seven stones are the same in the two lists, but five are different.

Verse 21. These **stones** were to be engraved with the **names**

---

[4]Ovid R. Sellers, "Weights and Measures," in *The Interpreter's Dictionary of the Bible*, ed. George Arthur Buttrick (Nashville: Abingdon Press, 1962), 4:837–38.

[5]W. H. Gispen, *Exodus*, trans. Ed van der Maas, Bible Student's Commentary (Grand Rapids, Mich.: Regency Reference Library, Zondervan Publishing House, 1982), 267–68.

[6]John I. Durham, *Exodus*, Word Biblical Commentary, vol. 3 (Waco, Tex.: Word Books, 1987), 387.

of the sons of Israel, that is, the **twelve tribes**. Genesis 49:28 speaks of the twelve sons of Jacob as the "twelve tribes" of Israel. Descendants of these men, who were in the exodus from Egypt and who traveled to Sinai, were referred to as "tribes" (24:4; 28:21; 39:14). As they were numbered in the wilderness of Sinai (Num. 1) and given instructions for encamping around the tabernacle (Num. 2), the "twelve tribes" included Ephraim and Manasseh (in the place of their father, Joseph) and excluded Levi (the priestly tribe).

Verses 22–28. A system of **rings of gold** and **cords** were to be formed. They were to **bind the breastpiece** to **the ephod**, so **that the breastpiece** [would] **not come loose**. The instructions given here are detailed and complicated; one would find it difficult to use them to reproduce the breastpiece today. However, the first readers were probably very familiar with the high priest's garments and thus the instructions would likely have made good sense to them. Durham noted that the "curious mingling of repetition and terseness suggests that these instructions were set down for people who knew what was being described."[7]

Verse 29. The item was a **breastpiece of judgment**—a statement made at the beginning and at the end of its description (28:15, 29). The Hebrew word for "judgment" (**מִשְׁפָּט**, *mishpat*) seems to imply "making decisions"[8] and may refer to the role the breastpiece played in ascertaining God's will, particularly as the place where the Urim and the Thummim were kept.

The breastpiece served another function as well: Because the names of the sons of Israel were located on it, the high priest carried **the names of the sons of Israel . . . over his heart when he** [entered] **the holy place, for a memorial before the LORD continually**. In other words, every time the high priest entered the holy place, he brought before the Lord the whole of Israel, asking God to remember His people with blessings. "Bearing the tribes before YHWH" may mean "bearing their guilt" or "interceding for them in prayer."[9]

---

[7]Ibid., 384–85.
[8]Gispen, 266–67.
[9]Cole, 200.

Verse 30. The Urim (אוּרִים, *'urim*) and **the Thummim** (תֻּמִּים, *thummim*) were carried or kept **in the breastpiece** (Lev. 8:8). Concerning these two transliterated terms, R. Alan Cole noted,

> Their names mean "lights" and "perfections" which, if taken literally, might be a reference to the nature of the God whose will they reveal. But they may be used in the sense of "alpha and omega", beginning and ending (Rev. 1:8), since the words respectively begin with the first and last letters of the Hebrew alphabet [**א**, *aleph*; **ת**, *tav*].[10]

By equating them with "judgment" or decision-making, the text implies that the Urim and the Thummim had an "oracular" purpose: They indicated God's answers to questions (Num. 27:21; 1 Sam. 28:6) or were connected with revelations from God in some other way. Walter C. Kaiser, Jr., wrote that they "were used in times of crisis to determine the will of God."[11] Further, the possession of them was a sign that a man was truly the high priest (Deut. 33:8; Ezra 2:63; Neh. 7:65).

Beyond these facts, uncertainty exists as to exactly what the Urim and the Thummim were and how they were used. Most Bible students think that they were two stones like the "lots" that were cast in biblical times (1 Sam. 14:41, 42; Prov. 16:33; Mk. 15:24; Acts 1:26), or like a pair of dice. When consulted by being thrown down, or emptied out of the bag in which they were kept, they somehow gave a yes, no, or neutral answer. In this context the Israelites were *not* given instructions for making the Urim and the Thummim. This fact suggests that they already existed and were in use.[12]

---

[10]Ibid., 201.

[11]Kaiser, 467.

[12]Gispen cited an alternative view—that the Urim and the Thummim referred to the stones *on* the breastpiece—which he said he liked but did not endorse. (Gispen, 269–70.) Other possibilities exist. John J. Davis listed and discussed nine different views on the subject and concluded that "these objects only symbolized the special revelation to which the high priest had access." (John J. Davis, *Moses and the Gods of Egypt: Studies in Exodus*, 2d ed. [Grand Rapids, Mich.: Baker Book House, 1986], 285–87.)

THE ROBE (28:31–35)

[31]"You shall make the robe of the ephod all of blue. [32]There shall be an opening at its top in the middle of it; around its opening there shall be a binding of woven work, like the opening of a coat of mail, so that it will not be torn. [33]You shall make on its hem pomegranates of blue and purple and scarlet material, all around on its hem, and bells of gold between them all around: [34]a golden bell and a pomegranate, a golden bell and a pomegranate, all around on the hem of the robe. [35]It shall be on Aaron when he ministers; and its tinkling shall be heard when he enters and leaves the holy place before the LORD, so that he will not die."

Verses 31, 32. A **robe** was to be made of **blue** for the high priest to wear under the **ephod**. It was to be seamless, made of a single piece of cloth, and have an **opening** for the priest's head reinforced by **a binding of woven work**. No opening for the arms is mentioned, but it may be assumed that there were slits in the cloth for the hands and arms.[13] John 19:23 mentions that Jesus' robe was seamless, an indirect way of "pointing to Christ's high-priestly position."[14]

Verses 33–35. Its **hem** was to be decorated with alternating **pomegranates** and **bells**. A "pomegranate," the red fruit of a small tree, is about the size of an orange and produces a refreshing juice. Pomegranates have multiple symbolic meanings in the Old Testament.[15] Most commentators assume that the pomegranates were woven into the hem of the high priest's robe, but some believe that they were three-dimensional representations which were hung on the hem, as were the bells. The **tinkling** of the bells would be **heard** from outside the tabernacle while **Aaron** ministered within; in fact, it had to be heard **so that** Aaron would **not die**!

---

[13]Davis, 287.

[14]Cole, 201.

[15]Megan Bishop Moore, "Pomegranate," in *Eerdmans Dictionary of the Bible*, ed. David Noel Freedman (Grand Rapids, Mich.: Wm. B. Eerdmans Publishing Co., 2000), 1070.

What the bells had to do with the high priest's living or dying is difficult to say. One purpose that the bells served was to enable the people to follow his activities, even though they could not see him, by listening to the ringing of the bells. The sound was a sign that God had accepted the high priest's offering for the people's sin and they would be assured of forgiveness. Consequently, "the sound of the bells as the priest left the tabernacle called for great rejoicing for the atonement that had been completed."[16] If the bells could not be heard, the people would presume that the high priest had done something wrong, or that for some other reason God had not accepted his intercession for them, and so the high priest had died, leaving the people still in their sins. Another possibility is that "the warning about death pertains not only to the bells but to all the strict demands of the priestly ritual."[17]

THE GOLD PLATE, TUNIC, TURBAN, AND SASH (28:36–39)

[36]"You shall also make a plate of pure gold and shall engrave on it, like the engravings of a seal, 'Holy to the Lord.' [37]You shall fasten it on a blue cord, and it shall be on the turban; it shall be at the front of the turban. [38]It shall be on Aaron's forehead, and Aaron shall take away the iniquity of the holy things which the sons of Israel consecrate, with regard to all their holy gifts; and it shall always be on his forehead, that they may be accepted before the Lord.

[39]"You shall weave the tunic of checkered work of fine linen, and shall make a turban of fine linen, and you shall make a sash, the work of a weaver."

Verse 36. Four items were necessary to complete Aaron's wardrobe—the **plate of pure gold**, the "turban" to put it on

[16]Davis, 287.

[17]Peter Enns, *Exodus*, The NIV Application Commentary (Grand Rapids, Mich.: Zondervan, 2000), 531. This idea was suggested by Haran, 218, and Nahum M. Sarna, *Exodus*, The JPS Torah Commentary (New York: Jewish Publication Society, 1991), 183.

(28:37, 38), the "tunic," and the "sash" (28:39). The word rendered "plate" (צִיץ, *tsits*) means "flower."[18] The NRSV translates the word "rosette," while the REB has "medallion" and the NJB has "flower." Probably, this was a golden plate in the shape of a flower, on which were to be engraved the words **Holy to the Lord**. Both the high priest and the people he represented were "set apart" for the Lord's service.

Verse 37. The plate was to be attached to the high priest's **turban**, which is identified in 39:30 as the "holy crown" or "sacred diadem" (NIV).

Verse 38. Wearing the golden plate with its inscription identified **Aaron** as the high priest. As such, he had both the privilege and the responsibility of making intercession for the people and **tak**[ing] **away the iniquity of the holy things**, including the iniquity of the holy people of God. As previously indicated in verse 35, Aaron had to wear the proper attire in order to atone for the sins of the nation.

Verse 39. The **tunic** was a tight-fitting garment longer than the robe and worn underneath it. Kaiser described it as "a long white linen coat worn over the linen drawers or breeches (v. 42), which . . . reached down to the ankles and was close-fitted."[19] Josephus said that this linen vestment reached down to the feet, sat close to the body, and had sleeves that were tied fast to the arms. It was "girded to the breast a little above the elbows, by a girdle . . . so loosely woven, that you would think it were the skin of a serpent."[20] The high priest's tunic differed from that of other priests. Even though all the tunics were made of **fine linen**, the high priest's tunic was made of **checkered work** while the others were plain.

The **sash** was something like an ornamental belt worn around the waist. The material of which it was to be made is not specified. Most likely, the same kind of material used in making the veil of the tabernacle was used for the high priest's sash.

The difference between the uniforms of the high priest and

---

[18]Durham 382, 384.
[19]Kaiser, 467.
[20]Josephus *Antiquities* 3.7.2.

the priests lay in the fact that the high priest's clothes were more elaborate: In addition to the high priest's tunic of **checkered work** (28:4), he had the sash which was **the work of a weaver**, and a **turban** instead of a "cap" (28:40). The high priest had the regular garments worn by all the priests, and he also wore the robe, the ephod, the breastpiece, and the golden plate on his turban.

TUNICS, SASHES, CAPS, AND LINEN BREECHES (28:40–43)

[40]"For Aaron's sons you shall make tunics; you shall also make sashes for them, and you shall make caps for them, for glory and for beauty. [41]You shall put them on Aaron your brother and on his sons with him; and you shall anoint them and ordain them and consecrate them, that they may serve Me as priests. [42]You shall make for them linen breeches to cover their bare flesh; they shall reach from the loins even to the thighs. [43]They shall be on Aaron and on his sons when they enter the tent of meeting, or when they approach the altar to minister in the holy place, so that they do not incur guilt and die. It shall be a statute forever to him and to his descendants after him."

Verses 40–43. Instructions for making the priestly garments conclude with directions for making the clothes which the other priests were to wear while serving in the tabernacle: **tunics**, **sashes**, **caps**, and **linen breeches**.

Four facts are pointed out in the text regarding the other priests and their garments. (1) Like the garments for the high priest (28:2), the priests' garments were to be made **for glory** and **for beauty** (28:40), although theirs contained no gold, gemstones, or brilliant colors. (2) Clothing the priests with these garments was closely tied to their consecration **as priests** (28:41; see 40:13, 14). (3) The "linen breeches" which **cover**[ed] the priests' **bare flesh** when they ministered at the altar were necessary **so that they** [would] **not incur guilt and die** (28:42, 43). The priests, like the high priest, were involved in a high-risk occupation. To fail to do what God required while serving in God's house was a crime punishable by death. (4) The **statute** regarding their wearing the linen breeches was to be a perpetual requirement. Indeed, all of the laws regarding the priesthood were to be observed as long as the Law remained in effect.

APPLICATION

The Purpose of the Priesthood (Ch. 28)

Exodus 28 is one of those chapters in the Bible that a reader might be inclined to skip. It tells how the priestly garments were to be made. We may ask, "Why does it matter to us what kind of garments the priests wore?" While we do not need the information in Exodus 28 to make priestly garments today, the items that the priests wore can teach us something about the purpose of the priesthood. Learning about the role of the priests should help us to understand Christ's role as our high priest and every Christian's function as a priest. What was the purpose of a priest?

The Priest Represented Man to God. The priest served as an intermediary between man and God. This role required him to intercede for man before God. The priest took the people's sacrifices and presented them to God, led the tabernacle worship, and officiated at the rituals of atonement.

This aspect of the priestly work is highlighted in the garments that the high priest wore. The major feature of the high priest's uniform was an ephod—an intricately woven, colorful vest or apron-like garment worn over his robe. The most significant feature of the ephod was a breastpiece with twelve precious stones, each inscribed with the name of one of the twelve "sons of Israel." The ephod also had two shoulder pieces, on which were placed two onyx stones. Each onyx stone was engraved with the names of six of the twelve sons of Israel. When the high priest went into the most holy place to make atonement for the people, he symbolically carried the people with him. He wore a constant reminder of his role as the people's representative before God.

Today, Jesus is the Christian's high priest (Heb. 8:1). He represents us before God (1 Tim. 2:5; 1 Jn. 2:1). As our high priest,

He entered into the most holy place once for all time—unlike Israel's high priest, who went into the most holy place once yearly. Instead of the blood of animals, Christ took with Him His own blood to atone for our sins (Heb. 9:25, 26). The sacrifice of animals could not take away sins (Heb. 10:4), but Christ's sacrifice of Himself could and did. His work as our high priest did not end at the cross. He continues to make intercession for us (Heb. 7:25). As our merciful and faithful high priest, He can sympathize with our weaknesses (Heb. 4:14–16). Jesus, now at God's right hand, can plead our case with the Father because He lived as a man.

In addition, those who are Christians are priests (1 Pet. 2:9, 10). The church has no priestly class separate from "ordinary" Christians; there is no clergy / laity distinction. All Christians are priests. "All" includes women as well as men, the young and the old, preachers, elders, and deacons, along with "ordinary" members of all nations and races. In Israel, one had to be born into a certain family to become a priest. Now we can become priests by being born again into the family of God. The privilege of being a priest is available to everyone.

As priests, Christians have access to God. We can pray. We live in such a way as to make our lives a holy sacrifice to God (Rom. 12:1). We are cleansed by Christ's blood, but we appropriate His blood by "walk[ing] in the Light" (1 Jn. 1:7), which includes repenting of and confessing our sins (Acts 8:22; 1 Jn. 1:9). Based on the blood Christ shed on the cross, we can receive atonement without the help of any other human being.

Does that mean that priests in Christ's church have no intercessory role? While each priest (Christian) has the right to approach God on his or her own behalf, each one is also privileged to approach God on behalf of others. We are told to "pray for one another" (Jas. 5:16). There is great power in intercessory prayer!

The Priest Represented God to Man. The priestly garments also indicate the priest's close relationship to God. The text emphasizes that each priest was God's priest (28:3, 4, 41). The high priest wore on his turban a gold plate that proclaimed him "Holy to the LORD" (28:36). The high priest's garments were made "for glory and for beauty" (28:2, 40), suggesting the Lord's glory and beauty. The breastpiece contained "the Urim and the Thummim" (28:30), by which God made His will known to Israel.

The Israelites, God's priestly people (19:6), were to represent God to other nations. Through Israel, God intended for His name to be known and glorified among all nations. Israel was to be "a light of the nations" (Is. 49:6).

Our high priest, Jesus Christ—God in the flesh—came to the earth to represent God to man. To know Him is to know the Father (Jn. 14:6–9). He makes God's will known to us through His New Testament.

Christians have the responsibility, as God's priestly people, to represent God to man. We carry out our priestly duty by "letting our light shine" and by proclaiming the good news that our great high priest has made salvation (and priesthood) available to all (see 1 Pet. 2:9, 10).

Conclusion. What does it mean to be a priest? As priests, we have the right of access to God and the right to enter the holy place. We also have responsibilities: to intercede for others, to worship, and to be God's representatives on earth by making His will for the world known through our works and our words.

"Priestly Garments" Today (Ch. 28)

God was concerned about what His priests wore in Old Testament times. He is concerned about what His priests (Christians) wear today. What should we wear? God does not specify a certain kind of clothes or uniform that every Christian has to wear, but He does specify how we are to be clothed spiritually. We have "clothed [ourselves] with Christ" (Gal. 3:26, 27), and we must live like it (Col. 3:1–17).

Aaron' s Sons Sinned (28:1; Lev. 10:1, 2)

Like a number of God's great men in the Old Testament, Aaron had children who were unfaithful to God; two of his four sons died because of their sin (28:1; Lev. 10:1, 2). Being a good man and being a man of God will not guarantee that your children will be faithful to God. God did not, however, blame Aaron for his sons' failure.

Twelve Tribes—One People (28:9–11, 21)

Like the twelve loaves on the table in the holy place (25:30; Lev. 24:5–9), the twelve stones on the breastpiece and the twelve names on the two onyx stones represented all of Israel (28:9–11, 21). The fact that those twelve are put together suggests that God wanted to impress upon the people of Israel their essential unity. They were twelve tribes, but they were only one people. The church today needs to remember the essential unity of God's people. We are all one in Christ—one people (1 Cor. 12:12; Eph. 4:4).

Christians—"Holy to the LORD" (28:36)

The high priest wore on his turban a plate engraved with the words "Holy to the LORD" (28:36). Christ, the Christian's high priest, is holy, just as God is holy. Those who are Christians are also "holy to the Lord." In fact, the church is a "holy nation" (1 Pet. 2:9, 10). What does it mean to be holy? (1) Holiness is the state in which we as Christians find ourselves. We are "holy" in that we have been set apart, or sanctified, for God's use (1 Cor. 6:11). Having been "sanctified" or made "holy," we have become "saints" or "holy ones." All Christians are saints. You do not have to die and be made a saint by a council. You become a saint, a "holy one," a set-apart person, by becoming a Christian. "Holiness" is a condition received by people when they are saved. (2) Holiness is a goal towards which Christians continually strive (Heb. 12:14; NRSV). When used in this sense, what does "holiness" mean? It means striving to take upon ourselves the characteristics of God (1 Cor. 11:1; Eph. 5:1; 1 Pet. 1:15, 16; 2 Pet. 1:4). To become ever more like God is our lifetime responsibility and privilege. We have been sanctified, or made holy; but we are constantly striving to become ever more holy.

Chapter 29

Instructions for the Consecration Of the Priesthood

In chapter 29, Moses was told how the priests were to be consecrated for the work they were called to do. In connection with the consecration ceremony, animal sacrifices were to be presented (29:1–3). Moreover, Aaron and his sons were to be washed with water, clothed with the priestly garments, and anointed with oil (29:4–9).

Then the priests were to be ordained in ceremonies involving the sacrifice of a bull and two rams. The blood of these animals was to be placed on and around the altar, on the priests, and on their priestly garments (29:10–30). Meat provided by the sacrifices was to be eaten by the priests (29:31–34). The ordination was to take seven days (29:35–37).

A daily sacrifice of a lamb each morning and each evening was to be offered at the tabernacle until the end of the Mosaic age (29:38–42).

The chapter concludes with the assuring word that the result of following God's commands in the consecration of the tabernacle will be that God "will dwell" among the Israelites and they will know that He is "the Lord their God who brought them out of the land of Egypt" (29:43–46).

THE PRIESTLY GARMENTS (29:1–9)

1"Now this is what you shall do to them to consecrate them to minister as priests to Me: take one young bull and two rams without blemish, 2and unleavened bread and unleavened cakes mixed with oil, and unleavened wafers spread with oil; you

shall make them of fine wheat flour. [3]You shall put them in one basket, and present them in the basket along with the bull and the two rams. [4]Then you shall bring Aaron and his sons to the doorway of the tent of meeting and wash them with water. [5]You shall take the garments, and put on Aaron the tunic and the robe of the ephod and the ephod and the breastpiece, and gird him with the skillfully woven band of the ephod; [6]and you shall set the turban on his head and put the holy crown on the turban. [7]Then you shall take the anointing oil and pour it on his head and anoint him. [8]You shall bring his sons and put tunics on them. [9]You shall gird them with sashes, Aaron and his sons, and bind caps on them, and they shall have the priesthood by a perpetual statute. So you shall ordain Aaron and his sons."

Verses 1–3. The role of the **priests** was so important that the Lord not only described in detail what garments he had to wear and how they were to be made, but He also gave detailed instructions for the priests' ordination—for the formal ceremony that made a man officially a priest and began his work. In Exodus 40:12–15, these instructions are repeated in connection with the completion and consecration of the tabernacle. The actual ordination ceremony is described in Leviticus 8.

The instructions indicate that the priest's ordination was to begin with the presentation of the offerings that would accompany it: **one young bull**, **two rams**, **unleavened bread and unleavened cakes**, and **unleavened wafers** in a **basket**. Probably these offerings were to be presented with some ceremony within the courtyard of the completed tabernacle.

To whom were these presented? Perhaps to the Lord, represented by Moses. Moses presided at the first ordination (Lev. 8:6); most likely he is the person addressed as **you** in verse 1. After the first ordination, there would be other leaders and priests who could preside. The chapter will later describe how and when these sacrifices were to be offered.

Verse 4. The second step in the ordination process was to bring in the priests and **wash them with water**, undoubtedly in the laver for that purpose (30:18–21).

Verses 5, 6. Third, Moses was to dress **Aaron** in the official uniform of the high priest's office. Specifically, Aaron was to be dressed from the inside out—first **the tunic**, then **the robe**, then **the ephod** with **the breastpiece** attached, and finally the **turban** with the **holy crown** (or golden plate, 28:36). This procedure was also to be followed by the high priests who came after him.

Verse 7. Fourth, Aaron, as high priest, was to be **anoint**[ed] by having the **anointing oil . . . pour**[ed] **. . . on his head**. To be appointed to a task by being anointed, or having oil poured on one's head, happened on other occasions in Old Testament times. For example, Samuel anointed Saul as king (1 Sam. 10:1); later he anointed David to succeed Saul (1 Sam. 16:13). Instructions for making the anointing oil are given in 30:22–33, and the account of its manufacture is found in 37:29.

Verses 8, 9a. Then the text says that Aaron's **sons**, the other priests, were to be dressed in simpler garb—their **tunics**. Further, all of the priests were to be **gird**[ed] with **sashes**, which were to be used like belts to pull their clothes to them. Finally, the sons of Aaron were to wear **caps** on their heads.

Verse 9b. After Aaron's sons had been ordained to the priesthood, the Lord assured them that they would then possess it **by a perpetual statute**. The Hebrew word עוֹלָם (*'olam*), translated "perpetual," is found frequently in the Hebrew Bible. It is rendered in a number of ways by various versions, including "ever," "everlasting," "old," "ancient," "forever," "forevermore," and "perpetual." *'Olam* does not necessarily mean "eternally" or "until the end of time." The point of verse 9 is that as long as the law remained in force, no one from any tribe other than that of Levi or from any family other than that of Aaron was allowed to serve as a priest. The author of Hebrews argued that a change in the priesthood necessarily means a change in the law. He pointed out that Jesus Christ, our great high priest, descended from Judah and not from Levi. Jesus came after the order of Melchizedek, not the order of Aaron (Heb. 7:11–22). This passage in Exodus, combined with the one in Hebrews, makes it clear that when Exodus speaks of "forever" or "perpetual," it is talking about the age during which the law of Moses remained in effect.

THE CONSECRATION CEREMONY (29:10–37)

The Offering of the Bull (29:10–14)

[10]"Then you shall bring the bull before the tent of meeting, and Aaron and his sons shall lay their hands on the head of the bull. [11]You shall slaughter the bull before the LORD at the doorway of the tent of meeting. [12]You shall take some of the blood of the bull and put it on the horns of the altar with your finger; and you shall pour out all the blood at the base of the altar. [13]You shall take all the fat that covers the entrails and the lobe of the liver, and the two kidneys and the fat that is on them, and offer them up in smoke on the altar. [14]But the flesh of the bull and its hide and its refuse, you shall burn with fire outside the camp; it is a sin offering."

The fifth and final step in the consecration of the priests involved the offering and consumption of the sacrifices previously mentioned. The instructions are long and detailed but may be broken down into three parts, each having to do with one of the three animals spoken of at the first of the section.

Verse 10. Of the three animals brought, the **bull** is to be offered first as a "sin offering" (29:14). When **Aaron and his sons** placed **their hands on the head of the bull**, they identified themselves with the bull. In some sense, they transferred their sins and those of the people to the bull.

Verse 11. The bull was then to be **slaughter**[ed], suggesting the idea that it received the punishment that the people deserved. R. Alan Cole wrote, "This clearly means that the death of the animal is accepted as the equivalent of the death of the individual."[1]

Verse 12. Some of the blood of the bull was to be smeared **on the horns of the altar** and the rest was to be **pour**[ed] **out . . . at the base of the altar**, signifying that it was by the blood, or death, of the bull that the Israelites sought forgiveness.

---

[1]R. Alan Cole, *Exodus: An Introduction and Commentary*, Tyndale Old Testament Commentaries (Downers Grove, Ill.: Inter-Varsity Press, 1973), 203.

THE CONSECRATION CEREMONY OF THE PRIESTS IN EXODUS 29 & LEVITICUS 8[2] And the Recurring Phrase "just as the LORD had commanded Moses"[3]		
Exodus 29 Instructions for the Ceremony		**Leviticus 8** Implementation of the Ceremony
29:10–14	The Bull for a Sin Offering	8:14–17 *Phrase (8:17)*
29:15–18	The Ram for a Burnt Offering	8:18–21 *Phrase (8:21)*
29:19, 20 29:21 29:22–28	The Ram of Ordination and the Wave Offering and the Heave Offering	8:22–24 8:30 8:25–29 *Phrase (8:29)*
29:29, 30	Aaron's Garments for His Sons After Him	——
29:31–37	Eating the Consecrated Food	8:31–36 *Phrase (8:36)*

Verses 13, 14. The fat, liver, and **kidneys** of the bull were then to be burned **on the altar**, but the rest of **the bull** was to be **burn**[ed] **. . . outside the camp**. Commentators suggest that the remaining parts of the bull had become contaminated with the sin that had been transferred to the bull and thus had to be disposed of by being burned "outside the camp." W. H. Gispen compared the phrase "outside the camp" with Christ's death, as He "suffered outside the gate" (Heb. 13:11–13). Gispen then added, "Christ has become our sin offering in the fullest sense of the

[2]See also Exodus 40:9–16 for the ceremony briefly described.

[3]This thematic phrase appears seven times in Exodus 39 (vv. 1, 5, 7, 21, 26, 29, 31), and seven times in Exodus 40 (vv. 19, 21, 23, 25, 27, 29, 32). The phrase is also used earlier in Leviticus 8 (vv. 9, 13).

word."[4] Apparently the sacrifice of the bull was to signify that, before Aaron and his sons could be ordained as priests, atonement had to be made for them; their sins had to be taken away.

The Offering of the First Ram (29:15–18)

[15]"You shall also take the one ram, and Aaron and his sons shall lay their hands on the head of the ram; [16]and you shall slaughter the ram and shall take its blood and sprinkle it around on the altar. [17]Then you shall cut the ram into its pieces, and wash its entrails and its legs, and put them with its pieces and its head. [18]You shall offer up in smoke the whole ram on the altar; it is a burnt offering to the LORD: it is a soothing aroma, an offering by fire to the LORD."

Verses 15, 16. The second animal offered was to be **one** of the **ram**[s]. Again, **Aaron and his sons** placed **their hands** on the sacrificial animal and the blood was taken to the altar, where it was **sprinkl**[ed] **around on the altar**.

Verses 17, 18. Then, after the carcass was **cut** up and **wash**[ed], **the whole ram** was to be offered **on the altar**, as a **soothing aroma** and **an offering by fire to the LORD**. This sacrifice is called a **burnt offering**. The emphasis seems to be on sacrifice—a gift given to the Lord from which the giver received no benefit except the knowledge that what he had done pleased the Lord.

The Offering of the Second Ram (29:19–37)

The sacrifice of the second ram seems to be the most crucial aspect of this phase of the ordination ceremony. This ceremony is spoken of in verse 28 as part of the people's "peace offerings." The ram is called the "ram of ordination" (29:22, 26) because its blood was used, not only to make atonement, but primarily to ordain Aaron and his sons to the priesthood.

---

[4]W. H. Gispen, *Exodus*, trans. Ed van der Maas, Bible Student's Commentary (Grand Rapids, Mich.: Regency Reference Library, Zondervan Publishing House, 1982), 275.

Sacrificing Part of the Ram (29:19–28)

19"Then you shall take the other ram, and Aaron and his sons shall lay their hands on the head of the ram. 20You shall slaughter the ram, and take some of its blood and put it on the lobe of Aaron's right ear and on the lobes of his sons' right ears and on the thumbs of their right hands and on the big toes of their right feet, and sprinkle the rest of the blood around on the altar. 21Then you shall take some of the blood that is on the altar and some of the anointing oil, and sprinkle it on Aaron and on his garments and on his sons and on his sons' garments with him; so he and his garments shall be consecrated, as well as his sons and his sons' garments with him.

22"You shall also take the fat from the ram and the fat tail, and the fat that covers the entrails and the lobe of the liver, and the two kidneys and the fat that is on them and the right thigh (for it is a ram of ordination), 23and one cake of bread and one cake of bread mixed with oil and one wafer from the basket of unleavened bread which is set before the LORD; 24and you shall put all these in the hands of Aaron and in the hands of his sons, and shall wave them as a wave offering before the LORD. 25You shall take them from their hands, and offer them up in smoke on the altar on the burnt offering for a soothing aroma before the LORD; it is an offering by fire to the LORD.

26"Then you shall take the breast of Aaron's ram of ordination, and wave it as a wave offering before the LORD; and it shall be your portion. 27You shall consecrate the breast of the wave offering and the thigh of the heave offering which was waved and which was offered from the ram of ordination, from the one which was for Aaron and from the one which was for his sons. 28It shall be for Aaron and his sons as their portion forever from the sons of Israel, for it is a heave offering; and it shall be a heave offering from the sons of Israel from the sacrifices of their peace offerings, even their heave offering to the LORD."

Verses 19, 20. The ceremony was to begin, as before, with **Aaron and his sons** and their **lay**[ing] **their hands on the head**

of the ram and then **slaughter**[ing] it. In these instructions, however, the procedure changed; the ram's **blood** was to be **put**, not first on the altar, but **on the lobes of** the priests' **right ears, the thumbs of their right hands**, and **the big toes of their right feet.** These actions symbolized the dedication of the entire person to God. Then the blood was to be **sprinkle**[d] **. . . around on the altar**.

Verse 21. Next, along with the **anointing oil**, some of the **blood** was to be **sprinkle**[d] on the priests' **garments**.

Verses 22–25. Then part of the **ram**, along with some of the **unleavened bread . . . from the basket** (29:2, 3), was to be burned on the **altar** as a **burnt offering**.

It is noteworthy that in connection with the ordination ceremony, the three main types of sacrifice in the Old Testament are mentioned: (1) *The sin offering*. The primary purpose of the sin offering was to make atonement for sin.[5] (2) *The burnt offering*. In the burnt offering the whole animal was consumed on the altar. The idea behind the burnt offering was that the person making the sacrifice was dedicating himself fully to the Lord and giving the animal altogether to Him. (3) *The peace offering*. The peace offering, also known as a "fellowship offering" (NIV), sought and celebrated peace between man and God and between man and man. Its main feature was the fact that part of the animal was consumed on the altar but the rest of it was eaten by the worshipers. The "thank offering," the "vow offering," and the "freewill offering" were all types of peace offerings.[6]

Verses 26–28. Two other types of offerings are mentioned in the chapter: the **wave offering** and the **heave offering**. The "wave offering" indicates a type of ritual action; that which was offered was first "waved" in some symbolic way and then placed on the altar. *The New Oxford Annotated Bible* says that the expression translated in the NRSV as "elevation offering" ("wave offering";

---

[5]There was also a "guilt" or "trespass" offering. The different offerings are explained in a chart, "The Offerings in Leviticus," in William Sanford LaSor, David Allan Hubbard, and Frederic William Bush, *Old Testament Survey: The Message, Form, and Background of the Old Testament* (Grand Rapids, Mich.: Wm. B. Eerdmans Publishing Co., 1982), 154–55.

[6]Ibid.

NASB) refers "to the act of moving the sacrifice toward and away from the altar, to symbolize presenting the gift to God and receiving it back as a portion."[7]

The idea of the "heave offering," as seems evident from the text, is that it was dedicated to God. According to David P. Wright, "heave offering" is "an incorrect translation" for a word "whose proper meaning is 'dedication' or 'dedicated gift.'"[8] He continued,

> [The same word] is used of the animal thigh of the well-being offering [peace offering] (Lev. 7:32–34), the tithe (Num. 18:24–29), sanctuary building materials (Exod. 25:2), land (Ezek. 48:8–21), and several other sacred donations. . . . Dedication indicates the transference of an object from the owner to God. . . . [It] is not a ritual act done at the sanctuary but is a simple dedication effected outside its precincts.[9]

With these types of sacrifices, the parts of the ram that were not consumed on the altar—**the breast of Aaron's ram of ordination** and **the thigh of the heave offering**—were to be given to the priests.

Eating the Rest of the Ram (29:29–37)

29"The holy garments of Aaron shall be for his sons after him, that in them they may be anointed and ordained. 30For seven days the one of his sons who is priest in his stead shall put them on when he enters the tent of meeting to minister in the holy place.

31"You shall take the ram of ordination and boil its flesh in

---

7Note on Exodus 29:24, Bruce M. Metzger and Roland E. Murphy, eds., *The New Oxford Annotated Bible with the Apocrypha*, rev. and enl. (New York: Oxford University Press, 1991), 108.

8David P. Wright, "heave offering," in *Harper's Bible Dictionary*, ed. Paul J. Achtemeier (San Francisco: Harper & Row, 1985), 378.

9Ibid.

a holy place. [32]Aaron and his sons shall eat the flesh of the ram and the bread that is in the basket, at the doorway of the tent of meeting. [33]Thus they shall eat those things by which atonement was made at their ordination and consecration; but a layman shall not eat them, because they are holy. [34]If any of the flesh of ordination or any of the bread remains until morning, then you shall burn the remainder with fire; it shall not be eaten, because it is holy.

[35]"Thus you shall do to Aaron and to his sons, according to all that I have commanded you; you shall ordain them through seven days. [36]Each day you shall offer a bull as a sin offering for atonement, and you shall purify the altar when you make atonement for it, and you shall anoint it to consecrate it. [37]For seven days you shall make atonement for the altar and consecrate it; then the altar shall be most holy, and whatever touches the altar shall be holy."

Verses 29, 30. In addition to describing the sacrifices which were to be used to ordain the **priest**[s], the directions given in the chapter explain the significance of **the holy garments of Aaron** that the priests wear and indicate that the ceremonial acts of consecration are to last for **seven days** (29:30–37). The text emphasizes that "the holy garments," most likely the high priestly uniform, were to be worn by **his sons**. The son who replaced Aaron, who became the next high priest, was to wear these garments when **he enter**[ed] **the tent of meeting to minister in the holy place**. For the ordination ceremony, this requirement meant that they would be worn for "seven days," since the rituals involved in the priests' ordination were to continue for that long (29:35, 37).

Verses 31–34. After the proper ceremony, a **ram** was to be **boil**[ed] in **a holy place** and **eat**[en], along with the rest of the **bread** left **in the basket**, by the priests **at the doorway of the tent of meeting**. Those who were not priests **could not eat** of this **holy** food. **If any of the flesh** [of the ram] **of ordination or any of the bread** was left over after the priests had finished eating, it was to be **burn**[ed].

Verses 35–37. The rituals for the seven-day period involved offering **a bull as a sin offering** daily, using the blood of the bull to make **atonement** for **the altar**, and anointing it. Nothing is said about repeating the offering of the two rams; however, it is generally assumed that the entire ritual was repeated for seven days. Though it is not mentioned in chapter 29, the anointing oil would have been used to **anoint** [the altar] **to consecrate it** (see 40:9, 10). R. Alan Cole said, "All this ritual must be repeated daily for seven days, both to emphasize its sacred importance and to give the sense of completeness."[10] The result would be that the altar would be consecrated to the Lord and counted as **holy**. The seven-fold repetition of the cleansing act of sacrifice emphasized the importance of and need for the altar to be completely purified so that it could be set aside and used in God's service. The result of the altar's purification and dedication was that **whatever touches the altar**—that is, every sacrifice made on the altar—would be "holy."

THE CONTINUAL DAILY OFFERINGS (29:38–42)

38"Now this is what you shall offer on the altar: two one year old lambs each day, continuously. 39The one lamb you shall offer in the morning and the other lamb you shall offer at twilight; 40and there shall be one-tenth of an ephah of fine flour mixed with one-fourth of a hin of beaten oil, and one-fourth of a hin of wine for a drink offering with one lamb. 41The other lamb you shall offer at twilight, and shall offer with it the same grain offering and the same drink offering as in the morning, for a soothing aroma, an offering by fire to the Lord. 42It shall be a continual burnt offering throughout your generations at the doorway of the tent of meeting before the Lord, where I will meet with you, to speak to you there."

Verses 38, 39. Having discussed the consecration of **the altar**, the Lord turns to its regular function. The altar would not only be used for such ordination services as are described in this chapter, but it would also be used on a daily basis. **Each day**, as long

[10]Cole, 202–3.

as the age lasts, the priests were to offer **on the altar** burnt offerings of **two one year old lambs—one . . . in the morning** and **the other lamb . . . at twilight**.

Verses 40, 41. Flour, oil, and **wine** would accompany each **offering**. Cole explained that these cereal-offerings and wine libations were sacrificed alongside the animal in an auxiliary capacity. He further explained, "Perhaps the thought was that a complete burnt-offering to God ought to include every element of an ordinary domestic meal (meat, bread, wine)."[11]

Verse 42. These offerings would be made **at the doorway of the tent of meeting** on the altar of burnt offering. The expression "tent of meeting" in verses 42 and 44 refers to the tabernacle, whereas the "tent of meeting" in 33:7 refers to another tent set up "outside the camp." The offerings were to be presented **before the LORD**, that is, to Him and in His presence. The tabernacle was the place where God would **meet with** His people and **speak** to them. There God, throughout the wilderness period at least, continued to reveal His will to Israel.

THE RESULTS OF CONSECRATION: GOD'S PRESENCE (29:43–46)

[43]"I will meet there with the sons of Israel, and it shall be consecrated by My glory. [44]I will consecrate the tent of meeting and the altar; I will also consecrate Aaron and his sons to minister as priests to Me. [45]I will dwell among the sons of Israel and will be their God. [46]They shall know that I am the LORD their God who brought them out of the land of Egypt, that I might dwell among them; I am the LORD their God."

Verses 43–45. The consecration of the priests and the altar would bring about the accomplishment of the purpose for which the tabernacle was to be built: God's presence. At the beginning of the directions for the tabernacle, God told the Israelites to "construct a sanctuary for Me, that I may dwell among [you]" (25:8). In chapter 29, after giving instructions for the making of

[11]Ibid., 204–5.

the tabernacle, the priests' garments, and the consecration of the priests, God said that He **will meet there with the sons of Israel**, that He will **consecrate** the tabernacle with His **glory**, and that He **will dwell among the sons of Israel and will be their God**. Then in the last chapter of Exodus, when the tabernacle was completed and set up, "the cloud covered the tent of meeting, and the glory of the LORD filled the tabernacle" (40:34).

Thus Israel is told in chapter 29 that when God makes His presence known at the completion of the tabernacle, His people will have the assurance that the God who has blessed them in the past and who has manifested His ability to keep His promises, will be with them.

Verse 46. Furthermore, Israel will **know** with certainty that it was **the LORD their God who brought** [His people] **out of Egypt**. Probably, the meaning here is not so much that the Israelites would know that it was their God Yahweh who had delivered them, but that they would know more about their God Yahweh who delivered them. They would better understand His power, grace, holiness, and glory, and could better appreciate His constant presence. The chapter ends with the statement: **I am the LORD their God.** Cole said of this final sentence:

> The section concludes with the triumphant all-inclusive claim . . . *I am YHWH their God*. As in Exodus 20:2, such a pronouncement is adequate reason and justification for every claim and demand made by God on His people, for it sets out God's nature, and His relationship to us, expressed in gracious act. This verse, then, is the sum and crown of all that has gone before.[12]

Umberto Cassuto noted,

> Finally, as befits a king, who signs his name at the end of the declaration that he has issued, in order to validate it and accept full responsibility for its implementation, comes the solemn formula, *I am the Lord their God*, which

---

[12]Ibid., 205.

concludes the main part of the Divine communication concerning the tabernacle of God's glory.[13]

While the chapter deals primarily with the ceremonies by which the priesthood would be consecrated on one occasion after the tabernacle was completed, it also establishes precedents that would govern Israel's worship until the end of the Mosaic age. This passage is like the instructions for the Passover (chs. 12; 13) in this respect. In that case, as in this chapter, instructions were given for a single occasion, but they had validity for the rest of Israel's history as God's people. Among the principles which are established are the following:

(1) All priests (not just the priesthood at its inauguration) are to be ordained in the way given. In addition, the priests are to continue to function in the role suggested by this chapter throughout the age (29:9, 29).

(2) The types of sacrifices spoken of (sin offering, burnt offering, and peace offering) anticipate more detailed instructions of the types of sacrifices that will be continually required (see Lev. 1—7).

(3) The fact that the priests were allowed to eat part of the second ram offered (29:32–34) establishes a continuing precedent. In fact, their right to eat part of the sacrifices brought to the tabernacle was part of their payment for "services rendered." This policy provided, in part, the way they earned their living.

(4) The instructions given for the daily sacrifice of two lambs were intended to be valid throughout Israel's history. In fact, the morning and evening sacrifice continued to be offered as long as the tabernacle, and the temple which took its place, stood.

Not only is the chapter significant because it establishes precedents and sheds light on the rest of Israel's history. It is also significant for Christians because Jesus is the high priest of the new covenant (Heb. 8:1) and all Christians serve as priests (1 Pet. 2:5, 9).

---

[13]Umberto Cassuto, *A Commentary on the Book of Exodus*, trans. Israel Abrahams (Jerusalem: Magnes Press, 1997), 389.

APPLICATION

Prerequisites for the Priesthood (Ch. 29)

One of the most significant facts we learn from comparing the old covenant with the new is that, just as there was a priesthood then, so there is a priesthood now. But the priesthood today consists of all Christians (1 Pet. 2:9, 10). The New Testament teaches "the priesthood of all believers."

Thinking of ourselves as priests leads to the question: What did it take to become a priest under the old covenant? Probably the requirements for the priesthood now would be similar to the requirements for the priesthood then. Therefore, let us consider the prerequisites for the priesthood as they are presented in Exodus 29 and the counterpart of each in the New Testament.

To become a priest, a man had to be washed (29:4). The washing took place in a laver. That washing in the laver can be likened to the washing that occurs in baptism (Acts 22:16; Eph. 5:26; Heb. 10:22). To become a priest today, that is, to become a Christian, one must be washed (immersed) in the waters of baptism (Acts 2:38; Mk. 16:16). He who has not been washed does not qualify to be a priest.

To serve as a priest, a man had to put on the priestly garments (29:5, 6). Christians, who are priests, also need to wear special garments. We do not have to wear a special kind of uniform to advertise that we are Christians, as do some who profess Christianity. Rather, we must "put on Christ," as one puts on a garment; and we put on Christ when we are baptized (Gal. 3:26, 27). After we have become Christians, then we are to live like it—to take off the old sinful garments of our worldly life and to put on the new garments of righteousness (Col. 3:1–17). He who has not put on Christ does not qualify to be a priest.

To become a priest, a man had to be anointed (29:7). The anointing was very important in the ordination ceremony; the oil had to be made especially for that purpose and it could be used for nothing else (Ex. 30:22–33). Paul said, "He who establishes us with you in Christ and anointed us is God, who also sealed us and gave us the Spirit in our hearts as a pledge" (2 Cor. 1:21, 22). God "established us," "anointed us," "sealed us," and "gave us the Spirit." Our anointing, therefore, involves our receiving the Holy Spirit. God gives us the Holy Spirit when we become Christians (Acts 2:38; 5:32; Gal. 4:6). He who has not received the Holy Spirit does not qualify to be a priest (Rom. 8:9).

To become a priest, a man had to be sprinkled with blood (29:19–21). Essential to the process was the death of an animal and the sprinkling of the blood on the altar, the priest, and the priest's garments. This sprinkling of the blood signified two things. (1) Since the priests put their hands on the animal before it was killed, the death of the animal served as a sin offering. The priests transferred, as it were, their sin to the animal and the animal died in their place. (2) The blood was sprinkled on the priests' ears, thumbs, and toes (Ex. 29:20), suggesting that the priests were wholly dedicated to the Lord.

Similarly, before we could become priests, One had to die. Instead of our dying for our own sins, Christ died in our place, and so by the shedding of His blood we are saved (Heb. 9:22–28; Eph. 1:7). The blood is applied to our souls at the same time that we are washed in water (Rom. 6:3, 4; Heb. 10:22). When we are saved, we dedicate ourselves altogether to the Lord. Baptism, because it involves our total immersion and is done by someone else while we are passive, implies that we have given ourselves completely to God. No one can be a priest who has not been cleansed by the blood of Christ.

To serve as a priest, a man had to constantly offer sacrifices (29:22–46). Sacrifices were involved in the consecration of the priesthood, and then the offering of sacrifice became the continuing responsibility of the priests. In a similar way, we have become priests because of Christ's sacrifice, and we now are to continue to offer sacrifices to God. Among those sacrifices, we offer the service of our bodies (Rom. 12:1, 2), the praises of our lips, and the sharing of our goods (Heb. 13:15, 16). No one can serve acceptably as a priest unless he is willing to offer sacrifices constantly to God.

Conclusion. In at least two ways the process of becoming a priest then differed from the process of becoming a priest now. (1) Under the Law, priests were qualified to be priests by a physical birth, and (2) the priesthood was limited to men from the tribe of Levi. Today, (1) we qualify for the priesthood by a spiritual birth, by being born again (Jn. 3:3, 5), and (2) anyone—male or female, from any tribe or tongue or nation or race or place—can qualify for the priesthood. Whether or not you become a priest in God's house is up to you. It is your choice.

Aaron as a Type of Christ (Ch. 29)

Many similarities exist between Israel's first high priest, Aaron, and our great high priest over the church, Jesus Christ. Both of them were: (1) called (Ex. 29:4; Jn. 10:18; Heb. 5:4–6); (2) washed (Ex. 29:44; Mt. 3:13–16); (3) clothed (Ex. 29:5, 6; Is. 63:1, 2; Rev. 1:13); (4) anointed (Ex. 29:7; Acts 10:38; Heb. 1:9); (5) perpetual priests (Ex. 29:9; Heb. 7:16, 17).[14]

Several differences also existed between Aaron and Christ: (1) Christ did not need to sacrifice for His own sins, while Aaron did (Ex. 29:10, 15, 16; Heb. 7:26–28). (2) Christ never dies, although Aaron did die (Ex. 29:29; Heb. 7:23, 24). (3) Christ did not need to repeat His sacrifice daily, but Aaron had to do so (Ex. 29:38, 39; Heb. 10:11, 12).[15]

Consecrated Ears, Hands, and Feet (29:20)

As part of their consecration as priests, Aaron and his sons had blood put on their ears, thumbs, and big toes, signifying their complete dedication to the Lord. Similarly, as God's priests today, we need to be completely dedicated to the Lord. We need to dedicate our ears to hearing His word, our hands to doing His work, and our feet to going His way—especially going where He would want us to go to feed the hungry and teach the lost.

Eating from the Altar and Being Paid to Preach (29:28; 1 Cor. 9:13, 14)

The priests were allowed to eat of the sacrifices offered on the altar; this privilege was how, in part, they made their living. Paul used their example to prove that it was right for preachers

---

[14]Wilbur Fields, *Exploring Exodus*, Bible Study Textbook Series (Joplin, Mo.: College Press, 1976), 652.

[15]Ibid.

to be paid (1 Cor. 9:13). So today, as Paul said, "The Lord directed those who proclaim the gospel to get their living from the gospel" (1 Cor. 9:14).

Meeting with the Lord—Where? (29:43)

The Lord said that He would meet with the Israelites in the tabernacle (29:43) and that there He would dwell among them (29:43, 45). Where can Christians meet with the Lord today? For one thing, we meet with Him in the church. It is His church; He is always there; to be in Him, we must be in the church. For another, we meet with Him in the assembly (Mt. 18:20). But, third, we can also meet with Him at any time or in any place; we do not have to go anywhere special to meet with the Lord (see Jn. 4:21–24). If you are in the church, you are in the Lord and the Lord is in you. Thus, if you are a Christian, you always have access to Christ.

Chapter 30

Instructions for the Tabernacle (Part 4)

Chapter 30 concludes the Lord's instructions for making the various parts of the tabernacle. After describing the priests' garments, consecration, and work (chs. 28; 29), He gave instructions for making the altar of incense (30:1–10). Next, He commanded that the people be taxed to provide the funds needed for "the service" of the tabernacle (30:11–16). The final item of furniture described is the bronze laver (30:17–21). Then He gave instructions for the manufacture and use of the "holy anointing oil" (30:22–33) and the fragrant incense for the altar of incense (30:34–38).

THE ALTAR OF INCENSE (30:1–10)

**[1]"Moreover, you shall make an altar as a place for burning
incense; you shall make it of acacia wood. [2]Its length shall be
a cubit, and its width a cubit, it shall be square, and its height
shall be two cubits; its horns shall be of one piece with it. [3]You
shall overlay it with pure gold, its top and its sides all around,
and its horns; and you shall make a gold molding all around
for it. [4]You shall make two gold rings for it under its molding;
you shall make them on its two side walls—on opposite sides—
and they shall be holders for poles with which to carry it. [5]You
shall make the poles of acacia wood and overlay them with
gold. [6]You shall put this altar in front of the veil that is near
the ark of the testimony, in front of the mercy seat that is over
the ark of the testimony, where I will meet with you. [7]Aaron
shall burn fragrant incense on it; he shall burn it every morn-**

ing when he trims the lamps. [8]When Aaron trims the lamps at twilight, he shall burn incense. There shall be perpetual incense before the LORD throughout your generations. [9]You shall not offer any strange incense on this altar, or burnt offering or meal offering; and you shall not pour out a drink offering on it. [10]Aaron shall make atonement on its horns once a year; he shall make atonement on it with the blood of the sin offering of atonement once a year throughout your generations. It is most holy to the LORD."

The Lord delayed instructions for building the altar of incense until He had almost finished His description of the tabernacle. The other furnishings of the tabernacle were described earlier, in chapter 25. No reason for separating the altar of incense from the other items is obvious from the text. Perhaps the instructions for the altar were given in chapter 30 because they contain information relating to the priests' role, which was the subject of chapters 28 and 29. Just as the priest was to offer sacrifices twice daily (29:38, 39), he was to trim the lamps and offer incense twice a day (30:7, 8) and make atonement on the altar of incense once a year (30:10).

Verses 1–3. The placement of these directions for the **altar** may be confusing, but the description is easy to follow. It was to be made of **acacia wood** overlaid with **gold**, as was fitting for furniture so close to the most holy place. **Its length shall be a cubit** [18"], **and its width a cubit, it shall be square, and its height shall be two cubits** [3']. The altar was to have **horns**, that is, horn-like projections from the four corners. Finally, a **gold molding** was to be crafted around its top.

Verses 4, 5. Like the other furniture in the tabernacle, it was to be portable. Therefore, it needed **gold rings** and **poles**, which were made of **acacia wood** overlaid with **gold**. These poles made it possible to carry the altar without touching it.

Verse 6. God said that the **altar** of incense was to be placed **in front of the veil that is near the ark of the testimony** and **in front of the mercy seat that is over the ark of the testimony**. Commentators agree that this passage locates the altar in the holy place, just in front of the veil that separated the holy place from the most holy place.[1] During the erection of the tabernacle, Moses "placed the gold altar in the tent of meeting in front of the veil" (40:26). The view that the altar was in the holy place, rather than in the most holy place, is consistent with the fact that the priests were to burn incense on the altar daily (30:7, 8) but were forbidden to enter the most holy place except once a year on the Day of Atonement (Lev. 16:34; Heb. 9:7). Regarding that day, these instructions were given for the high priest:

> He shall take a firepan full of coals of fire from upon the altar before the LORD and two handfuls of finely ground sweet incense, and bring it inside the veil. He shall put the incense on the fire before the LORD, that the cloud of incense may cover the mercy seat that is on the ark of the testimony, otherwise he will die (Lev. 16:12, 13).

According to this passage, incense was to be burned within the veil (within the most holy place)—but on a "firepan," not on the altar.[2]

Hebrews 9:3, 4 indicates that the "golden altar of incense" and "the ark of the covenant" were placed "behind the second veil" in "the Holy of Holies." Some Jewish writings also seem to place the altar of incense in the most holy place. For example, some apocryphal literature (2 Baruch 6:7; 2 Maccabees 2:5) is interpreted to mean that this altar was in the most holy place. However, if the passage in 2 Baruch indicates that the altar of incense was in the holy of holies, it also suggests that the most holy place contained "the veil, the holy ephod, the mercy seat,

---

[1]Umberto Cassuto, *A Commentary on the Book of Exodus*, trans. Israel Abrahams (Jerusalem: Magnes Press, 1997), 391; R. Alan Cole, *Exodus: An Introduction and Commentary*, Tyndale Old Testament Commentaries (Downers Grove, Ill.: Inter-Varsity Press, 1973), 205; Nahum M. Sarna, *Exodus*, The JPS Torah Commentary (New York: Jewish Publication Society, 1991), 193; W. H. Gispen, *Exodus*, trans. Ed van der Maas, Bible Student's Commentary (Grand Rapids, Mich.: Regency Reference Library, Zondervan Publishing House, 1982), 281; John I. Durham, *Exodus*, Word Biblical Commentary, vol. 3 (Waco, Tex.: Word Books, 1987), 399.

[2]Louis Goldberg, "Leviticus," in *Evangelical Commentary on the Bible*, ed. Walter A. Elwell (Grand Rapids, Mich.: Baker Book House, 1989), 78.

the two tablets, [and] the holy raiment of the priests." Since the veil, the ephod, and the priestly garments were not found in the most holy place, it is unlikely that the altar of incense was found there either. In addition, since "the veil" actually separated the most holy place from the holy place, the author of 2 Baruch probably did not mean that the things he mentioned were found in the most holy place, but only that they pertained to it. Neither does the passage in 2 Maccabees actually say that the incense altar was in the holy of holies.

The evidence from the Old Testament favors the view that the altar of incense was placed near the veil but within the holy place. The passage in Hebrews may be understood to say that the "altar of incense" *pertained to*, or was closely connected with, the most holy place. This view is permissible since it speaks of "the Holy of Holies" as "having a golden altar of incense," rather than saying specifically that the incense altar was in that part of the tabernacle.[3]

Verses 7–9. The text explains how the altar was to be used. Each morning and each evening, a priest was to **burn fragrant incense** there. The instructions include two negatives. First, the priests were not to offer **any strange incense**. John I. Durham translated the phrase "profane incense" and then included the following note: "'strange incense,' i.e., incense made and used for ordinary purposes."[4] Other versions have "unauthorised incense" (NJB; NEB), "unholy incense" (NRSV), "any other incense" (NIV), and "profane incense" (NAB). They were to offer only the incense made especially for that purpose (30:34–38). Second, this altar was not to be used for **burnt offering**[s], **meal offering**[s], or **drink offering**[s]; the altar of burnt offering in the courtyard was for those sacrifices.

---

[3]This interpretation is favored by many commentators on Hebrews, several of whom are listed in Neil R. Lightfoot, *Jesus Christ Today: A Commentary on the Book of Hebrews* (Grand Rapids, Mich.: Baker Book House, 1976), 179. The placement of the altar of incense is discussed in F. F. Bruce, *The Epistle to the Hebrews*, The New International Commentary on the New Testament (Grand Rapids, Mich.: Wm. B. Eerdmans Publishing Co., 1964), 184–87.

[4]Durham, 398–99.

Verse 10. The incense altar was to be used on the annual Day of Atonement; on that day, the high priest was to **make atonement on it with the blood of the sin offering of atonement** (see Lev. 23:27). Because of its function, it would be **most holy to the Lord.**

The aroma of the incense must have filled the holy place with a unique fragrance, a sweet smell that also penetrated the most holy place. Therefore, the altar of incense was closely related to the most holy place, where God met with His people behind the veil (30:6). Its holiness was not to be compromised by offering "strange fire" on it (Lev. 10:1–3). The smoke from the burning incense would produce a cloud with the double effect of symbolizing the presence of God and protecting the high priest when He entered the most holy place (Lev. 16:13). In regard to the Christian age, this practice perhaps best represents prayer. In Revelation 8:3, 4, incense is associated with "the prayers of the saints."

THE TAX REQUIRED (30:11–16)

11The Lord also spoke to Moses, saying, 12"When you take a census of the sons of Israel to number them, then each one of them shall give a ransom for himself to the Lord, when you number them, so that there will be no plague among them when you number them. 13This is what everyone who is numbered shall give: half a shekel according to the shekel of the sanctuary (the shekel is twenty gerahs), half a shekel as a contribution to the Lord. 14Everyone who is numbered, from twenty years old and over, shall give the contribution to the Lord. 15The rich shall not pay more and the poor shall not pay less than the half shekel, when you give the contribution to the Lord to make atonement for yourselves. 16You shall take the atonement money from the sons of Israel and shall give it for the service of the tent of meeting, that it may be a memorial for the sons of Israel before the Lord, to make atonement for yourselves."

Verses 11 through 16 give five reasons for the contribution. (1) It was given by each man as a "ransom" (כֹּפֶר, *koper*) for himself (30:12). Durham translated the word "atonement money" and then added this note: "life-price, ransom, atoning payment."[5] Walter C. Kaiser, Jr., said that the word for "ransom" means "to deliver or redeem by a substitute."[6] (2) It was given so that there might "be no plague" among the Israelites when the census was taken (30:12). (3) It was given by the Israelites to "make atonement" for themselves and was therefore called "atonement money" (30:15, 16). (4) It was given "for the service of the tent of meeting" (30:16). (5) It would "be a memorial for the sons of Israel before the LORD" (30:16).

These ideas can be summarized as two reasons for the required contribution and two possible results. The Israelites were to "make atonement" for their sins, or to "ransom" themselves by giving the half-shekel. Also, this contribution was to help in "the service of the tent of meeting." If they failed to give, they would be struck with a plague because they had been disobedient and had obtained no atonement for their sins. If they gave as they were assessed, they would be remembered and blessed by the Lord.

Verses 11, 12. The emphasis of God's instruction changes again in 30:11–16, from what was to be built for the tabernacle to how the tabernacle service was to be funded.

The LORD told **Moses** that **a ransom** or tax would fund the tabernacle, which could be calculated according to a **census**. When did Israel take the census which resulted in the contributions mentioned in 38:26? The amount that was given correlates perfectly with the number of men twenty years old and over who were counted in the census spoken of in Numbers 1:45, 46: 603,550 men. However, Numbers 1:1 specifies that the Lord gave the commandment to take the census on "the first of the second month, in the second year after they had come out of the land of Egypt." This was after the tabernacle was completed and erected, "in the first month of the second year, on the first day of the month" (40:17). How could the silver received as a result of the

---

[5]Ibid., 401.

[6]Walter C. Kaiser, Jr., "Exodus," in *The Expositor's Bible Commentary*, vol. 2, *Genesis—Numbers* (Grand Rapids, Mich.: Zondervan, 1990), 473.

census be used in the building of the tabernacle if the census was not taken until after the tabernacle had been built?

The best answer is that there was a census taken before the one referred to in Numbers 1. This later counting was done for a different purpose: to indicate how many men were available to fight in Israel's army (Num. 1:2, 3). If there were two numberings, the fact that they resulted in the same count should not be surprising.

Verses 13, 14. While the method required by God in 30:11–16 is a tax, it is also called **a contribution to the Lord**. This tax, levied on every adult male **twenty years old and over**, was to be **half a shekel according to the shekel of the sanctuary**. A shekel was a measure of weight. "Half a shekel" would be the weight of a precious metal, probably silver. Ovid R. Sellers equated half a shekel with 5.7 grams, or 0.2 of an ounce.[7] The meaning of "the shekel of the sanctuary" is unclear; the phrase seems to imply that the shekel used for the sanctuary tax differed from the shekel used in other circumstances. (The expression is also used in 30:24; 38:25, 26.)

Verse 15. The passage emphasizes the equality of all before the Lord and the essential fairness of the requirement: **The rich shall not pay more and the poor shall not pay less.**[8] If someone objects that it is not fair for the rich and the poor to pay the same, since the rich can better afford it, the reply would be that the amount required was small enough that the poor could also afford it.

Verse 16. The tax was to be given for the **atonement** of the **sons of Israel**.[9] To **make atonement** (כִּפֶּר, *kipper*) suggests the idea of "covering" sins. However, in light of the fact that atonement was made for the altar of burnt offering (29:36), the word must have a broader meaning. It can also mean "to purify" or "to dedicate." That definition fits well in this context. Just as the

---

[7]Ovid R. Sellers, "Weights and Measures," in *The Interpreter's Dictionary of the Bible*, ed. George Arthur Buttrick (Nashville: Abingdon Press, 1962), 4:832–33.

[8]Durham, 403.

[9]The reason for this "atonement" is discussed in Gispen, 282–83.

priests were to be purified for the Lord's service (ch. 29), and as the altar was to be dedicated to the Lord, so the entire adult male population was to be ceremonially purified and dedicated to the Lord.

Verse 16 also says that the tax was **for the service** of the tabernacle. Was the contribution to be for the building of the tabernacle or for its continuing maintenance? The phrasing in verse 16 sounds as if the tax was to be given continually (perhaps annually) to support the tabernacle services. For example, the money for more than seven hundred sacrificial lambs each year (29:38, 39) had to be provided somehow. Indeed, there is evidence that such a tax became customary. R. Alan Cole wrote, "Later, the 'half-shekel' became an annual temple tax (Mt. 17:24). See Nehemiah 10:32 for its collection in the post-exilic period."[10] However, the fulfillment of this requirement in chapter 38 indicates that the money received from this contribution was used to build the tabernacle. One might, therefore, conclude that the tax levied was to be a one-time contribution for that purpose.[11] Perhaps the best solution to the problem is to say that, as 30:16 implies, the tax was to be taken regularly, but the first collection was used to build the tabernacle. After all, there was no need to finance the services of the tabernacle until there was a tabernacle.

THE BRONZE LAVER (30:17–21)

[17]The LORD spoke to Moses, saying, [18]"You shall also make a laver of bronze, with its base of bronze, for washing; and you shall put it between the tent of meeting and the altar, and you shall put water in it. [19]Aaron and his sons shall wash their hands and their feet from it; [20]when they enter the tent of meeting, they shall wash with water, so that they will not die; or when they approach the altar to minister, by offering up in smoke a fire sacrifice to the LORD. [21]So they shall wash their hands and their feet, so that they will not die; and it shall be a perpetual

[10]Cole, 206.

[11]This is the conclusion given in James Burton Coffman, *Commentary on Exodus, The Second Book of Moses* (Abilene, Tex.: ACU Press, 1985), 423.

statute for them, for Aaron and his descendants throughout their generations."

Verses 17, 18. Like the instructions for building the altar of incense (30:1–10), the directions for making the **laver** seem to be out of place. The laver stood in the courtyard of the tabernacle; the other item in the courtyard, the altar of burnt offering, was described in chapter 27, along with the fence around the court. A possible explanation for this is that the instructions regarding both the altar of incense and the laver were delayed until after the section relating to the priests' garments and consecration (chs. 28; 29). Both the incense altar and the laver were closely connected to priestly duties. The priests' role is emphasized in the description of both the altar and the laver (30:7, 8, 19–21).

The laver was to be made of **bronze**, just as the altar of burnt offering was overlaid with bronze. It was to be placed **between . . . the altar** of burnt offering and the entrance to the tabernacle. Its size is not given.

Verses 19–21. The laver was to be filled with water and used for ritual washings (see 29:4). Every time a priest **enter**[ed] the tabernacle or made a **sacrifice** on the **altar** of burnt offering, he was to **wash** his **hands** and his **feet**. Only when he had been cleansed in this way was it safe for him to enter the holy place. Without the purifying act of washing, he would be struck dead by God. The death penalty might seem extreme, but it emphasized the holiness of God and of the tabernacle, which was, in effect, God's house. It also stressed the necessity of complete obedience. The importance of washing is accented by the fact that the command was to be **a perpetual statute** for the priests.

The washing in the laver can be compared to baptism in the Christian age. James Burton Coffman spoke of such washing as "the forerunner of Christian baptism (Tit. 3:5; Eph. 5:26)."[12] Now, as then, those who would enter God's "holy place" must first be washed (immersed) in water (Acts 2:38; 22:16; Eph. 5:26; Heb. 10:22).

---

[12]Ibid., 425–26.

THE ANOINTING OIL (30:22–33)

[22]Moreover, the LORD spoke to Moses, saying, [23]"Take also for yourself the finest of spices: of flowing myrrh five hundred shekels, and of fragrant cinnamon half as much, two hundred and fifty, and of fragrant cane two hundred and fifty, [24]and of cassia five hundred, according to the shekel of the sanctuary, and of olive oil a hin. [25]You shall make of these a holy anointing oil, a perfume mixture, the work of a perfumer; it shall be a holy anointing oil. [26]With it you shall anoint the tent of meeting and the ark of the testimony, [27]and the table and all its utensils, and the lampstand and its utensils, and the altar of incense, [28]and the altar of burnt offering and all its utensils, and the laver and its stand. [29]You shall also consecrate them, that they may be most holy; whatever touches them shall be holy. [30]You shall anoint Aaron and his sons, and consecrate them, that they may minister as priests to Me. [31]You shall speak to the sons of Israel, saying, 'This shall be a holy anointing oil to Me throughout your generations. [32]It shall not be poured on anyone's body, nor shall you make any like it in the same proportions; it is holy, and it shall be holy to you. [33]Whoever shall mix any like it or whoever puts any of it on a layman shall be cut off from his people.'"

Directions are given both for making the anointing oil and for using it to anoint the tabernacle and the priests. Exodus 40:9–16 repeats the instructions for using the anointing oil and states that Moses obeyed them. Like the other instructions in this chapter, these are closely related to the work of the priests.

Verses 22–24. The manufacture of the oil required **the finest of spices—myrrh**, **cinnamon**, **fragrant cane**, **cassia**, and **olive oil**. Altogether, the amounts specified add up to "about sixteen pounds of cinnamon and spices and one gallon of olive oil," a total which led Peter Enns to speak of it as "an expensive and even extravagant recipe."[13] Cole said, "The spices used are rare,

[13]Peter Enns, *Exodus*, The NIV Application Commentary (Grand Rapids, Mich.: Zondervan, 2000), 541.

costly and aromatic, mostly coming from lands as far away as India by way of trade: for Arabia was not only a producer of spices, but also a great spice-mart."[14]

Verse 25. The careful giving of directions made it possible to manufacture more **anointing oil** after the first batch was depleted. The instructions given were to be regarded as the recipe for continuing to produce the oil, as is indicated by the fact that others were warned against using the same recipe to make oil for their own purposes (30:32, 33). It was to be **holy**, set apart for God's special purposes.

Verses 26–29. The passage specifies the purposes of the **anointing oil**. It was to be used to anoint the tabernacle and its furniture, along with the priests who served there. This oil was to be used in their consecration, to make them **most holy**. The priests were "most holy" in that they were especially set apart by God to serve in the tabernacle. This was the exclusive purpose of the anointing oil in perpetuity (30:31–33).

Verses 30–33. If anyone used the **anointing oil** for any other purpose or made any like it for personal use, that person was to be **cut off from his people**, or killed (see 12:15, 19; 31:14). Why would the Lord punish someone for misusing anointing oil? Enns provided an appropriate reply:

> Death is the expected penalty for not following God's directions fully. One may be tempted to ask, "What is the big deal about anointing oil and incense?" This is not a biblical question to ask. The fact of the matter is that the oil and incense *are* worthy of such respect on Israel's part.[15]

Anointing oil and **incense** were worthy of respect because God said they were.

THE INCENSE (30:34–38)

[34]Then the Lord said to Moses, "Take for yourself spices,

---

[14]Cole, 207.
[15]Enns, 541.

stacte and onycha and galbanum, spices with pure frankincense; there shall be an equal part of each. [35]With it you shall make incense, a perfume, the work of a perfumer, salted, pure, and holy. [36]You shall beat some of it very fine, and put part of it before the testimony in the tent of meeting where I will meet with you; it shall be most holy to you. [37]The incense which you shall make, you shall not make in the same proportions for yourselves; it shall be holy to you for the LORD. [38]Whoever shall make any like it, to use as perfume, shall be cut off from his people."

Verses 34, 35. The instructions for the building of the tabernacle and its furnishings, as well as the directions for the priests' garments, consecration, and work, conclude with instructions for making the **incense** to be burned on the altar of incense. The instructions are similar to the directions previously given regarding the anointing oil. (1) A detailed recipe is given (30:34–36). (2) The required **spices** were rare and expensive.[16] The specific spices to be used in making the incense cannot be identified with certainty. (3) The incense was to be regarded as **holy** (30:35, 36). (4) No one was to make incense like it for personal use (30:37). (5) If someone broke this rule, he was to be "cut off from his people" (30:38), or killed.

Verse 36. The text says that the spices were to be **beat**[en] **very fine** and placed **before the testimony in the tent of meeting** where God would **meet** with the people. The need to "beat," or pulverize, the spices probably implies that the mixture was kept in its "coarse resin-grain form" until it was ready to be used.[17] Putting this pulverized mixture "before the testimony in the tent of meeting" simply refers to its being offered on the altar of incense. Because of its proximity to the veil and the nature of its use, the altar of incense is closely related to the most holy place and its contents.

Verses 37, 38. The **incense** was not for personal use. This, too, was set apart as **holy . . . for the LORD.**

---

[16]Durham, 408.
[17]Ibid.

APPLICATION

The Privilege and Peril of the Priesthood (Chs. 29; 30)

Exodus 28—30 is about the priests and their service in the tabernacle. Chapter 29 describes their consecration, with the last part of the chapter beginning a discussion of the priest's work which continues in chapter 30. These passages suggest the privilege and the peril of serving as a priest under the old law. What parallel can be drawn for today, since we are under the new law?

The privilege of being a priest. According to Exodus 29 and 30, priests were privileged to do at least six things other Israelites could not do. (1) They offered sacrifices on the altar of burnt offering (29:38–46). A lamb was to be sacrificed twice daily. (2) They burned incense on the altar of incense (30:1–19) twice a day. (3) They made atonement for the people's sins (30:10). The altar of incense was used on the Day of Atonement. (4) They received and disbursed contributions from the people (30:12–16). The text does not specify the priests' role in connection with the census and the tax, but we may assume that the priests played a role both in collecting and using the money. (5) They washed in the laver (30:17–21). Instructions for building the laver were given in this context because the laver was so closely connected to the role and work of the priests. (6) They also used the anointing oil and the fragrant incense (30:22–38).

These activities represented great privileges. It was a privilege to offer sacrifices, to burn incense, to make atonement for sin, to serve at the tabernacle, to wash in the laver, and to use the oil and the incense.

In a similar way, we who are Christians today serve as priests (1 Pet. 2:5). We are continually washed in the blood of Jesus. We approach the throne of God confidently, intercede for others, offer sacrifices of praise, and engage in worship as part of the church (1 Tim. 2:1; Heb. 4:16; 10:25; 12:38; 13:15; 1 Jn. 1:7). These are great privileges! We should be thankful that God has given us these privileges. We must take advantage of them and never take them lightly or let them become merely routine.

The peril of being a priest. With the great privileges of priesthood came danger. God is holy; therefore, everything connected to God is holy. Being in the presence of an all-holy God could be dangerous (33:3). To look into or touch that which was holy without authorization invited death (1 Sam. 6:19; 2 Sam. 6:6, 7).

The priest's job could be likened to the job of an electrician. The electrician works with a great source of power. When that power is rightly used by the electrician, it brings abundant blessings to others and to the electrician himself. However, if the electrician makes a mistake—if he mishandles the power—the results can be disastrous for the electrician and for others. In a similar way, the priest mediated great power. If he mishandled the power, he could bring death to himself and disaster to the people.

That fact is emphasized in Exodus 30. Every section of the chapter stresses that there would be a penalty if the priests failed to do what they were told. That penalty, whether stated or implied, was death. The Lord specified that the census was to be taken so that there would be "no plague" among the people (30:12). With regard to the laver, the priests were to "wash their hands and their feet, so that they [would] not die" (30:21). Anyone who misused the anointing oil would be "cut off from his people" (30:33). With regard to the fragrant incense, the text says, "Whoever shall make any like it, to use as perfume, shall be cut off from his people" (30:38). To be "cut off from his people" was to receive the death sentence.

Interestingly, the only command in the chapter which does not specify that punishment would result from disobedience relates to the burning of incense on the altar. Exodus 30:9 simply says, "You shall not offer any strange incense on this altar." Nevertheless, the Lord made clear the punishment for failing to follow these instructions when He struck down Nadab and Abihu for offering "strange fire" on the altar (Lev. 10:1, 2).

The death sentence for failing to carry out rituals properly seems too severe. However, we should remember that God does not judge by human standards and accept His wisdom and His will. If His standard says that failing to follow His directions exactly is deserving of death, then it is. In addition, we can remind ourselves that great responsibilities come with great privileges. The priests, for whom the instructions in Exodus 30 were primarily given, knew what was required of them. To fail to meet those requirements could be construed as open rebellion against the God who gave the instructions. In any army, rebellion and refusal to obey a commander's orders is regarded as a crime punishable by death. How much more is that statement true when the commander is the all-holy God who created the universe!

Conclusion. The lesson for us is obvious. We may think that it makes no difference to God whether or not we follow His instructions exactly in worship, as long as we worship Him. The examples of the Old Testament indicate otherwise. Issues that seem small to us may not seem small to God. "Minor" matters related to worship may be "major" to God.

Lessons on Prayer from the Incense Altar (30:1–10)

The golden altar and the incense offered on it can be likened to prayer (Rev. 8:3, 4). (1) The incense was offered only by priests, and prayer is the special privilege of the priesthood of believers today. (2) The altar and the incense were closely connected with the most holy place. Even as the smoke and the aroma from the incense filled the most holy place, our prayers ascend into the presence of God. (3) The burning of incense was closely associated with atonement, and Christians offer prayers for forgiveness. (4) Incense was burned every morning and evening. In the same way, Christians ought to pray regularly. (5) The altar of incense was "most holy," and the regulations concerning the incense were described as a "perpetual statute." Prayer is "most holy"—a sacred privilege and responsibility. It is also a "perpetual statute"—a requirement for Christians until the return of Christ. (6) It was dangerous to misuse the altar and the incense (Lev. 10:1–3), and Christians should not misuse the right of prayer.

Equal Under God (30:15)

The Declaration of Independence states that "all men are created equal." Under the law of Moses, everyone was equal before God, and the same is true under the new covenant. When God called for the half-shekel tax, He told Moses, "The rich shall not pay more and the poor shall not pay less." In many ways, God expects the same of rich and poor, young and old, male and female today. With regard to giving, each Christian is to give as he or she has been prospered (1 Cor. 16:1, 2).

Likewise, all are required to obey the same gospel in order to become Christians (Gal. 3:26–28). Everyone who seeks salvation must believe the gospel message: ". . . that Christ died for our sins according to the Scriptures, and that He was buried, and that He was raised on the third day according to the Scriptures" (1 Cor. 15:3, 4). When we repent of our sins and have them washed away in baptism (Acts 2:38), we become children of God and fellow heirs with Christ (Jn. 1:12; Rom. 8:17; 1 Jn. 3:1). God makes no distinctions between Jew and Greek, male and female, slave and free: All who call on Him and obey His commands will be saved (Rom. 10:12, 13; Gal. 3:28).

CHAPTER 31

A SUMMARY OF GOD'S INSTRUCTIONS

Moses' meeting with God on Mount Sinai drew to a close in chapter 31. God concluded His giving of the Law to Moses by indicating that Bezalel and Oholiab would direct the construction of the tabernacle (31:1–6). He reviewed what was to be built (31:7–11) and reminded Moses that Israel must observe the Sabbath (31:12–17). The finality of the message is indicated by the statement that God "finished speaking" to Moses and "gave Moses the two tablets . . . written by the finger of God" (31:18). The Lord would have more to say after the sin which is recorded in chapter 32, but the initial revelation was completed.

THE BUILDERS AND THE BUILDING PLANS (31:1–11)

[1]Now the LORD spoke to Moses, saying, [2]"See, I have called by name Bezalel, the son of Uri, the son of Hur, of the tribe of Judah. [3]I have filled him with the Spirit of God in wisdom, in understanding, in knowledge, and in all kinds of craftsmanship, [4]to make artistic designs for work in gold, in silver, and in bronze, [5]and in the cutting of stones for settings, and in the carving of wood, that he may work in all kinds of craftsmanship. [6]And behold, I Myself have appointed with him Oholiab, the son of Ahisamach, of the tribe of Dan; and in the hearts of all who are skillful I have put skill, that they may make all that I have commanded you: [7]the tent of meeting, and the ark of testimony, and the mercy seat upon it, and all the furniture of the tent, [8]the table also and its utensils, and the pure gold

lampstand with all its utensils, and the altar of incense, [9]the altar of burnt offering also with all its utensils, and the laver and its stand, [10]the woven garments as well, and the holy garments for Aaron the priest, and the garments of his sons, with which to carry on their priesthood; [11]the anointing oil also, and the fragrant incense for the holy place, they are to make them according to all that I have commanded you."

Verses 1, 2. With the plans for the tabernacle in place, God designated **Bezalel** to lead the construction work. He apparently was the grandson of **Hur**, one of Moses' helpers (17:10; 24:14). He was also from **the tribe of Judah**.

Verse 3. Bezalel was well equipped for the task, since he had been **filled . . . with the Spirit of God in wisdom, in understanding, in knowledge, and in all kinds of craftsmanship**. In other words, Bezalel had all the skills necessary to supervise the project, and he had them because he had received them from God.

R. Alan Cole wrote, "In early Old Testament days, every form of skill and strength and excellence is directly and bluntly credited to 'the Spirit of God'. This is because God is rightly seen as the source of all wisdom."[1] S. R. Driver noted that the Spirit of God is "regarded in the [Old Testament] as the source of any *exceptional* power or activity of man, as well as of supernatural spiritual gifts" and added that here the expression is used "of exceptional *artistic* capacity."[2] J. Philip Hyatt defined the "Spirit" as "the outgoing power of God."[3]

Verses 4, 5. The range of Bezalel's abilities included making **artistic designs** to use with precious metals (**gold**, **silver**, and **bronze**), **cutting** gem **stones**, and **carving . . . wood**. This list serves as a brief summary of the many skills given to him by God. The breadth of his ability is emphasized by the repeated phrase **all kinds of craftsmanship** (31:3, 5).

---

[1]R. Alan Cole, *Exodus: An Introduction and Commentary*, Tyndale Old Testament Commentaries (Downers Grove, Ill.: Inter-Varsity Press, 1973), 210.

[2]S. R. Driver, *The Book of Exodus*, The Cambridge Bible for Schools and Colleges (Cambridge: University Press, 1953), 342.

[3]J. Philip Hyatt, *Exodus*, The New Century Bible Commentary (Grand Rapids, Mich.: Wm. B. Eerdmans Publishing Co., 1971), 297.

Verse 6. Bezalel was to be assisted by **Oholiab . . . of the tribe of Dan**. He is frequently mentioned along with Bezalel (35:30, 34; 36:1, 2; 38:22, 23), but always in a way that suggests that he was Bezalel's assistant (**with him**). Moreover, the text mentions others to whom God had also given **skill**. Bezalel and Oholiab would not have to do the work themselves, for God had given others the necessary ability to help them. The text emphasizes that whatever skills these craftsmen had, they received from God. Someone has said, "Where God guides, God provides." In the building of the tabernacle, God guided Moses in how to build and then provided the workers to do the building.

Verses 7–11. The Lord's instructions regarding the tabernacle conclude with a summary of what the builders were to make. Almost every item for which He had given directions in the previous six chapters is named. The intent of the passage was to have Moses impress upon the builders that they were to make everything that the Lord had **commanded**. This point is repeated for emphasis (31:6, 11).

DIRECTIONS (CHS. 25—30)	SUMMARY (CH. 31)
Ark of the Testimony (25:10–16)	Ark of the Testimony (31:7)
Mercy Seat (25:17–22)	Mercy Seat (31:7)
Table of Showbread (25:23–30)	Table (31:8)
Golden Lampstand (25:31–39)	Golden Lampstand (31:8)
Tabernacle (26:1–30)	Tent of Meeting (31:7)
Veil (26:31–35)	———
Screen (26:36, 37)	———
Bronze Altar (27:1–8)	Altar of Burnt Offering (31:9)
Court (27:9–19)	———
Oil for Lamp (27:20, 21)	———
Priestly Garments (28:1–43)	Priestly Garments (31:10)
Altar of Incense (30:1–10)	Altar of Incense (31:8)
Bronze Laver (30:17–21)	Laver (31:9)
Anointing Oil (30:22–33)	Anointing Oil (31:11)
Incense (30:34–38)	Fragrant Incense (31:11)

THE SABBATH COMMAND REPEATED (31:12–17)

[12]"The LORD spoke to Moses, saying, [13]"But as for you, speak to the sons of Israel, saying, 'You shall surely observe My sabbaths; for this is a sign between Me and you throughout your generations, that you may know that I am the LORD who sanctifies you. [14]Therefore you are to observe the sabbath, for it is holy to you. Everyone who profanes it shall surely be put to death; for whoever does any work on it, that person shall be cut off from among his people. [15]For six days work may be done, but on the seventh day there is a sabbath of complete rest, holy to the LORD; whoever does any work on the sabbath day shall surely be put to death. [16]So the sons of Israel shall observe the sabbath, to celebrate the sabbath throughout their generations as a perpetual covenant.' [17]It is a sign between Me and the sons of Israel forever; for in six days the LORD made heaven and earth, but on the seventh day He ceased from labor, and was refreshed."

Before God's message to Moses on the mountain concluded, God gave the Sabbath command again. It was previously given in connection with God's provision of manna (16:22–30) and as one of the Ten Commandments (20:8–11). It was also repeated near the end of the Book of the Covenant (23:12). The Sabbath command is found two more times before the end of Exodus (34:21; 35:1–3).

No one can say with certainty why the Sabbath command was the last of the laws given to Moses before he came down from the mountain, but there are at least two possibilities. Perhaps the repetition of the command fits well with the emphasis of the entire section. Since keeping the Sabbath has more to do with ritual than with morals and ethics, the command matches a section which is largely about the tabernacle and the priesthood. John I. Durham wrote,

> [The Sabbath instructions] are intended as a conclusion to the whole series of instructions concerning the media

> of worship, a conclusion designed to call attention to the importance of stopping to reflect on the reality of the Presence of Yahweh, of providing a regular time for honoring that Presence in worship.[4]

Another possibility is that, since the context is the building of the tabernacle, the people needed to be reminded that they were not to work on the Sabbath—even on the tabernacle.[5]

Verses 12, 13. The **sabbath** was a **sign** between **the Lord** and **Israel** (31:13, 17); it was the sign of the covenant that God made with Israel. As the rainbow was the sign of the Noahic covenant, and circumcision was the sign of the Abrahamic covenant, Sabbath-keeping was a sign of the Mosaic covenant. As long as the Israelites kept the Sabbath, they bore witness to the fact that they were God's people whom He delivered out of Egypt (Deut. 5:12–15).

Verse 14. The penalty for breaking the **sabbath** was **death**. In this passage, for the first time the law reveals that Sabbath-breaking was a capital offense. That fact is stated again in 35:2 and is illustrated in Numbers 15. God wanted His people to understand that they could not break any of His laws without consequences.

The passage appears to use "be put to death" interchangeably with **shall be cut off from among his people**. Therefore, apparently to "be cut off" is the equivalent of to "be put to death." Some scholars, however, differentiate between the two penalties, saying that to "be cut off" suggests being expelled from the community. If there was a difference, the punishment applied must have depended on the circumstances (for example, on whether or not the sin was committed intentionally).[6]

Verse 15. The law of the **sabbath** required **complete rest**. The Sabbath day was to be **holy**, or set apart, as the one day of the

---

[4]John I. Durham, *Exodus*, Word Biblical Commentary, vol. 3 (Waco, Tex.: Word Books, 1987), 412.

[5]Umberto Cassuto, *A Commentary on the Book of Exodus*, trans. Israel Abrahams (Jerusalem: Magnes Press, 1997), 403.

[6]Durham, 413.

week when the Israelites were not to do **any work**.

Verses 16, 17. The **sabbath** was to last throughout the Mosaic age: **throughout their generations as a perpetual covenant**. God said, "[This] **is a sign between Me and the sons of Israel forever.**" One might conclude from these verses that the Sabbath was to continue to the end of time and, therefore, should be observed today. However, two facts must be remembered. First, God spoke of Sabbath-keeping in terms of a covenant with Israel only. If these laws were still in effect, they would apply only to Israel. Because of Christ's coming, the old covenant is no longer in effect. Second, "forever" (עוֹלָם, *'olam*) in the Old Testament does not mean "for eternity" or even "until the end of time." Aaron's priesthood was established as a "perpetual statute" (29:9). Such passages make it clear that the expressions "forever," "throughout your generations," and "perpetual statute" mean "as long as this age lasts." As long as the Mosaic age endured, the Israelites, as God's covenant people, were to observe the Sabbath.

The Sabbath was to be observed in imitation of God, **for in six days the LORD made heaven and earth, but on the seventh day He ceased from labor, and was refreshed**. The Lord's resting on the seventh day was the reason given initially for observing the Sabbath (20:11). The fact that the Israelites were told here to rest "on the seventh day" as "a sign" of their relationship with God does not conflict with the first reason. The two are complementary, not contradictory. The Lord was Israel's Creator and Redeemer. For both reasons—because He had made the world and because He had redeemed Israel from Egyptian slavery—they were to keep the Sabbath (see comments on 31:12, 13).

Though sometimes viewed as repetitious, this passage is intentionally arranged in a poetic ABBA pattern:

A1: "You shall surely observe My sabbaths . . . [as] a sign . . . throughout your generations, that you may know that I am the LORD who sanctifies you" (31:13).

B1: "Observe the sabbath, for it is holy to you. Everyone who profanes it shall surely be put to death . . . whoever does any work on it . . . shall be cut off from among his people" (31:14).

B2: "On the seventh day there is a sabbath of complete rest, holy to the LORD; whoever does any work on the sabbath day shall surely be put to death" (31:15).

A2: "'So the sons of Israel shall observe the sabbath . . . throughout their generation as a perpetual covenant.' It is a sign between Me and the sons of Israel forever; for in six days the LORD made heaven and earth, but on the seventh day He ceased from labor, and was refreshed" (31:16, 17).

The two inner verses speak of the consequences of breaking the Sabbath. The outer verses give the command, tell how long it was to be in effect, and add a reason for keeping it.

THE CONCLUSION OF THE LAW (31:18)

18When He had finished speaking with him upon Mount Sinai, He gave Moses the two tablets of the testimony, tablets of stone, written by the finger of God.

Verse 18. The Law revealed on **Mount Sinai** was completed with this verse. The fact that God wrote what was on the **two tablets of the testimony** with His own **finger** makes the contents of the Law even more impressive. Men dare not disobey commands written by God Himself!

Apparently, what was written on the "two tablets" was the Ten Commandments. Moses must have brought down the rest of God's laws concerning the tabernacle and priestly garments either in his memory or in writing, perhaps on a scroll. The latter is more likely as Moses had previously recorded the Book of the Covenant in writing (24:4).

"The finger of God" is anthropomorphic language in that it attributes a human characteristic to God (see comments on 15:8–10). Some commentators think that "written by the finger of God" means that the Lord was simply the source of what was written.[7] However, the fact that the text emphasizes God's writing in this passage and in 32:16 and 34:1 suggests that He was uniquely and personally involved in engraving the "Ten Words" on the stone tablets.[8] At the end of the chapter, Moses was ready to come down from the mountain and present God's laws to the people.

APPLICATION

Bezalel, Man of Many Talents, Dedicated to the Lord (31:1–5)

Have you ever known anyone like Bezalel? This man could, it seems, do anything—"make artistic designs" in any medium, cut stones, and carve wood. He was an expert in "all kinds of craftsmanship." He must also have been a good leader and manager, since God put him in charge of building the tabernacle. God had given him these talents and had appointed him to the job. The best thing about Bezalel is that, as the rest of Exodus makes clear, he accepted the task, dedicated himself to the work, and did not quit until the work was done. Do you know any multitalented people? Are you one of them yourself? Do you realize that all those talents come from God? Are you willing to use them in God's service, to dedicate yourself to the work which God gives you to do—and not to quit until that work is done?

What About the Sabbath? (31:12–17)

Of all the commandments in the law of Moses, none is more controversial than the Sabbath commandment. It is one of the Ten Commandments (20:8–11; Deut. 5:12–15). Its importance is seen in the fact that it is commanded five other times in Exodus (16:4, 5, 22–30; 23:12; 34:21; 35:1–3). It was, in fact, so important that breaking the Sabbath was punishable by death (31:15; 35:2; Num. 15:32–36). There is no doubt that Israel was required to

---

[7]Cassuto, 405–6.

[8]Wilbur Fields, *Exploring Exodus,* Bible Study Textbook Series (Joplin, Mo.: College Press, 1976), 699–700. In addition, Psalm 8:3 speaks of the universe being produced by the "fingers" of God. In Exodus 8:19 the magicians said that a miracle was being performed by the "finger of God." (See also Lk. 11:20.)

keep the Sabbath. The Sabbath command was still being observed by the Jews in New Testament times, and it is still honored today.

The controversial question is: Should we observe the Sabbath today? If not, does the Sabbath command in the Law have any significance for us?

Not an Obligation. Some who profess Christianity believe that the Sabbath command is binding on us today, just as it was on the Jews. Are they right?

The Sabbath was a part of the old law, the law of Moses, which was fulfilled. The New Testament teaches that the Old Testament has been taken out of the way (Gal. 3:24, 25; Eph. 2:15; Heb. 7:11–22; 8:13; 9:11–28). Those who keep the Sabbath object that the law that has been taken away is the ceremonial law and not the Ten Commandments. However, they make a distinction which neither the New Testament nor the Old Testament makes. When the Bible speaks of "the Law," it is talking about the entire law, both the ceremonial law and the moral law. Romans 7:1–7 indicates that the Ten Commandments are part of that law, and also states that Christians are "released from the law." Ephesians 2:15 specifies that Christ abolished "the Law of commandments contained in ordinances." No one can separate the "commandments" of the law from the "ordinances" of the law.

The Sabbath was not a command from the beginning of creation, as some teach. There is no indication that the Sabbath was kept by the patriarchs before the time of Moses or that the Sabbath is a command for all ages, not dependent on the Law of Moses. While Genesis 2:3 says that God "blessed" and "sanctified" the seventh day, it does not specify that He did so *at that time.* Rather, Genesis is telling us that when the Sabbath command was given, the command to rest was based on God's resting on the seventh day.

The Sabbath commandment was given to Israel as a sign of the covenant between Israel and God, and not to Gentiles. Since we live under a new covenant today, the command does not apply to us.

The early church was not required to meet for worship on the Sabbath. Christian evangelists preached the gospel message to Jews on the Sabbath, but their preaching is not the same thing as holding Christian worship services on the Sabbath. Instead of meeting on the Sabbath, the day Christians observed was the first day of the week (Acts 20:7; 1 Cor. 16:1, 2), the day of Christ's resurrection. This day became known as "the Lord's day" (Rev. 1:10), and on this day local congregations met to observe the Lord's Supper. That the church met on the first day of the week for its worship assemblies is confirmed by the writings of the church fathers. There is no New Testament command to rest on the Lord's Day; from that standpoint, the first day of the week is not the Christian equivalent of the Jewish Sabbath, which was a day of rest.

The "Christian Sabbath" is not the seventh day but heaven. The only time the New Testament uses the word "Sabbath" (or a close equivalent) with regard to Christians is in Hebrews 4:9–11, which identifies the Christian "Sabbath" with heaven and urges them to enter it.

A Reminder. If we do not have to observe the Sabbath, what significance does the Sabbath have for Christians today? The Sabbath command should remind us of the need to:

(1) Remember. The Jews were reminded each Sabbath of what God had done in creating the world. We, too, need to remember what God has done for us, in creation, in redemption, and in revelation. One way we remember is to meet together on the Lord's Day to partake of the Lord's Supper.

(2) Rest. Jesus said, "The Sabbath was made for man" (Mk. 2:27). The implication is that resting one day of the week is good for human beings. Perhaps we need to internalize that idea; one of our biggest problems may be that we work too much and rest too little.

(3) Respond to the needs of others. The Sabbath was intended to provide a time of rest not only for the Israelites but also for those who were dependent on them—their slaves, the strangers who lived with them, and even their animals (23:12; Deut. 5:14). May the Sabbath command remind us of the need to have compassion on others.

(4) Redouble our efforts to get to heaven, to strive for that "Sabbath rest" which awaits us in heaven (Heb. 4:9–11).

Sabbath: The "Sign" of the Covenant (31:13, 17)

The Sabbath was the "sign" of the covenant between God and Israel. By means of that sign, Israel was constantly reminded of what God had done for them. In addition, the Sabbath served to distinguish Israel from all other peoples; the people of Israel were known as the people who kept the Sabbath. Has God given us a "sign" of the covenant He made with His people in this age? Perhaps the practice of baptism and the observance of the Lord's Supper serve as signs of the New Covenant, since these requirements identify those who participate in them as Christ's disciples. But perhaps the most important "sign" that we are Christians is the love we to have for one another (Jn. 13:34, 35).

Chapter 32

Apostasy: The Golden Calf

Exodus 32—34 is placed immediately after the account of the Lord's final instructions to Moses for the building of the tabernacle. This text relates the apostasy and renewal of the people. The covenant, made in chapter 19 and ratified in chapter 24, was broken in chapter 32 and renewed in chapter 34. The section emphasizes that, even though the Israelites were faithless and the covenant was broken, God was gracious and compassionate toward them.

As Moses "delayed" his return from the mountain, Aaron agreed to lead the people in building a golden calf for them to worship (32:1–6). God informed Moses of Israel's sin and threatened to destroy the people (32:7–10). When Moses interceded on behalf of the Israelites, God relented (32:11–14).

When Moses came down from the mountain and saw Israel's idolatry for himself, he broke the tablets of the Law (32:15–19). Then he ground up the golden calf, mixed it with water, and made the people drink from it (32:20). After hearing Aaron's account of how the idol was made (32:21–24), Moses enlisted the Levites to put to death several thousand of the rebellious Israelites (32:25–29). Moses offered to bear the people's sin (32:30–32), but God held the guilty accountable instead (32:33). God sent a plague upon Israel because of their sin (32:34, 35).

ISRAEL'S SIN: WORSHIPING A CALF IDOL (32:1–6)

1Now when the people saw that Moses delayed to come

down from the mountain, the people assembled about Aaron and said to him, "Come, make us a god who will go before us; as for this Moses, the man who brought us up from the land of Egypt, we do not know what has become of him." [2]Aaron said to them, "Tear off the gold rings which are in the ears of your wives, your sons, and your daughters, and bring them to me." [3]Then all the people tore off the gold rings which were in their ears and brought them to Aaron. [4]He took this from their hand, and fashioned it with a graving tool and made it into a molten calf; and they said, "This is your god, O Israel, who brought you up from the land of Egypt." [5]Now when Aaron saw this, he built an altar before it; and Aaron made a proclamation and said, "Tomorrow shall be a feast to the LORD." [6]So the next day they rose early and offered burnt offerings, and brought peace offerings; and the people sat down to eat and to drink, and rose up to play.

Verse 1. Israel's apostasy was triggered by **Moses'** forty-day stay on **the mountain** (24:18). Even though some scholars believe that the forty-day period should be understood in a figurative sense, such as "a round number for an indefinitely long time,"[1] the figure should be taken literally. Deuteronomy 9:11 speaks of the same period of time as "forty days and nights."

While Israel's sin cannot be excused, it was perhaps understandable. From the people's standpoint, they owed their escape from Egypt, their deliverance through the Red Sea, and their ability to exist in the wilderness to the man Moses. No doubt, they also credited the Lord God, Yahweh, with their blessings. However, if Moses disappeared, how could Yahweh benefit them? As they saw it, His blessings came only through Moses.

If Moses was gone, they reasoned, what they needed was another **god** (אֱלֹהִים, *'elohim*) to guide them through the wilderness. This plural term is sometimes used for the "God" of Israel, another "god," or multiple "gods." The NASB, along with other

[1]Note on Exodus 32:1, Bruce M. Metzger and Roland E. Murphy, eds., *The New Oxford Annotated Bible with the Apocrypha* (New York: Oxford University Press, 1991), 112.

translations (NAB; NJB), opted for the singular "god" in this case, while many versions chose the plural "gods" (KJV; NKJV; NRSV; ESV; REB; NIV). The fact that *'elohim* is followed by a plural verb suggests that they were seeking another god, not Yahweh; when *'elohim* refers to the Lord, the verb is usually singular.[2] They should have recognized that a god made by their own hands would be powerless to help them. However, they, like most of the people of the ancient Near East, failed to see the fallacy of their thinking.

Verses 2, 3. The participation of **Aaron** in this apostasy is very puzzling. How could the Israelites forget the Lord so quickly after pledging allegiance to Him (19:8; 24:3, 7)? Even more curious is that the brother of Moses would go along with the people's idolatrous request. How can Aaron's behavior be explained?

(1) Did Aaron have a different view than the people? They wanted him to make a "god" or "gods" (*'elohim*), referring to a god or gods other than the One whom Moses represented. Did Aaron, instead, make a calf and then proclaim a feast to the Lord (32:5)? Maybe Aaron was not, in making the calf, renouncing his faith in the one true God.

(2) Was Aaron weaker than he should have been? Confronted by a crowd bent on wickedness, he may have determined just to live through this situation and do better in the future.

Aaron told the men to collect **the gold rings** that were worn **in the ears** of their **wives**, **sons**, and **daughters**—a command which they eagerly obeyed. Apparently it was not uncommon for both genders to wear earrings among Semitic people (Judg. 8:24–26). In addition to being worn for decoration, these sometimes also had a spiritual purpose. R. K. Harrison believed that earrings were first worn by ancient people as "magical amulets designed to protect the ear openings from infiltration by evil spirits that were thought to be the cause of disease."[3] The con-

---

[2]John J. Davis, *Moses and the Gods of Egypt: Studies in Exodus*, 2d ed. (Grand Rapids, Mich.: Baker Book House, 1986), 292–93.

[3]R. K. Harrison, "Earring," in *The International Standard Bible Encyclopedia*, rev. ed., ed. Geoffrey W. Bromiley (Grand Rapids, Mich.: Wm. B. Eerdmans Publishing Co., 1982), 2:3.

nection between earrings and paganism is illustrated by the fact that Jacob's household got rid of them along with their idols (Gen. 35:2, 4).

Perhaps some of the Israelites' earrings used to make the calf came from the gifts given to them by the Egyptians just before they left Egypt (11:2; 12:35, 36). After the rebellion, the Israelites took off their ornaments as a sign of mourning and repentance (33:5, 6). Later, they generously gave of their earrings and other jewelry for the construction of the tabernacle, its furnishings, and the priestly garments (35:21, 22).

Verse 4. On this occasion, Aaron took the Israelites' earrings and made **a molten calf**. Some commentators have thought that the image was made of wood overlaid with gold.[4] The fact that the image was burned with fire (32:20) might suggest that possibility. However, the fact that the image is described as "molten" (מַסֵּכָה, *massekah*) two times (32:4, 8) implies that it was cast in solid gold and then finished by hand with an [en]**graving tool**. As James Burton Coffman pointed out, there was more than enough gold from the earrings of this vast multitude to use in the idol's construction.[5]

According to R. Alan Cole, "calf" is not a good translation of the Hebrew word עֵגֶל (*'egel*); rather, "a young bull in his first strength is meant."[6] Where did Aaron and the Israelites get the idea of making a god or representing God with the image of a bull? Since their people had been living in Egypt for 430 years, the Israelites were no doubt influenced by the Egyptians who worshiped the sacred bull of Apis.[7] Moreover, Nahum M. Sarna noted,

---

[4]See C. F. Keil and F. Delitzsch, *The Pentateuch*, vol. 2, trans. James Martin, Biblical Commentary on the Old Testament (Grand Rapids, Mich.: Wm. B. Eerdmans Publishing Co., n.d.), 222.

[5]See James Burton Coffman, *Commentary on Exodus, The Second Book of Moses* (Abilene, Tex.: ACU Press, 1985), 441.

[6]R. Alan Cole, *Exodus: An Introduction and Commentary*, Tyndale Old Testament Commentaries (Downers Grove, Ill.: Inter-Varsity Press, 1973), 214.

[7]See the Egyptian statue of a bull representing the god Apis in Alfred J. Hoerth, *Archaeology and the Old Testament* (Grand Rapids, Mich.: Baker Books, 1998), 175.

> The depiction of a god in the form of a bull was widespread throughout the entire ancient Near East. That animal was a symbol of lordship, strength, vital energy, and fertility, and was either deified and made an object of worship, or, on account of these sovereign attributes, was employed in representation of deity.[8]

Although the image was made by Aaron from molten gold taken from the people's earrings, God held the people responsible for the construction of the idol (32:8).

After Aaron made the idol, **they said, "This is your god, O Israel, who brought you up from the land of Egypt."** As in verse 1, the NASB translates *'elohim* as "god," while other versions have the plural rendering "gods." "They" may refer to the people, or their leaders, who spoke to Aaron (32:1) and who provided the gold rings used in making the image (32:3). If so, these people may have been proclaiming that the idol was some god other than the One whom Moses represented. If, on the other hand, "they" refers to Aaron and his sons, then (regardless of what the people intended in worshiping the calf), they were saying, "This is the God, Yahweh, who brought you out of the land of Egypt." This understanding seems likely in view of the fact that the next day Aaron proclaimed "a feast to the LORD" (32:5).

Sarna asserted that the people were not asking for another god but for a representation of the Lord, the God of Israel. He said, "It is all but certain that in demanding 'a god,' they intended nothing more than an appropriate object emblematic of the Divine Presence."[9] Aaron may have been trying to meet the people's needs. Since Moses was gone, they had no one and nothing to represent the Lord God; therefore, he made a representation of Yahweh. They may not have intended to break the first commandment by worshiping another god.

In any case, they were breaking the second commandment

---

[8]Nahum M. Sarna, *Exploring Exodus: The Origins of Biblical Israel* (New York: Schocken Books, 1996), 218.

[9]Ibid., 217.

by making a physical representation of the spiritual God and then worshiping it (32:8). The passage may illustrate the danger of trying to represent God with a physical image or object. While the image may be intended to turn the worshipers' attention to God so that He may be worshiped more meaningfully, the inevitable result of making such an image is that the image itself ultimately and inevitably becomes the object of worship, and thus becomes a god in its own right. Thus breaking the second commandment leads to breaking the first.

Later, Moses confessed to God that the people had made for themselves "a god of gold" (32:31). Nehemiah wrote that they made for themselves "a calf of molten metal and said, 'This is your God who brought you up from Egypt'" (Neh. 9:18). Psalm 106:19, 20 says, "They made a calf in Horeb and worshiped a molten image. Thus they exchanged their glory for the image of an ox that eats grass." In the New Testament, Stephen said of the incident, "They made a calf and brought a sacrifice to the idol, and were rejoicing in the works of their hands" (Acts 7:41). Paul declared that they were guilty of idolatry (1 Cor. 10:7).

Verse 5. The phrase **when Aaron saw this** suggests that Aaron was not party to the proclamation "This is your god" (32:4). However, seeing that the Israelites connected the calf with the God who had brought them out of Egypt, Aaron might have determined to make the best of the situation by proclaiming **a feast to the LORD**. Aaron intended for the image to represent the Lord—perhaps to figuratively serve as a seat or a throne from which He could rule. W. H. Gispen noted, "Some assume that the calf, rather than being a representation of the deity, was merely the visible pedestal on which the invisible deity stood."[10]

Verse 6. Therefore, on **the next day**, the people celebrated a feast to the Lord. The day began with religious ceremonies. They **offered burnt offerings** and **peace offerings**. These types of sacrifices predated the Law given to Moses (10:25; 18:12). Offerings

[10]W. H. Gispen, *Exodus*, trans. Ed van der Maas, Bible Student's Commentary (Grand Rapids, Mich.: Regency Reference Library, Zondervan Publishing House, 1982), 293. See the stele portraying the storm god Hadad standing on the back of a bull in Hoerth, 221.

had been made to God from the time of Cain and Abel (Gen. 4:3–5). During the intervening years, some sacrifices had come to be known as "burnt offerings" because the offering was completely burned up on the altar. Other sacrifices were called "peace offerings"; these were partly offered on the altar and the rest was eaten by those who made them.

Then, the text says that **the people sat down to eat and to drink, and rose up to play.** The fact that eating and drinking took place should not be surprising since the Israelites made "peace offerings." After all, Jethro had earlier feasted with the elders of Israel after making such sacrifices (18:12). However, the fact that they "rose up to play" suggests that they engaged in "coarse and excessive carousing" which "was a typical feature of pagan fertility festivals."[11] The word "play" (צָחַק, *tsachaq*) can mean "laugh," "jest," "make sport of," or "mock." Further, it can also be a way of referring to sexual activity (Gen. 26:8; 39:14, 17). The religious feast evidently became something of a sexual orgy involving singing and dancing (32:17–19). In the New Testament, the apostle Paul used this incident as an example to warn the Christians in Corinth against participating in pagan idolatry and revelry (1 Cor. 10:7).

GOD'S RESPONSE: THE THREAT TO DESTROY ISRAEL (32:7–10)

7Then the LORD spoke to Moses, "Go down at once, for your people, whom you brought up from the land of Egypt, have corrupted themselves. 8They have quickly turned aside from the way which I commanded them. They have made for themselves a molten calf, and have worshiped it and have sacrificed to it and said, 'This is your god, O Israel, who brought you up from the land of Egypt!'" 9The LORD said to Moses, "I have seen this people, and behold, they are an obstinate people. 10Now then let Me alone, that My anger may burn against them and

---

[11]John H. Walton and Victor H. Matthews, *Genesis—Deuteronomy*, The IVP Bible Backgrounds Commentary (Downers Grove, Ill.: InterVarsity Press, 1997), 135.

that I may destroy them; and I will make of you a great nation."

Verse 7. The Israelites had assumed that Moses and his God had forsaken them. Left without a divine representative, they made their own god. However, neither the Lord nor Moses had forsaken the people. Instead, the people had forsaken Moses and the Lord. On the mountain, **the Lord** told **Moses** to **go down** and deal with the situation. God's anger with Israel is evident by the fact that He spoke of them not as His people, but as Moses' **people** or "this people" (32:9). Since they had broken the covenant with God, they could, in reality, no longer be called His people.[12] God further said that the Israelites, who had been called to be "a holy nation" (19:6), had **corrupted themselves**.

Verse 8. The Lord leveled the charge that the people had **quickly turned aside** from His way. They had made a **molten calf** and had **worshiped it** and **sacrificed to it** as if it had delivered them from **Egypt**.

If the people's impatience is somewhat understandable, how much more is God's anger! These are the same people whom God had by His own grace and power rescued from Egypt. They had seen the wonders He had performed in Egypt and in the wilderness. They had experienced His awesome presence. They had even pledged to do everything that the Lord commanded (19:8). Even after they had heard God's commands, including the first and second commandments (20:3–6), they had agreed again to do all that God required of them (24:3, 7). Only forty days had passed since Moses had ascended the mountain, and the people had turned to the worship of a golden calf. No wonder God wanted to destroy them!

Verse 9. The Lord referred to Israel as **an obstinate people**. The word "obstinate" or "stubborn" (NEB; TEV) is used to translate קְשֵׁה־עֹרֶף (*qᵉsheh 'orep*), an idiom that is literally rendered "stiff-necked" (KJV; NKJV; ASV; RSV; NRSV; NIV). This idiom most likely originated because stubborn farm animals stiffened

[12]Ronald F. Youngblood, *Exodus*, Everyman's Bible Commentary (Chicago: Moody Bible Institute, 1983), 135.

their necks, refusing to wear the yoke. James K. Hoffmeier explained,

> For the Israelites, obedience to the covenant stipulations was bearing the yoke, while disobedience was breaking the yoke (Jer. 2:20; 5:5); therefore, to wear God's yoke was the ideal, but to break the yoke was apostasy and to stiffen the neck was a refusal to wear it.[13]

Exodus 32:9 marks the first usage of "stiff-necked" in the Old Testament. The phrase repeatedly occurs, indicating Israel's refusal to obey God's covenant and to heed the warnings of His prophets.

Verse 10. At that point, God threatened to **destroy** the people and to establish **a great nation** through Moses. God's anger was, of course, justified. The covenant which God had made with the people said that, as long as the people obeyed God, they would be His people. As long as they did His will, He would bless them. Since they had not done His will in this instance, God was justified in being angry and would have been justified if He had renounced His covenant with Israel and destroyed the nation.

While God would have been justified in destroying Israel, He would not have been God if He had abandoned His plan to raise up a great people as the means by which He would save mankind. He presented an alternative to Moses. His "Plan B" was to fulfill the promises He had made to Israel's forefathers through Moses.

MOSES' INTERCESSION (32:11–13)

[11]Then Moses entreated the LORD his God, and said, "O LORD, why does Your anger burn against Your people whom You have brought out from the land of Egypt with great power

---

[13]James K. Hoffmeier, "Stiff-necked; stiffen the neck," in *The International Standard Bible Encyclopedia*, rev. ed., ed. Geoffrey W. Bromiley (Grand Rapids, Mich.: Wm. B. Eerdmans Publishing Co., 1988), 4:619.

and with a mighty hand? [12]Why should the Egyptians speak, saying, 'With evil intent He brought them out to kill them in the mountains and to destroy them from the face of the earth'? Turn from Your burning anger and change Your mind about doing harm to Your people. [13]Remember Abraham, Isaac, and Israel, Your servants to whom You swore by Yourself, and said to them, 'I will multiply your descendants as the stars of the heavens, and all this land of which I have spoken I will give to your descendants, and they shall inherit it forever.'"

Verse 11. Moses took the side of the Israelites, as a lawyer in a courtroom comes to the defense of an accused client. His persuasive speaking on this occasion casts doubts on his earlier protest that he had "never been eloquent," but was "slow of speech and slow of tongue" (4:10). Eloquently, Moses presented three arguments to persuade **God** not to carry out His announced plan.[14]

The first argument was for God to *remember what He had done*. Moses hinted at this idea by speaking of God's people whom He had **brought out from the land of Egypt with great power and with a mighty hand.** Apparently, he wanted God to remember what He had done for Israel so that He might be less inclined to destroy the ones He had so graciously redeemed.

Verse 12. The second argument was for God to *consider what others would say*. Moses indicated that **the Egyptians** knew that Israel's God had delivered them; they had seen and would acknowledge His power. If God now destroyed Israel in the wilderness, they would doubt His good intentions. They might say, "He is a powerful but *evil* god." In effect, Moses said, "Think of Your reputation."

Verse 13. The third argument was for God *not to forget His promises*. God's promises had been made to **Abraham, Isaac, and Israel** (Jacob), and they included a multitude of **descendants** and a **land**. Moses seemed to be saying, "If You wipe out all the people, these specific promises will not be fulfilled."

---

[14]Coffman, 443–44.

GOD'S RECONSIDERATION (32:14)

[14]So the LORD changed His mind about the harm which He said He would do to His people.

Verse 14. According to the text, Moses' arguments apparently persuaded God; He **changed His mind** and went back to "Plan A." Moses was then ready to do what God had earlier instructed him to do: "Go down at once" (32:7).

While the meaning of the verse is clear, it raises this important question: How can God change His mind? After all, God is, as the Bible teaches, unchangeable. He said in Malachi 3:6, "For I, the LORD, do not change; therefore you, O sons of Jacob, are not consumed" (see Num. 23:19; Jas. 1:17). How is it possible, then, to say that God "changed His mind," as in 32:14?

The word נָחַם (*nacham*), rendered "changed His mind" (NASB; NRSV), is also translated "relented" (NKJV; NIV; NAB; NJB; ESV). The KJV has "repented," which has increased the confusion in the minds of Bible readers. One might ask, "How can an all-holy, sinless God repent?" Walter C. Kaiser, Jr., provided this helpful explanation:

> God's repentance or "relenting" is an anthropomorphism (a description of God in human forms) that aims at showing us that he can and does change in his actions and emotions to men when given proper grounds for doing so, and thereby he does not change in his basic integrity or character (cf. Pss 99:6; 106:45; Jer 18:8; Amos 7:3, 6; Jonah 3:10; James 5:16). The grounds for the Lord's repenting are three: (1) intercession (cf. Amos 7:1–6); (2) repentance of the people (Jer 18:3–11; Jonah 3:9–10); and (3) compassion (Deut 32:36; Judg 2:18; 2 Sam 24:16).[15]

While the Hebrew term *nacham* is frequently used for God's changing His mind, the more common word for man's repentance from sin is שׁוּב (*shub*).

---

[15]Walter C. Kaiser, Jr., "Exodus," in *The Expositor's Bible Commentary*, vol. 2, *Genesis—Numbers* (Grand Rapids, Mich.: Zondervan, 1990), 479.

"The LORD changed His mind" means that He changed His previously stated attitude or planned action toward Israel based on a change in circumstances. In this case, the new factor in the circumstances that produced God's change was Moses' intercession. However, God's changing His behavior toward someone does not detract from the fact that He remains unchangeable—in His character, His basic plan for mankind, and His purpose.

ISRAEL'S PUNISHMENT (32:15–35)

Drinking Polluted Water (32:15–24)

[15]Then Moses turned and went down from the mountain
with the two tablets of the testimony in his hand, tablets which
were written on both sides; they were written on one side and
the other. [16]The tablets were God's work, and the writing was
God's writing engraved on the tablets. [17]Now when Joshua
heard the sound of the people as they shouted, he said to Moses,
"There is a sound of war in the camp." [18]But he said,
"It is not the sound of the cry of triumph,
Nor is it the sound of the cry of defeat;
But the sound of singing I hear."
[19]It came about, as soon as Moses came near the camp, that he
saw the calf and the dancing; and Moses' anger burned, and
he threw the tablets from his hands and shattered them at the
foot of the mountain. [20]He took the calf which they had made
and burned it with fire, and ground it to powder, and scattered
it over the surface of the water and made the sons of Israel
drink it.

[21]Then Moses said to Aaron, "What did this people do to
you, that you have brought such great sin upon them?" [22]Aaron
said, "Do not let the anger of my lord burn; you know the
people yourself, that they are prone to evil. [23]For they said to
me, 'Make a god for us who will go before us; for this Moses,
the man who brought us up from the land of Egypt, we do not
know what has become of him.' [24]I said to them, 'Whoever has
any gold, let them tear it off.' So they gave it to me, and I threw
it into the fire, and out came this calf."

Verse 15. The **two tablets** were the tablets **of the testimony** (see 31:18). The idea of the laws as a "testimony" suggests that the laws witnessed to God's will for Israel and, if the laws were broken, witnessed against those who rejected God's will. It is usually assumed that the tablets contained only the Ten Commandments. Unlike the pictorial representations common today, these tablets were **written on both sides**.

Verse 16. Since **the tablets were God's work, and the writing was God's writing engraved on the tablets**, the people could not break His laws without being punished. As John I. Durham noted, the intention of this statement "is to confirm God as the source of the commandments and therefore the authority behind them."[16] The text emphasizes God's part in the production of the tablets, which were written by His own "finger" (31:18).

Verse 17. Joshua had gone part of the way up the mountain and there waited for Moses to return. As Moses came down from the top of the mountain, Joshua interpreted the sounds he heard coming from **the camp** as the **sound of war**—a sound which would require Moses, the commander-in-chief, to return.

Verse 18. Moses, however, knowing what God had told him, was able to interpret the noise more accurately as the **sound** of revelry. The NASB prints this verse as poetry, just as it does such poetic passages as 15:1–18.

Verse 19. Earlier in the narrative, God's anger was emphasized (32:10). Moses urged God not to destroy the people in His anger. Because of Moses' intercession, the reader may get the impression that Moses, the mediator, was so compassionate that he would have been willing to overlook the people's sin. Such a view would, however, misrepresent Moses' position. Moses never intended to excuse the people's sin. He did not ask that they go unpunished for what they had done. Rather, his purpose was to hold back the wrath of God, to keep God from utterly destroying the people He had redeemed.

When Moses reached **the foot of the mountain**, he witnessed the people's apostasy firsthand. His reaction mirrored God's

---

[16]John I. Durham, *Exodus*, Word Biblical Commentary, vol. 3 (Waco, Tex.: Word Books, 1987), 430.

(32:10); Moses became angry. He **threw** down **the tablets** on which were written the laws of the covenant. As a result, the tablets **shattered**, signifying that the covenant had been broken.[17]

Verse 20. Next, Moses **took the calf** and **burned it**. Then he **ground it to powder**, mixed it in **water**, and made the people **drink it**. This may have illustrated that their sin was shared; all who partook of the water were guilty of the idolatry. Some commentators have connected this act with the "water of jealousy" spoken of in Numbers 5:11–31. There a woman accused of adultery was forced to drink water mixed with dust from the floor of the tabernacle. If she were guilty of adultery, the drinking of the water made her guilt obvious. The similarity between that ritual and Israel's drinking of the water lies in the fact that Israel was in fact guilty of spiritual adultery because they worshiped the golden calf.[18]

Verse 21. Moses also confronted **Aaron** about the people's rebellion. Earlier, the people had been blamed for the making of the calf; in this verse Moses blamed Aaron for bringing a **great sin** upon the **people**. Obviously, everyone involved in the affair was guilty. Aaron should have stood firm for the Lord by refusing the people's request. Rather than giving in to their determination to do wrong, he should have led them to do right. Verse 25 says that Aaron had let the people get "out of control."

Verse 22. Aaron responded by blaming the existence of the idol on **the people**. He reminded Moses that the Israelites were **prone to evil**. Moses certainly had experienced their murmuring and complaining enough times to believe that they were inclined to faithlessness.

Verses 23, 24. Aaron's account of the incident when the **calf** was built was factual—to a point. Aaron rightfully admitted that he had cooperated with the people by taking their gold and throwing **it into the fire**, but then he claimed that the calf just mysteriously emerged. The assertion that the calf came fully formed from the fire is so ridiculous as to be humorous.

Neither Moses' reaction nor God's reaction to Aaron's expla-

---

[17]Sarna, 219; Cole, 212.
[18]Sarna, 219–20.

nation is recorded in Exodus. However, Deuteronomy 9:20 says that God was so angry with Aaron that, except for Moses' intercession, He would have killed him. Therefore, Aaron's life was spared in the ensuing slaughter of the idolaters.

Three Thousand Slain by the Levites (32:25–29)

[25]Now when Moses saw that the people were out of control—for Aaron had let them get out of control to be a derision among their enemies—[26]then Moses stood in the gate of the camp, and said, "Whoever is for the LORD, come to me!" And all the sons of Levi gathered together to him. [27]He said to them, "Thus says the LORD, the God of Israel, 'Every man of you put his sword upon his thigh, and go back and forth from gate to gate in the camp, and kill every man his brother, and every man his friend, and every man his neighbor.'" [28]So the sons of Levi did as Moses instructed, and about three thousand men of the people fell that day. [29]Then Moses said, "Dedicate yourselves today to the LORD—for every man has been against his son and against his brother—in order that He may bestow a blessing upon you today."

The punishment for the people's sin had already begun. They had seen the tablets broken, and they had drunk the water made bitter by the object of their idolatry. Now the punishment became more terrible; they learned firsthand that "the wages of sin is death" (Rom. 6:23) and that idolatry was a capital offense.

Verse 25. Moses had apparently left **Aaron** and Hur in charge of the camp in his absence (24:14). The fact that Aaron had failed in his responsibility as a leader over the people has already been noted (32:21–24). Now Aaron's failure is underscored by the statement that he **let them get out of control**. Due to their revelry, the Israelites would become **a derision among their enemies** (see 32:12; Deut. 28:37). The rare word "derision" (שִׁמְצָה, *shimtsah*) carries the idea of malicious whispering.

Verse 26. Moses offered to all Israel the opportunity to stand up for the Lord: **"Whoever is for the LORD, come to me!"** Only the Levites responded.

Verses 27, 28. There is no indication that the Levites understood what they would be asked to do; but when they were asked, they obeyed. They went throughout the camp killing others by the **sword**, regardless of their close earthly ties to those they executed—whether **brother**, **friend**, or **neighbor**. **About three thousand men** were put to death. While it is possible that these were the only people involved in the worship of the golden calf, it is more likely that these were the leaders of the apostasy.

Verse 29. After the punishment had been meted out, Moses commanded the Levites to **dedicate** themselves **to the Lord**. This decision to be for the Lord qualified the Levites for consecration. Because of this choice, they became the priestly tribe and were especially blessed by God.

Forgiveness and Punishment (32:30–35)

[30]On the next day Moses said to the people, "You yourselves have committed a great sin; and now I am going up to the Lord; perhaps I can make atonement for your sin." [31]Then Moses returned to the Lord, and said, "Alas, this people has committed a great sin, and they have made a god of gold for themselves. [32]But now, if You will, forgive their sin—and if not, please blot me out from Your book which You have written!" [33]The Lord said to Moses, "Whoever has sinned against Me, I will blot him out of My book." [34]"But go now, lead the people where I told you. Behold, My angel shall go before you; nevertheless in the day when I punish, I will punish them for their sin." [35]Then the Lord smote the people, because of what they did with the calf which Aaron had made.

Verse 30. God had already changed His mind about destroying the people (32:10, 14). Nevertheless, atonement was still required for the people's **great sin**; they still needed to be forgiven. **Moses** rebuked the people for their sin, but he volunteered to **make atonement** for them. To do so, he had to make another trip up the mountain to stand again in the presence of **the Lord**.

Verse 31. Moses' appeal to the Lord was succinct. Instead of offering excuses to God, he humbly confessed Israel's failure. He began with the interjection **Alas**, which denotes a passionate appeal; the people were indeed sorry for what they had done. Moses then stated that the people had **committed a great sin**. The emphatic Hebrew expression חֲטָאתֶם חֲטָאָה גְדֹלָה (*chᵃta'them chᵃta'ah gᵉdolah*) can be literally translated as "sinned a great sin" (KJV). This is the third time that the phrase "great sin" appears within the chapter (32:21, 30, 31). The grievous sin of idolatry was specifically named: **they have made a god of gold for themselves.**

Verse 32. Moses then asked God to **forgive their sin**. In Old Testament times God's redeemed people had a relationship with Him that included the opportunity to seek forgiveness. These prayers for forgiveness did not necessarily have to be associated with specific acts of sacrifice, but could be granted by God Himself on the basis of His gracious nature and His relationship with the one offering the prayer.

The style is interesting: Moses started a sentence but never finished it. Rather, he interrupted himself—as indicated by the dash—to make an alternative request. This figure of speech, called "aposiopesis," generally indicates strong feeling. It is defined as "the sudden breaking off of a thought before it is completed."[19] Moses was saying, "If you will forgive them, please do so; if not, **blot me out from Your book**." Moses' depth of feeling for his fellow Israelites is revealed in this request. His compassion anticipated that of Paul (Rom. 9:3) and even of Jesus, who was made to be sin for us (2 Cor. 5:21).

Moses' statement contains the first mention in the Bible of a book which presumably contains the names of those who are pleasing to God (see Ps. 69:28; Is. 4:3; Ezek. 13:9; Dan. 12:1; Mal. 3:16; Lk. 10:20; Phil. 4:3; Heb. 12:23; Rev. 3:5; 13:8; 17:8; 20:12, 15; 21:27). This imagery is probably derived from the practice of ancient cities possessing a register containing the names of their citizens. If a person lost his status as a citizen or died, his name would be removed from the registry.

---

[19]Edward P. Myers, "Interpreting Figurative Language," in *Biblical Interpretation—Principles and Practice*, ed. F. Furman Kearley, Edward P. Myers, and Timothy D. Hadley (Grand Rapids, Mich.: Baker Book House, 1986), 97.

Verse 33. The Lord responded to Moses' request by stating, **"Whoever has sinned against Me, I will blot him out of My book."** These words contain a general principle which has been true throughout the ages: People are held responsible only for their own sins. Ezekiel said, "The person who sins will die. . . . the wickedness of the wicked will be upon himself" (Ezek. 18:20).

In the Old Testament especially there is a sense of corporate guilt—the guilt of an individual makes the whole body guilty in some sense. Furthermore, the promise of blessings and the threat of curses which are connected to the covenant and the Law are intended for the nation as a whole, not for individuals within the nation. Nevertheless, only those who are actually guilty of sin are held accountable by God for their sins.

Verse 34. The text does not reveal whether or not, or to what extent, the Lord forgave the ones who sinned on that occasion. Forgiveness is evident in God's decision not to destroy the Israelites. However, God intended to punish His people. **In the day when I punish** may mean the day when Moses appealed to God on behalf of the people. If so, God was announcing His intention to **punish them** for their **sin**. On the other hand, the expression may refer to the future. In that case, God was saying that He would be with the people and that He would punish them whenever they needed punishment.

In connection with God's statement that He would punish the people, He repeated Moses' commission: **"Lead the people where I told you."** It was as if God were saying, "Do not worry about what I will do to the people. Do what I have told you to do." Then God added, **"My angel shall go before you."** By saying that His angel would go before Israel, the Lord assured the people that, in spite of their failure, He would bring them to the promised land. This angel has already been discussed (see comments on 23:20, 21). Sometimes the angel seems to be the equivalent of God's presence, but in this context the angel's going with the people is contrasted with God's unwillingness to be in their midst (33:2, 3). Therefore, in this passage the "angel" is not likely God Himself.

Verse 35. The chapter ends by saying that **the Lord smote**

the people. Apparently, this act was the third punishment for their sin. They had drunk of the idol-corrupted water, and three thousand leaders of the rebellion had been killed. Now God "smote the people" by sending a plague upon them (KJV; NKJV; NIV; ESV; NRSV). No further details are given about this punishment. Umberto Cassuto wrote that the plague need not have occurred immediately after the sin involving the golden calf. He further explained,

> The meaning is that the Lord smote the people with a plague, as a collective punishment, at some undefined time, visiting on the day that He visited. The Bible does not specify how and when the punishment was inflicted, but only alludes to the matter in order to conclude the subject of the preceding verse, and to inform us at this stage that as it had been announced previously, even so it came to pass.[20]

Exodus 32 illustrates the difference between God's wrath and His punishment, or chastisement. When the people sinned, God threatened to destroy them. If He had done so, His destruction of His people would have been an illustration of His wrath. He would have been justified in taking extreme measures and destroying the people who had disregarded His covenant and disobeyed His laws. However, He was dissuaded from exercising His wrath against His people. The people still were to be punished, or chastised, so that they might understand the seriousness of their sin against God. Therefore, He punished them without totally destroying them.

APPLICATION

The Breaking of the Covenant (Ch. 32)

Exodus 19 tells about *the making of the covenant*. In Exodus 20—23 we find the good laws that were part of this covenant.

---

[20]Umberto Cassuto, *A Commentary on the Book of Exodus*, trans. Israel Abrahams (Jerusalem: Magnes Press, 1997), 424.

Exodus 24 describes the ceremony to confirm the covenant. Then Moses went up on Mount Sinai for forty days to receive the Law (24:18). All was well for Israel. Next, in Exodus 32, we read about *the breaking of the covenant.*

The church today has much the same relationship with God that Israel had. They were His covenant people then, and we are His covenant people now. Just as they broke the covenant, we can also break the covenant today. Therefore, we can learn from Israel's mistakes.

What Was Their Sin? Idolatry—the substitution of another god for the Lord God! Idolatry is basic to many, if not most, of our sins today: We put someone or something else before God. That is idolatry.

What Were the Causes of Israel's Sin? (1) *Impatience* (32:1). The Israelites had spent four hundred years in Egypt, but they could not even wait forty days for the Law! (2) *A desire for a god they could see* (32:4). God is spirit (Jn. 4:24) and cannot be seen with human eyes. We are to walk by faith and not by sight; but from Moses' time to this, people have wanted a visible god or at least physical evidence that God is alive and well. (3) *Failure to remember and appreciate what God had done for them* (32:9). The Israelites were stubborn and inclined to forget what God had done for them; their forgetfulness and ingratitude led them into sin. (4) *Lust* (32:6, 19). The lustful activities that were almost certainly a part of this occasion go with a false view of God (32:23, 24; see Rom. 1:22–25). To reject the true God is to invite people to become ever more sinful. (5) *Poor leadership* (32:25). Aaron was in part responsible for their sin.

What Were the Immediate Effects of Their Sin? (1) God's initial reaction was an inclination to destroy them (32:9, 10). (2) Moses' initial reaction was that of a good leader; he interceded on their behalf and showed that he cared more for them than he did for himself (32:11–13). (3) God's second reaction is found in verse 14: "The LORD repented of the evil . . ." (KJV). What does this expression mean? God changed His mind. He did not change His mind about their wrongdoing, nor did He decide not to punish them at all. Rather, He changed His mind and did not cast them off altogether, in spite of His right to do so. (4) Moses' second reaction was to break the "two tablets of the testimony." He became angry. He burned the calf, threw its ashes into the water, and made the people drink it (32:15–20). (5) Aaron's reaction was to blame the making of the calf on the people and on some miraculous act by which the calf formed itself (32:21–24). (6) The Levites' reaction was to rally to Moses and then go throughout the camp, slaying the leaders of the rebellion (32:26–28). (7) Moses' third reaction was to bless the Levites, confess the Israelites' sin, and ask the Lord to forgive the people (32:29–32). (8) God's third reaction was to announce that He would punish only those who were guilty. After that, He sent a plague upon the people (32:33–35).

What should this episode teach us? (1) Sin—or the breaking of the covenant—is no light matter! Sin usually has effects that last beyond the moment. Later in Israel's history, Jeroboam's calves led to the destruction of the northern kingdom. (2) Sin also affects others, not just ourselves. What sin is so private that it would not somehow affect someone else negatively? (3) Sin is noticed by and punished by God Himself (32:33). God holds us responsible for our own sins, not for the sins of others; and He does not hold others guilty for our sins. (4) Sin has drastic consequences—even death.

What Was the Aftermath of Their Sin? The two chapters that follow emphasize the reestablishment of Israel's former relationship with God. We read about the renewal of the promise of land (33:1), the renewal of the promise of God's presence (33:14–16), and the renewal of the covenant (34:1, 6; see 34:7, 9, 10). Even though Israel fell, God did not cast Israel off. He welcomed His people back. That is good news for sinners. We speak of falling away, but we can never fall so far away that we cannot return if we are willing to do so (1 Jn. 1:9).

The message for today is this: Other gods always tempt us. The world invites, entices, urges, begs, and pleads with us to serve other gods. However, if we break our covenant with the Lord, we can and should expect punishment. There is always a price to pay for sin, but there is always a way back. God can forgive the prodigal. Yes, God can and will forgive us, even if we have sinned as did the Israelites when they broke the covenant.

Three Uses for Our Treasures (32:2–4; 33:4–6; 35:22)

Three times in Exodus the people's jewelry is mentioned. They gave their earrings to build the golden calf; they took off their ornaments to show their penitence; and they willingly gave their golden jewelry to build the tabernacle. These three uses of their jewelry suggest three ways we can use our "gold"—our "treasures," our material possessions, in general. First, we should not use our material possessions to promote evil, as they did when they gave to build the golden calf (32:2–4). Second, we can use what we have to show our penitence, as did the Israelites when they took off their ornaments or, on other occasions, tore their clothes. We can do so by, for instance, giving up ill-gotten gains, restoring what we have stolen, and the like (33:4–6). Third, we can gladly give our treasures to build up the kingdom of God, as they did when they gave to build the tabernacle (35:22).

Moses, the Ideal Shepherd (32:7–35)

Moses was chosen by God to deliver the Israelites from Egypt and bring them to the promised land. God prepared Moses for the task by providentially arranging for him to serve forty years as a shepherd. In the golden calf incident Moses displayed the primary quality that a shepherd needs: concern for the sheep. Moses was so concerned for the sheep that he interceded with God when God said that He would destroy them and make of Moses a great nation (32:7–14). Moses was so concerned for the sheep and their spiritual welfare that he was outraged because of their sin and saw that those who led them into sin were admonished and punished (32:15–29). Moses' anger and the punishment he administered was also evidence of his love for the people. Moses was so concerned for the sheep that he sought to make atonement for the sheep, even to the point of being willing to experience condemnation in their place (32:30–35; see Rom. 9:1–3; 2 Cor. 5:21). Shepherds (elders) today need to learn from Moses that their primary job is to be concerned for the sheep (the church) they lead (see Jn. 10:1–18).

Hard Choices (32:10)

Was it hard for Moses to turn down the offer to become the

progenitor (like Abraham) of a line of people who would be God's people? Nevertheless, He did. Why? He cared for the people He was leading, and He cared for the things of God. He wanted God to be successful in the task He had undertaken. When we have hard choices to make, a concern for others and for God will help us make the right decision.

Can Humans Make God Change His Mind? (32:14)

"The LORD changed His mind" after hearing Moses' arguments. While this is a difficult concept to understand, this passage holds out hope for us that when we earnestly entreat the Lord, He may "change His mind" (in the same sense that He did in Ex. 32) and accept our petitions. Another way we can "change God's mind" is by repenting, as did the people of Nineveh (Jon. 3:10).

Ridiculous Excuses—
Aaron's Miraculous Calf (32:21–24)

When Moses rebuked Aaron for making the calf, Aaron told the most ridiculous story anyone has ever heard: He threw the gold into the fire and out walked the calf. Do we also offer excuses for our sins? Are some of our excuses just as ridiculous as Aaron's? Maybe they sound reasonable to us but ridiculous to God.

"A Great Sin" (32:21, 30, 31)

Moses called Israel's worship of the golden calf "a great sin" three times. Warren W. Wiersbe wrote,

> It was a great sin because of who committed it: the nation of Israel, the chosen people of God. . . . It was great because of when and where they committed it: at Mt. Sinai after they had heard God's Law declared and seen God's glory revealed. . . . It was a great sin because of what they had already experienced of the power and mercy of God: the judgments against Egypt, the deliverance at the Red Sea, the provision of food and water, and

> the gracious leading of God by the pillar of cloud and fire.[21]

As God's people saved by grace, Christians today should guard against committing "great" sins.

"Who Is on the LORD's Side?" (32:26; KJV)

As Moses made ready to administer God's punishment for the sin of idolatry, he asked, "Who is on the LORD's side? let him come unto me" (32:26; KJV). The NASB has "Whoever is for the LORD, come to me!" The Levites responded, did the Lord's will, and were blessed as a result. Mankind is confronted with the same question today: "Who is on the Lord's side?" Each of us must decide whether we will be on the Lord's side or not, whether we will be for Him or against Him.

---

[21]Warren W. Wiersbe, *Be Delivered* (Colorado Springs, Colo.: Victor, 1998), 165.

Chapter 33

Restoration: God's Promise of His Presence

After Israel's apostasy (ch. 32), the people prepared to move again toward the promised land. God renewed His command to go up to the land which He had promised to their ancestors, assuring them that He would drive out the Canaanites before them. He added that He would not go with them because He might destroy these obstinate people on their journey (33:1–3). Instead, an angel would go before them. The people were sorrowful because of this announcement; at God's request, they removed their ornaments (33:4–6).

God continued to communicate with the people by speaking with Moses face to face at the tent set up outside the camp. When Moses left the tent, Joshua remained there (33:7–11).

Moses sought a more intimate knowledge of God (33:12, 13), and God responded that His presence would indeed go with Israel (33:14). Moses then asked God for some evidence of His presence that would distinguish Israel from all other peoples (33:15, 16). God granted his request (33:17).

Moses asked that he might see the glory of the Lord, and God agreed to show Himself to Moses (33:18, 19). Since "no man can see [God] and live," Moses would have to stand in the cleft of the rock, and God would cover him until He had passed by. Then Moses would be allowed to see God's back (33:20–23).

GOD'S WITHDRAWAL FROM THE PEOPLE (33:1–6)

1Then the Lord spoke to Moses, "Depart, go up from here,

you and the people whom you have brought up from the land of Egypt, to the land of which I swore to Abraham, Isaac, and Jacob, saying, 'To your descendants I will give it.'
[2]I will send an angel before you and I will drive out the Canaanite, the Amorite, the Hittite, the Perizzite, the Hivite and the Jebusite.
[3]Go up to a land flowing with milk and honey; for I will not go up in your midst, because you are an obstinate people, and I might destroy you on the way."

[4]When the people heard this sad word, they went into mourning, and none of them put on his ornaments.
[5]For the LORD had said to Moses, "Say to the sons of Israel, 'You are an obstinate people; should I go up in your midst for one moment, I would destroy you. Now therefore, put off your ornaments from you, that I may know what I shall do with you.'"
[6]So the sons of Israel stripped themselves of their ornaments, from Mount Horeb onward.

Verses 1, 2. After the plague with which **the LORD** punished Israel, He reminded them of His instructions for **Moses** to lead **the people** He had delivered from **Egypt** to the promised land. God further assured them of the leadership of **an angel** (see comments on 23:20, 21; 32:34), as well as His own assistance in removing pagan peoples from the land. He again named six of the nations which the Israelites were to drive out of the land (see comments on 3:8b).

Verse 3. God added the disturbing news that, while they were traveling to a good **land flowing with milk and honey**, He would not **go** with them. He refused to accompany them because they were **an obstinate people** and He **might destroy** [them] **on the way**.

God's absence was another consequence of Israel's apostasy. Israel had shown themselves to be "obstinate"—a stubborn and rebellious people determined to disobey God (see comments on 32:9). God's absence would, in a way, be a blessing to Israel, since the presence of a holy God among a rebellious people would surely put them at risk. Almost certainly, if God remained among them, they would sin and He would destroy them. According to R. Alan Cole, "This refusal is protective. If YHWH is too close to

Israel when they sin, His wrath will blaze out and they will die."[1]

Verse 4. The **people** obviously did not view the prospect of God's withdrawal from their midst as a blessing. On the contrary, **they went into mourning**, removing their **ornaments** to indicate their repentance. The significance of this act may be heightened by the fact that earrings were used in making the golden calf and that they were sometimes associated with pagan idolatry (see comments on 32:2, 3).

Verses 5, 6. The narrative backs up to explain that the removal of ornaments occurred at God's command. Through **Moses, the LORD** had accused **Israel** of being **an obstinate**, rebellious **people** and had spoken to them of what would happen if He accompanied them on their journey. Then He had commanded the Israelites to take **off** [their] **ornaments**, implying that He had not yet decided what to do with them. Faced with the possibility that God might decide to destroy them, the Israelites **stripped themselves of their ornaments**. They refrained from wearing their jewelry **from Mount Horeb onward**, that is, throughout their years in the wilderness.

ASSURANCE THAT GOD WOULD MANIFEST HIMSELF (33:7–23)

How God Previously Manifested Himself (33:7–11)

[7]Now Moses used to take the tent and pitch it outside the camp, a good distance from the camp, and he called it the tent of meeting. And everyone who sought the LORD would go out to the tent of meeting which was outside the camp. [8]And it came about, whenever Moses went out to the tent, that all the people would arise and stand, each at the entrance of his tent, and gaze after Moses until he entered the tent. [9]Whenever Moses entered the tent, the pillar of cloud would descend and stand at the entrance of the tent; and the LORD would speak

---

[1]R. Alan Cole, *Exodus: An Introduction and Commentary*, Tyndale Old Testament Commentaries (Downers Grove, Ill.: Inter-Varsity Press, 1973), 222.

with Moses. [10]When all the people saw the pillar of cloud standing at the entrance of the tent, all the people would arise and worship, each at the entrance of his tent. [11]Thus the LORD used to speak to Moses face to face, just as a man speaks to his friend. When Moses returned to the camp, his servant Joshua, the son of Nun, a young man, would not depart from the tent.

Verse 7. This section provides information about where and how **Moses** was to communicate with **the LORD**. He would receive revelations from God in **the tent of meeting** which he set up **outside the camp**—in fact, **a good distance from the camp**. Those who wanted to know God's will would go **outside the camp** and seek it at this tent.

"The tent of meeting" in this context should not be confused with the tabernacle that was later constructed—even though the tabernacle is frequently referred to by that designation elsewhere in the book (27:21; 28:43; 29:4; 30:16; 31:7; 35:21; 39:32; 40:2). This tent was pitched by Moses himself, but the tabernacle was too large a tent to be transported and set up by one individual. In addition, the Levites had a special responsibility for moving and setting up the tabernacle. While this tent was set up "outside the camp," the tabernacle was set up in the center of the camp (Num. 2:1, 2). Also, the purpose of this tent seems to differ from the purpose of the tabernacle. The Lord periodically met with Moses at this tent, whereas the tabernacle was to become a more permanent dwelling place. This tent functioned as a place of revelation, whereas the tabernacle primarily served as a place of sacrifice and worship.

Verse 8. The Israelites gave special honor to **Moses** when he **went out to the tent** to meet with God. Within the camp, **the people** would **arise and stand** and **gaze** at him **until he entered the tent**. In this way, they demonstrated their reverence and awe for the divine encounter.

Verses 9, 10. There, **the LORD** came down in **the pillar of cloud** and communicated His word to **Moses**. Earlier in Exodus, "the pillar of cloud" guided the Israelites through the wilderness and shielded them from the Egyptian army (13:21, 22; 14:19). At this point, it displayed God's visitation to the leader of His people. As God descended in **the pillar, the people** watched and **worship**[ed], each man standing **at the entrance of his** [own] **tent**.

Verse 11. During those days **the Lord** spoke **face to face** with **Moses**. This description portrays the close communication that Moses shared with God, in contrast to the rest of the Israelites. The Lord had spoken "face to face" with the Israelites at the base of Mount Sinai, but they begged Moses that God speak through him instead (Deut. 5:4, 23–27). The direct communication that God shared with Moses is contrasted to the revelation He gave to other prophets in dreams and visions: "'Not so, with My servant Moses, he is faithful in all My household; with him I speak mouth to mouth, even openly, and not in dark sayings, and he beholds the form of the Lord'" (Num. 12:7, 8; see Deut. 34:10).

The phrase **just as a man speaks to his friend** further portrays the close relationship between Moses and God. Other great men of faith such as Enoch and Noah are described as having "walked with God" (Gen. 5:22, 24; 6:9). Moreover, Abraham was called "the friend of God" (Jas. 2:23; see 2 Chron. 20:7; Is. 41:8).

Joshua took care of the tent when **Moses** was not there. John I. Durham pointed out that Joshua's presence at the tent should not be understood as "an intermediary function before Yahweh" in Moses' absence, but rather "his role in the Tent is probably that of a guard."[2] Joshua is described as Moses' **servant** and **a young man** (see 17:9–14; 24:13; 32:17).

How does the account of the "tent of meeting" in 33:7–11 relate to the surrounding context? There are at least two possibilities. One possibility is that the passage is parenthetical.[3] The text may be a record of something that happened on a continuing basis, but not necessarily immediately after the events just

---

[2]John I. Durham, *Exodus*, Word Biblical Commentary, vol. 3 (Waco, Tex.: Word Books, 1987), 443.

[3]W. H. Gispen noted that these verses may be parenthetical, referring "to something Moses did repeatedly (NIV)." However, he favored the view that they referred "to what Moses did after the events described in verses 1–6." (W. H. Gispen, *Exodus*, trans. Ed van der Maas, Bible Student's Commentary [Grand Rapids, Mich.: Regency Reference Library, Zondervan Publishing House, 1982], 305–7.)

recounted in 33:1–6. If so, the story pauses for this description of how the Lord communicated His will to Israel in the wilderness. Although God had, in the previous verses, threatened to withdraw His presence from Israel, that threat was never carried out. God was, in the days and months that followed, present in the tent of meeting. Moses met with Him there, and the people had the privilege of observing God's presence by seeing the cloud over the tent. The theme of this paragraph and the next, then, is the presence of God with His people.

If this interpretation of the passage is correct, perhaps it is best to see this "tent of meeting" as the place where Israel (specifically Moses) met with God until the tabernacle was completed,[4] several months after the golden calf incident. Then the tabernacle took over the functions that this temporary tent served.

Another possible way this account relates to the context is that Moses set up "his" tent "outside the camp" because the camp was polluted by the people's sin. The Septuagint, rather than referring to "the" tent, says "his," suggesting that what Moses set up outside the camp was his own tent.

God had withdrawn His presence from the camp because of the Israelites' sin. In that case, setting up this "tent of meeting" may have been Moses' wise and righteous maneuver to continue to maintain contact with God in spite of the people's guilt. Gispen explained,

> At this point Moses was the only one with whom the Lord had fellowship. By means of this tent, Moses wanted to attempt to get the Lord to go back on His resolve, and to continue to meet with him and through him with His people. This is an initiative worthy of a mediator! And thus this tent, while acknowledging the separation between the Lord and His people . . . is a visible prayer, based on the mourning of the people (vv. 4, 6). Pitching this tent only for himself and outside the camp are two

---

[4]Walter C. Kaiser, Jr., "Exodus," in *The Expositor's Bible Commentary*, vol. 2, *Genesis—Numbers* (Grand Rapids, Mich.: Zondervan, 1990), 483.

> proofs of Moses' acknowledgment of what the Lord had said (vv. 1–3, 5): the matter between the Lord and Israel had not yet been settled in Israel's favor.[5]

If this explanation is correct, then the completion and setting up of the tabernacle signaled the end of the pollution. The descent of God's glory upon the tabernacle (40:34, 35) proclaimed that God would once more be present with the people; no longer would they have to go "outside the camp" to meet with Him.

How God Would Manifest Himself (33:12–23)

[12]Then Moses said to the LORD, "See, You say to me, 'Bring up this people!' But You Yourself have not let me know whom You will send with me. Moreover, You have said, 'I have known you by name, and you have also found favor in My sight.' [13]Now therefore, I pray You, if I have found favor in Your sight, let me know Your ways that I may know You, so that I may find favor in Your sight. Consider too, that this nation is Your people." [14]And He said, "My presence shall go with you, and I will give you rest." [15]Then he said to Him, "If Your presence does not go with us, do not lead us up from here. [16]For how then can it be known that I have found favor in Your sight, I and Your people? Is it not by Your going with us, so that we, I and Your people, may be distinguished from all the other people who are upon the face of the earth?"

[17]The LORD said to Moses, "I will also do this thing of which you have spoken; for you have found favor in My sight and I have known you by name." [18]Then Moses said, "I pray You, show me Your glory!" [19]And He said, "I Myself will make all My goodness pass before you, and will proclaim the name of the LORD before you; and I will be gracious to whom I will be gracious, and will show compassion on whom I will show compassion." [20]But He said, "You cannot see My face, for no man can see Me and live!" [21]Then the LORD said, "Behold, there is a place by Me, and you shall stand there on the rock; [22]and it

---

[5]Gispen, 306.

will come about, while My glory is passing by, that I will put you in the cleft of the rock and cover you with My hand until I have passed by. [23]Then I will take My hand away and you shall see My back, but My face shall not be seen."

Following the discussion of the ornaments and the tent of meeting, the narrative resumes. Verse 12 continues the story left off at verse 3 with an extended dialogue between Moses and the Lord. Moses spoke three times (33:12, 13, 15, 16, 18), and the Lord answered him three times (33:14, 17, 19–23). If the Lord's words at the beginning of the chapter are counted (33:1–3), then the Lord spoke four times, beginning and ending the conversation.

Verses 12, 13. The Lord had told Moses, "Depart, go up from here . . . to the land of which I swore to Abraham, Isaac, and Jacob" (33:1). At this point, Moses replied by making several requests.

First, **Moses** requested by implication that someone go with him as he led the people to Canaan. His request sounds like a complaint. He said to God, **"You say to me, 'Bring up this people!' But You Yourself have not let me know whom You will send with me."** Probably, implied here was a request for God not to withdraw His presence from His people.

Second, Moses asked for a more intimate knowledge of God. He quoted God's words **"I have known you by name"** and then requested, **"Let me know Your ways that I may know You."** Moses said, in effect, "If that is how You feel about me, You should reveal Yourself more fully to me." He hoped that, as a result, he could be even more pleasing to God.

A third request may be implied in Moses' words: **"Consider too, that this nation is Your people."** Perhaps Moses was asking God to reconsider His threat not to be in the midst of the Israelites as they traveled to the promised land. Moses indirectly suggested two reasons: (1) Without God, Israel would be doomed, and (2) since the Israelites were God's people, He would not want to see them lost.

Verse 14. God's response was short and to the point: **"My presence shall go with you, and I will give you rest."** In other words, God was revoking the threat to withdraw His presence

(33:3). The Lord would be with Israel just as He had been with them since their deliverance from Egypt. Further, He would bring them to the land where they were going and there would give them "rest." This term refers to an inheritance in the land, as well as security from their enemies (Deut. 12:10; 25:19; Josh. 11:23; 21:44).

Verse 15. Moses affirmed God's statement. Without the Lord's **presence**, Israel might as well stay where they were—or even have stayed in Egypt. Without God's direction, wisdom, and protection, Israel could not succeed (see Ps. 124).

Verse 16. However, Moses perceived another need: the evidence of God's presence. He reasoned that the only way for others to know that he and the people were still in God's **favor** was by His **going with** them. His presence, in fact, would distinguish Israel **from all the other people who are upon the face of the earth.** This striking statement affirms the unique status of Israel under the Law. Moses wanted not only for God to assure him and Israel of their special standing in God's sight, but also to provide irrefutable evidence of that standing.

Verse 17. God indicated His willingness to provide proof of Moses and Israel's special status because Moses had **found favor in** [His] **sight and** [He had] **known** [Moses] **by name**. According to the NASB, this verse begins a new paragraph. However, the thought in verse 17 follows so closely what was said in verse 16 that other versions (REB; NAB; NJB) end the paragraph with verse 17. The NIV probably best represents the conversational form of the text by starting a new paragraph with each new speaker.

Verse 18. The dialogue in this section moves quickly from one speaker to another, each speech building on what had been said before. The scene reaches a climax in this verse, where **Moses** specified what he wanted as evidence: **"Show me Your glory!"** If Moses could see God's glory, then he would have a more intimate knowledge of God. He would also have assurance that God would go with him, that Israel would survive, and that all would know of his (and Israel's) special status in God's eyes. This request bordered on the presumptuous.

Verse 19. God graciously agreed to do what Moses had asked.

The Lord said that **He** would **make all** [His] **goodness pass before** Moses. He added that He would **proclaim the name of the LORD before** Moses. To "proclaim the name of the LORD" meant not merely to pronounce His name, but to describe His person; the revelation of His name is the revelation of His nature. In the Old Testament, a person's "name" was synonymous with the person. Therefore, "the name of the LORD" was equivalent to "the Lord."

Next, Moses was given a preview of what proclaiming His name meant: It would include a statement that the Lord would **be gracious** and would **show compassion** to all those to whom He decided to show compassion (see Rom. 9:15). When the Lord revealed Himself to Moses in 34:6, 7, He proclaimed His nature more fully, specifically declaring Himself to be "compassionate" and "gracious."

Verse 20. One obstacle remained in the way of Moses' receiving the wonderful revelation God had in mind for him. God said, **"You cannot see My face, for no man can see Me and live!"** There is no contradiction between this statement and verse 11, where the text says that God spoke with Moses "face to face, just as a man speaks to his friend." Verse 11 means that God communicated more freely with Moses than with any other man; it does not suggest that Moses actually "saw" God as He is. Interestingly, those who are said to have seen God saw only something related to God: Moses saw His back but not His face (33:23); the elders of Israel saw the pavement under His feet (24:10); Isaiah saw "the train of His robe filling the temple" (Is. 6:1).

Verses 21–23. If God is so holy that no man can see Him and live, then how could He do what Moses had asked? **The LORD** provided the solution: He would place Moses in a **cleft** [or opening] **of the rock** and would **cover** him with His **hand** as He **passed by**. Then God would **take** [His] **hand away** after He had passed by, so that Moses could see His **back** but not His **face**. Cole wrote, "In vivid pictorial language, the passage says that man may see only where God has passed by (verses 22, 23) and so know Him by His past doings and acts."[6]

---

[6]Cole, 225.

Obviously, God was speaking in anthropomorphic terms. No being in a human form could cover Moses with his hand and pass by at the same time. Nevertheless, Moses was privileged to see God in a close, personal way, as probably no human being since Adam and Eve had seen Him. Moses' close association with the Lord after God appeared to him and renewed the covenant changed Moses' physical appearance: "The skin of his face shone because of his speaking with Him" (34:29).

APPLICATION

God's Absence and Israel's Anxiety (Ch. 33)

Exodus 33 tells a suspenseful story. Israel had sinned by making an idol and worshiping it. God changed His mind about destroying the people, but He did punish them (ch. 32). Israel's future remained uncertain. Their destiny depended on the answers to three questions.

Will Israel still be allowed to enter the promised land? From the time God first made plans to deliver Israel, He intended to bring them into the land which He had promised to the patriarchs. Not only was He delivering them *from* Egypt, but He was also delivering them *to* the promised land. The Israelites, by their sin, had broken the covenant and forfeited their right to Canaan. Would God forgive the nation and allow them to enter the land?

In spite of their rebellion, God told Moses that He would still allow the Israelites to enter the land (33:1–3). He would send "an angel" to go before them, and He would drive out the inhabitants of the land.

Will God be with Israel on the way? At the same time that God promised to bring Israel into the land, He also said He would not be in their midst (33:3). His absence would, in a sense, be for their good: "I will not go up in your midst, because . . . I might destroy you on the way." Because of their sinfulness, if God were among them, He would be obligated to destroy them. Therefore, for their safety, He would not continue to be "in [their] midst."

These were alarming words to the Israelites. They "went into mourning, and none of them put on his ornaments" (33:4). Moses implored God to be with him and the people. He wanted to know whom God would send with him. He wanted to know God's ways and find favor in God's sight. Moses let God know that he longed for His presence. He asked God to continue to be with His people (33:12, 13).

God said that His presence would go with Israel (33:14). Moses answered, "If Your presence does not go with us, do not lead us up from here" (33:15). Moses was saying, "If You are not going with us, then it would be better for us not to go!" Moses made it clear that our first priority is being with God and having Him with us.

Is that not a powerful statement of the need for God? We sing, "Anywhere with Jesus I can safely go."[7] If Moses lived today, he might say, "Anywhere *without* the Lord, I will *not* go." We can apply that thought by saying, "If Jesus cannot go with me on this trip [or to this activity], then I will not go." His presence is crucial.

How can Israel know that God will be with them? Moses asked that the Lord, as a sign of His agreement to go with the people, allow him to see God's glory (33:18). God replied favorably to Moses' audacious request, saying, "I . . . will proclaim the name of the LORD before you." Although He could not allow Moses to see His face, He agreed to show Moses His back (33:19–23). God indeed gave Moses evidence of His presence.

As Christians go through life, we may wonder, "How can we know that God is with us?" God does not appear to us as He did to Moses. Nevertheless, He gives us abundant evidence of His presence. We have the evidence of the created world and the evidence of answered prayer. We have evidence of His providence working in our lives. We have the Word of God, the Bible, in which He said, "I will never desert you, nor will I ever forsake you" (Heb. 13:5). God is always faithful (1 Cor. 10:13), and He always keeps His promises.

We can remember, from when we were very young, how important it was for our parents to be near. When a parent left

---

[7]Jessie Brown Pounds, "Anywhere with Jesus," *Songs of Faith and Praise,* comp. and ed. Alton H. Howard (West Monroe, La.: Howard Publishing Co., 1994).

the room, we experienced "separation anxiety" until that parent returned. As children of God, we ought to experience "separation anxiety" when we are separated from the Lord by sin (Is. 59:1, 2). If that has happened to us, we must take steps to close the distance between us and the Lord. We can come home, as the prodigal did in Luke 15, and God will run to meet us.

Man's Greatest Desire and Greatest Need:
To Know God and To Be Known by God (33:12–17)

Human beings have always desired to know God, yet even those who attempt to get in touch with the supernatural realm often reject the one true God. This passage focuses on knowing God. (1) God knows man (33:12, 17). (2) Man needs to know God (33:13). When one can say he knows God's ways, then he knows God; when he knows God, then he can "find favor" in God's sight. (3) God makes it possible for man to know Him (33:13, 17). (4) When people "know" God, they have a relationship with Him that makes it obvious that they are known by Him; they become His people, "distinguished from all the other people" (33:16). When God's people know God and are known by God, they are obviously different from the world about them.

Hidden in the "Cleft of the Rock" (33:22)

God hid Moses in the "cleft of the rock" while He passed by so that Moses would not see His face, for no human can see God's face and live (33:20). Augustus M. Toplady, the author of "Rock of Ages," had this passage in mind when he penned the words to that song:

> Rock of Ages, cleft for me,
> Let me hide myself in Thee;
> Let the water and the blood,
> From Thy wounded side which flowed,
> Be of sin the double cure,
> Save from wrath and make me pure.[8]

---

[8]Augustus M. Toplady, "Rock of Ages," as quoted in Robert J. Morgan, *Then Sings My Soul* (Nashville: Thomas Nelson Publishers, 2003), 75.

The Christian's "Rock of Ages" is Christ. God is referred to as a "rock" in numerous passages in the Old Testament (see Ps. 18:2; 19:14; 28:1; 31:3; 42:9). In 1 Corinthians 10:4, Christ is referred to as the "spiritual rock" which followed the Israelites in the wilderness. In His death, Christ shed His blood to protect us from the wrath of God. Otherwise, we would be destroyed—justly—because of our sins.

Chapter 34

Restoration: God's Renewal of the Covenant

Chapter 34 concludes the account of Israel's restoration after their apostasy. God called Moses to come up on the mountain, where He would again write out the Ten Commandments on two stone tablets (34:1–4). God proclaimed Himself to be a gracious God who also punishes the guilty (34:5–7). Moses asked God to forgive the people (34:8, 9), and God said that He would make a covenant with Israel and drive out the nations of Canaan before them (34:10, 11). They were to make no covenant with those idolatrous nations (34:12–17).

God repeated some of the laws and statutes He had already given to Moses, emphasizing regulations for worship (34:18–26). Moses wrote down God's words while he was on the mountain for forty days and forty nights (34:27, 28). As he descended from the mountain, his face shone from being in the presence of God (34:29, 30, 33–35). He then recounted the words of the Law to the people (34:31, 32).

After Israel's sin, an act of reconciliation with God was needed. Chapter 34 describes a virtual reenactment of the covenant ratification ceremony recorded in chapter 24. Both covenant ratification ceremonies were preceded by Moses' making a trip up the mountain and God's appearance to him there. Both times, God gave Moses a series of laws, and those laws were written down and then presented to the people. The major difference between the two covenant ratification ceremonies is that the latter one lacked any statement that the Israelites pledged themselves to obey the Law. Perhaps their public acceptance of the commands in 34:32 is to be understood.

Liberal scholars who are committed to the belief that the Pentateuch was derived from different sources believe that chapters 24 and 34 are two accounts of the same event. However, the text makes better sense if the similarities are understood as the result of a purposeful and meaningful reenactment of the original event. The similarities leave no doubt that, though Israel flagrantly violated the covenant, God had forgiven them by renewing the covenant.

GOD'S WILLINGNESS TO RENEW THE COVENANT (34:1–4)

1Now the LORD said to Moses, "Cut out for yourself two stone tablets like the former ones, and I will write on the tablets the words that were on the former tablets which you shattered. 2So be ready by morning, and come up in the morning to Mount Sinai, and present yourself there to Me on the top of the mountain. 3No man is to come up with you, nor let any man be seen anywhere on the mountain; even the flocks and the herds may not graze in front of that mountain." 4So he cut out two stone tablets like the former ones, and Moses rose up early in the morning and went up to Mount Sinai, as the LORD had commanded him, and he took two stone tablets in his hand.

The covenant renewal began with Moses' being summoned up the mountain. His stay on the mountain had two purposes. (1) God responded to Moses' request to see His glory (33:18), which had been prompted by God's threat to withdraw His presence from Israel (33:3). This was a means of assuring Moses and Israel of their special status before Him (33:16). (2) God reaffirmed the Law and the covenant which had been broken by Israel when they had worshiped the golden calf (32:1–10).

Verse 1. What **Moses** received was not a new set of laws. Instead, God was renewing the covenant He had made with the people earlier. **The words that were on the former tablets** refers to the Ten Commandments that God had previously given to Israel (34:28; Deut. 4:13; 5:22; 10:4). The fact that the former tablets had been **shattered** by Moses symbolically illustrated that the Israelites had broken the covenant that the Lord had made with them (32:19).

Verses 2, 3. God's instructions to Moses included the time (**morning**) and the place (the **top** of **Mount Sinai**) where they would meet. God told Moses to make sure that the people and animals stayed away from the **mountain**, just as He had warned before giving the Law the first time (19:12, 13). God would be present on the mountain while Moses was there, which made the ensuing experience even more spectacular.

Verse 4. Moses did as God had commanded, **cut**[ting] **out two stone tablets** and taking them with him when he went up on the mountain the next **morning**.

GOD'S NAME AND NATURE PROCLAIMED (34:5–9)

5The Lord descended in the cloud and stood there with him as he called upon the name of the Lord. 6Then the Lord passed by in front of him and proclaimed, "The Lord, the Lord God, compassionate and gracious, slow to anger, and abounding in lovingkindness and truth; 7who keeps lovingkindness for thousands, who forgives iniquity, transgression and sin; yet He will by no means leave the guilty unpunished, visiting the iniquity of fathers on the children and on the grandchildren to the third and fourth generations." 8Moses made haste to bow low toward the earth and worship. 9He said, "If now I have found favor in Your sight, O Lord, I pray, let the Lord go along in our midst, even though the people are so obstinate, and pardon our iniquity and our sin, and take us as Your own possession."

Verse 5. On the mountain, Moses **called upon the name of the Lord**; he prayed and worshiped God. God responded by coming down **in the cloud**, which was the sign of His presence. Moreover, God **stood there with him**.

Verse 6. What happened next was a climactic event anticipated since God's announcement that He would not go with Israel (33:3): **The Lord passed by in front of** Moses. This revelation of God was a momentous occasion as He condescended to make Himself known to Moses. From that time forward Moses was marked as one who had seen God. Evidence of that experience was visible in his face, according to 34:29–35.

God not only appeared to Moses, but He also "proclaimed" His name and His nature (33:19). He stated that His personal name is **the Lord** ("Yahweh"). This name represents God, with all of His divine characteristics. Next, with repetition, He affirmed that He is **the Lord God.** Israel had a powerful Deity, the one true God, whose name is "Yahweh."

God went on to describe His nature by listing five attributes.[1] (1) He is **compassionate** or "merciful" (KJV), a "God of tenderness" (NJB). He deeply cares for His people as a father cares for his children. (2) He is **gracious**, showing favor to those who are undeserving. (3) He is **slow to anger**, that is, "longsuffering" (KJV) and "patient" (CEV). (4) He is **abounding in lovingkindness** or "faithful love" (NJB). (5) He is also abounding in **truth** or "faithfulness" (NIV). God remains true to His covenant when His people have disappointed and even deserted Him.

Verse 7. God also **keeps lovingkindness for thousands** (see 20:6) and **forgives iniquity, transgression and sin**. His practice of showing lovingkindness to thousands expresses the broad scope of His love, especially of the mercy He extended to those who were in a covenant relationship with Him. The news that God forgives must have brought great comfort to Moses and Israel, for the people had committed grievous sins and needed much forgiveness (32:30–32). The depth of God's mercy is emphasized by the use of three terms for disobedience: "iniquity," "transgression," and "sin."

At the same time, God is just as well as merciful: **He will by no means leave the guilty unpunished, visiting the iniquity of fathers on the children and on the grandchildren to the third and fourth generations** (see comments on 20:5). His justice demands that He punish the "guilty."

Verse 8. After God's revelation of Himself to Moses, Moses fell down and **worship**[ed] the Lord. The appropriate response

---

[1]God's self-disclosure on this occasion became a kind of creedal statement in Israel (Num. 14:18; Neh. 9:17; Ps. 86:15; Jon. 4:2).

to an encounter with the true and living God is (1) humility, brought on by a sense of one's sinfulness and unworthiness in comparison to Him, and (2) worship, acknowledging His great power and goodness with praise.

Verse 9. Moses asked again for God's presence and **pardon**. He requested that **the Lord** (אֲדֹנָי, *'Adonay*) remain in the **midst** of **the people** of Israel as they traveled on to Canaan, something which God had earlier said He did not intend to do (33:3). Moses did not deny or excuse Israel's sinfulness, but rather he confessed that they were **obstinate** or "stiff-necked" (see comments on 32:9). Moses then begged for God's forgiveness, and asked that He renew His covenant with them and take them back as His **own possession** (see 19:5).

THE COVENANT RENEWED (34:10)

10Then God said, "Behold, I am going to make a covenant. Before all your people I will perform miracles which have not been produced in all the earth nor among any of the nations; and all the people among whom you live will see the working of the LORD, for it is a fearful thing that I am going to perform with you."

Verse 10. God agreed to Moses' request, saying that He would **make a covenant**. The covenant enunciated here can be seen as an elaboration on the covenant God had made with Israel earlier (19:5, 6; see Deut. 9; 10). R. Alan Cole noted, "This 'renewal' aspect may account for much repetition of thought, if not words (e.g. in the revelation of God, in verses 5–7, and the terms of the covenant, in verses 12–25)."[2]

God explained what being His special **people** meant: Because the Israelites belonged to Him, He would **perform** for them spectacular **miracles which have not been produced in all the earth nor among any of the nations**. Precisely what God meant when He spoke of these "miracles" or "wonders" (NIV) is unclear.

---

[2]R. Alan Cole, *Exodus: An Introduction and Commentary*, Tyndale Old Testament Commentaries (Downers Grove, Ill.: Inter-Varsity Press, 1973), 226.

Israel had already witnessed miracles in the wilderness, but others were yet to come. Perhaps God was predicting the miracles connected with the conquest of Canaan. The nations had never before witnessed anything like Israel's crossing of the Jordan River on dry ground or God's demolition of the walls of Jericho (Josh. 3; 6). His actions on Israel's behalf would be **a fearful thing**, that is, "an awesome thing" (NRSV). The nations were to experience wholesale destruction meted out by God—sometimes by miraculous means.[3]

THE LAW REISSUED (34:11–26)

God's Warning Against a Covenant With Any Nation (34:11–17)

[11]"Be sure to observe what I am commanding you this day: behold, I am going to drive out the Amorite before you, and the Canaanite, the Hittite, the Perizzite, the Hivite and the Jebusite. [12]Watch yourself that you make no covenant with the inhabitants of the land into which you are going, or it will become a snare in your midst. [13]But rather, you are to tear down their altars and smash their sacred pillars and cut down their Asherim [14]—for you shall not worship any other god, for the LORD, whose name is Jealous, is a jealous God— [15]otherwise you might make a covenant with the inhabitants of the land and they would play the harlot with their gods and sacrifice to their gods, and someone might invite you to eat of his sacrifice, [16]and you might take some of his daughters for your sons, and his daughters might play the harlot with their gods and cause your sons also to play the harlot with their gods. [17]You shall make for yourself no molten gods."

Verses 11, 12. While God assured Israel that He would fulfill His part of the covenant, He also told them how to meet their

---

[3]Cole, giving a somewhat different view, wrote, "Here the nature of the 'marvel' in question is explained as the expulsion of the Canaanites and the gift of the land of Canaan to Israel." (Ibid., 229.)

obligations. The covenant they were renewing with the Lord was exclusive. They were not allowed to enter into a **covenant** relationship with the peoples of **the land** to which they were traveling, whether **Amorite, Canaanite, Hittite, Perizzite, Hivite**, or **Jebusite** (see 3:8, 17; 13:5; 23:23; 33:2). Why? Because it was God's intention to "completely destroy" these peoples (23:23) and **drive** [them] **out** of the promised land. Moreover, such a covenant would **become a snare** for God's people, leading them to sin and destruction (see comments on 10:7; 23:33).

Verse 13. In order to ensure that the Israelites did not make a covenant with the Canaanite nations, they were to **tear down their altars** which were used to sacrifice to their gods. Further, the Israelites were to **smash their sacred pillars and cut down their Asherim** (see comments on 23:24). "Asherim" is the plural form of "Asherah," evidently "a carved pole resembling the goddess [by that name] or her sacred tree"; such an item was "apparently made of wood (Judg 6:25–26; 1 Kgs 15:13) and stood beside an altar."[4]

Verse 14. This requirement was based on the first two of the Ten Commandments: **You shall not worship any other god** (see 20:3) and "You shall make for yourself no molten gods" (34:17; see 20:4). God described Himself as **jealous** in the sense that He would not permit anyone or anything to be His rival in Israel's life. The people would be condemned if they worshiped other gods (see comments on 20:5).

Verses 15, 16. Making **covenant**[s] with the people of **the land** might lead Israel to **sacrifice to their gods**, to **eat of . . . sacrifice**[s] offered to idols. Intermarriage with these nations would cause Israel to **play the harlot with their gods**. This expression refers primarily to the spiritual adultery of forsaking the Lord, Israel's true "husband," and going after "lovers," or false gods (Ezek. 16; Hos. 2). However, sexual activities were often part of the religious ceremonies of the notoriously promiscuous pagan peoples.

Israel's need for this warning is evident from the nation's later history. Israel frequently, in spite of the teaching of the Law

---

[4]Ibid., 230.

and warnings by the prophets, made alliances with other peoples that led to disastrous consequences. One example of what God was warning against is found in Numbers 25:1–3. Later, the text indicates that sexual immorality was involved in the sin of Israel on that occasion (Num. 25:6–8).

Verse 17. The paragraph ends with this command: **"You shall make for yourself no molten gods."** Verses 14 through 17 evidence a chiastic (ABBA) pattern:

A1: "You shall not worship any other god" (34:14).
- B1: "You might make a covenant with the inhabitants of the land and they would play the harlot with their gods and sacrifice to their gods, and someone might invite you to eat of his sacrifice" (34:15).
- B2: "You might take some of his daughters for your sons, and his daughters might play the harlot with their gods and cause your sons also to play the harlot with their gods" (34:16).

A2: "You shall make for yourself no molten gods" (34:17).

Verse 17 parallels verse 14; taken together, these verses forbid the production and worship of idols. Verse 17 is worded slightly differently than the second commandment (20:4). It forbids "molten gods" instead of "graven images." In this way, the command speaks specifically against the sin which made the renewal of the covenant necessary—namely, the worship of a "molten calf" (32:4; see 20:23).

God's Emphasis on Israel's Responsibilities In Worship (34:18–26)

18"You shall observe the Feast of Unleavened Bread. For seven days you are to eat unleavened bread, as I commanded you, at the appointed time in the month of Abib, for in the month of Abib you came out of Egypt.

19"The first offspring from every womb belongs to Me, and all your male livestock, the first offspring from cattle and sheep.
20You shall redeem with a lamb the first offspring from a don-

key; and if you do not redeem it, then you shall break its neck. You shall redeem all the firstborn of your sons. None shall appear before Me empty-handed.

21"You shall work six days, but on the seventh day you shall rest; even during plowing time and harvest you shall rest. 22You shall celebrate the Feast of Weeks, that is, the first fruits of the wheat harvest, and the Feast of Ingathering at the turn of the year. 23Three times a year all your males are to appear before the Lord GOD, the God of Israel. 24For I will drive out nations before you and enlarge your borders, and no man shall covet your land when you go up three times a year to appear before the LORD your God.

25"You shall not offer the blood of My sacrifice with leavened bread, nor is the sacrifice of the Feast of the Passover to be left over until morning.

26"You shall bring the very first of the first fruits of your soil into the house of the LORD your God.

"You shall not boil a young goat in its mother's milk."

The text moves from Israel's obligation regarding the people and the gods of Canaan (34:11–17) to general statutes related to the worship of the Lord (34:18–26). This section repeats laws which were given (1) in a listing of ordinances from God (23:12–19) and (2) in the description concerning the firstborn at the time of the exodus (13:12, 13). The emphasis in these statutes is on the feasts and special days that the Israelites were commanded to observe, and on what the Israelites were required to give to the Lord.

Why are these ordinances included here? The most likely answer to this question is that the laws regarding worship and sacrifice were especially appropriate after Israel's rejection of God in favor of a golden idol. Israel's problem was perverted worship. These laws presented a picture of true worship as God would have it. Following the directions given here would keep Israel from repeating the mistake they made when they bowed down to the "molten calf."

Verse 18. The first law required Israel to **observe the Feast of Unleavened Bread**, a feast observed in connection with the

Passover (see 13:3–10; 23:15). Participants ate unleavened bread to commemorate Israel's hurried exit from Egypt, when the dough was without yeast because they "did not have time to prepare food for themselves" (12:39; NIV). The feast was timed to correlate with the first anniversary of Israel's deliverance from Egyptian bondage.

Verses 19, 20. In connection with the Feast of Unleavened Bread, the people were commanded to give the **first**[born] of their families and their animals to the Lord (see 13:1, 2, 11–15). Since **a donkey** was unclean and could not be offered as a sacrifice, it could be **redeem**[ed] **with a lamb**, or else it was to be killed (see 13:13). The owner of the donkey was not allowed to profit from the firstborn of his domestic animals at the Lord's expense. The firstborn **sons** were also to be **redeem**[ed]; money was to be given to the Lord as a substitute for sacrificing the firstborn sons to God. At first glance, the command **"None shall appear before Me empty-handed"** seems to indicate that the Feast of Unleavened Bread was the time of the year when the firstborn were presented to God. Another possible interpretation is that the expression refers to Israel's offering the first fruits of the barley harvest (see comments on 23:15; see Deut. 16:16, 17).

Verse 21. Next, the Lord reiterated the Sabbath commandment, stressing that the Israelites were to **rest** on **the seventh day** (see 23:12). For a farmer to postpone his work when his crop was ripe for **harvest** would require a great deal of faith. Cole commented that "to keep the sabbath was a test of faith in God's provision (Ex. 16:29)."[5]

Verse 22. Then the Lord repeated the commandment to observe the other two major feasts of Israel's religious calendar—**the Feast of Weeks** or "Pentecost," and **the Feast of Ingathering** or "Tabernacles" (see 23:16). The time for observing each feast is given. The Feast of Unleavened Bread was "in the month of Abib," when Israel had been delivered from Egypt (34:18). The Feast of Weeks occurred at the time of **the wheat harvest**. The name "Feast of Weeks" suggests that it happened forty-nine days (a week of weeks, 7 x 7) after the Feast of Unleavened Bread.

---

[5]Ibid., 231.

This is the average duration of harvest time. The Feast of Ingathering was observed **at the turn of the year**, meaning at the end of the agricultural calendar. If Israel had no other calendar, these few words would be enough to allow them to keep the feasts at the proper time.

Verses 23, 24. Israel's **males** were again commanded **to appear before the Lord God** at the **three** feasts (see 23:17). The place where the people would come before Him on these occasions is not specified here. Later, God said that He would choose a place for offerings to be made (Deut. 12:5–14). Prior to the monarchy, sacrifices were to be offered wherever the tabernacle and ark of the covenant were located. Ultimately, the place that God chose was Jerusalem where Solomon built a more permanent temple as God's dwelling place.

When the Israelites went to worship God together at a feast, they would not have to worry about their land being taken over by its previous inhabitants, for God would **drive out** [the] **nations** and **enlarge** [Israel's] **borders**. He said that **no man** would **covet** [their] **land** when they went up **to appear before the Lord**. Instead of the previous inhabitants, a less likely suggestion is that "no man" refers to Israelite neighbors who were less spiritual and did not attend the feast. These might be tempted to move the boundary stone (Deut. 19:14) of a more spiritual neighbor who had gone to worship God.[6]

Verse 25. Other individual ordinances were given in regard to sacrifices and offerings. (1) **Leavened bread** was **not** to be **offer**[ed] alongside an animal **sacrifice**. (2) The lamb slain on **Passover** night was to be eaten completely at the feast. Any part not eaten was to be burned; none was to be **left over until morning** (see comments on 23:18).

Verse 26. The **first fruits**—not only of the animals and the people, but also of the crops—were to be offered to God; they were to be brought **into the house of the Lord**. This ordinance anticipated the completion of the tabernacle, and later the temple (see 23:19).

The last requirement in the list, **"You shall not boil a young**

---

[6]Ibid.

goat in its mother's milk" must relate in some way to worship or sacrifice. No doubt, it was intended to keep Israel from engaging in a pagan ritual (see comments on 23:19). This law concludes the sampling of laws on worship repeated in chapter 34.

The regulations recorded in 34:18–26 are only a sampling of the laws which were given to Moses during his second forty-day stay on the mountain. These were of special interest to Moses and to those who first read the book (or heard it read) because they related to the kind of activity in which the Israelites had been sinfully engaging. Through these laws, the Lord was reemphasizing how His people were to worship Him acceptably.

Liberal scholars tend to view the laws found in this chapter (either 34:10–26; 34:14–26; or 34:17–26) as a "ritual decalogue" that stands in contrast to the "ethical decalogue" found in 20:1–17.[7] This view usually accompanies the idea that the covenant-making narrative of chapter 34 is an alternative account of that found in chapters 20 through 24.

While there is no doubt that the laws found in chapter 34 deal primarily with ritual, they do not appear to be a set of laws which could be seen as an alternative to the Ten Commandments. In fact, only by unlikely manipulation can the "ritual laws" found in this passage be forced into anything resembling a decalogue—a set of ten commandments. Consequently, it is best to interpret the laws in this chapter as representative of the total body of laws given by God on Mount Sinai. These particular laws are recorded at this point in the book because of their relevance to Israel's situation.

THE TEN COMMANDMENTS GIVEN A SECOND TIME (34:27, 28)

27Then the LORD said to Moses, "Write down these words, for in accordance with these words I have made a covenant with you and with Israel." 28So he was there with the LORD forty

[7]For example, see J. Philip Hyatt, *Exodus*, The New Century Bible Commentary (Grand Rapids, Mich.: Wm. B. Eerdmans Publishing Co., 1971), 319–22.

days and forty nights; he did not eat bread or drink water. And he wrote on the tablets the words of the covenant, the Ten Commandments.

Verse 27. The Law was given by **the LORD**; it was He who declared it orally (34:10). In addition, God instructed **Moses** to **write** [it] **down** in order to teach and guide **Israel** in the future. It was by **these words** that He had renewed the **covenant** with His people.

Verse 28. Moses spent **forty days and forty nights** on the mountain receiving the Law from God and writing it down (see Deut. 10:10). During that time he fasted; **he did not eat bread or drink water.**[8] Moses was demonstrating Israel's repentance as their mediator with God. Deuteronomy 9:18 records,

> "I fell down before the LORD, as at the first [Deut. 9:9], forty days and nights; I neither ate bread nor drank water, because of all your sin which you had committed in doing what was evil in the sight of the LORD to provoke Him to anger."

There is much debate about the latter part of verse 28: **And he wrote on the tablets the words of the covenant, the Ten Commandments.** The natural antecedent of "he" would be Moses, who is the subject of the previous lines. The NASB favors this position by not capitalizing the pronoun. However, at the beginning of the chapter, God said that He would "write on the tablets the words that were on the former tablets" (34:1). Cole argued that, to the narrator, "the two statements meant the same thing; they were alternative ways of describing the same pattern of events."[9] According to Old Testament theology, whatever happened, God was responsible for its occurrence.

Another possibility, suggested by John I. Durham, is that the

---

[8]In this respect, as in others, Jesus was like Moses. In the wilderness, before Jesus was tempted by Satan, He fasted forty days and forty nights (Mt. 4:2).

[9]Cole, 227.

final sentence of the paragraph has God as its subject.[10] In this case, God wrote the Ten Commandments on the two tablets (just as He had said in 34:1), and Moses wrote the rest of the laws and statutes on other material (just as he did in 24:4). This interpretation is supported by the parallel passage in Deuteronomy 10:4, where Moses speaks of God: "He wrote on the tablets, like the former writing, the Ten Commandments which the LORD had spoken to you on the mountain from the midst of the fire on the day of the assembly; and the LORD gave them to me."

THE LORD'S GRANDEUR DISPLAYED (34:29–35)

29It came about when Moses was coming down from Mount Sinai (and the two tablets of the testimony were in Moses' hand as he was coming down from the mountain), that Moses did not know that the skin of his face shone because of his speaking with Him. 30So when Aaron and all the sons of Israel saw Moses, behold, the skin of his face shone, and they were afraid to come near him. 31Then Moses called to them, and Aaron and all the rulers in the congregation returned to him; and Moses spoke to them. 32Afterward all the sons of Israel came near, and he commanded them to do everything that the LORD had spoken to him on Mount Sinai. 33When Moses had finished speaking with them, he put a veil over his face. 34But whenever Moses went in before the LORD to speak with Him, he would take off the veil until he came out; and whenever he came out and spoke to the sons of Israel what he had been commanded, 35the sons of Israel would see the face of Moses, that the skin of Moses' face shone. So Moses would replace the veil over his face until he went in to speak with Him.

Verse 29. When **Moses** came back **down from the mountain** with **the two tablets**, he was unaware that His encounter with

---

[10]John I. Durham, *Exodus*, Word Biblical Commentary, vol. 3 (Waco, Tex.: Word Books, 1987), 462–63.

God had caused **the skin of his face** to shine.[11] The light which shone from Moses' face must be seen as the reflected glory of the Lord, a result of having been in His presence (2 Cor. 3:7).

Verse 30. Israel reacted to the sight of **Moses** with fear. Just as the people had been **afraid** when God spoke from the mountain (20:18, 19), they were also afraid when God's representative came near to them. God's holy presence is dangerous; those who approached God or the things of God uninvited were likely to be struck dead. In this instance the people were safe. Moses' changed appearance provided assurance that he had been with God and that God had spoken through **him**, but it posed no threat to the nation.

Verses 31, 32. Therefore, **Moses called to them, and Aaron and all the rulers . . . returned to him.** Then **Moses spoke to them**. Apparently, Moses did no more than calm their fears. Perhaps he related to them his experiences and set a time for the reading of the Law.

Later, **all the sons of Israel came near, and** [Moses] **commanded them to do everything that the LORD had spoken to him on Mount Sinai**. On this occasion, Moses must have read or recited to the people the laws which God had given him for Israel, just as he had done at the covenant ratification ceremony (24:3, 7). While the text does not say that the people again pledged themselves to keep the Law, they probably did, given the precedent of the earlier event.

Verse 33. The final verses of the chapter deal with God's ongoing revelations to Moses. They indicate that Moses' shining **face** was a continuing condition rather than a temporary one. His face, in fact, was so bright as to be distracting during the conduct of daily affairs; consequently, when he was not acting as God's spokesman, his face was covered with **a veil**.

Verses 34, 35. When **Moses** received a message from God, **he would take off the veil**. At this time, these revelations pre-

---

[11]Jesus' face also shone when He was transfigured on a mountain (Mt. 17:2). This event may suggest that Jesus, as God's spokesman "in these last days" (Heb. 1:1, 2), is "the mediator of a [new and] better covenant" (Heb. 8:6).

sumably took place in the tent of meeting (33:7–11). When Moses came out and transmitted God's word to the people, they would see **that the skin of Moses' face shone**. This emphasized to them that his words were from God.[12] The rest of the time, it was necessary for Moses to wear his **veil**.

APPLICATION

After Restoration, What Then? (Ch. 34)

Individual Christians, like Simon the Sorcerer, sometimes need to be restored (Acts 8:18–24; Gal. 6:1; Jas. 5:20). The letters to the seven churches of Asia suggest that sometimes an entire congregation must be restored (Rev. 2:5). What does restoration involve? Obviously, those who have fallen away must recognize their sinfulness and repent (Acts 8:22; Rev. 2:5), and God forgives them. Then what? How can the restored person avoid falling again? The answer is renewal.

Exodus illustrates this principle. In chapters 32 and 33, the Israelites sinned and were forgiven. Before they could continue their journey to the promised land, they needed renewal, rededication, and revival! That is exactly what Christians must have to be restored.

A renewal of our vision of God. Israel already knew God; the people had experienced His presence. Now they needed to renew their understanding of and faith in Him. To meet that need, God allowed Moses to see Him (34:1–9; see 33:18–23). More important, God described Himself to Moses and Israel. Exodus 34:6, 7 depicts Him as a God of love: "compassionate and gracious, slow to anger, and abounding in lovingkindness and truth; who keeps lovingkindness for thousands." As a loving God, He "forgives iniquity, transgression and sin." He is also a God who punishes sin: "He will by no means leave the guilty unpunished, visiting the iniquity of fathers on the children and on the grandchildren to the third and fourth generations." God is not only a loving

---

[12]Paul used the veil over Moses' face to illustrate how some people reject the gospel because they fail to see that the old covenant is removed in Christ (2 Cor. 3:12–18).

God, but He is also a God of wrath. He punishes unrepentant sinners (see Rom. 11:22). At this point in their history, Israel had to learn about these characteristics of God.

In order for us to be restored, we must see God as He is: compassionate and forgiving, but also stern and wrathful. How He will deal with us depends on whether or not we are willing to repent. Once restored, we must remember that the loving God who willingly forgave our sin will condemn us if we go back into the world.

A renewal of our covenant with God. Israel's original experience in Exodus involved their coming to know God—through Moses, the plagues, the deliverance through the sea, their wilderness journey, and their experiences at Sinai. Then they made a covenant with God, pledging to obey Him (ch. 19). After committing their great sin (ch. 32), they renewed their covenant with Him.

Much that is recorded in Exodus 34 is reminiscent of Israel's prior experiences. God revealed Himself to Moses, as before, and the Law was written on two new tablets. When Moses asked God to take the nation for His "own possession" (34:9), he used the same words that God had used in 19:5. The Ten Commandments are mentioned in verse 28. Again, Moses delivered the laws to the people (34:31, 32; see Ex. 24). Obviously, God was renewing His covenant with Israel (34:9, 10).

When we as Christians want to be restored, we must renew our covenant with God. A Christian's initial agreement with God is similar to that of Israel. By becoming Christians, we said, in effect, "All that the LORD has spoken we will do." When we fall into sin, we break that covenant. In order to return, we must renew the covenant and rededicate ourselves to doing God's will with a fresh determination to do *all* that the Lord requires!

A renewal of our understanding of God's requirements. Exodus 34 indicates that God repeated the laws which He had given previously. Israel needed to hear again the promise that God would bring them to the land of Canaan (34:10, 11). They had to be reminded that God demanded their absolute devotion. This devotion was to be manifested in their refusal to worship any other gods (34:12–17), in regular times of worship (34:18, 21–25), in giving (34:19, 20, 26), and in treating others right, according to the teaching of the Ten Commandments (34:28).

We, too, ought to take a fresh look at God's requirements. Our commitment to God requires that we dedicate ourselves altogether to doing God's will, both by loving God and by loving man. Restoration requires a renewal of our understanding of and our determination to keep God's laws. Unless our lives reflect that determination, our restoration is worthless.

Conclusion. After Israel's terrible sin, they had a new beginning. With the covenant renewed and with their sins forgiven by a gracious God, Israel built the tabernacle, demonstrating great generosity and careful obedience. May their experience encourage us to turn from sin and be restored, to rededicate ourselves to God's cause.

God Is Both Merciful and Wrathful (34:6–8)

This passage, perhaps more than any other in the Old Testament, reveals the nature of God. The saying in 34:6–8 became almost a creed. When God appeared to Moses, He revealed Himself as One who is loving, compassionate, and gracious, as well as just and wrathful. He forgives, but He does not "leave the guilty unpunished." To understand God as He is, we must understand both of these aspects of His nature (see Rom. 11:22). We should do as Moses did: Bow down and worship Him!

Make No Covenant with the World (34:11–17)

God told Israel that He would drive out the inhabitants of the promised land (34:11). He then warned them not to make covenants with these peoples; such alliances would turn the Israelites away from the true God to idolatry (34:12–17). We could find no more eloquent testimony to the dangers involved in a Christian's entangling himself with unbelievers—including, but not limited to, the alliance of marriage. Paul's warning to Christians is appropriate: "Do not be bound together with unbelievers; for what partnership have righteousness and lawlessness, or what fellowship has light with darkness?" (2 Cor. 6:14). Followers of Jesus should make no covenants—no binding agreements, no entangling alliances—with unbelievers that might lead them away from God and into sin (1 Cor. 15:33).

Righteous Jealousy (34:14)

God was jealous for His people with a righteous jealousy. He did not want them to be unfaithful to Him. Why? Not only would their unfaithfulness reflect badly on Him, but it was not good for them! Those who deserted Him would deprive themselves of all His blessings. God is jealous for His children in the same way today. He does not want us to leave Him and go after other gods because doing so is bad for us!

Transformed by God's Presence (34:29–35)

Moses' encounter with God in 34:29–35 caused His face to shine. His shining face then served to impress the people that He had been in the presence of God and was God's representative and spokesman. When Christians spend time in the presence of God, God transforms us as well (Rom. 12:1, 2; 2 Cor. 3:18). He does so in a way that is likely to be visible to others.

Moses' Shining Face, the Veil, and the New Covenant (34:29–35; 2 Cor. 3:7–18)

Paul explained that the glory of God that shone from Moses' face indicated that the Law was glorious (with a fading glory). However, he then noted that the new covenant is even more glorious (2 Cor. 3:7–18). The apostle added that the veil which concealed Moses' face has been taken away so that those who are in Christ can see God's glory. However, the veil remains for those who do not understand that the law of Moses has been taken away. They are blind to great spiritual truths.

CHAPTER 35

PREPARATIONS FOR BUILDING THE TABERNACLE

Chapter 35 begins a new section of the Book of Exodus (chs. 35—40).[1] By this time, the Israelites had sinned, had been punished, and had been restored. Moses had gone back up on the mountain for another forty days to receive God's law a second time. Upon returning, he "assembled" the people to do what he had intended to do when he came down from the mountain after the first forty days: to relay to them the law of God that he had received on Sinai (chs. 25—31), especially the requirements regarding the tabernacle. Exodus 35 and 36 indicate that he delivered the command to build the tabernacle along with the directions he had received for its construction.

Since the record of the tabernacle's construction repeats in almost the same words the instructions for its building, many scholars have concluded that this section must have been added at a later time by another writer. Umberto Cassuto countered,

> However, this conjecture is based on ignorance of the methods employed in the composition of books in the ancient East. The theme of the founding and building of a shrine was a stereotyped literary category in the early writings of the Eastern countries; and it was usual for such passages to record first the divine utterance describ-

---

[1]In this section, the text of the Septuagint differs significantly from the Hebrew text. For a good discussion in which the superiority of the Hebrew text is upheld, see Wilbur Fields, *Exploring Exodus*, Bible Study Textbook Series (Joplin, Mo.: College Press, 1976), 769–72.

> ing the plan of the sanctuary in minutest detail, and thereafter to give an account of the construction, which repeated in identical or similar phrasing the description given in the divine communication.[2]

As Israel prepared to begin the task of building, Moses gathered the people together to relay to them God's instructions. Regarding the working conditions for the job, Moses said that God forbade the people to work on the Sabbath (35:1–3). To obtain the building materials, he indicated that God wanted the Israelites to make a freewill offering (35:4–9). The people were then given a preview of the overall plan for the tabernacle which would be built (35:10–19). The people left the assembly and began to make the contribution, with the result that the building materials were made available (35:20–29). The chapter closes with the appointment of Bezalel to be the construction supervisor and of Oholiab to be his helper (35:30–35).

THE SABBATH COMMAND (35:1–3)

1Then Moses assembled all the congregation of the sons of Israel, and said to them, "These are the things that the Lord has commanded you to do:

2"For six days work may be done, but on the seventh day you shall have a holy day, a sabbath of complete rest to the Lord; whoever does any work on it shall be put to death. 3You shall not kindle a fire in any of your dwellings on the sabbath day."

Verse 1. To present the revelation he had received from God, **Moses** summoned the people to a solemn assembly. He then began his presentation of the Law saying, **"These are the things that the Lord has commanded you to do."**

Verses 2, 3. Again, he presented the requirement to keep the **sabbath**. Thus, for the sixth time, Exodus records the command

---

[2]Umberto Cassuto, *A Commentary on the Book of Exodus,* trans. Israel Abrahams (Jerusalem: Magnes Press, 1997), 453.

that Israel must observe the Sabbath (16:4, 5, 23–29; 20:8–11; 23:10–12; 31:12–17; 34:21; 35:1–3). To say the least, the original readers should have been impressed with the importance of keeping this command of the Lord. In this context, it may have been repeated because the Israelites' next responsibility was to build the tabernacle. Perhaps the people needed to be reminded as they set to work building God's house that they were not to break God's commands in doing so. They were to work to build the tabernacle, but they were not to work on the Sabbath.

It may be significant that the command to observe the Sabbath was the last command given before Israel's apostasy, just before Moses came down from the mountain (31:12–17), and the first command given after Israel's restoration, just after Moses came down from the mountain a second time (35:1–3). The story of Israel's idolatry is sandwiched between these two references to the Sabbath command.

The emphasis in 35:2, 3 is on two facts. First, the Sabbath was to be a day of **complete rest to the Lord** ("solemn rest"; NRSV) even to the extent that they were not to **kindle a fire in any of** [their] **dwellings on the sabbath day.** To "kindle a fire" may have been intended to serve as an example. Even as little work as was required to "kindle a fire" was not allowed on the Sabbath day. Therefore, any other work, no matter how small, was also forbidden.

Second, the punishment for breaking the Sabbath was **death** (see 31:14, 15). While modern readers may think that breaking the Sabbath ought not to have been a capital crime, they would do well to remember that God has the right to determine the punishment for disobedience to His commands. Apparently, in God's sight, an Israelite who refused to obey the Sabbath command was just as much a rebel as one who worshiped another god. Peter Enns wrote that, just as the tabernacle was "holy space," the Sabbath was "holy time."[3] One must not desecrate either time or space which God has made holy.

---

[3]Peter Enns, *Exodus*, The NIV Application Commentary (Grand Rapids, Mich.: Zondervan, 2000), 546.

CALL FOR A CONTRIBUTION (35:4–9)

[4]Moses spoke to all the congregation of the sons of Israel, saying, "This is the thing which the LORD has commanded, saying, [5]'Take from among you a contribution to the LORD; whoever is of a willing heart, let him bring it as the LORD's contribution: gold, silver, and bronze, [6]and blue, purple and scarlet material, fine linen, goats' hair, [7]and rams' skins dyed red, and porpoise skins, and acacia wood, [8]and oil for lighting, and spices for the anointing oil, and for the fragrant incense, [9]and onyx stones and setting stones for the ephod and for the breastpiece.'"

Verses 4–9. While the people were assembled, in keeping with God's call for a freewill offering (25:1–7), **Moses** reported to **the congregation** that **the LORD** sought a voluntary **contribution** of the material with which the tabernacle would be constructed. Needed were precious metals (**gold**, **silver**, and **bronze**) and various kinds of cloth (including **fine linen**, **rams' skins**, and **porpoise skins**). The list also included **acacia wood**, **oil**, **spices**, **incense**, and semi-precious **stones** for the priestly garments (see comments on 25:1–7). The results of this call for a contribution are reported in 35:21–29 and 36:1–7.

A SUMMONS TO BUILD THE TABERNACLE (35:10–19)

[10]"'Let every skillful man among you come, and make all that the LORD has commanded: [11]the tabernacle, its tent and its covering, its hooks and its boards, its bars, its pillars, and its sockets; [12]the ark and its poles, the mercy seat, and the curtain of the screen; [13]the table and its poles, and all its utensils, and the bread of the Presence; [14]the lampstand also for the light and its utensils and its lamps and the oil for the light; [15]and the altar of incense and its poles, and the anointing oil and the fragrant incense, and the screen for the doorway at the entrance of the tabernacle; [16]the altar of burnt offering with its bronze grating, its poles, and all its utensils, the basin and its stand; [17]the hang-

ings of the court, its pillars and its sockets, and the screen for the gate of the court; [18]the pegs of the tabernacle and the pegs of the court and their cords; [19]the woven garments for ministering in the holy place, the holy garments for Aaron the priest and the garments of his sons, to minister as priests.'"

Verse 10. Moses challenged the congregation to accomplish the task presented to them by the Lord. The statement in this verse serves as a preface to the rest of the chapter and the next three chapters. Moses told who was to do the building—**every skillful man among you**—and what they were to build—**all that the Lord has commanded**. As with the provision for the materials, the labor for the construction was to be supplied on a volunteer basis. Those called upon to do the actual construction were the "skillful" workmen. Obviously, while the Israelites were to contribute freely of their material wealth, they also had to contribute their time and use their talents in order to complete the project successfully. After the tabernacle had been built, Exodus says that Israel did indeed make "all that the Lord had commanded Moses" (39:32, 42).

Verses 11–19. Moses not only indicated here that Israel was to build all that the Lord required, but he also repeated what God wanted them to build. Verses 11 through 19 introduce the account of the actual construction of the tabernacle by listing the various items that Israel was to make:

1. **the tabernacle**, that is, the **tent** itself (35:11)
2. **the ark** of the covenant (35:12)
3. **the mercy seat** (35:12)
4. **the curtain of the screen** (35:12)
5. **the table** of showbread (35:13)
6. **the lampstand** (35:14)
7. **the altar of incense** (35:15)
8. **the anointing oil and the fragrant incense** (35:15)
9. **the screen** for the **entrance** to the tent (35:15)
10. **the altar of burnt offering** (35:16)
11. **the court** (35:17, 18)
12. the priestly **garments** (35:19).

Chapters 25 through 31 contain the directions Moses received for making all these items, and chapters 36 through 39 relate how they were made. The text also emphasizes that Israel made everything that the Lord required by including in 39:32–41 an inventory of all that had been made when the work was finished.

THE FREEWILL OFFERING (35:20–29)

**20Then all the congregation of the sons of Israel departed
from Moses' presence. 21Everyone whose heart stirred him and
everyone whose spirit moved him came and brought the Lord's
contribution for the work of the tent of meeting and for all its
service and for the holy garments. 22Then all whose hearts
moved them, both men and women, came and brought brooches
and earrings and signet rings and bracelets, all articles of gold;
so did every man who presented an offering of gold to the
Lord. 23Every man, who had in his possession blue and purple
and scarlet material and fine linen and goats' hair and rams'
skins dyed red and porpoise skins, brought them. 24Everyone
who could make a contribution of silver and bronze brought
the Lord's contribution; and every man who had in his possession acacia wood for any work of the service brought it. 25All
the skilled women spun with their hands, and brought what
they had spun, in blue and purple and scarlet material and in
fine linen. 26All the women whose heart stirred with a skill
spun the goats' hair. 27The rulers brought the onyx stones and
the stones for setting for the ephod and for the breastpiece;
28and the spice and the oil for the light and for the anointing
oil and for the fragrant incense. 29The Israelites, all the men
and women, whose heart moved them to bring material for all
the work, which the Lord had commanded through Moses to
be done, brought a freewill offering to the Lord.**

Verse 20. The result of Moses' call to give was a liberal contribution. After hearing the request for donations with which to build the tabernacle, the people **departed from Moses' presence**. The assembly was dismissed and each went to his or her own tent to put together what he or she could give.

Verses 21, 22a. After the Israelites "departed from Moses' presence," they **came and brought the LORD's contribution**. In Hebrew, verses 21 and 22 both begin with "And they came" (וַיָּבֹאוּ, *wayyabo'u*). Cassuto noted that the language suggests the swiftness of the Israelites' response. He commented, "As soon as Moses ended his address they left to fetch their gifts, and immediately returned with their offerings."[4]

Moses had said that "whoever is of a willing heart" (35:5) was to give. The text then says that **everyone whose heart stirred him** and **whose spirit moved him** and **all whose hearts moved them** made these contributions. The gifts then were given willingly, voluntarily, cheerfully, prompted not by external pressure but by inner impulses. If someone is tempted to think of the Old Testament law as external and of those who were under it as being motivated solely by fear of obliteration, he should reflect on the willing participation of the Israelites in the contribution for the tabernacle.

The word "all" in verse 22 specifically includes **women**, who, along with the men, gave their gold jewelry (35:22b). "The skilled women" also made material to be given to the cause (35:25, 26). The women had a contribution to make, and they made it. This was a contribution in which "all" could and did participate.

Verses 22b–28. Those who brought gifts and what they brought are summarized in the chart below.

THOSE WHO GAVE	GIFTS	SCRIPTURE
Men and women	gold jewelry	35:22b
Men	colored cloth and skins	35:23
Everyone	silver and bronze	35:24a
Every man	acacia wood	35:24b
Women	spun cloth	35:25, 26
Rulers	gemstones, spice, oil	35:27, 28

[4]Cassuto, 456.

The result was that all the different kinds of material God asked for were given (see 35:5–9).

Verse 29. The author concluded the paragraph with a summary sentence: **The Israelites . . . brought a freewill offering to the Lord.** Their obedience to God's commandments and their warm generosity were highlighted.

One question that might be asked is: Why were the Israelites so generous? Anyone who knows their story knows that to this point they had been forgetful, ungrateful, and rebellious. Why, suddenly, were they so generous and liberal in giving to the Lord? Perhaps the answer lies in their recent experience. They rebelled against God and were punished for their rebellion. More significantly, God threatened to abandon them altogether. They had been, as it were, to the brink of hell and only barely escaped its flames. Even after God forgave them, He threatened to withdraw His presence from them. Yet He extended to them a gracious offer: He said, in effect, that if they would build Him a house, then He would dwell with them. No wonder, then, that they were glad to contribute! People snatched from the jaws of hell and promised heaven are likely to be grateful and generous.

THE CONSTRUCTION FOREMEN (35:30–35)

30Then Moses said to the sons of Israel, "See, the Lord has called by name Bezalel the son of Uri, the son of Hur, of the tribe of Judah. 31And He has filled him with the Spirit of God, in wisdom, in understanding and in knowledge and in all craftsmanship; 32to make designs for working in gold and in silver and in bronze, 33and in the cutting of stones for settings and in the carving of wood, so as to perform in every inventive work. 34He also has put in his heart to teach, both he and Oholiab, the son of Ahisamach, of the tribe of Dan. 35He has filled them with skill to perform every work of an engraver and of a designer and of an embroiderer, in blue and in purple and in scarlet material, and in fine linen, and of a weaver, as performers of every work and makers of designs."

Verse 30. The Lord had concluded his instructions to **Moses**

regarding the building of the tabernacle by naming the men who were to lead in its construction (see comments on 31:1–6). As construction was ready to start, Moses repeated God's words to the people, telling them that **Bezalel** was to supervise the work (see 36:1, 2; 37:1; 38:22, 23).

Verse 31. Bezalel was qualified for the job because he was a skilled and versatile artisan, talented to work in all the areas required for the completion of the project. His skill, however, was not his own doing; rather, it came from **the Spirit of God**, which provided him with **wisdom**, **understanding**, and **knowledge** and enabled him **in all craftsmanship**. The idea of being **filled** with the "Spirit of God" is that God empowered Bezalel to do what he did.

Verses 32–35. Bezalel was to be assisted by **Oholiab**, who was also enabled by God. Their task, apparently, involved three things: (1) To do the work of craftsmen—to actually make some of the items in the tabernacle. (2) **To teach**—apparently to teach others to do the kind of skilled work they could do.[5] (3) To supervise the work. Probably most of the work was done by others (see 35:10; 36:1, 8). The job of Bezalel and of Oholiab was to make sure the work was done properly, to oversee the job until it was completed. Because they supervised the construction, Bezalel (with Oholiab mentioned as his helper) is spoken of as making "all that the LORD had commanded Moses" (38:22, 23).

APPLICATION

Building God's House, Part 1 (35:1—36:7)

From Exodus 25 until the end of the book, the business of Israel was building the tabernacle—God's house, His dwelling place. In a similar way, the Christian's business today is not just farming, selling, teaching school, or whatever he does for a living. He is also to be busy building up the church (Eph. 4:11, 12;

[5]They were given "a capability of training and guiding assistants who would work with these two [skilled artisans]." (Walter C. Kaiser, Jr., "Exodus" in *The Expositor's Bible Commentary*, vol. 2, *Genesis—Numbers* [Grand Rapids, Mich.: Zondervan, 1990], 490.)

1 Cor. 3:9, 10), which is God's dwelling (1 Cor. 3:16)—His house (1 Tim. 3:15), His temple (Eph. 2:19–22).

How can we succeed in building God's house? By following the example of God's people who successfully built the tabernacle. They succeeded because many of them had "a willing heart" (35:5). A willing heart is likewise the key to church-building and church growth today. Willing hearts led the Israelites to contribute toward the building of the tabernacle. Their giving is an example for us in four ways.

They gave voluntarily. God called upon each person with a "willing heart" to bring something "as the LORD's contribution: gold, silver, and bronze" (35:5). He went on to list other goods which the people could bring (35:6, 7). Each one was to bring what he or she had in order that it might be used in the building of the tabernacle. The people complied.

The willingness with which the people of Israel brought these gifts is impressive. The text attributes their liberality to their willing hearts and says over and over that they gave not because they had to, but because their spirits moved them to do so (35:21, 22, 26, 29).

They were united in their giving. The extent of the involvement of the people was impressive. The contribution was given not just by a few, but by many. The text emphasizes the involvement of "all" the people. Among those listed as givers were "everyone whose heart stirred him" (35:21), "all whose hearts moved them, both men and women" (35:22), "every man, who had in his possession blue and purple and scarlet material" (35:23), "everyone who could make a contribution of silver" (35:24), "all the skilled women" (35:25), "all the women whose heart stirred with a skill" (35:26), "the rulers" (35:27), and "the Israelites, all the men and women, whose heart moved them" (35:29).

They gave gladly. The variety of the gifts was also impressive. Some gave gold, while others gave silver or bronze. Some gave cloth or leather or acacia wood which they possessed. Some gave precious or semiprecious stones, spices, or oil. Some used the skill that God had given them to spin the cloth that would be needed in constructing the tent. Everyone gave according to his or her own ability, as their hearts moved them.

They gave generously. The amount given by the Israelites was especially impressive. Exodus 36:2–7 says that they continued bringing their gifts until the people who were doing the actual building had no time left for construction. They were spending all their time receiving the gifts that the people kept bringing. Eventually, the workmen talked to Moses about the problem, and Moses had to ask the people to stop giving. Their giving was so generous that they had to be asked to quit! Their liberality is also obvious from the account given later, telling how much was given for and used in the building of the tabernacle (38:21–31).

Conclusion. If the church is to grow today—spiritually and numerically—its members must be willing to give liberally. God wants us to give as the Israelites did. He wants us to give from willing hearts, voluntarily (2 Cor. 9:7). He wants us all to contribute (1 Cor. 16:1, 2); giving is not something that is to be done only by those who have a lot of money. Everyone can and should give. God wants us to give of what we have; each should give "as he may prosper" (1 Cor. 16:2). The "two small copper coins" of the widow in Luke 21:1–4, given sacrificially from a willing heart, were as precious to God as the rich gifts of the prosperous. Whether the gift is a few loaves of bread for Jesus to multiply, a donkey for Him to ride, or an expensive jar of ointment with which to anoint Him, the Lord is glad to receive whatever we can give Him. Every member should give liberally and generously in order to build up the church.

The only kind of giving approved by the Lord is voluntary, generous, liberal, sacrificial giving. We may be inclined to compare what we give with the stinginess of miserly people. Instead, we should compare it with the generous gifts we read about in the Bible. God gave His Son (Jn. 3:16). Jesus gave up heaven, came to earth, and died (see 2 Cor. 8:9; 9:15). The wise men gave expensive gifts to Jesus (Mt. 2:11). Mary anointed Jesus with costly perfume (Jn. 12:3). Early Christians sold their possessions to meet others' needs (Acts 2:44, 45). The liberality of the Macedonian churches was remarkable (2 Cor. 8:1–5). Then we have the example of the Israelites, who had to be "restrained from bringing any more" (Ex. 36:6).

How does our giving compare with these examples? Are we

giving liberally, as did the Israelites and others whose stories are found in the Bible? Should we not be even more willing to give than they were? The devil will always have plenty of funds to do his work. The question is, Will the Lord's church have enough to be able to do its work? Will we give liberally to build up the church?

God's People Had Willing Hearts (35:5)

In chapter 35, as in other passages in Exodus, the Bible provides evidence that Israelite religion involved the hearts, the minds, and the attitudes of the people. In fact, when the time came for the tabernacle to be built, the people were so grateful in their hearts for what God had done that they gave generously from willing hearts for its construction. New Testament religion also must be "from the heart" (Rom. 6:17, 18). Now, as then, God does not want His children simply to go through the motions; He wants us to do what He asks from the heart.

Chapter 36

The Construction Of the Tabernacle (Part 1)

In chapter 35 Moses prepared the people for the building of the tabernacle, whereas in chapter 36 the work of construction began.

Moses concluded his charge to Bezalel, Oholiab, and the other skilled workers who were called to build the tabernacle, and then he put them to work (36:1, 2). Next the writer records that the people gave materials so generously that they finally had to be "restrained from bringing any more" (36:3–7).

The rest of the chapter records the building of the tabernacle, that is, the tent itself. The text describes the making of the following items: the inner curtains (36:8–13), the curtains of goats' hair and coverings of rams' skins and porpoise skins (36:14–19), the boards (36:20–30), the bars (36:31–34), the veil which separated the two compartments (36:35, 36), and the screen for the door (36:37, 38).

CALL FOR WORKERS (36:1, 2)

1"Now Bezalel and Oholiab, and every skillful person in whom the LORD has put skill and understanding to know how to perform all the work in the construction of the sanctuary, shall perform in accordance with all that the LORD has commanded."

2Then Moses called Bezalel and Oholiab and every skillful person in whom the LORD had put skill, everyone whose heart stirred him, to come to the work to perform it.

Verse 1. This verse continues, without a break, where Exodus 35 ends; verse 1 should be thought of as the concluding sentence of the paragraph that began with 35:30.[1] These are the words of Moses spoken to the congregation about who will build the tabernacle—**Bezalel and Oholiab**, assisted by **every skillful person**. The previous verses (35:30–35) have indicated *who* are to lead in the work and have described why they are qualified for the job: God has endowed them with the skill they need. The first verse of this chapter tells *what* they are to do: They are to build the tabernacle **in accordance with all that the LORD has commanded**, following His instructions. Throughout the account of the tabernacle construction the emphasis is on the fact that the tabernacle was God's doing and was to be built exactly according to His directions.

Verse 2. The narrative shifts from describing what **Moses** said to recounting what he did. After telling the congregation about the individuals God had chosen to supervise the construction, Moses **called** those who were to do the work. In other words, he formally appointed them to the task; he set them to work.[2]

THE ABUNDANT OFFERING (36:3–7)

3They received from Moses all the contributions which the sons of Israel had brought to perform the work in the construction of the sanctuary. And they still continued bringing to him freewill offerings every morning. 4And all the skillful men who were performing all the work of the sanctuary came, each from the work which he was performing, 5and they said to Moses, "The people are bringing much more than enough for the construction work which the LORD commanded us to perform." 6So Moses issued a command, and a proclamation was

---

[1]The NASB indicates that a new paragraph begins with verse 2, suggesting that verse 1 is a part of the previous paragraph.

[2]A similar procedure was followed in the New Testament. God providentially prepared and selected people for a work—in some cases by prescribing the qualifications. Then they were formally "appointed" or set to work. Compare the selection of the seven men for the food distribution (Acts 6:1–6) and the selection of Paul and Barnabas for their missionary task (Acts 13:1–3).

circulated throughout the camp, saying, "Let no man or woman any longer perform work for the contributions of the sanctuary." Thus the people were restrained from bringing any more. [7]For the material they had was sufficient and more than enough for all the work, to perform it.

Verse 3. One of the first responsibilities of the builders was to receive **the contributions** of the people so that they would have materials with which to build. The people brought gifts, just as they had been asked to do. **Every morning** they brought **freewill offerings**. Apparently, the workers were spending so much time receiving the gifts that they had little time for building.

Verses 4–7. Consequently, they urged **Moses** to do something about the situation. They explained that they had **much more than enough** to do the job. The text says that Moses **issued a command** and **a proclamation was circulated** so that **the people were restrained from bringing any more**.

To modern readers who are accustomed to being asked to give more and more to the church or to various causes, this account sounds strange. It is difficult to imagine God's spokesman *commanding* people *not to give* any more because they had already given more than enough. This record demonstrates the grateful, obedient hearts of the Israelites at this point in their history.

THE TENT (36:8–38)

The account of the construction begins at 36:8 and continues through 38:23. The value of the materials used in its construction is estimated in 38:24–31. Chapter 39 continues the story of construction by telling of the making of the priestly garments; then the entire project is pronounced finished in 39:32. The narrative in 35:1—36:7 serves as a prelude to the story told beginning in 36:8. In fact, all of the information found in Exodus 25—31 and 35:1—36:7 can be thought of as preparing for the account of the building of the tabernacle which begins in 36:8.

Replica of the Tabernacle (Timna Park, Israel)

The Four Coverings (36:8–19)

**8All the skillful men among those who were performing the work made the tabernacle with ten curtains; of fine twisted linen and blue and purple and scarlet material, with cherubim,
the work of a skillful workman, Bezalel made them. 9The length of each curtain was twenty-eight cubits and the width of each curtain four cubits; all the curtains had the same measurements.
10He joined five curtains to one another and the other five curtains he joined to one another. 11He made loops of blue on the edge of the outermost curtain in the first set; he did likewise on the edge of the curtain that was outermost in the second set.
12He made fifty loops in the one curtain and he made fifty loops on the edge of the curtain that was in the second set; the loops were opposite each other. 13He made fifty clasps of gold and joined the curtains to one another with the clasps, so the tabernacle was a unit.**

14Then he made curtains of goats' hair for a tent over the

tabernacle; he made eleven curtains in all. [15]The length of each curtain was thirty cubits and four cubits the width of each curtain; the eleven curtains had the same measurements. [16]He joined five curtains by themselves and the other six curtains by themselves. [17]Moreover, he made fifty loops on the edge of the curtain that was outermost in the first set, and he made fifty loops on the edge of the curtain that was outermost in the second set. [18]He made fifty clasps of bronze to join the tent together so that it would be a unit. [19]He made a covering for the tent of rams' skins dyed red, and a covering of porpoise skins above.

The record of the building of the tabernacle does not follow the sequence of the directions given in chapters 25 through 31. Whereas the instructions begin with the furnishings of the tabernacle, the record of the building begins with the tabernacle—the tent in which the furnishings would be housed. The construction followed the directions in detail (see comments on 26:1–14).

Verses 8–19. The person credited with the construction of **the tabernacle** throughout this section of Exodus is **Bezalel.** He functioned as a construction foreman, the builder in charge of the project. The explanation that follows consistently uses the words **he made** or the equivalent, referring to Bezalel. He is again mentioned by name in 37:1, and the pronoun "he"—referring to Bezalel—continues to be the subject of the sentences through the completion of the work in 38:20. Not until 39:1 does the text use "they" as the subject in speaking of those who made the tabernacle and its furnishings.

The passage begins by saying that Bezalel made the **curtains.** The tabernacle itself was a tent, a portable sanctuary, which consisted of four coverings of material draped over a framework of boards. The inner covering was made of colorful **fine twisted linen** with representations of **cherubim** woven into the material (36:8). The covering above that one was made of **goats' hair** (36:14). These two inner coverings were prepared from a number of individual curtains sewn together into two larger coverings, which were joined by **loops** and **clasps**. These two coverings were then overlaid by coverings of **rams' skins** and **porpoise skins** (36:19).

The Walls: The Boards and the Bars (36:20–34)

[20]Then he made the boards for the tabernacle of acacia wood, standing upright. [21]Ten cubits was the length of each board and one and a half cubits the width of each board. [22]There were two tenons for each board, fitted to one another; thus he did for all the boards of the tabernacle. [23]He made the boards for the tabernacle: twenty boards for the south side; [24]and he made forty sockets of silver under the twenty boards; two sockets under one board for its two tenons and two sockets under another board for its two tenons. [25]Then for the second side of the tabernacle, on the north side, he made twenty boards, [26]and their forty sockets of silver; two sockets under one board and two sockets under another board. [27]For the rear of the tabernacle, to the west, he made six boards. [28]He made two boards for the corners of the tabernacle at the rear. [29]They were double beneath, and together they were complete to its top to the first ring; thus he did with both of them for the two corners. [30]There were eight boards with their sockets of silver, sixteen sockets, two under every board.

[31]Then he made bars of acacia wood, five for the boards of one side of the tabernacle, [32]and five bars for the boards of the other side of the tabernacle, and five bars for the boards of the tabernacle for the rear side to the west. [33]He made the middle bar to pass through in the center of the boards from end to end. [34]He overlaid the boards with gold and made their rings of gold as holders for the bars, and overlaid the bars with gold.

Verses 20–34. The account of the construction of the tabernacle moves from the coverings to **the boards** and **the bars** which made up the framework of the tent. The record of their construction in 36:20–34 closely accords with the directions given in 26:15–29. The coverings were laid over a framework of vertical boards made of **acacia wood** (36:20) and covered with **gold** (36:34). The boards were held in place by **tenons** and **sockets of silver**. They were held together by five horizontal bars, also overlaid with **gold** (36:34). **The middle bar** on each side **pass**[ed] **through in the center of the boards from end to end** (36:33).

The Veil and the Screen (36:35–38)

[35]Moreover, he made the veil of blue and purple and scar-
let material, and fine twisted linen; he made it with cherubim,
the work of a skillful workman. [36]He made four pillars of aca-
cia for it, and overlaid them with gold, with their hooks of gold;
and he cast four sockets of silver for them. [37]He made a screen
for the doorway of the tent, of blue and purple and scarlet mate-
rial, and fine twisted linen, the work of a weaver; [38]and he made
its five pillars with their hooks, and he overlaid their tops and
their bands with gold; but their five sockets were of bronze.

Verses 35–38. The chapter concludes with the making of **the veil** which separated the two compartments and **the screen** which served as the entrance to **the tent**. The story of the construction of the veil and the screen parallels the directions given in 26:31–37, except that the directions speak of the function and significance of the veil: It marked the boundary defining the most holy place.

APPLICATION

Plan the Work, and Work the Plan (Chs. 25—31; 36—40)

Whoever said, "Plan the work, and then work the plan," might have taken the idea from Exodus. In chapters 25 through 31, God gave the plan; He had planned the work. In chapters 36 through 40, the Israelites worked the plan. The text demonstrates the orderly, businesslike way God went about getting His house built. Perhaps God wants His people to learn a lesson from the systematic way He went about this building. Churches can be disorganized organizations. We need to learn that it is scriptural to be organized, to make plans and carry them out, to conduct the affairs of the church in an orderly way. At the same time, we must remember that we are in the soul-saving business, not in the money-saving or building-maintenance business.

Evidence suggests that Jesus conducted His mission on earth in a systematic way, that Paul had a certain mission strategy as he preached the gospel in the Roman world, and that early churches (such as the ones in Jerusalem and in Antioch) functioned in an orderly fashion. In a similar way, we as individual workers and as congregations should try to "plan the work, and work the plan"—being orderly and systematic in the way we approach our tasks.

Building Up the Lord's Church (35:1—36:7)

Christians are constantly building the church of the Lord, the house of God—building it from the beginning in new areas, and then building it up both in numbers and in spirituality. How can we successfully help to build the Lord's church? Paul told us to be wise builders in 1 Corinthians 3:9, 10. We would be wise to consider the example of the Israelites who built the tabernacle. How did they do it?

The explanation of building the tabernacle emphasizes Israel's use of their talents and abilities in its construction. The text points out that some of the offerings for the tabernacle consisted of cloth made by "skilled women" (35:25) or by women "whose heart stirred with a skill" (35:26).

The text also highlights the fact that the actual building of the tabernacle was done by people who used their special skills for that purpose. The Lord told Moses that He had called Bezalel to take charge of the actual construction of the tabernacle, saying that He had "filled him with the Spirit of God in wisdom, in understanding, in knowledge, and in all kinds of craftsmanship" (31:3). In addition, God called Oholiab and other skilled men to help in the building, giving them the skills they needed to do so (31:6). In Exodus 35 Bezalel and the other workers were actually appointed to the task. Again, Moses emphasized that it was the Lord who had called Bezalel and his assistants and had endowed them with the skill they needed (35:30–35). In Exodus 36:1 we read,

> [Moses said,] "Now Bezalel and Oholiab, and every skillful person in whom the LORD has put skill and understanding to know how to perform all the work in the construction of the sanctuary, shall perform in accordance with all that the LORD has commanded" (see 36:2).

The book goes on to credit Bezalel with the building of the tabernacle (38:22).

Three truths stand out in our consideration of the gifts used in building the tabernacle.

The skills these men and women possessed came from God. What kinds of gifts were involved? Their gifts were not that they became prophets, able to speak the word of the Lord eloquently. They were skills that were necessary *for building*: skills related to making artistic designs, cutting stones for settings, carving wood, engraving, embroidering, and weaving. We need to learn that all our abilities, whatever they are, come from God. He does not just give preaching or teaching or song leading or leadership skills; He also gives Christians the skills they need to do their work as carpenters, electricians, plumbers, and seamstresses. If you can repair a car, fix a broken faucet, or make a computer run properly, then you have that talent from God.

These individuals were willing to use their abilities in the service of God. The Bible does not emphasize their willingness, but there is no suggestion in the text that God forced them to dedicate themselves and their skills to this cause. God called them, and they were willing to answer His call.

The people who had the gifts were willing to give their time in using them. In a sense, three kinds of contributions were necessary to build the tabernacle: contributions of money, talents, and time. Gifted individuals were willing to invest more than six months of their lives in building the tabernacle. They worked consistently for months, six days a week, on this project. They stayed with it until they were done.

What does the church today need? More money? Generally speaking, members have enough money to do what is needed, but they may need to become more generous givers. More talents? As a rule, within the membership of almost any congregation, there is plenty of talent to enable the church to accomplish everything that God expects. What the church needs more than anything else in most places is *time*—that is, time that the members are willing to invest in the work of the Lord. What good are abilities if those who have them are unwilling to volunteer their time to use those abilities in God's service? We need to be willing to use our time serving God—studying the Bible, praying, worshiping God in the services of the church, visiting the sick, helping our neighbors, getting involved in the activities of the church, teaching our friends about Christ, and doing mission work.

For the church to be what God wants it to be, members need to give their abilities, their time, and their money to the task. If they will, the church can be built up wherever we go, in the same way the tabernacle was built. Then God will be pleased today, just as He was then.

God Gives Skills to People (36:1)

The skills which were used in the building of the tabernacle were God-given. In the same way today, every ability and talent we have comes from God: "Every good thing given and every perfect gift is from above, coming down from the Father of lights, with whom there is no variation or shifting shadow" (Jas. 1:17). We should not try to take credit for our talents or skills, but give credit to God. We should praise Him for giving them to us and use them to God's glory in His kingdom.

CHAPTER 37

THE CONSTRUCTION OF THE TABERNACLE (PART 2)

Chapter 37 continues the account of the tabernacle's construction begun in chapter 36. It describes how Bezalel made the furnishings of the tabernacle—the sacred items which were placed inside the tent. The chapter first relates the making of the contents that would occupy the most holy place: the ark of the covenant (37:1–5) and the mercy seat located on top of the ark (37:6–9). It then tells how the three items in the holy place were made, along with their utensils: the table of showbread (37:10–16), the lampstand (37:17–24), and the altar of incense (37:25–28). The chapter concludes by saying that Bezalel also made the anointing oil and the fragrant incense (37:29).

The account of the building of the tabernacle differs sequentially from the instructions for making it. The Lord gave directions for making the contents of the tent (25:10–40) before He told how the tent was to be built (26:1–37). In the construction account, the tent comes first (36:8–38) and its furnishings second (37:1–29).

Why the difference? Evidently, the instructions begin with the element that is most important from a theological standpoint—the ark of the covenant and the mercy seat symbolizing God's presence.[1] In the explanation of the actual construction, practical or logical considerations are foremost: Before the ark could be built, for example, it needed a place to be housed.

---

[1]Wilbur Fields, *Exploring Exodus*, Bible Study Textbook Series (Joplin, Mo.: College Press, 1976), 767. To say that the furnishings are more important does not suggest that the tent itself was unimportant.

Therefore, the building of the tabernacle preceded the account of making its furnishings.

John I. Durham offered an alternative view in which the accounts of the tabernacle's construction (36:8–38) and erection (40:1–33) were intentionally arranged to bracket the narrative. Further, Israel's response in the contribution (35:4—36:7) and the Lord's response to the completion of His commands (40:34–38) serve as outer brackets.[2]

THE ARK OF THE COVENANT (37:1–5)

[1]Now Bezalel made the ark of acacia wood; its length was two and a half cubits, and its width one and a half cubits, and its height one and a half cubits; [2]and he overlaid it with pure gold inside and out, and made a gold molding for it all around. [3]He cast four rings of gold for it on its four feet; even two rings on one side of it, and two rings on the other side of it. [4]He made poles of acacia wood and overlaid them with gold. [5]He put the poles into the rings on the sides of the ark, to carry it.

Verses 1–5. After describing the construction of the tent (ch. 36), the author tells about the making of its contents. Foremost among the furnishings of the tabernacle was **the ark** of the covenant, which was a box containing the stone tablets on which the Law was inscribed (25:16). No significant difference exists between the instructions for making the ark and the record of how it was constructed, except that the former account tells what the ark contained and the latter does not. (See comments on 25:10–16.)

THE MERCY SEAT (37:6–9)

[6]He made a mercy seat of pure gold, two and a half cubits long and one and a half cubits wide. [7]He made two cherubim of

---

[2]John I. Durham, *Exodus*, Word Biblical Commentary, vol. 3 (Waco, Tex.: Word Books, 1987), 480.

gold; he made them of hammered work at the two ends of the mercy seat; [8]one cherub at the one end and one cherub at the other end; he made the cherubim of one piece with the mercy seat at the two ends. [9]The cherubim had their wings spread upward, covering the mercy seat with their wings, with their faces toward each other; the faces of the cherubim were toward the mercy seat.

Verses 6–9. The text next speaks of the making of the **mercy seat**, which served as the lid of the ark. On each end, **of one piece with the mercy seat**, was a **cherub**. Both figures faced inward, with **their wings** overshadowing **the mercy seat**. Both **the mercy seat** and **the cherubim** were made of **pure gold**. Basically, the only difference between the instructions for making the mercy seat and the account of its construction is the fact that the instructions include a statement regarding the theological significance of the mercy seat in 25:22—a statement not found in the record of its building. (See comments on 25:17–22.)

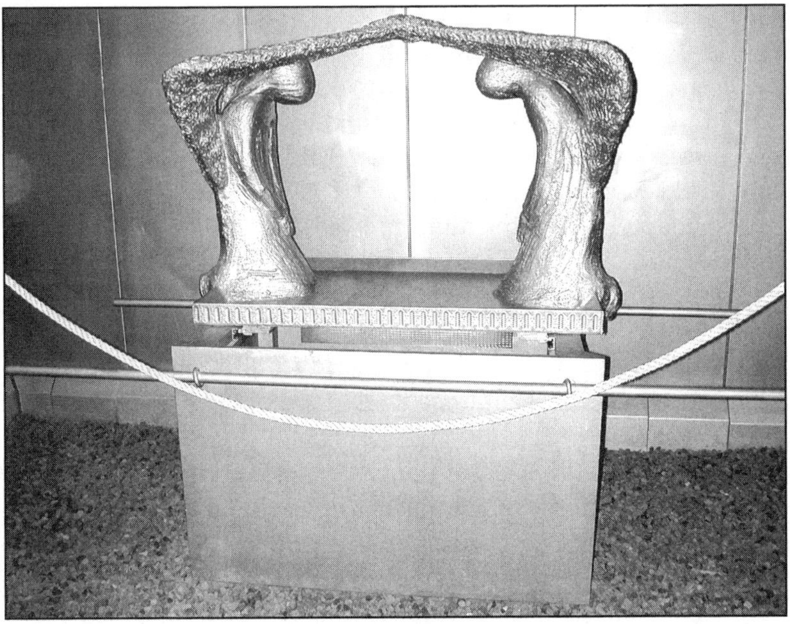

Replica of the Ark of the Covenant (Timna Park, Israel)

THE TABLE OF SHOWBREAD (37:10–16)

[10]Then he made the table of acacia wood, two cubits long and a cubit wide and one and a half cubits high. [11]He overlaid it with pure gold, and made a gold molding for it all around. [12]He made a rim for it of a handbreadth all around, and made a gold molding for its rim all around. [13]He cast four gold rings for it and put the rings on the four corners that were on its four feet. [14]Close by the rim were the rings, the holders for the poles to carry the table. [15]He made the poles of acacia wood and overlaid them with gold, to carry the table. [16]He made the utensils which were on the table, its dishes and its pans and its bowls and its jars, with which to pour out drink offerings, of pure gold.

After detailing the making of the furnishings for the most holy place, the writer turns to the construction of the objects found in the holy place. Each sacred item is described in turn: the table of showbread (37:10–16), the golden lampstand (37:17–24), and the altar of incense (37:25–28).

Although the two accounts of the making of the tabernacle (the instructions and the construction) differ in sequence, the individual items appear generally in the same order. One difference exists: In the directions for the building of these items, the table of showbread and lampstand (25:23–40) are separated by several chapters from the altar of incense (30:1–10). In contrast, all three of these objects are grouped together in this chapter.

Verses 10–16. The first item built for the holy place was **the table** of showbread. Like the ark, this table was made of **acacia wood** and **overlaid . . . with pure gold** (37:10, 11). It had **rings** attached to it, so that it could be carried from one place to another with **poles** (37:13–15). Along with the table, the workmen made **utensils** which were used in the tabernacle services (37:16).

The explanation of the building of the table does not differ significantly from the instructions given for its construction. However, as in other cases, the initial plan includes a statement of how the table was to be used in 25:30, which the later account omits. (See comments on 25:23–30.)

Replica of the Table of Showbread (Timna Park, Israel)

THE GOLDEN LAMPSTAND (37:17–24)

**17Then he made the lampstand of pure gold. He made the
lampstand of hammered work, its base and its shaft; its cups,
its bulbs and its flowers were of one piece with it. 18There were
six branches going out of its sides; three branches of the lampstand from the one side of it and three branches of the lampstand from the other side of it; 19three cups shaped like almond
blossoms, a bulb and a flower in one branch, and three cups
shaped like almond blossoms, a bulb and a flower in the other
branch—so for the six branches going out of the lampstand.
20In the lampstand there were four cups shaped like almond
blossoms, its bulbs and its flowers; 21and a bulb was under the
first pair of branches coming out of it, and a bulb under the
second pair of branches coming out of it, and a bulb under the
third pair of branches coming out of it, for the six branches
coming out of the lampstand. 22Their bulbs and their branches
were of one piece with it; the whole of it was a single ham-**

mered work of pure gold. [23]He made its seven lamps with its snuffers and its trays of pure gold. [24]He made it and all its utensils from a talent of pure gold.

Verses 17–24. The next furnishing which Bezalel made for the holy place was **the lampstand**. This item is often referred to by the Hebrew term מְנוֹרָה (*m*ᵉ*norah*). Unlike the other objects in the holy place, it was made of **pure gold** (37:17). The lampstand had a central **shaft** with **six branches** extending from it, **three** on each **side** (37:17, 18). Every part was ornately decorated with golden **bulbs** and **blossoms** (37:19–22). The central shaft and six branches culminated in seven lamp holders.

The Israelites also used **pure gold** in making the **seven lamps**, the **snuffers**, and other **utensils** needed in connection with the lampstand (37:23, 24). The purpose of the lampstand—"to shed light on the space in front of it" (25:37)—is explained in the command to build it, but not in the account of its building. (See comments on 25:31–40.)

Replica of the Lampstand (Timna Park, Israel)

THE ALTAR OF INCENSE (37:25–28)

[25]Then he made the altar of incense of acacia wood: a cubit long and a cubit wide, square, and two cubits high; its horns were of one piece with it. [26]He overlaid it with pure gold, its top and its sides all around, and its horns; and he made a gold molding for it all around. [27]He made two golden rings for it under its molding, on its two sides—on opposite sides—as holders for poles with which to carry it. [28]He made the poles of acacia wood and overlaid them with gold.

Verses 25–28. Like the table of showbread, **the altar of incense** was constructed from **acacia wood** and covered with **gold**. It had **horns**—projections from its four corners—and a **gold molding** around its top. The altar, like the other tabernacle furniture, was made with **rings** so it could be carried with **poles**. The instructions for building it include directions regarding its placement and its use (30:6–10), but the account of its building simply states that it was made. (See comments on 30:1–10.)

Replica of the Altar of Incense (Timna Park, Israel)

THE ANOINTING OIL AND INCENSE (37:29)

[29]And he made the holy anointing oil and the pure, fragrant incense of spices, the work of a perfumer.

Verse 29. The chapter concludes by saying that **he** [Bezalel] **made the holy anointing oil** and the **fragrant incense**. The placement of this statement after the account of the building of the altar of incense is logical, since the "fragrant incense" was made to be burned on the altar of incense. The recipe for the fragrant incense and instructions regarding its use are found in 30:34–38. The "anointing oil" was to be used in the consecration of the priests and of the tabernacle. Detailed instructions concerning its production and use are found in 30:22–33.

APPLICATION

The Blessings in God's Holy Place (Ch. 37)

The construction of the furnishings for the tabernacle is described in Exodus 37. Since the Mosaic law was a "shadow of the good things to come" (Heb. 10:1), it is legitimate to consider how those furnishings relate to the covenant under which Christians live. The church is God's holy place today. It was purchased with the blood of Christ (Acts 20:28) and is depicted as God's household (1 Tim. 3:15). It is compared to the temple or tabernacle (1 Cor. 3:16; Eph. 2:19–22). Can we find in the church today the things that could be found in the tabernacle then?

We have access to God's mercy. Exodus 37:1–9 tells of the building of the ark of the covenant and then goes on to describe the construction of the mercy seat and the cherubim. These were the furnishings of the most holy place, where God dwelt. The ark served as the repository for the tablets of the covenant. Between the cherubim on the mercy seat, on top of the ark, the high priest annually sprinkled blood to atone for the sins of the people. That is where God met with the people.

The most holy place is like heaven, the place where God dwells. It was a cube, and heaven is pictured in Revelation 21 as a cube. Just as the high priest could not enter the most holy place except through the holy place, so accountable people today cannot enter heaven except through the church, Christ's body of saved people (Eph. 5:23). The furnishings of the most holy place remind us that those in the church have access to God's mercy. As Christians, we have been cleansed by the atoning blood of Christ and are bound by a covenant to God.

We have a table, a light, and prayer as Christians. There were three items of furniture in the holy place: a table, a lampstand, and an altar of incense.

Exodus 37:10–16 relates the building of the table of showbread. Always on the table were twelve loaves of bread, the "bread of the Presence" (Ex. 25:30). The twelve loaves probably represented the twelve tribes of Israel, and their presence on the table may have signified that they belonged to God. In the church, Christians also have a table, the Lord's table (1 Cor. 10:21). The Lord's Supper does not serve exactly the same function as the table of showbread, but it does remind us that we are one and that together we belong to Christ.

Next, Exodus 37:17–24 tells how the lampstand was made. The golden lampstand had six branches and, with its central trunk, held seven lamps. These seven lamps were to be kept burning all the time; they provided the only light within the tabernacle. Symbolically, the lampstand may have functioned as a reminder that only God can provide light—the light from above that Israel needed to continue to exist. In the church, in a similar way, Christians have light—light from God, light from above. Christ is called the "Light of the world" (Jn. 8:12). God's Word gives light to the church (see Ps. 119:105). Without His guidance, we could not continue to be His church.

Third, Exodus 37:25–28 describes the construction of the altar of incense. On this altar, incense was burned morning and evening. As a result, the tabernacle must have been filled constantly with a sweet aroma. Surely, the fragrance of the incense also penetrated the most holy place, so that it presented a pleasing odor to the Lord. In the Christian age, the incense perhaps represents prayer. In Revelation 8:3, 4, incense is connected with "the prayers of the saints." We know that our prayers ascend to the throne of God. Our lives of service can also be a pleasing aroma before Him (see 2 Cor. 2:14, 15; Phil. 4:18).

Conclusion. In the church, as in the holy place, we have a table and a light. We are privileged to offer to God a fragrant aroma which enters into His very presence. Through the church, we have access to God, to His mercy, and to the benefits of the new covenant. These blessings are provided *only* for those who are in the church.

Sacred Items in the Tabernacle (Ch. 37)

Just as a sermon could be presented on each of the Ten Commandments, so one could preach on each of the individual items found or used in the tabernacle. For example, one could preach on "The Mercy Seat" and describe how people today can find mercy. A sermon on "The Table of Showbread" could focus on "The Lord's Table" today or on Christ as the "Bread of Life." A lesson on "The Altar of Incense" could tell of the need for Christians to pray constantly, just as incense was burned on the golden altar each morning and evening. In presenting "The Lampstand," one might discuss Christ as "The Light of the World" or talk about the light provided to the church by God's Word.

Vessels of Gold (37:16)

The utensils in the tabernacle were made of pure gold. If the tabernacle is like the church, then individual Christians can perhaps be compared to those utensils or to the materials of which the tabernacle was made. God's people are intrinsically "golden"; we are very valuable. However, it is up to us whether or not our value is realized. Let us make sure that we live so that we are like golden vessels that can stand the fire of testing (1 Cor. 3:13; 1 Pet. 1:7) and are made for honor (2 Tim. 2:20, 21).

The Lampstand and the Congregation (37:17–24)

The seven churches of Asia are compared to lampstands in Revelation 1:20. Just as the lampstand in the tabernacle provided light for the holy place, so local congregations should be the source of divine light for those in their communities. Any lampstand which fails to do its job is in danger of being removed from its place (Rev. 2:5).

Chapter 38

The Construction of the Tabernacle (Part 3)

Exodus 38 concludes the account of the construction of the tabernacle begun in 36:8.[1] The making of the tent and its furniture have already been described. This chapter finishes the story by relating the construction of the courtyard and its contents. It portrays the construction of the altar of burnt offering (38:1–7), the bronze laver (38:8), and the court that surrounded the tabernacle (38:9–20). In the rest of the chapter, the writer indicates the cost of the tabernacle (38:21–31). He describes "the number of the things for the tabernacle" (38:21), including both what was collected in the freewill offering (38:24) and what was received in the tax taken of all who were numbered (38:25).

THE BRONZE ALTAR (38:1–7)

[1]Then he made the altar of burnt offering of acacia wood, five cubits long, and five cubits wide, square, and three cubits high. [2]He made its horns on its four corners, its horns being of one piece with it, and he overlaid it with bronze. [3]He made all the utensils of the altar, the pails and the shovels and the basins, the flesh hooks and the firepans; he made all its utensils of bronze. [4]He made for the altar a grating of bronze network beneath, under its ledge, reaching halfway up. [5]He cast four rings on the four ends of the bronze grating as holders for the poles. [6]He made the poles of acacia wood and overlaid them

---

[1]This comment excludes the making of the priestly garments, which is depicted in chapter 39.

with bronze. 7He inserted the poles into the rings on the sides of the altar, with which to carry it. He made it hollow with planks.

Verses 1–7. The construction of **the altar of burnt offering** fulfilled the instructions given in 27:1–8. The person who is described as making the altar, identified by the pronoun **he**, is Bezalel. Beginning with 37:1, the text says that Bezalel made the ark, the table of showbread, the lampstand, and the altar of incense; here it indicates that he made the altar of burnt offering as well. For these statements to be true, Bezalel need not have been the artisan in every case. Others who were skilled workmen had been recruited to help him in the building (35:10–19). Bezalel **made** everything in the sense that he oversaw its construction. There are no significant differences between the instructions given for making the altar and the description of how those instructions were carried out. (See comments on 27:1–8.)

Replica of the Bronze Altar (Timna Park, Israel)

THE BRONZE LAVER (38:8)

[8]Moreover, he made the laver of bronze with its base of bronze, from the mirrors of the serving women who served at the doorway of the tent of meeting.

Verse 8. The account of the making of **the laver** requires only one sentence. Instructions for its construction (30:17–21) were the final directions given to Moses regarding the building of the tabernacle, except for instructions about the anointing oil.

A significant difference between the two passages is that 38:8 says the laver was constructed **from the mirrors of the serving women who served at the doorway of the tent of meeting.** The Old Testament mentions such women only one other time: In 1 Samuel 2:22 the text says that Eli's sons "lay with the women who served at the doorway of the tent of meeting."

Who these women were and how they "served" is unclear. The Hebrew word (צָבָא, *tsaba'*) suggests that they were organized for the service they performed; the same word is used for the Levitical priests' "service" (Num. 4:23; 8:24).[2] Commentators have suggested that they may have been a guild of women organized as cleaners to take care of the tabernacle complex, as singers and dancers who performed at religious festivals (see 15:20, 21), or as gatekeepers.[3] Because of 1 Samuel 2:22, some have even connected them with the cult prostitutes of the shrines used in Baal worship. However, this suggestion must be rejected since such a practice was unthinkable in God's plan for the tabernacle and its service.[4]

Some scholars believe that the reference to these women serving at the tent of meeting is an anachronism. They argue that the women are described as serving at the tabernacle prior to the

---

[2]John I. Durham, *Exodus*, Word Biblical Commentary, vol. 3 (Waco, Tex.: Word Books, 1987), 487.

[3]Various suggestions regarding the roles of these women are discussed in Durham, 487, and R. Alan Cole, *Exodus: An Introduction and Commentary*, Tyndale Old Testament Commentaries (Downers Grove, Ill.: Inter-Varsity Press, 1973), 236.

[4]Cole, 236.

time it was set up, making the statement unhistorical.[5] The most likely solution to this supposed difficulty is that these women served at the previous "tent of meeting" used by Moses (33:7) prior to donating their mirrors. Then, after the tabernacle was erected, they served there in the same capacity.

"Mirrors," made today of glass, were in ancient times made of burnished metal, making them valuable. Frederick W. Danker gave this description of such mirrors: "Some are simply round surfaces; others have handles, often shaped in the form of a female figure; others have pedestals and can be placed on furniture."[6] The donation of these mirrors by the serving women probably represented a considerable sacrifice. Perhaps this is the reason that their contribution was worthy of special note.

Replica of the Bronze Laver (Timna Park, Israel)

---

[5]For example, see J. Philip Hyatt, *Exodus*, The New Century Bible Commentary (Grand Rapids, Mich.: Wm. B. Eerdmans Publishing Co., 1971), 330.

[6]Frederick W. Danker, "Mirror," in *The International Standard Bible Encyclopedia*, rev. ed., ed. Geoffrey W. Bromiley (Grand Rapids, Mich.: Wm. B. Eerdmans Publishing Co., 1986), 3:382. This article has a bronze Egyptian mirror.

THE COURT (38:9–20)

**[9]Then he made the court: for the south side the hangings
of the court were of fine twisted linen, one hundred cubits;
[10]their twenty pillars, and their twenty sockets, made of bronze;
the hooks of the pillars and their bands were of silver. [11]For the
north side there were one hundred cubits; their twenty pillars
and their twenty sockets were of bronze, the hooks of the pil-
lars and their bands were of silver. [12]For the west side there
were hangings of fifty cubits with their ten pillars and their
ten sockets; the hooks of the pillars and their bands were of
silver. [13]For the east side fifty cubits. [14]The hangings for the one
side of the gate were fifteen cubits, with their three pillars and
their three sockets, [15]and so for the other side. On both sides
of the gate of the court were hangings of fifteen cubits, with
their three pillars and their three sockets. [16]All the hangings of
the court all around were of fine twisted linen. [17]The sockets
for the pillars were of bronze, the hooks of the pillars and their
bands, of silver; and the overlaying of their tops, of silver, and
all the pillars of the court were furnished with silver bands.
[18]The screen of the gate of the court was the work of the weaver,
of blue and purple and scarlet material and fine twisted linen.
And the length was twenty cubits and the height was five
cubits, corresponding to the hangings of the court. [19]Their four
pillars and their four sockets were of bronze; their hooks were
of silver, and the overlaying of their tops and their bands were
of silver. [20]All the pegs of the tabernacle and of the court all
around were of bronze.**

Verses 9–20. To say that this passage is about the construction of the courtyard may be misleading. The area around the tent became the tabernacle courtyard when it was enclosed by a fence. Exodus 27:9–19 gives the directions for the building of that fence, whereas 38:9–20 tells how those instructions were followed. The account of its construction in chapter 38 does not differ significantly from the instructions given earlier. The slight differences only emphasize that the latter passage is not simply an exact replica of the former. (See comments on 27:9–19.)

With the completion of the courtyard, in which both the altar of burnt offering and the laver stood, the construction of the tabernacle itself was finished.

THE COST OF THE TABERNACLE (38:21–31)

Next, the text provides information about what the tabernacle cost. It begins with those who led, either in collecting contributions or constructing the tabernacle (38:21–23) and then relates how much was given and how it was used (38:24–31).

The Leaders (38:21–23)

[21]This is the number of the things for the tabernacle, the tabernacle of the testimony, as they were numbered according to the command of Moses, for the service of the Levites, by the hand of Ithamar the son of Aaron the priest. [22]Now Bezalel the son of Uri, the son of Hur, of the tribe of Judah, made all that the LORD had commanded Moses. [23]With him was Oholiab the son of Ahisamach, of the tribe of Dan, an engraver and a skillful workman and a weaver in blue and in purple and in scarlet material, and fine linen.

Verse 21. The bookkeeper's summary starts with a sentence announcing the point of the section: to record the accounting of **the number of the things for the tabernacle** collected as tax from all those who were **numbered**. These revenues resulted from the census that had previously been commanded by God (30:11–16). In addition to the money required by the tax, the account also details the value of the miscellaneous goods given by the Israelites in the freewill offering (38:24, 29). The voluntary contribution called for in 25:1–7 was given in 35:21–29 and 36:3–7.

The expression **by the hand of Ithamar** indicates that the accounting was done under his direction.[7] Ithamar was one of the sons of Aaron and he served as a priest (6:23; 28:1; Lev. 10:6,

[7]Peter Enns, *Exodus*, The NIV Application Commentary (Grand Rapids, Mich.: Zondervan, 2000), 548.

12, 16). John I. Durham noted that Ithamar was "in charge of the inventory-taking" and referred to Numbers 7:1–8, where Ithamar was given responsibility for another supervisory task.[8]

The expression **for the service of the Levites** seems to be out of place, since the Levites had not yet begun their work in connection with the tabernacle. Therefore, some scholars conclude that "38:21–31 does not belong here, or that these verses refer to something that took place later."[9] However, the Levites had already distinguished themselves (32:26–28) and had already been dedicated to the Lord (32:29). It is reasonable, therefore, to assume that their service had indeed begun—that they, under Ithamar's oversight, had been given the task of accounting for the goods given for the tabernacle.

Verses 22, 23. The names of those most responsible for the building of the tent appear again: **Bezalel** and **Oholiab**. Bezalel was the leader in the work of building the tabernacle, while Oholiab served as his assistant (see comments on 31:1–6; 35:30–35).

The Amount Given (38:24–31)

**24All the gold that was used for the work, in all the work of the sanctuary, even the gold of the wave offering, was 29 talents and 730 shekels, according to the shekel of the sanctuary.
25The silver of those of the congregation who were numbered was 100 talents and 1,775 shekels, according to the shekel of the sanctuary; 26a beka a head (that is, half a shekel according to the shekel of the sanctuary), for each one who passed over to those who were numbered, from twenty years old and upward, for 603,550 men. 27The hundred talents of silver were for casting the sockets of the sanctuary and the sockets of the veil; one hundred sockets for the hundred talents, a talent for a socket. 28Of the 1,775 shekels, he made hooks for the pillars and overlaid their tops and made bands for them. 29The bronze**

[8]Durham, 489–90.

[9]W. H. Gispen, *Exodus*, trans. Ed van der Maas, Bible Student's Commentary (Grand Rapids, Mich.: Regency Reference Library, Zondervan Publishing House, 1982), 327.

of the wave offering was 70 talents and 2,400 shekels. [30]With it he made the sockets to the doorway of the tent of meeting, and the bronze altar and its bronze grating, and all the utensils of the altar, [31]and the sockets of the court all around and the sockets of the gate of the court, and all the pegs of the tabernacle and all the pegs of the court all around.

The precious metals given are presented in the order of their value, from the greatest to the least: gold, silver, and bronze. While the whole tabernacle complex was holy, items were made out of the material corresponding to their degree of holiness: bronze (holy), silver (holier), and gold (holiest).

Verse 24. The first precious metal, **gold**, was used extensively for the sacred furnishings of **the sanctuary**. The contributions are referred to as a **wave offering** (תְּנוּפָה, *theᵉnupah*) which, in this context, seems to be the equivalent of a "freewill offering." The record of this giving is found in 35:22: "Then all whose hearts moved them, both men and women, came and brought brooches and earrings and signet rings and bracelets, all articles of gold; so did every man who presented an offering of gold to the LORD."

Verses 25–28. Next, **silver** was given in the tax required of every adult Israelite male. This precious metal was used **for casting the sockets of the sanctuary and the sockets of the veil**, as well as making **hooks for the pillars**.

Peter Enns explained the mathematical relationship between the census and the amount of silver given:

> Each Israelite who crossed the Red Sea gave one beka (= 1/2 shekel). One hundred talents and 1,775 shekels comes to 301,775 shekels (one talent = 3000 shekels, hence 100 talents = 300,000 shekels). Since a beka is 1/2 a shekel the total number of Israelite men who crossed the sea (assuming "men" in v. 26 is to be taken literally) is twice the number of shekels, hence the number 603,550.[10]

---

[10]Enns, 549, n. 55.

This number is the same as that of the men counted in the census recorded in Numbers 1:46. Instructions for the census which resulted in the amount given are found in 30:11–16. This census was taken before the building of the tabernacle. The census in Numbers 1 was taken a month after the tabernacle was completed. Thus, the two censuses, taken several months apart, yielded the same data. Wilbur Fields suggested that the first census prepared for the second, which was apparently taken in a single day.[11]

Verses 29–31. The final precious metal listed is **bronze**, which was used for **the sockets to the doorway of the tent of meeting, the bronze altar** and its **utensils**, **the sockets of the court**, and **all the pegs of the tabernacle and all the pegs of the court.** As in the case of the gold, the contribution of bronze is also referred to as a **wave offering** (see comments on 38:24). Articles of bronze were given at the freewill offering (35:24).

The weight of the contributions of gold, silver, and bronze was also calculated by Enns:

> It takes 300 shekels to make one talent. The approximate weights of the material listed, in today's measures, are as follows: 2,193.25 pounds of gold, 7,544.38 pounds of silver, 5,310 pounds of bronze. To put it in perspective, the total weight in precious metals the Israelites carried out of Egypt was about 15,000 pounds. This may seem like an excessively heavy amount in the abstract but it comes to only approximately .025 pounds for every adult male Israelite—pocket change. There is no need to suggest, as some have done, that these weights are exaggerated numbers.[12]

While the gifts of gold and bronze emphasize the Israelites' generosity, the silver given demonstrates their obedience.

---

[11]Wilbur Fields, *Exploring Exodus*, Bible Study Textbook Series (Joplin, Mo.: College Press, 1976), 789–90.

[12]Enns, 548–49. For a similar reckoning, see Walter C. Kaiser, Jr., "Exodus," in *The Expositor's Bible Commentary*, vol. 2, *Genesis—Numbers* (Grand Rapids, Mich.: Zondervan, 1990), 495.

APPLICATION

"What Does It Cost?" (38:21–31)

What does it cost? In Australia, people say, "Emma Chizit?" ("How much is it?") That question is frequently asked about food, about clothing, about furniture, about houses. We should ask the same question in religion. How much does it cost to be a follower of Christ? Jesus encouraged people to count the cost of discipleship before they began to follow Him (Lk. 14:28–33). When the tabernacle was completed, someone determined how much it had cost to build.

Exodus 38:21–31 reads like an accountant's ledger. The construction of the parts for the tabernacle had been completed. All that was left to do was to make the priestly garments and then to erect the tent and put its furnishings in place. It seemed necessary to give an accounting of the goods that had been received from the people's freewill offering and from the half-shekel tax (30:13, 14). The accountant recorded how much gold was used, how much silver, and how much bronze. Since the silver came from the tax paid by all the assessed males, the account also indicates how many men were numbered in the census: 603,550 (38:26).

When this accounting was done, it probably served as an auditor's report; it demonstrated that what had been given had been properly used. For those who later read the words, the passage emphasized the liberality of the people. It also showed the value and importance of the tabernacle.

It costs nothing. What does it cost to be a Christian today? In one sense, it costs us nothing. That is not to say that salvation costs nothing. It cost Christ His life—His coming to earth, living a life of sorrow, and dying on the cross. He purchased the church "with His own blood" (Acts 20:28; see Eph. 5:25). Jesus gave "His life a ransom for many" (Mt. 20:28). He paid the ransom price demanded by God's justice to free us from sin. Consequently, salvation is free to us (Rev. 22:17); it is a gift (Rom. 6:23). Christ paid the price of our salvation.

It costs everything. In another sense, it costs us everything. When Jesus spoke of counting the cost of discipleship in Luke 14,

He plainly indicated that there was a cost involved in being a disciple. How much? The story of the rich young ruler answers that question. Jesus told him, "Go and sell all you possess and give to the poor, and you will have treasure in heaven; and come, follow Me" (Mk. 10:21). The rich young ruler is representative of all people. One who desires to follow Christ must be willing to give up anything that stands in the way of his being a disciple.

Giving Jesus everything means that we give ourselves to Him in obedience to His commands. Salvation is free. It is a gift, but it is a gift that must be accepted. We accept it when we believe in Jesus and trust Him enough to repent of our sins, confess His name, and be baptized for the forgiveness of sins. This does not add our merit to Christ's merit; we could never deserve the salvation He provides. We gratefully appropriate to ourselves the salvation which He freely offers.

Has being a Christian cost us very much? Are we doing our share of the work, or are we enjoying what is provided by others without paying any of the cost ourselves? The church cost Jesus His life. How much are we willing to give to advance the cause of that blood-bought body?

We Need an Ithamar! (38:21–31)

Every church and every good work needs an Ithamar! In every work that involves donated money or goods, an Ithamar, a good bookkeeper, is needed. The funds received should be accounted for in a way that will demonstrate that the money received was spent as it was intended and that none was wasted or misappropriated. Paul was very concerned about "taking precaution so that no one will discredit us in our administration of this generous gift; for we have regard for what is honorable, not only in the sight of the Lord, but also in the sight of men" (2 Cor. 8:18–21). We should have the same concern.

The Expensive Tabernacle
And Its Significance Today (38:21–31)

Does the fact that the tabernacle was expensive justify Christians today having an expensive lifestyle or building luxurious church buildings? (1) How about an expensive lifestyle? Christians need to understand that the Bible does not promise them prosperity. Furthermore, while some Christians may become rich (1 Tim. 6:17), they are not to covet riches (1 Tim. 6:9, 10). Each disciple must dedicate himself and his goods—however much or little he has—to the Lord.

(2) What about luxurious church buildings? The Bible is silent about church buildings. The tabernacle should not be used as an excuse to build magnificent buildings that are unnecessary for accomplishing the work of the Lord. Nevertheless, the tabernacle suggests that there is nothing wrong with building beautiful buildings which are also functional.

CHAPTER 39

THE MAKING OF THE PRIESTLY GARMENTS AND THE PRESENTATION OF THE TABERNACLE

Exodus 39 is composed of two parts. The first deals with the making of the priestly garments (39:1–31). These garments include the ephod and the onyx stones (39:1–7), the breastpiece (39:8–21), the robe (39:22–26), and the tunics, turban, caps, linen breeches, and gold plate (39:27–31). The second part (39:32–43) serves as a conclusion to the entire section on building the tabernacle (35:1—39:43). It emphasizes the completion of the construction work, the presentation of the finished product to Moses, and his approval (which implies God's approval).

THE MAKING OF THE PRIESTLY GARMENTS (39:1–31)

The first part of the chapter underscores the fact that Israel obeyed God by fashioning the priestly garments "just as the LORD had commanded Moses." This phrase appears at the end of each paragraph in this section (39:1, 5, 7, 21, 26, 29, 31). The original instructions for these garments appear in chapter 28.

INSTRUCTIONS	GARMENTS	CONSTRUCTION
28:6–14	Ephod	39:1–7
28:15–30	Breastpiece	39:8–21
28:31–35	Robe	39:22–26
28:36–38	Gold plate	39:30, 31
28:39–43	Tunics, turban, sashes, caps, breeches	39:27–29

The close similarity between Exodus 28 and 39 is noteworthy. The words used to describe the making of the garments often correspond almost exactly to the words given in the instructions. (For example, compare 28:17–21 and 39:10–14.)

Nevertheless, although the two descriptions of the priestly garments are similar, there are also interesting differences between them. One significant difference is that chapter 28 provides explanations—it gives the reasons "why"—which are not found in the story of the accomplishment of the task in chapter 39. There are several examples of these explanations. (1) Aaron's garments were to be made "for glory and for beauty" (28:2). (2) The breastpiece was to be a "breastpiece of judgment" that held "the Urim and the Thummim" (28:15, 29, 30). (3) The bells on the high priest's garment were put there so that their tinkling could be "heard when he enters and leaves the holy place before the LORD, so that he will not die" (28:35). (4) The linen breeches were to be made "to cover [the priests'] bare flesh" that they might "not incur guilt and die" when they serve at the altar (28:42, 43).

The similarities and differences between the two passages give an air of authenticity to them. They are exactly what one would expect to find. The similarities prove that there were not two differing and conflicting accounts of the same event; the differences prove that one account does not consist of a slavish imitation of the other.

The two accounts, then, though similar, have different emphases. Chapter 28 emphasizes what was to be done and why; it gives greater attention to the spiritual significance of the garments. Chapter 39 emphasizes the fact that the previous instructions were obeyed and, in some cases, how they were carried out. In chapter 39 the emphasis is not so much on the significance of the garments or of the priests who wore them, but on the fact that Moses and the Israelites followed God's directions exactly in the production of the garments.

The emphasis on Israel's obedience which permeates the section (chs. 35—39) stands in contrast to their gross disobedience in the golden calf incident (ch. 32). The text tells the reader: Though Israel fell, wholly and horribly, and God punished the nation, the people returned and God forgave them. As a result, the people, as evidence of their repentance, obeyed the Lord by doing exactly as He told them.

The Ephod and the Onyx Stones (39:1–7)

[1]Moreover, from the blue and purple and scarlet material, they made finely woven garments for ministering in the holy place as well as the holy garments which were for Aaron, just as the LORD had commanded Moses.

[2]He made the ephod of gold, and of blue and purple and scarlet material, and fine twisted linen. [3]Then they hammered out gold sheets and cut them into threads to be woven in with the blue and the purple and the scarlet material, and the fine linen, the work of a skillful workman. [4]They made attaching shoulder pieces for the ephod; it was attached at its two upper ends. [5]The skillfully woven band which was on it was like its workmanship, of the same material: of gold and of blue and purple and scarlet material, and fine twisted linen, just as the LORD had commanded Moses.

[6]They made the onyx stones, set in gold filigree settings; they were engraved like the engravings of a signet, according to the names of the sons of Israel. [7]And he placed them on the shoulder pieces of the ephod, as memorial stones for the sons of Israel, just as the LORD had commanded Moses.

Verse 1. This chapter begins, as do other sections of the book (see 40:1, 2, 17), with a summary of what follows. The writer said, in effect, "Next, I will describe how they made the priestly garments." Then he proceeded to do exactly that. A distinction is made between the **garments for ministering in the holy place** which were worn by the priests and **the holy garments which were for Aaron** and succeeding high priests.

Israel obeyed God by fashioning the priestly garments **just as the LORD had commanded Moses**. R. Alan Cole pointed out that this phrase appears seven times in this section (39:1, 5, 7, 21, 26, 29, 31), as well as in the next chapter (40:19, 21, 23, 25, 27, 29, 32). He explained that this intentional repetition points to "the faithfulness of Moses in carrying out God's instruction (Ex. 25:9)" and "the faithfulness of God" who "will still dwell among His people, in spite of their initial failure."[1]

Verses 2–5. First, **the ephod** was **made.** Note that verse 1 says that "they" made the garments, whereas verse 2 says that **he** made the ephod. In 39:1–31, the pronouns referring to the makers of the garments alternate between "they" (39:1, 3, 4, 6, 9, 10, 15, 16, 17, 18, 19, 20, 21, 24, 25, 27, 30, 31) and "he" (39:2, 7, 8, 22). "He" refers to Bezalel and "they" to the artisans who did the work on the tabernacle.[2]

The only additional information provided beyond that which is found in chapter 28 is the description of how **gold** was worked into the material for the ephod: **Then they hammered out gold sheets and cut them into threads to be woven in with the blue and the purple and the scarlet material, and the fine linen** (39:3). The priestly garments were made to be beautiful as well as functional and spiritually symbolic (28:2). (See comments on 28:6.)

Verses 6, 7. Next, the account says that **they made the onyx stones, set in gold filigree settings**. On these two stones were **engraved . . . the names of the** [twelve] **sons of Israel**, six on each stone (28:10). Moreover, the stones were set **on the shoulder pieces of the ephod**. When the high priest wore the ephod in his official duties, these stones served **as memorial stones**, symbolically indicating that he represented the entire people of Israel. (See comments on 28:7–14.)

The Breastpiece (39:8–21)

8He made the breastpiece, the work of a skillful workman, like the workmanship of the ephod: of gold and of blue and purple and scarlet material and fine twisted linen. 9It was square; they made the breastpiece folded double, a span long

---

[1]R. Alan Cole, *Exodus: An Introduction and Commentary*, Tyndale Old Testament Commentaries (Downers Grove, Ill.: Inter-Varsity Press, 1973), 233.

[2]John I. Durham, *Exodus*, Word Biblical Commentary, vol. 3 (Waco, Tex.: Word Books, 1987), 492.

and a span wide when folded double. 10And they mounted four rows of stones on it. The first row was a row of ruby, topaz, and emerald; 11and the second row, a turquoise, a sapphire and a diamond; 12and the third row, a jacinth, an agate, and an amethyst; 13and the fourth row, a beryl, an onyx, and a jasper. They were set in gold filigree settings when they were mounted. 14The stones were corresponding to the names of the sons of Israel; they were twelve, corresponding to their names, engraved with the engravings of a signet, each with its name for the twelve tribes. 15They made on the breastpiece chains like cords, of twisted cordage work in pure gold. 16They made two gold filigree settings and two gold rings, and put the two rings on the two ends of the breastpiece. 17Then they put the two gold cords in the two rings at the ends of the breastpiece. 18They put the other two ends of the two cords on the two filigree settings, and put them on the shoulder pieces of the ephod at the front of it. 19They made two gold rings and placed them on the two ends of the breastpiece, on its inner edge which was next to the ephod. 20Furthermore, they made two gold rings and placed them on the bottom of the two shoulder pieces of the ephod, on the front of it, close to the place where it joined, above the woven band of the ephod. 21They bound the breastpiece by its rings to the rings of the ephod with a blue cord, so that it would be on the woven band of the ephod, and that the breastpiece would not come loose from the ephod, just as the LORD had commanded Moses.

Verses 8–21. The description of the making of **the breastpiece** occupies more space than any other item of the priests' attire, just as more space was given to the instructions for the breastpiece in chapter 28. Although made separately, the breastpiece was attached to **the ephod** and was, therefore, essentially a part of the ephod. The most obvious feature of the breastpiece was the **four rows** of semiprecious **stones**, with three stones in each **row**. These twelve stones corresponded to **the names of the sons of Israel**; on each stone was engraved the name of one of those sons. The high priest's representation of the entire people—**the twelve tribes**—was therefore indicated in two ways: by the onyx stones on the ephod and by the twelve stones on the breastpiece. (See comments on 28:15–30.)

The detail that the breastpiece also held "the Urim and the Thummim" (28:30) is omitted here. No mention of them was necessary if they already existed and did not need to be made.

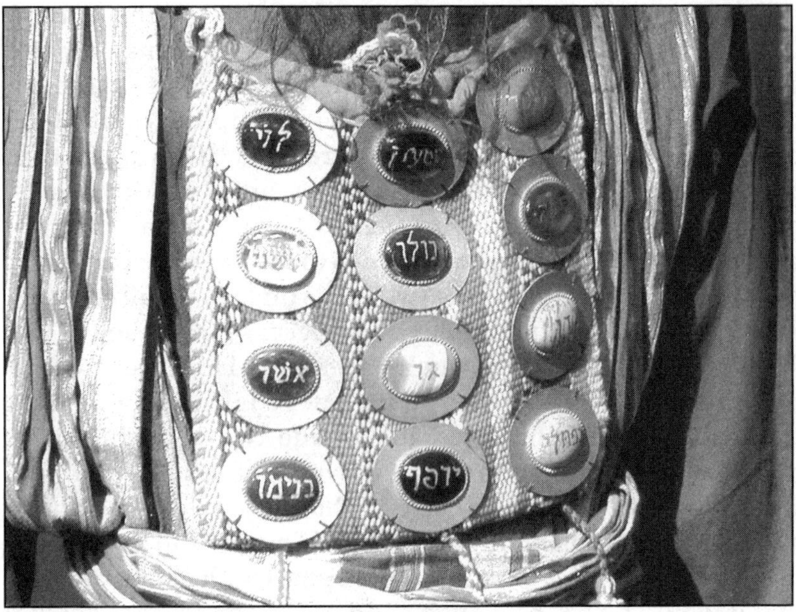

Replica of the Breastpiece (Timna Park, Israel)

The Robe (39:22–26)

**22Then he made the robe of the ephod of woven work, all
of blue; 23and the opening of the robe was at the top in the center, as the opening of a coat of mail, with a binding all around
its opening, so that it would not be torn. 24They made pome-
granates of blue and purple and scarlet material and twisted
linen on the hem of the robe. 25They also made bells of pure
gold, and put the bells between the pomegranates all around
on the hem of the robe, 26alternating a bell and a pomegranate
all around on the hem of the robe for the service, just as the
LORD had commanded Moses.**

Verses 22–26. The fact that the high priest's robe is called **the robe of the ephod** in 28:31 and 39:22 suggests that the ephod was the most important part of his apparel. This ephod, more than anything else, differentiated the high priest from the other priests and worshipers.

The robe was a plain **blue** garment worn under the ephod. The most unusual thing about it was the **pomegranates**, most likely woven into the hem, and the **bells** attached to the hem. (See comments on 28:31–35.)

The Tunics, Turban, Caps, Linen Breeches, and Gold Plate (39:27–31)

27They made the tunics of finely woven linen for Aaron and
his sons, 28and the turban of fine linen, and the decorated caps
of fine linen, and the linen breeches of fine twisted linen, 29and
the sash of fine twisted linen, and blue and purple and scarlet material, the work of the weaver, just as the LORD had commanded Moses.

30They made the plate of the holy crown of pure gold, and inscribed it like the engravings of a signet, "Holy to the LORD."
31They fastened a blue cord to it, to fasten it on the turban above, just as the LORD had commanded Moses.

Verses 27–29. This section continues the description of the making of the other priestly garments. **Aaron and his sons** all wore **tunics, linen breeches**, and **sash**[es]. These special garments distinguished them as priests from the rest of the Israelites. However, only Aaron (the high priest) wore **the turban**, whereas his sons wore **the decorated caps**. (See comments on 28:39–43.)

Verses 30, 31. The description concludes with an account of the manufacture of the golden **plate**, or **crown**. In the instructions of chapter 28, this plate precedes the tunics, caps, linen breeches, and sashes (28:36–38). The plate of gold was inscribed **Holy to the LORD** and was attached to the high priest's **turban**. The plate proclaimed that the high priest was "holy." According to John I. Durham, the inscription "refers not alone, indeed not even primarily to 'Aaron' and his successors. . . . It is Israel that is 'set apart for Yahweh.'"[3] Aaron and the high priests who followed him represented Israel when they wore their consecrated garments in God's presence. (See comments on 28:36–38.)

The importance of the priestly garments is obvious from the fact that so much space is given to their description. Undoubtedly, the different parts of the vestments also have symbolic significance. However, the text provides little information about the symbolism intended. These garments designed by God set apart the priests for the Lord's service.

Replica of the High Priest's Garments (Timna Park, Israel)

THE PRESENTATION OF THE TABERNACLE (39:32–43)

[32]Thus all the work of the tabernacle of the tent of meeting was completed; and the sons of Israel did according to all that

[3]Ibid, 388.

**the LORD had commanded Moses; so they did. [33]They brought
the tabernacle to Moses, the tent and all its furnishings: its
clasps, its boards, its bars, and its pillars and its sockets; [34]and
the covering of rams' skins dyed red, and the covering of por-
poise skins, and the screening veil; [35]the ark of the testimony
and its poles and the mercy seat; [36]the table, all its utensils, and
the bread of the Presence; [37]the pure gold lampstand, with its
arrangement of lamps and all its utensils, and the oil for the
light; [38]and the gold altar, and the anointing oil and the fra-
grant incense, and the veil for the doorway of the tent; [39]the
bronze altar and its bronze grating, its poles and all its uten-
sils, the laver and its stand; [40]the hangings for the court, its pil-
lars and its sockets, and the screen for the gate of the court, its
cords and its pegs and all the equipment for the service of the
tabernacle, for the tent of meeting; [41]the woven garments for
ministering in the holy place and the holy garments for Aaron
the priest and the garments of his sons, to minister as priests.
[42]So the sons of Israel did all the work according to all that the
LORD had commanded Moses. [43]And Moses examined all the
work and behold, they had done it; just as the LORD had com-
manded, this they had done. So Moses blessed them.**

Verse 32. Israel had finished their **work** on **the tabernacle**! This verse provides a suitable conclusion to chapter 39. It also serves as a climax to the entire story of the construction of the tabernacle found in Exodus 35—39. God gave the instructions in Exodus 25—31. All those instructions had been carried out. The text states that they **did according to all that the LORD had commanded Moses**. In this expression, "according to all that" replaces "just as" in the previous part of the chapter. This language serves to bracket the section (39:32, 42, 43).

Verses 33–41. The fact that **they brought the tabernacle to Moses** indicates that the parts of the tabernacle were made separately; they were put together after everything had been constructed. (Chapter 40 tells of the assembly of the various parts.) They brought the tabernacle and its furnishings to Moses for his approval. Since Moses was God's spokesman, they were seeking God's approval as well.

Verses 33 through 41 function as a checklist or inventory to demonstrate that everything on the Lord's "to do" list had been accomplished. The passage serves its function well. It emphasizes that Israel made *everything* that the Lord asked them to make.

THREE LISTINGS OF THE PARTS OF THE TABERNACLE BEING CONSTRUCTED[4]

Elements of the Tabernacle	*Summons to Build*	*Description of Construction*	*Presentation to Moses*
Tabernacle (tent)	35:11	36:8–34	39:33, 34
Inner veil	35:12	36:35, 36	39:34
Ark & mercy seat	35:12	37:1–9	39:35
Table of showbread	35:13	37:10–16	39:36
Lampstand	35:14	37:17–24	39:37
Altar of incense	35:15	37:25–29	39:38
Outer veil (screen)	35:15	36:37, 38	39:38
Bronze altar	35:16	38:1–7	39:39
Laver (basin)	35:16	38:8	39:39
Court	35:17, 18	38:9–20	39:40
Priestly garments	35:19	39:1–31	39:41

Verses 42, 43. These verses make explicit what had been implied by the previous list: **Israel** had done **all that the Lord** required of them in the construction of the tabernacle. **Moses** looked over the completed work, compared it with the Lord's blueprint—including what had been "shown" him on the mountain (25:40)—and approved of it.

Moses showed his approval by blessing those who had done the work. To "bless" someone means to praise or to congratulate him or her, or to wish an individual well. Moses praised the people for completing the task, indicating that, as God's representative, he was well pleased with their efforts. W. H. Gispen wrote, "Moses inspected and approved the work; to express his

---

[4]For a similar chart comparing God's original instructions and a summary, see comments on 31:7–11.

gratitude he rewarded the people by blessing them."[5]

Commentators point out that the expression **Moses blessed them** is reminiscent of Genesis 1:22, 28; 2:3: When all the parts of the creation were finished, "God blessed them." What Israel had done was like a new creation.[6] With the completion of this "new creation" the Israelites were ready to begin a new era of their history; all that remained was for the tabernacle to be set up and consecrated (ch. 40).

APPLICATION

"According to the Pattern" (Ch. 39)

In Exodus 25:8, 9, God told Moses to make the tabernacle "according to the pattern." Apparently, besides the instructions God gave Moses orally, He also showed Moses a picture, a vision, a visual representation or a model of the tabernacle. Then He told Moses to make the tabernacle according to that "pattern" (see 24:40; Heb. 8:5). As the writer of Hebrews alluded to this event, he indicated that there was a "heavenly" pattern which served as the model for the earthly tabernacle. That heavenly pattern, Hebrews says, was the present system, the Christian system.

In this lesson we want to focus on two things: (1) It was important for Moses and the Israelites to follow God's instructions in building the tabernacle. (2) If it was important for them to do so, then it is important for us to follow God's instructions in building God's "tabernacle," the church, today.

Israel was to follow God's "pattern" in building the tabernacle. We know it was important for Israel to follow God's instructions because God told them to do so (25:8, 9; see 19:5,6; 25:40; 31:11; Acts 7:44). For another, God gave detailed instructions, suggesting that He intended for them to be followed in detail. Further,

---

[5]W. H. Gispen, *Exodus*, trans. Ed van der Maas, Bible Student's Commentary (Grand Rapids, Mich.: Zondervan, 1978), 330.

[6]This idea has been expressed by several commentators, such as Peter Enns, *Exodus*, The NIV Application Commentary (Grand Rapids, Mich.: Zondervan, 2000), 550.

it is evident that following God's instructions to the letter was important for Israel because that is, in fact, what the Israelites did (39:1, 5, 7, 21, 26, 29, 31, 32, 42, 43). Apparently, Israel thought God meant what He said in giving the instructions for the tabernacle, because they followed those instructions carefully. Besides that, we know that God was pleased with their careful obedience because He blessed their efforts by entering into the tabernacle they had built "according to the pattern" (Ex. 40).

We should follow God's "pattern" today. The New Testament teaches that the message of God revealed through Christ and His apostles was intended to guide mankind until the end of time (Mt. 24:35; 28:18–20; Jn. 16:13; Gal. 1:8, 9; 2 Tim. 3:16,17; Jude 3). God has thus given those who desire to follow Christ a "pattern," just as He gave Israel a "pattern." Moreover, He intends for us to follow it, to obey His commands, just as He required obedience of Israel (Mt. 7:21–24). That continuing message involves the church, to which the saved are added (Acts 2:47). That church was built by Christ and saved by Christ (Mt. 16:18, 19; Eph. 5:23–25); Christ is the head of that church (Col. 1:18). When congregations were established as the result of the preaching of the gospel, they were guided by inspired men (Eph. 2:19, 20; 3:5). In this way, they were "built" according to the "pattern" which God had given them. None of those congregations were perfect; they were judged according to the God-given pattern by the apostles and other inspired writers of the New Testament.

Since those early churches were established in accordance with and then judged by a pattern given by God, Christians today are obligated to follow that same pattern when we establish or build churches. We must preach the gospel they preached and require of men today what they required of people to be saved. We must recognize the same standard of authority—namely the authority of Christ as found in the New Testament. In our congregations, we need to have the same worship and organization as was found in churches of the New Testament. We must require the same standards of Christian living that were required of believers in the first century. To follow that New Testament pattern is, in fact, what those involved in the Restoration Movement are trying to do and what we urge all others to do.

Sometimes people object to this aim, to what they like to call "pattern theology." They may say, (1) "God would surely not punish people for not following the New Testament." *Our reply*: If God punished people then for not following His pattern (see Lev. 10:1, 2), why would He not do so today? He is the same God and He requires obedience today just as He did then. (2) "But there was no discernible pattern in the New Testament, since the first-century churches differed from one another." *Our reply*: They may have differed from one another in some matters—in matters of expediency—but they were all to be alike in other ways—in matters of necessity. A pattern existed in the mind of God and was revealed to inspired men because all of the churches were judged by the same standard: the pattern which God revealed to the apostles. (3) "Surely, God does not care about the details; He will punish us only if we are wrong on major issues." *Our reply*: Maybe so, but who determines which matters are "major" to God and which are not? Exodus illustrates that some things we would call "minor" were considered by God to be "major," for He punished people accordingly.

Conclusion. God told Moses and Israel to "make all things according to the pattern." We need to follow the same principle today. If we do what people did in New Testament times to become Christians and to worship and live as Christians, then we will be Christians just as they were; and we will be pleasing to God.

We Can Come Back (39:1)

Some time ago a television commercial featured people saying, "I came back," referring to their decision to buy an older product which they once used over a newer product which they had found to be inferior. In Exodus 39:1, we learn that Israel "came back." Though Israel fell, wholly and horribly, and God punished the nation, the people returned and God forgave them. Then the people, as evidence of their repentance, obeyed the Lord by doing exactly as He told them. Just as Israel came back, so can we. No matter how sinful we have been, no matter what wrongs we have done, we can come back and become fully obedient. If God could accept the Israelites back, if Jesus could accept

Peter back, if Christ could make use of Saul the tormentor of the church, God can and will accept us back. Then we, like Israel, can do "just as the LORD commanded."

Leadership by Delegation (39:33)

The fact that "they brought the tabernacle to Moses" implies that Moses had not personally supervised the work; he had not been looking over the shoulders of the workmen to make sure every nail was driven in the right place, every board was exactly the right length, every stitch was straight. The work was overseen by workmen with special talents. Only after the work was finished was the completed product brought to Moses. Moses' leadership style provides a good example for leaders today.

"Moses Blessed Them"—
Blessings All Around (39:43)

Chapter 39 ends with these words: "So Moses blessed them." The work on the tabernacle had been completed. All that remained was for it to be set up and consecrated. Moses examined the work and saw that everything had been done well. He gave his approval of the work by blessing the people who had done it. Moses' blessing the people should remind us of some important truths. (1) God blessed His creation (Gen. 1:22, 28). The construction of the tabernacle was a kind of new creation. (2) We ought to "bless" others—that is, to praise them for the good that they do (1 Thess. 1:2, 3). (3) We have the opportunity to be blessed in this life (Mt. 5:3–12; Acts 20:35). (4) We have the hope of being blessed forever (Mt. 25:34; Rev. 14:13).

Chapter 40

Erecting and Consecrating The Tabernacle

Chapter 40 provides a fitting conclusion to the book. God had delivered Israel out of bondage in Egypt, brought His people to Sinai, made a covenant with them, and given them His law. In spite of the faithlessness of Israel, He had graciously granted them the privilege of building a place where He might "dwell among them" (25:8). The last chapter describes how the tabernacle was erected and then details the climactic moment of Israel's adventure: God's descent to dwell in His house among His people.

The chapter mirrors the literary structure of the entire section. In Exodus 25—31, God provided instructions about the building of the tabernacle. Exodus 36—39 tells how those instructions were carried out. In 40:1–15, God told how the tabernacle was to be erected and dedicated; 40:16–33 describes how Moses followed God's directions exactly. Then God descended upon the tabernacle, manifesting His presence in the form of a cloud that filled the structure (40:34, 35). Exodus concludes by indicating that the Lord provided continuing guidance for the Israelites during their time in the wilderness (40:36–38).

INSTRUCTIONS FOR ERECTING AND CONSECRATING THE TABERNACLE (40:1–15)

Directions for Setting Up The Tabernacle (40:1–8)

1Then the LORD spoke to Moses, saying, 2"On the first day

of the first month you shall set up the tabernacle of the tent of meeting. [3]You shall place the ark of the testimony there, and you shall screen the ark with the veil. [4]You shall bring in the table and arrange what belongs on it; and you shall bring in the lampstand and mount its lamps. [5]Moreover, you shall set the gold altar of incense before the ark of the testimony, and set up the veil for the doorway to the tabernacle. [6]You shall set the altar of burnt offering in front of the doorway of the tabernacle of the tent of meeting. [7]You shall set the laver between the tent of meeting and the altar and put water in it. [8]You shall set up the court all around and hang up the veil for the gateway of the court."

Verses 1, 2. As the chapter begins, a topic sentence states who (**the Lord**) was speaking to whom (**Moses**), what was to be done (**set up the tabernacle of the tent of meeting**), and when it was to happen (**on the first day of the first month**).

"The first day of the first month" refers to the first day of the second year of Israel's deliverance (40:17). The Israelites had reached Sinai "in the third month . . . on that very day" (exactly three months) after they had been delivered from Egypt (19:1). According to the text, Moses was "on the mountain forty days and forty nights" (24:18) before the golden calf tragedy. He spent another forty days and forty nights receiving the Law a second time (34:28). If Exodus 19:1 indicates that about ninety days had elapsed since Israel's exodus from Egypt, the other two periods of forty days each would make a total of 170 days, not counting the time required for additional events recorded in the narrative. Therefore, Israel apparently built the tabernacle in about six months.[1]

In contrast to a lengthy construction period of approximately six months, the tent could be put up in a day. That a specific day

---

[1]Walter C. Kaiser, Jr., "Exodus," in *The Expositor's Bible Commentary*, vol. 2, *Genesis—Numbers* (Grand Rapids, Mich.: Zondervan, 1990), 496. The same conclusion is given in C. F. Keil and F. Delitzsch, *The Pentateuch*, vol. 2, Commentary on the Old Testament (Grand Rapids, Mich.: Wm. B. Eerdmans Publishing Co., n.d.), 255.

was set for the erection of the tabernacle indicates that the construction of the tent was separate from its erection. This was in keeping with its nature as a portable place of worship. All of the items connected with the tabernacle had already been built. All that remained was a day of putting the parts together to make the whole.

The description "tabernacle of the tent of meeting" suggests that the function of Moses' "tent of meeting" (33:7) was transferred to the tabernacle. From that point on, the tabernacle was the "tent of meeting" where God met with the people or their representative[s]. It was also the place where the people would meet together to offer sacrifices and worship God.

Verse 3. After the tent was set up, the furnishings were to be placed in a logical order. To begin with, **the ark of the testimony** was to be put in the most holy place. The ark of the covenant is called the "ark of the testimony" because it contained the two stone tablets of the Law and bore witness to God's covenant with His people (25:16, 21; 40:20). Next, **the veil** separating the most holy place from the holy place was to be hung.

Verses 4, 5. After this, the furniture which belonged in the holy place was to be installed: **the table** with the bread of the Presence, **the lampstand** with **its** [seven] **lamps**, and **the gold altar of incense**. Then **the veil** or "screen" that covered the entrance to the holy place could be hung (see 40:21).

Verses 6–8. Next, attention turned to the court outside the tent. The first thing mentioned is the bronze **altar of burnt offering**, which was to be placed **in front of the doorway of the tabernacle of the tent of meeting.** The **laver** was to be set **between the tent of meeting and the altar**, and **water** was to be poured into it. Finally, the fence around **the court** was to be put up, and **the veil** which served as the entrance into the courtyard was to be hung.

**Directions for Consecrating
The Tabernacle and the Priests (40:9–15)**

9"Then you shall take the anointing oil and anoint the tabernacle and all that is in it, and shall consecrate it and all its fur-

nishings; and it shall be holy. [10]You shall anoint the altar of burnt offering and all its utensils, and consecrate the altar, and the altar shall be most holy. [11]You shall anoint the laver and its stand, and consecrate it. [12]Then you shall bring Aaron and his sons to the doorway of the tent of meeting and wash them with water. [13]You shall put the holy garments on Aaron and anoint him and consecrate him, that he may minister as a priest to Me. [14]You shall bring his sons and put tunics on them; [15]and you shall anoint them even as you have anointed their father, that they may minister as priests to Me; and their anointing will qualify them for a perpetual priesthood throughout their generations."

Verse 9. After providing directions for setting up the tabernacle, the Lord gave instructions for dedicating it to His use. These instructions are also prefaced by a statement summarizing what follows (see 40:1, 2). Moses was told to use **the anointing oil** to anoint everything connected with **the tabernacle**, including **all its furnishings.** The "furnishings" would include the ark of the covenant, the lampstand, the table of showbread, and the altar of incense.

In the anointing process, Moses would consecrate the tabernacle, setting it apart for God's purposes; the whole thing would become **holy**. It is noteworthy that "holiness" did not characterize the tabernacle, its furnishings, and the whole complex until after it was consecrated.[2] Furthermore, the tabernacle probably did not become truly holy until after God Himself visibly manifested His presence by the cloud that filled it (40:34).

Verses 10, 11. Next, Moses was instructed to **anoint the altar of burnt offering** which was located in the courtyard, along with **all its utensils.** He was also commanded to **anoint the laver and its stand.** As a result, these objects would become sacred to the Lord as well.

Verses 12–15. Then, Moses was instructed to turn his atten-

---

[2]This fact would explain why those who built the ark of the covenant were unharmed during its construction, while those who later looked into the ark were put to death by the Lord (1 Sam. 6:19).

tion to the priests, **Aaron and his sons**, and **wash them** at **the doorway of the tent of meeting**, no doubt at the laver that had just been consecrated (40:11, 31). As the high priest, **Aaron** was to be dressed with **the holy garments** and **anoint**[ed] with oil. Further, Aaron's **sons** were also to be dressed in their **tunics** and **anoint**[ed]. In this way, Aaron and his sons would be qualified to **minister as priests** to the Lord. He would establish **a perpetual priesthood** through them. (The consecration of priests is described in greater detail in chapter 29.)

SETTING UP THE TABERNACLE (40:16–33)

**[16]Thus Moses did; according to all that the LORD had com-
manded him, so he did.**

**[17]Now in the first month of the second year, on the first day
of the month, the tabernacle was erected. [18]Moses erected the
tabernacle and laid its sockets, and set up its boards, and
inserted its bars and erected its pillars. [19]He spread the tent
over the tabernacle and put the covering of the tent on top of
it, just as the LORD had commanded Moses. [20]Then he took the
testimony and put it into the ark, and attached the poles to the
ark, and put the mercy seat on top of the ark. [21]He brought the
ark into the tabernacle, and set up a veil for the screen, and
screened off the ark of the testimony, just as the LORD had com-
manded Moses. [22]Then he put the table in the tent of meeting
on the north side of the tabernacle, outside the veil. [23]He set
the arrangement of bread in order on it before the LORD, just
as the LORD had commanded Moses. [24]Then he placed the lamp-
stand in the tent of meeting, opposite the table, on the south
side of the tabernacle. [25]He lighted the lamps before the LORD,
just as the LORD had commanded Moses. [26]Then he placed the
gold altar in the tent of meeting in front of the veil; [27]and he
burned fragrant incense on it, just as the LORD had commanded
Moses. [28]Then he set up the veil for the doorway of the taber-
nacle. [29]He set the altar of burnt offering before the doorway
of the tabernacle of the tent of meeting, and offered on it the
burnt offering and the meal offering, just as the LORD had com-
manded Moses. [30]He placed the laver between the tent of meet-**

ing and the altar and put water in it for washing. [31]From it Moses and Aaron and his sons washed their hands and their feet. [32]When they entered the tent of meeting, and when they approached the altar, they washed, just as the LORD had commanded Moses. [33]He erected the court all around the tabernacle and the altar, and hung up the veil for the gateway of the court. Thus Moses finished the work.

Verses 16, 17. This section is again prefaced with a summary (see 40:1, 2, 9), highlighting the obedience of Moses in setting up the tabernacle. Just as Moses did with regard to the building of the tabernacle (39:32, 42, 43), so he did in connection with its erection and consecration: **Moses did; according to all that the LORD had commanded him**. The NASB and the NIV make verse 16 the closing sentence of the preceding paragraph. However, the sentence seems to work better as the introduction to a new paragraph, as in the NRSV. **The tabernacle was erected** at the exact time that God had commanded (40:2): **in the first month of the second year, on the first day of the month.**

Verses 18, 19. As with the directions given in 40:2–8, the actual setting up of the tabernacle follows a logical sequence. **Moses** began with **the tabernacle** itself, connecting the **sockets**, **boards**, **bars**, and **pillars** in order to make a framework. Next, **he spread the tent over the tabernacle and put the covering of the tent on top of it.** Moses' obedience is highlighted by the phrase **just as the LORD had commanded Moses**, which appears seven times in this section (see comments on 39:1).

Verses 20, 21. Next, the tablets of the Law (**the testimony**) were placed in **the ark**, the two **poles** were inserted into the rings, and **the mercy seat** was set **on top of the ark.** After this, **the ark** was brought **into the tabernacle**. The area where the ark was placed was then separated from the rest of the tent by the hanging of **a veil**; the most holy place was thus distinguished from the holy place.

Verses 22, 23. The furnishings were installed in the holy place. **The table** was set in place **on the north side of the tabernacle** and the **bread** was set out **before the LORD.**

Verses 24–27. Next, **the lampstand** was set up **on the south**

side of the tabernacle. Moses mounted the seven **lamps** in place and lit them **before the Lord.** After doing this, Moses put **the gold altar . . . in front of the veil.** Then **he burned fragrant incense on it** before the Lord.

Verse 28. In order to separate the holy place from the courtyard, Moses **set up the veil for the doorway of the tabernacle.**

Verse 29. At this point, he placed **the altar of burnt offering before the doorway** or in the courtyard and then sacrificed a **burnt offering** and a **meal** [grain] **offering** to the Lord.

Verses 30–32. Moses set up **the laver**, which was located **between the tent of meeting and the altar.** After **water** was poured into the laver, it was also put to use. **From it Moses and Aaron and his sons washed their hands and their feet**, purifying themselves.

Verse 33. Moses set up the fence, or **court, all around the tabernacle**. He also **hung up the veil** at the entrance to **the court.**

Finally, after the tabernacle had been constructed and erected, the writer could summarize the portion of the book which has to do primarily with the tabernacle by saying, **Thus Moses finished the work.**

Two questions might be raised about this section of the chapter. One deals with the dedication of the tabernacle. After the writer goes into considerable detail about how the newly constructed tabernacle is to be anointed and consecrated in 40:9–15, why did he not describe this anointing and consecration? A reader might conclude that Moses failed to carry out the Lord's orders at this point except for two facts: (1) The text says that Moses did what the Lord commanded (40:19, 21, 23, 25, 27, 29, 32). (2) The actual dedication service is described in Leviticus 8. This fact should serve to remind the reader that Exodus is part of a larger whole—the Pentateuch or Torah—and that the inspired writer of the Pentateuch did not always follow a strict chronological order in telling his story.

A second question might arise from this paragraph. If only the priests were to offer sacrifices, why was Moses allowed to light the lamps, burn incense, offer "the burnt offering and the meal offering," and wash in the laver (40:25, 27, 29, 31)? Several possibilities exist.

One possibility is that Moses, although not one of Aaron's descendants, served as a priest as well as a leader and lawgiver. He was, in fact, a member of the tribe of Levi; and he acted as a mediator between Israel and God, which was the chief function of a priest.[3]

Another possibility is that Moses' actions in this chapter occurred before the priestly order had begun to function officially. Until the priests were ordained, the rules regarding priesthood were not in effect. Thus, Moses did not break any laws when he performed actions later restricted to the priesthood.

A third possibility is that Moses himself did not actually make the offerings but rather caused them to be made.[4]

A final possibility is that the passages are to be taken as proleptic—speaking earlier of things which happened later. Perhaps the statements that Moses lit the lamps, burned incense, made offerings, and washed in the laver are not meant to be understood as happening at the time that the tabernacle was erected. Rather, they are to be understood as indicating what happened later in connection with the items of furniture described in the text. Verse 32 seems to provide evidence for this position, as it speaks of the washing in the laver which continued to occur; the verb "washed" is in the imperfect tense. Further, Umberto Cassuto asserted that the form of the verb used when the text says that "He lighted the lamps," indicated that the lighting "was not done as soon as the lampstand was put in its place, but after the completion of the erection and consecration of the Tabernacle."[5]

Whatever the explanation, one truth is certain: God was pleased with what Moses did.

---

[3]Umberto Cassuto, *A Commentary on the Book of Exodus*, trans. Israel Abrahams (Jerusalem: The Magnes Press, 1997), 483.

[4]R. Alan Cole, *Exodus: An Introduction and Commentary*, Tyndale Old Testament Commentaries (Downers Grove: Ill.: Inter-Varsity Press, 1973), 238.

[5]Cassuto, 482. He added that the same was true of the burning of the incense and the offering of the sacrifices. (Ibid., 482–83.)

THE TABERNACLE

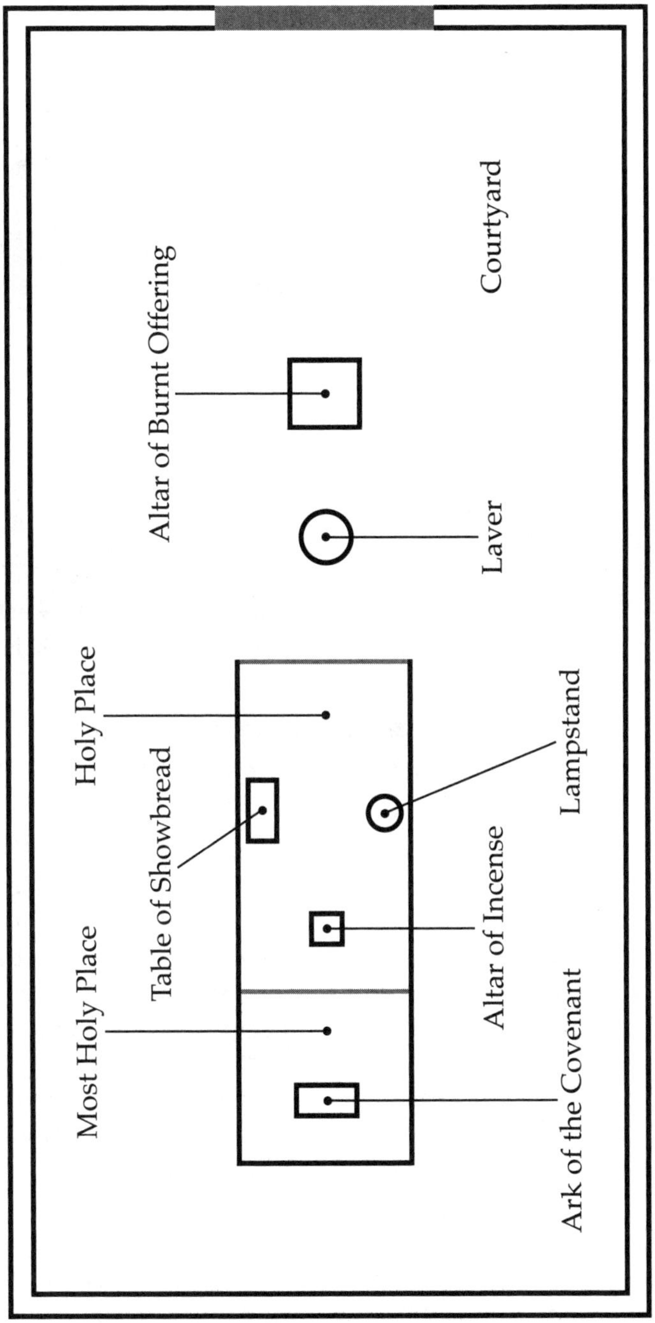

Replica of the Tabernacle and Courtyard (Timna Park, Israel)

THE LORD'S INDWELLING OF THE TABERNACLE (40:34–38)

34Then the cloud covered the tent of meeting, and the glory of the LORD filled the tabernacle. 35Moses was not able to enter the tent of meeting because the cloud had settled on it, and the glory of the LORD filled the tabernacle. 36Throughout all their journeys whenever the cloud was taken up from over the tabernacle, the sons of Israel would set out; 37but if the cloud was not taken up, then they did not set out until the day when it was taken up. 38For throughout all their journeys, the cloud of the LORD was on the tabernacle by day, and there was fire in it by night, in the sight of all the house of Israel.

Verses 34, 35. Exodus reaches its climax in these verses. The symphony of God's gracious dealings with Israel swelled to a crescendo as God came down to dwell with His people in **the**

tabernacle they had constructed for Him. Cassuto's comment on the passage is noteworthy:

> These verses, which are phrased in an elevated, poetic style, depict the manifestation of the Divine Glory in expressions that parallel those used at the end of chapter [24] to portray God's presence on Mount Sinai. The Tabernacle is a kind of miniature Sinai, which can be transported from place to place, in order to accompany the children of Israel in their wanderings and to serve as a palpable token of the Divine Presence in their midst throughout their journeyings.[6]

God's descent and His manifestation of His glory were intended to accomplish at least three things. (1) It demonstrated God's approval of the finished work of the tabernacle. (2) It symbolized that God was among His people and would always be with them to help and to guide them (see 40:36–38). (3) It emphasized the holiness of the tabernacle and everything connected with it. Since God was there, the tabernacle and its furnishings were holy and were not to be taken lightly. The presence of God was so holy that even **Moses** could not enter the tabernacle because of **the glory of the Lord**.

Moses' inability to enter the tabernacle was only temporary. John I. Durham wrote,

> As in the approach to Sinai following the covering of the cloud and the settling of the Glory (24:15–18), Moses must await Yahweh's invitation before he can draw nearer to the Presence. In the narrative of Exod 24, that invitation is given in v 17; here, that invitation comes farther along in the narrative, perhaps as Cassuto (484) suggests, in Lev 1:1. Another possibility is that it stands reflected at the end of the narrative of the ordination of Aaron and his sons, following Aaron's first sin-offering and atonement offering, after he had blessed Israel: "and then

---

[6]Cassuto, 484.

Moses and Aaron entered the Tent of Appointed Meeting" (Lev 9:23).[7]

God manifested Himself in a **cloud** a number of times in the Old Testament. On Mount Sinai, He said to Moses, "I will come to you in a thick cloud, so that the people may hear what I speak" (19:9). On the third day after that, there was a "thick cloud upon the mountain" (19:16) from which God spoke. When Moses entered the tent of meeting to receive revelations from God, God manifested His presence in a cloud (33:9). After the completion of the tabernacle, the Lord continued to make His presence known by means of a cloud by day which had fire in it by night (40:36–38). Much later, when the temple was completed, God made His presence known by means of a cloud which "filled the house of the LORD" (1 Kings 8:10, 11). God cannot be seen as He is, but He made His continual presence known to Israel by something that could be seen—a cloud.

Verses 36–38. Exodus ends on a hopeful, forward-looking note. God's promise that He would "dwell among the sons of Israel and . . . be their God" (29:45) had been fulfilled. Cole explained, "The theology of the presence of God has become the fact of His presence."[8]

However, Israel's story had not ended; it was just beginning. The people were on their way to the promised land. This passage emphasizes that Israel's history would continue and they would reach that goal. During that time, **throughout all their journeys**, God's presence would be with His people. **The cloud** and **fire** would be there to guide them. Just as **the sons of Israel** had followed God's directions in building the tabernacle, they followed God's guidance as they journeyed, determining whether to **set out** or to stay camped according to the movement of the cloud. As **all the house of Israel** looked forward to the future, they could expect **the cloud of the LORD** to continue to manifest His presence, His guidance, and His protection.

---

[7]John I. Durham, *Exodus*, Word Biblical Commentary, vol. 3 (Waco, Tex.: Word Books, 1987), 501.

[8]Cole, 239.

THE BUILDING OF THE TABERNACLE		
Exodus 25—31 What Was Required		**Exodus 35—40 What Was Done**
25:1–9	Offerings for the tabernacle	35:4–9, 20–29; 36:3–7
25:10–22	Ark of the covenant	37:1–9
25:23–30	Table of showbread	37:10–16
25:31–40	Golden lampstand	37:17–24
26:1–37	Curtains, boards, sockets, veil, screen	36:8–38
27:1–8	Bronze altar for burnt offerings	38:1–7
27:9–19	Court of the tabernacle	38:9–20
27:20, 21	Oil for lamp	[39:37]
28:1–43	Priestly garments	39:1–31
29:1–46	Consecration of the priests & offerings	
30:1–10	Altar of incense	37:25–28
30:11–16	Atonement money for the tabernacle	38:24–31
30:17–21	Bronze laver	38:8
30:22–38	Anointing oil & incense	37:29
31:1–11	The builders	35:10–19, 30–35; 36:1, 2; 38:21–23
31:12–17	Observing the Sabbath	
	Completion and setting up the tabernacle. The Lord enters it.	39:32–43; 40:1–38

APPLICATION

God's Presence (Ch. 40)

Exodus ends on a climactic note. The Israelites built the tabernacle. They set it up and prepared to dedicate it. Then came the climax: God's presence filled the tabernacle. In this way, God assured His people of His continued presence, protection, and guidance.

The Importance of His Presence. Throughout the Bible, the importance of God's presence is emphasized.

In Exodus. The idea of God's presence is a major theme in Exodus. When God called Moses, He said, "I have come down to deliver [Israel]" (3:7, 8). As Israel left Egypt, "The LORD was going before them in a pillar of cloud by day to lead them on the way, and in a pillar of fire by night" (13:21, 22; see 14:19, 20). The Israelites were told to build the tabernacle so God could "dwell among them" (25:8). God said, "I will dwell among the sons of Israel and will be their God. They shall know that I am the LORD their God who brought them out of the land of Egypt, that I might dwell among them; I am the LORD their God" (29:45, 46). The tabernacle represents the presence of God, especially the most holy place, where God met with the people. After Israel's sin, God threatened to withdraw His presence from the people (33:3); but He finally agreed to continue to be with them (33:14).

All of these passages suggest that the most crucial aspect of Israel's religion was not a list of rules, but the presence of God. Faith in God was essential, and obedience to God was necessary. However, these were just the means to an end: That end—the objective sought—was the presence of God!

In the remainder of the Old Testament, God's presence continues to be important. The Psalms frequently refer to the presence of God: "In Your presence is fullness of joy" (16:11); "Do not cast me away from Your presence" (51:11); "Let us come before His presence with thanksgiving" (95:2); "The upright will dwell in Your presence" (140:13).

In the New Testament, Christ came into the world as a manifestation of God. He was Immanuel, "God with us" (Is. 7:14; Mt. 1:23). He lived among men, and in Christ's presence one was in the very presence of God (Jn. 14:8–10). Jesus promised the presence of another comforter, the Holy Spirit (Jn. 14:16). As He concluded His earthly ministry, Christ said, "I am with you always" (Mt. 28:20).

Indeed, the New Testament affirms that Jesus Christ is present with Christians even while they live on earth (Col. 1:27). God is "in" us (Eph. 4:6); the Holy Spirit indwells saints (Rom. 8:9; Gal. 4:6). The Christian's body is "a temple of the Holy Spirit" (1 Cor. 6:19, 20), and the church is the temple in which God dwells (Eph. 2:19–22). Ultimately, the saved of all the ages will be in heaven—in the very presence of God (Rev. 21:1–4).

The Significance of His Presence for People Today. After learning what the Bible teaches about God's presence with Israel, we may be inclined to ask, "What does that mean for us?" The presence of God is significant today in at least two ways.

First, His presence in us is a present reality. Like the Israelites, we have a "holy place" in which God dwells. We are His dwelling place. (God dwells in us, whether we think of God's dwelling place as our individual bodies or as the corporate body, the church.) How should that knowledge affect us?

Our constant awareness of God's presence should affect everything we do. He should be constantly on our minds. Knowing that He is with us should govern all of our activities. It should cause us to keep ourselves pure (1 Cor. 6:19, 20). As with the Israelites, our religion should not be just a matter of rule-keeping. Rather, our primary aim should be to draw closer to God daily. Being with God and having Him with us must be at the heart of our religion.

Second, His presence is a future hope. We can look forward to the time when we will see God "as He is" (1 Jn. 3:2), when our flesh no longer stands between us and the presence of our Father (1 Cor. 15:50–57). One day, faith will become sight and hope will become reality. Of course, God is with us now, but we will be with Him then in a way which is not possible while we are in the world. Let us look forward to that day when we can experience God's presence and see Him in all His glory.

Conclusion. Some people cannot know His comforting presence. According to 2 Thessalonians 1:7–9, "those who do not know God and . . . do not obey the gospel of our Lord Jesus" will pay the penalty of "eternal destruction, away from the presence of the Lord and from the glory of His power." To be in His presence, therefore, you must be reconciled to God. He will be with you only if you are willing to believe in and obey Him.

"Moses Finished the Work" (40:33)

With the words "Moses finished the work," the story of the construction of the tabernacle ends. Imagine the feelings of those present on that occasion: feelings of relief, joy, and the satisfaction that comes from a job well done. Probably, they felt something like a writer feels when he finishes a book. Church members may have that feeling when they have been engaged for a long time in a building project and finally see it completed. How was the job finished? God blessed the work and made it possible, but the people involved worked hard for a long time; they persevered.

Each Christian, in a sense, is engaged in a great building project—to make himself fit for heaven, a person prepared for the presence of God. How can we succeed? God will make our success possible, but we must persevere (Heb. 12:1, 2). In completing our work, we will follow the example of our Lord, who cried out from the cross, "It is finished!" (Jn. 19:30; see 17:4). When we have finished our work, how wonderful it will be to say with Paul, "I have fought the good fight, I have finished the course, I have kept the faith. . . . there is laid up for me the crown of righteousness" (2 Tim. 4:7, 8)! How welcome will be the words "Well done, good and faithful slave" (Mt. 25:21)! We will enter into the very presence of God (Phil. 1:23; Rev. 21:3, 4), just as God entered the tabernacle when "Moses finished the work."

The Glory of God (40:35)

After the tabernacle was completed, God came and dwelt among His people. Exodus 40:35 notes that "the cloud . . . settled on it" and "the glory of the LORD filled the tabernacle." The Hebrew word שָׁכַן (*shakan*), translated "settled" (or "abode"; KJV), is behind the English term *Shekinah,* which refers to "the abiding presence of God" (see 24:16; 25:8). The presence of God's glory was so powerful that Moses was unable to enter the tabernacle!

Later in Jewish history, God's glory departed from the tabernacle due to the sin of the priests and the people (1 Sam. 4:21, 22). The ark of the covenant with the mercy seat—God's place for meeting with His people (Ex. 25:22)—was captured by the Philistines. As this tragic news spread in Israel, Eli died and his daughter-in-law gave birth to a son. She named the child Ichabod, meaning "the glory is gone." Later, when Solomon dedicated the temple he had built, God's glory returned to abide among His people (1 Kings 8:10, 11). Nevertheless, Israel's rebellion drove away God's glory once more (Ezek. 8:4; 9:3; 10:4, 18; 11:23).

In the fullness of time, God's glory returned to earth in the person of Jesus Christ (Jn. 1:14; Gal. 4:4). Interestingly, the Septuagint uses the same Greek word (ἐπισκιάζω, *episkiazō*) for "settled" in Exodus 40:35 as Luke 1:35 does for "overshadow." The angel told Mary, "'The Holy Spirit will come upon you, and the power of the Most High will *overshadow* you; and for that reason the holy Child shall be called the Son of God'" (Lk. 1:35; emphasis added). The virgin womb of Mary might be compared to the most holy place in the tabernacle; it was where God's glory dwelt in the person of His Son. Once again, many of God's people rejected His glory and eventually had Jesus nailed to a cross!

Today God's glory dwells in every true believer; each Christian is "a temple of the Holy Spirit" (1 Cor. 6:19, 20). Further, every local congregation is "a temple of God" in which "the Spirit of God dwells" (1 Cor. 3:10–23). Beyond this, the universal church is also "a holy temple in the Lord" (Eph. 2:20–22). One day the glory of God will be more fully realized in heaven by those who are faithful to Christ: "'Behold, the tabernacle of God is among men, and He will dwell with them, and they shall be His people, and God Himself will be among them'" (Rev. 21:3).[9]

---

[9]Adapted from Warren W. Wiersbe, *Be Delivered* (Colorado Springs, Colo.: Victor, 1998), 175–76.

APPENDIX

ADDITIONAL STUDIES

Study 1

The Author of Exodus

Moses has been traditionally regarded as the author of Exodus and the rest of the Pentateuch. Some, however, do not believe that Moses wrote these books. Bernhard W. Anderson noted that "many students who have pondered the Pentateuch carefully have become aware of repetitions, stylistic irregularities, and inconsistencies which can hardly be accounted for on the assumption of a single human author."[1]

Anderson described three major types of material in the Pentateuch and then concluded, "The dominant theory held by Jewish, Protestant, and Catholic scholars is that the Pentateuch is a composite work in which several traditions or 'sources' have been blended together."[2] He added that "these strands of tradition were woven together in various stages until the Pentateuch reached its present and final form about 400 B.C."[3]

Later, Anderson said that this is not the whole story, but that the documents were preceded by hundreds of years of oral traditions. Consequently, he wrote,

> The history of Pentateuchal traditions represents a long and dynamic process, from the time when the Israelite story was shaped orally and enriched with specific [narrative contributions] from the life of the people to the

---

[1]Bernhard W. Anderson, *Understanding the Old Testament*, 3d ed. (Englewood Cliffs, N.J.: Prentice-Hall, 1975), 18.

[2]Ibid., 19.

[3]Ibid.

> time when it was given literary formulation by various writers in their own circles, and finally to the time when these literary strands were brought together by the Priestly Writer into the canonical Pentateuch which we have received.[4]

According to this description, there were oral traditions, then various documents were written, and finally all the documents were put together by a priestly writer living in the fifth century B.C. This idea is a representation of the most popular alternative view to the Mosaic authorship, known as the Documentary Hypothesis. This hypothesis is the idea that the Pentateuch was put together by a series of redactors, or editors, over hundreds of years, using four basic documents. In the supposed order of their composition, the four documents that were used are the following:

(1) The earliest, which is said to be from the ninth century B.C., is the J document, or Yahwist Document. This document is so identified because of its predominant use of the name "Yahweh" (יהוה), or "Jehovah," for God. Its author is referred to as the Yahwist.

(2) Written next, perhaps during the eighth century B.C., was the E document, or Elohist document, which uses the name "Elohim" (אֱלֹהִים) for God. Its author is referred to as the Elohist.

(3) Written about the time of Josiah's reformation in the seventh century B.C., the next in line is the D document, or Deuteronomist document. This writing, named after Deuteronomy, is said to be composed largely of the contents of that book. Its author is known as the Deuteronomist.

(4) The last of the four, said to have been written during the sixth or fifth century B.C., is the P document, or Priestly document. This one is so-called because it supposedly was written or put together by priests and records "priestly" interests.[5]

---

[4]Ibid., 21.

[5]A description of the alleged documents and the process by which they became the Pentateuch is given in David Noel Freedman, "Documents," in *The Interpreter's Dictionary of the Bible*, ed. George Arthur Buttrick (Nashville: Abingdon Press, 1962), 1:860–61.

Overall, this theory suggests that the J document was written first and was later combined by an editor with the E document, resulting in a manuscript referred to as JE, which is said to have existed for a period of time. Later, the D document was added by another editor, so that JED made up the Pentateuch for a hundred years or more. Finally, theorists claim, a priest or group of priests added the P document, producing JEDP in its entirety. To claim that this process occurred is to accept that these editors, or redactors, not only added the successive documents to the original material as they found it, but also reworked the entire Pentateuch in accordance with their own special biases and purposes. The final result, then, would be the combination of the four documents plus the contributions of the editors who put the documents together.

This is a description of the Documentary Hypothesis as it reached its classical formulation by Julius Wellhausen toward the end of the nineteenth century. Since then, scholars have suggested a number of modifications to the original theory. Still, it is safe to say that most liberal scholars[6] accept some form of the Documentary Hypothesis, even if they do not accept the original version of the four sources (JEDP) in its entirety.

Those who embrace the Documentary Hypothesis believe they find in Exodus traces of three of the original four documents from which the Pentateuch was composed. Why, then, would we reject the Documentary Hypothesis and accept Mosaic authorship?[7]

First, evidence for the Documentary Hypothesis is not compelling. Proponents of the Documentary Hypothesis claim, for instance, that the use of different names for God provides evidence of different sources. In Genesis 1 "Elohim" is the name used for God; in Genesis 2 "Yahweh Elohim" ("Lord God") is used primarily.

---

[6]"Liberal" is used here to refer to one who has a lower view of the inspiration of the Scriptures and therefore doubts the verbal inspiration and inerrancy of the Bible, the reality of miracles, and the deity of Jesus (including questioning the virgin birth, the miracles, and the resurrection of Christ).

[7]The following arguments, and others, can be found in Gleason L. Archer, Jr., *A Survey of Old Testament Introduction*, rev. and exp. (Chicago: Moody Press, 1994), 113–40.

However, the use of different divine names may simply indicate that the author chose to use variety in referring to God. He may have favored a name with a certain connotation in one context and a name with a different connotation in another context. Perhaps the name "Yahweh" was used when God was thought of in His relationship with creation, with mankind, or with Israel in particular. "Yahweh" is the special covenant name of God.

Those who accept the Documentary Hypothesis note the presence of "doublets"—the same story related twice with varying details. For example, Abraham lied about his wife twice (Gen. 12:10–16; 20:1–18), and Isaac lied about his wife (Gen. 26:6–11). The theory holds that these are simply variations of one story found in different documents. Other explanations are possible, however. If Abraham benefited from lying once, he was more likely to lie a second time. Further, Isaac could have learned from the behavior of his father. The repetitions, irregularities, and inconsistencies mentioned by Anderson either do not exist or are easily explained.

Advocates of the Documentary Hypothesis also think they find anachronisms in the Pentateuch which indicate that it must have been written at a later date and could not have been written by Moses. One example given is that camels, which are mentioned frequently in Genesis (as in 12:16; 24:10), were not domesticated until later than Abraham's day. Another claim is that the Philistines, who are mentioned in the story of Abraham (Gen. 21:32), did not come into the land of Canaan until the thirteenth century B.C., long after Abraham's time. Critics claim that the mention of camels and Philistines indicates that the writer of Exodus lived long after the events he recorded. Such a writer would have made up the details of the story. However, the evidence put forward by the critics is in dispute. Some scholars believe that Philistines were in the land before the thirteenth century, and existing evidence suggests that camels could have been domesticated earlier.[8] In regard to naming the Philistines, it is possible that a later scribe updated the text by inserting the name of people who lived in the area at his time.

[8]Ibid., 180–81.

Other arguments for the Documentary Hypothesis can be dealt with in a similar way. In fact, the disinterested observer would conclude that the only thing that forces acceptance of the Documentary Hypothesis is an antisupernatural bias. Some people are simply determined to find a naturalistic explanation for everything, including the Torah.

Second, we have good reasons to believe that Moses is the author of the Pentateuch. These reasons include: (1) the long tradition that attributes the Pentateuch to Moses; (2) the fact that Moses is spoken of in the Pentateuch as writing; (3) the evidence of the New Testament, in which "the law" and "Moses" are equated (even by Jesus; John 5:46, 47); and (4) the fact that Moses had the time, the ability, the training, and the reason to write the Pentateuch. There is no better candidate to identify as author of the Pentateuch. The fact that Exodus refers to Moses in the third person does not disprove Mosaic authorship because other ancient authors wrote of themselves in the third person.

Since there are no compelling reasons to accept the Documentary Hypothesis, Moses should be considered the author of Exodus.

Study 2

The Date of the Exodus

Even among those who grant that the events recorded in the Book of Exodus actually happened—that Moses was a real person and that the exodus was a historical event—there are still questions about the date of the exodus. A number of dates have been proposed. According to the calculations of Archbishop Ussher, the exodus occurred in 1491 B.C.[1] Early in the twentieth century, C. R. Conder dated the exodus in 1520 B.C.[2] A more recent proposal by John J. Bimson suggested a date of 1470 B.C.[3] However, most scholars favor one of two other dates.

One of the widely accepted dates is 1290 B.C. (the late date). This dating was based largely on archaeological discoveries. The Merneptah Stela, which dates to about 1220 B.C., indicates that Israel as a nation was in the land of Canaan at that time. Therefore, they must have come into the land before then. A number of archaeological sites have shown evidence of widespread destruction which could be dated to about 1250 B.C. This has been interpreted as proof of the conquest of Canaan by the Israelites under Joshua. Such evidence is consistent with the Merneptah Stela, placing Israel in Canaan before 1220 B.C.

---

[1]Henry H. Halley, *Halley's Bible Handbook*, 24th ed., rev. (Grand Rapids, Mich.: Zondervan, 1965), 32.

[2]C. R. Conder, "The Exodus," in *The International Standard Bible Encyclopedia*, ed. James Orr (Grand Rapids, Mich.: Wm. B. Eerdmans Publishing Co., 1915), 2:1053.

[3]John H. Walton, "Exodus, Date of," in *Dictionary of the Old Testament: Pentateuch*, ed. T. Desmond Alexander and David W. Baker (Downers Grove, Ill.: InterVarsity Press, 2003), 260.

If Israel conquered Canaan about 1250 B.C., then counting forty years before that would make the date of the exodus 1290 B.C. That seems to be a likely date for other reasons. One of the store cities built by the Israelites during their slavery in Egypt was called Raamses, and Rameses II[4] began his reign as pharaoh of Egypt about 1290 B.C.

Furthermore, according to the Bible, the Israelites faced formidable opponents during their years in the wilderness. Archaeological surveys have suggested that the areas through which Israel traveled from Egypt to Canaan were uninhabited in the fifteenth century B.C. but were inhabited in the thirteenth century B.C. The exodus, then, more likely occurred in the thirteenth century than in the fifteenth.

The alternative to the 1290 B.C. date is based on the statement in 1 Kings 6:1, which places the exodus 480 years before Solomon's completion of the temple:

> In the four hundred and eightieth year after the sons of Israel came out of the land of Egypt, in the fourth year of Solomon's reign over Israel, in the month of Ziv, which is the second month, he began to build the house of the LORD.

If the temple was constructed about 965 B.C., as is usually estimated, then the exodus occurred about 1445 B.C. (the early date)[5] and the conquest about 1405 B.C. In Judges 11:26 Jephthah said that Israel had conquered the territory of Ammon three hundred years before his time. This would date the conquest at about 1400 B.C., since Jephthah lived about 1100 B.C., and place the

---

[4]Spellings, like dates, vary from one source to another. Historians refer to this pharaoh as "Rameses," "Ramesses," "Ramsses," or "Ramses." According to Exodus 1:11, one of the Egyptian storage cities was named "Raamses" (NASB; KJV) or "Rameses" (NIV; AB).

[5]The early date is favored in Gleason L. Archer, Jr., *A Survey of Old Testament Introduction*, rev. and exp. (Chicago: Moody Press, 1994), 239–52; Odis D. Duncan, "Dating the Exodus from Egypt: A Look at the Biblical Data," *The Journal of Biblical Interpretation and Application* 1 (July–September 2002): 79–92; and John J. Bimson and David Livingston, "Redating the Exodus," *Biblical Archaeology Review* 13 (September–October 1987): 40–53.

exodus at about 1440 B.C. Furthermore, even though Rameses was not pharaoh in the fifteenth century B.C., the name "Rameses" was known earlier than that and was used for the part of the land where Jacob settled his family when he moved them to Egypt (Gen. 47:11). Those who hold to the date of 1445 B.C. insist that arguments for the later date of 1290 B.C. are based on inadequate, outdated, or misinterpreted evidence.

Those who originally calculated the date of the exodus as 1290 B.C. held in high regard the Bible's historical accuracy. How did they deal with 1 Kings 6:1? They suggested that numbers are not always to be taken literally in the Old Testament, but sometimes are used as symbols—that is, that they represent concepts. They interpreted "forty years" as a generation. Just as the Israelites wandered in the wilderness for "forty years" until a whole generation was dead, so 1 Kings 6:1 was interpreted as speaking of twelve generations rather than a literal 480 years. However, a generation is more likely to be twenty-five years than forty years. If we count twelve generations averaging twenty-five years each, the total time represented is not a literal 480 years, but around three hundred years. If we add these years to 960 B.C., the result is 1260 B.C., which is close enough to 1290 to satisfy the requirements of the verse and the archaeological evidence.

Arguments regarding the date of the exodus are inconclusive and tend to cancel one another.[6] Both of these major alternatives, 1290 B.C. and 1445 B.C., have been accepted by some conservatives (people who believe fully in the inspiration of the Bible). For those who do not accept the inspiration of the Bible, discussion on the date of the exodus is irrelevant.

From a Christian standpoint, four facts are certain, whether the exodus is dated in the thirteenth century or in the fifteenth century B.C.:

(1) The events that are recorded in the Book of Exodus actually occurred.

---

[6]Principal arguments for and against the two main positions on the date of the exodus are presented in John H. Walton, *Chronological and Background Charts of the Old Testament*, rev. and exp. (Grand Rapids, Mich.: Zondervan Publishing House, 1994), 102–3.

(2) The exodus occurred during the New Kingdom era of Egyptian history—the period of time when Egypt reached the zenith of its power. Indeed, Egypt was the greatest power of the ancient Near East. In either case, God delivered Israel by defeating the greatest kingdom then in existence.

(3) The record of the events and the laws found in the book were almost certainly put in writing near the time when they occurred or were given.

(4) The inspired message of the Book of Exodus is the same, regardless of when the exodus occurred.

STUDY 3

THE LAND OF EGYPT

Egypt, the land of Israel's four-hundred-year sojourn, was one of the two oldest centers of civilization in the ancient Near East (the other being Mesopotamia). Long before Abraham was born, Egypt was a great nation with powerful pharaohs who had already built the great pyramids. In the fourth millennium B.C., the Egyptians became one of the first cultures to develop the ability to write; they used a form of picture-writing which became known as hieroglyphics. Just as modern-day tourists are fascinated by the pyramids, Abraham and the other patriarchs must have been amazed at the monuments, riches, and power of Egypt, which was already an ancient land when they visited there.

Its Name

The Hebrew name for Egypt is "Mizraim" (מִצְרַיִם, *Mitsrayim*), the name of a son of Ham (Gen. 10:6, 13). The Canaanites knew Egypt as "Misru," probably meaning "the fortified land." "Mizraim" is employed in the Hebrew Bible in a dual form, meaning "the two Egypts," probably referring to Upper and Lower Egypt.[1] The word "Egypt" may be derived from the Greek form of the name for Memphis (Αἴγυπτος, *Aiguptos*).[2] The ancient Egyptians did not themselves call their land "Mizraim"; rather, they called

---

[1]John D. Davis, *A Dictionary of the Bible*, 4th rev. ed. (Grand Rapids, Mich.: Baker Book House, 1957), 190.

[2]Charles F. Pfeiffer, ed., "Egypt," in *The Biblical World: A Dictionary of Biblical Archaeology* (Grand Rapids, Mich.: Baker Book House, 1966), 207; John A. Wilson, "Egypt," in *The Interpreter's Dictionary of the Bible*, ed. George Arthur Buttrick (Nashville: Abingdon Press, 1962), 2:39.

it simply "the Land" or "Two Lands," distinguishing the "Black Land" (the fertile silt deposited by the Nile River at flood stage) from the "Red Land" (the desert).[3]

Its Geography

Egypt has always been divided into two parts: Lower Egypt (in the north), comprising the Delta and a small part of the Nile valley to the south of Memphis, and Upper Egypt (in the south), which includes "the narrow valley [of the Nile] proper."[4] Israel settled originally in the delta area known as "Goshen" (Gen. 45:10, 11; 46:28). The cities of Pithom and Raamses (Ex. 1:11) were also located in this region.

The most important geographical feature of Egypt is the Nile River. Herodotus, in the fifth century B.C., spoke of Egypt as "the gift of the Nile." The Nile is one of the longest rivers in the world, flowing over a course of almost four thousand miles. It is among the few major rivers of the world that flow from south to north. The Nile makes Egypt habitable. Only the narrow strip of land on both sides of the river can be cultivated. Charles F. Pfeiffer said, "Ninety-nine percent of the population live on the four percent of the area which can be irrigated by the Nile water, and the rest is desert, with the exception of a few oases."[5] Rainfall is almost nonexistent there.

The most important physical fact about Egypt is that the Nile was generally predictable and benevolent. It could be counted on to flood each year, but not too much, making crops possible in an otherwise barren land. This flooding not only provided water, but also deposited a new layer of silt every year to replenish the fertility of the soil.[6]

---

[3]Pfeiffer, 207–9; Wilson, 39.

[4]H. W. Fairman, "Egypt," in James Hastings, *Dictionary of the Bible*, 2d ed., ed. Frederick C. Grant and H. H. Rowley (Edinburgh: T. & T. Clark, 1963), 231.

[5]Pfeiffer, 209.

[6]Kenneth A. Kitchen, "Egypt," in *Eerdmans' Handbook to the Bible*, ed. David Alexander and Pat Alexander (Grand Rapids, Mich.: Wm. B. Eerdmans Publishing Co., 1973), 151.

Among the consequences of Egypt's geography were the following:

(1) *National unity.* There were no natural barriers between the people of the north and the people of the south. In fact, the Nile provided a natural method of transportation and communication between the two parts of the land. (2) *Natural protection.* Compared to other countries, Egypt was relatively safe from invasion, having a sea on the north and desert surrounding the nation on the west, south, and east. (3) *Seasonal uniformity.* The mildness of the seasons, and especially of the Nile, affected the Egyptians' national psyche. They and their gods were different—more predictable and more benevolent—than the people and gods of Mesopotamia were.[7] (4) *Mineral wealth.* All kinds of precious stones and minerals and building materials were available in Egypt. Archaeological discoveries illustrate how rich the country was. However, Egypt lacked "good, firm wood for houses or ships."[8]

Its History

From the earliest recorded time, Egypt was divided into two kingdoms. This early division was retained in the name of the land and in its symbols. The country was united about 3000 B.C. by a great king known as Menes or Narmer. From that time on, more than any other country in the ancient Near East, Egypt remained one unified land. However, the Egyptian people never forgot the dual nature of their country: "The pharaohs were always 'King of Upper and Lower Egypt' and 'Lord of the Two Lands.'"[9]

About 280 B.C., the Egyptian priest Manetho divided the history of ancient Egypt into thirty dynasties. He identified three

---

[7]Jack P. Lewis wrote, "The uniformity of the Egyptian's world left its mark on his beliefs." (Jack P. Lewis, "Bible Archeology and Geography," in *The World and Literature of the Old Testament*, ed. John T. Willis [Austin, Tex.: Sweet Publishing Co., 1979], 94.)

[8]Wilson, 41.

[9]Kenneth A. Kitchen, "Egypt, Land of," in *The Zondervan Pictorial Encyclopedia of the Bible*, ed. Merrill C. Tenney (Grand Rapids, Mich.: Zondervan Publishing House, 1975), 2:227.

major periods of Egyptian power—the Old Kingdom, the Middle Kingdom, and the New Kingdom—plus intermediate periods of chaos and weakness. His work, though no longer extant, was cited by ancient historians and has been repeatedly adapted over the centuries. John H. Walton, citing the work of Kenneth A. Kitchen, presented the following dates for the eras of Egyptian history:[10]

Egyptian Chronology
Archaic Period (3000–2700 B.C.) *Dynasties 1, 2*
Old Kingdom (2700–2160 B.C.) *Dynasties 3–8*
First Intermediate Period (2160–2010 B.C.) *Dynasties 9, 10*
Middle Kingdom (2106–1786 B.C.) *Dynasties 11, 12*
Second Intermediate Period (1786–1550 B.C.) *Dynasties 13–17*
New Kingdom (1550–1069 B.C.) *Dynasties 18–20*
Third Intermediate Period (1069–656 B.C.) *Dynasties 21–25*
Saite-Persian Period (664–332 B.C.) *Dynasties 26–31**
*Dynasties 27 and 31 were Persian.

[10]John H. Walton, *Chronological and Background Charts of the Old Testament*, rev. and exp. (Grand Rapids, Mich.: Zondervan, 1994), 62–63; see Kenneth A. Kitchen, "Egypt, History of," in *Anchor Bible Dictionary*, ed. David Noel Freedman (New York: Doubleday, 1992), 2:328–30. Dates are approximate.

The great pyramids were built during the fourth dynasty, in the Old Kingdom era. After the New Kingdom era, Egyptian power waned:

> Egypt's real power swiftly sank. The Hebrew prophets rebuked their kings for relying on Egyptian support (see Isaiah 30, 31; Jeremiah 46). Egypt was no match for Assyria or Babylon, and with the rise of the Persian Empire indeed became a "lowly kingdom" (Ezekiel 29:15), losing her real national independence for ages to come.[11]

During the Second Intermediate Period, the Hyksos, foreign kings of Semitic origin, ruled Egypt. "According to Manetho, the [third]-century B.C. historian, the Hyksos took over Egypt by a violent invasion," a view which has more recently been challenged by scholars who claim that their ascension to the throne was the result of "an Amorite coup d'etat."[12]

The relationship between the Hyksos and the family of Jacob is unclear. Some have contended that the Hyksos were ruling Egypt when Joseph and his family arrived there, but an alternate view is that a native Egyptian was on the throne when Israel entered Egypt and it was the Hyksos who began to oppress Israel.[13] In either case, the following period, the era during which Israel escaped from Egypt, was the New Kingdom era (1550–1069 B.C.)—a time of expansion during which Egypt was the strongest power in the ancient Near East.

Its Rulers[14]

Hatshepsut (1486–1468 B.C.), who has been suggested as the

---

[11]Kitchen, *Eerdmans' Handbook*, 154.

[12]John J. Davis, *Moses and the Gods of Egypt: Studies in Exodus*, 2d ed. (Grand Rapids, Mich.: Baker Book House, 1986), 40.

[13]Gleason L. Archer, Jr., *A Survey of Old Testament Introduction*, rev. and exp. (Chicago: Moody Press, 1994), 221.

[14]These rulers are included here because historians have associated them with the events or the time period of the exodus. Dates for the pharaohs' reigns are from Wilson, 48–50. Ancient dates are approximate and vary from one source to another.

possible adoptive mother of Moses, was a female pharaoh.

> When Thutmose II died suddenly (ca. 1479 BCE), the regency for the infant Thutmose III was assumed by his stepmother Hatshepsut, his father's chief queen and a descendant of Ahmose. She eventually made herself king and reigned for nearly two decades alongside her stepson, presumably until her death. . . . Later in his reign, Thutmose III desecrated her monuments and defamed her memory.[15]

Thutmose III (1490–1436 B.C.) was described by John A. Wilson as "a man of great military and administrative ability" who "devoted seventeen campaigns to Asia, founded an Egyptian empire running up into [North] Syria, and introduced the military and civil controls to hold the area."[16] Gleason L. Archer, Jr., identified him as the pharaoh of the oppression. He noted that, other than Rameses II, only Thutmose III was on the throne long enough (fifty-four years, including the twenty-one years of Hatshepsut's regency) to have been reigning at the time of Moses' flight from Egypt. He would have died shortly before God called Moses at the burning bush, thirty to forty years later. Archer depicted this pharaoh as an "ambitious and energetic" ruler who achieved significant military victories and completed numerous building projects.[17]

Amenhotep IV (Akhenaton) ruled Egypt from 1369 to 1353 B.C. As a monotheist, he worshiped only the Sun-disc Aton and forced this exclusivistic faith on his subjects. He moved the capital from Thebes to a new city he built in middle Egypt, called Akhetaton ("Horizon of the Sun-disc"). At the same time, he changed his name from Amenhotep ("Amun" means "satisfied") to Akhenaton (meaning "He who is useful to the Sun-disc"). Nevertheless, his reforms were only temporary.

---

[15]David P. Silverman, ed., *Ancient Egypt* (New York: Oxford University Press, 1997), 32.

[16]Wilson, 48.

[17]Archer, 228.

> [His successor] Horemheb (1347–1318 B.C.E.) returned the capital to Thebes, closed the temples of the Sun-disc, and dismantled his buildings, using the blocks as fill in new projects. . . . Only time was needed before Akhenaton's monotheism fell by the wayside.[18]

Eventually, the Egyptians attempted to erase his influence altogether.

Documents known as the "Amarna Letters" have been dated to Akhenaton's reign. These letters were discovered at Tell el-Amarna, the modern name for the site of the ancient city Akhetaton, which was built by Akhenaton about 1365 B.C. but was soon abandoned. They were written in a cuneiform script in Akkadian, the "international diplomatic language of the age." Their content depicts "a situation of factionalism within the Egyptian sphere of influence in Syria-Palestine; local rulers accuse fellow vassals of treachery; requests of aid from the Egyptian overlord are frequent."[19]

The Amarna Letters speak of the Habiru people, who are mentioned in sources from the ancient Near East throughout the second millennium B.C. The Habiru are best described as a social group rather than an ethnic group. Wherever they are mentioned, they are characterized as "foreign" and in a relation of dependency upon the native population. The term "Habiru" seems to have been applied to any people without a settled home. The "Hebrews"—the Israelites who conquered Canaan—had some things in common with the Habiru, but the two groups cannot be equated since Habiru could be found in other parts of the ancient Near East at the time of the conquest.[20]

Tutankhamen (1352–1344 B.C.), also known as "King Tut," was

---

[18]John Keating Wiles, "Akhenaton," in *Mercer Dictionary of the Bible*, ed. Watson E. Mills (Macon, Ga.: Mercer University Press, 1991), 18–19.

[19]John Keating Wiles, "Amarna," in *Mercer Dictionary of the Bible*, ed. Watson E. Mills (Macon, Ga.: Mercer University Press, 1991), 22–23.

[20]Ibid. For more information on the Habiru, see Edward F. Campbell, Jr., "The Amarna Letters and the Amarna Period," *Biblical Archaeologist* 23 (February 1960): 2–22; and Niels Peter Lemche, "Habiru, Hapiru," in *Anchor Bible Dictionary*, ed. David Noel Freedman (New York: Doubleday, 1992), 3:6–10.

Akhenaton's son-in-law. He became pharaoh after Smenkhere (another son-in-law), who reigned 1355–1352 B.C., either sharing a co-regency with or succeeding Akhenaton. Neither Smenkhere nor Tutankhamen accepted their father-in-law's faith; they worshiped Amon, the sun god, rather than "the Aton, the life-giving disk of the sun."[21] Tutankhamen was young when he died, and his tomb was found intact in the 1920s. The richness of his unplundered tomb bears witness to the wealth of Egypt.

Rameses II (1290–1224 B.C.) was perhaps the greatest of the pharaohs. He served longer than any other, maintained Egypt's empire, and built great monuments. In addition, he "unscrupulously appropriated the monuments of his predecessors for himself."[22]

Merneptah (1224–1214 B.C.) was Rameses' successor. He conducted a military campaign against Egypt's enemies in Palestine and Syria and left a stele (dated about 1220 B.C.) commemorating his victories. Included on the Merneptah Stele are these words: "Israel is laid waste, he has no offspring."[23] This is the first mention of Israel in Egyptian literature and provides evidence that Israel was in Canaan by 1220 B.C.

Its Culture and Religion

While the pharaoh "was the keystone of society, as the intermediary between gods and men," Egypt's gods were viewed as "embodiments of the powers of nature, or its phenomena (sun, moon), or of concepts (just order)."[24] The pharaoh, the priests, and the government officials worshiped at great temples, where they sought the gods' blessings on Egypt through temple rites. Ordinary people worshiped household gods. "Magic flourished as an aspect of religion. . . . But 'black' magic was a punishable crime."[25]

Pharaoh's government was served by state officials and a

---

[21]Wilson, 50.
[22]Ibid., 51.
[23]Ibid., 52.
[24]Kitchen, *Eerdmans' Handbook*, 151–52.
[25]Ibid., 152.

bureaucracy of scribes. Priests had their own estates and administrations. From the New Kingdom onward, Egypt maintained an army equipped with chariots. Education took place in temple schools and as part of civil administration. Egypt developed a rich literature of stories and poetry, including wisdom-books (similar to Proverbs). Although Egypt was primarily a farming society, a large body of skilled artists and craftsmen served the pharaoh, producing magnificent monuments.

The Egyptians' belief in an afterlife led them to mummify bodies at death. Articles placed in tombs were intended to serve their owners in the realm of Osiris, god of the dead.[26]

Egypt and Israel[27]

Egypt has always had a prominent place in the history of Israel. Even before Israel was a nation, the Egyptian culture had an impact on God's people.

Old Testament. Abraham spent time in Egypt (Gen. 12:10–20), and Ishmael married an Egyptian woman (Gen. 21:21). Joseph was sold into Egypt (Gen. 37:25–28, 36) and eventually married an Egyptian woman (Gen. 41:45). Later, Jacob and the rest of the family went to live in Egypt. Moses had a name closely related to Egyptian names, as did other Israelites. From the time that the Israelites left their life of slavery, they identified themselves—and God identified them—as the people whom God had delivered out of Egypt (Ex. 19; 20; 32:1).[28]

After the Patriarchal age, in the days of Israel's kings, Egypt was an influential power—sometimes as a rival of Israel, and sometimes as an ally. Solomon married a daughter of Pharaoh (1 Kings 3:1) and traded with Egypt (1 Kings 10:28, 29). The "wisdom of Egypt" is mentioned in 1 Kings 4:30 (see Is. 19:12). Pharaoh captured Gezer (1 Kings 9:19), and Solomon's enemies found

[26]Ibid.

[27]Additional information about Egypt in relation to the Bible is given in Kitchen, *Eerdmans' Handbook*, 152–54.

[28]See Lev. 19:36; 26:13; Num. 20:15, 16; 24:8; Deut. 1:27; 5:6; 6:21; 16:1; 26:8; Josh. 9:9; 24:6; Judg. 2:1, 12; 6:8; 1 Sam. 8:8; 12:6; 2 Sam. 7:6; 1 Kings 8:9, 16, 21, 51; 2 Kings 17:7; 1 Chron. 17:21; 2 Chron. 5:10; Neh. 9:9, 18; Ps. 81:10.

refuge in Egypt (1 Kings 11:17–22, 40). Pharaoh attacked Rehoboam's kingdom (1 Kings 14:25, 26). Kings from Israel and Judah sought Egypt's aid (2 Kings 17:4), but the Assyrians warned them not to rely on Egypt (2 Kings 18:21). Josiah was killed by the Egyptian army (2 Kings 23:29). The Egyptians were defeated and lost all claim to Palestine (2 Kings 24:7). After Gedeliah's murder, some Israelites fled to Egypt, taking the prophet Jeremiah with them (2 Kings 25:26; Jer. 41—44).

Fine Egyptian linen is mentioned in Proverbs 7:16 (see Ezek. 27:7), and Isaiah 45:14 speaks of the "products of Egypt." The prophets prophesied against Egypt (see Is. 19; Jer. 46:2–26; Ezek. 29:2–20) and rebuked Israel for making an alliance with Egypt (Is. 30:1–5; 31:1). Once, when Egypt rescued Judah, Jeremiah warned that the relief was only temporary (Jer. 37:11; Ezek. 17:15). The prophet Uriah fled to Egypt, but he did not escape the king of Judah (Jer. 26:20–23).

New Testament. Soon after the birth of Jesus, His parents took Him to Egypt (Mt. 2:13–23). Stephen placed emphasis on Egypt in his speech in Acts 7. Apollos was from Alexandria, a major city of Egypt (Acts 18:24). Hebrews 11:26 speaks of the "treasures of Egypt." In Revelation, Egypt is depicted, along with Sodom, as a source of great wickedness (Rev. 11:8).

Non-Biblical References. While no secular record speaks of the Israelites as being in Egypt or escaping from Egypt, Egyptian writings and inscriptions give accounts of Semites going into Egypt and serving as slaves there. Existing evidence also indicates that Egyptians spent time in Canaan. Some of Egypt's literature closely resembles the Hebrew wisdom literature in the Bible. A colony of Hebrews built their own temple on Elephantine Island in Egypt in the sixth century B.C. and wrote letters to the governor of Judea during the Persian period in the fifth century B.C.[29] Later, a large colony of Jews lived in Alexandria, where the Septuagint (the Greek version of the Old Testament) was translated.

---

[29]Emil G. Kraeling, "Elephantine Papyri," in *The Interpreter's Dictionary of the Bible*, ed. George Arthur Buttrick (Nashville: Abingdon Press, 1962), 2:83–85.

Study 4

The Historicity of the Exodus

Critics doubt that the events connected with the exodus actually occurred. In an article in *Christianity Today,* Kevin D. Miller cited a number of "biblical minimalists" who doubt the historical basis of *most* of the Old Testament. He noted that this position is not new. Late in the 1800s, Julius Wellhausen led liberal scholars to the conclusion that the Law "was composed after the Jews had returned from their exile in Babylon only 450 years before Jesus."[1] William Albright and his students slowed the trend toward dismissing the historicity of Old Testament narratives in the mid-1900s by using archaeological discoveries to confirm Old Testament history. In 1981 John Bright said, "There can really be little doubt that ancestors of Israel had been slaves in Egypt and had escaped in some marvelous way. Almost no one today would question it."[2] "Biblical minimalists" have, however, questioned it repeatedly since then.

Some doubt that Israel was ever in Egypt and deny that there ever was an exodus. Others suggest that not all twelve tribes were in Egypt, but that only some of them lived there and were involved in the exodus. Still others believe that there was a historical person named Moses in Israel's distant past who had something to do with a God named "Yahweh." However, they

---

[1]Kevin D. Miller, "Did the Exodus Never Happen? How Two Egyptologists Are Countering Scholars Who Want to Turn the Old Testament into Myth," *Christianity Today* 42 (7 September 1998): 45.

[2]Ibid., 46. This statement also appears in John Bright, *A History of Israel* (Philadelphia: Westminster Press, 1959), 110.

believe that the details of Israel's religion, including its monotheism and its high ethical and moral standards, came from a much later date. They think that these religious principles were introduced by prophets who originated laws but attributed them to Moses and his God because Moses was already held in high regard by the people. In their opinion, Moses was credited with being the great lawgiver, even though the actual theological and moral laws came from prophets who lived long after his time.

What evidence is given for these views? (1) The critics who deny the authenticity of the exodus assert that scriptural references to the exodus do not prove that it occurred. They give no credence to what the Scriptures say unless external evidence supports the biblical statement. They practice what has been called a "hermeneutics of suspicion," claiming that anything the Bible says is suspect until other evidence confirms it.

(2) These critics argue that there is no external proof to support the sojourn in Egypt and the exodus. For instance, there is no mention of Moses' name or of the exodus in ancient Egyptian records. Doubters allege that the escape of more than a million slaves would have been a catastrophe of such magnitude that it would have to be recorded.

(3) Those who doubt the historicity of the exodus affirm that the record of miracles—including the ten plagues, the crossing of the Red Sea, manna from heaven, and water from a rock—makes the whole account suspect. Since they do not believe that miracles could happen, they deny that any account which includes miracles can be historical.

What reasons do we have to believe that the events recorded in Exodus actually occurred? (1) There are fallacies in the reasoning used by those who reject the historicity of the events in Exodus. It is illogical to disregard the Scriptures themselves as evidence. Since they are, to say the least, ancient documents, they should be accorded some value as evidence. Modern skeptics consider the events and people in the Old Testament mythical unless there is empirical [scientifically observable] proof for their existence. Since biblical records have proved to be accurate in many cases, it would be more reasonable to accept as true what the Bible says unless a biblical account were shown to be false.

The absence of direct evidence for the exodus does not prove that it did not happen. The Egyptians would likely not have recorded for posterity something as humiliating as the escape of a whole nation of slaves.

In addition, to say that the events could not have happened because they involved the miraculous is obviously to operate from antisupernatural assumptions. Such thinking must be rejected by anyone who admits that God is omnipotent and is involved in the affairs of men.

(2) There is evidence that the events occurred. The Bible provides such evidence. The Old Testament points to the exodus as the most important event in Israelite history. The New Testament speaks of Moses and the exodus as historical events. For Christians, that settles the matter. Those who believe the Bible believe that these events occurred.

Israel would not likely have fabricated such a background for itself. What people would want to invent as the central fact of their faith the story that they had begun as an enslaved people?[3]

(3) There is also evidence for the historicity of Israel's sojourn in and deliverance from Egypt. One source summarizes the evidence as follows:

> Although no direct historical evidence exists for either the oppression in Egypt or the escape, the indirect evidence is overwhelming. The Joseph story authentically reflects Egyptian life, customs, literature (especially in the northeast delta region), and even official titles as known from Egyptian records, lending great historical credence to the sojourn in Egypt. It is now known that great numbers of Semitic peoples were employed as state slaves on building projects near Thebes in the Eighteenth Dynasty and in the northeast delta during the Nineteenth Dynasty. Several Israelite names of the period, especially in Moses' family, are authentically Egyptian. Even the

[3]Bright, 110.

> escape of subject peoples from a major state is not without analogy in the ancient world.[4]

James K. Hoffmeier, an Egyptologist, subtitled his study "The Evidence for the Authenticity of the Exodus Tradition." After exploring the evidence in detail, he concluded that "the picture portrayed in Genesis 39 through Exodus 15" is "compatible with what is known from Egyptian history."[5]

The historicity of the exodus can, therefore, be accepted because the arguments against it are not convincing and the evidence for it is impressive.

---

[4]William Sanford LaSor, David Allan Hubbard, and Frederic William Bush, *Old Testament Survey: The Message, Form, and Background of the Old Testament* (Grand Rapids, Mich.: Wm. B. Eerdmans Publishing Co., 1982), 125.

[5]James K. Hoffmeier, *Israel in Egypt* (New York: Oxford University Press, 1996), 223.

Study 5

The Route of the Exodus

The Route Out of Egypt

Two important questions have been raised in regard to the route of the exodus. The first question focuses on how the Israelites exited Egypt. The text says that they did *not* go out by the way of the Philistines (13:17). This route would have taken them along the coastal road, the *Via Maris* ("the Way of the Sea"). This route was guarded by substantial fortifications, and the Israelites were unprepared for war. Instead, God led them "around by the way of the wilderness to the Red Sea" (13:18). Therefore, they followed a route which went south of the "way of the . . . Philistines" and involved camping at various locations:[1]

1. Rameses, the starting point (12:37)
2. Succoth (12:37)
3. Etham, on the edge of the wilderness (13:20)
4. Pi-hahiroth, by the Red Sea, near Migdol and Baal-zephon (14:2)
5. Through the Red Sea (chs. 14; 15; see 13:18; 15:4, 22)
6. Wilderness of Shur (15:22)
7. Marah, which was three days' journey into the wilderness (15:22, 23)
8. Elim, where there were twelve springs of water (15:27)
9. Wilderness of Sin, between Elim and Sinai (16:1)

---

[1]The same itinerary is found in Numbers 33:1–15, except that Numbers names other places where the Israelites camped on their way to Sinai (Num. 33:10–14).

10. Rephidim, also named Massah and Meribah (17:1, 7)
11. Wilderness, at the mount of God (18:5)
12. Wilderness of Sinai, from Rephidim, in front of the mountain (19:1, 2).

No one knows for sure where these places were, except that the first four listed are obviously in Egypt, west of the Red Sea. The others are east of the sea. Also, it is obvious that some names refer to specific places (for example, Elim), while others refer to larger areas (such as, the Wilderness of Sin). In addition, the names of some of the places were changed in the Israelites' vocabulary because of what happened there (for example, Marah, Massah, and Meribah; 15:23; 17:7). Of course, there is uncertainty about the route; the map below simply represents a consensus of the views of many commentators and map-makers.

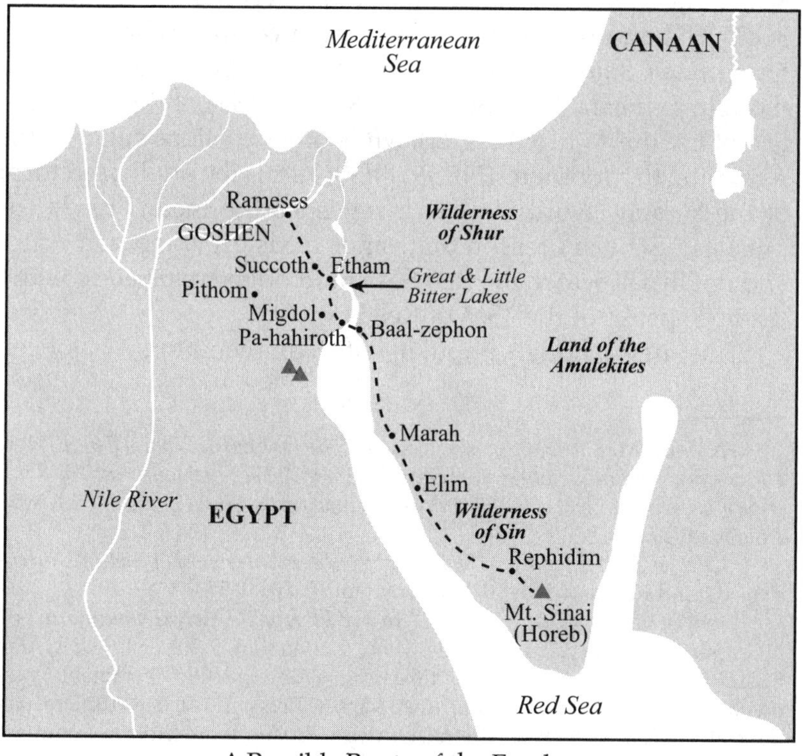

A Possible Route of the Exodus

Even the location of Mount Sinai is uncertain. Nahum M. Sarna noted that "thirteen distinct sites have been suggested for Mount Sinai in widely separated regions of the Sinai Peninsula and even in Moab and Edom."[2] The map indicates that the Israelites took the southern route through the Sinai peninsula and that the traditional Jebel Musa, or Gebel Musa (Arabic for "the mount of Moses"), is probably the site where the Law was given. Charles F. Pfeiffer pointed out that although "three ancient roads" traversed the land bridge between Egypt and Asia, "the Exodus did not take Israel along any of the well traveled roads."[3] Rather, Israel turned towards the south and so eventually came to Sinai, in the southern part of the land.

The Route Through the Red Sea

Another question is "Did Israel really go through the Red Sea, or did they cross marshy lakes somewhere north of the Red Sea?" The question arises, in part, because the Hebrew words יַם־סוּף (*Yam Sup*), translated "Red Sea" in most versions, are thought to mean "Reed Sea." The NJB has "Sea of Reeds" in the text of Exodus (13:18; 15:4, 22), while other versions suggest this rendering in a footnote (NRSV; NIV). *Yam* is the anglicized form of the Hebrew word for "sea"; *sup* is said to mean "reeds" or "rushes." Scholars reason that, since reeds grow in fresh water and not in salt water, the Red Sea could not be referred to when the text speaks of the "Sea of Reeds."

This view, though popular with commentators,[4] has been

---

[2]Nahum M. Sarna, *Exploring Exodus: The Origins of Biblical Israel* (New York: Schocken Books, 1996), 108; citing M. Har-El, *The Sinai Journeys: The Route of the Exodus in the Light of the Historical Geography of the Sinai Peninsula* (Tel-Aviv: Am Oved, 1973).

[3]Charles F. Pfeiffer, ed., *The Biblical World: A Dictionary of Biblical Archaeology* (Grand Rapids, Mich.: Baker Book House, 1966), 533.

[4]Walter C. Kaiser, Jr., "Exodus," in *The Expositor's Bible Commentary*, vol. 2, *Genesis—Numbers* (Grand Rapids, Mich.: Zondervan, 1990), 384, 389; R. Alan Cole, *Exodus: An Introduction and Commentary*, Tyndale Old Testament Commentaries (Downers Grove, Ill.: Inter-Varsity Press, 1973), 118–19. Durham translated it "sea of rushes." (John I. Durham, *Exodus*, Word Biblical Commentary, vol. 3 [Waco, Tex.: Word Books, 1987], 182, 185.)

refuted by scholars[5] who have pointed out that the same Hebrew words refer to the Red Sea in other contexts (Ex. 23:31; Num. 14:25; 21:4; 33:10; Deut. 1:40; 2:1; 1 Kings 9:26; Jer. 49:21).[6]

Those who doubt the miraculous deny that God parted the water and allowed the Israelites to cross through the main body of the sea, just as they deny all the other miracles connected with the exodus. Other skeptics see no reason to believe that the crossing of the sea was a real historical event; they view it as a mythological creation, equivalent to the myths of other peoples of the ancient Near East, which nevertheless served an important purpose in the religion of Israel. Bernard F. Batto wrote, "Biblical writers were less interested in reporting historical data than in symbolizing for their contemporaries the salvational significance of their traditions."[7] John J. Davis, in reply, pointed out that the prophets referred to actual historical events when they urged Israel to obey the Lord. He said, "The argument that historical facts are not important to Israel's theological values contradicts the plain language of the text and bankrupts the logic of prophetic preaching."[8]

Those who object to the miraculous crossing of the Red Sea on practical grounds find it difficult to understand how God could (1) divide the sea, (2) make the water stand back, (3) make it possible for Israel to cross on a sea bed newly exposed, (4) pro-

---

[5]Bernard F. Batto argued against the "Reed Sea" hypothesis. However, he assumed the validity of the documentary hypothesis and the unhistorical nature of the story of Israel's deliverance through the sea. (Bernard F. Batto, "The Reed Sea: *Requiescat in Pace*," *Journal of Biblical Literature* 102 [March 1983]: 27–35; Bernard F. Batto, "Red Sea or Reed Sea," *Biblical Archaeology Review* 10 [July–August 1984]: 56–63.)

[6]Sarna concluded that "the designation 'Sea of Reeds' was applied comprehensively" both to the lakes that existed in Egypt and to the body of water known today as the Red Sea. He added that this makes it difficult to know for sure what body of water is meant by the *Yam Sup* in Exodus 13—15, saying that "one scholar has noted that the *yam suf* that the Israelites crossed has been variously identified as no fewer than nine different bodies of water." (Sarna, 107–8; citing Har-El.)

[7]Batto, "Red Sea or Reed Sea," 63.

[8]John J. Davis, *Moses and the Gods of Egypt: Studies in Exodus*, 2d ed. (Grand Rapids, Mich.: Baker Book House, 1986), 182.

vide enough time for a large number of Israelites (600,000 men plus women and children) to pass through the sea in one night, and (5) then destroy an army which tried to follow. They prefer a more natural explanation. They believe that in a shallow area of a marshy lake—perhaps even an extension of the sea[9]—a low ebb tide could have combined with a strong wind to make a way for the Israelites to cross over to the other side. They accept that the return of the tide and the cessation of the wind could have caught the Egyptian army unawares, so that a relative few perished in the sea.

The problem with such an explanation is that it denies important aspects of the story as it is told in Exodus. Davis pointed out that "the biblical text does not speak of the ebb and flow of a tide."[10] Walter C. Kaiser, Jr., noted concerning the wall of water on the right and the left (14:22, 29), "The event, while incorporating the natural elements of the wind, has the element of the exceptional (cf. Deut 4:32, 34) accompanying it, as did the previous plagues. Thus it strongly suggests the presence of God in the event."[11]

We need not rule out the use of "natural means" in the working of this miracle, as long as we understand that God did something extraordinary. The text requires only that the reader accept that Israel crossed something known as the *Yam Sup*, the Red Sea, in an extraordinary manner and that Pharaoh's soldiers were drowned in the sea when the waters overwhelmed them.[12] These events made it obvious that God was saving Israel.

---

[9]Cole spoke of the possibility that these were "reedy salt-marshes, with a soft bottom, connected with the main gulf." (Cole, 121.)

[10]Davis, 172.

[11]Kaiser, 389.

[12]The text does not specify where they crossed the sea. Davis, after considering four views, said that the crossing probably occurred somewhere in the Bitter Lakes, north of the actual Red Sea. He based his opinion on the belief that this view best fits the biblical evidence and claimed that "the suggestion of a crossing in the Great Bitter Lake in no way diminishes the miraculous character of the event." He emphasized that, to drown the Egyptian army, "the waters crossed would have to exhibit substantial depth." (Davis, 176–80.)

Study 6

The Covenant

The concept of the "covenant" is a key to understanding Exodus, and, in fact, to understanding the entire Old Testament. The Hebrew word for "covenant," בְּרִית (b^e*rith*), appears 280 times in the Old Testament[1] and always means a treaty or an agreement.[2]

A covenant could be made between nations or individuals, or between God and men. Among covenants in the Old Testament were Abraham's covenant with Abimelech (Gen. 21:27, 32), Jonathan's covenant with David (1 Sam. 18:3), David's covenant with Abner (2 Sam. 3:12, 13), and Jehoiada's covenant with those who guarded the king's son (2 Kings 11:4). Political alliances also involved the making of covenants. Israel had a covenant with the Gibeonites (Josh. 9:6–15); the northern tribes became subservient to David by making a covenant with him (2 Sam. 5:1–3); Solomon made a covenant with King Hiram of Tyre (1 Kings 5:12); King Asa of Judah sought an alliance with Ben-hadad of Syria by asking him to break his covenant with King Baasha of Israel (1 Kings 15:19); and Ahab made a covenant with Ben-hadad after Ahab had defeated the Syrian army (1 Kings 20:34). Israel was warned against making covenants with other nations (Ex. 23:32; 34:12–15; Deut. 7:2). Even marriage was regarded as a cov-

[1]David T. Lusk, *God of the Covenant* (N.p.: By the author, 1994), 4.

[2]Some sources specify that the agreement involved in a covenant is a "formal agreement." Gary A. Herion defined "covenant" as "a solemn agreement between two or more parties, made binding by some sort of oath." (Gary A. Herion, "Covenant," in *Eerdmans Dictionary of the Bible*, ed. David Noel Freedman [Grand Rapids, Mich.: Wm. B. Eerdmans Publishing Co., 2000], 288.)

enant, in that it involved an agreement between husband and wife to remain together (Prov. 2:17; Mal. 2:14).

The history of God's dealings with man is, in a sense, a history of the covenants that God made with man. All of God's covenants involve blessings provided by God linked with responsibilities placed upon mankind.[3]

Background of Covenants in the Bible

God's initial covenant was with Adam, though the word "covenant" is not used. Adam was given certain privileges and responsibilities (Gen. 1:28, 29; 2:15–17). God's covenant with Noah (Gen. 6:18; 9:9–17) presumably remained in force for all but the descendants of Abraham throughout the Old Testament period. God made a special covenant with Abraham (Gen. 15:18; 17:2–8; Ex. 2:24), which included the promises that shaped biblical history. God then made a covenant with the people of Israel, the covenant which governed God's dealings with Israel for the rest of the Old Testament age. God later made a covenant with King David (2 Sam. 7:12, 13; 23:5), which consisted of a promise ultimately fulfilled in the Messiah. However, the Davidic covenant, while it contributed to the fulfillment of God's promises to Abraham, did not alter the terms of the Mosaic covenant. Finally, just as God had promised through Jeremiah (Jer. 31:31–34), He made a new covenant with His people when the Messiah, the Christ, came (see Mt. 26:28; Heb. 8:8–13).[4]

Covenants in History

Covenants were not unique to Israel; they were common

---

[3]Some covenants between God and man, such as the Abrahamic and Davidic covenants, are said to be unconditional covenants, since they did not require man's obedience. However, God's promises to Abraham were accepted by an active faith, and the promise that David's descendants would reign on the earthly throne of Israel was certainly conditional. It appears, therefore, that all of God's covenants with man have been, in some sense, conditional.

[4]Other covenants are mentioned, specifically one with Phinehas (Num. 25:11–13) concerning the priesthood. In that case, the word "covenant" seems to be used for a part of the covenant—the promises contained in the covenant—just as in other places the word "covenant" seems to refer only to the commandments, or requirements, found in the covenant.

throughout the ancient Near East. In general, two kinds of treaty-covenants could be made between peoples or nations. The first involved treaties between equals. These agreements often involved the exchange of gifts or a marriage arranged between the royal houses of the treaty partners. Probably, Solomon's dealings with Egypt and Tyre involved such treaties.

The other kind of treaty-covenant, known as a suzerain-vassal covenant, was between a greater power or king and a lesser power, such as a client king. Examples from the land of the Hittites (an ancient kingdom located in what is modern Turkey) are thought to be typical of such treaties throughout the Near East at that time. Those treaties included the following parts:

1. Preamble naming the author of the treaty.
2. Historical prologue setting out the relations between the parties prior to the signing of the treaty.
3. Stipulations explaining the mutual responsibilities of the partners.
4. A document clause describing the treaty document and arranging for the vassal to read it at regular intervals.
5. A list of gods witnessing the treaty.
6. Curses and blessings, threatening the vassal with illness, death, deportation, etc., if he breaks the treaty, but promising him prosperity and blessing if he remains faithful.[5]

The Mosaic Covenant

Similarities exist between the structure of ancient Hittite suzerain-vassal covenants and the structure of the covenant made between God and Israel. (1) In Exodus 19 God began by identifying Himself, the equivalent of the preamble. (2) Then He spoke of what He had done for Israel—the equivalent of a "historical prologue." (3) Next, He gave the stipulations: He said, "You must

---

[5]Gordon Wenham, "Covenants and Near Eastern Treaties," in *Eerdman's Handbook to the Bible*, ed. David Alexander and Pat Alexander (Grand Rapids, Mich.: Wm. B. Eerdmans Publishing Co., 1973), 198–99.

do everything I say." In other places in the Old Testament can be found the equivalent of (4) the document clause and (6) curses and blessings which relate to obeying or disobeying the covenant. However, neither here nor elsewhere in the Old Testament can be found the equivalent of (5) a list of gods witnessing the treaty.[6] Why? Because, obviously, Israel believed in only one God; therefore they would not accept the idea that a treaty they were a party to was witnessed by "gods" (plural).

The covenant found in Exodus 19 is very important. The rest of the Old Testament is to be understood on the basis of this agreement. This covenant governed Israel's relationship with God throughout the Mosaic era. For example, Jeremiah, in the sixth century B.C., asked why Jerusalem was to be destroyed. The answer to the question was "Because they forsook the covenant of the LORD their God" (Jer. 22:9). Further, when Jeremiah prophesied that God would make a new covenant with Israel, he said that it would not be "like the covenant which [God] made with their fathers in the day [He] took them by the hand to bring them out of the land of Egypt, [His] covenant which they broke" (Jer. 31:32). According to Jeremiah's understanding, the covenant made at Sinai would remain in effect until God gave the "new covenant."

Later parts of the Old Testament seem to say that Israel made a new covenant with the Lord (see Josh. 24:25; Ezra 10:3; Neh. 9:38). However, if the reader examines each passage, he will see that the reference is not to a different covenant but to the Mosaic covenant. Sometimes part of the covenant is spoken of as if it were the whole. "Commandments," though only part of the covenant, are sometimes synonymous with the word "covenant." In addition, people were sometimes said to "make a covenant" with the Lord when, in reality, they were either renewing their covenant vows or were voluntarily submitting to the covenant. That is, they were becoming a party to it by taking the same kind of oath that Israel took in Exodus 19.

Old Testament history demonstrates that, as long as the Israel-

---

[6]Although, in some cases, other "witnesses" were referred to (see Josh. 24:22, 27).

ites kept the covenant by obeying God, He blessed them. When they disobeyed (which happened more frequently), then God punished them. The Old Testament poets praised the Lord for His grace in condescending to make such a covenant with Israel, or they lamented Israel's failure to keep it. The prophets either urged Israel to keep the covenant or threatened doom because they had not kept it.

The New Covenant

The new covenant, like the old, is based on God's gracious acts—not on what men have done. It originates with God, not men. Human beings have the right to either accept or reject the covenant, but not to change its terms or conditions. The new covenant, like the old, involves blessings and curses. Those who fail to keep it will be condemned. Those who live up to the responsibilities of the new covenant will be blessed. We can be God's children under a new covenant (2 Cor. 3:6), and Jesus Himself is the mediator of this new covenant (Heb. 12:24).

Study 7

The Law of Moses

In the Old Testament, the expression "the Law," unless the phrase is further modified, refers to the laws given to Israel by God through Moses at Mount Sinai as well as all those given during the wilderness wanderings. When the prophets exhorted Israel to keep the Law or threatened Israel because they had broken the Law, they were referring to the law of Moses found in Exodus through Deuteronomy. The rest of the Old Testament, beyond the Pentateuch, does not add to the Law. Rather, it illustrates how the Law was being kept or broken.

Scholars today speak of the "moral law" and the "ritual law." Some suggest that "ritual law" has passed away, while "moral law" remains in effect. The Law itself made no such distinction. Even the Ten Commandments contain laws related to ritual or worship (the first four) and laws related to morality (the final six). In numerous Old Testament passages, the two types are intermingled, indicating no difference between them. In the New Testament, Paul settled the question of distinction between "commandments" (moral law) and "ordinances" (ritual law) by speaking of "the Law of commandments contained in ordinances" (Eph. 2:15).

The Law recorded in Exodus through Deuteronomy was given for the benefit of God's people. Various features of the Law made it in many respects a good law.

Its Comprehensive Nature

The law of Moses was comprehensive, dealing with every aspect of life. It provided Israel's religious and moral code. It also contained many regulations on the following topics:[1]

1. The family (Ex. 20:12; 21:15, 17; Deut. 21:15–21; 22:13–30; 24:1–4)
2. Agriculture (Ex. 23:10, 11; Lev. 19:9, 10)
3. Economics, business, and labor (Ex. 21:2–11; Lev. 19:13, 35, 36; Deut. 23:19, 20; 24:10–15)
4. Care for the poor (Lev. 19:9, 10; Deut. 23:24, 25; 24:19–22)
5. Health and sanitation (Deut. 23:12, 13; 24:8)
6. The judicial system (Ex. 20:16; 23:1–3; Lev. 19:15)
7. Taxes (Num. 18)
8. The conduct of war (Deut. 20)
9. Relationships with people living in the promised land (Ex. 23:23–33)
10. Education (Deut. 6:6–9)
11. Relationships between neighbors (Ex. 22:5, 6).

Every aspect of life was touched by its regulations. The Israelites were to see each part of their lives as having a religious or spiritual dimension.

The Law, to deal with all these topics, consisted of more than six hundred commandments.[2] However, even that many laws could not cover every possible situation that Israel would face. Therefore, the Law was "paradigmatic"[3]: It provided a paradigm—a model or example—for application to situations not precisely covered by individual laws.

Its Promises of Blessing and Threats of Cursing

The Law was characterized by promises of blessing and threats of cursing, depending on whether or not the people kept its commandments. Conditional blessings were specified in the

---

[1]The passages cited are examples and are not intended to represent all that the Pentateuch teaches on any subject.

[2]Gordon D. Fee and Douglas Stuart, *How to Read the Bible for All Its Worth*, 3d ed. (Grand Rapids, Mich.: Zondervan, 2003), 164.

[3]Ibid., 172.

original covenant God made with Israel (Ex. 19:5). Additional promises are scattered throughout the Law, along with numerous threats and examples of punishment for disobedience.

Two series of blessings and curses are found in Leviticus 26 and in Deuteronomy 27 and 28. In the very areas of life in which they would be blessed if they obeyed, God would curse them if they disobeyed (compare Deut. 28:5–13 with 28:17–26). These promises and threats of the Law were very different from those given in the New Testament in three ways:

They were national rather than individual. The Law spoke to Israel as a whole. Blessings were based on the nation's obedience to the Law, and God punished the nation because of the collective sins of the people (see 2 Kings 17).[4] Therefore, when punishment came, innocent people suffered with the guilty.

They were material rather than spiritual. Spiritual blessings were available in Old Testament times for those who obeyed the Lord, but the promises of the covenant focused on physical blessings: prosperity, victory over enemies, and the conquest of the land. Punishment for disobedience could include famine, pestilence, or even death. God designed the sacrificial system to deal with the sins of the individual as well as those of the nation, but the covenant blessings were primarily physical.

They were temporal rather than eternal. The promises and threats of the Law had their fulfillment in this world. While there may have been some concept of eternal rewards and punishment for individuals during the Old Testament era,[5] the Law did not make such promises explicit. This is in contrast to the new covenant, which offers the promise of eternal life.

---

[4]Individuals were held accountable for their own sins (see Deut. 24:16; Jer. 31:29, 30; Ezek. 18:20).

[5]It would be surprising if the people of Israel did not have some belief in life after death, since other peoples living about them—especially the Egyptians—did. Evidence of a knowledge of and belief in life after death is found in a few places in the Old Testament (see 1 Sam. 28:3–19; 2 Sam. 12:20–23; Job 19:25, 26; Is. 26:19; Dan. 12:2). The fact that many Jews believed in resurrection at the time of Jesus provides evidence that the Old Testament at least hinted at the idea.

Other Features of the Law

Not only was the Law comprehensive, with promises of blessings and threats of cursing, but it also had other important characteristics.

It was based on God's gracious acts, with reasons for obedience. The Israelites should have been eager to obey because the Lord God Himself—the One who had lovingly brought them out of Egypt—gave them the Law. God urged them to keep the Law for specific reasons (Ex. 22:21; 23:9).

It required righteous behavior. For example, it forbade murder, adultery, stealing, and lying. It encouraged obedience to parents and discouraged divorce, increasing family stability.

It governed thoughts and attitudes. Actions like stealing and murder were declared to be wrong, but the people were also taught not to hate or bear a grudge against a neighbor (Lev. 19:17, 18).

It valued life more than property. Human life was considered precious.

It prohibited personal revenge (Lev. 19:18). In contrast, it required a person to treat his enemies well (Ex. 23:4, 5).

It protected the defenseless. The Law provided for strangers, widows and orphans, the poor, and even slaves. God said that He Himself would enforce the rules which protected the unfortunate (Ex. 22:21–24).

It required fairness. The Law decreed that the punishment was to fit the crime ("eye for eye"; Ex. 21:24). One who maliciously took the life of another would himself be executed by the proper authorities. In court cases, each outcome had to be just or fair. The Law applied to everyone equally. Other codes of the ancient Near East differentiated between categories of people in pronouncing laws and their penalties, but not the law of Moses. All Israelites—from the least to the greatest—were subject to its provisions.

Conclusion. The Law was good and righteous (Rom. 7:12); however, it was not designed to take away sins (Heb. 8:7; 10:4). By its righteous demands, it proclaimed people to be sinners but provided no sacrifice adequate to save them from sin. The Law anticipated the cross.

Study 8

The Sabbath

The Meaning of the Word

The word "sabbath" in the English Bible is transliterated from the Hebrew word שַׁבָּת (*shabbath*), which means "cessation."[1] A closely related verb is defined as meaning "to rest from labour, to keep a sabbath."[2] One source defines the verb as meaning "to repose . . . to desist (from exertion), to cease, to leave off" and the noun as meaning "intermission, the Sabbath, the day of rest, the holy seventh day."[3]

Reasons to Keep the Sabbath Under the Old Law

"Remember the sabbath day to keep it holy" is one of the Ten Commandments (Ex. 20:8; see Deut. 5:12). Four reasons are given for its observance:

(1) *Creation.* In Exodus 20:8–11, the Israelites were told to observe the Sabbath as a day of rest because after God created the world in six days, he rested on the seventh day (see 31:17). Just as God rested after working for six days, so the Israelites were to rest after working for six days of the week.

(2) *Covenant.* In Exodus 31:12, the people were commanded

---

[1]Robert Young, *Analytical Concordance to the Bible* (Grand Rapids, Mich.: Eerdmans, n.d), 828. The Greek word translated "sabbath" in the New Testament is σάββατον (*sabbaton*), also a transliteration from the Hebrew.

[2]*Wilson's Old Testament Word Studies* (McLean, Va.: MacDonald Publishing Co., n.d.), 364.

[3]Spiros Zodhaites, Notes on *Shabath* and *Shabbath* in *The Hebrew-Greek Key Study Bible*, ed. Spiros Zodhiates (Grand Rapids, Mich.: Baker Book House, 1984), 1642.

to observe the Sabbath because it was a sign of the covenant between God and Israel—indeed, the day was to be celebrated "throughout their generations as a perpetual covenant" and was to be observed as "a sign between [God] and the sons of Israel forever" (31:16, 17).[4] The Sabbath day, in fact, served as a sign of the covenant: Its observance differentiated Israel, God's people, from all other nations throughout Israel's history.

(3) *Consideration.* In Deuteronomy 5:15, Moses urged the Israelites to consider what God had done for them as a reason for observing the Sabbath: "You shall remember that you were a slave in the land of Egypt, and the LORD your God brought you out of there by a mighty hand and by an outstretched arm; therefore the LORD your God commanded you to observe the sabbath day." Implied is the idea that one reason for keeping the command was Israel's gratitude for God's gracious deliverance of the nation out of Egyptian slavery.

(4) *Compassion.* The passage in Deuteronomy also suggests a humanitarian reason for observing the Sabbath. Not only were the Israelites to keep the Sabbath; they were also to see that the people and animals belonging to them kept it so that those who served the household might enjoy a day of rest:

> "In [the sabbath] you shall not do any work, you or your son or your daughter or your male servant or your female servant or your ox or your donkey or any of your cattle or your sojourner who stays with you, *so that your male servant and your female servant may rest as well as you*" (Deut. 5:14, emphasis added).

The Importance of the Sabbath In the Old Testament

The importance of the Sabbath in the Old Testament is evi-

---

[4]Paul A. Barker said, "The sabbath is the sign of the Mosaic covenant just as the rainbow is the sign of the Noahic covenant and circumcision is the sign of the Abrahamic covenant." (Paul A. Barker, "Sabbath, Sabbatical Year, Jubilee," in *Dictionary of the Old Tesament—Pentateuch,* ed. T. Desmond Alexander and David W. Baker [Downers Grove, Ill.: InterVarsity Press, 2003], 698.)

dent from the contexts in which the word is used or the idea is found.

The first mention of the observance of the Sabbath is found in Exodus 16:4, 5, 22–30, where the Israelites were instructed not to gather the manna on the Sabbath day. Genesis 2:1–3 says that "God blessed the seventh day and sanctified it," but does not indicate that the Sabbath began to be kept at that time. The mention of the Sabbath is probably proleptic—referring earlier to something that would happen later.[5] Abraham is said to have kept God's commandments (Gen. 26:5), but there is no indication in the text or anywhere else that those commandments included the Sabbath.

The significance of the command is emphasized by the fact that it is repeated six times in the Book of Exodus: in connection with the instructions for gathering the manna (16:4, 5, 22–30); as the fourth of the Ten Commandments (20:8–11); in the Book of the Covenant (23:12); and interspersed in the tabernacle narrative (31:12–17; 34:21; 35:1–3). It is found elsewhere in the Pentateuch in Leviticus 23:3 and Deuteronomy 5:12–15. It was, in fact, so important that the sin of breaking the Sabbath was punishable by death (31:15; 35:2; Num. 15:32–36).

After the giving of the Law, God's prophets and Israel's righteous leaders continued to stress the importance of the Sabbath requirement. In the eighth century B.C., Isaiah said that the man who keeps the Sabbath is happy (Is. 56:2) and that such people will be blessed (Is. 58:13, 14). In the seventh or sixth century B.C., Jeremiah commanded the people to keep the Sabbath day, promising blessings if they would and threatening destruction if they failed to do so (Jer. 17:19–27). In the sixth century B.C., Ezekiel condemned the people over and over for profaning the Sabbath throughout their history (Ezek. 20). Moreover, he blamed their impending doom, in part, on the fact that they had profaned the Sabbath (Ezek. 22:8, 15). In the fifth century B.C., Nehemiah said

---

[5]In other words, the author of Genesis, writing after the law of Moses had been given and while the Sabbath was being observed, tells his readers why they now observe the Sabbath: God blessed and hallowed the day in Moses' time because in the beginning He rested on the seventh day.

that God had brought disaster on the Jews and on Jerusalem because Israel's fathers had profaned the Sabbath day (Neh. 13:17, 18). Furthermore, as one of his reforms, Nehemiah required the enforcement of the Sabbath laws (Neh. 13:15–22).

How the Sabbath Was Observed

The Sabbath day that was observed by the Israelites was the seventh day of the week (Gen. 2:1–3). It was observed initially not as a day of worship[6] but as a day of rest;[7] Exodus 16:30 says, "So the people rested on the seventh day." One writer noted concerning the Sabbath laws found in the Pentateuch: "For the ordinary Israelite, no religious ceremony was commanded. Basically it was a day of rest. The dominant command or prohibition attached to the observance of the Sabbath day is 'You shall do no work.'"[8]

The commands and biblical examples connected with the Sabbath indicate the kind of activities that were prohibited on the Sabbath day: gathering manna (Ex. 16); any work (Ex. 20:10; 31:15; Deut. 5:14; Jer. 17:22, 24); plowing and harvesting (Ex. 34:21); kindling a fire in one's dwelling (Ex. 35:3); gathering wood (Num. 15:32–36); carrying a load or bringing anything into the city of Jerusalem (Jer. 17:21–27); "treading wine presses . . . bringing in sacks of grain and loading them on donkeys and [bringing] them into the city . . . [and selling] food" and buying food (Neh. 10:15–22). Isaiah summed up the requirements of the Sabbath by equating "trampling the sabbath" with "pursuing your own interests on my holy day" (Is. 58:13; NRSV). The Sabbath,

---

[6]The feast days were frequently connected with the Sabbath (see Lev. 16:31; 23:15). On those occasions the Sabbath became a day of worship; since the people met together to offer sacrifice and so to worship.

[7]The Sabbath was originally "observed simply by abstinence from labour." (Francis Brown, S. R. Driver, and Charles A. Briggs, *The Brown-Driver-Briggs Hebrew and English Lexicon* [Boston: Houghton, Mifflin and Co., 1906; reprint, Peabody, Mass.: Hendrickson Publishers, 1997], 992.)

[8]Barker, 698. A possible exception to this rule is Leviticus 23:3 which speaks of the sabbath as a "holy convocation." Since "convocation" (NASB) usually refers to an assembly, this passage may seem to call for a gathering each sabbath day. However, given the evidence found elsewhere, the word likely implies something different in this verse.

since it was devoted to God, was to be spent as He directed and not on one's "own interests."

The Sabbath was not only to be a day of rest for the Israelites but for every person and animal in their households. The command said that the Israelites were not to "do any work," but it added, "you or your son or your daughter, your male or your female servant or your cattle or your sojourner who stays with you" (20:10). Exodus 23:12 adds that on the seventh day the Israelites were to "cease from labor so that your ox and your donkey may rest" and that "your female slave, as well as your stranger, may refresh themselves" (see Deut. 5:14).

The fact that the Sabbath was a day of rest meant that it was a day to be enjoyed rather than endured, not a burden but a time of refreshment (Deut. 5:14). Isaiah said that Judah should "call the sabbath a delight and the holy day of the LORD honorable" (Is. 58:13; NRSV). Thus, Hosea wrote concerning the destruction of the Northern Kingdom, "I will also put an end to all her gaiety, her feasts, her new moons, her sabbaths and all her festal assemblies" (Hos. 2:11)—all of which were obviously thought of as joyful occasions. Likewise, when Jerusalem was destroyed, the fact that the Jews could no longer observe their feasts or keep the Sabbath was regarded as a tragedy (Lam. 2:6).

The prophets also indicated that keeping the Sabbath (or observing any of the ritual requirements of the Law[9]) legalistically—without the right attitude and apart from a life lived for God—was not by itself sufficient to please God. Amos spoke of and condemned those who longed to see the Sabbath ended so that they could continue to cheat people (Amos 8:5). Isaiah denounced in no uncertain terms those who observed the rituals of the law but neglected (what Jesus would later call) the "weightier matters" (Is. 1:10–17). He reported that the Lord said, among other things,

> When you come to appear before Me, who requires of you this trampling of My courts? Bring your worthless offerings no longer, incense is an abomination to Me. New

[9]See, for example, Isaiah's discussion of fasting (Is. 58).

> moon and sabbath, the calling of assemblies—I cannot endure iniquity and the solemn assembly. I hate your new moon festivals and your appointed feasts. . . . So when you spread out your hands in prayer . . . I will not listen. Your hands are covered with blood (Is. 1:12–15).

The command to rest on the Sabbath day was expanded to require the Israelites to allow the land to rest on the seventh year, the Sabbath or sabbatical year (Ex. 23:10, 11; Lev. 25:1–7). Seven-year periods of time, ending with the Sabbath year, were then called "sabbaths of years" (Lev. 25:8) and were used to define the Year of Jubilee, the fiftieth year (Lev. 25:8–34).

Later Developments Regarding the Sabbath

At some point in Israel's history, the custom arose of gathering together on the Sabbath for worship. That custom is evident in New Testament times, for Luke wrote that Jesus went into the synagogue on the Sabbath day as was his custom (Lk. 4:16); and New Testament evangelists preached to crowds of Jews and proselytes who were gathered together in synagogues on the Sabbath day (Acts 13:14, 15).

The requirement to keep the Sabbath day holy may have been emphasized even more as the period of history covered by the Old Testament came to an end. Nehemiah, one of the leaders in post-exilic Israel, emphasized the importance of the Sabbath.[10] Possibly the great concern for the Sabbath manifested by the post-exilic and intertestamental Jews stemmed from the fact that they were then living in a hostile world surrounded by Gentiles and keeping the Sabbath was essential to maintaining their identity as a people.

The Jews' great concern for the Sabbath later in their history is obvious from the writings they produced. "The Mishnah tractate Shabbath 7.2 lists thirty-nine classes of work, deduced from

---

[10]Note the great concern for the Sabbath manifested by the Jewish leaders who confronted Jesus.

the Scriptures, that were forbidden on the Sabbath."[11] The intentions of the rabbis in elaborating on the Sabbath command were good; they wanted to, as is often said, "build a fence" around the Law. The idea of a fence was that if the Jews kept those traditions—if they did not step over that fence which had been erected around the law—then they would not break the law itself. In the case of the requirement to keep the Sabbath holy by not working on that day, the command was too imprecise for them. What does it mean to "work"? What was "work" and what was not? To clarify what "work" was, they devised all kinds of specific laws, or traditions, which they then imposed on their countrymen.[12]

For instance, how far could one walk before his travel would be called "work"? Somehow the rabbis decided that if a Jew walked no more than about three-quarters of a mile, he had not worked; thus he had not broken the Sabbath. Consequently, a "sabbath day's journey" (Acts 1:12) was defined as about three-quarters of a mile. However, nowhere does the Law itself define a "sabbath day's journey." Uninspired Jewish teachers made that determination.

There was nothing wrong with the Jews attempting to determine what constituted "work" or even with their writing down the results of their deliberations. If anyone kept those traditions, chances are he would not, in fact, break the specific commands the traditions were intended to protect.

Jesus and the Sabbath

Jesus taught that the Jews' use of the traditions was sinful because, in observing the traditions, they broke the law of God "for the sake of [their] tradition" (Mt. 15:3). Thus He said that they worshiped God in vain, "teaching as doctrines the precepts of men" (Mt. 15:9).

---

[11]Everett Ferguson, *Backgrounds of Early Christianity*, 2d ed. (Grand Rapids, Mich.: Wm. B. Eerdmans Publishing Co., 1993), 522.

[12]See Stephen Westerholm, "Sabbath," in *Dictionary of Jesus and the Gospels*, ed. Joel B. Green and Scot McKnight (Downers Grove, Ill.: InterVarsity Press, 1992), 716.

From the story told in the Gospels. Jesus' attitude towards the Sabbath differed markedly from that of the Jewish leaders. He kept the Sabbath, just as He obeyed other commands of the Mosaic law under which He lived—just as He went up to Jerusalem to worship for the feast days, for instance.[13]

At the same time, Jesus obviously did not feel obligated to observe the traditions that had grown up around the Sabbath, any more than He felt obligated to keep other traditions. Consequently, He was accused of breaking the Sabbath (see Mk. 2:24). However, the accusation was based, not on what the law of Moses actually taught but on the traditions of the Jews.[14] Jesus responded to the accusation in several ways: (1) by citing the example of David who ate bread from the temple which was forbidden to any except to priests (Mt. 12:3, 4; Mk. 2:25, 26);[15] (2) by saying, "The Sabbath was made for man, and not man for the Sabbath" (Mk. 2:27); (3) by saying, "So the Son of Man is Lord even of the Sabbath" (Mk. 2:28; see Mt. 12:6–8); (4) by citing the example of the priests who "break the Sabbath" by working on the Sabbath in the performance of their duties and yet "are innocent" (Mt. 12:5).

The Sabbath and the Church

In the early church, there is no record of congregations meet-

---

[13]If Jesus had not kept the commandments of the Law, which was not taken away until His death, then He would have sinned; but the New Testament plainly states that He never sinned (Heb. 4:15). In Matthew 12:7, after being accused of breaking the Sabbath, Jesus specifically referred to Himself as "innocent" of the charge.

[14]Christ's enemies said that what His disciples did, as they plucked individual ears of grain while walking through a grainfield, was "not lawful on the sabbath" (Mk. 2:24). However, one could search the Old Testament from cover to cover and not find their actions prohibited. The disciples broke, not God's law, but rabbinic traditions.

[15]Jesus' use of David's example does not necessarily prove that David's actions were approved by Jesus. More likely, Jesus was using an *ad hominem* argument: Since his opponents approved of David's behavior (whether or not God approved of it), then why could they not accept as lawful the disciples' harmless act of plucking grain on the Sabbath?

ing for Christian worship on the Sabbath day,[16] or the seventh day. Instead, the day Christians observed was the first day of the week (Acts 20:7; 1 Cor. 16:1, 2), the day of Christ's resurrection, which became known as "the Lord's day" (Rev. 1:10). That early in church history Christians met on the first day of the week for their worship assemblies is confirmed by the writings of the church fathers. No rules are given in the New Testament for the observance of the Lord's Day except for the requirement to meet together to worship and observe the Lord's Supper. Certainly there is no New Testament command to rest on the Lord's Day; and, from that standpoint, the first day of the week (Sunday, or the Lord's Day) does not become the Christian equivalent of the Jewish Sabbath, the seventh day of the week.

The only time in the New Testament that the word "sabbath" (or a close equivalent) is used with regard to Christians is in Hebrews 4:9–11:

> So there remains a Sabbath rest for the people of God. For the one who has entered His rest has himself also rested from his works, as God did from His. Therefore, let us be diligent to enter that rest, so that no one will fall, through following the same example of disobedience.

In this passage, the Christian's "Sabbath rest" is heaven; and the Christian is to "strive" to enter it.

Observing the Sabbath Today

The major issue regarding the Sabbath today is this question: Are Christians required to observe the seventh day? Three facts indicate that the answer must be in the negative: (1) The Sabbath commandment was given to Israel as a sign of the covenant between Israel and God—and not to Gentiles or to the world at large. (2) The Sabbath was part of the Law, and the Law has been taken away (Rom. 7:1, 2; Gal. 3:24, 25; Eph. 2:15). (3) There is no

---

[16]Christian evangelists went into the Jewish synagogues to preach on the Sabbath day, but their actions do not provide a valid argument for the proposition that the church should meet for worship on the Sabbath day.

indication that the early church felt obligated to meet for worship on the Sabbath day. Therefore, it seems reasonable to conclude that individual Christians or congregations are not required to keep the Sabbath.[17]

[17]An individual Christian might decide that, since the Sabbath "was made for man," and since God seemed to feel that man needed to rest one day out of the week, he was going to rest every Sabbath, every Saturday. To rest on the seventh day would not break any New Testament requirements as long as one did not seek to make such an observance binding on all Christians.

SELECTED BIBLIOGRAPHY

GENERAL

Alexander, David and Pat Alexander, eds. *Eerdmans' Handbook to the Bible*. Grand Rapids, Mich.: Wm. B. Eerdmans Publishing Co., 1973.

Alexander, T. Desmond and David W. Baker, eds. *Dictionary of the Old Testament: Pentateuch*. Downers Grove, Ill.: InterVarsity Press, 2003.

Archer, Gleason L., Jr. *Encyclopedia of Bible Difficulties*. Grand Rapids, Mich.: Zondervan Publishing House, 1982.

__________. *A Survey of Old Testament Introduction*, rev. and exp. Chicago: Moody Press, 1994.

Bromiley, Geoffrey W., ed. *The International Standard Bible Encyclopedia*, rev. ed. 4 vols. Grand Rapids, Mich.: Wm. B. Eerdmans Publishing Co., 1979, 1982, 1986, 1988.

Brown, Francis, S. R. Driver, and Charles A. Briggs. *The Brown-Driver-Briggs Hebrew and English Lexicon*. Boston: Houghton, Mifflin and Co., 1906. Reprint, Peabody, Mass.: Hendrickson Publishers, 1997.

Brueggemann, Walter. "The Book of Exodus." In *The New Interpreter's Bible*, ed. Leander E. Keck, vol. 1. Nashville: Abingdon Press, 1994.

Bush, George. *Commentary on Exodus*. New York: M. H. Newman, 1843. Reprint, Grand Rapids, Mich.: Kregel Publications, 1993.

Buttrick, George Arthur, ed. *The Interpreter's Dictionary of the Bible*. Nashville: Abingdon Press, 1962.

Cassuto, Umberto. *A Commentary on the Book of Exodus*. Translated by Israel Abrahams. Jerusalem: Magnes Press, 1997.

Childs, Brevard S. *The Book of Exodus: A Critical, Theological Commentary*. The Old Testament Library. Louisville: Westminster Press, 1974.

Clements, Ronald E. *Exodus*. The Cambridge Bible Commentary. Cambridge: University Press, 1972.

Coffman, James Burton. *Commentary on Exodus, The Second Book of Moses*. Abilene, Tex.: ACU Press, 1985.

Cole, R. Alan. *Exodus: An Introduction and Commentary*. Tyndale Old Testament Commentaries. Downers Grove, Ill.: Inter-Varsity Press, 1973.

Davis, John J. *Moses and the Gods of Egypt: Studies in Exodus*, 2d ed. Grand Rapids, Mich.: Baker Book House, 1986.

Driver, S. R. *The Book of Exodus*. The Cambridge Bible for Schools and Colleges. Cambridge: University Press, 1953.

Durham, John I. *Exodus*. Word Biblical Commentary, vol. 3. Waco, Tex.: Word Books, 1987.

Ellison, H. L. *Exodus*. The Daily Study Bible Series. Philadelphia: Westminster Press, 1982.

Enns, Peter. *Exodus*. The NIV Application Commentary. Grand Rapids, Mich.: Zondervan, 2000.

Fields, Wilbur. *Exploring Exodus*. Bible Study Textbook Series. Joplin, Mo.: College Press, 1976.

Freedman, David Noel, ed. *The Eerdmans Dictionary of the Bible.* Grand Rapids, Mich.: Wm. B. Eerdmans Publishing Co., 2000.

Fretheim, Terence E. *Exodus*. Interpretation: A Bible Commentary for Teaching and Preaching. Louisville: John Knox Press, 1991.

Gispen, W. H. *Exodus*. Translated by Ed van der Maas. Bible Student's Commentary. Grand Rapids, Mich.: Regency Reference Library, Zondervan Publishing House, 1982.

Gray, John. "The Book of Exodus." In *The Interpreter's One-Volume Commentary on the Bible*, ed. Charles Laymon, 33-67. Nashville: Abingdon Press, 1971.

Hoffmeier, James K. "Exodus." In *Evangelical Commentary on the Bible*, ed. Walter A. Elwell, 38–63. Grand Rapids, Mich.: Baker Book House, 1989.

Hyatt, J. Philip. *Exodus*. The New Century Bible Commentary. Grand Rapids, Mich.: Wm. B. Eerdmans Publishing Co., 1971.

Janzen, Waldemar. *Exodus*. Believers Church Bible Commentary. Scottdale, Pa.: Herald Press, 2000.

Kaiser, Walter C., Jr., "Exodus." In *The Expositor's Bible Commentary*, vol. 2, *Genesis—Numbers*. Grand Rapids, Mich.: Zondervan, 1990.

Keil, C. F. and F. Delitzsch. *The Pentateuch*, vol. 2. Translated by James Martin. Biblical Commentary on the Old Testament. Grand Rapids, Mich.: Wm. B. Eerdmans Publishing Co., n.d.

LaSor, William Sanford, David Allan Hubbard, and Frederic William Bush. *Old Testament Survey: The Message, Form, and Background of the Old Testament.* Grand Rapids, Mich.: Wm. B. Eerdmans Publishing Co., 1982.

Noth, Martin. *Exodus.* Translated by J. S. Bowden. The Old Testament Library. Philadelphia: Westminster Press, 1962.

Pfeiffer, Charles F., ed. *The Biblical World: A Dictionary of Biblical Archaeology.* Grand Rapids, Mich.: Baker Book House, 1966.

Pritchard, James B., ed. *Ancient Near Eastern Texts: Relating to the Old Testament*, 3d ed. Princeton, N.J.: Princeton University Press, 1969.

Rawlinson, George. "Exodus." In *The Pulpit Commentary*, vol. 1, *Genesis and Exodus*, ed. H. D. M. Spence and Joseph S. Exell. Grand Rapids, Mich.: Wm. B. Eerdmans Publishing Co., 1950.

Sarna, Nahum M. *Exodus.* The JPS Torah Commentary. New York: Jewish Publication Society, 1991.

__________. *Exploring Exodus: The Origins of Biblical Israel.* New York: Schocken Books, 1996.

Walton, John H. and Victor H. Matthews. *Genesis—Deuteronomy.* The IVP Bible Background Commentary. Downers Grove, Ill.: InterVarsity Press, 1997.

Wiersbe, Warren W. *Be Delivered.* Colorado Springs, Colo.: Victor, 1998.

Youngblood, Ronald F. *Exodus.* Everyman's Bible Commentary. Chicago: Moody Bible Institute, 1983.

BIBLE TRANSLATIONS

The Amplified Bible. Grand Rapids, Mich.: Zondervan Publishing House, 1987.

The Holy Bible; American Standard Version. Thomas Nelson & Sons, 1901.

The Holy Bible; Authorized King James Version. Colorado Springs, Co.: International Bible Society, 1987.

The Holy Bible; Contemporary English Version. New York: American Bible Society, 1995.

The Holy Bible; English Standard Version. Wheaton, Ill.: Good News Publishers, 2001.

The Holy Bible; New Century Version. Dallas: Word Bibles, 1991.

The Holy Bible; New International Version. Grand Rapids, Mich.: Zondervan Publishing House, 1978.

The Holy Bible; New King James Version. New York: American Bible Society, 1990.

The Holy Bible; New Living Translation. Wheaton, Ill.: Tyndale House Publishers, 1996.

The Holy Bible; Revised Standard Version. Nashville: Thomas Nelson, Inc., 1972.

The Holy Bible; Today's English Version. New York: American Bible Society, 1976.

The New American Bible. New York: P. J. Kenedy, 1970.

New American Standard Bible. Anaheim, Calif.: Foundation Publications, 1995.

The New English Bible. New York: Oxford University Press, 1971.

The New Jerusalem Bible. Reader's Edition. New York: Doubleday, 1990.

The New Oxford Annotated Bible with the Apocrypha. Edited by Bruce M. Metzger and Roland E. Murphy, rev. and enl. New York: Oxford University Press, 1991.

The Revised English Bible. New York: Oxford University Press, 1989.

From the Editor

Have You Heard . . .
About Truth for Today?

What are the big missionary needs of our time? Those who study missionary evangelism point to two paramount needs that are ever present in the mission field.

THE BIG NEEDS OF WORLD EVANGELISM

First, they tell us that educating and maturing the national Christian man so that he can preach to his own people in their own language is of supreme importance. Giving this type of assistance to the national man will help to make our missionary efforts more self-supporting and more enduring. We appreciate one of our own preaching to us, and so do other peoples of the world. When we consider the work "our work," we approach it with greater care and will sacrifice more for it. This principle holds true in all cultures.

Christianity can flourish in any nation and culture, in any time or circumstance, if we will let it. When it is established through national preachers, it is far more likely to grow and blossom in the lives of the national people and not become an effort that is totally dependent upon American support.

After the Restoration Movement began in America, it did not take the early preachers long to realize that they had to teach young men to preach if the movement was really to grow. Thus very early in the history of the Restoration Movement schools were established. Wisdom suggested that route.

Christians should be grateful for every mission effort that is going on, such as campaigns, medical missions, and television presentations. However, we must not overlook the surpassing value of providing educational opportunities overseas that will assist a man in becoming capable of preaching effectively to his own people. This approach is absolutely vital to the ongoing success of the overall missionary work of the church.

Second, those who have researched missionary evangelism tell us that we need to make available biblical literature that provides an understanding of the Bible on the level of the people. Those whom the missionary is seeking to teach need their own copies of the Bible and assistance in understanding the Scriptures. They require guidance so they can grow quickly and accurately in their comprehension of the Bible. (See Acts 8:30, 31.)

When Tex Williams, the former director of World Bible School, was on Harding University's campus sometime ago, he spoke to students about mission work. As a guest lecturer, he told one of the mission classes that the greatest need of Africa is Christian literature. "Without this literature," he said, "they simply cannot become Christians and grow into Christian maturity as they should." There is possibly one exception to this principle. The exception would be places where there is the presence of well-grounded men of faith continually teaching and preaching. This exception obviously applies to only a few places around the world. Even then, biblical literature is needed to support the teaching done.

Let us all consider carefully these two obvious missionary needs. Our efforts must be geared to meeting them. Not to address them is to ignore the clear results of the research that has been done in mission evangelism.

ADDRESSING THESE NEEDS

An effort is currently being made to address both of these big missionary needs. It has been designated the Truth for Today World Mission School (TFTWMS). Started in 1990 as a work under the oversight of the Champions church of Christ in Houston, Texas, it has proven to be a wonderful way to combine three methods of evangelism and thus minister to these supreme needs.

First, TFTWMS is a unique preacher school. An education in the Scriptures is mailed to the national preacher. The work started with 1,460 native preachers enrolled from 110 nations. Now literature is mailed to 38,000 people in 136 nations. These preachers were recommended to the school by World Bible School teachers, missionaries, campaigners, and the national preachers themselves. The school has enjoyed amazing growth.

Second, it is a printed preacher school. Every three months, the men enrolled receive the equivalent of 450 pages of expository studies on the Scriptures. It is believed that the expository type of study crosses cultures better than other types of study. The materials sent give a thorough treatment of the New Testament book or Old Testament book being studied. It is designed to keep the national preacher enrolled in the school until he receives a study of each of the New Testament and Old Testament books, as well as several important special studies.

Picture three normal-sized books that are 150 pages in length, and you have the equivalent of the amount of material that is sent to these men every three months. The entire curriculum calls for these men to receive books that are 150 pages in size, that cover the entire Bible, and that include special studies on leadership, building sermons and Bible lessons, and soul-winning.

Third, in addition to sending expository studies to these men, a flexible, on-site preacher school is sometimes used as a follow-up to the printed material. This on-site school is literally taken to where the men are. Preachers and teachers go into a country and study with the national preachers in that location for two or three weeks. Students are provided with food and a syllabus for the classes they attend. They stay at that location day and night for the entire length of the school. They thus enjoy fellowship with other preaching brethren and are given opportunities to ask questions and receive feedback on problems they are facing.

The printed preacher school and the on-site school answer the big need of giving the national man an opportunity to prepare himself to preach to his own people in their own language. Since this work is accomplished to some extent through the printed page, it also answers the need of providing Christian literature for these teachers and preachers who are in desperate need of it.

THE STRONG POINTS

This unique missionary effort has strong points that should be immediately recognized. First, it provides an education to national men inexpensively. Expository materials can be sent to each of these men every two months in a cost-efficient way. Money for missions is hard to find or raise; what missionary money we have should be used to the maximum. TFTWMS sends an education to hundreds of national men with a small amount of money.

Second, the thrust of this work is to educate national men in their own land. Bringing these men to the United States for an education is very expensive. Often, when the national man tastes of the blessings of America, he does not want to return to his land. It is almost essential that a way be found through which the national preacher can receive an education in his own country.

Third, this effort can reach out to hundreds of national men quickly. All of these men are in need of assistance now! How can we get it to them? This method is one of the most practical ways of immediately getting materials to them.

Fourth, it allows the national man to receive an education over a period of time. Because the education comes in the form of printed matter, they have access to the material for months and even years. These men need time to comprehend and assimilate the studies. The printed page offers them that opportunity. They can read and re-read it. They can easily store it. They can share it with others. It can be retained in their possession for as long as ten to fifteen years.

PICTURING THE EFFECTIVENESS

Picture 38,000 men (and thousands more as the work grows) in 136 nations of the world, going out to preach in their own languages to their own people. They are committed to Christ but have had little teaching upon which to build. Furthermore, these men will never have the opportunity to study in the United States to enable them to preach more accurately and faithfully. They have few books, if any. Picture yourself in this type of situation. What would you need?

Can you imagine how these men would be assisted if they received materials on every Old Testament and New Testament book? Can you imagine how encouraging it would be to them to be able to attend a two- to three-week preacher school in their community? Can you picture them in a school, taking several courses in Bible studies, having fellowship with other preachers, having opportunities to have their questions answered, and getting assistance regarding the problems they are facing? Can you not see how these opportunities would increase their effectiveness in leading souls to Christ and in edifying those who have become Christians?

HELPING THOSE WHO HAVE NOT HEARD

In order to help those who have never heard the gospel to become Christians, a special book was designed in 1998 by TFTWMS. It contains three hundred plus pages on how to become a Christian. The reader of the book is introduced to God, Christ, the Holy Spirit, the Bible, the earthly life of Jesus, the death, burial, and resurrection of Jesus, the establishment of the church, and how one can live for Christ today as a member of His church. Then, in the last two hundred pages of the book, there is a complete copy of the New Testament (NASB).

Thousands of these books have been sent to Africa, the Eastern European countries, India, Latin America, and other places. The success rate has been very high—almost amazing. The book, 512 pages in length, can be printed and sent to someone in another country for $1.50. It is an attempt to bring together the very message that any Christian would want to provide for someone who has not heard the gospel.

In 2005 a ten-year plan was made to cover a large area of the earth each year with these books. Before printing, the book is culturally adapted for the specific area into which it is being sent and translated into the most prevalent languages of that area.

HOW CAN YOU HELP?

Your help is needed to maintain this missionary effort that has become one of the largest, most cost-effective and productive efforts. Here is a two-part challenge for every Christian:

First, would you challenge the church where you worship and with whom you work to give a one-time contribution to this work? Even a small contribution will go a long way in providing teaching materials and on-site training for these national preachers.

Second, could you give a one-time contribution to this work? This contribution, of course, would have to be above and beyond your regular contribution to the local congregation of which you are a part. We are not asking anyone to interrupt his commitment to the work of the local congregation. The church needs more works, not fewer works. This effort is designed to strengthen every missionary activity and does not seek to detract from any one of them.

You would be surprised how much can be done if we all do a little extra. No one person has a lot of light, but if we put our lights together, we can have a big light that will reach out into all of the world. Would you decide today to dig a little deeper and give a little extra for this wonderful method of world evangelization?

CONTRIBUTIONS NEEDED

Contributions should be made out to Truth for Today World Mission School and sent to 2209 S. Benton, Searcy, AR 72143. Will you assist us in providing study materials for national preachers? This work is under the oversight of the Champions church of Christ in Houston, Texas.

Eddie Cloer